ENGLISH PROSE SELECTIONS

英国散文名篇选注

鲍屡平 选注

2019年·北京

图书在版编目（CIP）数据

英国散文名篇选注 / 鲍屡平选注. —北京：商务印书馆，2019
ISBN 978-7-100-17171-7

Ⅰ. ①英… Ⅱ. ①鲍… Ⅲ. ①英语—高等学校—教材②散文集—英国 Ⅳ. ① H319.39

中国版本图书馆 CIP 数据核字（2019）第 042238 号

权利保留，侵权必究。

英国散文名篇选注
鲍屡平 选注

商务印书馆出版
（北京王府井大街 36 号 邮政编码 100710）
商务印书馆发行
北京冠中印刷厂印刷
ISBN 978-7-100-17171-7

2019 年 7 月第 1 版　　开本 880×1230　1/32
2019 年 7 月北京第 1 次印刷　印张 24 5/8
定价：98.00 元

选注者简介

鲍屡平教授 1915 年 2 月 28 日（农历元宵节）出生于安徽滁州职员之家，1995 年 2 月 14 日（农历元宵节）在杭州去世，享年 80 周岁。他是一位沉默寡言、好学不倦、一丝不苟、学博识广、严于律己、偏爱英语的教授。

1936 年他毕业于金陵大学农学院，获农学学士学位，并先后在金陵大学农学院、中国乡村建设学院任教。约 1943 年，重庆商务印书馆总管理处招聘 10 名英语研究生，鲍屡平获聘，考分居首，在商务印书馆总管理处编辑部任编译员，在馆中他受到馆长的器重和同事们的敬佩。1946 年他又以出色的成绩通过一项公费留学生考试（"中英庚子赔款公费留学生考试"），同年赴英公费留学。1948 年他毕业于英国爱丁堡大学文学院，获文学硕士学位，并按时毅然归国效劳。回国后，他受聘于浙江大学外文系任教。1952 年全国院系大调整，他随系调入浙江师范学院外语系任教；1958 年杭州大学建立，他调往杭州大学外语系任教，兼任外语系主任，直至退休。其间还兼任浙江省外文学会会长、名誉会长、中国外语教学研究会理事、中国英语教学研究会理事、中国外国文学学会理事。

他长期从事英国语言文学教学工作，曾讲授英语语音学、英语语法、英语精读、英汉翻译、英文写作、英语词汇专题、英语惯用法、英国散文、英国文学史、欧洲文学史、西方文艺批评等 10 多门课程；培养了大量外语人才，对杭州大学外语系的建设和发展及浙江省外语教学事业贡献突出。1992 年起享受国务院特殊津贴。

科研工作主要在英国诗文评论和英语习惯用法，且重视独创性与实用性。计有编著：《英文成语例解》、《续英文成语例解》、《英语精选成语例解》、《英文习用法举隅》等；译著：《魔沼》、《大都会的小故事》等；论著：《哲理诗人鲁克锐提乌斯》《英语同音词研究》《济慈叙事诗〈伊莎贝拉〉的分析研究》（曾获浙江省社会科学优秀成果一等奖和荣誉奖）、《赫兹利特〈初识诗人记〉简说》（英文）、《谈英文散文阅读》等；专著：《乔叟诗篇研究》；选注：《英国散文名篇选注》。此外，还有译稿"英国文学入门"，等等。

至此，鲍屡平教授的一些爱国、敬业、诚信、友善美德似可显见。

多读英文散文佳作

（前言）

我们研习英语的人，应多读一些现代、近代的英文散文。对于一篇一篇的佳作，如能用心阅读，深入揣摩，掌握其命意、布局、措辞和风格，就会增强理解英语的能力，而且在英语表达方面——特别是在写作上——会得到很大的帮助和有力的促进。我们可以为提高自己的英语水平而阅读英文散文，也可把英文散文当作专业研究的对象。

英文散文的范围至广，大致说来，以下几个方面的书籍或文章都可以读，也应当读：

1. 西方学术名著的英原文和英译文。

2. 较通俗的英文科技文章或书籍。选读一些内容新颖翔实、文字清晰可诵的英文科技文章，有利于我们吸收新知识，掌握现代英语。读这些文章时，不妨留意观察科技英语的特点，借以促进我们的教和学。

3. 英美时文。包括关于社会生活的报道，重要事物的说明，政治、经济诸方面的评论。

4. 英美小品文和其他文艺性散文。长篇小说、短篇小说、戏剧（非诗剧）、小品文，都是文艺性散文。前三种是文学的重要体裁，从中我们可以读到记叙文和描写文，还有说明文，甚至议论文，这就不用细说了。而小品文则是英文散文的一个特殊门类。一篇小品文字数不太多，笔调较明快，反映作者所处时代的风习、气氛，也表现了作者的性格和真实思想感情，很值得仔细阅读。

英国著名小品文家有培根（Francis Bacon, 1561-1626）、考利（Abraham Cowley, 1618-1667）、艾迪生（Joseph Addison, 1672-1719）、斯蒂尔（Richard Steele, 1672-1729）、哥尔斯密（Oliver Goldsmith, 1728-1774）、兰姆（Charles

Lamb，1775—1834）、赫兹利特（William Hazlitt，1778—1830）、利·亨特（Leigh Hunt，1784—1859）、史蒂文生（R. L. Stevenson，1850—1894）、吉辛（George Gissing，1857—1903）、卢卡斯（E. V. Lucas，1868—1938）、贝洛克（Hilaire Belloc，1870—1953）、切斯特顿（G. K. Chesterton，1874—1936），林德（Robert Lynd，1879—1949）等人。美国著名小品文家有欧文（Washington Irving，1783—1859）、爱默生（R. W. Emerson，1803—1882）、梭罗（H. D. Thoreau，1817—1862）、克罗瑟斯（S. M. Crothers，1857—1927）、雷普利尔（Agnes Repplier，1858—1950）、莫利（Christopher Morley，1890—1957）、怀特（E. B. White，1899—1985）等人。加拿大著名小品文家有利科克（Stephen Leacock，1869—1944）等人。

从文艺鉴赏的角度讲，我们读了一篇小品文后，要找出它的中心思想，考察作者处理题材的方式方法，研究作者所反映的时代特色、社会生活和他自己的性格。

5. 传记。英文中最著名的一部传记，是 18 世纪博斯韦尔所写的《塞缪尔·约翰逊博士传》（James Boswell, *The Life of Samuel Johnson*, 1791），此书详细记载文豪约翰逊的言和事，描述真实而传神。其次有 19 世纪洛克哈特所写的《沃尔特·司各特爵士传》（J. G. Lockhart, *The Life of Sir Walter Scott*, 1837—1838），此书详细描述小说家司各特的生活习惯和待人接物。福斯特所著《查尔斯·狄更斯传》（John Forster, *The Life of Charles Dickens*, 1872—1874），亦名世之作。20 世纪早期，斯特雷奇撰写了《维多利亚时代名人传》（Lytton Strachey, *Eminent Victorians*, 1918），此书较有想象成分，并常流露作者微讽的情态，开创出一种传记写作的新方法。

6. 日记。英国日记家中的佼佼者，有 17 世纪的伊夫林（John Evelyn，1620—1706）和皮普斯（Samuel Pepys，1633—1703），以及 18 世纪后期和 19 世纪前期的弗朗西斯（亦称范妮）·伯尼（Frances Burney or Fanny Burney，1752—1840）。伊夫林在日记中描述了他的游历经过和他的同代人，文字较雅；皮普斯的记录坦白、亲切，文字随便、活泼；范妮·伯尼是小说家，她的日记多报道宫廷生活中紧张而有趣的轶事。20 世纪早期，海军上校斯科特

（R. F. Scott, 1868-1912）写的日记于1913年出版，题名由编辑者定为《斯科特末次探险记》(*Scott's Last Expedition*)，记述他所领导的英国第二次南极探险队的活动（1910-1912），表现出艰苦奋斗的精神，很感人。

7. **书信**。英国历代尺牍家甚多，最著者似推蒙塔古夫人（Lady Mary Wortley Montagu, 1689-1762）、沃波尔（Horace Walpole, 1717-1797）、库珀（William Cowper, 1731-1800）。他们都是18世纪的作家，库珀还是诗人；其书信，言之有物，反映生活，表现性格，富有情趣，文辞清雅，娓娓动人。

8. **自传**。18世纪最著名的英文自传，出自美国政治家和科学家富兰克林（Benjamin Franklin, 1706-1790）之手，他写生活经历和重要事件，充满好见识和启蒙思想，文笔明洁、风趣。19世纪英国作家中写自传的很多，而且风格互异，如卡莱尔（Thomas Carlyle, 1795-1881）、纽曼（J. H. Newman, 1801-1890）、达尔文（Charles Darwin, 1809-1882）、特罗洛普（Anthony Trollope, 1815-1882）等。20世纪的自传，也是大量的，难于枚举；萧伯纳（Bernard Shaw, 1856-1950）、巴里（J. M. Barrie, 1860-1937）、韦尔斯（H. G. Wells, 1866-1946）、本内特（Arnold Bennett, 1867-1931）等名作家都曾涉猎。有两本极有特色的作品，就是戴维斯的《超级流浪汉自传》（W. H. Davies, *The Autobiography of a Super Tramp*, 1908）和赫德森的《远方与昔年》（W. H. Hudson, *Far Away and Long Ago*, 1918）：前者叙述诗人戴维斯的青年流浪生活，激起读者的同情；后者叙述作家赫德森童年时代在南美洲故乡的往事，充满对大自然的爱。

9. **游记**。19世纪政治家科贝特的《骑马乡行记》（William Cobbett, *Rural Rides*, 1830）描写了19世纪早期的英国，特别是乡村劳动者，真确有力，朴素清新。作家博罗的《圣经在西班牙》（George Borrow, *The Bible in Spain*, 1843）讲述他在西班牙的经历，坦率，诙谐。金莱克的《伊奥森》（A. W. Kinglake, *Eothen*, 1844）是作者的近东游记，颇有情趣和遐想。20世纪作家普里斯特利写的《英格兰游记》（J. B. Priestley, *English Journey*, 1934），也颇为生动有趣。

10. **历史**。英国史学家很多，声名显赫的至少须提三人：吉本（Edward

Gibbon, 1737-1794), 著有《罗马帝国衰亡史》(*The History of the Decline and Fall of the Roman Empire*, 1776-1788), 这是近代西方的史书杰作, 叙述罗马帝国的衰亡, 内容详赡准确, 风格端重优美; 麦考利 (T. B. Macaulay, 1800-1859), 著有《英国史》(*The History of England*, 1849-1855), 主要记17世纪末叶的英国史事, 有见解, 描述生动流畅; 格林 (J. R. Green, 1837-1883), 著有《英国人民简史》(*A Short History of the English People*, 1874), 讲英国人民的社会、政治、经济、文化史, 记叙简洁可诵。

11. 其他, 如演说、文论, 等等。

缩略语表

arch. = archaic
Bib. = Bible
c. = about (拉丁文 circa 的缩写，本书不用 ca.)
cf. = compare
colloq. = colloquial
dial. = dialect
fl. = flourish
fml. = formal
Fr. = French
Ger. = German
Gr. = Greek
Gr. myth. = Greek mythology

inf. = informal
Ir. = Irish
It. = Italian
Lat. = Latin
obs. = obsolete
phon. sp. = phonetic spelling
poet. = poetic
Rom. myth. = Roman mythology
Scot. = Scottish
sl. = slang
Span. = Spanish
Vulg. = Vulgar

目 录

1. JOHN LYLY (1554−1606) ·· 1
    EUPHUES' SPEECH TO LUCILLA ······················· 2
2. PHILIP SIDNEY (1554−1586) ································· 5
    SCENES IN ARCADIA ·· 7
    THE POET'S POWER ·· 9
3. FRANCIS BACON (1561−1626) ······························ 12
    OF TRUTH ·· 14
    OF DISCOURSE ·· 17
    OF STUDIES ··· 20
4. WILLIAM SHAKESPEARE (1564−1616) ················ 23
    SHYLOCK'S PASSIONATE SPEECH ···················· 25
    HAMLET'S ADVICE TO THE PLAYERS ··············· 28
5. BEN JONSON (1572−1637) ·· 30
    OF STYLE ··· 32
6. ROBERT BURTON (1577−1640) ······························· 34
    THE POWER OF LOVE ······································ 35
7. THOMAS OVERBURY (1581−1613) ························· 37
    A FAIR AND HAPPY MILKMAID ······················· 38
8. THOMAS HOBBES (1588−1679) ······························· 40
    OF SPEECH ··· 41
9. IZAAK WALTON (1593−1683) ································· 44
    THE MILKMAID AND HER SONG ····················· 45
10. JOHN EARLE (1601−1665) ······································ 48
    AN ANTIQUARY ·· 49

11. THOMAS BROWNE (1605–1682)	51
THE EMBLEMS OF MORTAL VANITIES	52
12. JOHN MILTON (1608–1674)	56
ON CENSORSHIP	58
13. ABRAHAM COWLEY (1618–1667)	62
OF MYSELF	63
14. JOHN EVELYN (1620–1706)	71
THE GREAT FIRE	72
15. JOHN BUNYAN (1628–1688)	76
VANITY FAIR	78
16. JOHN DRYDEN (1631–1700)	83
SHAKESPEARE, BEAUMONT AND FLETCHER, AND BEN JONSON	85
CHAUCER, THE FATHER OF ENGLISH POETRY	89
17. SAMUEL PEPYS (1633–1703)	92
HIS DIVERSE INTERESTS	94
18. DANIEL DEFOE (1660–1731)	98
THE SALVAGE FROM THE WRECK	100
19. JONATHAN SWIFT (1667–1745)	104
THE DIVERSIONS OF THE COURT OF LILLIPUT	106
20. RICHARD STEELE (1672–1729)	114
RECOLLECTIONS OF CHILDHOOD	116
THE SPECTATOR CLUB	120
A STAGE-COACH JOURNEY	126
21. JOSEPH ADDISON (1672–1719)	131
THE SPECTATOR'S ACCOUNT OF HIMSELF	133
SIR ROGER AT HOME	138
SIR ROGER IN LONDON	142
22. LADY MARY WORTLEY MONTAGU (1689–1762)	146
TO MRS. S. C.	147
23. PHILIP DORMER STANHOPE (1694–1773)	150
ON MAKING FRIENDS	151

24. HENRY FIELDING (1707–1754) ········ 154
    AN AFFRAY ········ 156
25. SAMUEL JOHNSON (1709–1784) ········ 160
    LETTER TO LORD CHESTERFIELD ········ 162
    SHAKESPEARE AND GENERAL NATURE ········ 164
26. THOMAS GRAY (1716–1771) ········ 168
    NETLEY ABBEY ········ 169
27. HORACE WALPOLE (1717–1797) ········ 171
    TO GEORGE MONTAGU, ESQ ········ 172
28. GILBERT WHITE (1720–1793) ········ 174
    GOSSAMER ········ 175
29. OLIVER GOLDSMITH (1728–1774) ········ 178
    FAMILY AMBITIONS ········ 179
    THE MAN IN BLACK ········ 184
30. EDMUND BURKE (1729–1797) ········ 188
    OBJECTIONS TO THE USE OF FORCE ········ 190
31. WILLIAM COWPER (1731–1800) ········ 198
    LETTER TO LADY HESKETH ········ 199
32. EDWARD GIBBON (1737–1794) ········ 202
    CONSTANTINE'S INVASION OF ITALY ········ 204
    A RETROSPECT ········ 207
33. JAMES BOSWELL (1740–1795) ········ 210
    A MORNING RAMBLE ········ 211
    CHARACTER OF GOLDSMITH ········ 213
    THE MEETING OF TWO FELLOW-COLLEGIANS ········ 216
34. RICHARD BRINSLEY SHERIDAN (1751–1816) ········ 221
    A SCENE FROM *THE SCHOOL FOR SCANDAL* ········ 222
35. WILLIAM COBBETT (1763–1835) ········ 236
    A RURAL RIDE ········ 237
36. SIR WALTER SCOTT (1771–1832) ········ 240
    THE ARCHERY CONTEST AT ASHBY ········ 242

37. SAMUEL TAYLOR COLERIDGE (1772–1834)	247
THE LYRICAL BALLADS	249
38. ROBERT SOUTHEY (1774–1843)	251
NELSON AND HIS MEN	252
39. JANE AUSTEN (1775–1817)	255
A FAMILY QUARREL	256
MR. AND MRS. JOHN DASHWOOD	262
40. CHARLES LAMB (1775–1834)	267
MACKERY END IN HERTFORDSHIRE	269
THE SUPERANNUATED MAN	275
41. WALTER SAVAGE LANDOR (1775–1864)	284
LOVE STRONG AS DEATH	285
42. WILLIAM HAZLITT (1778–1830)	289
ON GOING A JOURNEY	291
ON THE FEELING OF IMMORTALITY IN YOUTH	304
OF FAMILIAR STYLE	312
43. LEIGH HUNT (1784–1859)	321
A FEW THOUGHTS ON SLEEP	322
44. THOMAS DE QUINCEY (1785–1859)	329
ON THE KNOCKING AT THE GATE IN *MACBETH*	330
45. JOHN GIBSON LOCKHART (1794–1854)	335
SCOTT'S WAY WITH HIS CHILDREN	336
46. JOHN KEATS (1795–1821)	340
TO BENJAMIN BAILEY	341
47. THOMAS CARLYLE (1795–1881)	346
COLUMBUS	347
48. THOMAS BABINGTON MACAULAY (1800–1859)	349
OLIVER GOLDSMITH	351
LONDON COFFEE-HOUSES	369
49. JOHN HENRY CARDINAL NEWMAN (1801–1890)	373
THE VALUE OF A UNIVERSITY EDUCATION	374

50. GEORGE HENRY BORROW (1803–1881) 377
    AT AN INN 378
51. ELIZABETH CLEGHORN GASKELL (1810–1865) 383
    A PETITION 384
52. WILLIAM MAKEPEACE THACKERAY (1811–1863) 387
    THE BATTLE OF WATERLOO 388
    THE DUKE OF MARLBOROUGH 390
53. CHARLES DICKENS (1812–1870) 393
    THE ROAD TO DOVER 395
    MR. PICKWICK AND HIS FRIENDS ON THE ICE 404
54. CHARLOTTE BRONTË (1816–1855) 417
    SHIRLEY AND CAROLINE 418
55. GEORGE ELIOT (1819–1880) 422
    EPPIE REJECTS GODFREY'S OFFER 424
56. JOHN RUSKIN (1819–1900) 434
    THE TREASURES HIDDEN IN BOOKS 436
57. MATTHEW ARNOLD (1822–1888) 443
    CULTURE AND PERFECTION 444
58. THOMAS HENRY HUXLEY (1825–1895) 448
    LEARNING THE LAWS OF NATURE 449
59. FRANCIS KILVERT (1840–1879) 453
    EXTRACTS FROM *KILVERT'S DIARY* 454
60. THOMAS HARDY (1840–1928) 458
    HARVESTING 460
    A FACE ON WHICH TIME MAKES BUT LITTLE IMPRESSION 463
61. WILLIAM HENRY HUDSON (1841–1922) 468
    HER OWN VILLAGE 469
62. ROBERT LOUIS STEVENSON (1850–1894) 474
    THE OLD SEA DOG AT THE *ADMIRAL BENBOW* 475
    EL DORADO 481

63. LADY GREGORY (1852–1932)	484
THE RISING OF THE MOON	485
64. OSCAR WILDE (1854–1900)	496
THE HAPPY PRINCE	497
65. GEORGE BERNARD SHAW (1856–1950)	507
THE OPENING SCENE OF *MAJOR BARBARA*	509
SORROWS OF THE MILLIONAIRE	520
66. GEORGE GISSING (1857–1903)	522
EXTRACTS FROM *THE PRIVATE PAPERS OF HENRY RYECROFT*	523
67. JOSEPH CONRAD (1857–1924)	530
CAPTAIN MACWHIRR	531
68. HENRY WATSON FOWLER (1858–1933)	535
EXTRACTS FROM *A DICTIONARY OF MODERN ENGLISH USAGE*	536
69. JEROME KLAPKA JEROME (1859–1927)	540
A FISHY STORY	541
70. LOGAN PEARSALL SMITH (1865–1946)	549
THE ROSE	550
71. HERBERT GEORGE WELLS (1866–1946)	553
A DAY IN THE COUNTRY	555
THE LITERARY RENAISSANCE	558
72. ARNOLD BENNETT (1867–1931)	563
ST. LUKE'S SQUARE	564
73. JOHN GALSWORTHY (1867–1933)	570
ENCOUNTER	572
ACME	575
74. ROBERT FALCON SCOTT (1868–1912)	583
THE END OF THE STORY	584
75. ARTHUR CLUTTON-BROCK (1868–1924)	586
SUNDAY BEFORE THE WAR	587
76. EDWARD VERRALL LUCAS (1868–1938)	590
MEDITATIONS AMONG THE CAGES	591

	RIVALRY	596
	A FUNERAL	601
77.	ROBERT TRESSELL (1870–1911)	605
	PREFACE TO *THE RAGGED TROUSERED PHILANTHROPISTS*	606
78.	SAKI (PSEUDONYM OF HECTOR HUGH MUNRO, 1870–1916)	608
	THE OPEN WINDOW	609
79.	HILAIRE BELLOC (1870–1953)	613
	ON THINKING	614
	AN EXTRACT FROM *THE PATH TO ROME*	618
80.	MAX BEERBOHM (1872–1956)	625
	SEEING PEOPLE OFF	626
81.	HENRY MAJOR TOMLINSON (1873–1958)	631
	THE MASTER	632
82.	GILBERT KEITH CHESTERTON (1874–1936)	636
	WHAT I FOUND IN MY POCKET	637
	THE WORSHIP OF THE WEALTHY	641
83.	WILLIAM SOMERSET MAUGHAM (1874–1965)	645
	THE LUNCHEON	647
	LUCIDITY, SIMPLICITY, EUPHONY	652
84.	WINSTON LEONARD SPENCER CHURCHILL (1874–1965)	662
	THE NORMAN CONQUEST	663
	A FEW HOBBIES	669
85.	JAMES JEANS (1877–1946)	671
	THE FUTURE OF THE EARTH	672
86.	ROBERT LYND (1879–1949)	674
	BACK TO THE DESK	675
87.	LYTTON STRACHEY (1880–1932)	678
	GLADSTONE	679
88.	VIRGINIA WOOLF (*NÉE* ADELINE VIRGINIA STEPHEN, 1882–1941)	682
	MY FATHER: LESLIE STEPHEN	684

89. JAMES JOYCE (1882–1941) ... 691
    ARABY ... 693
90. ARTHUR STANLEY EDDINGTON (1882–1944) ... 700
    THE MILKY WAY AND BEYOND ... 701
91. DAVID HERBERT LAWRENCE (1885–1930) ... 711
    PAUL'S FIRST DAY AT JORDAN'S ... 713
92. KATHERINE MANSFIELD (PSEUDONYM OF KATHLEEN MANSFIELD BEAUCHAMP, 1888–1923) ... 722
    THE GARDEN PARTY ... 723
93. ROBIN GEORGE COLLINGWOOD (1889–1943) ... 738
    THE NATURE, OBJECT AND PURPOSE OF HISTORY ... 739
94. JOHN MIDDLETON MURRY (1889–1957) ... 741
    THREE MEANINGS OF THE WORD STYLE ... 742
95. ALDOUS LEONARD HUXLEY (1894–1963) ... 748
    GEORGE AND GEORGIANA ... 749
96. GEORGE ORWELL (1903–1950) ... 757
    WHY I WRITE ... 758

后记 ... 767

1

JOHN LYLY
(1554–1606)

John Lyly was an English novelist and dramatist. He was born in Kent about 1554, and graduated from Magdalen College, Oxford, in 1573. His prose romances, *Euphues: The Anatomy of Wit** (1578) and its sequel *Euphues and His England* (1580), were immensely popular works in the Elizabethan period. They contain little story but plenty of discourses on love and contemporary manners. They are remarkable for their highly mannered, ornate style, which is rich in parallelisms, antithesis, alliteration, allusions, and elaborate figures of speech. The term "euphuism" has generally been used to designate this affected style. Lyly's influential witty comedies, written in prose and interspersed with lyrics, include *Alexander, Campaspe, and Diogenes* (produced in 1584), *Endymion* (1588), *Midas* (about 1589), and *Mother Bombie* (about 1590). *The Woman in the Moon* (about 1594) was his only play in verse. Lyly served as a Member of Parliament from 1589 to 1601. He died in London in November 1606.

---

* 本书中黑斜体的文字用以强调重要的著作、正文中的重要内容及重要词汇。

EUPHUES' SPEECH TO LUCILLA

Gentlewoman, my acquaintance being so little, I am afraid my credit will be less, for that[1] they are commonly soonest believed that are best beloved, and they liked best whom we have known longest; nevertheless, the noble mind suspecteth no guile without cause, neither condemneth any wight[2] without proof; having therefore notice of your heroical heart[3], I am the better persuaded of my good hap. So it is, Lucilla, that coming to Naples but to fetch fire[4], as the byword is, not to make my place of abode, I have found such flames that I can neither quench them with the water of free-will, neither cool them with wisdom. For as the hop, the pole being never so high, groweth to the end, or as the dry beech kindled at the root, never leaveth until it come to the top; or as one drop of poison disperseth itself into every vein, so affection having caught hold of my heart, and the sparks of love kindled my liver[5], will suddenly, though secretly, flame up into my head, and spread itself into every sinew. It is your beauty (pardon my abrupt boldness), lady, that hath taken every part of me prisoner, and brought me into this deep distress, but seeing women when one praiseth them for their deserts, deem that he flattereth them to obtain his desire, I am here present to yield myself to such trial as your courtesy in this behalf shall require. Yet will you commonly object this to such as serve you, and starve to win your goodwill, that hot love is soon cold: that the bavin[6], though it burn bright, is but a blaze: that scalding water, if it stand awhile, turneth almost to ice: that pepper, though it be hot in the mouth, is cold in the maw: that the faith of men, though it fry in their words, it freezeth in their works: which things, Lucilla, albeit they be sufficient to reprove the lightness of some one, yet can they not convince everyone of lewdness: neither ought the constancy of all to be brought in question[7] through the subtlety of a few. For although the worm entereth into almost every wood, yet he eateth not the cedar-tree. Though the stone Cylindrus[8] at every thunder-clap roll from the hill, yet the pure, sleek stone[9] mounteth at the noise: though the rust fret the hardest steel, yet doth it not eat into the emerald: though the polypus[10] change his hue, yet the salamander keepeth his colour: though Proteus[11] transform himself into every shape, yet Pygmalion[12] retaineth his old form: though Aeneas were too fickle to Dido[13], yet Troilus was too faithful to Cressid[14]: though others seem counterfeit in their deeds, yet, Lucilla, persuade yourself that Euphues will be always current in his dealings. But as the true gold is tried by the touch, the pure flint by the stroke of the iron, so the loyal heart of the faithful lover is known by the trial of his lady: of the which trial, Lucilla, if you shall account Euphues worthy, assure yourself he will be as ready to offer himself a sacrifice for your sweet sake, as yourself shall be willing to employ him in your service. Neither doth he desire to be trusted in any way, until he shall be tried every way: neither doth he crave credit at the first, but a good countenance till his desire shall be made manifest by his deserts. Thus, not blinded by light affection, but dazzled with your rare perfection, and boldened by your exceeding courtesy, I have unfolded mine entire love, desiring you having so good leisure to give so friendly an answer, as I may receive comfort, and you commendation.

NOTES

1. **for that:** (obs.) because
2. **wight:** (arch.) person
3. **your heroical heart:** your noble heart
4. **fetch fire:** to make a short visit
5. **liver:** (arch.) seat of emotions
6. **bavin:** brushwood
7. **brought in question:** called in question; doubted; objected to
8. **Cylindrus:** the name of a precious stone
9. **sleek stone:** polishing stone
10. **polypus:** transparent jellyfish
11. **Proteus:** (in Gr. myth.) a marine demigod who had the gift of prophecy and the power of changing his shape
12. **Pygmalion:** (in Gr. legend) a sculptor who carved an ivory statue of a maiden and fell in love with it. After Venus at his request breathed life into it, he married the girl.

13. **though Aeneas were too fickle to Dido:** Aeneas, a Trojan prince, sailed for Italy but was driven by a storm to Africa, where he stayed for some time as the guest and lover of Dido, Queen of Carthage. He left Dido suddenly by order of the gods, and she killed herself.
14. **Troilus was too faithful to Cressid:** Troilus, a Trojan prince, was the forsaken lover of Cressid, the daughter of a priest.

2

PHILIP SIDNEY

(1554–1586)

Sir Philip Sidney was an English poet, critic, soldier, and statesman. Born in Kent on November 30, 1554, he was educated at Shrewsbury School, Shropshire, and Christ Church, Oxford. He became a brilliant member of Queen Elizabeth's court and a model of Renaissance chivalry. After serving on several diplomatic missions, he was elected a Member of Parliament in 1581, knighted in 1582, and appointed Governor of Flushing in 1585. On October 17, 1586, he died from a bullet wound that he had received twenty-five days before at the battle of Zutphen in Flanders.

Sidney's works include *Astrophel and Stella*, a collection of lyrics; *The Countess of Pembroke's Arcadia*, a rambling romance in heightened prose; and *A Defence of Poesy*, a critical essay. These were all published posthumously. *Astrophel and Stella*, written about 1582 and published in 1591, consists of 108 sonnets and 11 songs, and is one of the great Elizabethan sonnet sequences. The poet handles the Petrarchan sonnet form in a masterly fashion and displays the various feelings of Astrophel (the star-lover) in his unhappy love for Stella (the star). *Arcadia*, written about 1580 and published in 1590, is a pastoral-chivalric romance in five books, with an eclogue at the end of each book. The author's intention was to offer instruction as well as entertainment. *A Defence of Poesy*, also called *An Apology for Poetry*, was written about 1580 and published in 1595. It is one of the first important critical works in English. Sidney holds that the purpose of poetry should be to teach virtue, that there are different kinds of poetry, and that the poetic art can be improved by observing certain time-honoured principles.

SCENES IN ARCADIA[1]

There were hills which garnished their proud heights with stately trees; humble valleys whose base estate seemed comforted with refreshing of silver rivers; meadows enamelled with all sorts of eye-pleasing flowers; thickets which, being lined with most pleasant shade, were witnessed so to by the cheerful deposition[2] of many well-tuned birds; each pasture stored with sheep feeding with sober security, while the pretty lambs with bleating oratory craved the dams' comfort; here a shepherd's boy piping as though he should never be old; there a young shepherdess knitting and withal singing, and it seemed that her voice comforted her hands to work and her hands kept time to her voice's music. As for the houses of the country for many houses came under their eye they were all scattered, no two being one by the other, and yet not so far off as that it barred mutual succour; a show, as it were, of an accompanable[3] solitariness and of a civil[4] wildness....

The house itself was built of fair and strong stone, not affecting so much any extraordinary kind of fineness as an honourable representing of a firm stateliness. The lights[5], doors and stairs rather directed to the use of the guest than to the eye of the artificer; and yet as the one chiefly heeded, so the other not neglected; each place handsome without curiosity[6] and homely without loathsomeness; not so dainty as not to be trod on, nor yet slubbered up with good fellowship[7]; all more lasting than beautiful but that the consideration of the exceeding[8] lastingness made the eye believe it was exceeding beautiful. The servants, not so many in number as cleanly in apparel and serviceable in behaviour, testifying even in their countenances that their master took as well care to be served as of them that did serve....

This country Arcadia among all the provinces of Greece hath ever been had in singular reputation: partly for the sweetness of the air and other natural benefits, but principally for the well-tempered minds of the people who (finding that the shining title of glory, so much affected by other nations doth indeed help little to the happiness of life) are the only people which as by their justice and providence give neither cause nor hope to their neighbours to annoy them, so are they not stirred with false praise to trouble others' quiet, thinking it a small reward for the wasting of their own lives in ravening that their posterity should long after say they had done so. Even the Muses seem to approve their good determination by choosing this country for their chief repairing place[9], and by bestowing their perfections so largely here that the very shepherds have their fancies lifted to so high conceits, that the learned of other nations are content both to borrow their names and imitate their cunning[10].

NOTES

1. **Arcadia:** the pastoral district in central Peloponnese; the idealized rural setting of much pastoral poetry
2. **deposition:** testimony
3. **accompanable:** companionable
4. **civil:** civilized
5. **lights:** windows
6. **curiosity:** strangeness
7. **slubbered up with good fellowship:** made slovenly with revelry
8. **exceeding:** exceedingly
9. **their chief repairing place:** their chief place to repair to; their chief resort
10. **cunning:** knowledge, skill

THE POET'S POWER

I conclude, therefore, that he excelleth history[1] not only in furnishing the mind with knowledge, but in setting it forward to that which deserveth to be called and accounted good; which setting forward, and moving to well-doing, indeed setteth the laurel crown upon the poet as victorious, not only of the historian, but over the philosopher, howsoever in teaching it may be questionable. For suppose it be granted, (that which I suppose with great reason may be denied,) that the philosopher, in respect of his methodical proceeding, doth teach more perfectly than the poet, yet do I think that no man is so much ***philophilosophos***[2] as to compare the philosopher in moving with the poet. And that moving is of a higher degree than teaching, it may by this appear, that it is well nigh both the cause and the effect of teaching; for who will be taught, if he be not moved with desire to be taught? And what so much good doth that teaching bring forth (I speak still of moral doctrine,) as that it moveth one to do that which it doth teach? For, as Aristotle saith, it is not ***gnosis***[3] but ***praxis***[4] must be the fruit; and how ***praxis*** can be, without being moved to practise, it is no hard matter to consider. The philosopher showeth you the way, he informeth you of the particularities[5], as well of the tediousness of the way, as of the pleasant lodging you shall have when your journey is ended, as of the many by-turnings[6] that may divert you from your way; but this is to no man but to him that will read him, and read him with attentive, studious painfulness[7]; which constant desire whosoever hath in him, hath already passed half the hardness of the way, and therefore is beholding to the philosopher but for the other half. Nay, truly, learned men have learnedly thought, that where once reason hath so much overmastered passion as that the mind hath a free desire to do well, the inward light each mind hath in itself is as good as a philosopher's book; since in nature we know it is well to do well, and what is well and what is evil, although not in the words of art[8] which philosophers bestow upon us; for out of natural conceit[9] the philosophers drew it. But to be moved to do that which we know, or to be moved with desire to know, ***hoc opus, hic labor est***[10].

Now therein of all sciences[11] (I speak still of human, and according to the human conceit,) is our poet the monarch. For he doth not only show the way, but giveth so sweet a prospect into the way as will entice any man to enter into it. Nay, he doth, as if your journey should lie through a fair vineyard, at the very first give you a cluster of grapes, that full of that taste you may long to pass further. He beginneth not with obscure definitions, which must blur the margin with interpretations, and load the memory with doubtfulness. But he cometh to you with words set in delightful proportion, either accompanied with, or prepared for, the well-enchanting skill of music; and with a tale, forsooth, he cometh unto you, with a tale which holdeth children from play, and old men from the chimney-corner; and, pretending no more[12] doth intend[13] the winning of the mind from wickedness to virtue; even as the child is often brought to take most wholesome things, by hiding them in such other as have a pleasant taste,—which, if one should begin to tell them the nature of the aloes or rhubarb they should receive, would sooner take their physic at their ears than at their mouth. So is it in men, (most of which[14] are childish in the best things, till they be cradled in their graves,) glad they will be to hear the tales of Hercules[15], Achilles[16], Cyrus[17], Aeneas[18]; and, hearing them, must needs hear the right description of wisdom, valour, and justice; which, if they had been barely, (that is to say philosophically,) set out, they would swear they be brought to school again.

NOTES

1. **he excelleth history:** poetry surpasses history
2. ***philophilosophos*:** a lover of the philosopher
3. ***gnosis*:** theory
4. ***praxis*:** practice
5. **particularities:** details
6. **by-turnings:** byways
7. **painfulness:** labour, care
8. **the words of art:** the technical terms

9. **natural conceit:** intrinsic knowledge
10. ***hoc opus, hic labor est*:** This is the task, this the toil; This is the real difficulty (Virgil, *Aeneid*, VI. 129).
11. **sciences:** branches of knowledge
12. **pretending no more:** claiming to do no more
13. **and...doth intend:** and...he intends
14. **most of which:** most of whom
15. **Hercules:** (Roman name for) Heracles, a Greek hero of prodigious strength later worshipped as a god
16. **Achilles:** the principal hero of the *Iliad*, who slew Hector of Troy in battle and was killed by Paris with a poisoned arrow
17. **Cyrus:** Cyrus the Great (d. 529 B.C.), founder of the Persian Empire
18. **Aeneas:** Trojan hero and founder of the Roman state. His wanderings after the fall of Troy form the subject of Virgil's *Aeneid*.

3

FRANCIS BACON

(1561–1626)

Francis Bacon was an English statesman, philosopher, and essayist. He was born in London on January 22, 1561, attended Trinity College, Cambridge, from 1573 to 1575, and studied at Gray's Inn, London, in 1576 and 1579–1582. He was called to the bar in 1582, and elected to Parliament in 1584. Under James I, his political career prospered; he became Solicitor-General in 1607, Attorney-General in 1613, Lord Keeper in 1617, and Lord Chancellor in January 1618; and was created Baron Verulam in July 1618, and Viscount St. Alban in January 1621. Then in the spring of 1621, he was accused of taking bribes and found guilty by the House of Lords. The disgrace put an end to his public life. He devoted his last years to writing and died on April 9, 1626.

Bacon's *Novum Organum* (1620) is a treatise in Latin on the development of scientific method and the acquirement of knowledge by experience and experiment. Among his famous works in English are *The Advancement of Learning* (1605), *The History of the Reign of Henry VII* (1622), *The New Atlantis* (1626), and above all *The Essays or Counsels, Civil and Moral* (1597–1625). *The Advancement of Learning* is concerned with the pursuit of knowledge, and is notable for a terse and lucid style. *The History of the Reign of Henry VII* is a vigorous piece of explanatory narrative. *The New Atlantis* describes in clear and direct prose an imaginary community largely devoted to intellectual pursuits. Bacon published a slender volume of ten *Essays* in 1597; brought out an enlarged edition of the work in 1612, which contained the original pieces in revised forms and twenty-eight new essays; and further expanded the work and increased the essays to fifty-eight in the final edition of 1625. The essays treat of social and political problems, public and private conduct, human nature and modes of life, all showing practical wisdom. Their style is compact, neat, and vivid with imagery.

OF TRUTH

What is truth? said jesting Pilate[1], and would not stay for an answer. Certainly there be that[2] delight in giddiness[3], and count it a bondage to fix a belief, affecting[4] free will in thinking, as well as in acting. And though the sects of philosophers of that kind[5] be gone, yet there remain certain discoursing wits which are of the same veins, though there be not so much blood in them as was in those of the ancients. But it is not only the difficulty and labour which men take in finding out of truth, nor again that when it is found it imposeth upon[6] men's thoughts, that doth bring lies in favour, but a natural though corrupt love of the lie itself. One of the later schools of the Grecians[7] examineth the matter, and is at a stand to think what should be in it, that men should love lies, where neither they make for pleasure, as with poets, nor for advantage, as with the merchant, but for the lie's sake. But I cannot tell: this same truth is a naked and open daylight, that doth not show the masks[8] and mummeries and triumphs of the world, half so stately and daintily as candle-lights. Truth may perhaps come to the price of a pearl, that showeth best by day; but it will not rise to the price of a diamond or carbuncle, that showeth best in varied lights. A mixture of a lie doth ever add pleasure. Doth any man doubt, that if there were taken out of men's minds vain opinions, flattering hopes, false valuations, imaginations as one would, and the like, but it would leave the minds of a number of men poor shrunken things, full of melancholy and indisposition, and unpleasing to themselves? One of the Fathers, in great severity, called poesy ***vinum dæmonum***[9], because it filleth the imagination, and yet it is but with the shadow of a lie. But it is not the lie that passeth through the mind, but the lie that sinketh in and settleth in it, that doth the hurt; such as we spake of before. But howsoever these things are thus in men's depraved judgments and affections, yet truth, which only doth judge itself, teacheth that the inquiry of truth, which is the love-making or wooing of it, the knowledge of truth, which is the presence of it, and the belief of truth, which is the enjoying of it, is the sovereign good of human nature. The first creature[10] of God, in the works of the days, was the light of the sense, the last was the light of reason; and his sabbath work ever since is the illumination of His Spirit. First He breathed light upon the face of the matter or chaos; then He breathed light into the face of man; and still He breatheth and inspireth light into the face of his chosen. The poet that beautified the sect[11] that was otherwise inferior to the rest saith yet excellently well: *It is a pleasure to stand upon the shore, and to see ships tossed upon the sea; a pleasure to stand in the window of a castle, and to see a battle and the adventures[12] thereof below; but no pleasure is comparable to the standing upon the vantage ground of Truth* (a hill not to be commanded[13], and where the air is always clear and serene), *and to see the errors, and wanderings, and mists, and tempests, in the vale below*[14]; so always that[15] this prospect be with pity and not with swelling or pride. Certainly it is heaven upon earth to have a man's mind move in charity, rest in providence, and turn upon the poles of truth.

To pass from theological and philosophical truth to the truth of civil business, it will be acknowledged even by those that practise it not that clear and round dealing[16] is the honour of man's nature; and that mixture of falsehood is like allay[17] in coin of gold and silver, which may make the metal work the better, but it embaseth[18] it. For these winding and crooked courses are the goings of the serpent, which goeth basely upon the belly and not upon the feet. There is no vice that doth so cover a man with shame as to be found false and perfidious. And therefore Montaigne[19] saith prettily, when he inquired the reason, why the word of the lie should be such a disgrace and such an odious charge? Saith he, *If it be well weighed, to say that a man lieth, is as much to say, as that he is brave towards God and a coward towards men.* For a lie faces God and shrinks from man. Surely the wickedness of falsehood and breach of faith cannot possibly be so highly expressed, as in that it shall be the last peal[20] to call the judgments of God upon the generations of men, it being foretold that when Christ cometh, *he shall not find faith upon the earth*[21].

NOTES

1. **Pilate:** Pontius Pilate, the Roman governor of Judaea (A.D. 26–36) who ordered the

Crucification of Jesus
2. **there be that...:** there are those who...
3. **giddiness:** unsteadiness, fickleness
4. **affecting:** striving after, seeking
5. **the sects of philosophers of that kind:** the Greek Sceptics; the Sceptic school founded by Pyrrho of Elis (c. 360–270 B.C.)
6. **imposeth upon:** imposes an obligation on, restricts
7. **one of the later school of the Grecians:** Lucian (c. A.D. 120–190), Greek writer
8. **masks:** masques, dramatic entertainments in verse and song with lavish costumes and sets
9. *vinum dæmonum*: (Lat.) the wine of devils
10. **the first creature:** the first thing created
11. **the poet that beautified the sect:** Lucretius (c. 99–55 B.C.), the Roman philosophical poet who wrote *De Rerum Natura* ("Of the Nature of Things")
12. *adventures*: happenings
13. **commanded:** dominated, overtopped
14. *It is a pleasure...in the vale below*: Bacon's paraphrase of *De Rerum Natura*, Book II, lines 1-10
15. **so...that:** provided that; so long as
16. **round dealing:** honest conduct
17. **allay:** alloy
18. **embaseth:** debases
19. **Montaigne:** Michel Eyquem de Montaigne (1533–1592), French writer, author of the famous *Essais* (begun in 1571 and published in 1580)
20. **last peal:** last appeal
21. **it being foretold that when Christ cometh, *he shall not find faith upon the earth*:** The second sentence in Luke xviii. 8 reads, "Nevertheless when the Son of man cometh, shall he find faith on the earth?" This is not prophetic but interrogative, and the word *faith* does not mean fidelity or honesty but trust in God. Bacon misquotes and misapplies the sentence.

OF DISCOURSE

Some in their discourse[1] desire rather commendation of wit, in being able to hold all arguments, than of judgment, in discerning what is true; as if it were a praise to know what might be said, and not what should be thought. Some have certain commonplaces and themes wherein they are good, and want variety; which kind of poverty is for the most part tedious, and when it is once perceived, ridiculous. The honourablest part of talk is to give the occasion[2]; and again to moderate and pass to somewhat else; for then a man leads the dance. It is good, in discourse and speech of conversation, to vary and intermingle speech of the present occasion with arguments, tales with reasons, asking of questions with telling of opinions, and jest with earnest; for it is a dull thing to tire, and as we say now, to jade anything[3] too far. As for jest, there be certain things which ought to be privileged from it; namely, religion, matters of state, great persons, any man's present business of importance, and any case that deserveth pity. Yet there be some that think their wits have been asleep, except they dart out somewhat[4] that is piquant, and to the quick. That is a vein which would be bridled:

Parce, puer, stimulis, et fortius utere loris.[5]

And generally, men ought to find the difference between saltness and bitterness. Certainly, he that hath a satirical vein, as he maketh others afraid of his wit, so he had need be afraid of others' memory. He that questioneth much shall learn much, and content much[6]; but especially if he apply his questions to the skill of the persons whom he asketh; for he shall give them occasion to please themselves in speaking, and himself shall continually gather knowledge. But let his questions not be troublesome; for that is fit for a poser[7]. And let him be sure to leave other men their turns to speak. Nay, if there be any that would reign and take up all the time, let him find means to take them off, and to bring others on; as musicians use to do with those that dance too long galliards[8]. If you dissemble sometimes your knowledge of that you are thought to know, you shall be thought another time to know that you know not. Speech of a man's self[9] ought to be seldom, and well chosen. I knew one was wont to say in scorn, "He must needs be a wise man, he speaks so much of himself"; and there is but one case wherein a man may commend himself with good grace; and that is in commending virtue in another; especially if it be such a virtue whereunto himself pretendeth. Speech of touch toward others[10] should be sparingly used; for discourse ought to be as a field, without coming home to any man. I knew two noblemen, of the west part of England, whereof the one was given to scoff, but kept ever royal cheer in his house; the other would ask of those that had been at the other's table, "Tell truly, was there never a flout[11] or dry blow[12] given?" To which the guest would answer, "Such and such a thing passed." The lord would say, "I thought he would mar a good dinner." Discretion of speech is more than[13] eloquence; and to speak agreeably to him with whom we deal, is more than to speak in good words or in good order. A good continued speech, without a good speech of interlocution, shows slowness; and a good reply or second speech, without a good settled speech, showeth shallowness and weakness. As we see in beasts, that those that are weakest in the course[14] are yet nimblest in the turn; as it is betwixt the greyhound and the hare. To use too many circumstances[15] ere one come to the matter, is wearisome; to use none at all, is blunt.

NOTES

1. **discourse:** talk, conversation
2. **to give the occasion:** to suggest or introduce some topic of conversation
3. **to jade anything:** to overwork or weary anything
4. **dart out somewhat:** utter something suddenly and quickly
5. ***Parce, puer, stimulis, et fortius utere loris*:** (Lat.) Spare the whip, boy, and hold the reins more firmly. —Ovid, ***Metamorphoses***, ii. 127
6. **content much:** please much
7. **poser:** interrogator, examiner

8. **galliards:** A galliard was a gay and lively dance common in the sixteenth and seventeenth centuries.
9. **speech of a man's self:** speech concerning oneself
10. **speech of touch toward others:** speech touching or affecting others
11. **flout:** jeer
12. **dry blow:** sarcastic hit
13. **more than:** more important than; better than
14. **in the course:** in the hunt; in running
15. **circumstances:** details; introductory remarks

OF STUDIES

Studies serve for delight, for ornament, and for ability. Their chief use for delight is in privateness and retiring[1]; for ornament, is in discourse; and for ability, is in the judgment and disposition of business. For expert[2] men can execute and perhaps judge of particulars, one by one, but the general counsels and the plots and marshalling of affairs come best from those that are learned. To spend too much time in studies is sloth; to use them too much for ornament is affectation; to make judgment wholly by their rules is the humour[3] of a scholar. They perfect nature, and are perfected by experience, for natural abilities are like natural plants, that need proyning[4] by study; and studies themselves do give forth directions too much at large[5], except[6] they be bounded in by experience. Crafty men[7] contemn studies; simple men[8] admire[9] them; and wise men use them, for they teach not their own use, but that is a wisdom without[10] them and above them, won by observation. Read not to contradict and confute, nor to believe and take for granted, nor to find talk and discourse, but to weigh and consider. Some books are to be tasted, others to be swallowed, and some few to be chewed and digested; that is, some books are to be read only in parts; others to be read, but not curiously[11]; and some few to be read wholly and with diligence and attention. Some books also may be read by deputy, and extracts made of them by others, but that would be[12] only in the less important arguments[13] and the meaner sort of books; else distilled books[14] are like common distilled waters, flashy[15] things. Reading maketh a full man, conference[16] a ready man, and writing[17] an exact man. And therefore, if a man write little, he had need have[18] a great memory; if he confer little, he had need have a present wit[19]; and if he read little, he had need have much cunning[20], to seem to know that he doth not. Histories make men wise, poets witty[21] the mathematics subtile, natural philosophy[22] deep, moral grave, logic and rhetoric able to contend. *Abeunt studia in mores.*[23] Nay there is no stond[24] or impediment in the wit but may be wrought out by fit studies, like as diseases of the body may have appropriate exercises. Bowling is good for the stone and reins[25]; shooting for the lungs and breast; gentle walking for the stomach; riding for the head; and the like. So if a man's wit be wandering, let him study the mathematics, for in demonstrations, if his wit be called away never so little[26], he must begin again. If his wit be not apt[27] to distinguish or find differences, let him study the schoolmen[28], for they are *cymini sectores*[29]. If he be not apt to beat over matters[30], and to call up one thing to prove and illustrate another, let him study the lawyers' cases. So every defect of the mind may have a special receipt[31].

NOTES

1. **privateness and retiring:** privacy and retirement
2. **expert:** experienced
3. **humour:** whim, disposition
4. **proyning:** pruning
5. **too much at large:** too much unrestricted; too vague
6. **except:** unless
7. **crafty men:** those skilled in crafts or manual arts
8. **simple men:** ignorant men
9. **admire:** wonder at
10. **without:** beyond
11. **curiously:** carefully, attentively
12. **that would be:** that should be
13. **arguments:** subjects
14. **distilled books:** epitomes, summaries
15. **flashy:** insipid, tasteless
16. **conference:** consultation, conversation
17. **writing:** taking notes
18. **had need have:** would need to have
19. **present wit:** quick intelligence
20. **cunning:** skill
21. **witty:** imaginative

22. **natural philosophy:** (natural) science
23. ***Abeunt studia in mores.*:** (Lat.) Studies pass into character; Studies grow into habits.—Ovid
24. **stond:** block, hindrance
25. **the stone and reins:** the gallstone and kidneys
26. **never so little:** ever so little
27. **apt:** quick
28. **schoolmen:** philosophers and scholars of the Middle Ages
29. ***cymini sectores*:** (Lat.) splitters of cumin-seed; hair-splitters
30. **to beat over matters:** to examine matters thoroughly
31. **receipt:** prescription

WILLIAM SHAKESPEARE

(1564–1616)

William Shakespeare, playwright and poet, is regarded as the greatest of English writers. He was born at Stratford-on-Avon, Warwickshire, on about 23rd April, 1564. The eldest son of a prosperous merchant, he almost certainly attended the Stratford grammar school. In 1582 he married Anne Hathaway, a girl 8 years his senior, and they had three children. Nothing is known about his work in early manhood. Records show that by 1592 he was well established in London as a playwright and actor. He was attached to the Lord Chamberlain's Men, a successful company which became the King's Men on the accession of James I. He grew rich and in 1597 bought New Place, a large house in Stratford. He moved back to his native town about 1610, stopped writing in 1613, and died on 23rd April, 1616.

Shakespeare wrote some 37 plays, two narrative poems, and 154 sonnets. His plays fall into several categories: [1] Comedies, including ***A Midsummer Night's Dream*** (1595), ***The Merchant of Venice*** (1596), ***Much Ado About Nothing*** (1598), ***As You Like It*** (1599), and ***Twelfth Night*** (1599); [2] History plays, including ***Richard II*** (1595), ***Henry IV, Parts 1 and 2*** (1597), and ***Henry V*** (1598); [3] Tragedies, including ***Romeo and Juliet*** (1595), ***Julius Caesar*** (1599), ***Hamlet*** (1601), ***Othello*** (1604), ***King Lear*** (1605), ***Macbeth*** (1606), ***Antony and Cleopatra***

(1606), ***Coriolanous*** (1607); [4] Problem plays or "dark comedies", namely ***Troilus and Cressida*** (1601), ***All's Well That Ends Well*** (1603), and ***Measure for Measure*** (1604); [5] Romance plays or romantic tragi-comedies, namely ***Cymbeline*** (1609), ***The Winter's Tale*** (1610), and ***The Tempest*** (1611). (The dates of composition given in parentheses above are approximate.) His narrative poems ***Venus and Adonis*** and ***The Rape of Lucrece*** were published in 1593 and 1594 respectively. His sonnets were composed in the 1590's, and appeared in a volume in 1609.

Shakespeare's plays are written mainly in blank verse and with parts in prose. They are noted for his accurate reflection of many phases of life, his deep understanding of human nature, his vivid and subtle presentation of numerous characters, the wealth of his imagination, the power of his expression, and the richness of his language and imagery. His influence on later writers has been immense.

Shakespeare's prose is generally lucid and smooth, natural and easy.

SHYLOCK'S PASSIONATE SPEECH

ACT III

SCENE I. **Venice. A street.**

Enter Salanio **and** Salarino.

Salan. Now, what news on the Rialto[1]?

Salar. Why, yet it lives there unchecked that Antonio hath a ship of rich lading wrecked on the narrow seas; the Goodwins, I think they call the place; a very dangerous flat and fatal, where the carcases of many a tall ship lie buried, as they say, if my gossip Report be an honest woman of her word.

Salan. I would she were as lying a gossip in that as ever knapped ginger or made her neighbours believe she wept for the death of a third husband. But it is true, without any slips of prolixity or crossing the plain highway of talk, that the good Antonio, the honest Antonio, —O that I had a title good enough to keep his name company! —

Salar. Come, the full stop.

Salan. Ha! what sayest thou? Why, the end is, he hath lost a ship.

Salar. I would it might prove the end of his losses.

Salan. Let me say "amen" betimes, lest the devil cross my prayer, for here he comes in the likeness of a Jew.

Enter Shylock.

How now, Shylock! what news among the merchants?

Shy. You knew, none so well, none so well as you, of my daughter's flight[2].

Salar. That's certain: I, for my part, knew the tailor that made the wings she flew withal.

Salan. And Shylock, for his own part, knew the bird was fledged; and then it is the complexion³ of them all to leave the dam.

Shy. She is damned for it.

Salar. That's certain, if the devil may be her judge.

Shy. My own flesh and blood to rebel!

Salan. Out upon it,⁴ old carrion! rebels it at these years?⁵

Shy. I say, my daughter is my flesh and blood.

Salar. There is more difference between thy flesh and hers than between jet and ivory; more between your bloods than there is between red wine and rhenish⁶. But tell us, do you hear whether Antonio have had any loss at sea or no?

Shy. There I have another bad match⁷: a bankrupt, a prodigal, who dare scarce show his head on the Rialto; a beggar, that was used to come so smug upon the mart; let him look to his bond: he was wont to call me usurer; let him look to his bond: he was wont to lend money for a Christian courtesy; let him look to his bond.

Salar. Why, I am sure, if he forfeit, thou wilt not take his flesh: what's that good for?

Shy. To bait fish withal: if it will feed nothing else, it will feed my revenge. He hath disgraced me, and hindered me half a million; laughed at my losses, mocked at my gains, scorned my nation, thwarted my bargains, cooled my friends, heated mine enemies; and what's his reason? I am a Jew. Hath not a Jew eyes? hath not a Jew hands, organs, dimensions, senses, affections, passions? fed with the same food, hurt with the same weapons, subject to the same diseases, healed by the same means, warmed and cooled by the same winter and summer, as a Christian is? If you prick us, do we not bleed? if you tickle us, do we not laugh? if you poison us, do we not die? and if you wrong us, shall we not revenge? If we are like you in the rest, we will resemble you in that. If a Jew wrong a Christian, what is his humility? Revenge. If a Christian wrong a Jew, what should his sufferance⁸ be by Christian example? Why, revenge. The villany you teach me, I will execute, and it shall go hard but I will better the instruction.

Enter a Servant.

Serv. Gentlemen, my master Antonio is at his house and desires to speak with you both.

Salar. We have been up and down to seek him.

Enter Tubal.

Salan. Here comes another of the tribe: a third cannot be matched, unless the devil himself turn Jew.

[*Exeunt Salan., Salar., and Servant.*]

NOTES

1. **the Rialto:** a commercial centre in Venice, Italy
2. **my daughter's flight:** i.e. Jessica's elopement with Lorenzo
3. **complexion:** character, nature
4. **Out upon it:** an interjection of abhorrence
5. **rebels it at these years?:** Your flesh and blood rebels at your age? Salanio pretends to misunderstand Shylock's reference to his daughter as a reference to his own fleshly nature.
6. **rhenish:** white wine
7. **match:** compact, bargain
8. **sufferance:** an instance of suffering

HAMLET'S ADVICE TO THE PLAYERS

Hamlet. Speak the speech, I pray you, as I pronounced it to you, trippingly on the tongue; but if you mouth it[1], as many of your players do, I had as lief[2] the town-crier spoke my lines. Nor do not saw the air too much with your hand, thus; but use all gently[3]: for in the very torrent, tempest, and—as I may say—the whirlwind of passion, you must acquire and beget a temperance, that may give it smoothness. O! it offends me to the soul to hear a robustious[4] periwig-pated fellow tear a passion to tatters, to very rags, to split the ears of the groundlings[5], who for the most part are capable of nothing but inexplicable dumb-shows and noise: I would have such a fellow whipped for o'erdoing[6] Termagant[7]; it out-herods Herod[8]: pray you, avoid it.

First player. I warrant your honour.

Hamlet. Be not too tame neither, but let your own discretion be your tutor: suit the action to the word, the word to the action; with this special observance, that you o'erstep not the modesty[9] of nature; for anything so overdone is from the purpose[10] of playing, whose end, both at the first and now, was and is, to hold, as 'twere, the mirror up to nature; to show virtue her own feature, scorn[11] her own image, and the very age and body of the time[12] his form and pressure[13]. Now, this overdone, or come tardy off[14], though it make the unskilful[15] laugh, cannot but make the judicious grieve; the censure of the which one[16] must in your allowance[17] o'erweigh a whole theatre of others. O! there be players that I have seen play, and heard others praise, and that highly, not to speak it profanely, that, neither having the accent of Christians nor the gait of Christian, pagan, nor man, have so strutted and bellowed that I have thought some of nature's journeymen had made men and not made them well, they imitated humanity so abominably.

First player. I hope we have reformed that indifferently[18] with us.

Hamlet. O! reform it altogether. And let those that play your clowns speak no more than is set down for them; for there be of them that will themselves laugh, to set on some quantity of barren spectators to laugh too, though in the meantime some necessary question of the play be then to be considered; that's villainous, and shows a most pitiful ambition in the fool that uses it. Go, make you ready.

NOTES
1. **mouth it:** pronounce it too loudly
2. **I had as lief:** I would rather
3. **use all gently:** treat everything mildly
4. **robustious:** boisterous, violent
5. **the groundlings:** the poorer members of the audience who stood on the ground in the theatre, each paying only a penny for admission
6. **o'erdoing:** outdoing
7. **Termagant:** a supposed Saracen god, represented in miracle plays as a violent character
8. **it out-herods Herod:** The performance is even more violent than that of the Jewish tyrant Herod.
9. **modesty:** moderation
10. **from the purpose:** away from or contrary to the purpose
11. **scorn:** folly
12. **the very age and body of the time:** the present age and society
13. **pressure:** impression
14. **come tardy off:** imperfectly done
15. **the unskilful:** the uneducated
16. **the censure of the which one:** the criticism or judgement of the judicious
17. **in your allowance:** in your opinion
18. **indifferently:** to some extent

5

BEN JONSON

(1572–1637)

Ben Jonson was an English dramatist, poet, and critic. He was born in London in 1572, the posthumous son of a clergyman, and educated at Westminster School under the headmaster William Camden. He worked as a bricklayer in his stepfather's employ, saw military service in Flanders, and then became an actor and playwright. A powerful personality and influential writer, he was granted a pension by James I in 1616. The same year saw the publication of a folio edition of his **Works**. He died on 6th August 1637, and was buried in Westminster Abbey under a tombstone inscribed with the phrase "O rare Ben Jonson".

In drama Jonson was a classicist and moralist. His comedies are marked by a clear construction, a lively atmosphere, a satirical tone, a display of peculiar characters, and a brilliance of language; they include two important early works, **Every Man in His Humour** (1598) and **Every Man Out of His Humour** (1599), and four masterpieces, **Volpone, or The Fox** (1605 or 1606), **Epicoene, or The Silent Woman** (1609), **The Alchemist** (1610), and **Bartholomew Fair** (1614). His historical tragedies, **Sejanus** (1603) and **Catiline** (1611), show great learning and insight but lack creative passion. His pastoral play **The Sad Shepherd** was left unfinished. Jonson was virtually the creator of the masque; the best of his works in this genre are **The Masque of Beauty** (1608), **The**

Masque of Queens (1609), and ***Oberon, the Fairy Prince*** (1611).

Jonson also wrote a considerable number of non-dramatic poems. ***To Celia*** ("Drink to me only with thine eyes", 1616) and ***To the Memory of My Beloved Master William Shakespeare*** (1623) are particularly famous.

Jonson's principal prose work is ***Timber, or Discoveries***, printed posthumously in 1640 and containing notes and reflections on literary and other matters. His prose style is plain, neat, and vigorous.

OF STYLE

For a man to write well, there are required three necessaries: to read the best authors, observe the best speakers, and much exercise of his own style. In style, to consider what ought to be written, and after what manner, he must first think and excogitate his matter; then choose his words, and examine the weight of either. Then take care in placing and ranking[1] both matter and words, that the composition be comely; and to do this with diligence and often. No matter how slow the style be at first, so it be laboured and accurate; seek the best, and be not glad of the forward conceits or first words that offer themselves to us, but judge of what we invent, and order what we approve. Repeat[2] often what we have formerly written; which beside that it helps the consequence[3], and makes the juncture better, it quickens the heat of imagination, that often cools in the time of setting down, and gives it new strength, as if it grew lustier by the going back. As we see in the contention of leaping, they jump farthest, that fetch their race largest; or, as in throwing a dart or javelin, we force back our arms to make our loose[4] the stronger. Yet if we have a fair gale of wind, I forbid not the steering out of our sail, so the favour of the gale deceive us not. For all that we invent doth please us in the conception of birth[5], else we would never set it down. But the safest is to return to our judgement, and handle over again those things, the easiness of which might make them justly suspected. So did the best writers in their beginnings; they imposed upon themselves care and industry. They did nothing rashly. They obtained first to write well[6], and then custom made it easy and a habit. By little and little, their matter showed itself to 'em more plentifully; their words answered, their composition followed, and all, as in a well-ordered family, presented itself in the place. So that the sum of all is: ready writing makes not good writing, but good writing brings on ready writing; yet when we think we have got the faculty, it is even then good to resist it, as to give a horse a check sometimes with [a] bit, which doth not so much stop his course as stir his mettle. Again, whither a man's genius is best able to reach thither it should more and more contend, lift and dilate itself; as men of low stature raise themselves on their toes, and so oft-times get even, if not eminent. Besides, as it is fit for grown and able writers to stand of themselves[7], and work with their own strength, to trust and endeavour by their own faculties, so it is fit for the beginner and learner to study others and the best. For the mind and memory are more sharply exercised in comprehending another man's things than our own; and such as accustom themselves, and are familiar with the best authors, shall ever and anon find somewhat[8] of them in themselves, and in the expression of their minds, even when they feel it not; be able to utter something like theirs, which hath an authority above their own. Nay, sometimes it is the reward of a man's study, the praise of quoting another man fitly; and though a man be more prone, and able for one kind of writing than another, yet he must exercise all. For as in an instrument, so in style, there must be a harmony and consent[9] of parts.

NOTES

1. **ranking:** arranging
2. **repeat:** go over
3. **helps the consequence:** improve the effect
4. **our loose:** our act of loosing; our throw
5. **in the conception of birth:** when it is first conceived
6. **obtained first to write well:** aimed first at writing well
7. **stand of themselves:** stand on their own
8. **somewhat:** something
9. **consent:** coordination

6

ROBERT BURTON

(1577–1640)

Robert Burton was an English scholar and clergyman. He was born in Leicestershire on February 8, 1577. Educated at Brasenose College and Christ Church, Oxford, he was appointed vicar of St. Thomas Church in 1616, and became the Rector of Seagrave, Leicestershire, in 1630. He died on January 25, 1640.

Burton's fascinating compendium **The Anatomy of Melancholy** appeared in 1621, and it was an immediate success. He revised and expanded it several times. With his quotations and borrowings from numerous authors and his own comments and digressions, he made this work on the pathology of melancholy into a storehouse of strange tales and recondite learning. His prose style is rather loose and discursive, but sometimes rhetorical and eloquent.

THE POWER OF LOVE

Bocace[1] hath a pleasant tale to this purpose[2], which he borrowed from the Greeks, and which Beroaldus[3] hath turned into Latin, Bebelius[4] into verse, of Cimon and Iphigenia. This Cimon was a fool, a proper man of person, and the governor of Cyprus' son, but a very ass; insomuch that his father, being ashamed of him, sent him to a farm-house he had in the country to be brought up; where by chance, as his manner was, walking alone, he espied a gallant young gentlewoman named Iphigenia, a burgomaster's[5] daughter of Cyprus, with her maid, by a brook side in a little thicket, fast asleep in her smock, where she had newly bathed herself. When Cimon saw her, he stood leaning on his staff, gaping on her immoveable, and in a maze[6]. At last he fell so far in love with the glorious object, that he began to rouse himself up, to bethink what he was, would needs[7] follow her to the city, and for her sake began to be civil, to learn to sing and dance, to play on instruments, and got all those gentleman-like qualities and complements[8] in a short space, which his friends were most glad of. In brief, he became, from an idiot and a clown, to be one of the most complete gentlemen in Cyprus, did many valorous exploits, and all for the love of Mistress Iphigenia[9]. In a word, I may say this much of them all, let them be never so clownish, rude and horrid, Grobians[10] and sluts, if once they be in love, they will be most neat and spruce; for **Omnibus rebus, et nitidis nitoribus antevenit amor**[11]; they will follow the fashion, begin to trick up, and to have a good opinion of themselves; **venustatum enim mater Venus**;[12] a ship is not so long a rigging[13], as a young gentlewoman a trimming[14] up herself, against her sweetheart comes. A painter's shop, a flowery meadow, not so gracious an aspect in Nature's storehouse as a young maid, **nubilis puella**,[15] a Novitsa[16] or Venetian bride, that looks for a husband; or a young man that is her suitor; composed looks, composed gait, clothes, gestures, actions, all composed; all the graces, elegancies in the world are in her face. Their best robes, ribbons, chains, jewels, lawns, linens, laces, spangles, must come on, **praeter quam res patitur student elegantiae**,[17] they are beyond all measure coy, nice, and too curious on a sudden. 'Tis all their study, all their business, how to wear their clothes neat, to be polite and terse[18], and to set out themselves. No sooner doth a young man see his sweetheart coming, but he smugs up[19] himself, pulls up his cloak now fallen about his shoulders, ties his garters, points, sets his band, cuffs, slicks his hair, twirls his beard, etc.

NOTES

1. **Bocace:** Giovanni Boccaccio (1313-1375), Italian poet and story-writer. His chief works are: ***The Decameron*** (1348-1353), a collection of 100 short stories; ***Filocolo*** (1336-1338), a prose romance; ***Philostrato*** (c.1338) and ***Teseida*** (1339-1340), two long poems.
2. **a pleasant tale to this purpose:** the fifth story of the fifth day in the ***Decameron***
3. **Beroaldus:** François Béroalde de Verville (1558-1612), a French scholar
4. **Bebelius:** a Swabian scholar (fl. 1500)
5. **burgomaster:** member of the governing body of a town
6. **in a maze:** in confusion
7. **needs:** of necessity, inevitably
8. **complements:** accomplishments
9. **Mistress Iphigenia:** Miss Iphigenia
10. **Grobians:** boorish slovens
11. ***Omnibus rebus, et nitidis nitoribus antevenit amor***: In all things, even in glittering splendours, Love excels.
12. ***venustatum enim mater Venus***: For Venus is the mother of the graces—Plautus.
13. **a rigging:** a-rigging, on rigging
14. **a trimming:** on trimming
15. ***nubilis puella***: a girl of marriageable age
16. **Novitsa:** (It.) novizia or novizza, a bride
17. ***praeter quam res patitur student elegantiae***: They study elegance more than life allows (T. Balston's translation).
18. **terse:** (obs.) smooth, polished
19. **smugs up:** trims, makes neat

THOMAS OVERBURY

(1581–1613)

Sir Thomas Overbury was an English essayist and poet. He was born in Warwickshire and educated at Queen's College, Oxford, and the Middle Temple, London. A courtier himself, he became the victim of a court intrigue; he was imprisoned in the Tower and poisoned to death. His poem *A Wife* and twenty-one of his "Characters" were posthumously published in 1614. He is chiefly remembered for these Theophrastian character-sketches, which have for the most part a light and satirical tone and a pithy style. "A Fair and Happy Milkmaid", a memorable piece, is a description of an idealized type of character.

A FAIR AND HAPPY MILKMAID

A fair and happy milkmaid is a country wench that is so far from making herself beautiful by art, that one look of hers is able to put all face-physic out of countenance. She knows a fair look is but a dumb orator to commend virtue, therefore minds it not. All her excellences stand in her so silently, as if they had stolen upon her without her knowledge. The lining of her apparel, which is herself, is far better than outsides of tissue[1]; for though she be not arrayed in the spoil of the silkworm[2], she is decked in innocence, a far better wearing. She doth not, with lying long in bed, spoil both her complexion and conditions[3]; nature hath taught her, too, immoderate sleep is rust to the soul; she rises therefore with chanticleer, her dame's cock, and at night makes the lamb her curfew. In milking a cow, and straining the teats through her fingers, it seems that so sweet a milk-press makes the milk the whiter or sweeter; for never came almond-glove[4], or aromatic ointment on her palm to taint it. The golden ears of corn fall and kiss her feet when she reaps them, as if they wished to be bound and led prisoners by the same hand that felled them. Her breath is her own, which scents all the year long of June, like a new-made haycock. She makes her hand hard with labour, and her heart soft with pity; and when winter evenings fall early, sitting at her merry wheel[5], she sings defiance to the giddy wheel of fortune. She doth all things with so sweet a grace, it seems ignorance will not suffer her to do ill, being her mind is to do well. She bestows her year's wages at next fair, and in choosing her garments, counts no bravery in the world like decency. The garden and beehive are all her physic and surgery, and she lives the longer for it. She dares go alone and unfold sheep in the night, and fears no manner of ill, because she means none; yet, to say truth, she is never alone, but is still accompanied with old songs, honest thoughts, and prayers, but short ones; yet they have their efficacy, in that they are not palled[6] with ensuing idle cogitations. Lastly, her dreams are so chaste, that she dare tell them; only a Friday's dream is all her superstition; that she conceals for fear of anger. Thus lives she, and all her care is, she may die in the springtime, to have store of flowers stuck upon her winding-sheet.

NOTES
1. **tissue:** rich or gauzy fabric interwoven with gold or silver threads
2. **the spoil of the silkworm:** silk
3. **conditions:** (obs.) temper
4. **almond-glove:** almond-oil, cosmetic made of almonds
5. **her merry wheel:** her spinning-wheel
6. **palled:** made feeble

8

THOMAS HOBBES

(1588−1679)

    Thomas Hobbes was an English philosopher and man of letters. He was born in Wiltshire on April 5, 1588, the son of a country parson. In 1603 he entered Magdalen Hall, Oxford, where he graduated five years later. He served as tutor to several boys from noble families. He lived in Paris during 1640−1651, and instructed the Prince of Wales in mathematics from 1646 to 1648. On his return to England in 1652 he submitted to the Council of State. After the Restoration he was granted a pension by Charles Ⅱ. He died on December 4, 1679.

    Hobbes was a materialist and strongly opposed to supernaturalism. His chief works are **Leviathan** (1651) and **Of Liberty and Necessity** (1654). He held that the sovereign should have absolute power so as to give peace and security to the individuals. His prose is direct, concise, and scattered with metaphor and irony.

OF SPEECH

The invention of "printing", though ingenious, compared with the invention of "letters", is no great matter. But who was the first that found the use of letters is not known. He that first brought them into Greece, men say was Cadmus, the son of Agenor, king of Phoenicia. A profitable invention for continuing the memory of time past, and the conjunction of mankind, dispersed into so many and distant regions of the earth; and withal difficult, as proceeding from a watchful observation of the divers motions of the tongue, palate, lips, and other organs of speech; whereby to make as many differences of characters to remember them. But the most noble and profitable invention of all other was that of "speech", consisting of "names" or "appellations"[1], and their connexion; whereby men register their thoughts; recall them when they are past; and also declare them one to another for mutual utility and conversation; without which, there had been amongst men neither commonwealth, nor society, nor contract, nor peace, no more than amongst lions, bears, and wolves. The first author of speech was God himself, that instructed Adam how to name such creatures as he presented to his sight; for the scripture goeth no further in this matter. But this was sufficient to direct him to add more names as the experience and use of the creatures should give him occasion; and to join them in such manner by degrees, as to make himself understood; and so by succession of time, so much language might be gotten as he had found use for; though not so copious as an orator or philosopher has need of: for I do not find anything in the Scripture, out of which, directly or by consequence, can be gathered, that Adam was taught the names of all figures, numbers, measures, colours, sounds, fancies, relations, much less the names of words and speech, as **general, special, affirmative, negative, interrogative, optative, infinitive**, all which are useful; and least of all, of **entity, intentionality, quiddity**, and other insignificant words of the school.

But all this language gotten, and augmented by Adam and his posterity, was again lost at the Tower of Babel², when, by the hand of God, every man was stricken, for his rebellion, with an oblivion of his former language. And being hereby forced to disperse themselves into several parts of the world, it must needs be, that the diversity of tongues that now is, proceeded by degrees from them, in such manner as Need, the mother of all inventions, taught them; and in tract of time grew everywhere more copious.

  The general use of speech is to transfer our mental discourse into verbal; or the train of our thoughts into a train of words; and that for two commodities³, whereof one is the registering of the consequences of our thoughts; which being apt to slip out of our memory, and put us to a new labour, may again be recalled by such words as they were marked by. So that the first use of names is to serve for "marks" or "notes" of remembrance. Another is, when many use the same words, to signify, by their connexion and order, one to another, what they conceive or think of each matter; and also what they desire, fear, or have any other passion for. And for this use they are called "signs". Special uses of speech are these; first, to register, what by cogitation, we find to be the cause of anything, present or past; and what we find things present or past may produce, or effect; which, in sum, is acquiring of arts. Secondly, to show to others that knowledge which we have attained, which is, to counsel and teach one another. Thirdly, to make known to others our wills and purposes, that we may have the mutual help of one another. Fourthly, to please and delight ourselves and others, by playing with our words, for pleasure or ornament, innocently.

  To these uses, there are also four correspondent abuses. First, when men register their thoughts wrong, by the inconstancy of the signification of their words; by which they register for their conception that which they never conceived, and so deceive themselves. Secondly, when they use words metaphorically; that is, in other sense than that they are ordained for; and thereby deceive others. Thirdly, when by words they declare that to be their will, which is not. Fourthly, when they use them to grieve one another; for seeing Nature hath armed living creatures, some with teeth, some with horns, and some with hands, to grieve an enemy, it is but an abuse of speech to grieve him with the tongue, unless it be one whom we are obliged to govern; and then it is not to grieve, but to correct and amend.... In the right definition of names, lies the first use of speech; which is the acquisition of science. And in wrong or no definitions lies the first abuse; from which proceed all false and senseless tenets; which make those men that take their instruction from the authority of books, and not from their own meditation to be as much below the condition of ignorant men, as men endued with true science are above it. For between true science and erroneous doctrines, Ignorance is in the middle.

NOTES
1. **appellations:** identifying names or titles
2. **the Tower of Babel:** the tower built in an attempt to reach heaven, which God frustrated by confusing the languages of its builders so that they could not understand one another (Genesis X1: 1-9)
3. **commodities:** (obs.) advantages, conveniences

(9)

IZAAK WALTON

(1593–1683)

Izaak Walton was an English writer, a pioneer in biography and piscatory literature. He was born at Stafford on August 9, 1593. He was apprenticed to a London draper and iron-monger, worked as a shopkeeper in Fleet Street, and retired in 1644. His literary career must have begun when he was in business. He died at Winchester on December 15, 1683. Walton published the **Lives** of five churchmen, Donne (1640, 1658), Wotton (1651), Hooker (1665), Herbert (1670), and Sanderson (1678); they are full of intimate details and sympathetic in tone. **The Compleat Angler**, his most famous work, was published in 1653 and issued in an enlarged edition in 1655. Ostensibly a guide to the art of angling, it is really a charming idyll in praise of the English countryside and healthful pleasures. Walton's prose is limpid and natural.

THE MILKMAID AND HER SONG

Piscator[1]. But turn out of the way a little, good scholar[2]! towards yonder high honeysuckle hedge; there we'll sit and sing, whilst this shower falls so gently upon the teeming earth, and gives yet a sweeter smell to the lovely flowers that adorn these verdant meadows.

Look! under that broad beech-tree I sat down, when I was last this way a-fishing; and the birds in the adjoining grove seemed to have a friendly contention with an echo, whose dead[3] voice seemed to live in a hollow tree near to the brow of that primrose-hill. There I sat viewing the silver streams glide silently towards their centre, the tempestuous sea; yet sometimes opposed by rugged roots and pebble-stones, which broke their waves, and turned them into foam; and sometimes I beguiled time by viewing the harmless lambs; some leaping securely[4] in the cool shade, whilst others sported themselves in the cheerful sun; and saw others craving comfort from the swollen udders of their bleating dams. As I thus sat, these and other sights had so fully possest my soul with content, that I thought, as the poet has happily exprest it,

> I was for that time lifted above earth;
> And possest joys not promis'd in my birth.

As I left this place, and entered into the next field, a second pleasure entertained me; 'twas a handsome Milkmaid, that had not yet attained so much age and wisdom as to load her mind with any fears of many things that will never be, as too many men too often do; but she cast away all care, and sung like a nightingale. Her voice was good, and the ditty fitted for it; 'twas that smooth song which was made by Kit Marlowe[5], now at least fifty years ago; and the Milkmaid's mother sung an answer to it, which was made by Sir Walter Raleigh in his younger days[6].

They were old-fashioned poetry, but choicely good; I think much better than the strong lines that are now in fashion in this critical age. Look yonder! on my word, yonder, they both be a-milking again. I will give her the Chub, and persuade them to sing those two songs to us.

God speed you, good woman! I have been a-fishing; and am going to Bleak Hall[7] to my bed; and having caught more fish than will sup myself and my friend, I will bestow this upon you and your daughter, for I use to sell none.

Milk-Woman. Marry! God requite you, Sir, and we'll eat it cheerfully. And if you come this way a-fishing two months hence, a-grace of God! I'll give you a syllabub of new verjuice[8], in a new-made hay-cock, for it, and my Maudlin shall sing you one of her best ballads; for she and I both love all Anglers, they be such honest, civil, quiet men. In the mean time will you drink a draught of red cow's milk? You shall have it freely.

Piscator. No, I thank you; but, I pray, do us a courtesy that shall stand you and your daughter in nothing, and yet we will think ourselves still something in your debt; it is but to sing us a song that was sung by your daughter when I last passed over this meadow, about eight or nine days since.

Milk-Woman. What song was it, I pray? Was it "Come, Shepherds, deck your herds"? or, "As at noon Dulcina rested"? or, "Phillida flouts me"? or, "Chevy Chace"? or, "Johnny Armstrong"? or, "Troy Town"?

Piscator. No, it is none of those; it is a song that your daughter sung the first part, and you sung the answer to it.

Milk-Woman. O, I know it now; I learned the first part in my golden age, when I was about the age of my poor daughter; and the latter part, which indeed fits me best now, but two or three years ago, when the cares of the world began to take hold of me; but you shall, God willing, hear them both; and sung as well as we can, for we both love Anglers. Come, Maudlin, sing the first part to the gentlemen with a merry heart, and I'll sing the second, when you have done.

NOTES

1. **Piscator**: Angler, the chief character in **The Compleat Angler**
2. **good scholar**: Venator (or Hunter), who has become a pupil of Piscator

3. **dead:** dull, not resonant
4. **securely:** without care
5. **that smooth song which was made by Kit Marlowe:** Christopher Marlowe's poem, "The Passionate Shepherd to His Love", beginning with the line, "Come, live with me and be my love."
6. **an answer to it, which was made by Sir Walter Raleigh in his younger days:** Sir Walter Raleigh's poem, "The Nymph's Reply to the Shepherd", beginning with the line, "If all the world and love were young."
7. **Bleak Hall:** a rural inn on the bank of the River Lea
8. **a syllabub of new verjuice:** a dish of cream mixed with juice of unripe fruit

10

JOHN EARLE

(1601–1665)

John Earle was an English bishop and writer. He was born in York and educated at Merton College, Oxford. He became a tutor to Prince Charles in 1641, and during the latter's exile in France served as his chaplain. After the Restoration, he was appointed Bishop of Worcester in 1662 and translated to the see of Salisbury in 1663. His death occurred on November 17, 1665.

In 1628 appeared *Microcosmographie*, a famous collection of fifty-four Theophrastian character-sketches mostly by Earle's hand. He describes diverse social and moral types with sympathetic insight and ironical wit. His prose has a pointed style.

AN ANTIQUARY

He is a man strangely thrifty of time past, and an enemy indeed to his maw[1], whence he fetches out many things when they are now all rotten and stinking. He is one that hath that unnatural disease to be enamoured of old age and wrinkles, and loves all things (as Dutchmen do cheese), the better for being mouldy and worm-eaten. He is of our religion, because we say it is most ancient; and yet a broken statue would almost make him an idolater. A great admirer he is of the rust of old monuments, and reads only those characters, where time hath eaten out the letters. He will go you forty miles to see a saint's well or a ruined abbey; and if there be but a cross or stone foot-stool in the way, he'll be considering it so long, till he forgets his journey. His estate consists much in shekels[2], and Roman coins; and he hath more pictures of Caesar[3] than James[4] or Elizabeth[5]. Beggars cozen him with musty things which they have raked from dunghills, and he preserves their rags for precious relics. He loves no library, but where there are more spiders' volumes than authors', and looks with great admiration on the antique work of cob-webs. Printed books he contemns, as a novelty of this latter age, but a manuscript he pores on everlastingly, especially if the cover be all moth-eaten, and the dust make a parenthesis between every syllable. He would give all the books in his study (which are rarities all) for one of the old Roman binding, or six lines of Tully[6] in his own hand. His chamber is hung commonly with strange beasts' skins, and is a kind of charnel-house of bones extraordinary; and his discourse upon them, if you will hear him, shall last longer. His very attire is that which is the eldest out of fashion [and you may pick a criticism[7] out of his breeches]. He never looks upon himself till he is grey-haired, and then he is pleased with his own antiquity. His grave does not fright him, for he has been used to sepulchres, and he likes death the better, because it gathers him to his fathers.

NOTES

1. **his maw:** time's stomach
2. **shekels:** Jewish silver coins
3. **Caesar:** Gaius Julius Caesar (100–44 B.C.), Roman general and statesman
4. **James:** James Ⅰ (1566–1625), king of England (1603–1625) and (as James Ⅵ) king of Scotland (1567–1625)
5. **Elizabeth:** Elizabeth Ⅰ (1533–1603), queen of England (1558–1603)
6. **Tully:** familiar name for Marcus Tullius Cicero (106–43 B.C.), Roman statesman, orator and philosopher
7. **pick a criticism:** find something queer

111

THOMAS BROWNE

(1605–1682)

Sir Thomas Browne was an English physician and prose-writer. He was born in London on 19th October 1605, was educated at Winchester and Oxford, studied medicine abroad and earned an M.D. degree from Leyden University in 1633. From 1637 till the end of his life he practised the medical profession in Norwich. He was knighted in 1671 and died on 19th October, 1682.

Browne's best-known works are **Religio Medici** (1642, revised 1643) and **Hydriotaphia, Urn Burial** (1658). The first is a volume of personal reflections on matters of religious faith and on man's relations to his fellows; the second, a meditative account of burial methods in many nations. These books are admired for their rich, ornate style rather than the obscure or obvious thoughts contained in them. Browne's characteristic prose is elaborately wrought, full of learned words and phrases, stately periods, and sonorous cadences.

THE EMBLEMS OF MORTAL VANITIES

Now since these dead bones have already outlasted the living ones of Methuselah¹, and in a yard under ground, and thin walls of clay, out-worn all the strong and spacious buildings above it, and quietly rested under the drums and tramplings of three conquests²: what prince can promise such diuturnity³ unto his relics, or might not gladly say,

*Sic ego componi versus in ossa velim?*⁴

Time, which antiquates antiquities, and hath an art to make dust of all things, hath yet spared these minor monuments.

In vain we hope to be known by open and visible conservatories, when to be unknown was the means of their continuation, and obscurity their protection. If they died by violent hands, and were thrust into their urns, these bones become considerable, and some old philosophers would honour them, whose souls they conceived most pure, which were thus snatched from their bodies, and to retain a stronger propension⁵ unto them; whereas they weariedly left a languishing corpse, and with faint desires of reunion. If they fell by long and aged decay, yet wrapt up in the bundle of time, they fall into indistinction⁶, and make but one blot with infants. If we begin to die when we live, and long life be but a prolongation of death, our life is a sad composition; we live with death, and die not in a moment. How many pulses made up the life of Methuselah, were work⁷ for Archimedes⁸: common counters sum up the life of Moses his man⁹. Our days become considerable, like petty sums, by minute accumulations; where numerous fractions make up but small round numbers; and our days of a span long, make not one little finger¹⁰.

If the nearness of our last necessity¹¹ brought a nearer conformity into it, there were a happiness in hoary hairs, and no calamity in half-senses¹². But the long habit of living indisposeth us[13] for dying; when avarice makes us the sport of death, when even David[14] grew politicly[15] cruel, and Solomon[16] could hardly be said to be the wisest of men. But many are too early old, and before the date of age. Adversity stretcheth our days, misery makes Alcmena's nights[17], and time hath no wings unto it. But the most tedious being is that which can unwish itself, content to be nothing, or never to have been, which was beyond the malcontent of Job[18], who cursed not the day of his life, but his nativity; content to have so far been, as to have a title to future being, although he had lived here but in an hidden state of life, and as it were an abortion.

What song the Sirens sang, or what name Achilles assumed when he hid himself among women, though puzzling questions, are not beyond all conjecture[19]. What time the persons of these ossuaries entered the famous nations of the dead, and slept with princes and counselors, might admit a wide solution[20]. But who were the proprietaries of these bones, or what bodies these ashes made up, were a question above antiquarism; not to be resolved by man, nor easily perhaps by spirits, except we consult the provincial guardians[21], or tutelary observators[22]. Had they made as good provision for their names, as they have done for their relics, they had not so grossly erred in the art of perpetuation. But to subsist in bones, and be but pyramidally[23] extant, is a fallacy in duration. Vain ashes which in the oblivion of names, persons, times, and sexes, have found unto themselves a fruitless continuation, and only arise unto late posterity, as emblems of mortal vanities, antidotes against pride, vainglory, and madding vices. Pagan vainglories which thought the world might last for ever, had encouragement for ambition; and, finding no Atropos[24] unto the immortality of their names, were never damped with the necessity of oblivion. Even old ambitions had the advantage of ours, in the attempts of their vainglories, who acting early, and before the probable meridian of time, have by this time found great accomplishment of their designs, whereby the ancient heroes have already outlasted their monuments and mechanical preservations. But in this latter scene of time, we cannot expect such mummies unto our memories, when ambition may fear the prophecy of Elias[25], and Charles the Fifth[26] can never hope to live within two Methuselahs of Hector[27].

And therefore, restless unquiet for the diuturnity of our memories unto present considerations seems a vanity almost out of date, and superannuated piece of folly. We cannot hope to live so long in our names, as some have done in their persons. One face of Janus[28] holds no proportion unto the other. 'Tis too late to be ambitious. The great mutations of the world are acted, or time may be too short for our designs. To extend our memories by monuments whose death we daily pray for, and whose duration we cannot hope without injury to our expectations in the advent of the last day, were a contradiction to our beliefs. We whose generations are ordained in this setting part of time, are providentially taken off from such imaginations; and, being necessitated to eye the remaining particle of futurity, are naturally constituted unto thoughts of the next world, and cannot excusably decline the consideration of that duration which maketh pyramids pillars of snow, and all that's past a moment.

NOTES

1. **Methuselah:** a patriarch who is said to have lived 969 years (Genesis V. 27)
2. **three conquests:** the Roman, Saxon, and Norman Conquests of Celtic Britain
3. **diuturnity:** long life
4. *Sic ego componi versus in ossa velim*: Thus I, when turned to bones, should wish to rest (Tibullus).
5. **propension:** inclination, attraction
6. **indistinction:** indistinctness
7. **were work:** would be working
8. **Archimedes:** Greek mathematician and physicist (c. 287−212 B.C.)
9. **Moses his man:** Moses' man; the ordinary man. Psalm XC.10 says: " The days of our years are three-score years and ten."
10. **one little finger:** "According to the ancient arithmetic of the hand wherein the little finger of the right hand contracted, signified an hundred." (Browne's note)
11. **our last necessity:** our death
12. **half-senses:** weakened senses
13. **indisposeth us:** makes us unfit

14. **David:** the second king of the Hebrews (1015−975 B.C.)
15. **politicly:** (arch.) politically
16. **Solomon:** son of David and king of Israel (c. 970−933 B.C.)
17. **Alcmena's nights:** Alcmena in Greek mythology was the wife of Amphitryon. Zeus paid a surreptitious visit to her, and enjoyed it so much that he prevented the sun from rising, thus producing three nights in a row.
18. **the malcontent of Job:** Job was a prosperous good man whose patience and piety were tried by dreadful misfortunes. See "The Book of Job", iii. 3-12.
19. **not beyond all conjecture:** Tiberius ludicrously tested Grammarians with those "puzzling questions".
20. **a wide solution:** an approximate solution
21. **provincial guardians:** public angelic protectors
22. **tutelary observators:** personal angelic protectors
23. **pyramidally:** like a pyramid
24. **Atropos:** In Greek mythology there were three Fates: Clotho spun the thread of human life on her spindle, Lachesis measured it with her rod, and Atropos snipped it with her shears.
25. **the prophecy of Elias:** "That the world will last but six thousand years." (Browne's note)
26. **Charles the Fifth:** the Holy Roman Emperor, who was born in 1500, reigned during 1519−1556, and died in 1558
27. **Hector:** Hector in Greek legend was the principal hero of Troy.
28. **Janus:** (Roman myth.) Roman god of gates and doorways, represented with two faces looking in opposite directions

12

JOHN MILTON

(1608–1674)

John Milton was an English poet and prose polemicist. A scrivener's son, he was born in London on December 9, 1608, and was educated at St. Paul's School, London, and Christ's College, Cambridge. On receiving his M.A. degree from Cambridge in July 1632, he retired to his father's estate in Horton, Buckinghamshire, for a life of study. He travelled in Italy from June 1638, and returned to England in July 1639 to support the Puritan cause. In 1649, after the execution of Charles I, he was appointed Latin Secretary to the Commonwealth. It was his duty to put the state correspondence into Latin, and he also wrote many pamphlets defending the policy of the new government. In 1652 he became totally blind. After the Restoration in 1660 he went into retirement on the outskirts of London. He composed three great long poems by dictating them to his daughters and his friends. He died in Bunhill House in November 1674, and was buried in St. Giles' Church, with a monument erected to his memory in Westminster Abbey.

Milton's famous poetical works are the following: **L'Allegro** (1632) and **Il Penseroso** (1632), descriptive poems; **Comus** (1634), a masque; **Lycidas** (1637), a pastoral elegy; **Paradise Lost** (1667) and **Paradise Regained** (1671), epics; **Samson Agonistes** (1671), a tragedy. The last three poems are written in magnificent blank verse, and **Paradise Lost** is the only great epic in the English language.

Milton published numerous prose pamphlets during his middle life, including the following: ***On the Reformation in England*** (1641) and ***The Reason of Church Government Urged Against Prelaty*** (1642), which were anti-episcopal; ***The Doctrine and Discipline of Divorce*** (1643), which favoured divorce; ***Of Education*** (1644), which was concerned with humanist instruction; ***Areopagitica*** (1644), which was a passionate plea for the freedom of the press; ***The Tenures of Kings and Magistrates*** (1649) and ***The Ready and Easy Way to Establish a Free Commonwealth*** (1660), which dealt with political problems. These tracts reveal the impetuous idealist and staunch Parliamentarian. Milton's prose does not make easy reading, for it is laden with elaborate periods and learned vocabulary. But at its best it can be, as in ***Areopagitica***, lucid, eloquent, and powerful.

ON CENSORSHIP

Good and evil we know in the field of this world grow up together almost inseparably; and the knowledge of good is so involved and interwoven with the knowledge of evil, and in so many cunning resemblances hardly to be discerned, that those confused seeds[1] which were imposed upon Psyche as an incessant labour to cull out, and sort asunder, were not more intermixed. It was from out the rind of one apple tasted, that the knowledge of good and evil, as two twins cleaving together, leaped forth into the world. And perhaps this is that doom which Adam fell into of knowing good and evil, that is to say of knowing good by evil.

As therefore the state of man is, what wisdom can there be to choose, what continence to forbear without the knowledge of evil? He that can apprehend and consider vice with all her baits and seeming pleasures, and yet abstain, and yet distinguish, and yet prefer that which is truly better, he is the true warfaring Christian. I cannot praise a fugitive and cloistered virtue, unexercised and unbreathed, that never sallies out and sees her adversary, but slinks out of the race, where that immortal garland[2] is to be run for, not without dust and heat. Assuredly we bring not innocence into the world, we bring impurity much rather; that which purifies us is trial, and trial is by what is contrary. That virtue therefore which is but a youngling in the contemplation of evil, and knows not the utmost that vice promises to her followers, and rejects it, is but a blank virtue, not a pure; her whiteness is but an excremental[3] whiteness; which was the reason why our sage and serious poet Spenser[4], whom I dare be known to think a better teacher than Scotus[5] or Aquinas[6], describing true temperance under the person of Guyon[7], brings him in with his palmer through the cave of Mammon[8], and the bower of earthly bliss, that he might see and know, and yet abstain. Since therefore the knowledge and survey of vice is in this world so necessary to the constituting of human virtue, and the scanning of error to the confirmation of truth, how can we more safely, and with less danger, scout into the regions of sin and falsity than by reading all manner of tractates⁹ and hearing all manner of reason? And this is the benefit which may be had of books promiscuously read.

•   •   •   •   •   •   •

If we think to regulate printing, thereby to rectify manners, we must regulate all recreations and pastimes, all that is delightful to man. No music must be heard, nor song be set or sung, but what is grave and doric¹⁰. There must be licensing dancers, that no gesture, motion, or deportment be taught our youth but what by their allowance shall be thought honest; for such Plato¹¹ was provided of. It will ask more than the work of twenty licensers to examine all the lutes, the violins, and the guitars in every house; they must not be suffered to prattle as they do, but must be licensed what they may say. And who shall silence all the airs and madrigals that whisper softness in chambers? The windows also, and the balconies must be thought on; there are shrewd books with dangerous frontispieces set to sale; who shall prohibit them? Shall twenty licensers? The villages also must have their visitors to inquire what lectures the bagpipe and the rebec¹² reads, even to the ballatry and the gamut of every municipal fiddler, for these are the countryman's Arcadias and his Montemayors¹³. Next, what more national corruption, for which England hears ill abroad, than household gluttony? Who shall be the rectors of our daily rioting? And what shall be done to inhibit the multitudes that frequent those houses where drunkenness is sold and harboured? Our garments also should be referred to the licensing of some more sober work-masters to see them cut into a less wanton garb. Who shall regulate all the mixed conversation of our youth male and female together, as is the fashion of this country? Who shall still appoint what shall be discoursed, what presumed, and no further? Lastly, who shall forbid and separate all idle resort, all evil company? These things will be, and must be; but how they shall be least hurtful, how least enticing, herein consists the grave and governing wisdom of a state. To sequester out of the world into Atlantic and Utopian polities¹⁴, which never can be drawn into use, will not mend our condition; but to ordain wisely as in this world of evil, in the midst whereof God hath placed us unavoidably. Nor is it Plato's licensing of books will do this, which necessarily pulls along with it so many other kinds of licensing, as will make us all both ridiculous and weary, and yet frustrate; but those unwritten, or at least unconstraining laws of virtuous education, religious and civil nurture, which Plato there mentions as the bonds and ligaments of the commonwealth, the pillars and the sustainers of every written statute; these they be which will bear chief sway in such matters as these, when all licensing will be easily eluded. Impunity and remissness, for certain, are the bane of a commonwealth; but here the great art lies to discern in what the law is to bid restraint and punishment, and in what things persuasion only is to work. If every action which is good, or evil in man at ripe years, were to be under pittance[15] and prescription and compulsion, what were virtue but a name, what praise could be then due to well-doing, what gramercy[16] to be sober, just, or continent?

NOTES

1. **those confused seeds:** the heap of many kinds of seeds that Venus ordered Psyche to sort out
2. **that immortal garland:** the crown of true virtue
3. **excremental:** exterior, superficial
4. **Spenser:** Edmund Spenser (1552–1599), the great English poet whose works include *The Faerie Queene* (1590–1596), *The Shepherd's Calendar* (1579), *Amoretti* (1595), *Epithalamion* (1595), and *Prothalamion* (1596)
5. **Scotus:** John Duns Scotus (?1265–1308), a Scottish scholastic philosopher and an opponent to the theology of Thomas Aquinas
6. **Aquinas:** Thomas Aquinas (1225–1274), an Italian theologian and scholastic philosopher
7. **Guyon:** Book II of *The Faerie Queene* is concerned with "The Legend of Sir Guyon or of Temperance".
8. **Mammon:** riches; the devil of covetousness
9. **tractates:** treatises, tracts
10. **doric:** Dorian, (of music) simple and solemn
11. **Plato:** Plato (428 or 427–348 or 347 B.C.) was a famous Greek philosopher and the author of some 25 dialogues and *The Apology*. His dialogues include *Euthyphro*, *Crito*,

Phaedo, The Symposium, The Republic, and *The Laws*. He maintains in *The Republic* that writers of fiction must be banished from his ideal state and that no poetry can be admitted into it but hymns to the gods and songs in praise of great men.

12. **rebec:** medieval three-stringed fiddle with a lute-shaped body
13. **Montemayors:** Jorge de Montemayor (c. 1520–1561), who was a Spanish poet and the author of a pastoral romance called *Diana Enamorada*.
14. **Atlantic and Utopian polities:** Bacon's *New Atlantis* (1626) and More's *Utopia* (1516) describe imaginary and ideal states
15. **pittance:** small allowance, rationing
16. **gramercy:** (arch.) thanks, reward

13

ABRAHAM COWLEY

(1618–1667)

Abraham Cowley was an English poet and essayist. He was born in London in 1618, the seventh and posthumous son of a wealthy stationer, attended Westminster School, London, and studied at Trinity College, Cambridge, where he became a Fellow in 1640. On the outbreak of the Civil War he left Cambridge for Oxford. In 1644 he left Oxford for Paris, where he served the Royalist cause. He returned to England in 1654, was briefly imprisoned in 1655, and tried to ingratiate himself with the Commonwealth government with conciliatory remarks in the preface to his 1656 volume of **Poems**. After the Restoration, from which he derived no substantial benefits, he retired to the country. He died at Chertsey, Surrey, on July 28, 1667, and was buried in Westminster Abbey.

Cowley's principal poetical works are **The Mistress** (1647), a series of love poems; and the 1656 volume of **Poems**, which contains **Miscellanies** (1656), a collection of lyrics, **Davideis** (1656), an epic, and **Pindaric Odes** (1656). His verse is animated and witty, but deficient in passion. Among Cowley's prose works, the **Several Discourses by Way of Essays**, published posthumously in 1668, is an outstanding book. The essays reveal his mind and personality, and are marked by a smooth, easy, familiar style.

OF MYSELF

It is a hard and nice[1] subject for a man to write of himself; it grates his own heart to say anything of disparagement and the reader's ears to hear anything of praise from him. There is no danger from me of offending him in this kind; neither my mind, nor my body, nor my fortune allow me any materials for that vanity. It is sufficient for my own contentment that they have preserved me from being scandalous, or remarkable on the defective side. But besides that, I shall here speak of myself only in relation to the subject of these precedent discourses[2], and shall be likelier thereby to fall into the contempt than rise up to the estimation of most people. As far as my memory can return back into my past life, before I knew or was capable of guessing what the world, or glories, or business of it were, the natural affections[3] of my soul gave me a secret bent of aversion from them, as some plants are said to turn away from others, by an antipathy imperceptible to themselves and inscrutable to man's understanding. Even when I was a very young boy at school, instead of running about on holidays and playing with my fellows, I was wont to steal from them and walk into the fields, either alone with a book, or with some one companion, if I could find any of the same temper[4]. I was then, too, so much an enemy to all constraint, that my masters could never prevail on me, by any persuasions or encouragements, to learn without book the common rules of grammar, in which they dispensed with[5] me alone, because they found I made a shift to do the usual exercise out of my own reading and observation. That I was then of the same mind as I am now (which I confess I wonder at myself) may appear by the latter end of an ode[6] which I made when I was but thirteen years old, and which was then printed with many other verses. The beginning of it is boyish, but of this part which I here set down, if a very little were corrected, I should hardly now be much ashamed.

IX.

This only grant me, that my means may lie
Too low for envy, for contempt too high.
Some honour I would have,
Not from great deeds, but good alone.
The unknown are better than ill known.
Rumour can ope the grave;
Acquaintance I would have, but when 't depends
Not on the number, but the choice of friends.

X.

Books should, not business, entertain the light,
And sleep, as undisturbed as death, the night.
My house a cottage, more
Than palace, and should fitting be
For all my use, no luxury.
My garden painted o'er
With Nature's hand, not Art's; and pleasures yield,
Horace[7] might envy in his Sabine field[8].

XI.

Thus would I double my life's fading space,
For he that runs it well, twice runs his race.
And in this true delight,
These unbought sports, this happy state,
I would not fear, nor wish my fate,
But boldly say each night,
To-morrow let my sun his beams display,
Or in clouds hide them—I have lived to-day.

You may see by it I was even then acquainted with the poets (for the conclusion is taken out of Horace), and perhaps it was the immature and immoderate love of them which stamped first, or rather engraved, these characters in me. They were like letters cut into the bark of a young tree, which with the tree still grow proportionably. But how this love came to be produced in me so early is a hard question. I believe I can tell the particular little chance that filled my head first with such chimes of verse as have never since left ringing there. For I remember when I began to read, and to take some pleasure in it, there was wont to lie in my mother's parlour (I know not by what accident, for she herself never in her life read any book but of devotion), but there was wont to lie Spenser's works; this I happened to fall upon, and was infinitely delighted with the stories of the knights, and giants, and monsters, and brave houses, which I found everywhere there (though my understanding had little to do with all this); and by degrees with the tinkling of the rhyme and dance of the numbers, so that I think I had read him all over before I was twelve years old, and was thus made a poet as irremediably as a child is made an eunuch. With these affections of mind, and my heart wholly set upon letters, I went to the university[9], but was soon torn from thence by that violent public storm[10] which would suffer nothing to stand where it did, but rooted up every plant, even from the princely cedars to me, the hyssop. Yet I had as good fortune as could have befallen me in such a tempest; for I was cast by it into the family of one of the best persons[11], and into the court of one of the best princesses[12] of the world. Now though I was here engaged in ways most contrary to the original design of my life, that is, into much company, and no small business, and into a daily sight of greatness, both militant and triumphant, for that was the state then of the English and French courts; yet all this was so far from altering my opinion, that it only added the confirmation of reason to that which was before but natural inclination. I saw plainly all the paint[13] of that kind of life, the nearer I came to it; and that beauty which I did not fall in love with when, for aught I knew, it was real, was not like to bewitch or entice me when I saw that it was adulterate. I met with several great persons, whom I liked very well, but could not perceive that any part of their greatness was to be liked or desired, no more than I would be glad or content to be in a storm, though I saw many ships which rid safely and bravely in it. A storm would not agree with my stomach, if it did with my courage. Though I was in a crowd of as good company as could be found anywhere, though I was in business of great and honourable trust, though I ate at the best table, and enjoyed the best conveniences for present subsistence that ought to be desired by a man of my condition in banishment and public distresses, yet I could not abstain from renewing my old schoolboy's wish in a copy of verses to the same effect.

> Well then; I now do plainly see,
> This busy world and I shall ne'er agree, &c.[14]

And I never then proposed to myself any other advantage from His Majesty's happy restoration, but the getting into some moderately convenient retreat in the country, which I thought in that case I might easily have compassed, as well as some others, with no greater probabilities or pretences, have arrived to extraordinary fortunes. But I had before written a shrewd prophecy against myself, and I think Apollo[15] inspired me in the truth, though not in the elegance of it.

> Thou, neither great at court nor in the war,
> Nor at th' exchange shalt be, nor at the wrangling bar;
> Content thyself with the small barren praise,
> Which neglected verse does raise, &c.[16]

However, by the failing of the forces which I had expected, I did not quit the design which I had resolved on; I cast myself into it *A corps perdu*[17], without making capitulations or taking counsel of fortune. But God laughs at a man who says to his soul, "Take thy ease"[18]: I met presently not only with many little encumbrances and impediments, but with so much sickness (a new misfortune to me) as would have spoiled the happiness of an emperor as well as mine. Yet I do neither repent nor alter my course. ***Non ego perfidum dixi sacramentum***.[19]

Nothing shall separate me from a mistress which I have loved so long, and have now at last married, though she neither has brought me a rich portion, nor lived yet so quietly with me as I hoped from her.

> —*Nec vos, dulcissima mundi*
> *Nomina, vos Musae, libertas, otia, libri,*
> *Hortique sylvaeque anima remanente relinquam.*

> Nor by me e'er shall you,
> You of all names the sweetest, and the best,
> You Muses, books, and liberty, and rest;
> You gardens, fields, and woods forsaken be,
> As long as life itself forsakes not me.

But this is a very petty ejaculation. Because I have concluded all the other chapters with a copy of verses, I will maintain the humour to the last.

MARTIAL[20], LIB[21]. 10, EP. 47.

Vitam quae faciunt beatiorem, etc.

> SINCE, dearest friend, 'tis your desire to see
> A true receipt of happiness from me;
> These are the chief ingredients, if not all:
> Take an estate neither too great nor small,
> Which *quantum sufficit*[22] the doctors call;
> Let this estate from parents' care descend:
> The getting it too much of life does spend.
> Take such a ground, whose gratitude may be
> A fair encouragement for industry.
> Let constant fires the winter's fury tame,

And let thy kitchens be a vestal flame.[23]
Thee to the town let never suit at law,
And rarely, very rarely, business draw.
Thy active mind in equal temper keep,
In undisturbed peace, yet not in sleep.
Let exercise a vigorous health maintain,
Without which all the composition's vain.
In the same weight prudence and innocence take,
Ana[24] of each does the just mixture make.
But a few friendships wear, and let them be
By Nature and by Fortune fit for thee.
Instead of art and luxury in food,
Let mirth and freedom make thy table good.
If any cares into thy daytime creep,
At night, without wine's opium, let them sleep.
Let rest, which Nature does to darkness wed,
And not lust, recommend to thee thy bed.
Be satisfied, and pleased with what thou art;
Act cheerfully and well the allotted part.
Enjoy the present hour, be thankful for the past,
And neither fear, nor wish the approaches of the last.

MARTIAL, LIB. 10, EP. 96.

ME, who have lived so long among the great,
You wonder to hear talk of a retreat:
And a retreat so distant, as may show
No thoughts of a return when once I go.
Give me a country, how remote so e'er,
Where happiness a moderate rate does bear,
Where poverty itself in plenty flows

And all the solid use of riches knows.

The ground about the house maintains it there,

The house maintains the ground about it here.

Here even hunger's dear, and a full board

Devours the vital substance of the lord.

The land itself does there the feast bestow,

The land itself must here to market go.

Three or four suits one winter here does waste,

One suit does there three or four winters last.

Here every frugal man must oft be cold,

And little lukewarm fires are to you sold.

There fire's an element as cheap and free

Almost as any of the other three[25].

Stay you then here, and live among the great,

Attend their sports, and at their tables eat.

When all the bounties here of men you score:

The Place's bounty there, shall give me more.

NOTES

1. **hard and nice:** difficult and delicate
2. **these precedent discourses:** "Of Myself" is the 11th and last essay in *Several Discourses*.
3. **affections:** disposition
4. **of the same temper:** with the same disposition
5. **dispensed with:** excused
6. **an ode:** the poem *A Vote* in Cowley's *Sylva* (1636)
7. **Horace:** Quintus Horatius Flaccus (65–8 B.C.), the Roman poet who wrote *Satires, Epodes, Odes, Epistles,* and *Ars Poetica*
8. **his Sabine field:** Horace had a small farm on the Sabine hills.
9. **the university:** Cambridge University
10. **that violent public storm:** the Civil War between Charles I and the Parliamentarians

11. **one of the best persons:** Lord Jermyn, afterwards the Earl of St. Albans
12. **one of the best princesses:** Queen Henrietta Maria
13. **the paint:** the artificial nature
14. **Well then;…, &c.:** from *The Mistress*
15. **Apollo:** (Gr. myth.) the god of the sun, associated with music, poetry, and prophecy
16. **Thou, neither great…, &c.:** from the *Ode on Destiny*
17. *A corps perdu*: (Fr.) headlong
18. **"Take thy ease":** See Luke, xii. 19.
19. *Non ego perfidum dixi sacramentum*: (Lat.) I have sworn an oath that I will not break. —Horace
20. **MARTIAL:** Marcus Valerius Martialis (c. 40–104), Roman satiric poet
21. **LIB (abbreviation for *Liber*):** (Lat.) book
22. *quantum sufficit*: (Lat.) as much as is required
23. **a vestal flame:** a constant fire as on the altar of Vesta, the Roman goddess of the hearth
24. *Ana*: equal quantities of both ingredients
25. **the other three:** the other three elements than fire, i.e. earth, air, and water

14

JOHN EVELYN

(1620–1706)

John Evelyn was an English diarist and miscellaneous writer. He was born in Surrey on October 31, 1620, and educated at Balliol College, Oxford. A fine scholar as well as an extensive traveller and expert gardener, he helped to found the Royal Society. He published many practical works, including ***Fumifugium or The Inconvenience of the Air and Smoke of London Dissipated*** (1661), ***Sculptura*** (1662), ***Sylva*** (1664), and ***Navigation and Commerce*** (1674). For most of his life he kept a regular ***Diary***, which was published in an abridged edition by William Bray in 1818 and in a complete edition by E. S. de Beer (6 vols.) in 1955. He died in London on February 27, 1706.

Evelyn's ***Diary*** describes his private concerns, his travels abroad, his contemporaries, and the manners and public events of his time. It is a valuable record of English life in the second half of the 17th century. The book is readable with its simple, unadorned style.

THE GREAT FIRE

2nd September, 1666. This fatal night, about ten, began the deplorable fire, near Fish-street, in London.

3rd. I had public prayers at home. The fire continuing, after dinner, I took coach with my wife and son, and went to the Bankside in Southwark[1], where we beheld that dismal spectacle, the whole city in dreadful flames near the waterside; all the houses from the Bridge[2], all Thames-street, and upwards towards Cheapside, down to the Three Cranes[3], were now consumed; and so returned, exceeding[4] astonished what would become of the rest.

The fire having continued all this night (if I may call that night which was light as day for ten miles round about, after a dreadful manner), when conspiring with a fierce eastern wind in a very dry season, I went on foot to the same place; and saw the whole south part of the City burning from Cheapside to the Thames, and all along Cornhill (for it likewise kindled back against the wind as well as forward), Tower-street, Fenchurch-street, Gracious-street[5], and so along to Baynard's Castle, and was now taking hold of St. Paul's Church[6], to which the scaffolds[7] contributed exceedingly. The conflagration was so universal, and the people so astonished, that, from the beginning, I know not by what despondency, or fate, they hardly stirred to quench it; so that there was nothing heard, or seen, but crying out and lamentation, running about like distracted creatures, without at all attempting to save even their goods; such a strange consternation there was upon them, so as it burned both in breadth and length, the churches, public halls, Exchange[8], hospitals, monuments, and ornaments; leaping after a prodigious manner, from house to house, and street to street, at great distances one from the other. For the heat, with a long set[9] of fair and warm weather, had even ignited the air, and prepared the materials to conceive the fire, which devoured, after an incredible manner, houses, furniture, and everything. Here, we saw the Thames covered with goods floating, all the barges and boats laden with what some had time and courage to save, as, on the other side, the carts, &c., carrying out to the fields, which for many miles were strewed with moveables of all sorts, and tents erecting[10] to shelter both people and what goods they could get away. Oh, the miserable and calamitous spectacle! such as haply[11] the world had not seen since the foundation of it, nor can be outdone till the universal conflagration thereof. All the sky was of a fiery aspect, like the top of a burning oven, and the light seen above forty miles round-about for many nights. God grant mine eyes may never behold the like, who now saw above 10,000 houses all in one flame! The noise and cracking and thunder of the impetuous flames, the shrieking of women and children, the hurry of people, the fall of towers, houses, and churches, was like a hideous storm; and the air all about so hot and inflamed, that at the last one was not able to approach it, so that they were forced to stand still, and let the flames burn on, which they did, for near two miles in length and one in breadth. The clouds also of smoke were dismal, and reached, upon computation, near fifty miles in length. Thus, I left it this afternoon burning, a resemblance of Sodom[12], or the last day[13]. It forcibly called to my mind that passage—*non enim hic habemus stabilem civitatem*[14]: the ruins resembling the picture of Troy. London was, but is no more! Thus, I returned.

4th September. The burning still rages, and it is now gotten as far as the Inner Temple. All Fleet-street, the Old Bailey, Ludgate-hill, Warwick-lane, Newgate, Paul's-chain, Watling-street, now flaming, and most of it reduced to ashes; the stones of Paul's flew like grenados[15], the melting lead running down the streets in a stream, and the very pavements glowing with fiery redness, so as no horse, nor man, was able to tread on them, and the demolition had stopped all the passages, so that no help could be applied. The eastern wind still more impetuously driving the flames forward. Nothing but the Almighty power of God was able to stop them; for vain was the help of man.

5th. It crossed towards Whitehall[16]; but oh! the confusion there was then at that Court! It pleased his Majesty to command me, among the rest, to look after the quenching of Fetter-lane end, to preserve (if possible) that part of Holborn, whilst the rest of the gentlemen took their several posts, some at one part, and some at another (for now they began to bestir themselves, and not till now, who hitherto had stood as men intoxicated, with their hands across), and began to consider that nothing was likely to put a stop but the blowing up of so many houses as might make a wider gap than any had yet been made by the ordinary method of pulling them down with engines. This some stout seamen proposed early enough to have saved near the whole City, but this some tenacious and avaricious men, aldermen, &c., would not permit, because their houses must have been of the first. It was, therefore, now commended to be practised; and my concern being particularly for the Hospital of St. Bartholomew, near Smithfield, where I had many wounded and sick men, made me the more diligent to promote it; nor was my care for the Savoy[17] less. It now pleased God, by abating the wind, and by the industry of the people, when almost all was lost infusing a new spirit into them, that the fury of it began sensibly[18] to abate about noon, so as it came no farther than the Temple[19] westward, nor than the entrance of Smithfield, north; but continued all this day and night so impetuous towards Cripplegate and the Tower[20], as made us all despair. It also brake out again in the Temple; but the courage of the multitude persisting, and many houses being blown up, such gaps and desolations were soon made, as, with the former three days' consumption, the back fire did not so vehemently urge upon the rest as formerly. There was yet no standing near the burning and glowing ruins by near a furlong's space.

    The coal and wood-wharfs, and magazines of oil, rosin, &c., did infinite mischief, so as the invective[21] which a little before I had dedicated to his Majesty and published, giving warning what probably might be the issue of suffering those shops to be in the City was looked upon as a prophecy.

    The poor inhabitants were dispersed about St. George's Fields, and Moorfields, as far as Highgate, and several miles in circle, some under tents, some under miserable huts and hovels, many without a rag, or any necessary utensils, bed or board, who from delicateness, riches, and easy accommodations in stately and well-furnished houses, were now reduced to extremest misery and poverty.

    In this calamitous condition, I returned with a sad heart to my house, blessing and adoring the distinguishing mercy of God to me and mine, who, in the midst of all this ruin, was like Lot[22], in my little Zoar, safe and sound.

NOTES

1. **Southwark:** a borough in southeast London, on the south bank of the river Thames
2. **the Bridge:** the old London Bridge
3. **the Three Cranes:** a tavern in Upper Thames Street
4. **exceeding:** (arch., adv.) exceedingly
5. **Gracious-street:** now Gracechurch Street
6. **St. Paul's Church:** the great medieval church of "Old St. Paul's", burned down in the Great Fire of 1666. On its site was built the new St. Paul's Cathedral, begun in 1675 and completed in 1710, the masterpiece of Christopher Wren (1632–1723).
7. **the scaffolds:** St. Paul's Church was being repaired when the fire broke out.
8. **Exchange:** the Royal Exchange
9. **set:** tendency
10. **erecting:** being erected
11. **haply:** (arch.) perhaps
12. **Sodom:** an ancient city near the Dead Sea, destroyed, together with Gomorrah, by fire because of its wickedness (Genesis, xviii.-xix.)
13. **the last day:** the end of the world
14. ***non enim hic habemus stabilem civitatem***: (Lat.) For here have we no continuing city (Epistle to the Hebrews, xiii. 14).
15. **grenados:** grenades
16. **Whitehall:** the Royal Palace in London in Charles II's reign
17. **the Savoy:** the Savoy Hospital
18. **sensibly:** perceptibly
19. **the Temple:** the London Temple on whose site the two Inns of Court, called the Inner and the Middle Temple, now stand
20. **the Tower:** the Tower of London, a group of buildings on the north bank of the Thames that served first as a palace and then a prison and is now a museum
21. **invective:** a pamphlet that Evelyn published in 1661 under the title of "Fumifugium", in which he inveighed against the nuisance of the smoke in London and proposed expedients for its removal
22. **Lot:** Abraham's nephew who fled to Zoar to escape the fire of Sodom (Genesis, xix)

15

JOHN BUNYAN

(1628–1688)

John Bunyan was an English evangelist and allegorist. The son of a tinker, he was born at Elstow, Bedfordshire, on November 30, 1628, and had a brief education at the village school. He served in the Parliamentary Army in 1644–1646, practised the tinker's trade from 1646, joined a nonconformist church in Bedford in 1653, began preaching in 1656, and became well known as a travelling preacher. At the Restoration he was imprisoned for preaching without a license. He spent twelve years in Bedford gaol, doing manual work, studying and writing. After his release in 1672, he was appointed pastor at the nonconformist church in Bedford. He continued to preach and write until his death, which occurred on August 31, 1688.

Bunyan's principal works include ***Grace Abounding*** (1666), a spiritual autobiography; ***The Pilgrim's Progress*** (1st part, 1678; 2nd part, 1684), an allegorical narrative of the struggle and salvation of Christian; ***The Life and Death of Mr. Badman*** (1680), an allegorical biography of the wicked Badman; and ***The Holy War*** (1682), an allegorical account of the fall and rise of man. Of these ***The Pilgrim's Progress*** is Bunyan's most popular book. It is of interest both as a Puritan romance and as a social satire. We notice its lively narration of incident after incident happening to its hero, its vivid characterization of types of people, and its realistic description of country and town. We are especially delighted with its beautiful, simple language. As Bunyan was conversant with the English of the Bible and likewise the English of the people, he succeeded in combining the dignity of the one with the colloquial quality of the other. His style is plain, direct, pithy, and rich in imagery. ***The Pilgrim's Progress*** is the greatest prose allegory in English and has been translated into over a hundred languages.

VANITY FAIR

Then I saw in my dream, that when they were got out of the wilderness[1], they presently saw a town before them, and the name of that town is Vanity; and at the town there is a fair kept, called Vanity Fair: it is kept all the year long; it beareth the name of Vanity Fair, because the town where it is kept is lighter than vanity; and also because all that is there sold, or that cometh thither, is vanity. As is the saying of the wise, "all that cometh *is* vanity"[2].

This fair is no new-erected business, but a thing of ancient standing; I will show you the original of it.

Almost five thousand years agone, there were pilgrims walking to the Celestial City, as these two honest persons are: and Beelzebub, Apollyon, and Legion[3], with their companions, perceiving by the path that the pilgrims made, that their way to the city lay through this town of Vanity, they contrived here to set up a fair; a fair wherein should be sold all sorts of vanity, and that it should last all the year long: therefore at this fair are all such merchandise sold, as houses, lands, trades, places, honours, preferments, titles, countries, kingdoms, lusts, pleasures, and delights of all sorts, as whores, bawds, wives, husbands, children, masters, servants, lives, blood, bodies, souls, silver, gold, pearls, precious stones, and what not.

And, moreover, at this fair there is at all times to be seen juggling, cheats, games, plays, fools, apes, knaves, and rogues, and that of every kind.

Here are to be seen, too, and that for nothing, thefts, murders, adulteries, false swearers, and that of a blood-red colour.

And as in other fairs of less moment, there are the several rows and streets, under their proper names, where such and such wares are vended; so here likewise you have the proper places, rows, streets (viz. countries and kingdoms), where the wares of this fair are soonest to be found. Here is the Britain Row, the French Row, the Italian Row, the Spanish Row, the German Row, where several sorts of vanities are to be sold. But, as in other fairs, some one commodity is as the chief of all the fair, so the ware of Rome[4] and her merchandise is greatly promoted in this fair; only our English nation, with some others, have taken a dislike thereat.

Now, as I said, the way to the Celestial City lies just through this town where this lusty[5] fair is kept; and he that will go to the City, and yet not go through this town, must needs "go out of the world". The Prince of princes[6] himself, when here, went through this town to his own country, and that upon a fair day too; yea, and as I think, it was Beelzebub, the chief lord of this fair, that invited him to buy[7] of his vanities; yea, would have made him lord of the fair, would he but have done him reverence as he went through the town. Yea, because he was such a person of honour, Beelzebub had him from street to street, and showed him all the kingdoms of the world in a little time, that he might, if possible, allure the Blessed One to cheapen[8] and buy some of his vanities; but he had no mind to the merchandise, and therefore left the town, without laying out so much as one farthing upon these vanities. This fair, therefore, is an ancient thing, of long standing, and a very great fair. Now these pilgrims, as I said, must needs go through this fair. Well, so they did: but, behold, even as they entered into the fair, all the people in the fair were moved, and the town itself as it were in a hubbub about them; and that for several reasons: for—

First, the pilgrims were clothed with such kind of raiment as was diverse from the raiment of any that traded in that fair. The people, therefore, of the fair, made a great gazing upon them: some said they were fools, some they were bedlams[9], and some they are outlandish men.

Secondly, and as they wondered at their apparel, so they did likewise at their speech; for few could understand what they said; they naturally spoke the language of Canaan[10], but they that kept the fair were the men of this world; so that, from one end of the fair to the other, they seemed barbarians each to the other.

Thirdly, but that which did not a little amuse the merchandisers was, that these pilgrims set very light by all their wares; they cared not so much as to look upon them; and if they called upon them to buy, they would put their fingers in their ears, and cry, "Turn away mine eyes from beholding vanity"[11], and look upwards, signifying that their trade and traffic was in heaven.

One chanced mockingly, beholding the carriage of the men[12], to say unto them, What will ye buy? But they, looking gravely upon him, answered, "We buy the truth". At that there was an occasion taken to despise the men the more; some mocking, some taunting, some speaking reproachfully, and some calling upon others to smite them. At last things came to a hubbub and great stir in the fair, insomuch that all order was confounded. Now was word presently brought to the great one of the fair, who quickly came down, and deputed some of his most trusty friends to take these men into examination, about whom the fair was almost overturned. So the men were brought to examination; and they that sat upon them[13], asked them whence they came, whither they went, and what they did there, in such an unusual garb? The men told them that they were pilgrims and strangers in the world, and that they were going to their own country, which was the heavenly Jerusalem; and that they had given no occasion to the men of the town, nor yet to the merchandisers, thus to abuse them, and to let[14] them in their journey, except it was for that, when one asked them what they would buy, they said they would buy the truth. But they that were appointed to examine them did not believe them to be any other than bedlams and mad, or else such as came to put all things into a confusion in the fair. Therefore they took them and beat them, and besmeared them with dirt, and then put them into the cage, that they might be made a spectacle to all the men of the fair.

> Behold Vanity Fair! the Pilgrims there
> Are chained and stand beside:
> Even so it was our Lord passed here,
> And on Mount Calvary[15] died.

There, therefore, they lay for some time, and were made the objects of any man's sport, or malice, or revenge, the great one of the fair laughing still at all that befell them. But the men being patient, and not rendering railing for railing, but contrariwise, blessing, and giving good words for bad, and kindness for injuries done, some men in the fair that were more observing, and less prejudiced than the rest, began to check and blame the baser sort for their continual abuses done by them to the men; they, therefore, in angry manner, let fly at them again, counting them as bad as the men in the cage, and telling them that they seemed confederates, and should be made partakers of their misfortunes. The other replied, that for aught they could see, the men were quiet, and sober, and intended nobody any harm; and that there were many that traded in their fair that were more worthy to be put into the cage, yea, and pillory too, than were the men they had abused. Thus, after divers words had passed on both sides, the men behaving themselves all the while very wisely and soberly before them, they fell to some blows among themselves, and did harm one to another. Then were these two poor men brought before their examiners again, and there charged as being guilty of the late hubbub that had been in the fair. So they beat them pitifully, and hanged irons upon them, and led them in chains up and down the fair, for an example and a terror to others, lest any should speak in their behalf, or join themselves unto them. But Christian and Faithful behaved themselves yet more wisely, and received the ignominy and shame that was cast upon them, with so much meekness and patience, that it won to their side, though but few in comparison of the rest, several of the men in the fair. This put the other party yet into greater rage, insomuch that they concluded the death of these two men. Wherefore they threatened, that neither cage nor irons should serve their turn, but that they should die, for the abuse they had done, and for deluding the men of the fair.

Then were they remanded to the cage again, until further order should be taken with them. So they put them in, and made their feet fast in the stocks.

Here, therefore, they called again to mind what they had heard from their faithful friend Evangelist[16], and were the more confirmed in their way and sufferings, by what he told them would happen to them. They also now comforted each other, that whose lot it was to suffer, even he should have the best of it; therefore each man secretly wished that he might have that preferment: but committing themselves to the all-wise disposal of Him that ruleth all things, with much content, they abode in the condition in which they were, until they should be otherwise disposed of.

NOTES

1. **when they were got out of the wilderness:** when Christian and his companion Faithful had got out of the wilderness
2. **"all that cometh *is* vanity":** The sentence occurs in Ecclesiastes xi. 8.
3. **Beelzebub, Apollyon, and Legion:** devils
4. **Rome:** the Roman Catholic Church
5. **lusty:** joyous
6. **the Prince of princes:** Jesus Christ
7. **invited him to buy:** The reference is to the temptation of Jesus by the devil. See Matthew iv. 4-10.
8. **cheapen:** bargain for
9. **bedlams:** madmen
10. **Canaan:** the Promised Land of Israelites, the region later called Palestine
11. **"Turn away mine eyes from beholding vanity":** See Psalms cxix. 37.
12. **the carriage of the men:** the men's behaviour
13. **sat upon them:** sat in judgement on them
14. **to let:** (arch.) to hinder or obstruct
15. **Calvary:** the place near Jerusalem where Jesus was crucified
16. **Evangelist:** a friendly person that Christian and Faithful had met on the road to Vanity Fair

16

JOHN DRYDEN

(1631–1700)

John Dryden was an English poet, playwright, and critic. He was born into a Puritan family in Northamptonshire on August 9, 1631, and educated at Westminster School, London, and Trinity College, Cambridge. His first important poem, *Heroic Stanzas* (1658), was an elegy on the death of Cromwell. Later, however, he celebrated the Restoration with *Astraea Redux* (1660) and *Panegyric* (1661). Under Charles II, Dryden was appointed Poet Laureate in 1668 and Historiographer Royal in 1670. On the accession of James II in 1685 he became a Roman Catholic. He retained his new faith and lost the two posts when the Catholic James II was deposed in 1688 by the Protestant William III. He died on May 1, 1700, and was buried in Westminster Abbey.

Dryden wrote and excelled in many forms of literature. Among his major works may be mentioned: the satires *Absalom and Achitophel* (1681), *The Medal* (1682), and *Mac Flecknoe* (1682), all in heroic couplets; the Pindaric odes *A Song for Saint Cecilia's Day* (1687) and *Alexander's Feast* (1697); the tragedy *All for Love* (1678), adapted from Shakespeare's *Antony and Cleopatra* and expressed in blank verse; and the critical pieces *An Essay of Dramatic Poesy* (1668) and *Preface to Fables Ancient and Modern* (1700). *An Essay of Dramatic*

Poesy is Dryden's best critical writing: it not only sets forth the classical principles of play-writing but gives warm praise to the English dramatists Shakespeare, Fletcher, and Jonson; and it is typical of Dryden's prose, which is lucid and supple, easy and vigorous, natural and graceful.

SHAKESPEARE, BEAUMONT AND FLETCHER, AND BEN JONSON[1]

To begin, then, with Shakespeare. He was the man who of all modern, and perhaps ancient poets, had the largest and most comprehensive soul. All the images of nature were still present to him, and he drew them, not laboriously, but luckily; when he describes anything, you more than see it, you feel it too. Those who accuse him to have wanted learning, give him the greater commendation; he was naturally learned; he needed not the spectacles of books to read nature; he looked inwards, and found her there. I cannot say he is everywhere alike; were he so, I should do him injury to compare him with the greatest of mankind. He is many times flat, insipid; his comic wit degenerating into clenches[2], his serious swelling into bombast. But he is always great, when some great occasion is presented to him; no man can say he ever had a fit subject for his wit, and did not then raise himself as high above the rest of poets,

Quantum lenta solent inter viburna cupressi.[3]

The consideration of this made Mr. Hales of Eton[4] say, that there was no subject of which any poet ever wrote but he would produce it much better done in Shakespeare; and however others are now generally preferred before him, yet the age wherein he lived, which had contemporaries with him Fletcher[5] and Jonson, never equalled them to him in their esteem: and in the last king's[6] court, when Ben's reputation was at highest, Sir John Suckling[7], and with him the greater part of the courtiers, set our Shakespeare far above him.

Beaumont and Fletcher, of whom I am next to speak, had, with the advantage of Shakespeare's wit, which was their precedent, great natural gifts, improved by study: Beaumont especially being so accurate a judge of plays that Ben Jonson, while he lived, submitted all his writings to his censure, and, 'tis thought, used his judgement in correcting, if not contriving, all his plots. What value he had for him, appears by the verses he writ to him; and therefore I need speak no farther of it. The first play that brought Fletcher and him in esteem was their *Philaster*: for before that, they had written two or three very unsuccssfully, as the like is reported of Ben Jonson, before he wrote ***Every Man in His Humour***. Their plots were generally more regular than Shakespeare's, especially those which were made before Beaumont's death; and they understood and imitated the conversation of gentlemen much better; whose wild debaucheries, and quickness of wit in repartees, no poet before them could paint as they have done. Humour which Ben Jonson derived from particular persons they made it not their business to describe: they represented all the passions very lively, but above all, love. I am apt to believe the English language in them arrived to its highest perfection; what words have since been taken in, are rather superfluous than ornamental. Their plays are now the most pleasant and frequent entertainments of the stage; two of theirs being acted through the year for one of Shakespeare's or Jonson's: the reason is, because there is a certain gaiety in their comedies and pathos in their more serious plays, which suits generally with all men's humours. Shakespeare's language is likewise a little obsolete, and Ben Jonson's wit comes short of theirs.

As for Jonson, to whose character I am now arrived, if we look upon him while he was himself (for his last plays were but his dotages), I think him the most learned and judicious writer which any theatre ever had. He was a most severe judge of himself, as well as others. One cannot say he wanted wit, but rather that he was frugal of it. In his works you find little to retrench or alter. Wit, and language, and humour also in some measure, we had before him; but something of art was wanting to the drama, till he came. He managed his strength to more advantage than any who preceded him. You seldom find him making love in any of his scenes, or endeavouring to move the passions; his genius was too sullen and saturnine to do it gracefully, especially when he knew he came after those who had performed both to such a height. Humour was his proper sphere; and in that he was delighted most to represent mechanic people. He was deeply conversant in the ancients, both Greek and Latin, and he borrowed boldly from them: there is scarce a poet or historian among the Roman authors of those times whom he has not translated in ***Sejanus***[8] and ***Catiline***[9]. But he has done his robberies so openly, that one may see he fears not to be taxed by any law. He invades authors like a monarch; and what would be theft in other poets is only victory in him. With the spoils of these writers he so represents old Rome to us, in its rites, ceremonies, and customs, that if one of their poets had written either of his tragedies, we had seen less of it than in him. If there was any fault in his language, 'twas that he weaved it too closely and laboriously, in his comedies especially;[10] perhaps too, he did a little too much Romanize our tongue, leaving the words which he translated almost as much Latin as he found them: wherein, though he learnedly followed their language, he did not enough comply with the idiom of ours. If I would compare him with Shakespeare, I must acknowledge him the more correct poet, but Shakespeare the greater wit. Shakespeare was the Homer[11], or father of our dramatic poets; Jonson was the Virgil[12], the pattern of elaborate writing; I admire him, but I love Shakespeare. To conclude of him; as he has given us the most correct plays, so in the precepts which he has laid down in his ***Discoveries***, we have as many and profitable rules for perfecting the stage, as any wherewith the French can furnish us.

NOTES

1. **Shakespeare, Beaumont and Fletcher, and Ben Jonson:** The passage is a speech of Neander's in *An Essay of Dramatic Poesy* (1668), which is a critical essay in dialogue form by John Dryden. The four speakers (given classical names) represent Dryden himself ("Neander") and three of his friends.
2. **clenches:** clinches, puns, punning retorts
3. ***Quantum lenta solent inter viburna cupressi:*** (Lat.) As much as cypresses raise themselves among the drooping bushes. —Virgil
4. **Mr. Hales of Eton:** John Hales (1584–1656), a Fellow of Eton College
5. **Fletcher:** John Fletcher (1579–1625) wrote many plays, both by himself and in collaboration with other dramatists, especially Francis Beaumont (1584–1616). The plays by Beaumont and Fletcher include *The Knight of the Burning Pestle* (1609),

Philaster (1611), *The Maid's Tragedy* (1611), and *A King and No King* (1811).

6. **the last king:** Charles Ⅰ
7. **Sir John Suckling:** Suckling (1609–1642) was a playwright and poet.
8. *Sejanus*: a tragedy (1603) on the fall of the Roman Emperor Tiberius' favourite Sejanus
9. *Catiline*: a tragedy (1611) based on the conspiracy of the Roman politician Catiline in 65 B.C.
10. **in his comedies especially:** This is the reading of the second edition. The original phrase in the first edition, "in his serious plays", is more appropriate.
11. **Homer:** Homeros (c.9th century B.C.), the earliest of Greek poets and the reputed author of two great epics, the *Iliad* and the *Odyssey*
12. **Virgil:** Publius Vergilius Maro (70–19 B.C.), the Roman poet who wrote the *Eclogues* (42–37 B.C.), the *Georgics* (37–30 B.C.), and the *Aeneid* (30–19 B.C.)

CHAUCER, THE FATHER OF ENGLISH POETRY

It remains that I say somewhat of Chaucer[1] in particular. In the first place, as he is the father of English poetry, so I hold him in the same degree of veneration as the Grecians held Homer, or the Romans Virgil. He is a perpetual fountain of good sense; learned in all sciences[2]; and, therefore, speaks properly on all subjects. As he knew what to say, so he knows also when to leave off; a continence which is practised by few writers, and scarcely by any of the ancients, excepting Virgil and Horace[3]. One of our late great poets is sunk in his reputation, because he could never forgo any conceit which came in his way; but swept like a drag-net, great and small. There was plenty enough, but the dishes were ill sorted; whole pyramids of sweetmeats for boys and women, but little of solid meat for men. All this proceeded not from any want of knowledge, but of judgement; neither did he want that in discerning the beauties and faults of other poets, but only indulged himself in the luxury of writing; and perhaps knew it was a fault, but hoped the reader would not find it. For this reason, though he must always be thought a great poet, he is no longer esteemed a good writer; and for ten impressions, which his works have had in so many successive years, yet at present a hundred books are scarcely purchased once a twelvemonth; for, as my last Lord Rochester said, though somewhat profanely, "Not being of God, he could not stand."

Chaucer followed Nature everywhere, but was never so bold to go beyond her; and there is a great difference of being ***poeta*** and ***nimis poeta***[4], if we may believe Catullus[5], as much as betwixt a modest behaviour and affectation. The verse of Chaucer, I confess, is not harmonious to us[6], but 'tis like the eloquence of one whom Tacitus[7] commends, it was ***auribus istius temporis accommodata***[8]: they who lived with him, and some time after him, thought it musical; and it continues so, even in our judgement, if compared with the numbers of Lydgate[9] and Gower[10], his contemporaries: there is the rude sweetness of a Scotch tune in it, which is natural and pleasing, though not perfect. 'Tis true, I cannot go so far as he who published the last edition of him; for he would make us believe the fault is in our ears, and that there were really ten syllables in a verse where we find but nine: but this opinion is not worth confuting; 'tis so gross and obvious an error, that common sense (which is a rule in everything but matters of Faith and Revelation) must convince the reader, that equality of numbers, in every verse which we call **heroic**, was either not known, or not always practised, in Chaucer's age. It were an easy matter to produce some thousands of his verses, which are lame for want of half a foot, and sometimes a whole one, and which no pronunciation can make otherwise. We can only say, that he lived in the infancy of our poetry, and that nothing is brought to perfection at the first. We must be children before we grow men....

He must have been a man of a most wonderful comprehensive nature, because, as it has been truly observed of him, he has taken into the compass of his **Canterbury Tales** the various manners and humours (as we now call them) of the whole English nation, in his age. Not a single character has escaped him. All his pilgrims are severally[11] distinguished from each other; and not only in their inclinations, but in their very physiognomies and persons. Baptista Porta[12] could not have described their natures better, than by the marks which the poet gives them. The matter and manner of their tales, and of their telling, are so suited to their different educations, humours, and callings, that each of them would be improper in any other mouth. Even the grave and serious characters are distinguished by their several[13] sorts of gravity: their discourses are such as belong to their age, their calling, and their breeding; such as are becoming of them, and of them only. Some of his persons are vicious, and some virtuous; some are unlearned, or (as Chaucer calls them) lewd, and some are learned. Even the ribaldry of the low characters is different: the Reeve, the Miller, and the Cook, are several men, and distinguished from each other as much as the mincing Lady Prioress and the broad-speaking, gap-toothed Wife of Bath. But enough of this; there is such a variety of game springing up before me, that I am distracted in my choice, and know not which to follow. 'Tis sufficient to say, according to the proverb, that **here is God's plenty**. We have our forefathers and great-granddames all before us, as they were in Chaucer's days: their general characters are still remaining in mankind, and even in England, though they are called by other names than those of Monks and Friars, and Canons, and Lady Abbesses, and Nuns; for mankind is ever the same, and nothing lost out of Nature, though everything is altered.

NOTES

1. **Chaucer:** Geoffrey Chaucer (1342?–1400), the great English poet who wrote *The Canterbury Tales* (1387–1400), *Troylus and Criseyde* (1385), etc.
2. **all sciences:** all branches of knowledge
3. **Horace:** Quintus Horatius Flaccus (65–8 B.C.), Roman poet and satirist. His works include the *Satires*, *Odes*, *Epodes*, and *Ars Poetica*.
4. **being *poeta* and *nimis poeta*:** being a poet and being too much of a poet (the phrase is from Martial rather than Catullus)
5. **Catullus:** Gaius Valerius Catullus (c.84–c.54 B.C.), Roman poet. He wrote love poems, elegies, and satirical epigrams.
6. **not harmonious to us:** In Dryden's time the readers in general did not know how to pronounce Middle English properly and therefore could not feel the harmony of Chaucer's verse.
7. **Tacitus:** Publius Cornelius Tacitus (c.A.D.55–c.120), Roman historian and orator
8. ***auribus istius temporis accommodata*:** suited to the ears of another age
9. **Lydgate:** John Lydgate (?1370–1451), English poet
10. **Gower:** John Gower (?1330–1408), English poet and Chaucer's friend
11. **severally:** distinctly
12. **Baptista Porta:** Giambattista della Porta (c.1540–1615), Italian natural philosopher
13. **several:** different

17

SAMUEL PEPYS

(1633–1703)

Samuel Pepys was an English diarist. The son of a tailor, he was born in London on 23rd February, 1633 and was educated at St. Paul's School, London, and Magdalene College, Cambridge. He began to work in the navy office in 1660 and, because of his diligence and great ability, soon became one of its most important officials. While holding the posts of Clerk of the Acts (from 1660), Surveyor general of the Victualling Office (from 1665), and Secretary to the Admiralty (in 1672–1679 and 1684–1688), he laboured hard for the regeneration of the British navy. Besides, he served as M. P. in 1678–1679 and President of the Royal Society in 1684–1686. He went into retirement after the revolution of 1688, published his **Memoirs Relating to the State of the Royal Navy** in 1690, and died on 26th May, 1703. His valuable library of three thousand volumes was bequeathed to Magdalene College, Cambridge.

Pepys kept a *Diary* in cipher from January 1660 to May 1669. It was deciphered by John Smith, edited by Lord Braybrooke, and published with many omissions in 1825. A full edition by H. B. Wheatley (10 vols.) appeared in 1893–1899, and a complete edition by R. Latham and W. Matthews (11 vols.) in 1970–1983. The *Diary* of this busy man of affairs is a day-to-day record of what he did, what he saw, what he thought, and what he felt. He describes objectively and with the utmost candour his official duties and daily habits, his family and friends, his intellectual interests and aesthetic prejudices, his pleasures and worries, and the big events or scenes he witnessed. The whole thing constitutes an extraordinary document of historical value and psychological significance. It is written in plain, everyday English.

HIS DIVERSE INTERESTS

22nd November 1660. This morning came the carpenters to make me a door at the other side of my house, going into the entry. My wife and I walked to the Old Exchange, and there she bought her a white whisk[1], and put it on, and I a pair of gloves. To Mr. Fox's[2], where we found Mrs. Fox within, and an alderman of London paying £1000 or £1400 in gold upon the table for the King. Mr. Fox came in presently, and did receive us with a great deal of respect; and then did take my wife and I to the Queen's presence-chamber, where he got my wife placed behind the Queen's chair, and the two Princesses came to dinner. The Queen, a very little, plain old woman, and nothing more in her presence in any respect nor garb than any ordinary woman. The Princess of Orange I had often seen before. The Princess Henrietta is very pretty, but much below my expectation; and her dressing of herself with her hair frized short up to her ears did make her seem so much the less to me. But my wife standing near her with two or three black patches on, and well dressed, did seem to me much handsomer than she. Dinner being done, we went to Mr. Fox's again, where many gentlemen dined with us, and most princely dinner—all provided for me and my friends, but I bringing none but myself and wife, he did call the company to help to eat up so much good victuals. At the end of the dinner my Lord Sandwich's[3] health, in the gilt tankard that I did give to Mrs. Fox the other day.

28th January 1661. At the office all the morning. Dined at home. And after dinner to Fleet street with my sword to Mr. Brigden (lately made Captain of the Auxiliaries) to be refreshed. And with him to an alehouse, where I met Mr. Damport; and after some talk of Cromwell[4], Ireton[5] and Bradshaw's[6] bodies being taken out of their graves today, I went to Mr. Crew's and thence to the Theatre, where I saw again *The Lost Lady*, which doth now please me better than before. And here, I sitting behind in a dark place, a lady spat backward upon me by a mistake, not seeing me. But after seeing her to be a very pretty lady, I was not troubled at it at all. Thence to Mr. Crew's; and there met Mr. Moore, who came lately to town, and went with me to my father's and with him to Standing's—whither came to us Dr. Fairbrother[7], who I took and my father to the Bear and gave a pint of sack and a pint of claret. He doth still continue his expressions of respect and love to me. And tells me my brother John will make a good scholar.

Thence to see the Doctor at his lodgings at Mr. Holden's, where I bought a hat, cost me 35*s*. So home by moonshine and by the way was overtaken by the Comptroller's[8] coach; and so home to his house with him. So home and to bed. This noon I had my press set up in my chamber for papers to be put in.

26th August 1661. Casting up my father's accounts, and upon the whole, I find that all he hath in money of his own due to him in the world is £45, and he owes about the same sum; so that I cannot but think in what a condition he had left my mother, if he should have died before my uncle Robert. To the Theatre, and saw ***The Antipodes***[9], wherein there is much mirth, but no great matter else. I found a letter from my Lord Sandwich, who is now very well again of his feaver, but not yet gone from Alicante, where he lay sick, and was twice there bled. This letter dated the 22nd of July last, which puts me out of doubt of his being ill.

30th July 1666. Thence home; and to sing with my wife and Mercer[10] in the garden; and coming in, I find my wife plainly dissatisfied with me, that I can spend so much time with Mercer, teaching her to sing, and could never take the pains with her, which I acknowledge; but it is because that the girl doth take music mighty readily, and she doth not; and music is the thing of the world that I love most, and all the pleasure almost that I can now take. So to bed, in some little discontent, but no words from me.

6th May 1668. I understand that my Lord St. John is meant by Mr. Woodcocke in ***The Impertinents***. This morning the House is upon the City Bill, and they say hath passed it, though I am sorry that I did not think to put somebody in mind of moving for the churches to be allotted according to the convenience of the people, and not to gratify this Bishop, or that College. To Mr. Pierce's, where invited, and there was Knipp and Mrs. Foster; here dined, but a poor, sluttish dinner, as usual, and so I could not be heartily merry at it; here saw her girl's picture, but it is mighty far short of her boy's, and not like her, neither; but it makes Hales's picture of her boy appear a good picture. To the King's playhouse, and there saw **The Virgin Martyr**[11], and heard the music that I like so well, and intended to have seen Knipp, but I let her alone; and having there done, went to Mrs. Pierce's back again, where she was. And so to talk, and by and by did eat some curds and cream, and thence away home, and it being night, I did walk in the dusk up and down, round through our garden, over Tower Hill, and so through Crutched Friars, three or four times. Home to put up things against tomorrow's carrier for my wife; and, among others, a very fine salmon-pie, sent me by Mr. Steventon, W. Hewer's uncle.

30th November 1668. My wife, after dinner, went the first time abroad in her coach, calling on Roger Pepys[12], and visiting Mrs. Creed, and my cousin Turner. Thus ended this month, with very good content, but most expenseful to my purse on things of pleasure, having furnished my wife's closet and the best chamber, and a coach and horses, that ever I knew in the world; and I am put into the greatest condition of outward state that ever I was in, or hoped ever to be, or desired; and this at a time when we do daily expect great changes in this Office[13]; and by all reports we must, all of us, turn out. But my eyes are come to that condition that I am not able to work; and therefore that, and my wife's desire, make me have no manner of trouble in my thoughts about it. So God do his will in it!

NOTES

1. **whisk:** tippet or neckerchief worn by women
2. **Mr. Fox:** Steven Fox (1627-1716), a politician who supported the House of Stuart
3. **Lord Sandwich:** Edward Montagu (1625-1672), the Earl of Sandwich, who was Pepys's patron
4. **Cromwell:** Oliver Cromwell (1599-1658), leader of the Parliamentary troops in the Civil War and Lord Protector of the Commonwealth (1653-1658)
5. **Ireton:** Henry Ireton (1611-1651), Parliamentarian general
6. **Bradshaw:** John Bradshaw (1602-1659), English politician and president of the court which condemned Charles I

7. **Dr. Fairbrother:** William Fairbrother, who was Fellow of King's college, Cambridge
8. **the Comptroller:** the Comptroller of the Navy
9. ***The Antipodes*:** a comedy by Richard Brome (c. 1590−1652/3)
10. **Mercer:** Mary Mercer, Mrs. Pepys's companion
11. ***The Virgin Martyr*:** a religious play by Philip Massinger (1583−1640) and Thomas Dekker (?1570−1632)
12. **Roger Pepys:** Samuel's cousin
13. **this Office:** the Victualling Office where Pepys was Surveyor-general

18

DANIEL DEFOE

(1660-1731)

Daniel Defoe was an English novelist and journalist. The son of a butcher, he was born in London, and educated at Morton's Academy for Dissenters. After an unsuccessful commercial career, he took to journalism. His satirical poem *The True-Born Englishman* (1701), a defence of the new king William III, was very well received. His pamphlet *The Shortest Way with the Dissenters* (1702), an attack on the government's religious policy, caused him to be imprisoned and pilloried in 1703. In the next year he started *The Review*, a periodical which appeared three times weekly and in which he gave his opinions on current affairs and problems. It lasted till 1713.

A versatile and prolific writer, Defoe had more than five hundred publications to his credit, covering the fields of politics, political economy, social study, history, and fiction. He was the first of the English novelists and is chiefly remembered for his fictional works: **Robinson Crusoe** (1719), **Captain Singleton** (1720), **Moll Flanders** (1722), **A Journal of the Plague Year** (1722), **Colonel Jack** (1722), and **Roxana** (1724). In his fictional writing everything is described with realism so that the story has an air of authenticity about it and the central character appears to be a life-like individual. Defoe's novels, especially **Robinson Crusoe** and **Moll Flanders**, have been studied and appreciated by generation after generation of readers. Their perpetual charm is due to his powerful imagination of situation, his realistic handling of detail, and his plain, simple, matter-of-fact prose style.

THE SALVAGE FROM THE WRECK

A little after noon I found the sea very calm and the tide ebbed so far out that I could come within a quarter of a mile of the ship; and here I found a fresh renewing of my grief, for I saw evidently that if we had kept on board, we had been all safe[1], that is to say, we had all got safe on shore, and I had not been so miserable as to be left entirely destitute of all comfort and company, as I now was; this forced tears from my eyes again, but as there was little relief in that, I resolved, if possible, to get to the ship; so I pulled off my clothes, for the weather was hot to extremity, and took the water; but when I came to the ship, my difficulty was still greater to know how to get on board, for as she lay aground, and high out of the water, there was nothing within my reach to lay hold of; I swam round her twice, and the second time I spied a small piece of a rope which I wondered I did not see at first, hang down by the fore-chains so low as that with great difficulty I got hold of it, and by the help of that rope, got up into the forecastle of the ship. Here I found that the ship was bulged, and had a great deal of water in her hold, but that she lay so on the side of a bank of hard sand, or rather earth, that her stern lay lifted up upon the bank and her head low almost to the water; by this means all her quarter was free[2], and all that was in that part was dry; for you may be sure my first work was to search and to see what was spoiled and what was free; and first I found that all the ship's provisions were dry and untouched by the water, and being very well disposed to eat, I went to the bread-room and filled my pockets with biscuit, and ate it as I went about other things, for I had no time to lose; I also found some rum in the great cabin, of which I took a large dram, and which I had indeed need enough of to spirit me for what was before me. Now I wanted nothing but a boat to furnish myself with many things which I foresaw would be very necessary to me.

It was in vain to sit still and wish for what was not to be had, and this extremity roused my application. We had several spare yards and two or three large spars of wood and a spare topmast or two in the ship; I resolved to fall to work with these and I flung as many of them overboard as I could manage for their weight, tying every one with a rope that they might not drive away; when this was done I went down the ship's side, and pulling them to me, I tied four of them fast together at both ends as well as I could, in the form of a raft, and laying two or three short pieces of plank upon them crossways, I found I could walk upon it very well, but that it was not able to bear any great weight, the pieces being too light; so I went to work, and with the carpenter's saw I cut a spare topmast into three lengths and added them to my raft, with a great deal of labour and pains; but hope of furnishing myself with necessaries encouraged me to go beyond what I should have been able to have done upon another occasion.

My raft was now strong enough to bear any reasonable weight; my next care was what to load it with and how to preserve what I laid upon it from the surf of the sea; but I was not long considering this; I first laid all the planks or boards upon it that I could get, and having considered well what I most wanted, I first got three of the seamen's chests, which I had broken open and emptied, and lowered them down upon my raft; the first of these I filled with provisions, viz., bread, rice, three Dutch cheeses, five pieces of dried goat's flesh, which we lived much upon, and a little remainder of European corn which had been laid by for some fowls which we brought to sea with us, but the fowls were killed; there had been some barley and wheat together, but, to my great disappointment, I found afterwards that the rats had eaten or spoiled it all. As for liquors, I found several cases of bottles belonging to our skipper, in which were some cordial waters[3], and in all about five or six gallons of sack; these I stowed by themselves, there being no need to put them into the chest, nor no room for them. While I was doing this, I found the tide began to flow, though very calm, and I had the mortification to see my coat, shirt, and waistcoat which I had left on shore upon the sand, swim away; as for my breeches, which were only linen, and open-kneed, I swam on board in them, and my stockings. However, this put me upon rummaging for clothes, of which I found enough, but took no more than I wanted for present use, for I had other things which my eye was more upon, as first, tools to work with on shore; and it was after long searching that I found out the carpenter's chest, which was indeed a very useful prize to me, and much more valuable than a ship loading of gold would have been at that time; I got it down to my raft, even whole as it was, without losing time to look into it, for I knew in general what it contained.

My next care was for some ammunition and arms; there were two very good fowling pieces in the great cabin, and two pistols; these I secured first, with some powder horns[4], and a small bag of shot, and two old rusty swords; I knew there were three barrels of powder in the ship, but knew not where our gunner had stowed them, but with much search I found them, two of them dry and good, the third had taken water; those two I got to my raft with the arms. And now I thought myself pretty well freighted, and began to think how I should get to shore with them, having neither sail, oar, or rudder; and the least capful of wind[5] would have overset all my navigation.

I had three encouragements: 1. A smooth, calm sea. 2. The tide rising and setting in to the shore. 3. What little wind there was blew me towards the land; and thus, having found two or three broken oars belonging to the boat, and besides the tools which were in the chest, I found two saws, an axe, and a hammer, and with this cargo I put to sea. For a mile or thereabouts my raft went very well, only that I found it drive a little distant from the place where I had landed before, by which I perceived that there was some indraught[6] of the water, and consequently I hoped to find some creek or river there which I might make use of as a port to get to land with my cargo.

As I imagined, so it was; there appeared before me a little opening of the land, and I found a strong current of the tide set into it, so I guided my raft as well as I could to keep in the middle of the stream. But here I had like to have suffered[7] a second shipwreck, which, if I had, I think verily would have broke my heart; for knowing nothing of the coast, my raft run aground at one end of it upon a shoal, and not being aground at the other end, it wanted but a little that all my cargo had slipped off towards that end that was afloat, and so fallen into the water. I did my utmost by setting my back against the chests to keep them in their places, but could not thrust off the raft with all my strength, neither durst I stir from the posture I was in, but holding up the chests with all my might, stood in that manner near half an hour, in which time the rising of the water brought me a little more upon a level; and a little after, the water still rising, my raft floated again, and I thrust her off with the oar I had, into the channel, and then driving up higher, I at length found myself in the mouth of a little river, with land on both sides, and a strong current or tide running up; I looked on both sides for a proper place to get to shore, for I was not willing to be driven too high up the river, hoping in time to see some ship at sea and therefore resolved to place myself as near the coast as I could.

At length I spied a little cove on the right shore of the creek, to which with great pain and difficulty I guided my raft, and at last got so near as that, reaching ground with my oar, I could thrust her directly in; but here I had like to have dipped all my cargo in the sea again; for that shore lying pretty steep, that is to say, sloping, there was no place to land, but where one end of my float, if it run on shore, would lie so high and the other sink lower as before, that it would endanger my cargo again. All that I could do was to wait till the tide was at the highest, keeping the raft with my oar like an anchor to hold the side of it fast to the shore, near a flat piece of ground, which I expected the water would flow over; and so it did. As soon as I found water enough (for my raft drew about a foot of water), I thrust her on upon that flat piece of ground and there fastened or moored her by sticking my two broken oars into the ground, one on one side near one end, and one on the other side near the other end; and thus I lay till the water ebbed away and left my raft and all my cargo safe on shore.

NOTES

1. **if we had kept on board, we had been all safe:** if we had remained in the ship, we would have been all safe
2. **all her quarter was free:** all her quarter was in good condition
3. **cordial waters:** drinks that stimulate the heart
4. **powder horns:** powder flasks made of horn
5. **the least capful of wind:** the least amount of wind
6. **indraught:** inward flow
7. **I had like to have suffered:** I had almost suffered

19

JONATHAN SWIFT

(1667–1745)

Jonathan Swift was a British satirist. He was born of English parentage in Dublin on 30th November, 1667, and educated at Kilkenny Grammar School and Trinity College, Dublin, at both of which he had a fellow student in William Congreve. In 1689 he went to England and worked as secretary to William Temple at Moor Park, Surrey. At Temple's house he met Esther Johnson ("Stella"), the girl who was to become his ever-loving and ever-beloved friend. After Temple's death in 1699, he returned to Ireland, and served as chaplain to the Earl of Berkeley in 1700 and as vicar of Laracor and prebend in St. Patrick's Cathedral, Dublin, in 1701. He made numerous visits to London and wrote political pamphlets in the service of the Whigs. He changed over to the Tories in 1710 and lived in London from 1710 to 1714, enjoying the prestige of an influential public figure and the friendship of Addison, Steele, Pope, Gay, and other men of letters. He was appointed dean of St. Patrick's in 1713, returned to Ireland in 1714, and became a leader of the Irish resistance movement in 1724. After having suffered from infirmities for a long time, he died on 19th October, 1745, and was buried in St. Patrick's by the side of "Stella", who had died in 1728.

Swift published a large number of satires and other works. His best-known books are: ***The Battle of the Books*** (written 1697, published

1704), a discussion of the comparative merits of the ancients and the moderns in literature; *A Tale of a Tub* (1704), a satire on corruptions in religion, especially in the Roman Church; *Journal to Stella* (written 1710-1713), Swift's letters to Esther Johnson about his daily life in London; *The Drapier's Letters* (1724), a protest against the Englishman Wood's monopoly of minting copper money in Ireland; *Gulliver's Travels* (1726), a satirical fable about human follies and absurdities; and *A Modest Proposal* (1729), a satirical pamphlet showing deep concern over the misery of the Irish poor under the English rule. Swift's power as one of the greatest satirists in English is found in his indignation at the irrational, his serious purpose of writing, his witty treatment of material, and his use of an impeccable prose. He conveys his thoughts and feelings in a delightful familiar style. His style has the cardinal virtues of clearness, directness, and vigour; yet it is not without finesse in the form of innuendo, irony, or paradox.

THE DIVERSIONS OF THE COURT OF LILLIPUT

The author[1] diverts the Emperor and his nobility of both sexes, in a very uncommon manner. The diversions of the court of Lilliput described. The author hath his liberty granted him upon certain conditions.

My gentleness and good behaviour had gained so far on the Emperor and his court, and indeed upon the army and people in general, that I began to conceive hopes of getting my liberty in a short time. I took all possible methods to cultivate this favourable disposition. The natives came by degrees to be less apprehensive of any danger from me. I would sometimes lie down, and let five or six of them dance on my hand. And at last the boys and girls would venture to come and play at hide and seek in my hair. I had now made a good progress in understanding and speaking their language. The Emperor had a mind one day to entertain me with several of the country shows, wherein they exceed all nations I have known, both for dexterity and magnificence. I was diverted with none so much as that of the rope-dancers, performed upon a slender white thread, extended about two foot, and twelve inches from the ground. Upon which I shall desire liberty, with the reader's patience, to enlarge a little.

This diversion is only practised by those persons who are candidates for great employments, and high favour, at court. They are trained in this art from their youth, and are not always of noble birth, or liberal education. When a great office is vacant either by death or disgrace (which often happens) five or six of those candidates petition the Emperor to entertain his Majesty and the court with a dance on the rope, and whoever jumps the highest without falling, succeeds in the office. Very often the chief ministers themselves are commanded to show their skill, and to convince the Emperor that they have not lost their faculty. Flimnap[2], the Treasurer, is allowed to cut a caper on the strait rope, at least an inch higher than any other lord in the whole empire. I have seen him do the summerset several times together upon a trencher fixed on the rope, which is no thicker than a common packthread in England. My friend Reldresal, principal Secretary for Private Affairs, is, in my opinion, if I am not partial, the second after the Treasurer; the rest of the great officers are much upon a par.

These diversions are often attended with fatal accidents, whereof great numbers are on record. I myself have seen two or three candidates break a limb. But the danger is much greater when the ministers themselves are commanded to show their dexterity; for by contending to excel themselves and their fellows, they strain so far, that there is hardly one of them who hath not received a fall, and some of them two or three. I was assured that a year or two before my arrival, Flimnap would have infallibly broke his neck, if one of the King's cushions[3], that accidentally lay on the ground, had not weakened the force of his fall.

There is likewise another diversion, which is only shown before the Emperor and Empress, and first minister, upon particular occasions. The Emperor lays on a table three fine silken threads of six inches long. One is blue, the other red, and the third green[4]. These threads are proposed as prizes for those persons whom the Emperor hath a mind to distinguish by a peculiar mark of his favour. The ceremony is performed in his Majesty's great chamber of state, where the candidates are to undergo a trial of dexterity very different from the former, and such as I have not observed the least resemblance of in any other country of the old or the new world. The Emperor holds a stick in his hands, both ends parallel to the horizon, while the candidates, advancing one by one, sometimes leap over the stick, sometimes creep under it backwards and forwards several times, according as the stick is advanced or depressed. Sometimes the Emperor holds one end of the stick, and his first minister the other; sometimes the minister has it entirely to himself. Whoever performs his part with most agility, and holds out the longest in leaping and creeping, is rewarded with the blue-coloured silk; the red is given to the next, and the green to the third, which they all wear girt twice round about the middle; and you see few great persons about this court who are not adorned with one of these girdles.

The horses of the army, and those of the royal stables, having been daily led before me, were no longer shy, but would come up to my very feet without starting. The riders would leap them over my hand as I held it on the ground, and one of the Emperor's huntsmen, upon a large courser, took my foot, shoe and all; which was indeed a prodigious leap. I had the good fortune to divert the Emperor one day after a very extraordinary manner. I desired he would order several sticks of two foot high, and the thickness of an ordinary cane, to be brought me; whereupon his Majesty commanded the master of his woods to give directions accordingly, and the next morning six woodmen arrived with as many carriages, drawn by eight horses to each. I took nine of these sticks, and fixing them firmly in the ground in a quadrangular figure, two foot and a half square, I took four other sticks, and tied them parallel at each corner, about two foot from the ground; then I fastened my handkerchief to the nine sticks that stood erect, and extended it on all sides till it was as tight as the top of a drum; and the four parallel sticks, rising about five inches higher than the handkerchief, served as ledges on each side. When I had finished my work, I desired the Emperor to let a troop of his best horse, twenty-four in number, come and exercise upon this plain. His Majesty approved of the proposal, and I took them up one by one in my hands, ready mounted and armed, with the proper officers to exercise them. As soon as they got into order, they divided into two parties, performed mock skirmishes, discharged blunt arrows, drew their swords, fled and pursued, attacked and retired, and in short discovered the best military discipline I ever beheld. The parallel sticks secured them and their horses from falling over the stage; and the Emperor was so much delighted, that he ordered this entertainment to be repeated several days, and once was pleased to be lifted up, and give the word of command; and, with great difficulty, persuaded even the Empress her self to let me hold her in her close chair[5] within two yards of the stage, from whence she was able to take a full view of the whole performance. It was my good fortune that no ill accident happened in these entertainments, only once a fiery horse that belonged to one of the captains pawing with his hoof struck a hole in my handkerchief, and his foot slipping, he overthrew his rider and himself; but I immediately relieved them both, and covering the hole with one hand, I set down the troop with the other, in the same manner as I took them up. The horse that fell was strained in the left shoulder, but the rider got no hurt, and I repaired my handkerchief as well as I could; however, I would not trust to the strength of it any more in such dangerous enterprises.

About two or three days before I was set at liberty, as I was entertaining the court with these kinds of feats, there arrived an express to inform his Majesty that some of his subjects, riding near the place where I was first taken up, had seen a great black substance lying on the ground, very oddly shaped, extending its edges round as wide as his Majesty's bedchamber, and rising up in the middle as high as a man; that it was no living creature, as they at first apprehended, for it lay on the grass without motion, and some of them had walked round it several times; that by mounting upon each other's shoulders, they had got to the top, which was flat and even, and stamping upon it they found it was hollow within; that they humbly conceived it might be something belonging to the Man-Mountain, and if his Majesty pleased, they would undertake to bring it with only five horses. I presently knew what they meant, and was glad at heart to receive this intelligence. It seems upon my first reaching the shore after our shipwreck, I was in such confusion, that before I came to the place where I went to sleep, my hat, which I had fastened with a string to my head while I was rowing, and had stuck on all the time I was swimming, fell off after I came to land; the string, as I conjecture, breaking by some accident which I never observed, but thought my hat had been lost at sea. I intreated his Imperial Majesty to give orders it might be brought to me as soon as possible, describing to him the use and the nature of it; and the next day the waggoners arrived with it, but not in a very good condition; they had bored two holes in the brim, within an inch and half of the edge, and fastened two hooks in the holes; these hooks were tied by a long cord to the harness, and thus my hat was dragged along for above half an English mile; but the ground in that country being extremely smooth and level, it received less damage than I expected.

Two days after this adventure, the Emperor having ordered that part of his army which quarters in and about his metropolis to be in a readiness, took a fancy of diverting himself in a very singular manner. He desired I would stand like a colossus, with my legs as far asunder as I conveniently could. He then commanded his general (who was an old experienced leader, and a great patron of mine) to draw up the troops in close order, and march them under me, the foot by twenty-four abreast, and the horse by sixteen, with drums beating, colours flying, and pikes advanced. This body consisted of three thousand foot, and a thousand horse. His Majesty gave orders, upon pain of death, that every soldier in his march should observe the strictest decency with regard to my person; which, however, could not prevent some of the younger officers from turning up their eyes as they passed under me. And, to confess the truth, my breeches were at that time in so ill a condition, that they afforded some opportunities for laughter and admiration.

  I had sent so many memorials and petitions for my liberty, that his Majesty at length mentioned the matter, first in the cabinet, and then in a full council; where it was opposed by none, except Skyresh Bolgolam[6], who was pleased, without any provocation, to be my mortal enemy. But it was carried against him by the whole board, and confirmed by the Emperor. That minister was **Galbet**, or Admiral of the Realm, very much in his master's confidence, and a person well versed in affairs, but of a morose and sour complexion[7]. However, he was at length persuaded to comply; but prevailed that the articles and conditions upon which I should be set free, and to which I must swear, should be drawn up by himself. These articles were brought to me by Skyresh Bolgolam in person, attended by two under-secretaries, and several persons of distinction. After they were read, I was demanded to swear to the performance of them; first in the manner of my own country, and afterwards in the method prescribed by their laws; which was to hold my right foot in my left hand, to place the middle finger of my right hand on the crown of my head, and my thumb on the tip of my right ear. But because the reader may perhaps be curious to have some idea of the style and manner of expression peculiar to that people, as well as to know the articles upon which I recovered my liberty, I have made a translation of the whole instrument word for word, as near as I was able, which I here offer to the public.

  Golbasto Momaren Evlame Gurdilo Shefin Mully Ully Gue, most mighty

Emperor of Lilliput, delight and terror of the universe, whose dominions extend five thousand *blustrugs* (about twelve miles in circumference) to the extremities of the globe; monarch of all monarchs, taller than the sons of men; whose feet press down to the center, and whose head strikes against the sun; at whose nod the princes of the earth shake their knees; pleasant as the spring, comfortable as the summer, fruitful as autumn, dreadful as winter. His most sublime Majesty proposeth to the Man-Mountain, lately arrived at our celestial dominions, the following articles, which by a solemn oath he shall be obliged to perform.

First, The Man-Mountain shall not depart from our dominions, without our licence under our great seal.

Secondly, He shall not presume to come into our metropolis, without our express order; at which time the inhabitants shall have two hours' warning to keep within their doors.

Thirdly, The said Man-Mountain shall confine his walks to our principal high roads, and not offer to walk or lie down in a meadow or field of corn.

Fourthly, As he walks the said roads, he shall take the utmost care not to trample upon the bodies of any of our loving subjects, their horses, or carriages, nor take any of our said subjects into his hands, without their own consent.

Fifthly, If an express requires extraordinary dispatch, the Man-Mountain shall be obliged to carry in his pocket the messenger and horse a six days' journey once in every moon, and return the said messenger back (if so required) safe to our Imperial Presence.

Sixthly, He shall be our ally against our enemies in the island of Blefuscu[8], and do his utmost to destroy their fleet, which is now preparing to invade us.

Seventhly, That the said Man-Mountain shall, at his times of leisure, be aiding and assisting to our workmen, in helping to raise certain great stones, towards covering the wall of the principal park, and other our royal buildings.

Eighthly, That the said Man-Mountain shall, in two moons' time, deliver in an exact survey of the circumference of our dominions by a computation of his own paces round the coast.

Lastly, That upon his solemn oath to observe all the above articles, the said

Man-Mountain shall have a daily allowance of meat and drink, sufficient for the support of 1728 of our subjects, with free access to our Royal Person, and other marks of our favour. Given at our palace at Belfaborac the twelfth day of the ninety-first moon of our reign.

  I swore and subscribed to these articles with great cheerfulness and content, although some of them were not so honourable as I could have wished; which proceeded wholly from the malice of Skyresh Bolgolam the High Admiral; whereupon my chains were immediately unlocked, and I was at full liberty; the Emperor himself in person did me the honour to be by at the whole ceremony. I made my acknowledgements by prostrating myself at his Majesty's feet; but he commanded me to rise; and after many gracious expressions, which, to avoid the censure of vanity, I shall not repeat, he added, that he hoped I should prove a useful servant, and well deserve all the favours he had already conferred upon me, or might do for the future.

  The reader may please to observe, that in the last article for the recovery of my liberty, the Emperor stipulates to allow me a quantity of meat and drink sufficient for the support of 1728 Lilliputians. Some time after, asking a friend at court how they came to fix on that determinate number, he told me, that his Majesty's mathematicians, having taken the height of my body by the help of a quadrant[9], and finding it to exceed theirs in the proportion of twelve to one, they concluded from the similarity of their bodies, that mine must contain at least 1728 of theirs, and consequently would require as much food as was necessary to support that number of Lilliputians. By which the reader may conceive an idea of the ingenuity of that people, as well as the prudent and exact economy of so great a prince.

NOTES

1. **the author:** Lemuel Gulliver, the ostensive narrator of ***Gulliver's Travels***, written by Swift
2. **Flimnap:** a caricature of Robert Walpole, the Whig politician
3. **one of the King's cushions:** This designates the Duchess of Kendall, mistress of

George I, who helped to restore Walpole to power in 1721 after his resignation in 1717.
4. **One is blue, the other red, and the third green:** The reference is to the Orders of the Garter, the Bath, and the Thistle.
5. **close chair:** sedan chair
6. **Skyresh Bolgolam:** a caricature of the Earl of Nottingham, the Tory politician
7. **complexion:** disposition
8. **Blefuscu:** This represents France.
9. **quadrant:** instrument for measuring heights

20

RICHARD STEELE

(1672–1729)

Richard Steele was a British essayist and dramatist. He was born in Dublin, Ireland, in March 1672, the son of an attorney; attended Charterhouse School, London, where he began his life-long friendship with Joseph Addison; and studied at Merton College, Oxford, but left the University without taking a degree. He became a soldier, took to politics, entered Parliament, and wrote for the Whigs. He was knighted in 1715, retired to Wales in 1724, and died at Carmarthen on September 1, 1729.

Steele began his literary career by writing sentimental comedies, *The Funeral* (1701), *The Lying Lover* (1703), and *The Tender Husband* (1705). Many years were to pass before his last and best comedy, *The Conscious Lovers* (1722), was written. He turned from his first plays to journalism. In April 1709 he founded *The Tatler*, a periodical which appeared three times every week till January 1711. One of the most important early organs of English journalism, it contained essays mainly on daily life, good manners, and social conduct. Of the 271 numbers, 188 were by Steele, by his old school-fellow Joseph Addison, and 36 their joint products. During March 1711–December 1712 the two friends ran *The Spectator*, which appeared daily except Sunday. This periodical was concerned with manners, morals, philosophical ideas, and literary criticism. Of the 555 papers, about 240 were attributed to Steele and 274 to Addison. After ***The Spectator*** Steele conducted ***The Guardian*** (March October 1713), ***The Englishman*** (1713–1714), ***The Plebeian*** (1718), ***The Theatre*** (1720), etc. Steele's essays show a predilection for social amelioration, a leaning towards sentiment, a striking inventive power, and a genial humour. They are written in a plain, natural style, which is marked by lightness and ease, freedom and flexibility.

RECOLLECTIONS OF CHILDHOOD

Dies ni fallor, adest, quem semper acerbum,
Semper honoratum, sic dii voluistis, habebo.[1]
—Virg, *Aen.* v. 49

There are those among mankind, who can enjoy no relish of their being, except the world is made acquainted with all that relates to them, and think everything lost that passes unobserved; but others find a solid delight in stealing by the crowd, and modelling their life after such a manner as is as much above the approbation as the practice of the vulgar. Life being too short to give instances great enough of true friendship or goodwill, some sages have thought it pious to preserve a certain reverence for the Manes of their deceased friends; and have withdrawn themselves from the rest of the world at certain seasons, to commemorate in their own thoughts such of their acquaintance who have gone before them out of this life. And indeed, when we are advanced in years, there is not a more pleasing entertainment, than to recollect in a gloomy moment the many we have parted with that have been dear and agreeable to us, and to cast a melancholy thought or two after those with whom, perhaps, we have indulged ourselves in whole nights of mirth and jollity. With such inclinations in my heart I went to my closet yesterday in the evening, and resolved to be sorrowful[2]; upon which occasion I could not but look with disdain upon myself, that though all the reasons which I had to lament the loss of many of my friends are now as forcible as at the moment of their departure, yet did not my heart swell with the same sorrow which I felt at that time; but I could, without tears, reflect upon many pleasing adventures I have had with some, who have long been blended with common earth[3]. Though it is by the benefit of nature that length of time thus blots out the violence of afflictions; yet, with tempers too much given to pleasure, it is almost necessary to revive the old places of grief in our memory; and ponder step by step on past life, to lead the mind into that sobriety of thought which poises the heart, and makes it beat with due time, without being quickened by desire, or retarded with despair, from its proper and equal motion. When we wind up a clock that is out of order, to make it go well for the future, we do not immediately set the hand to the present instant, but we make it strike the round of all its hours, before it can recover the regularity of its time. Such, thought I, shall be my method this evening; and since it is that day of the year which I dedicate to the memory of such in another life as I much delighted in when living, an hour or two shall be sacred to sorrow and their memory, while I run over all the melancholy circumstances of this kind which have occurred to me in my whole life.

The first sense of sorrow I ever knew was upon the death of my father[4], at which time I was not quite five years of age; but was rather amazed at what all the house meant than possessed with a real understanding why nobody was willing to play with me. I remember I went into the room where his body lay, and my mother sat weeping alone by it. I had my battledore in my hand, and fell a-beating the coffin, and calling papa; for, I know not how, I had some slight idea that he was locked up there. My mother catched[5] me in her arms, and, transported beyond all patience of the silent grief she was before in, she almost smothered me in her embraces; and told me in a flood of tears, "Papa could not hear me, and would play with me no more[6], for they were going to put him under ground, whence he could never come to us again". She was a very beautiful woman, of a noble spirit, and there was a dignity in her grief amidst all the wildness of her transport which, methought, struck me with an instinct of sorrow, that, before I was sensible of what it was to grieve, seized my very soul, and has made pity the weakness of my heart[7] ever since. The mind in infancy is, methinks, like the body in embryo; and receives impressions so forcible, that they are as hard to be removed by reason as any mark with which a child is born is to be taken away by any future application[8]. Hence it is that good-nature in me is no merit; but having been so frequently overwhelmed with her tears before I knew the cause of any affliction, or could draw defences from my own judgment[9], I imbibed commiseration, remorse, and an unmanly gentleness of mind, which has since insnared me into ten thousand calamities; from whence I can reap no advantage, except it be that, in such a humour as I am now in, I can the better indulge myself in the softness of humanity, and enjoy that sweet anxiety which arises from the memory of past afflictions.

We, that are very old, are better able to remember things which befell us in our distant youth than the passages[10] of later days. For this reason it is that the companions of my strong and vigorous years present themselves more immediately to me in this office of sorrow[11]. Untimely and unhappy deaths are what we are most apt to lament; so little are we able to make it indifferent when a thing happens, though we know it must happen. Thus we groan under life, and bewail those who are relieved from it. Every object that returns to our imagination raises different passions, according to the circumstance of their departure. Who can have lived in an army, and in a serious hour reflect upon the many gay and agreeable men that might long have flourished in the arts of peace, and not join with the imprecations of the fatherless and widow on the tyrant to whose ambition they fell sacrifices? But gallant men, who are cut off by the sword, move rather our veneration than our pity; and we gather relief enough from their own contempt of death, to make that no evil, which was approached with so much cheerfulness, and attended with so much honour. But when we turn our thoughts from the great parts of life on such occasions, and instead of lamenting those who stood ready to give death to those from whom they had the fortune to receive it; I say, when we let our thoughts wander from such noble objects, and consider the havoc which is made among the tender and the innocent, pity enters with an unmixed softness, and possesses all our souls at once.

Here (were there words to express such sentiments with proper tenderness) I should record the beauty, innocence, and untimely death of the first object my eyes ever beheld with love. The beauteous virgin! How ignorantly did she charm[12], how carelessly excel! Oh Death! thou hast right to the bold, to the ambitious, to the high, and to the haughty; but why this cruelty to the humble, to the meek, to the undiscerning, to the thoughtless? Nor age, nor business, nor distress can erase the dear image from my imagination. In the same week, I saw her dressed for a ball, and in a shroud. How ill did the habit of death[13] become the pretty trifler! I still behold the smiling earth[14]—a large train of disasters were coming on to my memory, when my servant knocked at my closet-door, and interrupted me with a letter, attended with a hamper of wine, of the same sort with that which is to be put to sale on Thursday next at Garraway's coffee-house[15]. Upon the receipt of it I sent for three of my friends. We are so intimate that we can be company in whatever state of mind we meet, and can entertain each other without expecting always to rejoice. The wine we found to be generous and warming, but with such a heat as moved us rather to be cheerful than frolicsome. It revived the spirits, without firing the blood. We commended it until two of the clock this morning; and having to-day met a little before dinner, we found that, though we drank two bottles a man, we had much more reason to recollect than forget what had passed the night before.

NOTES

1. ***Dies, ni fallor, adest, quem semper acerbum, / Semper honoratum, sic dii voluistis, habebo.*:** And now the rising day renews the year, /A day for ever sad, for ever dear (Dryden's version).
2. **resolved to be sorrowful:** resolved to indulge in memories of dead friends
3. **blended with common earth:** dead and buried
4. **the death of my father:** Steele's father, an attorney, died when the son "was not quite five years of age"
5. **catched:** caught
6. **Papa could not hear me, and would play with me no more:** i.e. Papa could not hear you, and would play with you no more
7. **the weakness of my heart:** my strongest emotion
8. **application:** healing lotion
9. **draw defences from my own judgment:** check my emotions by my reason
10. **passages:** occurrences
11. **this office of sorrow:** this sorrowful duty
12. **How ignorantly did she charm:** How little did she know that she attracted people.
13. **the habit of death:** the shroud
14. **the smiling earth:** the smile on the dead person's face
15. **Garraway's coffee-house:** a coffee-house in Change Alley, Cornhill

THE SPECTATOR CLUB

Ast alii sex
Et plures uno conclamant ore.[1]
Juv. Sat vii. ver. 167

The first of our society[2] is a gentleman of Worcestershire[3], of ancient descent, a baronet, his name Sir Roger de Coverley. His great-grandfather was inventor of that famous country-dance which is called after him. All who know that shire are very well acquainted with the parts and merits of Sir Roger. He is a gentleman that is very singular in his behaviour, but his singularities proceed from his good sense, and are contradictions to the manners of the world, only as he thinks the world is in the wrong. However, this humour creates him no enemies, for he does nothing with sourness or obstinacy; and his being unconfined to modes and forms, makes him but the readier and more capable to please and oblige all who know him. When he is in town, he lives in Soho Square[4]. It is said, he keeps himself a bachelor by reason he was crossed in love by a perverse beautiful widow of the next county to him. Before this disappointment, Sir Roger was what you call a fine gentleman, had often supped with my Lord Rochester[5] and Sir George Etherege[6], fought a duel upon his first coming to town, and kicked Bully Dawson[7] in a public coffee-house for calling him youngster. But being ill-used by the above-mentioned widow, he was very serious for a year and a half; and though, his temper being naturally jovial, he at last got over it, he grew careless of himself, and never dressed afterwards; he continues to wear a coat and doublet of the same cut that were in fashion at the time of his repulse, which, in his merry humours, he tells us, has been in and out twelve times since he first wore it....He is now in his fifty-sixth year, cheerful, gay, and hearty; keeps a good house in both town and country; a great lover of mankind; but there is such a mirthful cast in his behaviour, that he is rather beloved than esteemed. His tenants grow rich, his servants look satisfied, all the young women profess love to him, and the young men are glad of his company. When he comes into a house he calls the servants by their names, and talks all the way upstairs to a visit. I must not omit that Sir Roger is a justice of the quorum[8]; that he fills the chair at a quarter-session with great abilities, and three months ago, gained universal applause by explaining a passage in the Game-Act.

The gentleman next in esteem and authority among us, is another bachelor, who is a member of the Inner Temple[9]; a man of great probity, wit, and understanding; but he has chosen his place of residence rather to obey the direction of an old humoursome[10] father, than in pursuit of his own inclinations. He was placed there to study the laws of the land, and is the most learned of any of the house in those of the stage. Aristotle[11] and Longinus[12] are much better understood by him than Littleton[13] or Coke[14]. The father sends up every post questions relating to marriage-articles, leases, and tenures, in the neighbourhood; all which questions he agrees with an attorney to answer and take care of in the lump. He is studying the passions themselves, when he should be inquiring into the debates among men which arise from them. He knows the argument of each of the orations of Demosthenes[15] and Tully[16], but not one case in the reports of our own courts. No one ever took him for a fool, but none, except his intimate friends, know he has a great deal of wit[17]. This turn[18] makes him at once both disinterested and agreeable: as few of his thoughts are drawn from business, they are most of them fit for conversation. His taste of books is a little too just for the age he lives in; he has read all, but approves of very few. His familiarity with the customs, manners, actions, and writings of the ancients, makes him a very delicate observer of what occurs to him in the present world. He is an excellent critic, and the time of the play is his hour of business; exactly at five he passes through New Inn[19], crosses through Russel Court[20], and takes a turn[21] at Will's till the play begins; he has his shoes rubbed and his periwig powdered at the barber's as you go into the Rose[22]. It is for the good of the audience when he is at a play, for the actors have an ambition to please him.

The person of next consideration is Sir Andrew Freeport, a merchant of great eminence in the city of London; a person of indefatigable industry, strong reason, and great experience. His notions of trade are noble and generous, and (as every rich man has usually some sly way of jesting, which would make no great figure were he not a rich man) he calls the sea the British Common. He is acquainted with commerce in all its parts, and will tell you that it is a stupid and barbarous way to extend dominion by arms; for true power is to be got by arts and industry. He will often argue, that if this part of our trade were well cultivated, we should gain from one nation; and if another, from another. I have heard him prove that diligence makes more lasting acquisitions than valour, and that sloth has ruined more nations than the sword. He abounds in several frugal maxims, amongst which the greatest favourite is, "A penny saved is a penny got." A general trader of good sense is pleasanter company than a general scholar; and Sir Andrew having a natural unaffected eloquence, the perspicuity of his discourse gives the same pleasure that wit would in another man. He has made his fortunes himself; and says that England may be richer than other kingdoms, by as plain methods as he himself is richer than other men; though at the same time I can say this of him, that there is not a point in the compass, but blows home a ship in which he is an owner.

Next to Sir Andrew in the club-room sits Captain Sentry, a gentleman of great courage, good understanding, but invincible modesty. He is one of those that deserve very well, but are very awkward at putting their talents within the observation of such as should take notice of them. He was some years a captain, and behaved himself with great gallantry in several engagements, and at several sieges; but having a small estate of his own, and being next heir to Sir Roger, he has quitted a way of life in which no man can rise suitably to his merit, who is not something of a courtier, as well as a soldier. I have heard him often lament, that in a profession where merit is placed in so conspicuous a view, impudence should get the better of modesty. When he has talked to this purpose, I never heard him make a sour expression, but frankly confess that he left the world[23], because he was not fit for it. A strict honesty and an even regular behaviour, are in themselves obstacles to him that must press through crowds who endeavour at the same end with himself, the favour of a commander. He will, however, in his way of talk, excuse generals, for not disposing according to men's desert, or inquiring into it; for, says he, that great man who has a mind to help me, has as many to break through to come at me, as I have to come at him; therefore he will conclude, that the man who would make a figure, especially in a military way, must get over all false modesty, and assist his patron against the importunity of other pretenders, by a proper assurance in his own vindication. He says it is a civil cowardice to be backward in asserting what you ought to expect, as it is a military fear to be slow in attacking when it is your duty. With this candour does the gentleman speak of himself and others. The same frankness runs through all his conversation. The military part of his life has furnished him with many adventures, in the relation of which he is very agreeable to the company; for he is never overbearing, though accustomed to command men in the utmost degree below him; nor ever too obsequious, from a habit of obeying men highly above him.

But that our society may not appear a set of humourists[24] unacquainted with the gallantries and pleasures of the age, we have among us the gallant Will Honeycomb, a gentleman who, according to his years, should be in the decline of his life, but having ever been very careful of his person, and always had a very easy fortune, time has made but a very little impression, either by wrinkles on his forehead, or traces in his brain. His person is well turned, and of a good height. He is very ready at that sort of discourse with which men usually entertain women. He has all his life dressed very well, and remembers habits as others do men. He can smile when one speaks to him, and laughs easily. He knows the history of every mode, and can inform you from which of the French king's wenches our wives and daughters had this manner of curling their hair, that way of placing their hoods; whose frailty was covered by such a sort of petticoat, and whose vanity to show her foot made that part of the dress so short in such a year. In a word, all his conversation and knowledge has been in the female world: as other men of his age will take notice to you what such a minister said upon such and such an occasion, he will tell you when the Duke of Monmouth[25] danced at court, such a woman was then smitten, another was taken with him at the head of his troop in the Park[26]. In all these important relations, he has ever about the same time received a kind glance or a blow of a fan, from some celebrated beauty, mother of the present

Lord such-a-one. If you speak of a young Commoner that said a lively thing in the House, he starts up, "He has good blood in his veins, Tom Mirabell begot him, the rogue cheated me in that affair; that young fellow's mother used me more like a dog than any woman I ever made advances to." This way of talking of his, very much enlivens the conversation among us of a more sedate turn; and I find there is not one of the company but myself, who rarely speak at all, but speaks of him as of that sort of man, who is usually called a well-bred fine gentleman. To conclude his character, where women are not concerned, he is an honest worthy man.

I cannot tell whether I am to account him whom I am next to speak of, as one of our company; for he visits us but seldom, but when he does, it adds to every man else a new enjoyment of himself. He is a clergyman, a very philosophic man, of general learning, great sanctity of life, and the most exact good breeding. He has the misfortune to be of a very weak constitution, and consequently cannot accept of such cares and business as preferments in his function would oblige him to: he is therefore among divines what a chamber-counsellor[27] is among lawyers. The probity of his mind, and the integrity of his life, create him followers, as being eloquent or loud advances others. He seldom introduces the subject he speaks upon; but we are so far gone in years that he observes when he is among us, an earnestness to have him fall on some divine topic, which he always treats with much authority, as one who has no interests in this world, as one who is hastening to the object of all his wishes, and conceives hope from his decays and infirmities. These are my ordinary companions.

NOTES

1. ***Ast alii sex/Et plures uno conclamant ore.*:** But six more at least shout with one voice.
2. **our society:** the imaginary Spectator Club
3. **Worcestershire:** a former county of west central England, now part of Hereford and Worcester
4. **Soho Square:** a fashionable quarter in central London
5. **Lord Rochester:** John Wilmot (1647–1680), the second Earl of Rochester, who was a poet and a rake

6. **Sir George Etherege:** George Etherege (1634?–1691) was like John Wilmot in character and accomplishments
7. **Bully Dawson:** a notorious card-sharper and ruffian
8. **a justice of the quorum:** a Justice of the Peace, one of the county magistrates
9. **the Inner Temple:** one of the four inns of court or legal societies in London (the other three being the Middle Temple, Lincoln's Inn, and Gray's Inn)
10. **humoursome:** eccentric
11. **Aristotle:** the great Greek philosopher (384–322 B.C.) whose best-known works are *Ethics*, *Politics*, and *Poetics*
12. **Longinus:** a Greek philosopher and rhetorician (1st century A.D.) who wrote the treatise *On the Sublime*
13. **Littleton:** Thomas Littleton (1422?–1481), a famous English judge and the author of *Tenures*
14. **Coke:** Edward Coke (1552–1634), a famous English judge and the author of a commentary on Littleton's *Tenures*
15. **Demosthenes:** the best-known Greek orator (385–322 B.C.)
16. **Tully:** Marcus Tullius Cicero (106–43 B.C.), Roman orator and writer
17. **wit:** intellect, understanding
18. **turn:** proclivity, characteristic
19. **New Inn:** a place near the Middle Temple
20. **Russel Court:** a narrow passage from Drury Lane
21. **takes a turn:** spends a short time
22. **the Rose:** a tavern in Russell Street, Covent Garden, and near the Drury Lane Theatre
23. **left the world:** retired from public life
24. **humourists:** eccentric people
25. **the Duke of Monmouth:** James Stuart, the Duke of Monmouth, who was Charles II's illegitimate son. He headed a rebellion in 1685 against James II but was defeated and executed.
26. **the Park:** Hyde Park, in west central London
27. **a chamber-counsellor:** a consulting barrister; a barrister who does not go into court

A STAGE-COACH JOURNEY

Qui, aut tempus quid postulet non videt, aut plura loquitur, aut se ostentat, aut eorum quibuscum est rationem non habet, is ineptus esse dicitur.[1]—Tull[2]

Having notified to my good friend Sir Roger that I should set out for London the next day, his horses were ready at the appointed hour in the evening; and, attended by one of his grooms, I arrived at the county-town at twilight, in order to be ready for the stage-coach[3] the day following. As soon as we arrived at the inn, the servant, who waited upon me, inquired of the chamberlain[4] in my hearing, what company he had for the coach? The fellow answered, "Mrs.[5] Betty Arable, the great fortune, and the widow her mother; a recruiting officer (who took a place because they were to go); young Squire Quickset, her cousin (that her mother wished her to be married to); Ephraim[6] the Quaker[7], her guardian; and a gentleman that had studied himself dumb[8] from Sir Roger de Coverley's[9]." I observed by what he said of myself, that according to his office he dealt much in intelligence; and doubted not but there was some foundation for his reports of the rest of the company, as well as for the whimsical account he gave of me. The next morning at daybreak we were called; and I, who know my own natural shyness, and endeavour to be as little liable to be disputed with as possible, dressed immediately, that I might make no one wait. The first preparation for our setting-out was, that the captain's half-pike[10] was placed near the coachman, and a drum behind the coach. In the meantime the drummer, the captain's equipage[11], was very loud, that none of the captain's things should be placed so as to be spoiled; upon which his cloak-bag[12] was fixed in the seat of the coach[13]; and the captain himself, according to a frequent, though invidious[14] behaviour of military men, ordered his man to look sharp, that none but one of the ladies should have the place he had taken fronting to the coach-box.

We were in some little time fixed in our seats, and sat with that dislike which people not too good-natured usually conceive of each other at first sight. The coach jumbled us insensibly into some sort of familiarity; and we had not moved above two miles, when the widow asked the captain what success he had in his recruiting? The officer, with a frankness he believed very graceful, told her, that indeed he had but very little luck, and had suffered much by desertion, therefore should be glad to end his warfare in the service of her or her fair daughter. "In a word," continued he, "I am a soldier, and to be plain is my character; you see me, madam, young, sound, and impudent; take me yourself, widow, or give me to her, I will be wholly at your disposal. I am a soldier of fortune, ha!" This was followed by a vain laugh of his own, and a deep silence of all the rest of the company. I had nothing left for it but to fall fast asleep, which I did with all speed. "Come," said he, "resolve upon it, we will make a wedding at the next town; we will wake this pleasant companion who is fallen asleep, to be the brideman[15], and " (giving the Quaker a clap on the knee) he concluded, "This sly saint, who, I'll warrant, understands what's what[16] as well as you or I, widow, shall give the bride as father." The Quaker, who happened to be a man of smartness, answered, "Friend, I take it in good part[17] that thou hast given me the authority of a father over this comely and virtuous child; and I must assure thee, that if I have the giving her[18], I shall not bestow her on thee. Thy mirth, friend, savoureth of folly; thou art a person of a light mind; thy drum is a type of thee, it soundeth because it is empty. Verily, it is not from thy fullness, but thy emptiness that thou hast spoken this day. Friend, friend, we have hired this coach in partnership with thee, to carry us to the great city; we cannot go any other way. This worthy mother must hear thee if thou wilt needs utter thy follies; we cannot help it, friend, I say: if thou wilt we must hear thee; but, if thou wert a man of understanding, thou wouldst not take advantage of thy courageous countenance[19] to abash us children of peace. Thou art, thou sayest, a soldier; give quarter to[20] us, who cannot resist thee. Why didst thou fleer[21] at our friend, who feigned himself asleep? He said nothing; but how dost thou know what he containeth? If thou speakest improper things in the hearing of this virtuous young virgin, consider it as an outrage against a distressed person that cannot get from thee: to speak indiscreetly what we are obliged to hear, by being hasped up[22] with thee in this public vehicle, is in some degree assaulting on the high road."

Here Ephraim paused, and the captain with a happy and uncommon impudence (which can be convicted and support itself at the same time) cries, "Faith, friend, I thank thee; I should have been a little impertinent if thou hadst not reprimanded me. Come, thou art, I see, a smoky[23] old fellow, and I'll be very orderly the ensuing part of the journey. I was going to give myself airs, but, ladies, I beg pardon."

The captain was so little out of humour, and our company was so far from being soured by this little ruffle[24], that Ephraim and he took a particular delight in being agreeable to each other for the future; and assumed their different provinces in the conduct[25] of the company. Our reckonings, apartments, and accommodation, fell under Ephraim; and the captain looked to all disputes on the road, as the good behaviour of our coachman, and the right we had of taking place as going to London of all vehicles[26] coming from thence. The occurrences we met with were ordinary, and very little happened which could entertain by the relation of them; but when I considered the company we were in, I took it for no small good fortune, that the whole journey was not spent in impertinences, which to one part of us might be an entertainment, to the other a suffering. What therefore Ephraim said when we were almost arrived at London, had to me an air not only of good understanding but good breeding. Upon the young lady's expressing her satisfaction in the journey, and declaring how delightful it had been to her, Ephraim delivered himself as follows: "There is no ordinary part of human life which expresseth so much a good mind, and a right inward[27] man, as his behaviour upon meeting with strangers, especially such as may seem the most unsuitable companions to him: such a man, when he falleth in the way with persons of simplicity and innocence, however knowing he may be in the ways of men, will not vaunt himself thereof; but will the rather[28] hide his superiority to them, that he may not be painful unto them. My good friend," (continued he, turning to the officer) "thee and I[29] are to part by and by, and peradventure we may never meet again: but be advised by a plain man; modes and apparel are but trifles to the real man, therefore do not think such a man as thyself terrible for thy garb, nor such a one as me contemptible for mine. When two such as thee and I meet, with affections[30] such as we ought to have towards each other, thou shouldst rejoice to see my peaceable demeanour, and I should be glad to see thy strength and ability to protect me in it."

NOTES

1. **the Motto in Latin:** That man is guilty of impertinence, who does not see what the occasion demands and who talks too much, or is boastful, or pays no regard to the company he is in.
2. **Tull:** Tully, the former English name for Marcus Tullius Cicero
3. **stage-coach:** (hist.) horse-drawn coach that ran regularly with passengers from stage to stage between two places
4. **chamberlain:** upper servant
5. **Mrs.:** Mistress; a title applied in the 17th–19th centuries to unmarried as well as married women
6. **Ephraim:** a generic name for Quakers
7. **Quaker:** member of the Society of Friends; a Christian sect founded by George Fox about 1650 and distinguished by peaceful principles and plain manners
8. **dumb:** uncommunicative
9. **Sir Roger de Coverley's:** Sir Roger de Coverley's house which was in Worcestershire
10. **half-pike:** short pike; short lance
11. **equipage:** train; (here) attendant
12. **clock-bag:** portmanteau
13. **in the seat of the coach:** under the seat of the coach; in the well of the coach
14. **invidious:** offensive, disagreeable
15. **the brideman:** the best man
16. **what's what:** (colloq.) the true state of affairs
17. **take it in good part:** take it with good humour
18. **the giving her:** the giving of her
19. **countenance:** bearing, behaviour
20. **give quarter to:** show mercy to

21. **fleer:** jeer, gibe
22. **hasped up:** shut up
23. **smoky:** (sl.) shrewd
24. **ruffle:** annoyance, disturbance
25. **conduct:** guidance
26. **taking place...of all vehicles:** taking the best part of the road while the opposite vehicles had to stop
27. **inward:** pious
28. **will the rather:** will rather
29. **thee and I:** thou and I. The Friends generally used *thee* for *thou*.
30. **affections:** feelings

21

JOSEPH ADDISON

(1672–1719)

Joseph Addison was an English essayist, poet, and politician. He was born in Wiltshire on May 1, 1672, the son of a church dean, and was educated at Charterhouse School, London, where he began a life-long friendship with Richard Steele, and at Magdalen College, Oxford, where he was made a Fellow in 1693. After travelling on the Continent on a scholarship, he pursued a political career in the service of the Whigs. He became an Under-Secretary of State in 1706, served as an M.P. from 1708 to 1719, held the post of Secretary of State in the Sunderland cabinet in 1717–1718, and died on June 17, 1719.

Addison published in 1703 *The Campaign*, a poem in heroic couplets celebrating the victory of Blenheim, and had his neo-classical blank-verse tragedy *Cato* produced in 1713. He contributed 42 (46?) essays to Richard Steele's *Tatler* (April 1709–January 1711), a thrice-weekly periodical; edited, in conjunction with Steele, *The Spectator* (March 1711–December 1712), a daily, and wrote 274 essays for it; and revived *The Spectator* alone in 1714, when 80 numbers were issued, of which 24 came from his pen. His high reputation has always been based on his periodical essays. These are chiefly concerned with the art of living, with the cultivation of rational life, practical virtue and good taste. They contain his sympathetic observation of humanity, sound critical judgement, and pervading kindly humour, all expressed in plain, natural English, in a style marked by clearness, simplicity, order, precision, and grace. Addison's prose was acclaimed by Dr. Johnson as "the model of the middle style", "an English style, familiar but not coarse, and elegant but not ostentatious".

THE SPECTATOR'S ACCOUNT OF HIMSELF

Non fumum ex fulgore, sed ex fumo dare lucem
Cogitat, ut speciosa dehine miracula promat.[1]
                                        Hor. *Ars Poet.* ver. 143

    I have observed, that a reader seldom peruses a book with pleasure till he knows whether the writer of it be a black[2] or a fair man, of a mild or choleric disposition, married or a bachelor, with other particulars of the like nature, that conduce very much to the right understanding of an author. To gratify this curiosity, which is so natural to a reader, I design this paper, and my next, as prefatory discourses to my following writings, and shall give some account in them of the several persons that are engaged in this work. As the chief trouble of compiling, digesting, and correcting will fall to my share, I must do myself the justice to open the work with my own history.

    I was born to a small hereditary estate, which, according to the tradition of the village where it lies, was bounded by the same hedges and ditches in William the Conqueror's[3] time that it is at present, and has been delivered down from father to son whole and entire, without the loss or acquisition of a single field or meadow, during the space of six hundred years. There runs a story in the family, that, some time before my birth, my mother dreamt that her child was to be a judge. Whether this might proceed from a lawsuit which was then depending[4] in the family, or my father's being a justice of the peace, I cannot determine; for I am not so vain as to think it presaged any dignity that I should arrive at in my future life, though that was the interpretation which the neighbourhood put upon it. The gravity of my behaviour at my very first appearance in the world, and afterwards, seemed to favour my mother's dream: for, as she has often told me, I threw away my rattle before I was two months old, and would not make use of my coral[5] till they had taken away the bells from it.

As for the rest of my infancy, there being nothing in it remarkable, I shall pass it over in silence. I find that, during my nonage, I had the reputation of a very sullen youth, but was always a favourite of my schoolmaster, who used to say, *that my parts were solid, and would wear well*. I had not been long at the university, before I distinguished myself by a most profound silence: for, during the space of eight years, excepting in the public exercises[6] of the college, I scarce uttered the quantity of a hundred words; and indeed do not remember that I ever spoke three sentences together in my whole life. Whilst I was in this learned body, I applied myself with so much diligence to my studies, that there are very few celebrated books, either in the learned or the modern tongues[7], which I am not acquainted with.

Upon the death of my father I was resolved to travel into foreign countries, and therefore left the university, with the character of an odd unaccountable fellow, that had a great deal of learning, if I would but show it. An insatiable thirst after knowledge carried me into all the countries of Europe, in which there was anything new or strange to be seen; nay, to such a degree was my curiosity raised, that having read the controversies of some great men concerning the antiquities of Egypt[8], I made a voyage to Grand Cairo, on purpose to take the measure of a pyramid; and, as soon as I had set myself right in that particular, returned to my native country with great satisfaction.

I have passed my latter years in this city, where I am frequently seen in most public places, though there are not above half a dozen of my select friends that know me; of whom my next paper shall give a more particular account. There is no place of general resort wherein I do not often make my appearance; sometimes I am seen thrusting my head into a round of politicians at Will's[9] and listening with great attention to the narratives that are made in those little circular audiences. Sometimes I smoke a pipe at Child's[10]; and, while I seem attentive to nothing but the *Postman*[11], overhear the conversation of every table in the room. I appear on Sunday nights at St. James's Coffee-house[12], and sometimes join the little committee of politics in the inner room, as one who comes there to hear and improve. My face is likewise very well known at the Grecian[13], the Cocoa-Tree[14], and in the theatres both of Drury Lane[15] and the Haymarket[16]. I have been taken for a merchant upon the Exchange[17] for above these ten years, and sometimes pass for a Jew in the assembly of stock-jobbers at Jonathan's[18]. In short, wherever I see a cluster of people, I always mix with them, though I never open my lips but in my own club.

Thus I live in the world, rather as a spectator of mankind, than as one of the species; by which means I have made myself a speculative statesman[19], soldier, merchant, and artisan, without ever meddling with any practical part in life. I am very well versed in the theory of a husband or a father, and can discern the errors in the economy[20], business, and diversion of others, better than those who are engaged in them; as standers-by discover blots[21], which are apt to escape those who are in the game. I never espoused any party with violence, and am resolved to observe an exact neutrality between the Whigs and Tories[22], unless I shall be forced to declare myself by the hostilities of either side. In short, I have acted in all the parts of my life as a looker-on, which is the character I intend to preserve in this paper.

I have given the reader just so much of my history and character, as to let him see I am not altogether unqualified for the business I have undertaken. As for other particulars in my life and adventures, I shall insert them in following papers, as I shall see occasion. In the meantime, when I consider how much I have seen, read, and heard, I begin to blame my own taciturnity; and since I have neither time nor inclination to communicate the fulness of my heart in speech, I am resolved to do it in writing; and to print myself out, if possible, before I die. I have been often told by my friends that it is a pity so many useful discoveries which I have made, should be in the possession of a silent man. For this reason, therefore, I shall publish a sheet full of thoughts every morning, for the benefit of my contemporaries; and if I can any way contribute to the diversion or improvement of the country in which I live, I shall leave it, when I am summoned out of it, with the secret satisfaction of thinking that I have not lived in vain.

There are three very material points which I have not spoken to[23] in this paper, and which, for several important reasons, I must keep to myself, at least for some time: I mean, an account of my name, my age, and my lodgings. I must confess

I would gratify my reader in anything that is reasonable; but as for these three particulars, though I am sensible they might tend very much to the embellishment of my paper, I cannot yet come to a resolution of communicating them to the public. They would indeed draw me out of that obscurity which I have enjoyed for many years, and expose me in public places to several salutes and civilities, which have been always very disagreeable to me; for the greatest pain I can suffer, is the being talked to, and being stared at. It is for this reason likewise, that I keep my complexion and dress, as very great secrets; though it is not impossible, but I may make discoveries[24] of both in the progress of the work I have undertaken.

After having been thus particular upon myself, I shall in to-morrow's paper give an account of those gentlemen who are concerned with me in this work. For, as I have before intimated, a plan of it is laid and concerted[25] (as all other matters of importance are) in a club. However, as my friends have engaged me to stand in the front, those who have a mind to correspond with me, may direct their letters to the ***Spectator***, at Mr. Buckley's[26], in Little Britain[27]. For I must further acquaint the reader, that though our club meets only on Tuesdays and Thursdays, we have appointed a committee to sit every night, for the inspection of all such papers as may contribute to the advancement of the public weal.

NOTES

1. **the Motto in Latin:** He thinks not of the flash ending in smoke but of light emerging from the smoke, and he hopes to create a dazzling miracle.
2. **black:** dark
3. **William the Conqueror:** i.e. William Ⅰ (1028–1087), Duke of Normandy (1035–1087) and King of England (1066–1087)
4. **depending:** pending, not settled
5. **my coral:** my toy made of polished coral
6. **public exercises:** scholastic disputations, academic discussions
7. **the learned...tongues:** Greek and Latin
8. **the controversies of some great men concerning the antiquities of Egypt:** Addison is alluding to John Greaves's ***Pyramidographia or a Discourse on the Pyramids of***

Egypt published in the middle of the 17th century and a pamphlet on the same subject published in the early 18th century.

9. **Will's:** Will's Coffee-house in Russell Street, Covent Garden, patronized especially by men of letters
10. **Child's:** Child's Coffee-house in St. Paul's Churchyard, frequented especially by clergymen, doctors, and scientists
11. *Postman*: a weekly newspaper of the day
12. **St. James's Coffee-house:** The Coffee-house in St. James's Street used to be the favourite resort of Whig politicians.
13. **the Grecian:** The Grecian Coffee-house in the Strand was the first coffee-house opened in London and was patronized by lawyers and scholars.
14. **the Cocoa-Tree:** a chocolate-house in St. James's Street
15. **Drury Lane:** Drury Lane Theatre, which was built in 1674 and burnt down in 1809
16. **the Haymarket:** the Haymarket Theatre which was built in 1705
17. **the Exchange:** The Royal Exchange, a building in the heart of the City of London, was a meeting place for merchants and bankers to conduct their business.
18. **Jonathan's:** Jonathan's Coffee-house in Cornhill, where stock brokers and business men gathered
19. **a speculative statesman:** a statesman given to speculation or theory
20. **the economy:** (here) the management of a household
21. **blots:** mistakes
22. **the Whigs and Tories:** the two leading political parties of England, the Liberals and Conservatives
23. **spoken to:** referred to, discussed
24. **discoveries:** disclosures, revelations
25. **concerted:** agreed upon
26. **Mr. Buckley's:** Samuel Buckley was the printer of *The Spectator*.
27. **Little Britain:** a short street in London which was in Addison's day the regular booksellers' quarter.

SIR ROGER AT HOME

Hic tibi copia Manabit ad plenum,
Benigno Ruris honorum opulenta cornu.[1]

Hor. *Od*. 1. 17.

Having often received an invitation from my friend Sir Roger de Coverley to pass away a month with him in the country, I last week accompanied him thither, and am settled with him for some time at his country-house, where I intend to form several of my ensuing speculations. Sir Roger, who is very well acquainted with my humour[2], lets me rise and go to bed when I please; dine at his own table or in my chamber as I think fit, sit still and say nothing without bidding me be merry. When the gentlemen of the country come to see him, he only shows me at a distance: as I have been walking in his fields I have observed them stealing a sight of me over a hedge, and have heard the knight desiring them not to let me see them, for that[3] I hated to be stared at.

I am the more at ease in Sir Roger's family, because it consists of sober and staid persons: for as the knight is the best master in the world, he seldom changes his servants; and as he is beloved by all about him, his servants never care for leaving him; by this means his domestics are all in years, and grown old with their master. You would take his valet-de-chambre for his brother, his butler is grey-headed, his groom is one of the gravest men that I have ever seen, and his coachman has the looks of a privy-counsellor. You see the goodness of the master even in the old house-dog, and in a grey pad[4] that is kept in the stable with great care and tenderness out of regard to his past services, though he has been useless for several years.

I could not but observe with a great deal of pleasure the joy that appeared in the countenance of these ancient domestics upon my friend's arrival at his country-seat. Some of them could not refrain from tears at the sight of their old master; every one of them pressed forward to do something for him, and seemed discouraged if they were not employed. At the same time the good old knight, with a mixture of the father and the master of the family, tempered the inquiries after his own affairs with several kind questions relating to themselves. This humanity and good nature engages everybody to him, so that when he is pleasant upon[5] any of them, all his family are in good humour, and none so much as the person whom he diverts himself with: on the contrary, if he coughs, or betrays any infirmity of old age, it is easy for a stander by to observe a secret concern in the looks of all his servants.

My worthy friend has put me under the particular care of his butler, who is a very prudent man, and, as well as the rest of his fellow-servants, wonderfully desirous of pleasing me, because they have often heard their master talk of me as of his particular friend.

My chief companion, when Sir Roger is diverting himself in the woods or the fields, is a very venerable man who is ever with Sir Roger, and has lived at his house in the nature of a chaplain above thirty years. This gentleman is a person of good sense and some learning, of a very regular life and obliging conversation[6]: he heartily loves Sir Roger, and knows that he is very much in the old knight's esteem, so that he lives in the family rather as a relation than a dependant.

I have observed in several of my papers, that my friend Sir Roger, amidst all his good qualities, is something of a humorist[7]; and that his virtues, as well as imperfections, are, as it were, tinged by a certain extravagance, which makes them particularly his, and distinguishes them from those of other men. This cast of mind, as it is generally very innocent in itself, so it renders his conversation highly agreeable, and more delightful than the same degree of sense and virtue would appear in their common or ordinary colours. As I was walking with him last night, he asked me how I liked the good man whom I have just now mentioned; and, without staying for my answer, told me that he was afraid of being insulted with Latin and Greek at his own table; for which reason he desired a particular friend of his at the university to find him out a clergyman rather of plain sense than much learning, of a good aspect, a clear voice, a sociable temper: and, if possible, a man that understood a little of back-gammon. "My friend," says Sir Roger, "found me out this gentleman, who, besides the endowments required of him, is, they tell me, a good scholar, though he does not show it: I have given him the parsonage of the parish; and because I know his value, have settled upon him a good annuity for life. If he outlives me, he shall find that he was higher in my esteem than perhaps he thinks he is. He has now been with me thirty years; and though he does not know I have taken notice of it, has never in all that time asked anything of me for himself, though he is every day soliciting me for something in behalf of one or other of my tenants, his parishioners. There has not been a law-suit in the parish since he has lived among them; if any dispute arises they apply themselves to him for the decision; if they do not acquiesce in his judgment, which I think never happened above once or twice at most, they appeal to me. At his first settling with me, I made him a present of all the good sermons which have been printed in English, and only begged of him that every Sunday he would pronounce one of them in the pulpit. Accordingly, he has digested them into such a series, that they follow one another naturally, and make a continued system of practical divinity[8]."

As Sir Roger was going on in his story, the gentleman we were talking of came up to us; and upon the knight's asking him who preached to-morrow (for it was Saturday night) told us, the Bishop of St. Asaph[9] in the morning, and Dr. South[10] in the afternoon. He then showed us his list of preachers for the whole year, where I saw with a great deal of pleasure Archbishop Tillotson[11], Bishop Saunderson[12], Dr. Barrow[13], Dr. Calamy[14], with several living authors who have published discourses of practical divinity. I no sooner saw this venerable man in the pulpit, but I very much approved of my friend's insisting upon the qualifications of a good aspect and a clear voice; for I was so charmed with the gracefulness of his figure and delivery, as well as with the discourses he pronounced, that I think I never passed any time more to my satisfaction. A sermon repeated after this manner, is like the composition of a poet in the mouth of a graceful actor.

I could heartily wish that more of our country clergy would follow this example; and instead of wasting their spirits in laborious compositions of their own, would endeavour after a handsome elocution, and all those other talents that are proper to enforce what has been penned by greater masters. This would not only be more easy to themselves, but more edifying to the people.

NOTES
1. **the Motto in Latin:** Here, Plenty, rich in the honours of the quiet plain, shall shower upon you copious gifts from her bounteous horn (C. B. Wheeler's translation).
2. **humour:** inclination, disposition
3. **for that:** because
4. **pad:** easy-paced horse
5. **is pleasant upon:** makes a joke about
6. **conversation:** behaviour
7. **humorist:** eccentric person
8. **practical divinity:** practical theology, the application of religious precepts to practical life
9. **the Bishop of St. Asaph:** William Fleetwood (1656–1723), a bishop and pulpit orator
10. **Dr. South:** Robert South (1634–1716), a court preacher with a homely style
11. **Archbishop Tillotson:** John Tillotson (1630–1694), Archbishop of Canterbury
12. **Bishop Saunderson:** Robert Saunderson (1587–1663), Bishop of Lincoln and professor of Divinity at Oxford
13. **Dr. Barrow:** Issac Barrow (1630–1677), a mathematician, classical scholar, and divine
14. **Dr. Calamy:** Edmund Calamy (1600–1666), one of the leading Presbyterian ministers under the Commonwealth

SIR ROGER IN LONDON

Aevo rarissima nostro Simplicitas.[1]

Ovid, *Ares. Am.* i. 241

I was this morning surprised with a great knocking at the door, when my landlady's daughter came up to me, and told me, that there was a man below desired to speak with me. Upon my asking her who it was, she told me it was a very grave elderly person, but that she did not know his name. I immediately went down to him, and found him to be the coachman of my worthy friend Sir Roger de Coverley. He told me that his master came to town last night, and would be glad to take a turn with me in Gray's Inn walks[2]. As I was wondering in myself what had brought Sir Roger to town, not having lately received any letter from him, he told me that his master was come up to get a sight of Prince Eugene[3], and that he desired I would immediately meet him.

I was not a little pleased with the curiosity of the old knight, though I did not much wonder at it, having heard him say more than once in private discourse, that he looked upon Prince Eugenio (for so the knight always calls him) to be a greater man than Scanderbeg[4].

I was no sooner come into Gray's Inn walks, but I heard my friend upon the terrace hemming twice or thrice to himself with great vigour, for he loves to clear his pipes in good air (to make use of his own phrase), and is not a little pleased with any one who takes notice of the strength which he still exerts in his morning hems.

I was touched with a secret joy at the sight of the good old man, who before he saw me was engaged in conversation with a beggar man that had asked an alms of him. I could hear my friend chide him for not finding out some work; but at the same time saw him put his hand into his pocket and give him sixpence.

Our salutations were very hearty on both sides, consisting of many kind shakes of the hand, and several affectionate looks which we cast upon one another. After which the knight told me, my good friend his chaplain was very well, and much at my service, and that the Sunday before he had made a most incomparable sermon out of Dr. Barrow. "I have left," says he, "all my affairs in his hands, and being willing to lay an obligation upon him, have deposited with him thirty marks, to be distributed among his poor parishioners."

He then proceeded to acquaint me with the welfare of Will Wimble[5]. Upon which he put his hand into his fob, and presented me in his name with a tobacco-stopper, telling me, that Will had been busy all the beginning of the winter in turning great quantities of them; and that he made a present of one to every gentleman in the country who has good principles, and smokes. He added, that poor Will was at present under great tribulation, for that Tom Touchy[6] had taken the law of him for cutting some hazel sticks out of one of his hedges.

Among other pieces of news which the knight brought from his country-seat, he informed me that Moll White[7] was dead; and that about a month after her death the wind was so very high, that it blew down the end of one of his barns. "But for my own part," says Sir Roger, "I do not think that the old woman had any hand in it."

He afterwards fell into an account of the diversions which had passed in his house during the holidays; for Sir Roger, after the laudable custom of his ancestors, always keeps open house at Christmas. I learned from him, that he had killed eight fat hogs for this season; that he had dealt about his chines very liberally amongst his neighbours; and that in particular he had sent a string of hog's puddings[8] with a pack of cards to every poor family in the parish. "I have often thought," says Sir Roger, "it happens very well that Christmas should fall out in the middle of winter. It is the most dead and uncomfortable time of the year, when the poor people would suffer very much from their poverty and cold, if they had not good cheer, warm fires, and Christmas gambols to support them. I love to rejoice their poor hearts at this season, and to see the whole village merry in my great hall. I allow a double quantity of malt to my small beer, and set it a running for twelve days to every one that calls for it. I have always a piece of cold beef and a mince-pie upon the table, and am wonderfully pleased to see my tenants pass away a whole evening in playing their innocent tricks, and smutting one another. Our friend Will Wimble is as merry as any of them, and shows a thousand roguish tricks upon these occasions."

I was very much delighted with the reflection of my old friend, which carried so much goodness in it. He then launched out into the praise of the late act of Parliament for securing the Church of England[9], and told me, with great satisfaction, that he believed it already began to take effect, for that a rigid dissenter, who chanced to dine at his house on Christmas day had been observed to eat very plentifully of his plum-porridge.

After having dispatched all our country matters, Sir Roger made several inquiries concerning the club, and particularly of his old antagonist Sir Andrew Freeport[10]. He asked me with a kind of smile, whether Sir Andrew had not taken the advantage of his absence to vent among them some of his republican doctrines; but soon after, gathering up his countenance into a more than ordinary seriousness, "Tell me truly," said he, "don't you think Sir Andrew had a hand in the Pope's procession[11]?"—but without giving me time to answer him, "Well, well," says he, "I know you are a wary man, and do not care for talking of public matters."

The knight then asked me if I had seen Prince Eugenio, and made me promise to get him a stand in some convenient place where he might have a full sight of that extraordinary man, whose presence does so much honour to the British nation. He dwelt very long on the praises of this great general, and I found that, since I was with him in the country, he had drawn many observations together out of his reading in Baker's Chronicle[12], and other authors, who always lie in his hall window, which very much redound to the honour of this prince.

Having passed away the greatest part of the morning in hearing the knight's reflections, which were partly private and partly political, he asked me if I would smoke a pipe with him over a dish of coffee at Squire's[13]. As I love the old man, I take delight in complying with everything that is agreeable to him, and accordingly waited on him to the coffee-house, where his venerable aspect drew upon us the eyes of the whole room. He had no sooner seated himself at the upper end of the high table, but he called for a clean pipe, a paper of tobacco, a dish of coffee, a wax-candle, and the *Supplement*[14], with such an air of cheerfulness and good humour, that all the boys in the coffee-room (who seemed to take pleasure in serving him) were at once employed on his several errands, insomuch that nobody else could come at a dish of tea, till the knight had got all his conveniences about him.

NOTES

1. **the Motto in Latin:** simplicity, found all too seldom in our times—Ovid (C. B. Wheeler's translation)
2. **Gray's Inn walks:** a fashionable promenade on the north side of Holborn
3. **Prince Eugene:** François Eugene de Savoic-Carignan (1663–1736), the French-born Austrian general, was associated with Marlborough in the War of the Spanish Succession. They defeated the French at Blenheim (1704), Oudenaarde (1708), and Malplaquet (1709).
4. **Scanderbeg:** George Castriota (1404?–1466), the Albanian commander who led his people in resisting the progress of the Turks
5. **Will Wimble:** a fictitious character—a country gentleman "extremely well versed in all the little handicrafts of an idle man"
6. **Tom Touchy:** a fictitious character—a fellow "famous for taking the law of everybody"
7. **Moll White:** a fictitious character—an old woman labelled as a witch
8. **hog's puddings:** large sausages
9. **the late act of Parliament for securing the Church of England:** the *Occasional Conformity Act* (1710)
10. **Sir Andrew Freeport:** a merchant and member of the fictitious Spectator Club
11. **the Pope's procession:** the annual procession (on November 17) in which the Pope's head in effigy was carried—a Whig demonstration to show opposition to the Roman Catholic Church
12. **Baker's Chronicle:** Sir Richard Baker (1568–1645) wrote *A Chronicle of the Kings of England* (1643), which could not have mentioned Prince Eugene.
13. **Squire's:** Squire's Coffee-house in Holborn
14. **the *Supplement*:** a newspaper of the day, an alternative edition of *The Postboy*

22

LADY MARY WORTLEY MONTAGU

(1689–1762)

Lady Mary Wortley Montagu was an English letter-writer. She was born in London, the eldest daughter of Evelyn Pierrepont, fifth Earl and first Duke of Kingston. Well-educated and witty, she moved in London's literary and social circles. In 1712 she married Edward Wortley Montagu, an M.P. In 1716 she accompanied her husband to Constantinople, where he worked as British ambassador to Turkey. She stayed there until 1718, when she returned to London. She lived by herself in Italy and France from 1739 to 1762, and died in London shortly after her return. Her letters, mostly written from abroad, are rich in matter; they describe her experiences and feelings, the people and scenes she saw; they also discuss literature, science, education, and politics. Her shrewd observations and sound opinions are conveyed in lucid, easy, vivid prose.

TO MRS. S. C.[1]

Adrianople[2], April 1, O.S.[3] 1717

In my opinion, dear S., I ought rather to quarrel with you for not answering my Nimeguen[4] letter of August till December, than to excuse my not writing again till now. I am sure there is on my side a very good excuse for silence, having gone such tiresome land-journeys, though I don't find the conclusion of them so bad as you seem to imagine. I am very easy here, and not in the solitude you fancy me. The great number of Greeks, French, English, and Italians, that are under our protection[5], make their court to me from morning till night; and, I'll assure you, are many of them very fine ladies; for there is no possibility for a Christian to live easily under this government but by the protection of an ambassador—and the richer they are, the greater is their danger.

Those dreadful stories you have heard of the *plague* have very little foundation in truth. I own I have much ado to reconcile myself to the sound of a word which has always given me such terrible ideas, though I am convinced there is little more in it than in a fever. As a proof of this, let me tell you that we passed through two or three towns most violently infected. In the very next house where we lay (in one of those places) two persons died of it. Luckily for me I was so well deceived that I knew nothing of the matter; and I was made believe, that our second cook had only a great cold. However, we left our doctor to take care of him, and yesterday they both arrived here in good health; and I am now let into the secret that he has had the *plague*. There are many that escape it; neither is the air ever infected. I am persuaded that it would be as easy a matter to root it out here as out of Italy and France; but it does so little mischief, they are not very solicitous about it, and are content to suffer this distemper instead of our variety, which they are utterly unacquainted with.

A propos of distempers, I am going to tell you a thing that will make you wish yourself here. The small-pox, so fatal, and so general amongst us, is here entirely harmless by the invention of ***ingrafting***[6], which is the term they give it. There is a set of old women who make it their business to perform the operation every autumn, in the month of September, when the great heat is abated. People send to one another to know if any of their family has a mind to have the small-pox: they make parties for this purpose, and when they are met (commonly fifteen or sixteen together), the old woman comes with a nut-shell full of the matter of the best sort of small-pox, and asks what vein you please to have opened. She immediately rips open that you offer to her with a large needle (which gives you no more pain than a common scratch), and puts into the vein as much matter as can lie upon the head of her needle, and after that binds up the little wound with a hollow bit of shell; and in this manner opens four or five veins. The Grecians have commonly the superstition of opening one in the middle of the forehead, one in each arm, and one on the breast, to mark the sign of the cross; but this has a very ill effect, all these wounds leaving little scars, and is not done by those that are not superstitious, who choose to have them in the legs, or that part of the arm that is concealed. The children or young patients play together all the rest of the day, and are in perfect health to the eighth[7]. Then the fever begins to seize them, and they keep their beds two days, very seldom three. They have very rarely above twenty or thirty[8] in their faces, which never mark; and in eight days' time they are as well as before their illness. Where they are wounded, there remain running sores during the distemper, which I don't doubt is a great relief to it. Every year thousands undergo this operation; and the French ambassador says pleasantly, that they take the small-pox here by way of diversion, as they take the waters[9] in other countries. There is no example of any one that has died in it; and you may believe I am well satisfied of the safety of this experiment, since I intend to try it on my dear little son.

  I am patriot enough to take pains to bring this useful invention into fashion in England[10]; and I should not fail to write to some of our doctors very particularly about it, if I knew any one of them that I thought had virtue enough to destroy such a considerable branch of their revenue for the good of mankind. But that distemper is too beneficial to them, not to expose to all their resentment the hardy wight that should undertake to put an end to it. Perhaps, if I live to return, I may, however, have courage to war with them. Upon this occasion admire the heroism in the heart of your friend, etc., etc.

NOTES

1. **S. C.:** Sarah Chiswell
2. **Adrianople:** a town in northwest Turkey, now called Edirne
3. **O. S.:** Old Style; according to the Julian Calendar. England did not adopt the New Style, i.e. the Gregorian Calendar until 1752.
4. **Nimeguen:** a city of Gelderland in the east Netherlands
5. **under our protection:** under the protection of the British Embassy in Turkey
6. *ingrafting*: inoculation
7. **to the eighth:** to the eighth day
8. **twenty or thirty:** twenty or thirty pimples
9. **take the waters:** go to a spa and drink the mineral waters
10. **I am patriot enough to take pains to bring this useful invention into fashion in England:** Lady Mary Wortley Montagu recounted the Turkish practice of inoculation for small-pox in 1717 and introduced the treatment into England in 1718.

23

PHILIP DORMER STANHOPE

(1694-1773)

Philip Dormer Stanhope, fourth Earl of Chesterfield, was an English statesman, diplomatist, and letter writer. He was born in London and educated at Trinity College, Cambridge. He entered the House of Commons in 1715 and the House of Lords in 1726, and served as ambassador to The Hague from 1728 to 1732, Lord Lieutenant of Ireland in 1745-1746, and Secretary of State in 1746-1748. This man of high culture is chiefly remembered as the author of **Letters to His Son**, letters which he wrote to his natural son Philip Stanhope (1732-1768) from 1737 onwards and which were published by his son's widow in 1774. In them he taught good breeding and worldly wisdom, for he believed that polite behaviour and social harmony were of paramount importance. His descriptions and prescriptions are given in flowing, elegant prose.

ON MAKING FRIENDS

London, October 9, O.S[1]. 1747

Dear Boy,

People of your age have commonly an unguarded frankness about them, which makes them the easy prey and bubbles[2] of the artful and the experienced: they look upon every knave, or fool, who tells them that he is their friend, to be really so; and pay that profession of simulated friendship with an indiscreet and unbounded confidence, always to their loss, often to their ruin. Beware, therefore, now that you are coming into the world, of these proffered friendships. Receive them with great civility, but with great incredulity, too; and pay them with compliments, but not with confidence. Do not let your vanity and self-love make you suppose that people become your friends at first sight, or even upon a short acquaintance. Real friendship is a slow growth; and never thrives, unless ingrafted upon a stock of known and reciprocal merit. There is another kind of nominal friendship, among young people, which is warm for the time, but, by good luck, of short duration. This friendship is hastily produced by their being accidentally thrown together, and pursuing the same course of riot and debauchery. A fine friendship, truly! and well cemented by drunkenness and lewdness. It should rather be called a conspiracy against morals and good manners, and be punished as such by the civil Magistrate. However, they have the impudence and the folly to call this confederacy a friendship. They lend one another money for bad purposes; they engage in quarrels, offensive and defensive, for their accomplices; they tell one another all they know, and often more, too; when, of a sudden, some accident disperses them, and they think no more of each other, unless it be to betray and laugh at their imprudent confidence. Remember to make a great difference between companions and friends; for a very complaisant and agreeable companion may, and often does, prove a very improper and a very dangerous friend. People will, in a great degree, and not without reason, form their opinion of you upon that which they have of your friends; and there is a Spanish proverb, which says very justly, ***Tell me whom you live with, and I will tell you who you are.*** One may fairly suppose that a man who makes a knave or a fool his friend, has something very bad to do, or to conceal. But, at the same time that you carefully decline the friendship of knaves and fools, if it can be called friendship, there is no occasion to make either of them your enemies, wantonly and unprovoked; for they are numerous bodies; and I would rather choose a secure neutrality, than alliance or war, with either of them. You may be a declared enemy to their vices and follies, without being marked out by them as a personal one. Their enmity is the next dangerous thing to their friendship. Have a real reserve with almost everybody; and have a seeming reserve with almost nobody; for it is very disagreeable to seem reserved, and very dangerous not to be so. Few people find the true medium; many are ridiculously mysterious and reserved upon trifles; and many imprudently communicative of all they know.

The next thing to the choice of your friends is the choice of your company. Endeavour, as much as you can, to keep company with people above you. There you rise, as much as you sink with people below you; for (as I have mentioned before) you are whatever the company you keep is. Do not mistake, when I say company above you, and think that I mean with regard to their birth; that is the least consideration: but I mean with regard to their merit, and the light in which the world considers them.

There are two sorts of good company; one which is called the ***beau monde***[3], and consists of those people who have the lead in Courts, and in the gay part of life; the other consists of those who are distinguished by some peculiar merit, or who excel in some particular and valuable art or science. For my own part, I used to think myself in company as much above me, when I was with Mr. Addison and Mr. Pope[4], as if I had been with all the princes in Europe. What I mean by low company, which should by all means be avoided, is the company of those who, absolutely insignificant and contemptible in themselves, think they are honored by being in your company, and who flatter every vice and every folly you have, in order to engage you to converse with them. The pride of being the first of the company is but too common; but it is very silly, and very prejudicial. Nothing in the world lets down a character more than that wrong turn[5].

You may possibly ask me whether a man has it always in his power to get into the best company? and how? I say, Yes, he has, by deserving it; provided he is but in circumstances which enable him to appear upon the footing of a gentleman. Merit and good breeding will make their way everywhere. Knowledge will introduce him, and good breeding will endear him to the best companies; for, as I have often told you, politeness and good breeding are absolutely necessary to adorn any or all other good qualities or talents. Without them, no knowledge, no perfection whatsoever, is seen in its best light. The Scholar, without good breeding, is a Pedant; the Philosopher, a Cynic; the Soldier, a Brute; and every man disagreeable.

I long to hear from my several correspondents at Leipsic[6], of your arrival there, and what impression you make on them at first; for I have Arguses[7], with a hundred eyes each, who will watch you narrowly, and relate to me faithfully. My accounts will certainly be true; it depends upon you entirely of what kind they shall be. Adieu.

NOTES

1. **O. S.:** Old Style; according to the Julian Calendar. In 1751, thanks to Lord Chesterfield's exertions, the English Parliament decided to adopt the Gregorian Calendar ("New Style") in place of the Julian Calendar ("Old Style") from the beginning of 1752, and enacted that 2 September 1752 should be followed by 14 September 1752, with the omission of 11 days which had been lost under the old system.
2. **bubble(s):** (arch.) dupe, gull; plaything
3. **the *beau monde*:** (Fr.) the fashionable world
4. **Mr. Pope:** Alexander Pope (1688-1744), the poet who wrote ***An Essay on Criticism*** (1711), ***The Rape of the Lock*** (1712), ***Winsor Forest*** (1713), etc.
5. **that wrong turn:** that wrong tendency
6. **Leipsic:** Leipzig, a city in southeast Germany
7. **Argus(es):** (in Gr. Myth.) Argus was a giant with a hundred eyes. Hera set him to watch Io, of whom she was jealous. After he was slain by Hermes, Hera transferred his eyes to the peacock's tail.

24

HENRY FIELDING

(1707–1754)

Henry Fielding was an English novelist and dramatist. He was born in Somerset on April 22, 1707, attended Eton College in 1719–1725, studied law at the University of Leyden in 1728–1729, entered the Middle Temple in 1737, and was called to the bar in 1740. His literary career lasted all his mature life, and his professional work was as a lawyer from 1740 and a Justice of the Peace for Westminster from 1748. On August 7, 1754, he set off with his wife and a daughter for Lisbon in the hope of improving his failing health, but unfortunately he died there two months later, on October 8. *The Journal of a Voyage* (published posthumously in 1755) describes this journey.

In his youth Fielding wrote twenty-odd comedies, of which the most successful was **Tom Thumb** (1730) or its revised version **The Tragedy of Tragedies** (1731), a farce ridiculing the fashionable bombastic tragedies of the time. Later he published novels, e.g. **Joseph Andrews** (1742), a book of adventure; **Jonathan Wild the Great** (1743), a satire on the "Great Man" in the form of a narrative of the villainies of a scoundrel; **Tom Jones** (1749), a true "comic epic" in prose; and **Amelia** (1752), the story of a good wife. **Tom Jones**, his masterpiece, is one of the few greatest novels in the English language. Here he paints a faithful picture of English life in town and country in the eighteenth century, and displays his realism, imagination, and humour at their best. Fielding played an important part in the development of the English novel. His writing is realistic, lively, and vigorous. Except for a few archaic words, his style is fresh and clear.

AN AFFRAY

The clock had now struck twelve, and every one in the house were in their beds, except the sentinel who stood to guard Northerton[1], when Jones softly opening his door, issued forth in pursuit of his enemy, of whose place of confinement he had received a perfect description from the drawer. It is not easy to conceive a much more tremendous figure than he now exhibited. He had on, as we have said, a light-coloured coat, covered with streams of blood. His face, which missed that very blood, as well as twenty ounces more drawn from him by the surgeon, was pallid. Round his head was a quantity of bandage, not unlike a turban. In the right hand he carried a sword, and in the left a candle. So that the bloody Banquo[2] was not worthy to be compared to him. In fact, I believe a more dreadful apparition was never raised in a churchyard, nor in the imagination of any good people met in a winter evening over a Christmas fire in Somersetshire[3].

When the sentinel first saw our hero approach, his hair began to lift up his grenadier cap; and in the same instant his knees fell to blows with each other. Presently his whole body was seized with worse than an ague fit. He then fired his piece, and fell flat on his face.

Whether fear or courage was the occasion of his firing, or whether he took aim at the object of his terror, I cannot say. If he did, however, he had the good fortune to miss his man.

Jones seeing the fellow fall, guessed the cause of his fright, at which he could not forbear smiling, not in the least reflecting on the danger from which he had just escaped. He then passed by the fellow, who still continued in the posture in which he fell, and entered the room where Northerton, as he had heard, was confined. Here, in a solitary situation, he found—an empty quart pot standing on the table, on which some beer being spilt. It looked as if the room had lately been inhabited; but at present it was entirely vacant.

Jones then apprehended it might lead to some other apartment; but upon searching all around it, he could perceive no other door than that at which he entered, and where the sentinel had been posted. He then proceeded to call Northerton several times by his name; but no one answered; nor did this serve to any other purpose than to confirm the sentinel in his terrors, who was now convinced that the volunteer was dead of his wounds, and that his ghost was come in search of the murderer: he now lay in all the agonies of horror; and I wish, with all my heart, some of those actors who are hereafter to represent a man frighted out of his wits had seen him, that they might be taught to copy nature, instead of performing several antic[4] tricks and gestures for the entertainment and applause of the galleries[5].

Perceiving the bird was flown, at least despairing to find him, and rightly apprehending that the report of the firelock would alarm the whole house, our hero now blew out his candle, and gently stole back again to his chamber, and to his bed; whither he would not have been able to have gotten undiscovered, had any other person been on the same staircase, save only one gentleman who was confined to his bed by the gout; for before he could reach the door to his chamber, the hall where the sentinel had been posted was half full of people, some in their shirts, and others not half dressed, all very earnestly inquiring of each other what was the matter.

The soldier was now found lying in the same place and posture in which we just now left him. Several immediately applied themselves to raise him, and some concluded him dead; but they presently saw their mistake, for he not only struggled with those who laid their hands on him, but fell a roaring like a bull. In reality, he imagined so many spirits or devils were handling him; for his imagination being possessed with the horror of an apparition, converted every object he saw or felt into nothing but ghosts and spectres.

At length he was overpowered by numbers, and got upon his legs; when candles being brought, and seeing two or three of his comrades present, he came a little to himself; but when they asked him what was the matter? he answered, "I am a dead man, that's all, I am a dead man, I can't recover it, I have seen him."— "What hast thou seen, Jack?" says one of the soldiers. —"Why, I have seen the young volunteer that was killed yesterday." He then imprecated the most heavy curses on himself, if he had not seen the volunteer, all over blood, vomiting fire out of his mouth and nostrils, pass by him into the chamber where Ensign Northerton was, and then seizing the ensign by the throat, fly away with him in a clap of thunder.

This relation met with a gracious reception from the audience. All the women present believed it firmly, and prayed Heaven to defend them from murder. Amongst the men too, many had faith in the story; but others turned it into derision and ridicule; and a sergeant who was present answered very coolly, "Young man, you will hear more of this, for going to sleep and dreaming on your post."

The soldier replied, "You may punish me if you please; but I was as broad awake as I am now; and the devil carry me away, as he hath the ensign, if I did not see the dead man, as I tell you, with eyes as big and fiery as two large flambeaux."

The commander of the forces, and the commander of the house, were now both arrived; for the former being awake at the time, and hearing the sentinel fire his piece, thought it his duty to rise immediately, though he had no great apprehensions of any mischief; whereas the apprehensions of the latter were much greater, lest her spoons and tankards should be upon the march, without having received any such orders from her.

Our poor sentinel, to whom the sight of this officer was not much more welcome than the apparition, as he thought it, which he had seen before, again related the dreadful story, and with many additions of blood and fire; but he had the misfortune to gain no credit with either of the last-mentioned persons; for the officer, though a very religious man, was free from all terrors of this kind; besides, having so lately left Jones in the condition we have seen, he had no suspicion of his being dead. As for the landlady, though not over religious, she had no kind of aversion to the doctrine of spirits; but there was a circumstance in the tale which she well knew to be false, as we shall inform the reader presently.

But whether Northerton was carried away in thunder or fire, or in whatever other manner he was gone, it was now certain that his body was no longer in custody. Upon this occasion, the lieutenant formed a conclusion not very different from what the sergeant is just mentioned to have made before, and immediately ordered the sentinel to be taken prisoner. So that, by a strange reverse of fortune (though not very uncommon in a military life), the guard became the guarded.

NOTES
1. **Northerton:** a character in *Tom Jones*— an ensign with whom Jones wants to fight over a quarrel
2. **the bloody Banquo:** In Shakespeare's *Macbeth*, Banquo is also murdered after Duncan's tragic death, and his ghost becomes twice visible to Macbeth.
3. **Somersetshire:** a county of Southwest England; Fielding was born there
4. **antic:** (arch.) fantastic
5. **the galleries:** the cheapest parts of the theatre

25

SAMUEL JOHNSON

(1709–1784)

Samuel Johnson was an English critic, essayist, poet, and lexicographer. He was born in Lichfield, Staffordshire, on September 18, 1709, the son of a country bookseller. After fourteen months of attendance at Pembroke College, Oxford, he was forced by poverty to leave the University in December 1729. He did school teaching for a few years, and then migrated to London in 1735. He gradually achieved eminence in literature. In 1764 he founded The Club, later known as The Literary Club, whose members included the painter Joshua Reynards, the statesman Edmund Burke, the writer Oliver Goldsmith, and the celebrated actor David Garrick. He was awarded an honorary M.A. degree by Oxford University in 1755, and the LL.D. degree by Trinity College, Dublin, in 1765 and by Oxford in 1775. He died in London on December 13, 1784, and was buried in Westminster Abbey.

As the dominant literary figure of his time, Johnson's achievement is, indeed, high and wide. His satires **London** (1738) and **The Vanity of Human Wishes** (1749) are admirable poems. **A Dictionary of the English Language**, on which he had expended seven years of labour, was published in 1755; it is the first great work in the history of English lexicography. His best criticism is contained in the Preface to his Edition of **The Plays of Shakespeare** (1765) and in his **Lives of the Poets**

(1779–1781). Johnson wrote a large number of essays; those for *The Rambler* (1750–1752) and those in a series entitled "The Idler" (1758–1760) contributed to *The Universal Chronicle* are the most notable. His periodical essays, which include discussions on ethical issues, personal reflections on life, character sketches, fables, and critical articles, display a moral gravity and an emotional force. He published two other famous prose works: *Rasselas* (1750), a philosophical romance; and *A Journey to the Western Islands of Scotland* (1775), a volume of travel notes. Johnson frequently uses an elaborate, elegant, and dignified prose. It strikes one as a stilted, pompous style, full of big words, rounded periods, and balanced phrases. At times, however, he can be straightforward and simple.

LETTER TO LORD CHESTERFIELD

To the Right Honourable the Earl of Chesterfield
February 7th, 1755

My Lord,

I have been lately informed, by the proprietor of ***The World***[1], that two papers, in which my Dictionary[2] is recommended to the public, were written by your Lordship. To be so distinguished is an honour, which, being very little accustomed to favours from the great, I know not well how to receive, or in what terms to acknowledge.

When, upon some slight encouragement, I first visited your Lordship, I was overpowered, like the rest of mankind, by the enchantment of your address, and could not forbear to wish that I might boast myself *Le vainqueur du vainqueur de la terre*[3]; that I might obtain that regard for which I saw the world contending; but I found my attendance so little encouraged, that neither pride nor modesty would suffer me to continue it. When I had once addressed your Lordship in public, I had exhausted all the art of pleasing which a retired and uncourtly scholar can possess. I had done all that I could; and no man is well pleased to have his all neglected, be it ever so little[4].

Seven years, my Lord, have now past[5], since I waited in your outward rooms, or was repulsed from your door; during which time I have been pushing on my work through difficulties, of which it is useless to complain, and have brought it, at last, to the verge of publication, without one act of assistance, one word of encouragement, or one smile of favour. Such treatment I did not expect, for I never had a Patron before.

The shepherd in Virgil grew at last acquainted with Love, and found him a native of the rocks[6].

Is not a Patron, my Lord, one who looks with unconcern on a man struggling for life in the water, and, when he has reached ground, encumbers him with help? The notice which you have been pleased to take of my labours, had it been early, had been kind; but it has been delayed till I am indifferent, and cannot enjoy it; till I am solitary[7], and cannot impart it; till I am known, and do not want it. I hope it is no very cynical asperity not to confess obligations where no benefit has been received, or to be unwilling that the public should consider me as owing that to a Patron, which Providence has enabled me to do for myself.

Having carried on my work thus far with so little obligation to any favourer of learning, I shall not be disappointed though I should conclude it, if less be possible, with less; for I have been long wakened from that dream of hope, in which I once boasted myself with so much exultation, my Lord,

Your Lordship's most humble,
Most obedient servant,
Sam. Johnson

NOTES

1. ***The World*:** a weekly periodical in London between 1753 and 1756. Its editor was Edward Moore (1712–1757).
2. **my Dictionary:** *A Dictionary of the English Language* (1755), compiled by Samuel Johnson
3. ***Le vainqueur du vainqueur de la terre*:** (Fr.) the conqueror of the conqueror of the world
4. **be it ever so little:** however little it may be
5. **have now past:** have now passed
6. **a native of the rocks:** one living among the hills. In Virgil's *Eclogues*, the shepherd thought Love was a god but later found him to be a native of the hills, an uncouth or hard-hearted person.
7. **till I am solitary:** till I am alone. Here Johnson is referring to the loss of his wife; she died in March, 1752.

SHAKESPEARE AND GENERAL NATURE

The poet of whose works I have undertaken the revision may now begin to assume the dignity of an ancient and claim the privilege of established fame and prescriptive veneration. He has long outlived his century, the term commonly fixed as the test of literary merit. Whatever advantages he might once derive from personal allusions, local customs, or temporary opinions, have for many years been lost; and every topic of merriment or motive of sorrow which the modes of artificial life afforded him now only obscure the scenes which they once illuminated. The effects of favour and competition are at an end; the tradition of his friendships and his enmities has perished; his works support no opinion with arguments nor supply any faction with invective; they can neither indulge vanity nor gratify malignity; but are read without any other reason than the desire of pleasure, and are therefore praised only as pleasure is obtained; yet, thus unassisted by interest or passion, they have passed through variations of taste and changes of manners, and, as they devolved from one generation to another, have received new honours at every transmission.

But because human judgment, though it be gradually gaining upon certainty, never becomes infallible, and approbation, though long continued, may yet be only the approbation of prejudice or fashion, it is proper to inquire by what peculiarities of excellence Shakespeare has gained and kept the favour of his countrymen.

Nothing can please many, and please long, but just representations of general nature. Particular manners can be known to few, and therefore few only can judge how nearly they are copied. The irregular combinations of fanciful invention may delight awhile by that novelty of which the common satiety of life sends us all in quest; but the pleasures of sudden wonder are soon exhausted, and the mind can only repose on the stability of truth.

Shakespeare is, above all writers, at least above all modern writers, the poet of nature, the poet that holds up to his readers a faithful mirror of manners and of life[1].

His characters are not modified by the customs of particular places, unpractised by the rest of the world; by the peculiarities of studies or professions which can operate but upon small numbers; or by the accidents of transient fashions or temporary opinions: they are the genuine progeny of common humanity, such as the world will always supply, and observation will always find. His persons act and speak by the influence of those general passions and principles by which all minds are agitated and the whole system of life is continued in motion. In the writings of other poets a character is too often an individual; in those of Shakespeare it is commonly a species.

It is from this wide extension of design that so much instruction is derived. It is this which fills the plays of Shakespeare with practical axioms and domestic wisdom. It was said of Euripides[2] that every verse was a precept; and it may be said of Shakespeare that from his works may be collected a system of civil and economical prudence. Yet his real power is not shown in the splendour of particular passages, but by the progress of his fable[3] and the tenor of his dialogue; and he that tries to recommend him by select quotations will succeed like the pedant in Hierocles[4], who, when he offered his house to sale, carried a brick in his pocket as a specimen.

It will not easily be imagined how much Shakespeare excels in accommodating his sentiments to real life but by comparing him with other authors. It was observed of the ancient schools of declamation that the more diligently they were frequented, the more was the student disqualified for the world, because he found nothing there which he should ever meet in any other place. The same remark may be applied to every stage but that of Shakespeare. The theatre, when it is under any other direction, is peopled by such characters as were never seen, conversing in a language which was never heard, upon topics which will never arise in the commerce of mankind. But the dialogue of this author is often so evidently determined by the incident which produces it, and is pursued with so much ease and simplicity, that it seems scarcely to claim the merit of fiction, but to have been gleaned by diligent selection out of common conversation and common occurrences.

Upon every other stage the universal agent is love, by whose power all good and evil is distributed and every action quickened or retarded. To bring a lover, a lady, and a rival into the fable; to entangle them in contradictory obligations, perplex them with oppositions of interest, and harass them with violence of desires inconsistent with each other; to make them meet in rapture, and part in agony; to fill their mouths with hyperbolical joy and outrageous sorrow; to distress them as nothing human ever was distressed; to deliver them as nothing human ever was delivered, is the business of a modern dramatist. For this, probability is violated, life is misrepresented, and language is depraved. But love is only one of many passions; and as it has no great influence upon the sum of life, it has little operation in the dramas of a poet who caught his ideas from the living world and exhibited only what he saw before him. He knew that any other passion, as it was regular or exorbitant, was a cause of happiness or calamity.

Characters thus ample and general were not easily discriminated and preserved; yet perhaps no poet ever kept his personages more distinct from each other. I will not say with Pope[5] that every speech may be assigned to the proper speaker, because many speeches there are which have nothing characteristical; but, perhaps, though some may be equally adapted to every person, it will be difficult to find any that can be properly transferred from the present possessor to another claimant. The choice is right, when there is reason for choice.

Other dramatists can only gain attention by hyperbolical or aggravated characters, by fabulous and unexampled excellence or depravity, as the writers of barbarous romances invigorated the reader by a giant and a dwarf; and he that should form his expectations of human affairs from the play, or from the tale, would be equally deceived. Shakespeare has no heroes[6]; his scenes are occupied only by men, who act and speak as the reader thinks that he should himself have spoken or acted on the same occasion. Even where the agency is supernatural, the dialogue is level with life. Other writers disguise the most natural passions and most frequent incidents so that he who contemplates them in the book will not know them in the world. Shakespeare approximates the remote and familiarizes the wonderful; the event which he represents will not happen, but, if it were possible, its effects would probably be such as he has assigned; and it may be said that he has not only shown human nature as it acts in real exigences, but as it would be found in trials to which it cannot be exposed.

This, therefore, is the praise of Shakespeare, that his drama is the mirror of life; that he who has mazed his imagination in following the phantoms which other writers raise up before him, may here be cured of his delirious ecstasies by reading human sentiments in human language, by scenes from which a hermit may estimate the transactions of the world and a confessor predict the progress of the passions.

—*The Preface to Shakespeare*

NOTES

1. **holds up to his readers a faithful mirror of manners and of life:** cf. Hamlet's words in Shakespeare's *Hamlet*, III. ii: "...the purpose of playing, whose end both at the first, and now, was and is, to hold as 'twere the mirror up to nature..."
2. **Euripides:** a Greek tragedian (c. 480–406 B.C.) and the author of 19 extant plays including *Alcestis, Medea,* and *The Trojan Women*
3. **the progress of his fable:** the development of his story or plot
4. **Hierocles:** Hierocles of Alexandria, a Neo-Platonic philosopher of the fifth century and the reputed author of an extant commentary on the *Golden Verses* of Pythagoras
5. **Pope:** Pope published his edition of Shakespeare's plays in 1725.
6. **Shakespeare has no heroes:** Shakespeare has no heroes of the hyperbolical kind.

26

THOMAS GRAY

(1716–1771)

Thomas Gray was an English poet and letter-writer. He was born in London on 26 December, 1716, the son of a scrivener, and educated at Eton and Cambridge. After his two-year tour of France and Italy, he stayed in London in 1741 studying law. In 1742 he moved to Cambridge and began to write poetry in English instead of Latin. His poetry was so generally admired that in 1757 he was offered the laureateship, which he declined. In 1768 he was appointed Regius Professor of Modern History at Cambridge. He died on 30 July 1771, and was buried in the churchyard of Stoke Poges, Buckinghamshire, beside his mother.

Gray's best poetical work comprises some of his Pindaric odes—***Ode on a Distant Prospect of Eton College*** (1747), ***The Progress of Poetry*** (1753), ***The Bard*** (1757)—and his ***Elegy Written in a Country Churchyard*** (1751). The ***Elegy*** is one of the most famous poems in the English language. Gray's poetry is marked by an intense yet controlled sentiment, a genuine love of nature, and a deep understanding of life and history.

Gray was also one of the best letter-writers of the 18th century. His letters are full of observation and erudition, warm feeling and subtle humour. His prose style is witty, natural, and elegant.

NETLEY ABBEY[1]

I received your letter at Southampton, and as I would wish to treat everybody according to their own rule and measure of good breeding, have, against my inclination, waited till now before I answered it, purely out of fear and respect, and an ingenuous diffidence of my own abilities. If you will not take this as an excuse, accept it at least as a well-turned period, which is always my principal concern.

So I proceed to tell you, that my health is much improved by the sea; not that I drank it, or bathed in it, as the common people do: no! I only walked by it, and looked upon it. The climate is remarkably mild, even in October and November; no snow has been seen to lie there for these thirty years past, the myrtles grow in the ground against the houses, and Guernsey lilies[2] bloom in every window. The town, clean and well-built, surrounded by its old stone walls, with their towers and gateways, stands at the point of a peninsula, and opens full south to an arm of the sea, which, having formed two beautiful bays on each hand of it, stretches away in direct view till it joins the British Channel[3]; it is skirted on either side with gently-rising grounds, clothed with thick wood; and directly across its mouth rise the high lands of the Isle of Wight[4], at distance, but distinctly seen. In the bosom of the woods (concealed from profane eyes) lie hid the ruins of Netley Abbey: there may be richer and greater houses of religion, but the abbot is content with his situation. See there, at the top of that hanging meadow, under the shade of those old trees that bend into a half circle about it, he is walking slowly (good man!) and bidding his beads for the souls of his benefactors interred in that venerable pile that lies beneath him. Beyond it (the meadow still descending) nods a thicket of oaks that mask the building, and have excluded a view too garish and luxuriant for a holy eye: only, on either hand, they leave an opening to the blue glittering sea. Did you not observe how, as that white sail shot by and was lost, he turned and crossed himself to drive the tempter from him that had thrown that distraction in his way. I should tell you that the ferryman who rowed me, a lusty young fellow, told me that he would not for all the world pass a night at the Abbey (there were such things seen near it), though there was a power of money hid there. From thence I went to Salisbury[5], Wilton[6], and Stonehenge[7]; but of these things I say no more, they will be published at the University press[8].

PS. I must not close my letter without giving you one principal event of my history; which was, that (in the course of my late tour) I set out one morning before five o'clock, the moon shining through a dark and misty autumnal air, and got to the sea-coast time enough to be at the sun's levee. I saw the clouds and dark vapours open gradually to right and left, rolling over one another in great smoky wreaths, and the tide (as it flowed gently in upon the sands) first whitening, then slightly tinged with gold and blue; and all at once a little line of insufferable brightness that (before I can write these five words) was grown to half an orb, and now to a whole one, too glorious to be distinctly seen. It is very odd it makes no figure on paper; yet I shall remember it as long as the sun, or at least as long as I endure. I wonder whether anybody ever saw it before? I hardly believe it.

NOTES

1. **Netley Abbey:** a Cistercian abbey (founded in 1239) whose ruins lie three miles S. E. of Southampton, Hampshire
2. **Guernsey lilies:** a kind of amraryllis (***Nerine Sarniensis***) with scarlet umbellate flowers
3. **the British Channel:** the English Channel, the channel between England and France
4. **the Isle of Wight:** an island off the south coast of England
5. **Salisbury:** a city in S. E. Wiltshire, S. England
6. **Wilton:** a town in Wiltshire
7. **Stonehenge:** a prehistoric stone monument—a circular group of huge standing stones—in Wiltshire on Salisbury Plain
8. **the University press:** i.e. Cambridge University Press

27

HORACE WALPOLE

(1717–1797)

Horace Walpole was an English writer and connoisseur. He was born in London on September 24, 1717, the fourth son of the powerful statesman Robert Walpole, studied at Eton College from 1727 to 1734, and at King's College, Cambridge, from 1735 to 1739, and travelled in France and Italy with the poet Thomas Gray from 1739 to 1741. He dabbled in politics as an M.P. for 26 years (1641–1667). In 1747 he settled in a villa at Twickenham, Middlesex. The house was subsequently renamed Strawberry Hill, transformed into "a little Gothic castle", and filled with his collections of art; naturally it attracted numerous visitors. He became the fourth Earl of Oxford in 1791 and died on March 2, 1797.

Horace Walpole passed his life as a dilettante, attempting different forms of literature. His ***Anecdotes of Painting in England*** (1762), based on the famous engraver George Vertue's notebooks, is a valuable work on English art before 1750. His gothic novel ***The Castle of Otranto*** (1764) and blank-verse tragedy ***The Mysterious Mother*** (1768) are romantic works of terror. His literary fame, however, rests chiefly on his letters, about 4000 in all. These letters, covering a wide range of subjects and interests, may be considered an informal but intimate social history of 18th-century England as well as an informal but substantial autobiography of a man of taste. They are noted for the writer's lively observation, witty manner, and limpid expression.

TO GEORGE MONTAGU[1], ESQ

Strawberry Hill[2], July 28, 1765

The less one is disposed, if one has any sense, to talk of oneself to people that inquire only out of compliment, and do not listen to the answer, the more satisfaction one feels in indulging in a self-complacency, by sighing to those that really sympathise with our griefs. Do not think it is pain that makes me give this low-spirited air to my letter. No, it is the prospect of what is to come, not the sensation of what is passing, that affects me. The loss of youth is melancholy enough; but to enter into old age through the gate of infirmity most disheartening. My health and spirits make me take but slight notice of the transition, and, under the persuasion of temperance being a talisman, I marched boldly on towards the descent of the hill, knowing I must fall at last, but not suspecting that I should stumble by the way. This confession explains the mortification I feel. A month's confinement to one who never kept his bed a day is a stinging lesson, and has humbled my insolence to almost indifference. Judge, then, how little I interest myself about public events. I know nothing of them since I came hither, where I had not only the disappointment of not growing better, but a bad return in one of my feet[3], so that I am still wrapped up and upon a couch. It was the more unlucky as Lord Hertford is come to England for a very few days. He has offered to come to me; but as I then should see him only for some minutes, I propose being carried to town to-morrow. It will be so long before I can expect to be able to travel, that my French journey will certainly not take place so soon as I intended, and if Lord Hertford goes to Ireland, I shall be still more fluctuating; for though the Duke and Duchess of Richmond will replace them at Paris, and are as eager to have me with them, I have had so many more years heaped upon me within this month, that I have not the conscience to trouble young people, when I can no longer be as juvenile as they are. Indeed I shall think myself decrepit, till I again saunter into the garden in my slippers and without my hat in all weathers, —a point I am determined to regain if possible; for even this experience cannot make me resign my temperance and my hardiness. I am tired of the world, its politics, its pursuits, and its pleasures; but it will cost me some struggles before I submit to be tender and careful. Christ! Can I ever stoop to the regimen of old age? I do not wish to dress up a withered person, nor drag it about to public places; but to sit in one's room, clothed warmly, expecting visits from folks I don't wish to see, and tended and flattered by relations impatient for one's death! Let the gout do its worst as expeditiously as it can; it would be more welcome in my stomach than in my limbs. I am not made to bear a course of nonsense and advice, but must play the fool in my own way to the last, alone with all my heart, if I cannot be with the very few I wished to see: but, to depend for comfort on others, who would be no comfort to me; this surely is not a state to be preferred to death; and nobody can have truly enjoyed the advantages of youth, health, and spirits, who is content to exist without the two last, which alone bear any resemblance to the first.

You see how difficult it is to conquer my proud spirit: low and weak as I am, I think my resolution and perseverance will get the better, and that I shall still be a gay shadow[4]; at least, I will impose any severity upon myself, rather than humour the gout, and sink into that indulgence with which most people treat it. Bodily liberty is as dear to me as mental, and I would as soon flatter any other tyrant as the gout, my Whiggism[5] extending as much to my health as to my principles, and being as willing to part with life, when I cannot preserve it, as your uncle Algernon when his freedom was at stake. Adieu!

NOTES

1. **George Montagu:** George Montagu, M.P., was one of Walpole's intimate friends.
2. **Strawberry Hill:** a small property at Twickenham, a town on the Thames near London
3. **a bad return in one of my feet:** a bad return of the gout in one of my feet
4. **shadow:** person wasted away
5. **Whiggism:** progressiveness, liberalism

28

GILBERT WHITE

(1720–1793)

Gilbert White was an English naturalist. He was born at Selborne, a village in Hampshire, and educated at Oriel College, Oxford. A curate by profession, he lived most of his time in his native village, observing the plant, animal and bird life there. He communicated his observations and reflections in letters to other naturalists, especially Thomas Pennant and Daines Barrington. These letters formed the basis of his famous work ***The Natural History and Antiquities of Selborne*** (1789), which displays his curiosity about wild life and his love of nature. The book has become a classic, for it combines natural history with literary quality. Its style is lucid and elegant.

GOSSAMER

Selborne, June 8th, 1775

Dear Sir,

On September the 21st, 1741, being then on a visit, and intent on field-diversions, I rose before daybreak: when I came into the enclosures, I found the stubbles and clover-grounds matted all over with a thick coat of cobweb, in the meshes of which a copious and heavy dew hung so plentifully, that the whole face of the country seemed, as it were, covered with two or three setting-nets[1] drawn one over another. When the dogs attempted to hunt, their eyes were so blinded and hoodwinked that they could not proceed, but were obliged to lie down and scrape the incumbrances from their faces with their fore-feet, so that, finding my sport interrupted, I returned home musing in my mind on the oddness of the occurrence.

As the morning advanced, the sun became bright and warm, and the day turned out one of those most lovely ones which no season but the autumn produces; cloudless, calm, serene, and worthy of the South of France itself.

About nine an appearance very unusual began to demand our attention, a shower of cobwebs, falling from very elevated regions, and continuing, without any interruption, till the close of the day. These webs were not single filmy threads, floating in the air in all directions, but perfect flakes or rags; some near an inch broad, and five or six long, which fell with a degree of velocity which showed they were considerably heavier than the atmosphere.

On every side, as the observer turned his eyes, might he behold a continual succession of fresh flakes falling into his sight, and twinkling like stars as they turned their sides towards the sun.

How far this wonderful shower extended would be difficult to say; but we know that it reached Bradley, Selborne, and Alresford[2], three places which lie in a sort of triangle, the shortest of whose sides is about eight miles in extent.

At the second of those places there was a gentleman (for whose veracity and intelligent turn we have the greatest veneration) who observed it the moment he got abroad; but concluded that, as soon as he came upon the hill above his house, where he took his morning rides, he should be higher than this meteor[3], which he imagined might have been blown, like thistledown, from the common above: but, to his great astonishment, when he rode to the most elevated part of the down, 300 feet above his fields, he found the webs in appearance still as much above him as before; still descending into sight in a constant succession, and twinkling in the sun, so as to draw the attention of the most incurious.

Neither before nor after was any such fall observed; but on this day the flakes hung in the trees and hedges so thick, that a diligent person sent out might have gathered baskets full.

The remark that I shall make on these cobweb-like appearances, called gossamer, is, that, strange and superstitious as the notions about them were formerly, nobody in these days doubts but that they[4] are the real production of small spiders, which swarm in the fields in fine weather in autumn, and have a power of shooting out webs from their tails so as to render themselves buoyant, and lighter than air. But why these apterous[5] insects should ***that day*** take such a wonderful aerial excursion, and why their webs should at once become so gross and material as to be considerably more weighty than air, and to descend with precipitation, is a matter beyond my skill. If I might be allowed to hazard a supposition, I should imagine that those filmy threads, when first shot, might be entangled in the rising dew, and so drawn up, spiders and all, by a brisk evaporation, into the region where clouds are formed: and if the spiders have a power of coiling and thickening their webs in the air, as Dr. Lister[6] says they have, then, when they were become heavier than the air, they must fall.

Every day in fine weather, in autumn chiefly, do I see those spiders shooting out their webs and mounting aloft: they will go off from your finger, if you will take them into your hand. Last summer one alighted on my book as I was reading in the parlour; and, running to the top of the page, and shooting out a web, took its departure from thence. But what I most wondered at was, that it went off with considerable velocity in a place where no air was stirring; and I am sure that I did not assist it with my breath. So that these little crawlers seem to have, while mounting, some locomotive power without the use of wings, and to move in the air faster than the air itself.

NOTES

1. **setting-nets:** nets for trapping
2. **Bradley, Selborne, and Alresford:** three villages in Hampshire
3. **meteor:** meteor-like phenomenon, dazzling but short-lived thing
4. **nobody in these days doubts but that they...:** nobody in these days doubts that they...
5. **apterous:** wingless
6. **Dr. Lister:** Martin Lister (1638?–1712), an English zoologist and expert on spiders

29

OLIVER GOLDSMITH

(1728–1774)

Oliver Goldsmith was a British novelist, dramatist, poet, and essayist. The second son of an Anglo-Irish clergyman, he was born at Pallas, Longford, or Elphin, Roscommon, on November 10, 1728, and educated at Trinity College, Dublin, in 1745–1749. After desultory studies and Continental travels, he landed up in London to carve out a literary career for himself. He wrote and excelled in several genres, and was one of the founder-members of Dr. Johnson's Literary Club. He died on April 4, 1774.

Among Goldsmith's numerous works, we can name at least four masterpieces: ***The Vicar of Wakefield*** (1766), a novel telling with idyllic charm the story of an innocent-minded priest and his family; ***The Deserted Village*** (1770), a poem describing in graceful heroic couplets the changes in country life; ***She Stoops to Conquer*** (1773), a comedy of situation shining with hearty pleasantry and verbal dexterity; and ***The Citizen of the World*** (1762), a collection of letters or essays providing shrewd comments on English people and fashions. These works were enthusiastically received by his contemporaries and have remained popular classics. Goldsmith produced a vast amount of prose. In all he wrote, particularly in his essays, inside and outside ***The Citizen of the World***, there is an exquisite, high quality. This quality stands for his good nature, kindly humour, simple wisdom, and lucid style. His style is easy and natural, limpid and delicate.

FAMILY AMBITIONS

I[1] now began to find that all my long and painful lectures upon temperance, simplicity, and contentment were entirely disregarded. The distinctions lately paid us by our betters awakened that pride which I had laid asleep, but not removed. Our windows again, as formerly, were filled with washes[2] for the neck and face. The sun was dreaded as an enemy to the skin without doors, and the fire as a spoiler of the complexion within. My wife[3] observed that rising too early would hurt her daughters' eyes, that working after dinner would redden their noses; and she convinced me that the hands never looked so white as when they did nothing. Instead therefore of finishing George's[4] shirts, we now had them new-modelling their old gauzes, or flourishing[5] upon catgut[6]. The poor Miss Flamboroughs, their former gay companions, were cast off as mean[7] acquaintance, and the whole conversation ran upon high life, and high-lived company, with pictures, taste, Shakespeare, and the musical glasses[8].

But we could have borne all this, had not a fortune-telling gipsy come to raise us into perfect sublimity. The tawny sibyl[9] no sooner appeared, than my girls came running to me for a shilling a-piece to cross her hand with silver[10]. To say the truth, I was tired of being always wise, and could not help gratifying their request, because I loved to see them happy. I gave each of them a shilling; though for the honour of the family it must be observed, that they never went without money themselves, as my wife always generously let them have a guinea each, to keep in their pockets, but with strict injunctions never to change it. After they had been closeted up[11] with the fortune-teller for some time, I knew by their looks, upon their returning, that they had been promised something great. "Well, my girls, how have you sped[12]? Tell me, Livy[13], has the fortune-teller given thee a pennyworth?"—"I protest, papa," says the girl, "I believe she deals with somebody that's not right; for she positively declared, that I am to be married to a Squire in less than a twelvemonth! "—"Well, now Sophy[14], my child," said I, "and what sort of a husband are you to have?"—"Sir," replied she, "I am to have a Lord soon after my sister has married the Squire."—"How!" cried I, "is that all you are to have for your two shillings? Only a Lord and a Squire for two shillings? You fools, I could have promised you a Prince and a Nabob[15] for half the money."

This curiosity of theirs, however, was attended with very serious effects: we now began to think ourselves designed by the stars[16] to something exalted, and already anticipated our future grandeur.

It has been a thousand times observed, and I must observe it once more, that the hours we pass with happy prospects in view, are more pleasing than those crowned with fruition. In the first case, we cook the dish to our own appetite; in the latter, Nature cooks it for us. It is impossible to repeat the train of agreeable reveries we called up for our entertainment. We looked upon our fortunes as once more rising; and, as the whole parish asserted that the Squire was in love with my daughter, she was actually so with him; for they persuaded her into the passion. In this agreeable interval my wife had the most lucky dreams in the world, which she took care to tell us every morning with great solemnity and exactness. It was one night a coffin and cross-bones, the sign of an approaching wedding; at another time she imagined her daughters' pockets filled with farthings, a certain sign of their being shortly stuffed with gold. The girls themselves had their omens. They felt strange kisses on their lips; they saw rings in the candle; purses bounced from the fire, and true-love-knots lurked in the bottom of every teacup.

Towards the end of the week we received a card from the two ladies, in which, with their compliments, they hoped to see all our family at church the Sunday following. All Saturday morning I could perceive, in consequence of this, my wife and daughters in close conference together, and now and then glancing at me with looks that betrayed a latent plot. To be sincere, I had strong suspicions that some absurd proposal was preparing[17] for appearing with splendour the next day. In the evening they began their operations in a very regular manner, and my wife undertook to conduct the siege. After tea, when I seemed in spirits[18], she began thus: "I fancy, Charles, my dear, we shall have a great deal of good company at our church to-morrow."—"Perhaps we may, my dear," returned I, "though you need be under no uneasiness about that; you shall have a sermon whether there be or not."—"That is what I expect," returned she; "but I think, my dear, we ought to appear there as decently as possible, for who knows what may happen?"—"Your precautions," replied I, "are highly commendable. A decent behaviour and appearance in church is what charms me. We should be devout and humble, cheerful and serene."—"Yes," cried she, "I know that; but I mean we should go there in as proper a manner as possible; not altogether like the scrubs[19] about us."—"You are quite right, my dear," returned I, "and I was going to make the very same proposal. The proper manner of going is to go there as early as possible, to have time for meditation before the service begins."—"Phoo[20], Charles," interrupted she, "all that is very true; but not what I would be at. I mean, we should go there genteelly. You know the church is two miles off, and I protest I don't like to see my daughters trudging up to their pew all blowzed[21] and red with walking, and looking for all the world as if they had been winners at a smock race[22]. Now, my dear, my proposal is this: there are our two plough-horses, the Colt that has been in our family these nine years, and his companion Blackberry, that has scarcely done an earthly thing for this month past. They are both grown fat and lazy. Why should not they do something as well as we? And let me tell you, when Moses[23] has trimmed them a little, they will cut a very tolerable figure."

To this proposal I objected that walking would be twenty times more genteel than such a paltry conveyance, as Blackberry was wall-eyed[24], and the Colt wanted the tail; that they had never been broke[25] to the rein[26], but had a hundred vicious tricks; and that we had but one saddle and pillion in the whole house. All these objections, however, were overruled; so that I was obliged to comply. The next morning I perceived them not a little busy in collecting such materials as might be necessary for the expedition; but, as I found it would be a business of time[27], I walked on to the church before, and they promised speedily to follow. I waited near an hour in the reading desk for their arrival; but not finding them come as expected, I was obliged to begin, and went through the service, not without some uneasiness at finding them absent. This was increased when all was finished, and no appearance of the family. I therefore walked back by the horse-way, which was five miles round, though the foot-way was but two, and, when I got about half-way home, perceived the procession marching slowly forwards towards the church; my son, my wife, and the two little ones, exalted on one horse, and my two daughters upon the other. I demanded the cause of their delay; but I soon found by their looks they had met with a thousand misfortunes on the road. The horses had at first refused to move from the door, till Mr. Burchell[28] was kind enough to beat them forward for about two hundred yards with his cudgel. Next, the straps of my wife's pillion broke down, and they were obliged to stop to repair them before they could proceed. After that, one of the horses took it into his head to stand still, and neither blows nor entreaties could prevail with him to proceed. He was just recovering from this dismal situation when I found them; but perceiving everything safe, I own their present mortification did not much displease me, as it would give me many opportunities of future triumph, and teach my daughters more humility.

NOTES

1. **I:** Charles Primrose, the central character and narrator of *The Vicar of Wakefield*
2. **washes:** liquid preparations for beautifying skin, cleansing hair, etc.
3. **my wife:** Deborah Primrose
4. **George:** Dr. Primrose's eldest son
5. **flourishing:** (arch.) putting forth flowers
6. **catgut:** coarse corded cloth
7. **mean:** poor or shabby
8. **musical glasses:** glasses which chink when struck
9. **sibyl:** fortune-teller
10. **to cross her hand with silver:** to give her money
11. **closeted up:** shut up in a small private room
12. **how have you sped?:** How have you been getting along?
13. **Livy:** Olivia, Dr. Primrose's daughter
14. **Sophy:** Sophia, Dr. Primrose's second daughter
15. **a Nabob:** a European who has made a fortune in India
16. **the stars:** luck

17. **preparing:** being prepared
18. **in spirits:** in high spirits
19. **scrubs:** insignificant or mean persons
20. **Phoo:** phew
21. **blowzed:** flushed; dishevelled
22. **smock race:** race for the prize of a smock
23. **Moses:** the Vicar's fourth child and second son
24. **wall-eyed:** very light grey in the eyes or in one eye
25. **broke:** broken
26. **they had never been broke to the rein:** they had never been trained to wear reins
27. **it would be a business of time:** it would take a considerable time
28. **Mr. Burchell:** an eccentric gentleman who admires Sophia

THE MAN IN BLACK

Though fond of many acquaintances, I desire an intimacy only with a few. The Man in Black, whom I have often mentioned, is one whose friendship I could wish to acquire, because he possesses my esteem. His manners, it is true, are tinctured with some strange inconsistencies; and he may be justly termed a humorist in a nation of humorists. Though he is generous even to profusion, he affects to be thought a prodigy of parsimony and prudence; though his conversation be replete with the most sordid and selfish maxims, his heart is dilated with the most unbounded love. I have known him profess himself a man-hater, while his cheek was glowing with compassion; and, while his looks were softened into pity, I have heard him use the language of the most unbounded ill-nature. Some affect humanity and tenderness, others boast of having such dispositions from Nature; but he is the only man I ever knew who seemed ashamed of his natural benevolence. He takes as much pains to hide his feelings as any hypocrite would to conceal his indifference; but on every unguarded moment the mask drops off, and reveals him to the most superficial observer.

In one of our late excursions into the country, happening to discourse upon the provision that was made for the poor in England, he seemed amazed how any of his countrymen could be so foolishly weak as to relieve occasional objects of charity, when the laws had made such ample provision for their support. "In every parish-house[1]," says he, "the poor are supplied with food, clothes, fire, and a bed to lie on; they want no more, I desire no more myself; yet still they seem discontented. I'm surprised at the inactivity of our magistrates in not taking up[2] such vagrants, who are only a weight upon the industrious; I'm surprised that the people are found to relieve them, when they must be at the same time sensible that it, in some measure, encourages idleness, extravagance, and imposture. Were I to advise any man for whom I had the least regard, I would caution him by all means not to be imposed upon by their false pretences: let me assure you, Sir, they are impostors, every one of them; and rather merit a prison than relief."

He was proceeding in this strain earnestly, to dissuade me from an imprudence of which I am seldom guilty, when an old man, who still had about him the remnants of tattered finery, implored our compassion. He assured us that he was no common beggar, but forced into the shameful profession to support a dying wife and five hungry children. Being prepossessed against such falsehoods, his story had not the least influence upon me; but it was quite otherwise with the Man in Black; I could see it visibly operate upon his countenance, and effectually interrupt his harangue. I could easily perceive that his heart burned to relieve the five starving children, but he seemed ashamed to discover[3] his weakness to me. While he thus hesitated between compassion and pride, I pretended to look another way, and he seized this opportunity of giving the poor petitioner a piece of silver, bidding him at the same time, in order that I should hear, go work for his bread, and not tease passengers with such impertinent falsehoods for the future.

As he had fancied himself quite unperceived, he continued, as we proceeded, to rail against beggars with as much animosity as before; he threw in some episodes on[4] his own amazing prudence and economy, with his profound skill in discovering impostors; he explained the manner in which he would deal with beggars, were he a magistrate, hinted at enlarging some of the prisons for their reception, and told two stories of ladies that were robbed by beggarmen. He was beginning a third to the same purpose, when a sailor with a wooden leg once more crossed our walks, desiring our pity, and blessing our limbs. I was for going on without taking any notice, but my friend, looking wistfully upon the poor petitioner, bid me stop, and he would show me with how much ease he could at any time detect an impostor.

He now, therefore, assumed a look of importance, and in an angry tone began to examine the sailor, demanding in what engagement he was thus disabled and rendered unfit for service. The sailor replied in a tone as angrily as he, that he had been an officer on board a private ship of war, and that he had lost his leg abroad, in defence of those who did nothing at home. At this reply, all my friend's importance vanished in a moment; he had not a single question more to ask; he now only studied what method he should take to relieve him unobserved. He had, however, no easy part to act, as he was obliged to preserve the appearance of ill-nature before me, and yet relieve himself by relieving the sailor. Casting, therefore, a furious look upon some bundles of chips which the fellow carried in a string at his back, my friend demanded how he sold his matches; but not waiting for a reply, desired in a surly tone to have a shilling's worth. The sailor seemed at first surprised at his demand, but soon recollecting himself, and presenting his whole bundle— "Here, master," says he, "take all my cargo, and a blessing into the bargain."

It is impossible to describe with what an air of triumph my friend marched off with his new purchase; he assured me that he was firmly of opinion that those fellows must have stolen their goods who could thus afford to sell them for half value. He informed me of several different uses to which those chips might be applied; he expatiated largely upon the savings that would result from lighting candles with a match instead of thrusting them into the fire. He averred that he would as soon have parted with a tooth as his money to those vagabonds, unless for some valuable consideration. I cannot tell how long this panegyric upon frugality and matches might have continued, had not his attention been called off by another object more distressful than either of the former. A woman in rags, with one child in her arms, and another on her back, was attempting to sing ballads, but with such a mournful voice that it was difficult to determine whether she was singing or crying. A wretch, who in the deepest distress still aimed at good humour, was an object my friend was by no means capable of withstanding: his vivacity and his discourse were instantly interrupted; upon this occasion his very dissimulation had forsaken him. Even in my presence, he immediately applied his hands to his pockets, in order to relieve her; but guess his confusion, when he found he had already given away all the money he carried about him to former objects. The misery painted in the woman's visage was not half so strongly expressed as the agony in his. He continued to search for some time, but to no purpose, till, at length, recollecting himself, with a face of ineffable good-nature, as he had no money, he put into her hands his shilling's worth of matches.

NOTES

1. **parish-house:** poor-house
2. **taking up:** arresting
3. **to discover:** to reveal, to disclose
4. **threw in some episodes on:** told a few little stories about

30

EDMUND BURKE

(1729-1797)

Edmund Burke was a British statesman and writer. He was born in Dublin on January 12, 1729, attended Abraham Shackleton's school in Ballitore from 1741 to 1743, and studied at Trinity College, Dublin, from 1744 to 1748. He went over to England and entered the Middle Temple, London, in 1750, but left the law for literature in 1755. *A Philosophical Enquiry into the Origin of Our Ideas of the Sublime and the Beautiful* (1757), an essay in aesthetics, was his first notable work. Burke was a Whig M.P. from 1765 to 1794 and one of the most brilliant orators in the House of Commons, but never held very high office. He stood for reason, toleration and justice in most of his political works, e.g. the essay *Thoughts on the Cause of the Present Discontents* (1770) and the speeches *On American Taxation* (1774), *On Conciliation with the Colonies* (1775), and *On the Nabob of Arcot's Private Debts* (1785). He advocated moderation and opposed radical change, as can be seen in his famous *Reflections on the Revolution in France* (1790). Many of his essays and speeches owe their eloquence to a combination of qualities—solid substance, passionate conviction, great learning, and splendid rhetoric. His style, rich in imagery, allusion and irony and warm with fervour, has great vividness and vigour. Burke retired from Parliament in 1794 and was given a government pension, for which he was criticized by a couple of peers, against whom he defended himself ably in *A Letter to a Lord* (1796), a masterpiece of English prose. He died on July 9, 1797.

OBJECTIONS TO THE USE OF FORCE

I am sensible, Sir, that all which I have asserted in my detail, is admitted in the gross, but that quite a different conclusion is drawn from it. America, gentlemen say, is a noble object. It is an object well worth fighting for. Certainly it is, if fighting a people be the best way of gaining them. Gentlemen in this respect will be led to their choice of means by their complexions[1] and their habits. Those who understand the military art will of course have some predilection for it. Those who wield the thunder of the state[2] may have more confidence in the efficacy of arms. But I confess, possibly for want of this knowledge, my opinion is much more in favour of prudent management than of force, considering force not as an odious, but a feeble instrument for preserving a people so numerous, so active, so growing, so spirited as this in a profitable and subordinate connection with us.

First, Sir, permit me to observe that the use of force alone is but *temporary*. It may subdue for a moment, but it does not remove the necessity of subduing again; and a nation is not governed which is perpetually to be conquered.

My next objection is its *uncertainty*. Terror is not always the effect of force, and an armament is not a victory. If you do not succeed, you are without resource; for, conciliation failing, force remains, but, force failing, no further hope of reconciliation is left. Power and authority are sometimes bought by kindness, but they can never be begged as alms by an impoverished and defeated violence.

A further objection to force is, that you *impair the object* by your very endeavours to preserve it. The thing you fought for is not the thing which you recover, but depreciated, sunk, wasted, and consumed in the contest. Nothing less will content me than *whole America*. I do not choose to consume its strength long with our own, because in all parts it is the British strength that I consume. I do not choose to be caught by a foreign enemy at the end of this exhausting conflict; and still less in the midst of it. I may escape, but I can make no assurance against such an event. Let me add, that I do not choose wholly to break the American spirit, because it is the spirit that has made the country.

Lastly, we have no sort of *experience* in favour of force as an instrument in the rule of our colonies. Their growth and their utility has been owing to methods altogether different. Our ancient indulgence has been said to be pursued to a fault[3]. It may be so. But we know, if feeling is evidence, that our fault was more tolerable than our attempt to mend it, and our sin far more salutary than our penitence.

These, Sir, are my reasons for not entertaining that high opinion of untried force by which many gentlemen, for whose sentiments in other particulars[4] I have great respect, seem to be so greatly captivated. But there is still behind a third consideration concerning this object, which serves to determine my opinion on the sort of policy which ought to be pursued in the management of America, even more than its population and its commerce—I mean its *temper and character*.

In this character of the Americans, a love of freedom is the predominating feature which marks and distinguishes the whole; and as an ardent is always a jealous affection, your colonies become suspicious, restive, and untractable whenever they see the least attempt to wrest from them by force or shuffle from them by chicane[5] what they think the only advantage worth living for. This fierce spirit of liberty is stronger in the English colonies probably than in any other people of the earth; and this from a great variety of powerful causes, which, to understand the true temper of their minds and the direction which this spirit takes, it will not be amiss to lay open somewhat more largely.

First, the people of the colonies are descendants of Englishmen. England, Sir, is a nation which still I hope respects, and formerly adored, her freedom. The colonists emigrated from you when this part of your character was most predominant, and they took this bias and direction the moment they parted from your hands. They are therefore not only devoted to liberty, but to liberty according to English ideas and on English principles. Abstract liberty, like other mere abstractions, is not to be found. Liberty inheres in some sensible object[6]; and every nation has formed to itself some favourite point, which by way of eminence becomes the criterion of their happiness. It happened you know, Sir, that the great contests for freedom in this country were from the earliest times chiefly upon the question of taxing. Most of the contests in the ancient commonwealths turned primarily on the right of election of magistrates, or on the balance among the several orders of the state. The question of money was not with them so immediate. But in England it was otherwise. On this point of taxes the ablest pens and most eloquent tongues have been exercised; the greatest spirits have acted and suffered. In order to give the fullest satisfaction concerning the importance of this point, it was not only necessary for those who in argument defended the excellence of the English constitution to insist on this privilege of granting money as a dry point of fact, and to prove that the right had been acknowledged in ancient parchments and blind usages to reside in a certain body called a House of Commons. They went much further; they attempted to prove, and they succeeded, that in theory it ought to be so, from the particular nature of a House of Commons, as an immediate representative of the people, whether the old records had delivered this oracle or not. They took infinite pains to inculcate, as a fundamental principle, that in all monarchies the people must in effect themselves, mediately or immediately, possess the power of granting their own money, or no shadow of liberty could subsist. The colonies draw from you, as with their life-blood, these ideas and principles. Their love of liberty, as with you, fixed and attached on this specific point of taxing. Liberty might be safe or might be endangered in twenty other particulars, without their being much pleased or alarmed. Here they felt its pulse, and as they found that beat they thought themselves sick or sound. I do not say whether they were right or wrong in applying your general arguments to their own case. It is not easy indeed to make a monopoly of theorems and corollaries. The fact is, that they did thus apply those general arguments; and your mode of governing them, whether through lenity or indolence, through wisdom or mistake, confirmed them in the imagination that they, as well as you, had an interest in these common principles.

  They were further confirmed in this pleasing error by the form of their provincial legislative assemblies. Their governments are popular in a high degree, some are merely popular, in all the popular representative is the most weighty, and this share of the people in their ordinary government never fails to inspire them with lofty sentiments and with a strong aversion from whatever tends to deprive them of their chief importance.

If anything were wanting to this necessary operation of the form of government, religion would have given it a complete effect. Religion, always a principle of energy, in this new people is no way worn out or impaired, and their mode of professing it is also one main cause of this free spirit. The people are Protestants, and of that kind which is the most adverse to all implicit submission of mind and opinion. This is a persuasion[7] not only favourable to liberty, but built upon it. I do not think, Sir, that the reason of this averseness in the dissenting churches, from all that looks like absolute government, is so much to be sought in their religious tenets as in their history. Every one knows that the Roman Catholic religion is at least coeval with most of the governments where it prevails, that it has generally gone hand in hand with them, and received great favour and every kind of support from authority. The Church of England[8], too, was formed from her cradle under the nursing care of regular government. But the dissenting interests have sprung up in direct opposition to all the ordinary powers of the world, and could justify that opposition only on a strong claim to natural liberty. Their very existence depended on the powerful and unremitted assertion of that claim. All Protestantism, even the most cold and passive, is a sort of dissent. But the religion most prevalent in our northern colonies is a refinement on the principle of resistance; it is the dissidence of dissent and the Protestantism of the Protestant religion. This religion, under a variety of denominations agreeing in nothing but in the communion of the spirit of liberty, is predominant in most of the northern provinces, where the Church of England, notwithstanding its legal rights, is in reality no more than a sort of private sect, not composing most probably the tenth of the people. The colonists left England when this spirit was high, and in the emigrants was the highest of all; and even that stream of foreigners, which has been constantly flowing into these colonies, has, for the greatest part, been composed of dissenters from the establishments of their several countries, and have brought with them a temper and character far from alien to that of the people with whom they mixed.

Sir, I can perceive by their manner that some gentlemen object to the latitude of this description; because in the southern colonies the Church of England forms a large body and has a regular establishment. It is certainly true. There is, however, a circumstance attending these colonies which, in my opinion, fully counterbalances this difference, and makes the spirit of liberty still more high and haughty than in those to the northward. It is, that in Virginia and the Carolinas[9] they have a vast multitude of slaves. Where this is the case in any part of the world, those who are free are by far the most proud and jealous of their freedom. Freedom is to them not only an enjoyment, but a kind of rank and privilege. Not seeing there that freedom, as in countries where it is a common blessing and as broad and general as the air, may be united with much abject toil, with great misery, with all the exterior of servitude, liberty looks amongst them like something that is more noble and liberal. I do not mean, Sir, to commend the superior morality of this sentiment, which has at least as much pride as virtue in it; but I cannot alter the nature of man. The fact is so; and these people of the southern colonies are much more strongly, and with a higher and more stubborn spirit, attached to liberty than those to the northward. Such were all the ancient commonwealths, such were our Gothic ancestors, such in our days were the Poles, and such will be all masters of slaves who are not slaves themselves. In such a people, the haughtiness of domination combines with the spirit of freedom, fortifies it, and renders it invincible.

Permit me, Sir, to add another circumstance in our colonies, which contributes no mean part towards the growth and effect of this untractable spirit. I mean their education. In no country perhaps in the world is the law so general a study. The profession itself is numerous and powerful, and in most provinces it takes the lead. The greater number of the deputies sent to the congress were lawyers. But all who read, and most do read, endeavour to obtain some smattering in that science. I have been told by an eminent bookseller that in no branch of his business, after tracts of popular devotion, were so many books as those on the law exported to the plantations. The colonists have now fallen into the way of printing them for their own use. I hear that they have sold nearly as many of Blackstone's[10] Commentaries in America as in England. General Gage[11] marks out this disposition very particularly in a letter on your table. He states that all the people in his government are lawyers, or smatterers in law, and that in Boston they have been enabled, by successful chicane, wholly to evade many parts of one of your capital penal constitutions. The smartness of debate will say, that this knowledge ought to teach them more clearly the rights of legislature, their obligations to obedience, and the penalties of rebellion. All this is mighty well. But my honourable and learned friend[12] on the floor, who condescends to mark what I say for animadversion, will disdain that ground. He has heard, as well as I, that when great honours and great emoluments do not win over this knowledge to the service of the state, it is a formidable adversary to government. If the spirit be not tamed and broken by these happy methods, it is stubborn and litigious. ***Abeunt studia in mores***[13]. This study renders men acute, inquisitive, dexterous, prompt in attack, ready in defence, full of resources. In other countries, the people, more simple and of a less mercurial cast[14], judge of an ill principle in government only by an actual grievance; here they anticipate the evil and judge of the pressure of the grievance by the badness of the principle. They augur misgovernment at a distance, and snuff the approach of tyranny in every tainted breeze.

The last cause of this disobedient spirit in the colonies is hardly less powerful than the rest, as it is not merely moral, but laid deep in the natural constitution of things. Three thousand miles of ocean lie between you and them. No contrivance can prevent the effect of this distance in weakening government. Seas roll, and months pass, between the order and the execution, and the want of a speedy explanation of a single point is enough to defeat a whole system. You have, indeed, winged ministers of vengeance[15], who carry your bolts in their pounces[16] to the remotest verge of the sea. But there a power steps in that limits the arrogance of raging passions and furious elements, and says, "So far shalt thou go, and no farther." Who are you, that should fret and rage and bite the chains of nature? Nothing worse happens to you than does to all nations who have extensive empire; and it happens in all the forms into which empire can be thrown. In large bodies, the circulation of power must be less vigorous at the extremities. Nature has said it. The Turk cannot govern Egypt, and Arabia, and Curdistan, as he governs Thrace;

nor has he the same dominion in Crimea and Algiers which he has at Brusa[17] and Smyrna[18]. Despotism itself is obliged to truck and huckster[19]. The Sultan gets such obedience as he can. He governs with a loose rein that he may govern at all; and the whole of the force and vigour of his authority in his centre is derived from a prudent relaxation in all his borders. Spain, in her provinces, is, perhaps, not so well obeyed as you are in yours. She complies too, she submits, she watches times. This is the immutable condition, the eternal law, of extensive and detached empire.

Then, Sir, from these six capital sources: of descent, of form of government, of religion in the northern provinces, of manners in the southern, of education, of the remoteness of situation from the first mover of government—from all these causes a fierce spirit of liberty has grown up. It has grown with the growth of the people in your colonies, and increased with the increase of their wealth; a spirit that unhappily meeting with an exercise of power in England which, however lawful, is not reconcilable to any ideas of liberty, much less with theirs, has kindled this flame that is ready to consume us.

NOTES

1. **complexions:** temperaments
2. **the thunder of the state:** the thunderbolt of the state; the military force of the state
3. **to a fault:** excessively
4. **in other particulars:** in other respects
5. **chicane:** chicanery, trickery, deception
6. **some sensible object:** some perceptible material thing
7. **a persuasion:** an established religious belief
8. **the Church of England:** the protestant church of the United Kingdom created by law in the 16th century with the sovereign as its secular head
9. **the Carolinas:** North Carolina and South Carolina
10. **Blackstone:** William Blackstone (1723–1780), English jurist and author of the *Commentaries on the Laws of England* (1765–1769)
11. **General Gage:** Thomas Gage (1721–1787), British General in the American Revolution
12. **my honourable and learned friend:** i.e. the Attorney-General

13. *Abeunt studia in mores*: (Lat.) Pursuits influence character.
14. **of a less mercurial cast:** of a less lively character
15. **winged ministers of vengeance:** winged avenging agents, referring, here, to British warships
16. **who carry your bolts in their pounces:** who carry your thunderbolts in their claws
17. **Brusa:** a city in northwest Turkey, now called Bursa
18. **Smyrna:** a seaport in west Turkey, now called Izmir
19. **to truck and huckster:** to barter and bargain; to change and adapt

31

WILLIAM COWPER

(1731–1800)

William Cowper was an English poet and letter-writer. The son of a rector, he was born at Great Berkhamstead in Hertfordshire, and educated at Westminster School, London. After a period of study in the Middle Temple, he was called to the bar in 1754. Subject to fits of melancholia, he lived in the country and busied himself with literary work. He is remembered principally for his charming letters and such of his poems as: **The Diverting History of John Gilpin** (1785), an inimitable comic ballad; **The Task** (1785), a work in six books of blank verse describing the landscapes, seasons, people, and pleasures of the rural world he knew; **On the Receipt of My Mother's Picture out of Norfolk** (1790), **To Mary Unwin** (1793), and **The Castaway** (1799), lyrics. His letters record in a lively manner his uneventful life in a provincial town. Whether he delineates a friend or neighbour or tells a good story, he unconsciously reveals his personality, his benignity and delicate humour. His prose style is admirably clear.

LETTER TO LADY HESKETH

TO LADY HESKETH[1]

Oct. 12, 1785

My Dear Cousin,

It is no new thing with you to give pleasure; but I will venture to say, that you do not often give more than you gave me this morning. When I came down to breakfast, and found upon the table a letter franked[2] by my uncle, and when opening that frank I found that it contained a letter from you, I said within myself—"This is just as it should be. We are all grown young again, and the days that I thought I should see no more, are actually returned." You perceive, therefore, that you judged well when you conjectured, that a line from you would not be disagreeable to me. It could not be otherwise than, as in fact it proved, a most agreeable surprise, for I can truly boast of an affection for you, that neither years, nor interrupted intercourse, have at all abated. I need only recollect how much I valued you once, and with how much cause, immediately to feel a revival of the same value: if that can be said to revive, which at the most has only been dormant for want of employment, but I slander it when I say that it has slept. A thousand times have I recollected a thousand scenes, in which our two selves have formed the whole of the drama, with the greatest pleasure; at times, too, when I had no reason to suppose that I should ever hear from you again. I have laughed with you at the *Arabian Nights' Entertainment*[3], which afforded us, as you well know, a fund of merriment that serves never to be forgot. I have walked with you to Netley Abbey[4], and have scrambled with you over hedges in every direction, and many other feats we have performed together, upon the field of my remembrance, and all within these few years. Should I say within this twelvemonth, I should not transgress the truth. The hours that I have spent with you were among the pleasantest of my former days, and are therefore chronicled in my mind so deeply, as to feel no erasure. Neither do I forget my poor friend, Sir Thomas. I should remember him, indeed, at any rate, on account of his personal kindness to myself; but the last testimony that he gave of his regard for you endears him to me still more. With his uncommon understanding (for with many peculiarities he had more sense than any of his acquaintance), and with his generous sensibilities, it was hardly possible that he should not distinguish you as he has done. As it was the last, so it was the best proof, that he could give, of a judgement that never deceived him, when he would allow himself leisure to consult it.

You say that you have often heard of me: that puzzles me. I cannot imagine from what quarter, but it is no matter. I must tell you, however, my cousin, that your information has been a little defective. That I am happy in my situation is true; I live, and have lived these twenty years, with Mrs. Unwin, to whose affectionate care of me, during the far greater part of that time, it is, under Providence, owing that I live at all. But I do not account myself happy in having been for thirteen of those years in a state of mind that has made all that care and attention necessary; an attention, and a care, that have injured her health, and which, had she not been uncommonly supported, must have brought her to the grave. But I will pass to another subject; it would be cruel to particularise only to give pain, neither would I by any means give a sable hue to the first letter of a correspondence so unexpectedly renewed.

I am delighted with what you tell me of my uncle's good health. To enjoy any measure of cheerfulness at so late a day is much; but to have that late day enlivened with the vivacity of youth, is much more, and in these postdiluvian times a rarity indeed. Happy, for the most part, are parents who have daughters. Daughters are not apt to outlive their natural affections, which a son has generally survived, even before his boyish years are expired. I rejoice particularly in my uncle's felicity, who has three female descendants from his little person, who leave him nothing to wish for upon that head.

My dear cousin, dejection of spirits, which I suppose may have prevented many a man from becoming an author, made me one. I find constant employment necessary, and therefore take care to be constantly employed. Manual occupations do not engage the mind sufficiently, as I know by experience, having tried many. But composition, especially of verse, absorbs it wholly. I write, therefore, generally three hours in a morning, and in an evening I transcribe. I read also, but less than I write, for I must have bodily exercise, and therefore never pass a day without it.

You ask me where I have been this summer. I answer at Olney. Should you ask me where I spent the last seventeen summers, I should still answer, at Olney. Ay, and the winters also; I have seldom left it, and except when I attended my brother in his last illness, never I believe a fortnight together.

Adieu, my beloved cousin, I shall not always be thus nimble in reply, but shall always have great pleasure in answering you when I can.

> Yours, my dear friend, and cousin,
> W. C.

NOTES

1. **Lady Hesketh:** Lady Hesketh, née Harriet Cowper, who was William Cowper's cousin
2. **franked:** sent free of charge
3. **Arabian Nights' Entertainment:** a collection of oriental folk stories and fairy tales written in Arabic and dating from the 10th century. It is also called *The Thousand and One Nights*.
4. **Netley Abbey:** a ruined abbey in the village of Netley in Southampton

32

EDWARD GIBBON

(1737–1794)

Edward Gibbon was an English historian. He was born in Putney, London, on 27 April, 1737; educated at Westminster School, London (1749–1750), and Magdalen College, Oxford (1752–1753); and devoted to the study of history and French and Latin classics in Lausanne (1753–1758). From 1759 to 1770 he served in the Hampshire militia; in 1772 he settled in London and began to write his Roman history. He joined Dr. Johnson's Literary Club and became Professor of Ancient History at the Royal Academy in 1774, acted as an M.P. in 1774–1783, and held the office of Commissioner of Trade and Plantations in 1779–1782. From 1783 to 1793 he lived in Lausanne, where he completed his history. Shortly after his final return to England, he died in London on January 16, 1794.

Gibbon's reputation rests primarily on *The History of the Decline and Fall of the Roman Empire*, his *magnum opus* in six volumes published during the period 1776–1788, and secondarily on his interesting *Memoirs,* arranged and published by his friend the Earl of Sheffield (John Baker Holroyd) in 1796. *The Decline and Fall* treats the history of Rome from the second to the fifteenth century. The long narrative has an imposing quality derived from the author's deep learning, accurate information, lively description, powerful organization, ironic wit, and grand manner. Gibbon's prose is of an elaborate type, making constant use of an elevated diction and a periodic or symmetric or tripartite syntax. This dignified style is commensurate with his tremendous subject. It is weighty, but still lucid and supple. ***The Decline and Fall of the Roman Empire*** is not only the most celebrated history written in English but also a great work of art.

CONSTANTINE'S INVASION OF ITALY

While Constantine[1] signalized his conduct and valour in the field, the sovereign of Italy appeared insensible of the calamities and danger of a civil war which raged in the heart of his dominions. Pleasure was still the only business of Maxentius[2]. Concealing, or at least attempting to conceal, from the public knowledge the misfortunes of his arms, he indulged himself in vain confidence which deferred the remedies of the approaching evil, without deferring the evil itself. The rapid progress of Constantine was scarcely sufficient to awaken him from this fatal security; he flattered himself that his well-known liberality, and the majesty of the Roman name, which had already delivered him from two invasions, would dissipate with the same facility the rebellious army of Gaul. The officers of experience and ability who had served under the banners of Maximian[3] were at length compelled to inform his effeminate son of the imminent danger to which he was reduced; and, with a freedom that at once surprised and convinced him, to urge the necessity of preventing his ruin by a vigorous exertion of his remaining power. The resources of Maxentius, both of men and money, were still considerable. The Praetorian guards felt how strongly their own interest and safety were connected with his cause; and a third army was soon collected, more numerous than those which had been lost in the battles of Turin[4] and Verona[5]. It was far from the intention of the emperor to lead his troops in person. A stranger to the exercises of war, he trembled at the apprehension of so dangerous a contest; and, as fear is commonly superstitious, he listened with melancholy attention to the rumours of omens and presages which seemed to menace his life and empire. Shame at length supplied the place of courage, and forced him to take the field. He was unable to sustain the contempt of the Roman people. The circus[6] resounded with their indignant clamours, and they tumultuously besieged the gates of the palace, reproaching the pusillanimity of their indolent sovereign, and celebrating the heroic spirit of Constantine. Before Maxentius left Rome, he consulted the Sibylline books[7]. The guardians of these ancient oracles were as well versed in the arts of this world, as they were ignorant of the secrets of fate; and they returned him a very prudent answer, which might adapt itself to the event, and secure their reputation whatever should be the chance of arms.

The celerity of Constantine's march has been compared to the rapid conquest of Italy by the first of the Caesars; nor is the flattering parallel repugnant to the truth of history, since no more than fifty-eight days elapsed between the surrender of Verona and the final decision of the war. Constantine had always apprehended that the tyrant would obey the dictates of fear, and perhaps of prudence; and that, instead of risking his last hopes in a general engagement, he would shut himself up within the walls of Rome. His ample magazines secured him against the danger of famine; and, as the situation of Constantine admitted not of delay, he might have been reduced to the sad necessity of destroying with fire and sword the Imperial city, the noblest reward of his victory, and the deliverance of which had been the motive, or rather indeed the pretence, of the civil war. It was with equal surprise and pleasure that, on his arrival at a place called Saxa Rubra, about nine miles from Rome, he discovered the army of Maxentius prepared to give him battle. Their long front filled a very spacious plain, and their deep array reached to the banks of the Tiber[8], which covered their rear, and forbade their retreat. We are informed, and we may believe, that Constantine disposed his troops with consummate skill, and that he chose for himself the post of honour and danger. Distinguished by the splendour of his arms, he charged in person the cavalry of his rival; and his irresistible attack determined the fortune of the day. The cavalry of Maxentius was principally composed either of unwieldy cuirassiers[9] or of light Moors[10] and Numidians[11]. They yielded to the vigour of the Gallic horse, which possessed more activity than the one, more firmness than the other. The defeat of the two wings left the infantry without any protection on its flanks, and the undisciplined Italians fled without reluctance from the standard of a tyrant whom they had always hated, and whom they no longer feared. The Praetorians, conscious that their offences were beyond the reach of mercy, were animated by revenge and despair. Notwithstanding their repeated efforts, those brave veterans were unable to recover the victory: they obtained, however, an honourable death; and it was observed that their bodies covered the same ground which had been occupied by their ranks. The confusion then became general, and the dismayed troops of Maxentius, pursued by an implacable enemy, rushed by thousands into the deep and rapid stream of the Tiber. The emperor himself attempted to escape back into the city over the Milvian bridge, but the crowds which pressed together through that narrow passage forced him into the river, where he was immediately drowned by the weight of his armour. His body, which had sunk very deep into the mud, was found with some difficulty the next day. The sight of his head, when it was exposed to the eyes of the people, convinced them of their deliverance, and admonished them to receive with acclamations of loyalty and gratitude the fortunate Constantine, who thus achieved by his valour and ability the most splendid enterprise of his life.

NOTES

1. **Constantine:** Flavius Valerius Aurelius Constantine (280?–337), called Constantine the Great, was the first Christian Roman Emperor (306–337). In 312 he crossed the Alps from Gaul, won a great victory over Maxentius near Rome, and entered the city in triumph. Soon he changed his capital to Byzantium and renamed it Constantinople (330).
2. **Maxentius:** Marcus Aurelius Valerius was a Roman Emperor (306–312), who ruled Italy. He was defeated by Constantine at Saxa Rubra in 312 and was drowned while trying to escape into the city of Rome over the Milvian Bridge.
3. **Maximian:** Marcus Aurelius Valerius Maximianus was Roman Emperor (286–305) and father of Maxentius.
4. **Turin:** a city in Northwest Italy
5. **Verona:** a city in North Italy
6. **circus:** open-air stadium
7. **Sibylline books:** prophetic books supposedly bought from the Cumaean Sibyl
8. **the Tiber:** a river in central Italy flowing through Rome
9. **cuirassiers:** horse-soldiers wearing cuirasses
10. **Moors:** Muslim people of North Africa
11. **Numidians:** people of Numidia, an ancient country of North Africa corresponding roughly to modern Algeria

A RETROSPECT

When I contemplate the common lot of mortality, I must acknowledge that I have drawn a high prize in the lottery of life. The far greater part of the globe is overspread with barbarism or slavery; in the civilised world the most numerous class is condemned to ignorance and poverty; and the double fortune of my birth in a free and enlightened country, in an honourable and wealthy family, is the lucky chance of a unit against millions. The general probability is about three to one that a new-born infant will not live to complete his fiftieth year. I have now passed that age, and may fairly estimate the present value of my existence in the three-fold division of mind, body, and estate.

1. The first and indispensable requisite of happiness is a clear conscience, unsullied by the reproach or remembrance of any unworthy action.

—Hic murus aheneus esto,
Nil conscire sibi, nullâ pallescere culpâ[1].

I am endowed with a cheerful temper, a moderate sensibility, and a natural disposition to repose rather than to activity: some mischievous appetites and habits have perhaps been corrected by philosophy or time. The love of study, a passion which derives fresh vigour from enjoyment, supplies each day, each hour, with a perpetual source of independent and rational pleasure; and I am not sensible of any decay of the mental faculties. The original soil has been highly improved by labour and manure[2]; but it may be questioned whether some flowers of fancy, some grateful errors, have not been eradicated with the weeds of prejudice.

2. Since I have escaped from the long perils of my childhood, the serious advice of a physician has seldom been requisite. "The madness of superfluous health"[3] I have never known, but my tender constitution has been fortified by time, and the inestimable gift of the sound and peaceful slumbers of infancy may be imputed

both to the mind and body. 3. I have already described the merits of my society and situation; but these enjoyments would be tasteless or bitter if their possession were not assured by an annual and adequate supply. According to the scale of Switzerland[4] I am a rich man; and I am indeed rich, since my income is superior to my expense, and my expense is equal to my wishes. My friend Lord Sheffield[5] has kindly relieved me from the cares to which my taste and temper are most adverse: shall I add that, since the failure of my first wishes, I have never entertained any serious thoughts of a matrimonial connection?

I am disgusted with the affectation of men of letters, who complain that they have renounced a substance for a shadow, and that their fame (which sometimes is no insupportable weight) affords a poor compensation for envy, censure, and persecution. My own experience, at least, has taught me a very different lesson: twenty happy years have been animated by the labour of my ***History***[6], and its success has given me a name, a rank, a character in the world to which I should not otherwise have been entitled. The freedom of my writings has indeed provoked an implacable tribe; but, as I was safe from the stings, I was soon accustomed to the buzzing of the hornets: my nerves are not tremblingly alive, and my literary temper is so happily framed that I am less sensible of pain than of pleasure. The rational pride of an author may be offended, rather than flattered, by vague indiscriminate praise; but he cannot, he should not, be indifferent to the fair testimonies of private and public esteem. Even his moral sympathy may be gratified by the idea that now, in the present hour, he is imparting some degree of amusement or knowledge to his friends in a distant land; that one day his mind will be familiar to the grandchildren of those who are yet unborn. I cannot boast of the friendship or favour of princes; the patronage of English literature has long since been devolved on our booksellers, and the measure of their liberality is the least ambiguous test of our common success. Perhaps the golden mediocrity[7] of my fortune has contributed to fortify my application.

The present is a fleeting moment, the past is no more; and our prospect of futurity is dark and doubtful. This day may possibly be my last: but the laws of probability, so true in general, so fallacious in particular, still allow about fifteen years. I shall soon enter into the period which, as the most agreeable of his long life, was selected by the judgment and experience of the sage Fontenelle[8]. His choice is approved by the eloquent historian of nature, who fixes our moral happiness to the mature season, in which our passions are supposed to be calmed, our duties fulfilled, our ambition satisfied, our fame and fortune established on a solid basis. In private conversation, that great and amiable man added the weight of his own experience; and this autumnal felicity might be exemplified in the lives of Voltaire, Hume, and many other men of letters. I am far more inclined to embrace than to dispute this comfortable doctrine. I will not suppose any premature decay of the mind or body; but I must reluctantly observe that two causes, the abbreviation of time, and the failure of hope, will always tinge with a browner shade the evening of life.

(The Autobiography)
(Memoirs)

NOTES

1. ***Hic murus aheneus esto, /Nil conscire sibi, nullâ pallescere culpâ***: This shall be one's brazen wall, to feel no consciousness of guilt, nor grow pale through misconduct.
2. **labour and manure:** cultivation
3. **"The madness of superfluous health":** Pope, *Essay on Man* III. 3
4. **Switzerland:** Gibbon lived in Switzerland for five years (1753–1758) in his youth.
5. **Lord Sheffield:** John Baker Holroyd (1735–1821), the Earl of Sheffield, was Gibbon's friend.
6. **my *History*:** *The History of the Decline and Fall of the Roman Empire* (1776–1788)
7. **golden mediocrity:** golden mean
8. **Fontenelle:** Bernard le Bovier de Fontenelle (1657–1757), who was a French thinker and writer.

33

JAMES BOSWELL

(1740–1795)

James Boswell was a Scottish lawyer, biographer, and miscellaneous writer. He was born in Edinburgh and educated at the Universities of Edinburgh, Glasgow, and Utrecht. He was called to the Scottish bar in 1766, and practised law from 1769. His aspirations, however, were directed towards literature and the pursuit of great men. His best-known works are his masterpiece *The Life of Samuel Johnson, LL.D.* (1791, revised 1793) and his entertaining travel book *The Journal of a Tour to the Hebrides* (1785). Boswell, the hero-worshipper, made the acquaintance of Johnson in 1763, and during a period of twenty-one years he paid frequent visits to the master in London. Based on his personal knowledge of his subject and the numerous relevant documents, letters, and statements he had collected, he composed the monumental *Life of Samuel Johnson*, giving a complete account of Johnson's activities and habits, writings and conversations, opinions and sentiments. Here lives for all posterity the great writer, talker and moralist. The narrative is also noteworthy for its limpid and vivacious style. This *Life* is generally recognized as the first classic of English biography.

A MORNING RAMBLE

One night, when Beauclerk[1] and Langton[2] had supped at a tavern in London, and sat till about three in the morning, it came into their heads to go and knock up Johnson, and see if they could prevail on him to join them in a ramble[3]. They rapped violently at the door of his chambers in the Temple[4], till at last he appeared in his shirt with his little black wig on the top of his head, instead of a night-cap, and a poker in his hand, imagining, probably, that some ruffians were coming to attack him. When he discovered who they were, and was told their errand, he smiled, and with great good humour agreed to their proposal: "What, is it you, you dogs! I'll have a frisk with you!" He was soon dressed, and they sallied forth together into Covent-Garden, where the green-grocers and fruiterers were beginning to arrange their hampers, just come in from the country. Johnson made some attempts to help them; but the honest gardeners stared so at his figure and manner, and odd interference, that he soon saw his services were not relished. They then repaired to one of the neighbouring taverns, and made a bowl of that liquor called **Bishop**[5], which Johnson had always liked; while in joyous contempt of sleep, from which he had been roused, he repeated the festive lines,

> "Short, O short, then be thy reign,
> And give us to the world again!"

They did not stay long, but walked down to the Thames, took a boat, and rowed to Billingsgate. Beauclerk and Johnson were so well pleased with their amusement, that they resolved to persevere in dissipation for the rest of the day; but Langton deserted them, being engaged to breakfast with some young ladies. Johnson scolded him for "leaving his social friends to go and sit with a set of wretched **un-idea'd** girls." Garrick[6] being told of this ramble, said to him smartly, "I heard of your frolick t'other night. You'll be in the 'Chronicle.'"[7] Upon which

Johnson afterwards observed, "*He* durst not do such a thing. His *wife* would not *let* him!"

NOTES

1. **Beauclerk:** Topham Beauclerk (1739-1780), an English book-collector and an intimate friend of Samuel Johnson
2. **Langton:** Bennet Langton (1737-1801), an English Greek scholar and an intimate friend of Samuel Johnson
3. **a ramble:** Boswell was inaccurate in placing the event under the year 1752, for it could not have taken place before 1760.
4. **the Temple:** Johnson lived in Inner Temple Lane between 1760 and 1765.
5. *Bishop*: a mixture of wine, oranges, and sugar
6. **Garrick:** David Garrick (1717-1779), the most famous English actor of the 18th century
7. **the Chronicle:** *The London Chronicle*, a Tory paper

CHARACTER OF GOLDSMITH

As Dr. Oliver Goldsmith will frequently appear in this narrative, I shall endeavour to make my readers in some degree acquainted with his singular character. He was a native of Ireland, and a contemporary with Mr. Burke[1], at Trinity College, Dublin, but did not then give much promise of future celebrity. He, however, observed to Mr. Malone[2], that "though he made no great figure in mathematics, which was a study in much repute there, he could turn an Ode of Horace into English better than any of them." He afterwards studied physic at Edinburgh, and upon the Continent: and, I have been informed, was enabled to pursue his travels on foot, partly by demanding, at Universities, to enter the lists as a disputant, by which, according to the custom of many of them, he was entitled to the premium of a crown, when, luckily for him, his challenge was not accepted; so that, as I once observed to Dr. Johnson, he *disputed* his passage through Europe. He then came to England, and was employed successively in the capacities of an usher to an academy, a corrector of the press, a reviewer, and a writer for a newspaper. He had sagacity enough to cultivate assiduously the acquaintance of Johnson, and his faculties were gradually enlarged by the contemplation of such a model. To me and many others it appeared that he studiously copied the manner of Johnson, though, indeed, upon a smaller scale.

At this time I think he had published nothing with his name, though it was pretty generally known that *one Dr. Goldsmith* was the author of "An Inquiry into the Present State of Polite Learning in Europe," and of "The Citizen of the World," a series of letters supposed to be written from London by a Chinese. No man had the art of displaying with more advantage, as a writer, whatever literary acquisitions he made. *"Nihil quod tetigit non ornavit."*[3] His mind resembled a fertile but thin soil. There was a quick, but not a strong, vegetation, of whatever chanced to be thrown upon it. No deep could be struck. The oak of the forest did not grow there; but the elegant shrubbery and the fragrant parterre[4] appeared in gay succession. It has been generally circulated and believed that he was a mere fool in conversation; but, in truth, this has been greatly exaggerated. He had, no doubt, a more than common share of that hurry of ideas which we often find in his countrymen, and which sometimes produces a laughable confusion in expressing them. He was very much what the French call **un étourdi**[5], and from vanity and an eager desire of being conspicuous wherever he was, he frequently talked carelessly without knowledge of the subject, or even without thought. His person as short, his countenance coarse and vulgar, his deportment that of a scholar awkwardly affecting the easy gentleman. Those who were in any way distinguished, excited envy in him to so ridiculous an excess, that the instances of it are hardly credible. When accompanying two beautiful young ladies, with their mother, on a tour in France, he was seriously angry that more attention was paid to them than to him; and once at the exhibition of the **Fantoccini**[6] in London, when those who sat next him observed with what dexterity a puppet was made to toss a pike, he could not bear that it should have such praise, and exclaimed, with some warmth, "Pshaw! I can do it better myself."

He, I am afraid, had no settled system of any sort, so that his conduct must not be strictly scrutinised; but his affections were social and generous, and when he had money he gave it away very liberally. His desire of imaginary consequence predominated over his attention to truth. When he began to rise into notice, he said he had a brother who was Dean of Durham, a fiction so easily detected, that it is wonderful how he should have been so inconsiderate as to hazard it. He boasted to me at this time of the power of his pen in commanding money, which I believe was true in a certain degree, though in the instance he gave he was by no means correct. He told me that he had sold a novel for four hundred pounds. This was his "Vicar of Wakefield." But Johnson informed me that he had made the bargain for Goldsmith, and the price was sixty pounds. "And, Sir," said he, "a sufficient price too, when it was sold; for then the fame of Goldsmith had not been elevated, as it afterwards was, by his 'Traveller'; and the bookseller had such faint hopes of profit by his bargain, that he kept the manuscript by him a long time, and did not publish it till after the 'Traveller' had appeared. Then, to be sure, it was accidentally worth more money."

Mrs. Piozzi[7] and Sir John Hawkins[8] have strangely mis-stated the history of Goldsmith's situation and Johnson's friendly interference, when this novel was sold. I shall give it authentically from Johnson's own exact narration:

"I received one morning a message from poor Goldsmith that he was in great distress, and, as it was not in his power to come to me, begging that I would come to him as soon as possible. I sent him a guinea, and promised to come to him directly. I accordingly went as soon as I was dressed, and found that his landlady had arrested him for his rent, at which he was in a violent passion. I perceived that he had already changed my guinea, and had got a bottle of Madeira and a glass before him. I put the cork into the bottle, desired he would be calm, and began to talk to him of the means by which he might be extricated. He then told me that he had a novel ready for the press, which he produced to me. I looked into it, and saw its merit; told the landlady I should soon return; and, having gone to a bookseller, sold it for sixty pounds. I brought Goldsmith the money, and he discharged his rent, not without rating his landlady in a high tone for having used him so ill."

NOTES

1. **Mr. Burke:** Edmund Burke (1729–1797), who was a British Whig statesman and a conservative orator and writer
2. **Mr. Malone:** Edmond Malone (1741–1812), literary critic and editor of Shakespeare
3. *Nihil quod tetigit non ornavit*: He touched nothing which he did not adorn.
4. **parterre:** flower-bed, garden plot
5. **un étourdi:** (Fr.) a thoughtless fellow
6. *Fantoccini*: (It.) puppets
7. **Mrs. Piozzi:** Mrs. Hester Thrale (1741–1821) after Thrale's death married Gabriel Piozzi, an Italian musician. She was Dr. Johnson's friend and the author of *Anecdotes of the Late Samuel Johnson* (1786).
8. **Sir John Hawkins:** John Hawkins (1719–1789), a friend of Dr. Johnson's, who published *a life of Johnson* in 1787–1789

THE MEETING OF TWO FELLOW-COLLEGIANS

And now I am to give a pretty full account of one of the most curious incidents in Johnson's life[1], of which he himself has made the following minute on this day: "In my return from church, I was accosted by Edwards, an old fellow-collegian, who had not seen me since 1729. He knew me, and asked if I remembered one Edwards; I did not at first recollect the name, but gradually as we walked along, recovered it, and told him a conversation that had passed at an alehouse between us. My purpose is to continue our acquaintance."

It was in Butcher-row that this meeting happened. Mr. Edwards, who was a decent-looking elderly man in grey clothes, and a wig of many curls, accosted Johnson with familiar confidence, knowing who he was, while Johnson returned his salutation with a courteous formality, as to a stranger. But as soon as Edwards had brought to his recollection their having been at Pembroke College[2] together nine-and-forty years ago, he seemed much pleased, asked where he lived, and said he should be glad to see him in Bolt Court[3]. EDWARDS. "Ah, Sir! we are old men now." JOHNSON, (who never liked to think of being old:) "Don't let us discourage one another." EDWARDS. "Why, Doctor, you look stout and hearty, I am happy to see you so; for the newspapers told us you were very ill." JOHNSON. "Ah, Sir, they are always telling lies of *us old fellows*."

Wishing to be present at more of so singular a conversation as that between two fellow-collegians, who had lived forty years in London without ever having chanced to meet, I whispered to Mr. Edwards that Dr. Johnson was going home, and that he had better accompany him now. So Edwards walked along with us, I eagerly assisting to keep up the conversation. Mr. Edwards informed Dr. Johnson that he had practised long as a solicitor in Chancery[4], but that he now lived in the country upon a little farm, about sixty acres, just by Stevenage in Hertfordshire[5], and that he came to London (to Barnard's Inn, No. 6,) generally twice a week. Johnson appearing to me in a reverie, Mr. Edwards addressed himself to me, and expatiated on the pleasure of living in the country. BOSWELL. "I have no notion of this, Sir. What you have to entertain you, is, I think, exhausted in half an hour." EDWARDS. "What? don't you love to have hope realized? I see my grass, and my corn, and my trees growing. Now, for instance, I am curious to see if this frost has not nipped my fruit-trees." JOHNSON, (who we did not imagine was attending:) "You find, Sir, you have fears as well as hopes."—So well did he see the whole, when another saw but the half of a subject.

When we got to Dr. Johnson's house, and were seated in his library, the dialogue went on admirably. EDWARDS. "Sir, I remember you would not let us say *prodigious* at College. For even then, Sir, (turning to me) he was delicate[6] in language, and we all feared him." JOHNSON, (to Edwards:) "From your having practised the law long, Sir, I presume you must be rich." EDWARDS. "No, Sir; I got a good deal of money; but I had a number of poor relations to whom I gave a great part of it." JOHNSON. "Sir, you have been rich in the most valuable sense of the word." EDWARDS. "But I shall not die rich." JOHNSON. "Nay, sure, Sir, it is better to *live* rich, than to *die* rich." EDWARDS. "I wish I had continued at College." JOHNSON. "Why do you wish that, Sir?" EDWARDS. "Because I think I should have had a much easier life than mine has been. I should have been a parson, and had a good living, like Bloxham and several others, and lived comfortably." JOHNSON. "Sir, the life of a parson, of a conscientious clergyman, is not easy. I have always considered a clergyman as the father of a larger family than he is able to maintain. I would rather have Chancery suits upon my hands than the cure of souls. No, Sir, I do not envy a clergyman's life as an easy life, nor do I envy the clergyman who makes it an easy life."—Here taking himself up all of a sudden, he exclaimed, "O! Mr. Edwards! I'll convince you that I recollect you. Do you remember our drinking together at an alehouse near Pembroke gate. At that time, you told me of the Eton[7] boy, who, when verses on our SAVIOUR's turning water into wine were prescribed as an exercise, brought up a single line, which was highly admired:

'Vidit et erubuit lympha pudica DEUM.'[8]

and I told you of another fine line in 'Camden's **Remains**[9],' an eulogy upon one of our Kings, who was succeeded by his son, a prince of equal merit:

'Mira cano, Sol occubuit, nox nulla secuta est.''[10]

EDWARDS. "You are a philosopher, Dr. Johnson. I have tried too in my time to be a philosopher; but, I don't know how, cheerfulness was always breaking in." —Mr. Burke, Sir Joshua Reynolds, Mr. Courtenay, Mr. Malone, and, indeed, all the eminent men to whom I have mentioned this, have thought it an exquisite trait of character. The truth is, that philosophy, like religion, is too generally supposed to be hard and severe, at least so grave as to exclude all gaiety.

EDWARDS. "I have been twice married, Doctor. You, I suppose, have never known what it was to have a wife." JOHNSON. "Sir, I have known what it was to have a wife, and (in a solemn tender faultering tone) I have known what it was to *lose a wife*. —It had almost broke my heart."

EDWARDS. "How do you live, Sir? For my part, I must have my regular meals, and a glass of good wine. I find I require it." JOHNSON. "I now drink no wine, Sir. Early in life I drank wine; for many years I drank none. I then for some years drank a great deal." EDWARDS. "Some hogsheads, I warrant you." JOHNSON. "I then had a severe illness, and left it off, and I have never begun it again. I never felt any difference upon myself from eating one thing rather than another, nor from one kind of weather rather than another. There are people, I believe, who feel a difference; but I am not one of them. And as to regular meals, I have fasted from the Sunday's dinner to the Tuesday's dinner, without any inconvenience. I believe it is best to eat just as one is hungry; but a man who is in business, or a man who has a family, must have stated meals. I am a straggler. I may leave this town and go to Grand Cairo, without being missed here or observed there." EDWARDS. "Don't you eat supper, Sir?" JOHNSON. "No, Sir." EDWARDS. "For my part, now, I consider supper as a turn-pike through which one must pass, in order to get to bed."

JOHNSON. "You are a lawyer, Mr. Edwards. Lawyers know life practically. A bookish man should always have them to converse with. They have what he wants." EDWARDS. "I am grown old: I am sixty-five." JOHNSON. "I shall be sixty-eight next birthday. Come, Sir, drink water, and put in for a hundred."

Mr. Edwards mentioned a gentleman who had left his whole fortune to Pembroke College. JOHNSON. "Whether to leave one's whole fortune to a College be right, must depend upon circumstances. I would leave the interest of the fortune I bequeathed to a College to my relations or my friends, for their lives. It is the same thing to a College, which is a permanent society, whether it gets the money now or twenty years hence; and I would wish to make my relations or friends feel the benefit of it."

This interview confirmed my opinion of Johnson's most humane and benevolent heart. His cordial and placid behaviour to an old fellow collegian, a man so different from himself; and his telling him that he would go down to his farm and visit him, showed a kindness of disposition very rare at an advanced age. He observed, "how wonderful it was that they had both been in London forty years, without having ever once met, and both walkers in the street too!" Mr. Edwards, when going away, again recurred to his consciousness of senility, and looking full in Johnson's face, said to him, "You'll find in Dr. Young[11],

'O my coevals! remnants of yourselves.'"

Johnson did not relish this at all; but shook his head with impatience. Edwards walked off seemingly highly-pleased with the honour of having been thus noticed by Dr. Johnson. When he was gone, I said to Johnson, I thought him but a weak man. JOHNSON. "Why, yes, Sir. Here is a man who has passed through life without experience: yet I would rather have him with me than a more sensible man who will not talk readily. This man is always willing to say what he has to say." Yet Dr. Johnson had himself by no means that willingness which he praised so much, and I think so justly; for who has not felt the painful effect of the dreary void, when there is a total silence in a company, for any length of time; or, which is as bad, or perhaps worse, when the conversation is with difficulty kept up by a perpetual effort?

NOTES

1. **one of the most curious incidents in Johnson's life:** The incident occurred on April 17, 1778.
2. **Pembroke College:** one of the colleges in Oxford University
3. **Bolt Court:** Dr. Johnson lived in Bolt Court from 1776 to 1784.
4. **Chancery:** Lord Chancellor's Court
5. **Hertfordshire:** a county of South England
6. **delicate:** fastidious
7. **Eton:** Eton College, a public school for boys in Berkshire, South England, founded in 1440
8. ***Vidit et erubuit lympha pudica DEUM***: (Lat.) The crystal water blushed when she saw the Master.
9. **Camden's *Remains*:** William Camden (1551–1623) who was an English antiquarian and historian; among his several works is his ***Remains***, a book on historic relics.
10. ***Miro cano, Sol occubuit, nox nulla secuta est***: (Lat.) I tell a tale of wonder. The sun sank, but no night followed.
11. **Dr. Young:** Edwrad Young (1683–1765), English poet and dramatist

34

RICHARD BRINSLEY SHERIDAN

(1751–1816)

R. B. Sheridan was an Irish dramatist and politician. He was born in Dublin in the autumn of 1751, of literary parents, and educated at Harrow School, London. In 1773 he married Eliza Linley, the girl he loved, under romantic circumstances. To improve his means of living, he wrote in 1774 a play, **The Rivals**, which was produced at Covent Garden in 1775 with great success. This was followed by *St. Patrick's Day* (1775), *The Duenna* (1775), *A Trip to Scarborough* (1777), *The School for Scandal* (1777), and *The Critic* (1779), all warmly received by the audience. Sheridan became manager of the Drury Lane Theatre in 1776 and its sole proprietor in 1779. In 1777 he was elected a member of Johnson's Club. Sheridan liked politics even better than the theatre. He entered Parliament in 1780, soon gained a reputation as a brilliant orator, and later held several governmental offices. He died in July 1816, and was buried in Westminster Abbey, near the actor and playwright David Garrick. Sheridan is chiefly remembered for his three superb comedies of manners, **The Rivals**, **The School for Scandal**, and **The Critic**. Their plots are ingenious, their characters are memorable, and their dialogue is sparkling.

A SCENE FROM
THE SCHOOL FOR SCANDAL

ACT I

Scene I—Lady Sneerwell's[1] *House.*
Discovered Lady Sneerwell at the dressing-table; Snake[2] *drinking chocolate.*

Lady Sneer. The paragraphs, you say, Mr. Snake, were all inserted?

Snake. They were, madam; and as I copied them myself in a feigned hand, there can be no suspicion whence they came.

Lady Sneer. Did you circulate the report of Lady Brittle's[3] intrigue with Captain Boastall[4]?

Snake. That's in as fine a train[5] as your ladyship could wish. In the common course of things[6], I think it must reach Mrs. Clackitt's[7] ears within four and twenty hours; and then, you know, the business is as good as done.

Lady Sneer. Why, truly, Mrs. Clackitt has a very pretty talent, and a great deal of industry.

Snake. True, madam, and has been tolerably successful in her day. To my knowledge she has been the cause of six matches being broken off, and three sons disinherited; of four forced elopements, and as many close confinements[8]; nine separate maintenances[9], and two divorces. Nay, I have more than once traced her causing a *tête-à-tête* in the **Town and Country Magazine**[10], when the parties, perhaps, had never seen each other's face before in the course of their lives.

Lady Sneer. She certainly has talents, but her manner is gross.

Snake. 'Tis very true. —She generally designs well, has a free tongue[11] and a bold invention; but her colouring is too dark, and her outlines often extravagant. She wants that delicacy of tint, and mellowness of sneer, which distinguishes your ladyship's scandal.

Lady Sneer. You are partial, Snake.

Snake. Not in the least—everybody allows that Lady Sneerwell can do more with a word or a look than many can with the most laboured detail, even when they happen to have a little truth on their side to support it.

Lady Sneer. Yes, my dear Snake; and I am no hypocrite to deny the satisfaction I reap from the success of my efforts. Wounded myself in the early part of my life by the envenomed tongue of slander, I confess I have since known no pleasure equal to the reducing others to the level of my own injured reputation.

Snake. Nothing can be more natural. But, Lady Sneerwell, there is one affair in which you have lately employed me, wherein, I confess, I am at a loss to guess your motives.

Lady Sneer. I conceive you mean with respect to my neighbour, Sir Peter Teazle[12], and his family?

Snake. I do. Here are two young men[13], to whom Sir Peter has acted as a kind of guardian since their father's death; the eldest possessing the most amiable character, and universally well spoken of; the youngest, the most dissipated and extravagant young fellow in the kingdom, without friends or character: the former an avowed admirer of your ladyship's, and apparently your favourite; the latter attached to Maria, Sir Peter's ward, and confessedly beloved by her. Now, on the face of these circumstances, it is utterly unaccountable to me why you, the widow of a City knight[14], with a good jointure[15], should not close with the passion of[16] a man of such character and expectations as Mr. Surface[17]; and more so why you should be so uncommonly earnest to destroy the mutual attachment subsisting between his brother Charles and Maria.

Lady Sneer. Then at once to unravel this mystery, I must inform you, that love has no share whatever in the intercourse between Mr. Surface and me.

Snake. No!

Lady Sneer. His real attachment is to Maria, or her fortune; but finding in his brother a favoured rival, he has been obliged to mask his pretensions, and profit by my assistance.

Snake. Yet still I am more puzzled why you should interest yourself in his success.

Lady Sneer. How dull you are! Cannot you surmise the weakness which I hitherto, through shame, have concealed even from you? Must I confess, that Charles, that libertine, that extravagant, that bankrupt in fortune and reputation, that he it is for whom I'm thus anxious and malicious, and to gain whom I would sacrifice everything?

Snake. Now, indeed, your conduct appears consistent; but how came you and Mr. Surface so confidential?

Lady Sneer. For our mutual interest. I have found him out a long time since. I know him to be artful, selfish, and malicious—in short, a sentimental knave[18]; while with Sir Peter, and indeed with all his acquaintance, he passes for a youthful miracle of prudence, good sense, and benevolence.

Snake. Yes; yet Sir Peter vows he has not his equal in England—and above all, he praises him as a man of sentiment[19].

Lady Sneer. True—and with the assistance of his sentiment and hypocrisy, he has brought Sir Peter entirely into his interest with regard to Maria; while poor Charles has no friend in the house, though, I fear, he has a powerful one in Maria's heart, against whom we must direct our schemes.

Enter Servant.

Serv. Mr. Surface.
Lady Sneer. Show him up. (*Exit Servant.*

Enter Joseph Surface.

Joseph S. My dear Lady Sneerwell, how do you do to-day? Mr. Snake, your most obedient[20].

Lady Sneer. Snake has just been rallying me on our mutual attachment; but I have informed him of our real views. You know how useful he has been to us, and, believe me, the confidence is not ill placed.

Joseph S. Madam, it is impossible for me to suspect a man of Mr. Snake's sensibility and discernment.

Lady Sneer. Well, well, no compliments now; but tell me when you saw your mistress, Maria—or, what is more material to me, your brother.

Joseph S. I have not seen either since I left you; but I can inform you that they never meet. Some of your stories have taken a good effect on Maria.

Lady Sneer. Ah! my dear Snake! the merit of this belongs to you; but do your brother's distresses[21] increase?

Joseph S. Every hour. I am told he has had another execution[22] in the house yesterday. In short, his dissipation and extravagance exceed anything I have ever heard of.

Lady Sneer. Poor Charles!

Joseph S. True, madam; notwithstanding his vices one can't help feeling for him. Poor Charles! I'm sure I wish it were in my power to be of any essential service to him; for the man who does not share in the distresses of a brother, even though merited by his own misconduct, deserves—

Lady Sneer. O Lud![23] you are going to be moral, and forget that you are among friends.

Joseph S. Egad[24], that's true!—I'll keep that sentiment till I see Sir Peter; —however, it certainly is a charity to rescue Maria from such a libertine, who, if he is to be reclaimed, can be so only by a person of your ladyship's superior accomplishments and understanding.

Snake. I believe, Lady Sneerwell, here's company coming; I'll go and copy the letter I mentioned to you. —Mr. Surface, your most obedient. (*Exit Snake.*

Joseph S. Sir, your very devoted[25]. —Lady Sneerwell, I am very sorry you have put any farther confidence in that fellow.

Lady Sneer. Why so?

Joseph S. I have lately detected him in frequent conference with old Rowley, who was formerly my father's steward, and has never, you know, been a friend of mine.

Lady Sneer. And do you think he would betray us?

Joseph S. Nothing more likely: —take my word for't[26], Lady Sneerwell, that fellow hasn't virtue enough to be faithful even to his own villany. —Ah! Maria!

Enter Maria.

Lady Sneer. Maria, my dear, how do you do?—What's the matter?

Maria. Oh! there is that disagreeable lover of mine, Sir Benjamin Backbite[27], has just called at my guardian's, with his odious uncle, Crabtree[28]; so I slipt out, and ran hither to avoid them.

Lady Sneer. Is that all?

Joseph S. If my brother Charles had been of the party, madam, perhaps you would not have been so much alarmed.

Lady Sneer. Nay, now you are severe; for I dare swear the truth of the matter is, Maria heard *you* were here. —But, my dear, what has Sir Benjamin done, that you would avoid him so?

Maria. Oh, he has done nothing—but 'tis for what he has said: his conversation is a perpetual libel on all his acquaintance.

Joseph S. Aye, and the worst of it is, there is no advantage in not knowing him—for he'll abuse a stranger just as soon as his best friend; and his uncle's as bad.

Lady Sneer. Nay, but we should make allowance[29]—Sir Benjamin is a wit and a poet.

Maria. For my part, I confess, madam, wit loses its respect with me, when I see it in company with malice. —What do you think, Mr. Surface?

Joseph S. Certainly, madam; to smile at the jest which plants a thorn in another's breast is to become a principal in the mischief[30].

Lady Sneer. Pshaw!—there's no possibility of being witty without a little ill nature; the malice of a good thing is the barb that makes it stick. —What's your opinion, Mr. Surface?

Joseph S. To be sure, madam; that conversation, where the spirit of raillery is suppressed, will ever appear tedious and insipid.

Maria. Well, I'll not debate how far scandal may be allowable; but in a man, I am sure, it is always contemptible. We have pride, envy, rivalship, and a thousand motives to depreciate each other; but the male slanderer must have the cowardice of a woman before he can traduce one.

Enter Servant.

Serv. Madam, Mrs. Candour[31] is below, and if your ladyship's at leisure, will leave her carriage.
Lady Sneer. Beg her to walk in.—(*Exit Servant.*—Now, Maria, here is a character to your taste; for though Mrs. Candour is a little talkative, everybody allows her to be the best-natured and best sort of woman.
Maria. Yes,—with a very gross affectation of good nature and benevolence, she does more mischief than the direct malice of old Crabtree.
Joseph S. I'faith[32] that's true, Lady Sneerwell: whenever I hear the current running against the characters of my friends, I never think them in such danger as when Candour undertakes their defence.
Lady Sneer. Hush!—here she is!

Enter Mrs. Candour.

Mrs. Can. My dear Lady Sneerwell, how have you been this century?—Mr. Surface, what news do you hear? —though indeed it is no matter, for I think one hears nothing else but scandal.
Joseph S. Just so, indeed, ma'am.
Mrs. Can. O Maria! child, —what, is the whole affair off between you and Charles? His extravagance, I presume—the town talks of nothing else.
Maria. Indeed! I am very sorry, ma'am, the town is not better employed.
Mrs. Can. True, true, child; but there's no stopping people's tongues. I own I was hurt to hear it, as I indeed was to learn, from the same quarter, that your guardian, Sir Peter, and Lady Teazle have not agreed lately as well as could be wished.

Maria. 'Tis strangely impertinent for people to busy themselves so.

Mrs. Can. Very true, child; —but what's to be done? People will talk—There's no preventing it. Why, it was but yesterday I was told that Miss Gadabout[33] had eloped with Sir Filigree Flirt[34]. —But, Lord! There's no minding what one hears; though, to be sure, I had this from very good authority.

Maria. Such reports are highly scandalous.

Mrs. Can. So they are, child—shameful, shameful! But the world is so censorious, no character escapes. —Lord, now who would have suspected your friend, Miss Prim[35], of an indiscretion? Yet such is the ill-nature of people, that they say her uncle stopt her last week, just as she was stepping into the York diligence[36] with her dancing-master.

Maria. I'll answer for't there are no grounds for that report.

Mrs. Can. Ah, no foundation in the world, I dare swear; no more, probably, than for the story circulated last month, of Mrs. Festino's[37] affair with Colonel Cassino[38]; —though, to be sure, that matter was never rightly cleared up.

Joseph S. The licence of invention some people take is monstrous indeed.

Maria. 'Tis so, —but, in my opinion, those who report such things are equally culpable.

Mrs. Can. To be sure they are; tale-bearers are as bad as the tale-makers—'tis an old observation, and a very true one: but what's to be done, as I said before? how will you prevent people from talking? To-day, Mrs. Clackitt assured me, Mr. and Mrs. Honeymoon[39] were at last become mere man and wife, like the rest of their acquaintance. She likewise hinted that a certain widow, in the next street, had got rid of her dropsy and recovered her shape in a most surprising manner. And at the same time, Miss Tattle[40], who was by, affirmed, that Lord Buffalo[41] had discovered his lady at a house of no extraordinary fame; and that Sir H. Bouquet[42] and Tom Saunter[43] were to measure swords[44] on a similar provocation. —But, Lord, do you think I would report these things? —No, no! tale-bearers, as I said before, are just as bad as the tale-makers.

Joseph S. Ah! Mrs. Candour, if everybody had your forbearance and good-nature!

Mrs. Can. I confess, Mr. Surface, I cannot bear to hear people attacked behind their backs; and when ugly circumstances come out against our acquaintance, I own I always love to think the best. —By-the-by, I hope 'tis not true that your brother is absolutely ruined?

Joseph S. I am afraid his circumstances are very bad indeed, ma'am.

Mrs. Can. Ah! I heard so—but you must tell him to keep up his spirits; everybody almost is in the same way—Lord Spindle[45], Sir Thomas Splint, Captain Quinze[46], and Mr. Nickit[47]—all up, I hear, within this week; so if Charles is undone, he'll find half his acquaintance ruined too, and that, you know, is a consolation.

Joseph S. Doubtless, ma'am—a very great one.

Enter Servant.

Serv. Mr. Crabtree and Sir Benjamin Backbite.

Lady Sneer. So, Maria, you see your lover pursues you; positively you shan't escape.

Enter Crabtree and Sir Benjamin Backbite.

Crabt. Lady Sneerwell, I kiss your hand—Mrs. Candour, I don't believe you are acquainted with my nephew, Sir Benjamin Backbite? Egad! ma'am, he has a pretty wit, and is a pretty poet too; isn't he, Lady Sneerwell?

Sir Benj. B. Oh, fie, uncle!

Crabt. Nay, egad, it's true; I back him at a rebus or a charade against the best rhymer in the kingdom. —Has your ladyship heard the epigram he wrote last week on Lady Frizzle's[48] feather catching fire? —Do, Benjamin, repeat it, or the charade you made last night extempore at Mrs. Drowzie's conversazione[49]. Come now; —your first is the name of a fish, your second a great naval commander, and—

Sir Benj. B. Uncle, now—prythee[50]—

Crabt. I'faith, ma'am, 'twould surprise you to hear how ready he is at all these fine sort of things.

Lady Sneer. I wonder, Sir Benjamin, you never publish anything.

Sir Benj. B. To say truth, ma'am, 'tis very vulgar to print; and as my little productions are mostly satires and lampoons on particular people, I find they circulate more by giving copies in confidence to the friends of the parties. However, I have some love elegies, which, when favoured with this lady's smiles, I mean to give the public.

Crabt. 'Fore Heaven[51], ma'am, they'll immortalize you! —you will be handed down to posterity, like Petrarch's Laura[52], or Waller's Sacharissa[53].

Sir Benj. B. Yes, madam, I think you will like them, when you shall see them on a beautiful quarto page[54], where a neat rivulet of text shall meander through a meadow of margin. 'Fore Gad, they will be the most elegant things of their kind!

Crabt. But, ladies, that's true—have you heard the news?

Mrs. Can. What, sir, do you mean the report of—

Crabt. No, ma'am, that's not it—Miss Nicely is going to be married to her own footman.

Mrs. Can. Impossible!

Crabt. Ask Sir Benjamin.

Sir Benj. B. 'Tis true very, ma'am; everything is fixed, and the wedding liveries bespoke[55].

Crabt. Yes—and they do say there were pressing reasons for it.

Lady Sneer. Why, I have heard something of this before.

Mrs. Can. It can't be—and I wonder any one should believe such a story, of so prudent a lady as Miss Nicely.

Sir Benj. B. O Lud! ma'am, that's the very reason 'twas believed at once. She has always been so cautious and so reserved, that everybody was sure there was some reason for it at bottom.

Mrs. Can. Why, to be sure, a tale of scandal is as fatal to the credit of a prudent lady of her stamp, as a fever is generally to those of the strongest constitutions. But there is a sort of puny sickly reputation, that is always ailing, yet will outlive the robuster characters of a hundred prudes.

Sir Benj. B. True, madam, —there are valetudinarians in reputation as well as constitution; who, being conscious of their weak part, avoid the least breath of air, and supply their want of stamina by care and circumspection.

Mrs. Can. Well, but this may be all a mistake. You know, Sir Benjamin, very trifling circumstances often give rise to the most injurious tales.

Crabt. That they do, I'll be sworn, ma'am. O Lud! Mr. Surface, pray is it true that your uncle, Sir Oliver, is coming home?

Joseph S. Not that I know of, indeed, sir.

Crabt. He has been in the East Indies a long time. You can scarcely remember him, I believe? Sad comfort whenever he returns, to hear how your brother has gone on!

Joseph S. Charles has been imprudent, sir, to be sure; but I hope no busy people have already prejudiced Sir Oliver against him. He may reform.

Sir Benj. B. To be sure he may; for my part, I never believed him to be so utterly void of principle as people say; and though he has lost all his friends, I am told nobody is better spoken of by the Jews[56].

Crabt. That's true, egad, nephew. If the Old Jewry[57] was a ward[58], I believe Charles would be an alderman; —no man more popular there, 'fore Gad! I hear he pays as many annuities as the Irish tontine[59]; and that whenever he is sick, they have prayers for the recovery of his health in all the synagogues.

Sir Benj. B. Yet no man lives in greater splendour. They tell me, when he entertains his friends he will sit down to dinner with a dozen of his own securities[60]; have a score of tradesmen waiting in the antechamber, and an officer[61] behind every guest's chair.

Joseph S. This may be entertainment to you, gentlemen, but you pay very little regard to the feelings of a brother.

Maria. Their malice is intolerable. —Lady Sneerwell, I must wish you a good morning: I'm not very well.

(Exit Maria.

Mrs. Can. Oh dear! she changes colour very much.

Lady Sneer. Do, Mrs. Candour, follow her; she may want assistance.

Mrs. Can. That I will, with all my soul, ma'am. —Poor dear girl, who knows what her situation may be!

(Exit Mrs. Candour.

Lady Sneer. 'Twas nothing but that she could not bear to hear Charles reflected on, notwithstanding their difference.

Sir Benj. B. The young lady's ***penchant*** [62] is obvious.

Crabt. But, Benjamin, you must not give up the pursuit for that; —follow her, and put her into good humour. Repeat her some of your own verses. Come, I'll assist you.

Sir Benj. B. Mr. Surface, I did not mean to hurt you; but depend on't[63] your brother is utterly undone.

Crabt. O Lud, ay! undone as ever man was. —Can't raise a guinea! —

Sir Benj. B. And everything sold, I'm told, that was movable.

Crabt. I have seen one that was at his house. Not a thing left but some empty bottles that were over-looked, and the family pictures, which I believe are framed in the wainscots—

Sir Benj. B. And I'm very sorry, also, to hear some bad stories against him.

*(**Going.***

Crabt. Oh! he has done many mean things, that's certain.

Sir Benj. B. But, however, as he's your brother—

*(**Going.***

Crabt. We'll tell you all another opportunity.

*(**Exit Crabtree and Sir Benjamin.***

Lady Sneer. Ha! ha! 'tis very hard for them to leave a subject they have not quite run down.

Joseph S. And I believe the abuse was no more acceptable to your ladyship than Maria.

Lady Sneer. I doubt[64] her affections are farther engaged than we imagine. But the family are to be here this evening, so you may as well dine where you are, and we shall have an opportunity of observing farther; in the meantime, I'll go and plot mischief, and you shall study sentiment.

*(**Exeunt.***

NOTES

1. **Sneerwell:** a name suggesting one who speaks in a sneering manner
2. **Snake:** a name suggesting evil and deceit
3. **Brittle:** a name suggesting a weak personality
4. **Boastall:** a name suggesting boastfulness
5. **in as fine a train:** in as good a condition; going as well
6. **in the common course of things:** in the natural development of events
7. **Clackitt:** a name suggesting a clatterer
8. **close confinements:** cases of having girls strictly shut up in their chambers to prevent elopement or secret meetings with their lovers
9. **separate maintenances:** separations in which the husband provides for the wife
10. **the *Town and Country Magazine*:** an 18th-century magazine which often reported scandals
11. **has a free tongue:** talks irresponsibly
12. **Teazle:** a name suggesting the tendency to tease people
13. **two young men:** Joseph Surface and his brother Charles
14. **a City knight:** a merchant of the City of London
15. **a good jointure:** a good estate settled upon a woman at her marriage and to be used by her after her husband's death
16. **close with the passion of:** accept the love of
17. **Surface:** a name suggesting superficiality
18. **a sentimental knave:** a rogue given to the affectation of fine feelings
19. **a man of sentiment:** a man of refined feelings
20. **your most obedient**: I am your most obedient servant.
21. **distresses:** cases of the distraining of goods
22. **execution:** execution of a court order for the seizure of a debtor's goods
23. **O Lud!:** O Lord!
24. **Egad:** Ah, God!
25. **your very devoted:** I am your very devoted servant.
26. **take my word for't:** take my word for it; believe me

27. **Backbite:** a name suggesting one who speaks ill of others behind their backs
28. **Crabtree:** a name suggesting crabbiness or perversity
29. **make allowance:** take mitigating circumstances into account
30. **a principal in the mischief:** a person primarily responsible for the injury
31. **Candour:** an ironic name suggesting that Mrs. Candour pretends to be candid but is not really so
32. **I'faith:** in faith
33. **Gadabout:** a name suggesting that Miss Gadabout goes about idly
34. **Filigree Flirt:** a name suggesting that the man is ostentatious and flippant
35. **Prim:** a name suggesting a prudish personality
36. **the York diligence:** the stage-coach to York
37. **Festino:** a name suggesting an entertainer
38. **Cassino:** a name suggesting a gambler
39. **Honeymoon:** a name suggesting initial enthusiasm
40. **Tattle:** a name suggesting idle gossip
41. **Buffalo:** a name suggesting physical strength
42. **Bouquet:** a name suggesting a bunch of flowers
43. **Saunter:** a name suggesting one who strolls aimlessly
44. **to measure swords:** to fight a duel
45. **Spindle:** a name suggesting a tall and thin person
46. **Quinze:** a name suggesting a card game
47. **Nickit:** a name suggesting a correct guess or a winning throw at dice
48. **Frizzle:** a name suggesting a small curl
49. **conversazione:** (It.) evening assembly for cards and conversations
50. **prythee:** I pray thee.
51. **'Fore Heaven:** Before Heaven
52. **Petrarch's Laura:** the woman Laura eulogized in the Italian poet Petrarch's verses
53. **Waller's Sacharissa:** the woman Sacharissa praised in the 17th-century English poet Waller's verses
54. **a quarto page:** a page about 12 × 9 inches
55. **and the wedding liveries bespoke:** and the clothes to be worn by servants at the

wedding are bespoken or ordered
56. **the Jews:** the money-lending Jews
57. **the Old Jewry:** the Jews' quarter in London
58. **ward:** administrative division especially for elections
59. **the Irish tontine:** an Irish scheme by which a number of people subscribed to a common fund and then received annuities during their lifetime
60. **securities:** people who guarantee the payment of a loan
61. **an officer:** a sheriff's officer or bailiff
62. *penchant*: (Fr.) strong inclination, partiality
63. **depend on't:** depend on it
64. **I doubt:** I suspect

35

WILLIAM COBBETT

(1763–1835)

William Cobbett was an English journalist and a political leader of the English working class. The son of a farmer, he was born at Farnham, Surrey, on March 9, 1763, and was largely self-educated. He served in the army from 1784 to 1791, emigrated in 1792 to America, where he took to journalism, returned to England in 1800 and began his active political career. He served as an M. P. in 1832–1834, and died on June 18, 1835. His best-known work is ***Rural Rides,*** accounts of his journeys on horseback through England. They had appeared for several years in his weekly ***Political Register*** before they were published in book form in 1830. In them he observed that the rural labourers did not get their fair share of what the land produced. His other famous works are ***A Grammar of the English Language*** (1818), ***A History of Protestant "Reformation" in England and Ireland*** (1826–1827), and ***Advice to Young Men*** (1829). He wrote with clarity and vigour, in a plain, straightforward, lively style.

A RURAL RIDE

In quitting Tilford[1] we came on to the land belonging to Waverley Abbey[2], and then, instead of going on to the town of Farnham[3], veered away to the left towards Wrecclesham, in order to cross the Farnham and Alton[4] turnpike-road, and to come on by the side of Crondall to Odiham. We went a little out of the way to go to a place called the Bourn, which lies in the heath at about a mile from Farnham. It is a winding narrow valley, down which, during the wet season of the year, there runs a stream beginning at the Holt Forest, and emptying itself into the Wey[5] just below Moor Park, which was the seat of Sir William Temple[6] when Swift was residing with him. We went to this Bourn in order that I might show my son the spot where I received the rudiments of my education. There is a little hop-garden in which I used to work when from eight to ten years old; from which I have scores of times run to follow the hounds, leaving the hoe to do the best that it could to destroy the weeds; but the most interesting thing was a sandhill which goes from a part of the heath down to the rivulet. As a due mixture of pleasure with toil, I, with two brothers, used occasionally to disport ourselves, as the lawyers call it, at this sandhill. Our diversion was this: we used to go to the top of the hill, which was steeper than the roof of a house; one used to draw his arms out of the sleeves of his smock-frock, and lay himself down with his arms by his sides; and the others, one at the head, and the other at the feet, sent him rolling down the hill like a barrel or a log of wood. By the time he got to the bottom his hair, eyes, ears, nose, and mouth were all full of this loose sand; then the others took their turn, and at every roll there was a monstrous spell of laughter. I had often told my sons of this while they were very little, and now I took one of them to see the spot. But, that was not all. This was the spot where I was receiving my education; and this was the sort of education; and I am perfectly satisfied that if I had not received such an education, or something very much like it—that, if I had been brought up a milksop, with a nursery-maid everlastingly at my heels, I should have been at this day as great a fool, as inefficient a mortal, as any of those frivolous idiots that are turned out from Winchester[7] and Westminster School[8], or from any of those dens of dunces called Colleges and Universities. It is impossible to say how much I owe to that sandhill; and I went to return it my thanks for the ability which it probably gave me to be one of the greatest terrors to one of the greatest and most powerful bodies of knaves and fools that ever were permitted to afflict this or any other country.

From the Bourn we proceeded on to Wrecclesham, at the end of which we crossed what is called the River Wey. Here we found a parcel of labourers at parish work. Amongst them was an old playmate of mine. The account they gave of their situation was very dismal. The harvest was over early. The hop-picking is now over; and now they are employed by the parish—that is to say, not absolutely digging holes one day and filling them up the next; but, at the expense of half-ruined farmers and tradesmen and landlords, to break stones into very small pieces to make nice smooth roads lest the jolting, in going along them, should create bile in the stomachs of the over-fed tax-eaters. I call upon mankind to witness this scene and to say whether ever the like of this was heard of before. It is a state of things where all is out of order; where self-preservation, that great law of nature, seems to be set at defiance; for here are farmers unable to pay men for working for them, and yet compelled to pay them for working in doing that which is really of no use to any human being. There lie the hop-poles unstripped. You see a hundred things in the neighbouring fields that want doing. The fences are not nearly what they ought to be. The very meadows, to our right and our left in crossing this little valley, would occupy these men advantageously until the setting in of the frost; and here are they, not, as I said before, actually digging holes one day and filling them up the next, but, to all intents and purposes, as uselessly employed. Is this Mr. Canning's[9] "sun of prosperity"? Is this the way to increase or preserve a nation's wealth? Is this a sign of wise legislation and of good government? Does this thing "work well," Mr. Canning? Does it prove that we want no change? True, you were born under a Kingly Government; and so was I as well as you; but I was not born under Six Acts[10]; nor was I born under a state of things like this. I was not born under it, and I do not wish to live under it; and, with God's help, I will change it if I can.

    We left these poor fellows, after having given them, not "religious tracts," which would, if they could, make the labourer content with half-starvation, but something to get them some bread and cheese and beer, being firmly convinced that it is the body that wants filling and not the mind. However, in speaking of their low wages, I told them that the farmers and hop-planters were as much objects of compassion as themselves, which they acknowledged.

    We immediately after this crossed the road, and went on towards Crondall upon a soil that soon became stiff loam and flint at top, with a bed of chalk beneath. We did not go to Crondall, but kept along over Slade Heath, and through a very pretty place called Well. We arrived at Odiham about half after eleven, at the end of a beautiful ride of about seventeen miles, in a very fine and pleasant day.

NOTES

1. **Tilford:** a village in Surrey three miles southeast of Farnham
2. **Waverley Abbey:** the earliest Cistercian House in England (founded in 1129), two miles southeast of Farnham
3. **Farnham:** a town in Surrey
4. **Alton:** a town in Southampton
5. **the Wey:** a river in Southeast England flowing to the Thames
6. **Sir William Temple:** William Temple (1628–1699) was an English diplomat and essayist.
7. **Winchester:** Winchester College, a public school (founded in 1382) in Hampshire
8. **Westminster School:** a public school (founded in 1560) in London
9. **Mr. Canning:** George Canning (1770–1827) was a British statesman; he served as Foreign Secretary (1822–1827) and Prime Minister (1827).
10. **Six Acts:** the six measures sponsored by the Liverpool Ministry in 1819 to curb radical agitation

36

SIR WALTER SCOTT

(1771–1832)

Walter Scott was a Scottish novelist, poet, and critic. He was born in Edinburgh on August 15, 1771, the son of a lawyer. Educated at the High School of Edinburgh and at the University, he was called to the Scottish bar in 1792. His writing career began in 1796. He served as Sheriff of Selkirkshire from 1799 to 1832, and as Clerk of the Court of Session from 1806 to 1830, and was created a baronet in 1820. In 1799 he joined the Ballantyne brothers in a printing and publishing business in Edinburgh, and for many years he contributed capital and literary material to it. The firm tumbled into ruin in 1826, and Scott found himself liable for a debt of £130,000. He refused to go through bankruptcy and determined to pay the debt by his pen. He worked strenuously and had cleared off £70,000 before he died. His creditors were paid in full after his death by the sale of his copyrights. He died at his home of Abbotsford near Melrose on September 21, 1832.

Scott's literary output was enormous. His first important publication was *The Minstrelsy of the Scottish Border* (1802–1803), three volumes of ballads that he had collected, collated and adapted. Then he produced a succession of romantic narrative poems which made him famous; they included *The Lay of the Last Minstrel* (1805), *Marmion* (1808), *The Lady of the Lake* (1810), and *Rokeby* (1813). Between 1814 and

1831 he published more than twenty novels, the more notable of them being **Waverley** (1814), **Guy Mannering** (1815), **The Antiquary** (1816), **Old Mortality** (1816), **Rob Roy** (1817), **The Heart of Midlothian** (1818), **Ivanhoe** (1819), **Kenilworth** (1821), **Quentin Durward** (1823), **Redgauntlet** (1824), and **The Fair Maid of Perth** (1828). Scott is good at story-telling, characterization, and description of scenes, but his narrative style is rather stilted. His influence as one who established the form of the historical novel was incalculable.

THE ARCHERY CONTEST AT ASHBY[1]

A target was placed at the upper end of the southern avenue which led to the lists. The contending archers took their station in turn, at the bottom of the southern access; the distance between that station and the mark allowing full distance for what was called a shot at rovers[2]. The archers, having previously determined by lot their order of precedence, were to shoot each three shafts in succession. The sports were regulated by an officer of inferior rank, termed the provost of the games; for the high rank of the marshals of the lists would have been held degraded had they condescended to superintend the sports of the yeomanry.

One by one the archers, stepping forward, delivered their shafts yeomanlike and bravely. Of twenty-four arrows shot in succession, ten were fixed in the target, and the others ranged so near it that, considering the distance of the mark, it was accounted good archery. Of the ten shafts which hit the target, two within the inner ring were shot by Hubert, a forester in the service of Malvoisin, who was accordingly pronounced victorious.

"Now, Locksley," said Prince John to the bold yeoman, with a bitter smile, "wilt thou try conclusions with Hubert, or wilt thou yield up bow, baldric, and quiver to the provost of the sports?"

"Sith[3] it be no better," said Locksley, "I am content to try my fortune; on condition that when I have shot two shafts at yonder mark of Hubert's he shall be bound to shoot one at that which I shall propose."

"That is but fair," answered Prince John, "and it shall not be refused thee. If thou dost beat this braggart, Hubert, I will fill the bugle with silver pennies for thee."

"A man can do but his best," answered Hubert; "but my grandsire drew a good long bow at Hastings[4], and I trust not to dishonour his memory."

The former target was now removed, and a fresh one of the same size placed in its room. Hubert, who, as victor in the first trial of skill, had the right to shoot first, took his aim with great deliberation, long measuring the distance with his eye, while he held in his hand his bended bow, with the arrow placed on the string. At length he made a step forward, and raising the bow at the full stretch of his left arm, till the centre or grasping-place was nigh[5] level with his face, he drew his bowstring to his ear. The arrow whistled through the air, and lighted within the inner ring of the target, but not exactly in the centre.

"You have not allowed for the wind, Hubert," said his antagonist, bending his bow, "or that had been[6] a better shot."

So saying, and without showing the least anxiety to pause upon his aim, Locksley stept to the appointed station, and shot his arrow as carelessly in appearance as if he had not even looked at the mark. He was speaking almost at the instant that the shaft left the bowstring, yet it alighted in the target two inches nearer to the white spot which marked the centre than that of Hubert.

"By the light of Heaven!" said Prince John to Hubert, "an[7] thou suffer that runagate knave to overcome thee, thou art worthy of the gallows!"

Hubert had but one set speech for all occasions. "An your Highness were to hang me," he said, "a man can but do his best. Nevertheless, my grandsire drew a good bow—"

"The foul fiend on thy grandsire and all his generation!" interrupted John. "Shoot, knave, and shoot thy best, or it shall be the worse for thee!"

Thus exhorted, Hubert resumed his place, and not neglecting the caution which he had received from his adversary, he made the necessary allowance for a very light air of wind which had just arisen, and shot so successfully that his arrow alighted in the very centre of the target.

"A Hubert! a Hubert!" shouted the populace, more interested in a known person than in a stranger. "In the clout[8]!—in the clout! Hubert forever!"

"Thou canst not mend that shot, Locksley," said the Prince, with an insulting smile.

"I will notch his shaft for him, however," replied Locksley.

And letting fly his arrow with a little more precaution than before, it lighted right upon that of his competitor, which it split to shivers. The people who stood around were so astonished at his wonderful dexterity that they could not even give vent to their surprise in their usual clamour. "This must be the devil, and no man of flesh and blood," whispered the yeomen to each other; "such archery was never seen since a bow was first bent in Britain."

"And now," said Locksley, "I will crave your Grace's permission to plant such a mark as is used in the North Country; and welcome every brave yeoman who shall try a shot at it to win a smile from the bonny lass he loves best."

He then turned to leave the lists. "Let your guards attend me," he said, "if you please; I go but to cut a rod from the next willow-bush."

Prince John made a signal that some attendants should follow him in case of his escape; but the cry of "Shame! Shame!" which burst from the multitude induced him to alter his ungenerous purpose.

Locksley returned almost instantly with a willow wand about six feet in length, perfectly straight and rather thicker than a man's thumb. He began to peel this with great composure, observing at the same time that to ask a good woodsman to shoot at a target so broad as had hitherto been used, was to put shame upon his skill. "For his own part," he said, "and in the land where he was bred, men would as soon take for their mark King Arthur's round table[9], which held sixty knights around it. A child of seven years old," he said, "might hit yonder target with a headless shaft; but," added he, walking deliberately to the other end of the lists, and sticking the willow wand upright in the ground, "he that hits that rod at fivescore yards, I call him an archer fit to bear both bow and quiver before a king, and it were the stout King Richard himself."

"My grandsire," said Hubert, "drew a good bow at the battle of Hastings, and never shot at such a mark in his life—and neither will I. If this yeoman can cleave that rod, I give him the bucklers; or rather, I yield to the devil that is in his jerkin, and not to any human skill; a man can but do his best, and I will not shoot where I am sure to miss. I might as well shoot at the edge of our parson's whittle, or at a wheat straw, or at a sunbeam, as at a twinkling white streak which I can hardly see."

"Cowardly dog!" said Prince John. "Sirrah Locksley, do thou shoot; but, if thou hittest such a mark, I will say thou art the first man ever did so. Howe'er it be, thou shalt not crow over us with a mere show of superior skill."

"I will do my best, as Hubert says," answered Locksley; "no man can do more."

So saying, he again bent his bow, but on the present occasion looked with attention to his weapon, and changed the string, which he thought was no longer truly round, having been a little frayed by the two former shots. He then took his aim with some deliberation, and the multitude awaited the event in breathless silence. The archer vindicated their opinion of his skill: his arrow split the willow rod against which it was aimed. A jubilee of acclamations followed; and even Prince John, in admiration of Locksley's skill, lost for an instant his dislike to his person. "These twenty nobles," he said, "which, with the bugle, thou hast fairly won, are thine own; we will make them fifty if thou wilt take livery and service with us as a yeoman of our body-guard, and be near to our person. For never did so strong a hand bend a bow or so true an eye direct a shaft."

"Pardon me, noble Prince," said Locksley; "but I have vowed that, if ever I take service, it should be with your royal brother King Richard. These twenty nobles I leave to Hubert, who has this day drawn as brave a bow as his grandsire did at Hastings. Had his modesty not refused the trial, he would have hit the wand as well as I."

Hubert shook his head as he received with reluctance the bounty of the stranger; and Locksley, anxious to escape further observation, mixed with the crowd, and was seen no more.

NOTES

1. **Ashby:** a town in the county of Leicester, England
2. **a shot at rovers:** shooting at a long range
3. **sith:** (arch.) since
4. **Hastings:** Hastings is a town on the coast of Sussex, England. At the Battle of Hastings (1066) William of Normandy defeated the English under Harold II.
5. **nigh:** (arch.) nearly

6. **or that had been:** or that would have been
7. **an:** (arch.) if
8. **clout:** white target; centre of the target
9. **King Arthur's round table:** King Arthur of Britain was probably a chieftain or general in the 5th or 6th century. He had a huge table around which he and his valiant knights had their seats.

37

SAMUEL TAYLOR COLERIDGE

(1772–1834)

S. T. Coleridge was an English poet and critic. The youngest son of a vicar, he was born in Devon, on October 21, 1772, attended Christ's Hospital, London, where he began a life-long friendship with Charles Lamb, and studied two years at Jesus College, Cambridge. In 1794 he met Robert Southey at Oxford, and together they planned to found an ideal community, named "Pantisocracy", in America, but the scheme fell through. In 1797 Coleridge met Wordsworth in Dorset and their close association began. Coleridge wrote and lectured, but in general he led a restless life, labouring under the use of opium. He left his wife and children to the charity of Southey, his brother-in-law. In the spring of 1816 he was received into the household of the sympathetic Dr. Gillman at Highgate, London. There he remained in contentment till his death on July 25, 1834.

The Lyrical Ballads which Coleridge and Wordsworth jointly published in 1798 marked a break with 18th-century traditions in poetry and a starting-point of the English Romantic Movement. Coleridge is well known to the general reader for four great poems: *The Rime of the Ancient Mariner* (1798), a narrative in the ballad measure of a sailor's offence against nature and its expiation; *Christabel* (written in 1797 and 1800 and published in 1816), an unfinished tale of the evil enchantress

Geraldine; ***Kubla Khan*** (written in 1797 and published in 1816), an unfinished poem consisting of a series of visionary views; and ***Dejection: An Ode*** (1802), a poem bewailing among other things the author's loss of poetic inspiration. Coleridge wrote a good number of prose works. Outstanding among them is ***Biographia Literaria*** (1817), a book of romantic criticism as well as a philosophical autobiography. His thoughts are always noteworthy though his prose style is rather involved.

THE LYRICAL BALLADS

During the first year that Mr. Wordsworth and I were neighbours[1], our conversations turned frequently on the two cardinal points of poetry, the power of exciting the sympathy of the reader by a faithful adherence to the truth of nature, and the power of giving the interest of novelty by the modifying colours of imagination. The sudden charm which accidents of light and shade, which moonlight or sunset, diffused over a known and familiar landscape, appeared to represent the practicability of combining both. These are the poetry of nature. The thought suggested itself (to which of us I do not recollect) that a series of poems might be composed of two sorts. In the one, the incidents and agents were to be in part at least, supernatural; and the excellence aimed at was to consist in the interesting of the affections[2] by the dramatic truth of such emotions, as would naturally accompany such situations, supposing them real. And real in this sense they have been to every human being who, from whatever source of delusion, has at any time believed himself under supernatural agency. For the second class, subjects were to be chosen from ordinary life; the characters and incidents were to be such as will be found in every village and its vicinity where there is a meditative and feeling mind to seek after them, or to notice them when they present themselves.

In this idea originated the plan of the "Lyrical Ballads"; in which it was agreed that my endeavours should be directed to persons and characters supernatural, or at least romantic; yet so as to transfer from our inward nature a human interest and a semblance of truth sufficient to procure for these shadows of imagination that willing suspension of disbelief for the moment, which constitutes poetic faith. Mr. Wordsworth, on the other hand, was to propose to himself as his object, to give the charm of novelty to things of every day, and to excite a feeling analogous to the supernatural, by awakening the mind's attention from the lethargy of custom, and directing it to the loveliness and the wonders of the world before us; an inexhaustible treasure, but for which, in consequence of the film of familiarity and selfish solicitude, we have eyes, yet see not, ears that hear not, and hearts that neither feel nor understand.

With this view I wrote the "Ancient Mariner," and was preparing among other poems, the "Dark Ladie,"[3] and the "Christabel," in which I should have more nearly realised my ideal than I had done in my first attempt. But Mr. Wordsworth's industry had proved so much more successful, and the number of his poems so much greater[4], that my compositions, instead of forming a balance, appeared rather an interpolation of heterogeneous matter. Mr. Wordsworth added two or three poems written in his own character, in the impassioned, lofty, and sustained diction which is characteristic of his genius. In this form the "Lyrical Ballads" were published; and were presented by him as an experiment, whether subjects, which from their nature rejected the usual ornaments and extracolloquial style of poems in general, might not be so managed in the language of ordinary life as to produce the pleasurable interest which it is the peculiar business of poetry to impart.

NOTES

1. **During the first year that Mr. Wordsworth and I were neighbours:** In 1797 when Wordsworth and Coleridge were living respectively at Alfoxden and Nether Stowey in Somerset.
2. **the interesting of the affections:** the exciting of the emotions
3. **the "Dark Ladie":** "The Ballad of the Dark Ladie"
4. **But Mr. Wordsworth's industry had proved so much more successful, and the number of his poems so much greater:** The first edition of *The Lyrical Ballads*, published anonymously in 1798, contained 19 poems by Wordsworth (including "Lines Written a Few Miles Above Tintern Abbey") and four poems by Coleridge (including "The Rime of the Ancient Mariner").

38

ROBERT SOUTHEY

(1774–1843)

Robert Southey was an English poet and biographer. He was born at Bristol, the son of a linen-draper, and educated at Westminster School, London, and Balliot College, Oxford. He was a generous man and a diligent writer. His literary output was prodigious. He wrote several long poems, which were much admired in his own day but are almost forgotten now. Poetically he is remembered for a few short pieces, such as **The Battle of Blenheim** and **The Inchcape Rock**. Among his voluminous prose works the most famous are **The Life of Nelson** (1813), a deservedly popular classic, and **The Three Bears**, a beautiful fairy tale. Southey's prose style is lucid and firm.

NELSON[1] AND HIS MEN

Never was any commander more beloved. He governed men by their reason and their affections[2]: they knew that he was incapable of caprice or tyranny; and they obeyed him with alacrity and joy, because he possessed their confidence as well as their love. "Our Nel,"[3] they used to say, "is as brave as a lion, and as gentle as a lamb." Severe discipline he detested, though he had been bred in a severe school: he never inflicted corporal punishment if it were possible to avoid it, and when compelled to enforce it, he, who was familiar with wounds and death, suffered like a woman. In his whole life Nelson was never known to act unkindly towards an officer. If he was asked to prosecute one for ill-behaviour, he used to answer: "That there was no occasion for him to ruin a poor devil, who was sufficiently his own enemy to ruin himself." But in Nelson there was more than the easiness and humanity of a happy nature: he did not merely abstain from injury; his was an active and watchful benevolence, ever desirous not only to render justice, but to do good. During the peace he had spoken in Parliament upon the abuses respecting prize-money, and had submitted plans to Government for more easily manning the navy, and preventing desertion from it, by bettering the condition of the seamen. He proposed that their certificates should be registered, and that every man who had served, with a good character, five years in war, should receive a bounty of two guineas[4] annually after that time, and of four guineas after eight years. "This," he said, "might, at first sight, appear an enormous sum for the state to pay; but the average life of a seaman is, from hard service, finished at forty-five; he cannot, therefore, enjoy the annuity many years; and the interest of the money saved by their not deserting would go far to pay the whole expense."

To his midshipmen he ever showed the most winning kindness, encouraging the diffident, tempering the hasty, counselling and befriending both. "Recollect," he used to say, "that you must be a seaman to be an officer; and also, that you cannot be a good officer without being a gentleman." A lieutenant wrote to him, to say that he was dissatisfied with his captain. Nelson's answer was in that spirit of perfect wisdom and perfect goodness which regulated his whole conduct toward those who were under his command. "I have just received your letter, and I am truly sorry that any difference should arise between your captain, who has the reputation of being one of the bright officers of the service, and yourself, a very young man, and a very young officer, who must naturally have much to learn; therefore the chance is that you are perfectly wrong in the disagreement. However, as your present situation must be very disagreeable, I will certainly take an early opportunity of removing you, provided your conduct to your present captain be such that another may not refuse to receive you." The gentleness and benignity of his disposition never made him forget what was due to discipline. Being on one occasion applied to, to save a young officer from a court-martial which he had provoked by his misconduct, his reply was: "That he would do everything in his power to oblige so gallant and good an officer as Sir John Warren," in whose name the intercession had been made: "But what," he added, "would he do if he were here? —Exactly what I have done, and am still willing to do. The young man must write such a letter of contrition as would be an acknowledgment of his great fault; and with a sincere promise, if his captain will intercede to prevent the impending court-martial, never to so misbehave again. On his captain's inclosing me such a letter, with a request to cancel the order for the trial, I might be induced to do it; but the letters and reprimand will be given in the public order-book[5] of the fleet, and read to all the officers. The young man has pushed himself forward to notice, and he must take the consequence. It was upon the quarter-deck, in the face of the ship's company, that he treated his captain with contempt; and I am in duty bound to support the authority and consequence of every officer under my command. A poor ignorant seaman is for ever punished for contempt to his superiors."

NOTES

1. **Nelson:** Horatio Nelson (1758–1805) was a British naval commander. He won his greatest victory at Trafalgar on 21st October 1805, when he defeated the combined French and Spanish fleets and was himself killed.

2. **their affections:** their emotions
3. **Nel:** pet form for Nelson
4. **two guineas:** A guinea is an old British gold coin or unit of money worth 21 shillings (=now £1.05).
5. **order-book:** book for entering the special orders of a commanding officer

39

JANE AUSTEN

(1775–1817)

Jane Austen was an English novelist. She was born at Steventon, Hampshire, on December 16, 1775, the seventh child of the rector of the parish. Educated largely at home, she lived with her family at Steventon until 1801, when they moved to Bath. Her father died in 1805, and she and her mother moved to Southampton in 1806. Then they moved to Chawton, Hampshire, in 1809. Here she remained until May 1817. Her life was uneventful and she never married. She wrote stories from an early age. She died of consumption in Winchester on July 18, 1817.

Of Jane Austen's major novels four were published during her lifetime and two after her death: *Sense and Sensibility* (1811), *Pride and Prejudice* (1813), *Mansfield Park* (1814), *Emma* (1816), *Northanger Abbey* (posthumously,1817) and *Persuasion* (1818). Three of them, *Pride and Prejudice*, *Sense and Sensibility* and *Northanger Abbey*, were written in her early twenties, whereas the rest in her late thirties. Her novels deal with middle-class life in the country. Within this limited scope she displays a finished realism with consummate art. She is incomparable for her convincing characterization, moral penetration, structural precision, and quiet ironic humour. She is clever in producing controlled dialogue appropriate to her characters, and her narrative style is clear though slightly formal. She is regarded as one of the greatest English novelists.

A FAMILY QUARREL

I

It is a truth universally acknowledged, that a single man in possession of a good fortune must be in want of a wife.

However little known the feelings or views of such a man may be on his first entering a neighbourhood, this truth is so well fixed in the minds of the surrounding families, that he is considered as the rightful property of some one or other of their daughters.

"My dear Mr. Bennet[1]," said his lady to him one day, "have you heard that Netherfield Park[2] is let at last?"

Mr. Bennet replied that he had not.

"But it is," returned she; "for Mrs. Long[3] has just been here, and she told me all about it."

Mr. Bennet made no answer.

"Do not you want to know who has taken it?" cried his wife impatiently.

"*You* want to tell me, and I have no objection to hearing it."

This was invitation enough.

"Why, my dear, you must know, Mrs. Long says that Nether field is taken by a young man of large fortune from the north of England; that he came down on Monday in a chaise and four[4] to see the place, and was so much delighted with it that he agreed with Mr. Morris[5] immediately; that he is to take possession before Michaelmas[6], and some of his servants are to be in the house by the end of next week."

"What is his name?"

"Bingley."

"Is he married or single?"

"Oh! single, my dear, to be sure! A single man of large fortune; four or five thousand a year[7]. What a fine thing for our girls!"

"How so? how can it affect them?"

"My dear Mr. Bennet," replied his wife, "how can you be so tiresome! You must know that I am thinking of his marrying one of them."

"Is that his design in settling here?"

"Design! nonsense, how can you talk so! But it is very likely that he *may* fall in love with one of them, and therefore you must visit him as soon as he comes."

"I see no occasion for that. You and the girls may go, or you may send them by themselves, which perhaps will be still better, for as you are as handsome as any of them, Mr. Bingley might like you the best of the party."

"My dear, you flatter me. I certainly *have* had my share of beauty, but I do not pretend to be anything extraordinary now. When a woman has five grown-up daughters, she ought to give over thinking of her own beauty."

"In such cases, a woman has not often much beauty to think of."

"But, my dear, you must indeed go and see Mr. Bingley when he comes into the neighbourhood."

"It is more than I engage for[8], I assure you."

"But consider your daughters. Only think what an establishment it would be for one of them. Sir William and Lady Lucas[9] are determined to go, merely on that account, for in general you know they visit no new-comers. Indeed you must go, for it will be impossible for *us* to visit him if you do not."

"You are over-scrupulous, surely. I dare say Mr. Bingley will be very glad to see you; and I will send a few lines by you to assure him of my hearty consent to his marrying whichever he chooses of the girls; though I must throw in a good word for my little Lizzy[10]."

"I desire you will do no such thing. Lizzy is not a bit better than the others; and I am sure she is not half so handsome as Jane[11], nor half so good humoured as Lydia[12]. But you are always giving *her* the preference."

"They have none of them much to recommend them," replied he; "they are all silly and ignorant, like other girls; but Lizzy has something more of quickness[13] than her sisters."

"Mr. Bennet, how can you abuse your own children in such a way? You take delight in vexing me. You have no compassion on my poor nerves."

"You mistake me, my dear. I have a high respect for your nerves. They are my old friends. I have heard you mention them with consideration these twenty years at least."

"Ah! you do not know what I suffer."

"But I hope you will get over it, and live to see many young men of four thousand a year come into the neighbourhood."

"It will be no use to us, if twenty such should come, since you will not visit them."

"Depend upon it, my dear, that when there are twenty, I will visit them all."

Mr. Bennet was so odd a mixture of quick parts[14], sarcastic humour, reserve, and caprice, that the experience of three and twenty years had been insufficient to make his wife understand his character. *Her* mind was less difficult to develop. She was a woman of mean understanding, little information, and uncertain temper. When she was discontented, she fancied herself nervous. The business of her life was to get her daughters married; its solace was visiting and news.

II

Mr. Bennet was among the earliest of those who waited on Mr. Bingley. He had always intended to visit him, though to the last always assuring his wife that he should not go; and till the evening after the visit was paid she had no knowledge of it. It was then disclosed in the following manner. Observing his second daughter employed in trimming a hat, he suddenly addressed her with,

"I hope Mr. Bingley will like it, Lizzy."

"We are not in a way to know *what* Mr. Bingley likes," said her mother resentfully, "since we are not to visit."

"But you forget, mamma," said Elizabeth, "that we shall meet him at the assemblies[15], and that Mrs. Long has promised to introduce him."

"I do not believe Mrs. Long will do any such thing. She has two nieces of her own. She is a selfish, hypocritical woman, and I have no opinion of her[16]."

"No more have I," said Mr. Bennet, "and I am glad to find that you do not depend on her serving you."

Mrs. Bennet deigned not to make any reply; but, unable to contain herself, began scolding one of her daughters.

"Don't keep coughing so, Kitty[17], for heaven's sake! Have a little compassion on my nerves. You tear them to pieces."

"Kitty has no discretion in her coughs," said her father; "she times them ill."

"I do not cough for my own amusement," replied Kitty fretfully. "When is your next ball to be, Lizzy?"

"To-morrow fortnight."

"Aye, so it is," cried her mother, "and Mrs. Long does not come back till the day before; so, it will be impossible for her to introduce him, for she will not know him herself."

"Then, my dear, you may have the advantage of your friend, and introduce Mr. Bingley to *her*."

"Impossible, Mr. Bennet, impossible, when I am not acquainted with him myself; how can you be so teasing?"

"I honour your circumspection. A fortnight's acquaintance is certainly very little. One cannot know what a man really is by the end of a fortnight. But if *we* do not venture, somebody else will; and after all, Mrs. Long and her nieces must stand their chance; and therefore, as she will think it an act of kindness, if you decline the office, I will take it on myself."

The girls stared at their father. Mrs. Bennet said only, "Nonsense, nonsense!"

"What can be the meaning of that emphatic exclamation?" cried he. "Do you consider the forms of introduction, and the stress that is laid on them, as nonsense? I cannot quite agree with you *there*. What say you, Mary[18]? for you are a young lady of deep reflection I know, and read great books, and make extracts."

Mary wished to say something very sensible, but knew not how.

"While Mary is adjusting her ideas," he continued, "let us return to Mr. Bingley."

"I am sick of Mr. Bingley." cried his wife.

"I am sorry to hear *that*; but why did not you tell me so before? If I had known as much this morning I certainly would not have called on him. It is very unlucky; but as I have actually paid the visit, we cannot escape the acquaintance now."

The astonishment of the ladies was just what he wished; that of Mrs. Bennet perhaps surpassing the rest; though when the first tumult of joy was over, she began to declare that it was what she had expected all the while.

"How good it was in you, my dear Mr. Bennet. But I knew I should persuade you at last. I was sure you loved your girls too well to neglect such an acquaintance. Well, how pleased I am! and it is such a good joke, too. that you should have gone this morning, and never said a word about it till now."

"Now, Kitty, you may cough as much as you choose," said Mr. Bennet; and, as he spoke, he left the room, fatigued with the raptures of his wife.

"What an excellent father you have, girls." said she, when the door was shut. "I do not know how you will ever make him amends for his kindness; or me either, for that matter. At our time of life it is not so pleasant, I can tell you, to be making new acquaintance every day; but for your sakes, we would do anything. Lydia, my love, though you *are* the youngest, I dare say Mr. Bingley will dance with you at the next ball."

"Oh!" said Lydia stoutly, "I am not afraid; for though I *am* the youngest, I'm the tallest."

The rest of the evening was spent in conjecturing how soon he would return Mr. Bennet's visit, and determining when they should ask him to dinner.

NOTES

1. **Mr. Bennet:** a characer in *Pride and Prejudice*
2. **Netherfield Park:** (in the novel) a large house in Longbourn, Hertfordshire
3. **Mrs. Long:** a neighbour of the Bennets
4. **a chaise and four:** a light close carriage drawn by four horses
5. **Mr. Morris:** the owner of Netherfield Park

6. **Michaelmas:** the festival of St. Michael, September 29, one of the four quarter days
7. **four or five thousand a year:** with an income of four or five thousand pounds a year
8. **than I engage for**: than I can promise
9. **Sir William and Lady Lucas:** neighbours of the Bennets
10. **Lizzy:** (pet form for) Elizabeth, the second daughter of Mr. and Mrs. Bennet
11. **Jane:** the eldest daughter of Mr. and Mrs. Bennet
12. **Lydia:** the fifth and youngest daughter of Mr. and Mrs. Bennet
13. **quickness:** ready-wittedness, cleverness
14. **quick parts**: intellectual talents, wit
15. **assemblies:** established assembly-rooms for social gatherings
16. **have no opinion of her:** have no good opinion of her
17. **Kitty:** (pet form for) Catherine, the fourth daughter of Mr. and Mrs. Bennet
18. **Mary:** the third daughter of Mr. and Mrs. Bennet

MR. AND MRS. JOHN DASHWOOD

Mrs. John Dashwood[1] did not at all approve of what her husband intended to do for his sisters. To take three thousand pounds from the fortune of their dear little boy, would be impoverishing him to the most dreadful degree. She begged him to think again on the subject. How could he answer it to himself to rob his child, and his only child too, of so large a sum? And what possible claim could the Miss Dashwoods[2], who were related to him only by half blood, which she considered as no relationship at all, have on his generosity to so large an amount? It was very well known that no affection was ever supposed to exist between the children of any man by different marriages; and why was he to ruin himself, and their poor little Harry, by giving away all his money to his half-sisters?

"It was my father's last request to me," replied her husband, "that I should assist his widow and daughters."

"He did not know what he was talking of, I dare say; ten to one but he was light-headed at the time. Had he been in his right senses, he could not have thought of such a thing as begging you to give away half your fortune from your own child."

"He did not stipulate for any particular sum, my dear Fanny[3]; he only requested me, in general terms, to assist them, and make their situation more comfortable than it was in his power to do. Perhaps it would have been as well if he had left it wholly to myself. He could hardly suppose I should neglect them. But as he required the promise, I could not do less than give it: at least I thought so at the time. The promise, therefore, was given, and must be performed. Something must be done for them whenever they leave Norland[4] and settle in a new home."

"Well, then, *let* something be done for them; but *that* something need not be three thousand pounds. Consider," she added, "that when the money is once parted with, it never can return. Your sisters will marry, and it will be gone for ever. If, indeed, it could ever be restored to our poor little boy...."

"Why, to be sure," said her husband, very gravely, "that would make a great difference. The time may come when Harry will regret that so large a sum was parted with. If he should have a numerous family, for instance, it would be a very convenient addition."

"To be sure it would."

"Perhaps, then, it would be better for all parties if the sum were diminished one half. Five hundred pounds would be a prodigious increase to their fortunes."

"Oh, beyond anything great! What brother on earth would do half so much for his sisters, even if *really* his sisters! And as it is—only half blood! —But you have such a generous spirit!"

"I would not wish to do anything mean," he replied. "One had rather, on such occasions, do too much than too little. No one, at least, can think I have not done enough for them: even themselves, they can hardly expect more."

"There is no knowing what *they* may expect," said the lady, "but we are not to think of their expectations: the question is, what you can afford to do."

"Certainly, and I think I may afford to give them five hundred pounds apiece. As it is, without any addition of mine, they will each have above three thousand pounds on their mother's death: a very comfortable fortune for any young woman."

"To be sure it is: and, indeed, it strikes me that they can want no addition at all. They will have ten thousand pounds divided amongst them. If they marry, they will be sure of doing well; and if they do not, they may all live very comfortably together on the interest of ten thousand pounds."

"That is very true, and, therefore, I do not know whether, upon the whole, it would not be more advisable to do something for their mother while she lives rather than for them; something of the annuity kind I mean. My sisters would feel the good effects of it as well as herself. A hundred a year would make them all perfectly comfortable."

His wife hesitated a little, however, in giving her consent to this plan.

"To be sure," said she, "it is better than parting with fifteen hundred pounds at once. But then, if Mrs. Dashwood should live fifteen years, we shall be completely taken in."

"Fifteen years! my dear Fanny; her life cannot be worth half that purchase."

"Certainly not; but if you observe, people always live for ever when there is any annuity to be paid them; and she is very stout and healthy, and hardly forty. An annuity is a very serious business; it comes over and over every year, and there is no getting rid of it. You are not aware of what you are doing. I have known a great deal of the trouble of annuities; for my mother was clogged with the payment of three to old superannuated servants by my father's will, and it is amazing how disagreeable she found it. Twice every year, these annuities were to be paid; and then there was the trouble of getting it to them; and then one of them was said to have died, and afterwards it turned out to be no such thing. My mother was quite sick of it. Her income was not her own, she said, with such perpetual claims on it; and it was the more unkind in my father, because, otherwise, the money would have been entirely at my mother's disposal, without any restriction whatever. It has given me such an abhorrence of annuities, that I am sure I would not pin myself down to the payment of one for all the world."

"It is certainly an unpleasant thing," replied Mr. Dashwood, "to have those kind of yearly drains on one's income. One's fortune, as your mother justly says, is **not** one's own. To be tied down to the regular payment of such a sum, on every rent day, is by no means desirable: it takes away one's independence."

"Undoubtedly; and, after all, you have no thanks for it. They think themselves secure, you do no more than what is expected, and it raises no gratitude at all. If I were you, whatever I did should be done at my own discretion entirely. I would not bind myself to allow them anything yearly. It may be very inconvenient some years to spare a hundred, or even fifty pounds, from our own expenses."

"I believe you are right, my love; it will be better that there should be no annuity in the case; whatever I may give them occasionally will be of far greater assistance than a yearly allowance, because they would only enlarge their style of living if they felt sure of a larger income, and would not be sixpence the richer for it at the end of the year. It will certainly be much the best way. A present of fifty pounds, now and then, will prevent their ever being distressed for money, and will, I think, be amply discharging my promise to my father."

"To be sure it will. Indeed, to say the truth, I am convinced within myself, that your father had no idea of your giving them any money at all. The assistance he thought of, I dare say, was only such as might be reasonably expected of you; for instance, such as looking out for a comfortable small house for them, helping them to move their things, and sending them presents of fish and game, and so forth, whenever they are in season. I'll lay my life that[5] he meant nothing further; indeed, it would be very strange and unreasonable if he did. Do but consider, my dear Mr. Dashwood, how excessively comfortable your mother-in-law and her daughters may live on the interest of seven thousand pounds, besides the thousand pounds belonging to each of the girls, which brings them in fifty pounds a year apiece, and, of course, they will pay their mother for their board out of it. Altogether, they will have five hundred a year amongst them, and what on earth can four women want for more than that? They will live so cheap! Their housekeeping will be nothing at all. They will have no carriage, no horses, and hardly any servants; they will keep no company, and can have no expenses of any kind! Only conceive how comfortable they will be! Five hundred a year! I am sure I cannot imagine how they will spend half of it; and as to your giving them more, it is quite absurd to think of it. They will be much more able to give you something."

"Upon my word," said Mr. Dashwood, "I believe you are perfectly right. My father certainly could mean nothing more by his request to me than what you say. I clearly understand it now, and I will strictly fulfil my engagement by such acts of assistance and kindness to them as you have described. When my mother removes into another house, my services shall be readily given to accommodate her as far as I can. Some little present of furniture, too, may be acceptable then."

"Certainly," returned Mrs. John Dashwood. "But, however, **one** thing must be considered. When your father and mother moved to Norland, though the furniture of Stanhill was sold, all the china, plate, and linen was saved, and is now left to your mother. Her house will therefore be almost completely fitted up as soon as she takes it."

"That is a material consideration, undoubtedly. A valuable legacy indeed! And yet some of the plate would have been a very pleasant addition to our own stock here."

"Yes; and the set of breakfast china is twice as handsome as what belongs to this house. A great deal too handsome, in my opinion, for any place ***they*** can ever afford to live in. But, however, so it is. Your father thought only of ***them***. And I must say this: that you owe no particular gratitude to him, nor attention to his wishes, for we very well know that if he could, he would have left almost everything in the world to ***them***."

This argument was irresistible. It gave to his intentions whatever of decision was wanting before; and he finally resolved, that it would be absolutely unnecessary, if not highly indecorous, to do more for the widow and children of his father, than such kind of neighbourly acts as his own wife pointed out.

NOTES

1. **Mrs. John Dashwood:** a character in *Sense and Sensibility*
2. **the Miss Dashwoods:** Mrs. Henry Dashwood's daughters and John Dashwood's half-sisters—Elinor, Marianne, and Margaret
3. **Fanny:** Fanny Dashwood, John Dashwood's wife
4. **Norland:** After her husband's death, Mrs. Dashwood with her three daughters remained for some time in Norland Park, their old house in Surrey. Her stepson's wife, Mrs. John Dashwood, had, however, installed herself mistress of Norland.
5. **I'll lay my life that...:** I am absolutely sure that...

CHARLES LAMB

(1775–1834)

Charles Lamb was an English essayist and critic. He was born in London on February 10, 1775, the third child and second son of a lawyer's clerk, and was educated at Christ's Hospital, London, during the period 1782–1789. He worked in the office of a city merchant in 1790, in the Examiner's Office of the South Sea House in 1791–1792, and in the Accountant's Office of the East India Company from 1792 to 1825. In 1796 his elder sister Mary in a sudden frenzy killed their mother, and thereafter he took charge of his sister, who was liable to intermittent fits of insanity. He began to write early, and was a life-long friend of Coleridge, Wordsworth, and Hazlitt. He died a bachelor, on December 27, 1834.

Lamb's writing career began with poetry, but his poems are now little read except a few, such as "The Old Familiar Faces" and "On an Infant Dying as soon as Born". He wrote with Mary Lamb *Tales from Shakespeare* (1807), a very popular children's book. In 1808 appeared his critical anthology, *Specimens of English Dramatic Poets Who Lived About the Time of Shakespeare*. His critical essays "On the Tragedies of Shakespeare" and "On the Genius and Character of Hogarth" were published in Leigh Hunt's *The Reflector* in 1811. Many of his illuminating remarks on literature are scattered in his articles and letters.

Lamb's best-known works are ***The Essays of Elia*** (1823) and ***The Last Essays of Elia*** (1833). In these familiar essays he discourses about personal experiences and impressions, peculiar characters and comical events, everyday trifles and problems of art. They show his gentleness, whimsicality, humour, and shrewdness. His thoughts are original, but his style is highly mannered and quaintly archaic with echoes of 17th-century prose masters.

MACKERY END IN HERTFORDSHIRE[1]

BRIDGET ELIA[2] has been my housekeeper for many a long year. I have obligations to Bridget, extending beyond the period of memory. We house together, old bachelor and maid, in a sort of double singleness; with such tolerable comfort, upon the whole, that I, for one, find in myself no sort of disposition to go out upon the mountains, with the rash king's offspring[3], to bewail my celibacy. We agree pretty well in our tastes and habits—yet so, as "with a difference."[4] We are generally in harmony, with occasional bickerings—as it should be among near relations. Our sympathies are rather understood, than expressed; and once, upon my dissembling[5] a tone in my voice more kind than ordinary, my cousin burst into tears, and complained that I was altered. We are both great readers in different directions. While I am hanging over (for the thousandth time) some passage in old Burton[6], or one of his strange contemporaries, she is abstracted in some modern tale or adventure, whereof our common reading-table is daily fed with assiduously fresh supplies. Narrative teases me. I have little concern in the progress of events. She must have a story—well, ill, or indifferently told—so there be life stirring in it, and plenty of good or evil accidents. The fluctuations of fortune in fiction—and almost in real life—have ceased to interest, or operate but dully upon me. Out-of-the-way humours and opinions—heads with some diverting twist in them—the oddities of authorship please me most. My cousin has a native disrelish of anything that sounds odd or bizarre. Nothing goes down with her[7], that is quaint, irregular, or out of the road of common sympathy. She "holds Nature more clever[8]." I can pardon her blindness to the beautiful obliquities of the ***Religio Medici***[9]; but she must apologize to me for certain disrespectful insinuations, which she has been pleased to throw out latterly, touching the intellectuals[10] of a dear favourite of mine, of the last century but one—the thrice noble, chaste, and virtuous,—but again somewhat fantastical, and original-brained, generous Margaret Newcastle[11].

It has been the lot of my cousin, oftener perhaps than I could have wished, to have had for her associates and mine, free-thinkers—leaders, and disciples, of novel philosophies and systems; but she neither wrangles with, nor accepts, their opinions. That which was good and venerable to her, when a child, retains its authority over her mind still. She never juggles or plays tricks with her understanding.

We are both of us inclined to be a little too positive; and I have observed the result of our disputes to be almost uniformly this—that in matters of fact, dates, and circumstances, it turns out that I was in the right, and my cousin in the wrong. But where we have differed upon moral points; upon something proper to be done, or let alone; whatever heat of opposition or steadiness of conviction, I set out with, I am sure always, in the long-run, to be brought over to her way of thinking.

I must touch upon the foibles of my kinswoman with a gentle hand, for Bridget does not like to be told of her faults. She hath an awkward trick (to say no worse of it) of reading in company; at which times she will answer *yes* or *no* to a question, without fully understanding its purport—which is provoking, and derogatory in the highest degree to the dignity of the putter of the said question. Her presence of mind is equal to the most pressing trials of life, but will sometimes desert her upon trifling occasions. When the purpose requires it, and is a thing of moment, she can speak to it greatly; but in matters which are not stuff of the conscience, she hath been known sometimes to let slip a word less seasonably.

Her education in youth was not much attended to; and she happily missed all that train of female garniture, which passeth by the name of accomplishments. She was tumbled early, by accident or design, into a spacious closet of good old English reading, without much selection or prohibition, and browsed at will upon that fair and wholesome pasturage. Had I twenty girls, they should be brought up exactly in this fashion. I know not whether their chance in wedlock might not be diminished by it; but I can answer for it, that it makes (if the worst come to the worst) most incomparable old maids.

In a season of distress, she is the truest comforter; but in the teasing accidents, and minor perplexities, which do not call out the *will* to meet them, she sometimes maketh matters worse by an excess of participation. If she does not always divide your trouble, upon the pleasanter occasions of life she is sure always to treble your satisfaction. She is excellent to be at a play[12] with, or upon a visit; but best, when she goes a journey with you.

We made an excursion together a few summers since into Hertfordshire, to beat up the quarters of[13] some of our less-known relations in that fine corn country.

The oldest thing I remember is Mackery End—or Mackarel End, as it is spelt, perhaps more properly, in some old maps of Hertfordshire—a farm-house, delightfully situated within a gentle walk from Wheathampstead. I can just remember having been there, on a visit to a great-aunt[14], when I was a child, under the care of Bridget; who, as I have said, is older than myself by some ten years. I wish that I could throw into a heap the remainder of our joint existences, that we might share them in equal division. But that is impossible. The house was at that time in the occupation of a substantial yeoman, who had married my grandmother's sister. His name was Gladman. My grandmother was a Bruton, married to a Field. The Gladmans and the Brutons are still flourishing in that part of the county, but the Fields are almost extinct. More than forty years had elapsed since the visit I speak of; and, for the greater portion of that period, we had lost sight of the other two branches also. Who or what sort of persons inherited Mackery End—kindred or strange folk—we were afraid almost to conjecture, but determined some day to explore.

By somewhat a circuitous route, taking the noble park at Luton in our way from Saint Albans, we arrived at the spot of our anxious curiosity about noon. The sight of the old farm-house, though every trace of it was effaced from my recollection, affected me with a pleasure which I had not experienced for many a year. For though *I* had forgotten it, *we* had never forgotten being there together, and we had been talking about Mackery End all our lives, till memory on my part became mocked with a phantom of itself, and I thought I knew the aspect of a place, which, when present, O how unlike it was to *that*, which I had conjured up so many times instead of it!

Still the air breathed balmily about it; the season was in the "heart of June[15]," and I could say with the poet—

> But thou[16], that didst appear so fair
> To fond imagination,
> Dost rival in the light of day
> Her delicate creation!

Bridget's was more a waking bliss[17] than mine, for she easily remembered her old acquaintance again—some altered features, of course, a little grudged at. At first, indeed, she was ready to disbelieve for joy; but the scene soon reconfirmed itself in her affections—and she traversed every outpost of the old mansion, to the wood-house, the orchard, the place where the pigeon-house had stood (house and birds were alike flown) —with a breathless impatience of recognition, which was more pardonable perhaps than decorous at the age of fifty odd. But Bridget in some things is behind her years[18].

The only thing left was to get into the house—and that was a difficulty which to me singly would have been insurmountable; for I am terribly shy in making myself known to strangers and out-of-date kinsfolk. Love, stronger than scruple, winged my cousin in without me; but she soon returned with a creature that might have sat to a sculptor for the image of Welcome. It was the youngest of the Gladmans; who, by marriage with a Bruton, had become mistress of the old mansion. A comely brood are the Brutons. Six of them, females, were noted as the handsomest young women in the county. But this adopted Bruton, in my mind, was better than they all—more comely. She was born too late to have remembered me. She just recollected in early life to have had her cousin Bridget once pointed out to her, climbing a stile. But the name of kindred, and of cousinship, was enough. Those slender ties, that prove slight as gossamer in the rending atmosphere of a metropolis, bind faster, as we found it, in hearty, homely, loving Hertfordshire. In five minutes we were as thoroughly acquainted as if we had been born and bred up together; were familiar, even to the calling each other by our Christian names. So Christians should call one another. To have seen Bridget, and her—it was like the meeting of the two scriptural cousins[19]! There was a grace and dignity, an amplitude of form and stature, answering to her mind, in this farmer's wife, which would have shined in a palace—or so we thought it. We were made welcome by husband and wife equally—we, and our friend that was with us—I had almost forgotten him—but B.F.[20] will not so soon forget that meeting, if peradventure he shall read this on the far distant shores where the kangaroo haunts[21]. The fatted calf was made ready[22], or rather was already so, as if in anticipation of our coming; and, after an appropriate glass of native wine, never let me forget with what honest pride this hospitable cousin made us proceed to Wheathampstead, to introduce us (as some new found rarity) to her mother and sister Gladmans, who did indeed know something more of us, at a time when she almost knew nothing. —With what corresponding kindness we were received by them also—how Bridget's memory, exalted by the occasion, warmed into a thousand half-obliterated recollections of things and persons, to my utter astonishment, and her own—and to the astoundment of B. F., who sat by, almost the only thing that was not a cousin there—old effaced images of more than half-forgotten names and circumstances still crowding back upon her, as words written in lemon[23] come out upon exposure to a friendly warmth, —when I forget all this, then may my country cousins forget me; and Bridget no more remember, that in the days of weakling infancy I was her tender charge—as I have been her care in foolish manhood since—in those pretty pastoral walks, long ago, about Mackery End, in Hertfordshire.

NOTES

1. **Hertfordshire:** a county of South England
2. **BRIDGET ELIA:** Lamb's elder sister, Mary Lamb
3. **the rash king's offspring:** Jephthah's daughter, who "went with her companions, and bewailed her celibacy upon the mountains" (Judges xi.38)
4. **"with a difference":** from *Hamlet* IV. v.182 — "O! you must wear your rue with a difference."
5. **dissembling:** simulating
6. **Burton:** Robert Burton (1577-1640), author of *The Anatomy of Melancholy* (1621)
7. **goes down with her:** is accepted or appreciated by her

8. **"holds Nature more clever"**: a proverbial expression
9. *Religio Medici*: a work (1642) by Thomas Browne (1605–1682)
10. **intellectuals**: intellectual powers, intellect
11. **Margaret Newcastle**: Margaret, Duchess of Newcastle (1624–1674), wrote a life of her husband, an autobiography, and many other works
12. **to be at a play**: to play a card game
13. **to beat up the quarters of**: (military) to make a sudden attack upon
14. **a great-aunt**: Lamb's grandmother Mrs. Field, née Mary Bruton
15. **"heart of June"**: from Ben Jonson, *Epithalamium for Mrs. Hierome Weston*
16. **But thou...**: from Wordsworth, *Yarrow Visited*, LL. 41-44
17. **a waking bliss**: a substantial happiness
18. **behind her years**: younger than her years
19. **the two scriptural cousins**: the Virgin Mary and Elizabeth, the mother of John the Baptist (Luke i. 39-40)
20. **B. F.**: Barron Field (1786–1846), an English barrister
21. **on the far distant shores where the kangaroo haunts**: on the remote shores of Australia
22. **The fatted calf was made ready**: a sumptuous feast was prepared. The phrase "fatted calf" occurs in the Parable of the Prodigal Son in Luke, xv. 23 and 30.
23. **words written in lemon**: words written in lemon juice

THE SUPERANNUATED MAN

Sera tamen respexit Libertas.[1]
　　　　　　　　　　　Virgil

A Clerk I was in London gay. —O'Keefe[2]

If peradventure, Reader, it has been thy lot to waste the golden years of thy life—thy shining youth—in the irksome confinement of an office; to have thy prison days prolonged through middle age down to decrepitude and silver hairs, without hope of release or respite; to have lived to forget that there are such things as holidays, or to remember them but as the prerogatives of childhood; then, and then only, will you be able to appreciate my deliverance.

It is now six-and-thirty years[3] since I took my seat at the desk in Mincing Lane[4]. Melancholy was the transition at fourteen from the abundant playtime, and the frequently-intervening vacations of school days, to the eight, nine, and sometimes ten hours' a day attendance at the counting-house. But time partially reconciles us to anything. I gradually became content—doggedly contented, as wild animals in cages.

It is true I had my Sundays to myself; but Sundays, admirable as the institution of them is for purposes of worship, are for that very reason the very worst adapted for days of unbending and recreation. In particular, there is a gloom for me attendant upon a city Sunday, a weight in the air. I miss the cheerful cries of London, the music, and the ballad-singers—the buzz and stirring murmur of the streets. Those eternal bells depress me. The closed shops repel me. Prints, pictures, all the glittering and endless succession of knacks and gewgaws, and ostentatiously displayed wares of tradesmen, which make a week-day saunter through the less busy parts of the metropolis so delightful—are shut out. No bookstalls deliciously to idle over—no busy faces to recreate the idle man who contemplates them ever passing by—the very face of business a charm by contrast to his temporary relaxation from it. Nothing to be seen but unhappy countenances—or half-happy at best—of emancipated 'prentices[5] and little tradesfolks, with here and there a servant-maid that has got leave to go out, who, slaving all the week, with the habit has lost almost the capacity of enjoying a free hour; and livelily expressing the hollowness of a day's pleasuring. The very strollers in the fields on that day look anything but comfortable.

But besides Sundays, I had a day at Easter, and a day at Christmas, with a full week in the summer to go and air myself in my native fields of Hertfordshire[6]. This last was a great indulgence; and the prospect of its recurrence, I believe, alone kept me up through the year, and made my durance tolerable. But when the week came round, did the glittering phantom of the distance keep touch with me? Or rather was it not a series of seven uneasy days, spent in restless pursuit of pleasure, and a wearisome anxiety to find out how to make the most of them? Where was the quiet, where the promised rest? Before I had a taste of it, it was vanished, I was at the desk again, counting upon the fifty-one tedious weeks that must intervene before such another snatch would come. Still the prospect of its coming threw something of an illumination upon the darker side of my captivity. Without it, as I have said, I could scarcely have sustained my thraldom.

Independently of the rigours of attendance, I have ever been haunted with a sense (perhaps a mere caprice) of incapacity for business. This, during my latter years, had increased to such a degree, that it was visible in all the lines of my countenance. My health and my good spirits flagged. I had perpetually a dread of some crisis, to which I should be found unequal. Besides my daylight servitude, I served over again all night in my sleep, and would awake with terrors of imaginary false entries, errors in my accounts, and the like. I was fifty years of age, and no prospect of emancipation presented itself. I had grown to my desk, as it were; and the wood had entered into my soul.

My fellows in the office would sometimes rally me upon the trouble legible in my countenance; but I did not know that it had raised the suspicions of any of my employers, when, on the fifth of last month, a day ever to be remembered by me, L—[7], the junior partner in the firm, calling me on one side, directly taxed me with my bad looks, and frankly inquired the cause of them. So taxed, I honestly made confession of my infirmity, and added that I was afraid I should eventually be obliged to resign his service. He spoke some words of course to hearten me, and there the matter rested. A whole week I remained labouring under the impression that I had acted imprudently in my disclosure; that I had foolishly given a handle against myself, and had been anticipating my own dismissal. A week passed in this manner, the most anxious one, I verily believe, in my whole life, when on the evening of the 12th of April, just as I was about quitting my desk to go home (it might be about eight o'clock), I received an awful summons to attend the presence of the whole assembled firm in the formidable back parlour. I thought now my time is surely come, I have done for myself, I am going to be told that they have no longer occasion for me, L—, I could see, smiled at the terror I was in, which was a little relief to me, —when to my utter astonishment B—[8], the eldest partner, began a formal harangue to me on the length of my services, my very meritorious conduct during the whole of the time (the deuce thought I, how did he find out that? I protest I never had the confidence to think as much). He went on to descant on the expediency of retiring at a certain time of life (how my heart panted!), and asking me a few questions as to the amount of my own property, of which I have a little, ended with a proposal, to which his three partners nodded a grave assent, that I should accept from the house, which I had served so well, a pension for life to the amount of two-thirds of my accustomed salary—a magnificent offer! I do not know what I answered between surprise and gratitude, but it was understood that I accepted their proposal, and I was told that I was free from that hour to leave their service. I stammered out a bow, and at just ten minutes after eight I went home—for ever. This noble benefit— gratitude forbids me to conceal their names—I owe to the kindness of the most munificent firm in the world—the house of Boldero, Merryweather, Bosanquet, and Lacy.

*Esto perpetua!*⁹

For the first day or two I felt stunned, overwhelmed. I could only apprehend my felicity; I was too confused to taste it sincerely. I wandered about, thinking I was happy, and knowing that I was not. I was in the condition of a prisoner in the old Bastile, suddenly let loose after a forty years' confinement. I could scarce trust myself with myself. It was like passing out of Time into Eternity—for it is a sort of Eternity for a man to have his Time all to himself. It seemed to me that I had more time on my hands than I could ever manage. From a poor man, poor in Time, I was suddenly lifted up into a vast revenue; I could see no end of my possessions; I wanted some steward, or judicious bailiff, to manage my estates in Time for me. And here let me caution persons grown old in active business, not lightly, nor without weighing their own resources, to forego their customary employment all at once, for there may be danger in it. I feel it by myself, but I know that my resources are sufficient; and now that those first giddy raptures have subsided, I have a quiet home-feeling of the blessedness of my condition. I am in no hurry. Having all holidays, I am as though I had none. If Time hung heavy upon me, I could walk it away; but I do not walk all day long, as I used to do in those old transient holidays, thirty miles a day, to make the most of them. If Time were troublesome, I could read it away; but I do not read in that violent measure, with which, having no Time in my own but candlelight Time, I used to weary out my head and eyesight in bygone winters. I walk, read, or scribble (as now), just when the fit seizes me. I no longer hunt after pleasure; I let it come to me. I am like the man

>   —that's born¹⁰, and has his years come to him,
>   In some green desert.

"Years!" you will say; "what is this superannuated simpleton calculating upon? He has already told us he is past fifty."

I have indeed lived nominally fifty years, but deduct out of them the hours which I have lived to other people and not to myself, and you will find me still a young fellow. For that is the only true Time, which a man can properly call his own, that which he has all to himself; the rest, not his. The remnant of my poor days, long or short, is at least multiplied for me threefold. My ten next years, if I stretch so far, will be as long as any preceding thirty. 'Tis a fair rule-of-three sum.

Among the strange fantasies which beset me at the commencement of my freedom, and of which all traces are not yet gone, one was, that a vast tract of time had intervened since I quitted the Counting House. I could not conceive of it as an affair of yesterday. The partners, and the clerks with whom I had for so many years, and for so many hours in each of the year, been closely associated—being suddenly removed from them—they seemed as dead to me. There is a fine passage, which may serve to illustrate this fancy, in a Tragedy by Sir Robert Howard[11], speaking of a friend's death: —

>—'Twas but just now he went away;
>I have not since had time to shed a tear;
>And yet the distance does the same appear
>As if he had been a thousand years from me.
>Time takes no measure in Eternity.

To dissipate this awkward feeling, I have been fain to go among them once or twice since; to visit my old deskfellows—my co-brethren of the quill—that I had left below in the state militant. Not all the kindness with which they received me could quite restore to me that pleasant familiarity, which I had heretofore enjoyed among them. We cracked some of our old jokes, but methought they went off but faintly. My old desk; the peg where I hung my hat, were appropriated to another. I knew it must be, but I could not take it kindly. D—l take me[12], if I did not feel some remorse—beast, if I had not—at quitting my old compeers, the faithful partners of my toils for six-and-thirty years, that smoothed for me with their jokes and conundrums the ruggedness of my professional road. Had it been so rugged then, after all? or was I a coward simply? Well, it is too late to repent; and I also know that these suggestions are a common fallacy of the mind on such occasions. But my heart smote me. I had violently broken the bands betwixt us. It was at least not courteous. I shall be some time before I get quite reconciled to the separation. Farewell, old cronies, yet not for long, for again and again I will come among ye, if I shall have your leave. Farewell, Ch—[13], dry, sarcastic, and friendly! Do—[14], mild, slow to move, and gentlemanly! Pl—[15], officious to do, and to volunteer, good services! —and thou, thou dreary pile, fit mansion for a Gresham[16] or a Whittington[17] of old, stately house of Merchants; with thy labyrinthine passages and light-excluding, pent-up offices, where candles for one-half the year supplied the place of the sun's light; unhealthy contributor to my weal, stern fosterer of my living, farewell! In thee remain, and not in the obscure collection of some wandering bookseller, my "works"! There let them rest, as I do from my labours, piled on thy massy shelves, more MSS. in folio than ever Aquinas[18] left, and full as useful! My mantle I bequeath among ye[19].

A fortnight has passed since the date of my first communication. At that period I was approaching to tranquillity, but had not reached it. I boasted of a calm indeed, but it was comparative only. Something of the first flutter was left; an unsettling sense of novelty; the dazzle to weak eyes of unaccustomed light. I missed my old chains, forsooth, as if they had been some necessary part of my apparel. I was a poor Carthusian, from strict cellular discipline suddenly by some revolution returned upon the world. I am now as if I had never been other than my own master. It is natural to me to go where I please, to do what I please. I find myself at eleven o'clock in the day in Bond Street, and it seems to me that I have been sauntering there at that very hour for years past. I digress into Soho, to explore a book-stall. Methinks I have been thirty years a collector. There is nothing strange nor new in it. I find myself before a fine picture in the morning. Was it ever otherwise? What is become of Fish Street Hill? Where is Fenchurch Street? Stones of old Mincing Lane, which I have worn with my daily pilgrimage for six-and-thirty years, to the footsteps of what toil-worn clerk are your everlasting flints now vocal? I indent the gayer flags of Pall Mall. It is 'Change time[20], and I am strangely among the Elgin marbles[21]. It was no hyperbole when I ventured to compare the change in my condition to a passing into another world. Time stands still in a manner to me. I have lost all distinction of season. I do not know the day of the week or of the month. Each day used to be individually felt by me in its reference to the foreign post days; in its distance from, or propinquity to, the next Sunday. I had my Wednesday feelings[22], my Saturday nights' sensations. The genius of each day was upon me distinctly during the whole of it, affecting my appetite, spirits, etc. The phantom of the next day, with the dreary five to follow, sate as a load upon my poor Sabbath recreations. What charm has washed that Ethiop white? What is gone of Black Monday[23]? All days are the same. Sunday itself—that unfortunate failure of a holiday, as it too often proved, what with my sense of its fugitiveness, and overcare to get the greatest quantity of pleasure out of it—is melted down into a week day. I can spare to go to church now, without grudging the huge cantle[24] which it used to seem to cut out of the holiday, I have Time for everything, I can visit a sick friend. I can interrupt the man of much occupation when he is busiest. I can insult over him with an invitation to take a day's pleasure with me to Windsor this fine May-morning. It is Lucretian pleasure[25] to behold the poor drudges, whom I have left behind in the world, carking[26] and caring; like horses in a mill, drudging on in the same eternal round—and what is it all for? A man can never have too much Time to himself, nor too little to do. Had I a little son, I would christen him Nothing-to-do; he should do nothing. Man, I verily believe, is out of his element as long as he is operative. I am altogether for the life contemplative. Will no kindly earthquake come and swallow up those accursed cotton mills? Take me that lumber of a desk there, and bowl it down

As low as to the fiends[27].

I am no longer..., clerk to the Firm of, etc. I am Retired Leisure. I am to be met with in trim gardens. I am already come to be known by my vacant face and careless gesture, perambulating at no fixed pace, nor with any settled purpose. I walk about; not to and from. They tell me, a certain ***cum dignitate***[28] air, that has been buried so long with my other good parts, has begun to shoot forth in my person. I grow into gentility perceptibly. When I take up a newspaper, it is to read the state of the opera. ***Opus operatum est***[29]. I have done all that I came into this world to do. I have worked task-work, and have the rest of the day to myself.

NOTES

1. ***Sera tamen respexit Libertas***: It was late ere Freedom cast her eyes on me. (C. B. Wheeler's translation)
2. **O'Keefe:** John O'Keefe (1747–1833), an Irish dramatist who wrote many comedies
3. **six-and-thirty years:** Lamb was employed as a clerk in the office of Joseph Paice in 1790, in the South Sea House in 1791, and in the East India House from 1792 to 1825.
4. **Mincing Lane:** a street near the Tower of London and the centre of the tea trade
5. **'prentices:** apprentices
6. **my native fields of Hertfordshire:** Lamb was a native of London, but he spent his childhood holidays with his grandmother at Blakesware, near Hertford.
7. **L—:** Lacy, a fictitious name
8. **B—:** Boldero, a fictitious name
9. ***Esto perpetua!***: May it last for ever! (C. B. Wheeler's translation)
10. **that's born...:** from Middleton (1570–1627), ***The Mayor of Quinborough*** (1661), I.i. 101-3
11. **a Tragedy by Sir Robert Howard:** ***The Vestal Virgin, or the Roman Ladies*** (1665), by Robert Howard (1626–1698).
12. **D—l take me:** Devil takes me (an oath).
13. **Ch—:** John Chambers
14. **Do—:** Henry Dodwell
15. **Pl—:** W. D. Plumley
16. **Gresham:** Thomas Gresham (1519–1579), founder of the Royal Exchange
17. **Whittington:** Richard Whittington (c. 1358–1423), three times Lord Mayor of London (1397–1398, 1406–1407, 1419–1420)
18. **Aquinas:** Thomas Aquinas (c. 1225–1274), Italian theologian and philosopher
19. **My mantle I bequeath among ye:** cf. *The Bible*, 2 Kings ii. 8-15
20. **'Change time:** business hours at the Exchange
21. **the Elgin marbles:** a collection of Greek sculptures acquired by the 7th Earl of Elgin

and sold to the British Government in 1816

22. **Wednesday feelings:** a reference to Lamb's Wednesday evening parties
23. **Black Monday:** the first schoolday after a vacation
24. **cantle:** slice, fragment
25. **Lucretian pleasure:** an allusion to Lucretius' *De Rerum Natura*, ii. 1-10
26. **carking:** concerned
27. **As low as to the fiends:** *Hamlet*, II. ii. 527
28. *cum dignitate*: (Lat.) with dignity
29. *Opus operatum est*: (Lat.) My work is finished.

WALTER SAVAGE LANDOR

(1775–1864)

Walter Savage Landor was an English poet and prose-writer. He was born in Warwick on January 30, 1775, the son of a doctor, and educated at Rugby School and at Trinity College, Oxford, where he was rusticated in 1794 as the "mad Jacobin". He fought in Spain against Napoleon in 1808, and lived in Italy from 1815 to 1835. His violent temper involved him in an action for libel in 1858, and he left England to settle in Florence, where he died on September 17, 1864.

Landor's epic *Gebir* (1798) and tragedy *Count Julian* (1812) are hardly read today. Some of his lyrics, e.g. "Rose Aylmer" and "On His Seventy-Fifth Birthday", are clear and elegant, and have remained favourites with the general reader. His famous prose works are ***Imaginary Conversations of Literary Men and Statesmen*** (1824–1829), ***Pericles and Aspasia*** (1836), ***The Pentameron*** (1837), and ***Imaginary Conversations of Greeks and Romans*** (1853). They are concerned with political, social, and literary questions. His style is elevated and exquisitely finished.

LOVE STRONG AS DEATH

Rhodope.[1] Never shall I forget the morning when my father, sitting in the coolest part of the house, exchanged his last measure of grain for a chlamys of scarlet cloth fringed with silver. He watched the merchant out of the door, and then looked wistfully into the corn chest. I, who thought there was something worth seeing, looked in also, and finding it empty, expressed my disappointment, not thinking, however, about the corn. A faint transient smile came over his countenance at the sight of mine. He unfolded the chlamys[2], stretched it out with both hands before me, and then cast it over my shoulders. I looked down on the glittering fringe and screamed with joy. He then went out; and I know not what flowers he gathered, but he gathered many; and some he placed in my bosom, and some in my hair. But I told him with captious pride, first, that I could arrange them better, and again, that I would have only the white. However, when he had selected all the white, and I had placed a few of them according to my fancy, I told him (rising in my slipper) he might crown me with the remainder. The splendour of my apparel gave me a sensation of authority. Soon as the flowers had taken their station on my head, I expressed a dignified satisfaction at the taste displayed by my father, just as if I could have seen how they appeared! But he knew that there was at least as much pleasure as pride in it, and perhaps we divided the latter (alas! not both) pretty equally. He now took me into the market place, where a concourse of people was waiting for the purchase of slaves. Merchants came and looked at me; some commending, others disparaging; but all agreeing that I was slender and delicate, that I could not live long, and that I should give much trouble. Many would have bought the chlamys, but there was something less saleable in the child and flowers.

Aesop. Had thy features been coarse and thy voice rustic, they would all have patted thy cheeks and found no fault in thee.

Rhodope. As it was, every one had bought exactly such another in time past, and been a loser by it. At these speeches I perceived the flowers tremble slightly on my bosom, from my father's agitation. Although he scoffed at them, knowing my healthiness, he was troubled internally, and said many short prayers, not very unlike imprecations, turning his head aside. Proud was I, prouder than ever, when at last several talents were offered for me, and by the very man who in the beginning had undervalued me the most, and prophesied the worst of me. My father scowled at him and refused the money. I thought he was playing a game, and began to wonder what it could be, since I had never seen it played before. Then I fancied it might be some celebration because plenty had returned to the city, insomuch that my father had bartered the last of the corn he hoarded. I grew more and more delighted at the sport. But soon there advanced an elderly man, who said gravely, "Thou hast stolen this child; her vesture alone is worth above a hundred drachmas. Carry her home again to her parents, and do it directly, or Nemesis[3] and the Eumenides[4] will overtake thee." Knowing the estimation in which my father had always been holden by his fellow-citizens, I laughed again, and pinched his ear. He, although naturally choleric, burst forth into no resentment at these reproaches, but said calmly, "I think I know thee by name, O guest! Surely thou art Xanthus the Samian[5]. Deliver this child from famine."

  Again I laughed aloud and heartily; and thinking it was now my part of the game, I held out both my arms and protruded my whole body towards the stranger. He would not receive me from my father's neck, but he asked me with benignity and solicitude if I was hungry; at which I laughed again and more than ever; for it was early in the morning, soon after the first meal, and my father had nourished me most carefully and plentifully in all the days of the famine. But Xanthus, waiting for no answer, took out of a sack, which one of his slaves carried at his side, a cake of wheaten bread and a piece of honeycomb, and gave them to me. I held the honeycomb to my father's mouth, thinking it the most of a dainty. He dashed it to the ground; but seizing the bread, he began to devour it ferociously. This also I thought was in play; and I clapped my hands at his distortions. But Zanthus looked on him like one afraid, and smote the cake from him, crying aloud, "Name the price." My father now placed me in his arms, naming a price much below what the other had offered, saying, "The gods are ever with thee, O Xanthus! therefore to thee do I consign my child." But while Xanthus was counting out the silver, my father seized the cake again, which the slave had taken up and was about to replace in the wallet. His hunger was exasperated by the taste and the delay. Suddenly there arose much tumult. Turning round in the old woman's bosom who had received me from Xanthus, I saw my beloved father struggling on the ground, livid and speechless. The more violent my cries, the more rapidly they hurried me away; and many were soon between us. Little was I suspicious that he had suffered the pangs of famine long before; alas! and he had suffered them for me. Do I weep while I am telling you they ended? I could not have closed his eyes, I was too young; but I might have received his last breath[6], the only comfort of an orphan's bosom. Do you now think him blamable, O Aesop?

Aesop. It was sublime humanity: it was forbearance and self-denial which even the immortal gods have never shewn us. He could endure to perish by those torments which alone are both acute and slow; he could number the steps of death and miss not one; but he could never see thy tears, nor let thee see his. O weakness above all fortitude! Glory to the man who rather bears a grief corroding his breast, than permits it to prowl beyond, and to prey on the tender and compassionate! Women commiserate the brave, and men the beautiful. The dominion of pity has usually this extent, no wider. Thy father was exposed to the obloquy not only of the malicious, but also of the ignorant and thoughtless, who condemn in the unfortunate what they applaud in the prosperous. There is no shame in poverty or in slavery, if we neither make ourselves poor by our improvidence nor slaves by our venality. The lowest and the highest of the human race are sold: most of the intermediate are also slaves, but slaves who bring no money into the market.

—*Imaginary Conversations*

NOTES

1. **Rhodope:** Rhodopia (fl.c. 600 B.C.) a Greek woman whom Landor calls Rhodope, and Aesop (c. 620–560 B.C.), the Greek fabulist, were at first both slaves of Iadmon of Samos. Later, Rhodopia was taken to Naucratis in Egypt, became a slave of Xanthus,

and was ransomed by Charaxus, Sappho's brother. Aesop won his freedom from Iadmon, owing to his keen wit.

2. **chlamys:** short mantle or cloak for men
3. **Nemesis:** the goddess of vengeance
4. **the Eumenides:** the Fates or Furies
5. **Samian:** native or inhabitant of the Isle of Samos in the Aegean Sea
6. **his last breath:** his last whisper

42

WILLIAM HAZLITT

(1778–1830)

William Hazlitt was an English essayist and critic. He was born in Kent on April 10, 1778, the son of a Unitarian minister, and lived with his family in the United States from 1783 to 1787 and in Wem, Shropshire, from 1783 to 1805. He divided his time between Wem and London during the period 1805–1808, settled in Winterslow, Wiltshire, in 1808, and returned to London in 1812. Mainly self-educated, he began to write in 1792 and to lecture in 1812. As a staunch supporter of revolutionary principles, he had many quarrels and controversies with other men of letters. He died on September 18, 1830.

Hazlitt began life as a student of philosophy and painting, but soon switched to literature as a career. He read widely in English literature and felt keenly about what he read. He was a leading Romantic critic who could do justice to many English writers, past and contemporary. Some of his famous critical works are: "Characters of Shakespeare's Plays" (1817), "Lectures on the English Poets" (1818), "Lectures on the English Comic Writers" (1819), "Lectures Chiefly on the Dramatic Literature of the Age of Elizabeth" (1820), and "The Spirit of the Age" (1825). For general readers the most interesting part of his work is to be found in his essays, of which the best-known volumes are "Table Talk" (1821–1822) and "The Plain Speaker" (1826). His essays deal with a wide range of subjects. He describes his experiences and impressions and carries over his emotions to his readers. His astute observation, his incisive judgement, and his zest for life are all exhilarating. His style is clear and graphic, lively and vigorous.

ON GOING A JOURNEY

One of the pleasantest things in the world is going a journey; but I like to go by myself. I can enjoy society in a room; but out of doors, nature is company enough for me. I am then never less alone than when alone.

> The fIelds his study, nature was his book.[1]

I cannot see the wit of walking and talking at the same time. When I am in the country I wish to vegetate like the country. I am not for criticising hedge-rows and black cattle. I go out of town in order to forget the town and all that is in it. There are those who for this purpose go to watering-places, and carry the metropolis with them. I like more elbowroom and fewer encumbrances. I like solitude, when I give myself up to it, for the sake of solitude; nor do I ask for

> a friend in my retreat,
> Whom.I may whisper solitude is sweet.[2]

The soul of a journey is liberty, perfect liberty, to think, feel, do, just as one pleases. We go a journey chiefly to be free of all impediments and of all inconveniences; to leave ourselves behind, much more to get rid of others. It is because I want a little breathing-space to muse on indifferent matters, where Contemplation

> May plume her feathers and let grow her wings,
> That in the various bustle of resort
> Were all too ruffled, and sometimes impair'd,[3]

that I absent myself from the town for a while, without feeling at a loss the moment I am left by myself. Instead of a friend in a postchaise or in a Tilbury[4], to exchange good things with, and vary the same stale topics over again, for once let me have a truce with impertinence. Give me the clear blue sky over my head, and the green turf beneath my feet, a winding road before me, and a three hours' march to dinner—and then to thinking! It is hard if I cannot start some game on these lone heaths. I laugh, I run, I leap, I sing for joy. From the point of yonder rolling cloud I plunge into my past being, and revel there, as the sun-burnt Indian plunges headlong into the wave that wafts him to his native shore. Then long-forgotten things, like "sunken wrack and sumless treasuries[5]," burst upon my eager sight, and I begin to feel, think, and be myself again. Instead of an awkward silence, broken by attempts at wit or dull common-places, mine is that undisturbed silence of the heart which alone is perfect eloquence. No one likes puns, alliterations, antitheses, argument, and analysis better than I do; but I sometimes had rather be without them. "Leave, oh, leave me to my repose[6]!" I have just now other business in hand, which would seem idle to you, but is with me "very stuff o'the conscience[7]." Is not this wild rose sweet without a comment? Does not this daisy leap to my heart set in its coat of emerald? Yet if I were to explain to you the circumstance that has so endeared it to me, you would only smile. Had I not better then keep it to myself, and let it serve me to brood over, from here to yonder craggy point, and from thence onward to the far-distant horizon? I should be but bad company all that way, and therefore prefer being alone. I have heard it said that you may, when the moody fit comes on, walk or ride on by yourself, and indulge your reveries. But this looks like a breach of manners, a neglect of others, and you are thinking all the time that you ought to rejoin your party. "Out upon such half-faced fellowship[8]," say I. I like to be either entirely to myself, or entirely at the disposal of others; to talk or be silent, to walk or sit still, to be sociable or solitary. I was pleased with an observation of Mr. Cobbett's[9], that "he thought it a bad French custom to drink our wine with our meals, and that an Englishman ought to do only one thing at a time." So I cannot talk and think, or indulge in melancholy musing and lively conversation by fits and starts. "Let me have a companion of my way," says Sterne[10], "were it but to remark how the shadows lengthen as the sun declines." It is beautifully said; but, in my opinion, this continual comparing of notes interferes with the involuntary impression of things upon the mind, and hurts the sentiment. If you only hint what you feel in a kind of dumb show, it is insipid: if you have to explain it, it is making a toil of a pleasure. You cannot read the book of nature without being perpetually put to the trouble of translating it for the benefit of others. I am for this synthetical method on a journey in preference to the analytical. I am content to lay in a stock of ideas then, and to examine and anatomise them afterwards. I want to see my vague notions float like the down of the thistle before the breeze, and not to have them entangled in the briars and thorns of controversy. For once, I like to have it all my own way; and this is impossible unless you are alone, or in such company as I do not covet. I have no objection to argue a point with any one for twenty miles of measured road, but not for pleasure. If you remark the scent of a bean-field crossing the road, perhaps your fellow-traveller has no smell. If you point to a distant object, perhaps he is short-sighted, and has to take out his glass to look at it. There is a feeling in the air, a tone in the colour of a cloud, which hits your fancy, but the effect of which you are unable to account for. There is then no sympathy, but an uneasy craving after it, and a dissatisfaction which pursues you on the way, and in the end probably produces ill-humour. Now I never quarrel with myself, and take all my own conclusions for granted till I find it necessary to defend them against objections. It is not merely that you may not be of accord on the objects and circumstances that present themselves before you—these may recall a number of objects, and lead to associations too delicate and refined to be possibly communicated to others. Yet these I love to cherish, and sometimes still fondly clutch them, when I can escape from the throng to do so. To give way to our feelings before company seems extravagance or affectation; and, on the other hand, to have to unravel this mystery of our being at every turn, and to make others take an equal interest in it (otherwise the end is not answered), is a task to which few are competent. We must "give it an understanding, but no tongue[11]." My old friend Coleridge, however, could do both. He could go on in the most delightful explanatory way over hill and dale a summer's day, and convert a landscape into a didactic poem or Pindaric ode[12]. "He talked far above singing.[13]" If I could so clothe my ideas in sounding and flowing words, I might perhaps wish to have some one with me to admire the swelling theme; or I could be more content, were it possible for me still to hear his echoing voice in the woods of All-Foxden[14]. They had "that fine madness in them which our first poets had[15]"; and if they could have been caught by some rare instrument, would have breathed such strains as the following[16]: —

> Here be woods as green
> As any, air likewise as fresh and sweet
> As when smooth Zephyrus[17] plays on the fleet
> Face of the curled streams, with flow'rs as many
> As the young spring gives, and as choice as any;
> Here be all new delights, cool streams and wells,
> Arbours o'ergrown with woodbines, caves and dells;
> Choose where thou wilt, whilst I sit by and sing,
> Or gather rushes to make many a ring
> For thy long fingers; tell thee tales of love,
> How the pale Phoebe[18], hunting in a grove,
> First saw the boy Endymion[19], from whose eyes
> She took eternal fire that never dies;
> How she convey'd him softly in a sleep,
> His temples bound with poppy, to the steep
> Head of old Latmos[20], where she stoops each night,
> Gilding the mountain with her brother's light,
> To kiss her sweetest.

Had I words and images at command like these, I would attempt to wake the thoughts that lie slumbering on golden ridges in the evening clouds: but at the sight of nature my fancy, poor as it is, droops and closes up its leaves, like flowers at sunset. I can make nothing out on the spot: I must have time to collect myself.

In general, a good thing spoils out-of-door prospects: it should be reserved for Table-talk. Lamb is for this reason, I take it, the worst company in the world out of doors; because he is the best within. I grant there is one subject on which it is pleasant to talk on a journey, and that is, what one shall have for supper when we get to our inn at night. The open air improves this sort of conversation or friendly altercation, by setting a keener edge on appetite. Every mile of the road heightens the flavour of the viands we expect at the end of it. How fine it is to enter some old town, walled and turreted, just at approach of nightfall, or to come to some straggling village, with the lights streaming through the surrounding gloom; and then, after inquiring for the best entertainment that the place affords, to "take one's ease at one's inn[21]"! These eventful moments in our lives' history are too precious, too full of solid, heartfelt happiness to be frittered and dribbled away in imperfect sympathy. I would have them all to myself, and drain them to the last drop: they will do to talk of or to write about afterwards. What a delicate speculation it is, after drinking whole goblets of tea—

The cups that cheer, but not inebriate[22]—

and letting the fumes ascend into the brain, to sit considering what we shall have for supper-eggs and a rasher, a rabbit smothered in onions, or an excellent veal-cutlet! Sancho[23] in such a situation once fixed on cow-heel; and his choice, though he could not help it, is not to be disparaged. Then, in the intervals of pictured scenery and Shandean[24] contemplation, to catch the preparation and the stir in the kitchen [getting ready for the gentleman in the parlour]. **Procul, O procul este profani!**[25] These hours are sacred to silence and to musing, to be treasured up in the memory, and to feed the source of smiling thoughts hereafter. I would not waste them in idle talk; or if I must have the integrity of fancy broken in upon, I would rather it were by a stranger than a friend. A stranger takes his hue and character from the time and place; he is a part of the furniture and costume of an inn. If he is a Quaker, or from the West Riding[26] of Yorkshire, so much the better. I do not even try to sympathise with him, and he breaks no squares[27]. [How I love to see the camps of the gypsies, and to sign my soul into that sort of life. If I express this feeling to another, he may qualify and spoil it with some objection.] I associate nothing with my travelling companion but present objects and passing events. In his ignorance of me and my affairs, I in a manner forget myself. But a friend reminds one of other things, rips up old grievances, and destroys the abstraction of the scene. He comes in ungraciously between us and our imaginary character. Something is dropped in the course of conversation that gives a hint of your profession and pursuits; or from having some one with you that knows the less sublime portions of your history, it seems that other people do. You are no longer a citizen of the world; but your "unhoused free condition is put into circumspection and confine[28]." The incognito of an inn is one of its striking privileges— "lord of one's self, uncumbered with a name[29]." Oh! it is great to shake off the trammels of the world and of public opinion—to lose our importunate, tormenting, everlasting personal identity in the elements of nature, and become the creature of the moment, clear of all ties—to hold to the universe only by a dish of sweetbreads, and to owe nothing but the score of the evening—and no longer seeking for applause and meeting with contempt, to be known by no other title than ***the Gentleman in the parlour***! One may take one's choice of all characters in this romantic state of uncertainty as to one's real pretensions, and become indefinitely respectable and negatively right-worshipful. We baffle prejudice and disappoint conjecture; and from being so to others, begin to be objects of curiosity and wonder even to ourselves. We are no more those hackneyed common-places that we appear in the world; an inn restores us to the level of nature and quits scores with society! I have certainly spent some enviable hours at inns—sometimes when I have been left entirely to myself, and have tried to solve some metaphysical problem, as once at Witham Common[30], where I found out the proof that likeness is not a case of the association of ideas—at other times, when there have been pictures in the room, as at St. Neot's[31] (I think it was), where I first met with Gribelin's engravings of the Cartoons[32], into which I entered at once, and at a little inn on the borders of Wales, where there happened to be hanging some of Westall's[33] drawings, which I compared triumphantly (for a theory that I had, not for the admired artist) with the figure of a girl who had ferried me over the Severn, standing up in a boat between me and the twilight—at other times I might mention luxuriating in books, with a peculiar interest in this way, as I remember sitting up half the night to read ***Paul and Virginia***[34], which I picked up at an inn at Bridgewater[35], after being drenched in the rain all day; and at the same place I got through two volumes of Madame D'Arblay's[36] ***Camilla***. It was on the 10th of April 1798 that I sat down to a volume of the ***New Eloise***[37], at the inn at Llangollen, over a bottle of sherry and a cold chicken. The letter I chose was that in which St. Preux describes his feelings as he first caught a glimpse from the heights of the Jura of the Pays de Vaud[38], which I had brought with me as a ***bon bouche***[39] to crown the evening with. It was my birthday, and I had for the first time come from a place in the neighbourhood to visit this delightful spot. The road to Llangollen[40] turns off between Chirk[41] and Wrexham[42]; and on passing a certain point you come all at once upon the valley, which opens like an amphitheatre, broad, barren hills rising in majestic state on either side, with "green upland swells that echo to the bleat of flocks"[43] below, and the river Dee babbling over its stony bed in the midst of them. The valley at this time "glittered green with sunny showers," and a budding ash-tree dipped its tender branches in the chiding stream. How proud, how glad I was to walk along the high road that overlooks the delicious prospect, repeating the lines which I have just quoted from Mr. Coleridge's poems! But besides the prospect which opened beneath my feet, another also opened to my inward sight, a heavenly vision, on which were written, in letters large as Hope could make them, these four words, LIBERTY, GENIUS, LOVE, VIRTUE; which have since faded into the light of common day, or mock my idle gaze.

The beautiful is vanished, and returns not.[44]

Still I would return some time or other to this enchanted spot; but I would return to it alone. What other self could I find to share that influx of thoughts, of regret, and delight, the fragments of which I could hardly conjure up to myself, so much have they been broken and defaced. I could stand on some tall rock, and overlook the precipice of years that separates me from what I then was. I was at that time going shortly to visit the poet whom I have above named. Where is he now? Not only I myself have changed; the world, which was then new to me, has become old and incorrigible. Yet will I turn to thee in thought, O sylvan Dee[45], in joy, in youth and gladness as thou then wert; and thou shalt always be to me the river of Paradise, where I will drink of the waters of life freely!

    There is hardly anything that shows the short-sightedness or capriciousness of the imagination more than travelling does. With change of place we change our ideas; nay, our opinions and feelings. We can by an effort indeed transport ourselves to old and long-forgotten scenes, and then the picture of the mind revives again; but we forget those that we have just left. It seems that we can think but of one place at a time. The canvas of the fancy is but of a certain extent, and if we paint one set of objects upon it, they immediately efface every other. We cannot enlarge our conceptions, we only shift our point of view. The landscape bares its bosom to the enraptured eye, we take our fill of it, and seem as if we could form no other image of beauty or grandeur. We pass on, and think no more of it: the horizon that shuts it from our sight also blots it from our memory like a dream. In travelling through a wild barren country I can form no idea of a woody and cultivated one. It appears to me that all the world must be barren, like what I see of it. In the country we forget the town, and in town we despise the country. "Beyond Hyde Park," says Sir Fopling Flutter[46], "all is a desert." All that part of the map that we do not see before us is blank. The world in our conceit of it is not much bigger than a nutshell. It is not one prospect expanded into another, county joined to county, kingdom to kingdom, land to seas, making an image voluminous and vast; —the mind can form no larger idea of space than the eye can take in at a single glance. The rest is a name written in a map, a calculation of arithmetic. For instance, what is the true signification of that immense mass of territory and population known by the name of China to us? An inch of pasteboard on a wooden globe, of no more account than a China orange! Things near us are seen of the size of life: things at a distance are diminished to the size of the understanding. We measure the universe by ourselves, and even comprehend the texture of our being only piecemeal. In this way, however, we remember an infinity of things and places. The mind is like a mechanical instrument that plays a great variety of tunes, but it must play them in succession. One idea recalls another, but it at the same time excludes all others.

In trying to renew old recollections, we cannot as it were unfold the whole web of our existence; we must pick out the single threads. So in coming to a place where we have formerly lived, and with which we have intimate associations, every one must have found that the feeling grows more vivid the nearer we approach the spot, from the mere anticipation of the actual impression: we remember circumstances, feelings, persons, faces, names that we had not thought of for years; but for the time all the rest of the world is forgotten! —To return to the question I have quitted above: —

I have no objection to go to see ruins, aqueducts, pictures, in company with a friend or a party, but rather the contrary, for the former reason reversed. They are intelligible matters, and will bear talking about. The sentiment here is not tacit, but communicable and overt. Salisbury Plain is barren of criticism, but Stonehenge[47] will bear a discussion antiquarian, picturesque, and philosophical. In setting out on a party of pleasure, the first consideration always is where we shall go to: in taking a solitary ramble, the question is what we shall meet with by the way. "The mind is its own place[48]"; nor are we anxious to arrive at the end of our journey. I can myself do the honours indifferently well to works of art and curiosity. I once took a party to Oxford with no mean éclat[49]—showed them that seat of the Muses at a distance,

> With glistering spires and pinnacles adorn'd[50]—

descanted on the learned air that breathes from the grassy quadrangles and stone walls of halls and colleges—was at home in the Bodleian[51]; and at Blenheim[52] quite superseded the powdered Cicerone[53] that attended us, and that pointed in vain with his wand to commonplace beauties in matchless pictures. As another exception to the above reasoning, I should not feel confident in venturing on a journey in a foreign country without a companion. I should want at intervals to hear the sound of my own language. There is an involuntary antipathy in the mind of an Englishman to foreign manners and notions that requires the assistance of social sympathy to carry it off. As the distance from home increases, this relief, which was at first a luxury, becomes a passion and an appetite. A person would almost feel stifled to find himself in the deserts of Arabia without friends and countrymen: there must be allowed to be something in the view of Athens or old Rome that claims the utterance of speech; and I own that the Pyramids are too mighty for any single contemplation. In such situations, so opposite to all one's ordinary train of ideas, one seems a species by one's-self, a limb torn off from society, unless one can meet with instant fellowship and support. Yet I did not feel this want or craving very pressing once, when I first set my foot on the laughing shores of France. Calais was peopled with novelty and delight. The confused, busy murmur of the place was like oil and wine poured into my ears; nor did the mariners' hymn, which was sung from the top of an old crazy vessel in the harbour, as the sun went down, send an alien sound into my soul. I only breathed the air of general humanity. I walked over "the vine-covered hills and gay regions of France[54]," erect and satisfied; for the image of man was not cast down and chained to the foot of arbitrary thrones: I was at no loss for language, for that of all the great schools of painting was open to me. The whole is vanished like a shade. Pictures, heroes, glory, freedom, all are fled: nothing remains but the Bourbons[55] and the French people!—There is undoubtedly a sensation in travelling into foreign parts that is to be had nowhere else; but it is more pleasing at the time than lasting. It is too remote from our habitual associations to be a common topic of discourse or reference, and, like a dream or another state of existence, does not piece into our daily modes of life. It is an animated but a momentary hallucination. It demands an effort to exchange our actual for our ideal identity; and to feel the pulse of our old transports revive very keenly, we must "jump[56]" all our present comforts and connections. Our romantic and itinerant character is not to be domesticated. Dr. Johnson remarked how little foreign travel added to the facilities of conversation in those who had been abroad. In fact, the time we have spent there is both delightful, and in one sense instructive; but it appears to be cut out of our substantial, downright existence, and never to join kindly on to it. We are not the same, but another, and perhaps more enviable individual, all the time we are out of our own country. We are lost to ourselves, as well as our friends. So the poet somewhat quaintly sings:

> Out of my country and myself I go.

Those who wish to forget painful thoughts, do well to absent themselves for a while from the ties and objects that recall them; but we can be said only to fulfil our destiny in the place that gave us birth. I should on this account like well enough to spend the whole of my life in travelling abroad, if I could anywhere borrow another life to spend afterwards at home!

NOTES
1. **The fields his study, nature was his book:** from Robert Bloomfield's poem *The Farmer's Boy, Spring*, l. 32
2. **a friend in my retreat,/Whom I may whisper solitude is sweet:** from Cowper's poem *Retirement*, ll. 741-2
3. **May plume her feathers…:** from Milton's *Comus*, ll. 378-80
4. **a Tilbury:** a small two-wheeled open carriage
5. **sunken wrack and sumless treasuries:** from *Henry V*, I. ii. 163-5
6. **Leave, oh, leave me to my repose!:** the closing line of some stanzas in Gray's *Descent of Odin*
7. **very stuff o'the conscience:** from *Othello*, I. ii. 2
8. **Out upon such half-faced fellowship:** from *Henry IV*, Part 1, I. iii. 208
9. **Mr. Cobbett's:** William Cobbett (1763–1835) was the editor of *Cobbett's Political Register* and the author of *Rural Rides*.
10. **Sterne:** Laurence Sterne (1713–1768) was the author of *Tristram Shandy*, a whimsical novel.
11. **give it an understanding, but no tongue:** *Hamlet*, I. ii. 249.
12. **Pindaric ode:** an ode in the style of the Greek lyric poet Pindar (522–443 B.C.); an ode in an irregular and changeful metre
13. **He talked far above singing:** from Beaumont and Fletcher, *Philaster*, V. v
14. **All-Foxden:** In 1798 Hazlitt visited Coleridge at All-Foxden, near Nether-Stowey,

Somersetshire.

15. **that fine madness in them which our first poets had:** from Michael Drayton's *Elegy to Henry Reynolds*
16. **such strains as the following:** the quotation is from Fletcher's pastoral play, *The Faithful Shepherdess*, i. 3
17. **Zephyrus:** (Gr. myth.) god of the west wind
18. **pale Phoebe:** the moon; goddess of the moon
19. **the boy Endymion:** the Latmian shepherd Endymion
20. **Latmos:** a mountain in the southwest of Asia Minor
21. **take one's ease at one's inn:** from *Henry IV*, Part 1, III. iii. 91-92
22. **the cups that cheer, but not inebriate:** Cowper, *The Task*, IV. 39-40
23. **Sancho:** a humorous character in Cervantes' story *Don Quixote*
24. **Shandean:** in the manner of Tristram Shandy; carefree
25. **Procul, O procul este profani!:** (Virgil, *Aeneid*, vi. 258) Away, away, ye uninitiated.
26. **the West Riding:** an administrative division of Yorkshire, contained since 1974 in West Yorkshire
27. **he breaks no squares:** he does no harm.
28. **unhoused free condition is put into circumspection and confine:** from *Othello*, I. ii. 26-27
29. **lord of one's self, uncumbered with a name:** Dryden, *Epitaph to My Honoured Kinsman, John Driden*, I. 18
30. **Witham Common:** a tract of public ground in Witham, a town in Essex
31. **St. Neot's:** St. Neots, a town in Huntingdonshire
32. **Gribelin's engravings of the Cartoons:** Simon Gribelin (1661-1733) engraved a set of the cartoons of Raphael on a small scale in 1707.
33. **Westall:** Richard Westall (1765-1836) was a historical painter and book illustrator.
34. **Paul and Virginia:** a French romance (1788) by Benardin de St. Pierre (1737-1814)
35. **Bridgewater:** a town in Somerset
36. **Madame D'Arblay:** Frances Burney (1752-1840) was an English novelist who was the author of *Evelina* (1778), *Cecilia* (1782), and *Camilla* (1796).
37. **the *New Eloise*:** a novel (*La Nouvelle Heloise*, 1761) by J. J. Rousseau (1712-1778)

38. **the Jura of the Pays de Vaud:** the mountain in the western canton of Switzerland
39. ***bon bouche*:** (Fr.) ***bonne bouche***, dainty morsel
40. **Llangollen:** a town in northwest Wales
41. **Chirk:** a town in north Wales
42. **Wrexham:** a town in north Wales
43. **green upland swells that echo to the bleat of flocks:** from Coleridge's ***Ode to the Departing Year***, St. 7
44. **The beautiful is vanished, and returns not:** Coleridge, ***The Death of Wallenstein***, V. i. 68
45. **O sylvan Dee:** The Dee is a river in North Wales and NW England.
46. **Sir Fopling Flutter:** the hero in ***The Man of Mode*** (1676), a comedy by George Etherege (?1634–1691)
47. **Stonehenge:** a prehistoric group of monumental stones on Salisbury Plain
48. **The mind is its own place:** Milton, ***Paradise Lost***, i. 254
49. **éclat:** (Fr.) splendour, distinction
50. **With glistering spires and pinnacles adorn'd:** from ***Paradise Lost***, iii. 550
51. **the Bodleian:** the Oxford University Library
52. **at Blenheim:** at Blenheim Palace (which had been built for the Duke of Marlborough) near Oxford
53. **powdered Cicerone:** guide wearing a powdered wig
54. **the vine-covered hills and gay regions of France:** a line from a song by William Roscoe (1753–1831)
55. **the Bourbons:** the Royal house that ruled in France from 1589 to 1793 and from 1830 to 1848
56. **jump:** risk

ON THE FEELING OF IMMORTALITY IN YOUTH

No young man believes he shall ever die. It was a saying of my brother's[1] and a fine one. There is a feeling of Eternity in youth which makes us amends for everything. To be young is to be as one of the *Immortals*. One half of time indeed is *spent*—the other half remains in store for us, with all its countless treasures, for there is no line drawn, and we see no limit to our hopes and wishes. We make the coming age our own—

"The vast, the unbounded prospect lies before us."[2]

Death, old age, are words without a meaning, *a dream, a fiction, with which we have nothing to do*. Others may have undergone, or may still *undergo* them—we "bear a charmed life[3]," which laughs to scorn all such *idle* fancies. As, in setting out on a delightful journey, we strain our eager *sight* forward,

"Bidding the lovely scenes at distance hail[4],"

and see no end to *prospect after prospect*, new objects presenting themselves as we advance, so in the *outset* of life we *see no end* to our desires nor to the *opportunities* of gratifying them. We have as yet found no obstacle, no disposition to flag, and it seems that we can go on so for ever. We look round in a new world, full of life and motion, and ceaseless progress, and feel in ourselves all the vigor and spirit to keep pace with it, and do not foresee from any present *signs* how we shall be left behind in the *race*, decline into old age, and drop into the grave. It is the simplicity and, as it were, abstractedness of our feelings in youth that (so to speak) identifies us with nature and (our experience being *weak* and our passions strong) *makes us fancy ourselves* immortal like it. Our short-lived connection with *being*, we fondly flatter ourselves, is an indissoluble and lasting union. As infants smile and sleep, we are rocked in the cradle of our *desires*, and *hushed into fancied security* by the roar of the universe around us—we quaff the cup of life with eager *thirst* without draining it, *and joy and hope seem ever mantling*[5] *to the brim*—objects press around us, filling the mind with their magnitude and with the throng of desires that wait upon them, so that there is no room for the thoughts of death. We are too much dazzled by the *gorgeousness and novelty of the bright waking dream about* us to *discern the dim shadow lingering for us in the distance.* Nor would the hold that life has taken of us permit us to detach our thoughts *that way*, even if we could. *We are too much absorbed* in present objects and pursuits. While the spirit of youth remains unimpaired, ere "the wine of life is *drunk*[6]," we are like people intoxicated or in a fever, who are hurried away by the violence of their own sensations; it is only as present objects begin to pall upon the sense, as we have been disappointed in our favorite pursuits, cut off from our closest ties, that we by degrees become weaned from the world, that passion loosens its hold upon *futurity*, and that *we begin* to contemplate as in a glass darkly the possibility of parting with it for good. Till then, the example of others has no effect upon us. Casualties we *avoid*; the slow *approaches* of age we play at hide-and-seek with[7]. Like the foolish fat scullion in Sterne[8], *who* hears that Master Bobby is dead, our only reflection is, "So am not I!" The idea of death, instead of staggering our confidence, *only* seems to strengthen and enhance *our sense of the possession* and enjoyment of life. Others may fall around us like leaves, or be mowed down by the scythe of Time *like grass*: these are but *metaphors* to the unreflecting, *buoyant* ears and overweening presumption of youth. It is not till we see the flowers of Love, Hope, and Joy withering around us, that we *give up the flattering delusions that before led us on, and* that the emptiness and dreariness of the prospect before us reconciles us *hypothetically* to the *silence* of the grave.

Life is indeed a strange gift, and its privileges are most *mysterious*. *No wonder when* it is first granted to us, that our gratitude, our admiration and our delight should prevent us from reflecting on our own nothingness, or from thinking it will ever be recalled. Our first and strongest impression are *borrowed* from the mighty scene that is opened to us, and we *unconsciously* transfer its durability as well as ***its splendor*** to ourselves. So newly found, we cannot ***think of*** parting with it yet, ***or*** at least put off that consideration ***sine die***[9]. Like a ***rustic*** at a fair, we are full of amazement and rapture, and have no thought of going home, or that it will soon be night. We know our existence only ***by ourselves, and confound our knowledge with the objects of it. We and Nature are therefore one.*** Otherwise the ***illusion***, the "feast of reason and the flow of soul[10]," to which ***we are*** invited, ***is*** a mockery and a cruel insult. We do not go from a play till the ***last act*** is ended, and the lights are ***about*** to be extinguished. But the ***fairy*** face of ***Nature*** still shines on: shall we be called away before the curtain falls, or ere we have scarce had a glimpse of what is going on? Like children, our stepmother Nature holds us up to see the raree-show[11] of the universe, and then, as if ***we*** were a burden ***to her*** to support, lets us ***fall*** down again. Yet what brave sublunary things does not ***this pageant present, like a ball or fête of the universe!***

    To see the golden sun, the azure sky, the outstretched ocean; to walk upon the green earth, and be lord of a thousand creatures; to look down ***yawning*** precipices or over distant ***sunny*** vales; to see the world spread out under one's ***feet on*** a map; to bring the stars near; to view the smallest insects ***through*** a microscope; to read history, and ***consider*** the revolutions of empire and the successions of generations; to hear of the glory ***of Tyre***[12], ***of Sidon***[13], ***of Babylon***[14], ***and of Susa***[15], and to say all these were ***before me*** and are now nothing; ***to say I*** exist in such a point of time, and in such a ***point*** of space; to be ***a spectator*** and a part of ***its ever-moving*** scene; to ***witness the change*** of season, of spring and autumn, ***of winter and summer***; to feel ***hot*** and cold, pleasure and pain, [beauty and deformity,] right and wrong; [to be sensible to the accidents of nature; to consider the mighty world of eye and ear[16];] ***to listen to the*** stock-dove's[17] ***notes*** amid the forest deep; ***to journey over moor and mountain***; ***to hear*** the midnight ***sainted*** choir; to visit lighted halls, or the ***cathedral's*** gloom, or sit in crowded theatres and see life itself mocked; to study the works of art and refine the sense of beauty to agony; to worship fame, and to dream of immortality; [to look upon the Vatican,[18]] and to read Shakespeare; [to gather up the wisdom of the ancients, and to pry into the future; to listen to the trump of war, the shout of victory; to question history as to the movements of the human heart; to seek for truth; to plead the cause of humanity; to overlook the world as if time and Nature poured their treasures at our feet—] to be and to do all this, and then in a moment to be nothing—to have it all snatched from *us by a juggler's trick* or a phantasmagoria! There is something in this transition *from all to nothing that shocks us and damps the enthusiasm of youth new flushed with hope and pleasure, and we cast the comfortless thought as far from us as we can.* In the first enjoyment of the estate of life we discard the fear of debts and duns, and never think of the final payment of our great debt to Nature. Art, we know, is long; life, we flatter ourselves, should be so too. We see no end of the difficulties and delays we have to encounter: perfection is slow of attainment, and we must have time to accomplish it in. The fame of the great names we look up to is immortal; and shall not we who contemplate it imbibe a portion of ethereal fire, the *divinoe particula auroe*[19], which nothing can extinguish? A wrinkle in Rembrandt[20] or in Nature takes whole days to resolve itself into its component parts, its softenings and its sharpnesses; we refine upon our perfections, and unfold the intricacies of Nature. What a prospect for the future! What a task have we not begun! And shall we be arrested in the middle of it? We do not count our time thus employed lost, or our pains thrown away; we do not flag or grow tired, but gain new vigour at our endless task. Shall Time, then, grudge us to finish what we have begun, and have formed a compact with Nature to do! Why not fill up the blank that is left us in this manner? I have looked for hours at a Rembrandt without being conscious of the flight of time, but with ever new wonder and delight, have thought that not only my own but another existence I could pass in the same manner. This rarefied, refined existence seemed to have no end, nor stint, nor principle of decay in it. The print would remain long after I who looked on it had become the prey of worms. The thing seems in itself out of all reason: health, strength, appetite, are opposed to the idea of death, and we are not ready to credit it till we have found our illusions vanished and our hopes grown cold. Objects in youth, from novelty, &c., are stamped upon the brain with such force and integrity that one thinks nothing can remove or obliterate them. They are riveted there, and appear to us as an element of our nature. It must be a mere violence that destroys them, not a natural decay.

In the very strength of this persuasion we seem to enjoy an age by anticipation. We melt down years into a single moment of intense sympathy, and by anticipating the fruits defy the ravages of time. If then, a single moment of our lives is worth years, shall we set any limits to its total value and extent? Again, does it not happen that so secure do we think ourselves of an indefinite period of existence, that at times, when left to ourselves, and impatient of novelty, we feel annoyed at what seems to us the slow and creeping progress of time, and argue that if it always moves at this tedious snail's-pace it will never come to an end? How ready are we to sacrifice any space of time which separates us from a favorite object, little thinking that before long we shall find it move too fast!

For my part, I started in life with the French Revolution, and I have lived, alas! to see the end of it[21]. But I did not foresee this result. My sun arose with the first dawn of liberty, and I did not think how soon both must set. The new impulse to ardor given to men's minds, imparted a congenial warmth and glow to mine; we were strong to run a race together, and I little dreamed that long before mine was set, the sun of liberty would turn to blood, or set once more in the night of despotism. Since then, I confess, I have no longer felt myself young, for with that my hopes fell.

I have since turned my thoughts to gathering up some of the fragments of my early recollections, and putting them into a form to which I might occasionally revert. The future was barred to my progress, and I turned for consolation and encouragement to the past. It is thus that, *while* we find our personal and substantial identity vanishing from us, we strive to gain a reflected and *vicarious* one in our thoughts: we do not like to perish wholly, and wish to bequeath our names, at least, to posterity. As long as we can *make* our cherished thoughts and nearest interests *live* in the minds of others, we do not appear to have retired altogether from the stage. We still occupy *the breasts of others, and exert an influence and power* over them, and it is only our bodies that are *reduced to dust and powder.* Our *favorite* speculations still find encouragement, and we make as *great* a figure in the *eye of the world, or* perhaps *a greater,* than in our lifetime. The demands of our self-love are *thus* satisfied [,and these are the most imperious and unremitting]. Besides, if by *our* intellectual superiority we survive ourselves in this world, by *our virtues and faith* we *may attain* an interest in another and a higher state of being, and *may thus be recipients* at the same time of men and of angels.

> "E'en from the tomb the voice of Nature cries,
> E'en in our ashes live their wonted fires."[22]

As we *grow old, our sense* of the value of time *becomes vivid.* Nothing else, indeed, seems of any consequence. We can never *cease* wondering *that* that which has ever been should cease to be. We find many things remain the same: why, then, should there be change in us? *This adds a convulsive grasp of whatever is*, a sense of a fallacious hollowness in all we see. Instead of the full, pulpy feeling of youth, [tasting existence and every object in it,] *all* is flat and *vapid*, —a whited sepulchre, fair without, but full of ravening and all uncleanness within. The world is a *witch* that puts us off with false shows and *appearances*. The *simplicity* of youth, *the confiding expectation, the boundless raptures,* are *gone*; [we only think of getting out of it as well as we can, and without any great mischance or annoyance. The flush of illusion, even the complacent retrospect of past joys and hopes, is over;] if we can slip out of *life* without *indignity,* can *escape with little* bodily infirmity, and frame our minds to the *calm and respectable* composure of *still-life* before we *return to physical nothingness*, it is as much as we can expect. We do not *die wholly at our deaths*: we have mouldered away gradually long before. Faculty after faculty, [interest after interest,] attachment after attachment, *disappear*: we are torn from ourselves while living, year after year *sees us no longer the same,* and death only consigns the last fragment of what we were to the grave. That we should *wear out by slow stages*, and dwindle *at last* into nothing, is not *wonderful,* when even in our prime *our* strongest impressions leave *little trace but for the moment, and we are the creatures of petty circumstance*. How little effect is *made* on us *in our best days* by the books we have read, the scenes we have witnessed, the *sensations* we have gone through! Think only of *the feelings* we experience in reading a *fine* romance [one of Sir Walter's[23], for instance;] what beauty, what sublimity, what *interest*, what heart-rending emotions! You would suppose *the feelings you then experienced* would last for ever, or subdue the mind to *their own harmony and tone: while we are reading*, it seems as if nothing could ever *put us out of our way or trouble us:* —the first splash of mud that we get on entering the street, the *first twopence we are cheated out of*, *the feeling* vanishes clean out of our *minds*, and we become *the prey of petty* and annoying circumstance. The mind *soars* to the lofty: it is at home in the groveling, the disagreeable, and the little. [And yet we wonder that age should be feeble and querulous, —that the freshness of youth should fade away. Both worlds would hardly satisfy the extravagance of our desires and of our presumption.]

NOTES

1. **my brother:** i.e. John Hazlitt, a portrait painter
2. **The vast, the unbounded prospect lies before us:** from Addison's *Cato*, V. i. 13
3. **bear a charmed life:** from *Macbeth*, V. viii. 12
4. **Bidding the lovely scenes at distance hail:** from Collins's *The Passions, An Ode for Music*, l. 32— "And bade the lovely scenes at distance hail!"
5. **mantling:** frothing
6. **the wine of life is drunk:** from *Macbeth*, II . iii. 100— "The wine of life is drawn..."
7. **play at hide-and-seek with:** trifle with
8. **the foolish fat scullion in Sterne:** See Laurence Sterne's *Tristram Shandy*, Book V, Chapter VII.
9. **sine die:** (Lat.) indefinitely
10. **the "feast of reason and flow of soul":** Pope's *Imitations of Horace*, Satire I. l. 128
11. **raree-show:** spectacle
12. **Tyre:** the ancient Phoenician seaport on the southwest coast of Lebanon
13. **Sidon:** the chief city of ancient Phoenicia
14. **Babylon:** the chief city of ancient Mesopotamia on the Euphrates
15. **Susa:** an ancient city north of the Persian Gulf, capital of the Persian Empire
16. **the mighty world of eye and ear:** Wordsworth's *Tintern Abbey*, ll. 105-6

17. **stock-dove:** small kind of wood pigeon
18. **the Vatican:** the Pope's palace and official residence on Vatican Hill in Rome
19. *divinoe particula auroe*: (Lat.) divine particle of life
20. **Rembrandt:** Rembrandt Harmensz van Rijn (1606–1669), the great Dutch painter
21. **I started in life with the French Revolution, and I have lived, alas! to see the end of it:** Hazlitt was one of the most loyal English supporters of the French Revolution.
22. **"E'en from the tomb the voice of Nature cries,/E'en in our ashes live their wonted fires.":** from Gray's *Elegy Written in a Country Churchyard*, ll. 91-92
23. **Sir Walter:** Sir Walter Scott (1771–1832), Scottish historical novelist and romantic poet

OF FAMILIAR STYLE

It is not easy to write a familiar style. Many people mistake a familiar for a vulgar style, and suppose that to write without affectation is to write at random. On the contrary, there is nothing that requires more precision, and, if I may so say, purity of expression, than the style I am speaking of. It utterly rejects not only all unmeaning pomp, but all low, cant phrases, and loose, unconnected, ***slipshod*** allusions. It is not to take the first word that offers, but the best word in common use; it is not to throw words together in any combinations we please, but to follow and avail ourselves of the true idiom of the language. To write a genuine familiar or truly English style, is to write as any one would speak in common conversation, who had a thorough command and choice of words, or who could discourse with ease, force, and perspicuity, setting aside all pedantic and oratorical flourishes. Or to give another illustration, to write naturally is the same thing in regard to common conversation, as to read naturally is in regard to common speech. It does not follow that it is an easy thing to give the true accent and inflection to the words you utter, because you do not attempt to rise above the level of ordinary life and colloquial speaking. You do not assume indeed the solemnity of the pulpit, or the tone of stage declamation: neither are you at liberty to gabble on at a venture[1], without emphasis or discretion, or to resort to vulgar dialect or clownish pronunciation. You must steer a middle course. You are tied down to a given and appropriate articulation, which is determined by the habitual associations between sense and sound, and which you can only hit by entering into the author's meaning, as you must find the proper words and style to express yourself by fixing your thoughts on the subject you have to write about. Any one may mouth out a passage with a theatrical cadence, or get upon stilts to tell his thoughts; but to speak or write with propriety and simplicity is a more difficult task. Thus it is easy to affect a pompous style, to use a word twice as big as the thing you want to express: it is not so easy to pitch upon the very word that exactly fits it. Out of eight or ten words equally common, equally intelligible, with nearly equal pretensions, it is a matter of some nicety and discrimination to pick out the very one, the preferableness of which is scarcely perceptible, but decisive. The reason why I object to Dr. Johnson's style is, that there is no disrimination, no variety in it. He uses none but "tall, opaque words,"[2] taken from the "first row of the rubric"[3]: words with the greatest number of syllables, or Latin phrases with merely English terminations. If a fine style depended on this sort of arbitrary pretension, it would be fair to judge of an author's elegance by the measurement of his words, and the substitution of foreign circumlocutions (with no precise associations) for the mother tongue. How simple it is to be dignified without ease, to be pompous without meaning! Surely, it is but a mechanical rule for avoiding what is low to be always pedantic and affected. It is clear you cannot use a vulgar English word, if you never use a common English word at all. A fine tact is shown in adhering to those which are perfectly common, and yet never falling into any expressions which are debased by disgusting circumstances, or which owe their signification and point to technical or professional allusions. A truly natural or familiar style can never be quaint or vulgar, for this reason, that it is of universal force and applicability, and that quaintness and vulgarity arise out of the immediate connection of certain words with coarse and disagreeable, or with confined ideas. The last form what we understand by *cant* or *slang* phrases. To give an example of what is not very clear in the general statement, I should say that the phrase ***To cut with a knife***, or ***To cut a piece of wood***, is perfectly free from vulgarity, because it is perfectly common; but *to cut an acquaintance* is not quite unexceptionable, because it is not perfectly common or intelligible, and has hardly yet escaped out of the limits of slang phraseology. I should hardly therefore use the word in this sense without putting it in italics as a license of expression, to be received ***cum grano salis***[4]. All provincial or bye-phrases come under the same mark of reprobation-all such as the writer transfers to the page from his fireside or a particular ***coterie***, or that he invents for his own sole use and convenience. I conceive that words are like money, not the worse for being common, but that it is the stamp of custom alone that gives them circulation or value. I am fastidious in this respect, and would almost as soon coin the currency of the realm as counterfeit the King's English. I never invented or gave a new and unauthorized meaning to any word but one single one (the term ***impersonal*** applied to feelings) and that was in an abstruse metaphysical discussion to express a very difficult distinction. I have been (I know) loudly accused of reveling in vulgarisms and broken English. I cannot speak to that point; but so far I plead guilty to the determined use of acknowledged idioms and common elliptical expressions. I am not sure that the critics in question know the one from the other, that is, can distinguish any medium between formal pedantry and the most barbarous solecism. As an author, I endeavor to employ plain words and popular modes of construction, as, were I a chapman and dealer, I should common weights and measures.

The proper force of words lies not in the words themselves, but in their application. A word may be a fine-sounding word of an unusual length, and very imposing from its learning and novelty, and yet in the connection in which it is introduced, may be quite pointless and irrelevant. It is not pomp or pretension, but the adaptation of the expression to the idea that clenches a writer's meaning: as it is not the size or glossiness of the materials, but their being fitted each to its place, that gives strength to the arch; or as the pegs and nails are as necessary to the support of the building as the large timbers, and more so than the mere showy, unsubstantial ornaments. I hate anything that occupies more space than it is worth. I hate to see a load of bandboxes go along the street, and I hate to see a parcel of big words without anything in them. A person who does not deliberately dispose of all his thoughts alike in cumbrous draperies and flimsy disguises, may strike out twenty varieties of familiar everyday language, each coming somewhat nearer to the feeling he wants to convey, and at last not hit upon that particular and only one, which may be said to be identical with the exact expression in his mind. This would seem to show that Mr. Cobbett[5] is hardly right in saying that the first word that occurs is always the best. It may be a very good one; and yet a better may present itself on reflection or from time to time. It should be suggested naturally, however, and spontaneously, from a fresh and lively conception of the subject. We seldom succeed by trying at improvement, or by merely substituting one word for another that we are not satisfied with, as we cannot recollect the name of a place or person by merely plaguing ourselves about it. We wander farther from the point by persisting in a wrong scent, but it starts up accidentally in the memory when we least expected it, by touching some link in the chain of previous association.

There are those who hoard up and make a cautious display of nothing but rich and rare phraseology: ancient medals, obscure coins, and Spanish pieces of eight[6]. They are very curious to inspect; but I myself would neither offer nor take them in the course of exchange. A sprinkling of archaisms is not amiss; but a tissue of obsolete expressions is more fit *for keep than wear*. I do not say I would not use any phrase that had been brought into fashion before the middle or the end of the last century; but I should be shy of using any that had not been employed by any approved author during the whole of that time. Words, like clothes, get old-fashioned, or mean and ridiculous, when they have been for some time laid aside. Mr. Lamb[7] is the only imitator of old English style I can read with pleasure; and he is so thoroughly imbued with the spirit of his authors, that the idea of imitation is almost done away. There is an inward unction, a marrowy vein[8] both in the thought and feeling, an intuition, deep and lively, of his subject, that carries off any quaintness or awkwardness arising from an antiquated style and dress. The matter is completely his own, though the manner is assumed. Perhaps his ideas are altogether so marked and individual, as to require their point and pungency to be neutralized by the affectation of a singular but traditional form of conveyance. Tricked out in the prevailing costume, they would probably seem more startling and out of the way. The old English authors, Burton[9], Fuller[10], Coryate[11], Sir Thomas Browne[12], are a kind of mediators between us and the more eccentric and whimsical modern, reconciling us to his peculiarities. I do not, however, know how far this is the case or not, till he condescends to write like one of us. I must confess that what I like best of his papers under the signature of Elia (still I do not presume, amidst such excellence, to decide what is most excellent) is the account of **Mrs. Battle's Opinions on Whist**, which is also the most free from obsolete allusions and turns of expressions—

A well of native English undefiled[13].

To those acquainted with his admired prototypes, these **Essays** of the ingenious and highly gifted author have the same sort of charm and relish that Erasmus's ***Colloquies***[14] or a fine piece of modern Latin have to the classical scholar. Certainly, I do not know any borrowed pencil that has more power or felicity of execution than the one of which I have here been speaking.

 It is as easy to write a gaudy style without ideas as it is to spread a pallet of showy colors, or to smear in a flaunting transparency[15]. "What do you read?" — "Words, words, words."[16] — "What is the matter?" — "***Nothing***," it might be answered. The florid style is the reverse of the familiar. The last is employed as an unvarnished medium to convey ideas; the first is resorted to as a spangled veil to conceal the want of them. When there is nothing to be set down but words, it costs little to have them fine. Look through the dictionary, and cull out a ***florilegium***[17], rival the ***tulipomania***[18]. ***Rouge*** high enough, and never mind the natural complexion. The vulgar, who are not in the secret, will admire the look of preternatural health and vigor; and the fashionable, who regard only appearances, will be delighted with the imposition. Keep to your sounding[19] generalities, your tinkling phrases, and all will be well. Swell out an unmeaning truism to a perfect tympany of style[20]. A thought, a distinction is the rock on which all this brittle cargo of verbiage splits at once. Such writers have merely ***verbal*** imaginations, that retain nothing but words. Or their puny thoughts have dragon-wings[21], all green and gold. They soar far above the vulgar failing of the ***Sermo humi obrepens***[22]— their most ordinary speech is never short of an hyperbole, splendid, imposing, vague, incomprehensible, magniloquent, a cento[23] of sounding commonplaces. If some of us, whose "ambition is more lowly," pry a little too narrowly into nooks and corners to pick up a number of "unconsidered trifles," they never once direct their eyes or lift their hands to seize on any but the most gorgeous, tarnished, threadbare patchwork set of phrases, the left-off finery of poetic extravagance, transmitted down through successive generations of barren pretenders. If they criticize actors and actresses, a huddled phantasmagoria of feathers, spangles, floods of light, and oceans of sound float before their morbid sense, which they paint in the style of Ancient Pistol[24]. Not a glimpse can you get of the merits or defects of the performers: they are hidden in a profusion of barbarous epithets and willful rhodomontade. Our hypercritics are not thinking of these little fantoccini beings[25]—

>That strut and fret their hour upon the stage[26]—

but of tall phantoms of words, abstractions, ***genera*** and ***species***, sweeping clauses, periods that unite the Poles[27], forced alliterations, astounding antitheses—

>And on their pens ***Fustian*** sits plumed[28].

If they describe kings and queens, it is an Eastern pageant. The Coronation at either House is nothing to it. We get at four repeated images—a curtain, a throne, a scepter, and a footstool. These are with them the wardrobe of a lofty imagination; and they turn their servile strains to servile uses. Do we read a description of pictures? It is not a reflection of tones and hues which "nature's own sweet and cunning hand laid on,[29]" but piles of precious stones, rubies, pearls, emeralds, Golconda's[30] mines, and all the blazonry of art. Such persons are in fact besotted with words, and their brains are turned with the glittering, but empty and sterile phantoms of things. Personifications, capital letters, seas of sunbeams, visions of glory, shining inscriptions, the figures of a transparency, Britannia with her shield, or Hope leaning on an anchor, make up their stock in trade. They may be considered as ***hieroglyphical*** writers. Images stand out in their minds isolated and important merely in themselves, without any groundwork of feeling—there is no context in their imaginations. Words affect them in the same way, by the mere sound, that is, by their possible, not by their actual application to the subject in hand. They are fascinated by first appearances, and have no sense of consequences. Nothing more is meant by them than meets the ear: they understand or feel nothing more than meets their eye. The web and texture of the universe, and of the heart of man, is a mystery to them: they have no faculty that strikes a chord in unison with it. They cannot get beyond the daubings of fancy, the varnish of sentiment. Objects are not linked to feelings, words to things, but images revolve in splendid mockery, words represent themselves in their strange rhapsodies. The categories of such a mind are pride and ignorance—pride in outside show, to which they sacrifice everything, and ignorance of the true worth and hidden structure both of words and things. With a sovereign contempt for what is familiar and natural, they are the slaves of vulgar affection—of a routine of highflown phrases. Scorning to imitate realities, they are unable to invent anything, to strike out one original idea. They are not copyists of nature, it is true; but they are the poorest of all plagiarists, the plagiarists of words. All is farfetched, dear-bought, artificial, oriental in subject and allusion: all is mechanical, conventional, vapid, formal, pedantic in style and execution. They startle and confound the understanding of the reader, by the remoteness and obscurity of their illustrations: they soothe the ear by the monotony of the same everlasting round of circuitous metaphors. They are the **mock school** in poetry and prose. They flounder about between fustian in expression, and bathos in sentiment. They tantalize the fancy but never reach the head nor touch the heart. Their Temple of Fame is like a shadowy structure raised by Dullness to Vanity, or like Cowper's description of the Empress of Russia's palace of ice, "as worthless as in show 'twas glittering"[31]—

It smiled, and it was cold![32]

NOTES

1. **at a venture:** by chance
2. **tall, opaque words:** exaggerated, obscure words (quoted from Sterne's ***Tristram Shandy***)
3. **the "first row of the rubric":** the title of a book printed in red letters
4. ***cum grano salis*:** (Lat.) with a grain of salt; with reservation
5. **Mr. Cobbett:** William Cobbett (1762–1835), political writer, author of ***Rural Rides, A Grammar of the English Language***, etc.

6. **Spanish pieces of eight:** Spanish coins each worth eight reals
7. **Mr. Lamb:** Charles Lamb (1775–1834), essayist and critic, author of *Essays of Elia* and *Last Essays of Elia*
8. **a marrowy vein:** a vital strain
9. **Burton:** Robert Burton (1577–1640), English clergyman and author of *The Anatomy of Melancholy*
10. **Fuller:** Thomas Fuller (1608–1661), English clergyman and author of *The Holy State*, *The Profane State*, and *The Worthies of England*
11. **Coryate:** Thomas Coryate (1577–1617), English traveller and author of *Coryate's Crudities*
12. **Sir Thomas Browne:** author of *Religio Medici* and *Hydirotaphia*
13. **A well of native English undefiled.:** from Spenser's *The Pairie Queene*, IV. ii. 32— Dan Chaucer, well of native English undefiled
14. **Erasmus's *Colloquies*:** Desiderius Erasmus (1467–1536) was a great Dutch humanist. His Latin *Colloquia* is a vivid and entertaining account of the manners of his time.
15. **a flaunting transparency:** a gaudy picture on some transparent material
16. **"What do you read?"—"Words, words, words.":** from *Hamlet*, II.ii
17. *florilegium*: flower-picking; (here) showy word or expression
18. *tulipomania*: craze for tulips
19. **sounding:** having more sound than sense
20. **a perfect tympany of style:** a pomposity of style
21. **dragon-wings:** dragon-flies
22. *Sermo humi obrepens*: speech that crawls upon the ground, from Horace, *Ep.*, II. i
23. **cento:** patchwork composition
24. **Ancient Pistol:** ensign Pistol, a braggart and swaggerer in Shakespeare's *Henry IV* and *Henry V*
25. **fantoccini beings:** puppets
26. **That strut and fret their hour upon the stage:** from *Macbeth*, V. v
27. **periods that unite the Poles:** periodic sentences long enough to connect the North and the South Pole
28. **And on their pens *Fustian* sits plumed:** a humorous imitation of Milton's expression—

"and on his crest/sat Horror plumed" (***Paradise Lost***, IV.988-989)
29. **nature's own sweet and cunning hand laid on:** from ***Twelfth Night***, I. v
30. **Golconda:** a city in South central India, noted for diamond-cutting in the 16th century
31. **As worthless as in show 'twas glittering:** Cowper's phrase reads "as worthless, as it seem'd/Intrinsically precious", ***The Task***, V. 174-5
32. **It smiled, and it was cold!:** from ***The Task***, V. 176

LEIGH HUNT

(1784–1859)

Leigh Hunt was an English journalist and poet. He was born in Middlesex on October 19, 1784, the son of an improvident clergyman. After an education at Christ's Hospital, London, he became a journalist. From 1813 to 1815 he was imprisoned for libelling the Prince Regent, and his fellow writers looked upon him as a hero. He was a friend of several eminent writers—Hazlitt, Lamb, Keats, and Shelley. A journalist all his life, he was granted a Civil List pension in 1847, and died on August 28, 1859.

Hunt's journalistic career was brilliant; he edited a series of periodicals: **The Examiner** (1808–1821), **The Reflector** (1810–1811), **The Indicator** (1819–1821), **The Liberal** (1822–1823), **The Companion** (1828), **The Chat of the Week** (1830), **The Tatler** (1830–1832), and **Leigh Hunt's London Journal** (1834–1835). His famous poems are *The Story of Rimini* (1816) and a few lyrics such as "Jenny Kissed Me" and "The River Nile". He wrote a large number of essays, which reflect his cheerful spirit and his love for literature and art. Some of them can still be read with pleasure. His most memorable work is his ***Autobiography*** (1850), which recounts a troubled and interesting career bound up with the literary history of the first half of the 19th century. Carlyle thought it "the best book of the autobiographic kind in the English language". Hunt's prose has sometimes a whimsical charm but is often heavily mannered.

A FEW THOUGHTS ON SLEEP

This is an article for the reader to think of when he or she is warm in bed, a little before he goes to sleep, the clothes at his ear, and the wind moaning in some distant crevice.

" Blessings," exclaimed Sancho[1], "on him that first invented sleep! It wraps a man all round like a cloak."[2] It is a delicious moment certainly—that of being well nestled in bed, and feeling that you shall drop gently to sleep. The good is to come, not past: the limbs have been just tired enough to render the remaining in one posture delightful: the labour of the day is done. A gentle failure of the perceptions comes creeping over one, the spirit of consciousness disengages itself more and more, with slow and hushing degrees, like a mother detaching her hand from that of her sleeping child; the mind seems to have a balmy lid closing over it, like the eye; — 'tis closing; — 'tis more closing; — 'tis closed. The mysterious spirit has gone to take its airy rounds.

It is said that sleep is best before midnight: and Nature herself, with her darkness and chilling dews, informs us so. There is another reason for going to bed betimes; for it is universally acknowledged that lying late in the morning is a great shortener of life. At least, it is never found in company with longevity. It also tends to make people corpulent. But these matters belong rather to the subject of early rising than of sleep.

Sleep at a late hour in the morning is not half so pleasant as the more timely one. It is sometimes, however, excusable, especially to a watchful or overworked head; neither can we deny the seducing merits of " t'other doze"[3], the pleasing wilfulness of nestling in a new posture, when you know you ought to be up, like the rest of the house. But then you cut up the day, and your sleep the next night.

In the course of the day few people think of sleeping, except after dinner; and then it is often rather a hovering and nodding on the borders of sleep than sleep itself. This is a privilege allowable, we think, to none but the old, or the sickly, or the very tired and care-worn; and it should be well understood before it is exercised in company. To escape into slumber from an argument; or to take it as an affair of course, only between you and your biliary duct; or to assent with involuntary nods to all that you have just been disputing, is not so well; much less, to sit nodding and tottering beside a lady; or to be in danger of dropping your head into the fruit-plate or your host's face; or of waking up, and saying "Just so" to the bark of a dog; or "Yes, madam," to the black[4] at your elbow.

Care-worn people, however, might refresh themselves oftener with day-sleep than they do; if their bodily state is such as to dispose them to it. It is a mistake to suppose that all care is wakeful. People sometimes sleep, as well as wake, by reason of their sorrow. The difference seems to depend upon the nature of their temperament; though in the *most* excessive cases, sleep is perhaps Nature's never-failing relief, as swooning is upon the rack[5]. A person with jaundice in his blood shall lie down and go to sleep at noonday, when another of a different complexion shall find his eyes as unclosable as a statue's, though he has had no sleep for nights together. Without meaning to lessen the dignity of suffering, which has quite enough to do with its waking hours, it is this that may often account for the profound sleeps enjoyed the night before hazardous battles, executions, and other demands upon an over-excited spirit.

The most complete and healthy sleep that can be taken in the day is in summer-time, out in a field. There is, perhaps, no solitary sensation so exquisite as that of slumbering on the grass or hay, shaded from the hot sun by a tree, with the consciousness of a fresh but light air running through the wide atmosphere, and the sky stretching far overhead upon all sides. Earth and heaven and a placid humanity seem to have the creation to themselves. There is nothing between the slumberer and the naked and glad innocence of nature.

Next to this, but at a long interval, the most relishing snatch of slumber out of bed is the one which a tired person takes before he retires for the night, while lingering in his sitting-room. The consciousness of being very sleepy, and of having the power to go to bed immediately, gives great zest to the unwillingness to move. Sometimes he sits nodding in his chair; but the sudden and leaden jerks of the head to which a state of great sleepiness renders him liable, are generally too painful for so luxurious a moment; and he gets into a more legitimate posture, sitting sideways with his head on the chair-back, or throwing his legs up at once on another chair, and half reclining. It is curious, however, to find how long an inconvenient posture will be borne for the sake of this foretaste of repose. The worst of it is, that on going to bed the charm sometimes vanishes; perhaps from the colder temperature of the chamber; for a fireside is a great opiate.

Speaking of the painful positions into which a sleepy lounger will get himself, it is amusing to think of the more fantastic attitudes that so often take place in bed. If we could add anything to the numberless things that have been said about sleep by the poets, it would be upon this point. Sleep never shows himself a greater leveller. A man in his waking moments may look as proud and self-possessed as he pleases. He may walk proudly, he may sit proudly, he may eat his dinner proudly; he may shave himself with an air of infinite superiority; in a word, he may show himself grand and absurd upon the most trifling occasions. But Sleep plays the petrifying magician. He arrests the proudest lord as well as the humblest clown in the most ridiculous postures: so that if you could draw a grandee from his bed without waking him, no limb-twisting fool[6] in a pantomime should create wilder laughter. The toy with the string between its legs is hardly a posture-master more extravagant. Imagine a despot lifted up to the gaze of his valets, with his eyes shut, his mouth open, his left hand under his right ear, his other twisted and hanging helplessly before him like an idiot's, one knee lifted up, and the other leg stretched out, or both knees huddled up together; —what a scarecrow to lodge majestic power in!

But Sleep is kindly even in his tricks, and the poets have treated him with proper reverence. According to the ancient mythologists he had even one of the Graces[7] to wife. He had a thousand sons, of whom the chief were Morpheus[8], or the Shaper; Icelos, or the Likely; Phantasus, the Fancy; and Phobetor, the Terror. His dwelling some writers place in a dull and darkling part of the earth; others, with greater compliment, in heaven; and others, with another kind of propriety, by the sea-shore. There is a good description of it in Ovid[9]; but in these abstracted tasks of poetry the moderns outvie the ancients; and there is nobody who has built his bower for him so finely as Spenser. Archimago[10], in the first book of the ***Faerie Queene*** (Canto I. st. 39), sends a little spirit down to Morpheus to fetch him a Dream:

> "He, making speedy way through spersed ayre,
> And through the world of waters, wide and deepe,
> To Morpheus' house doth hastily repaire.
> Amid the bowels of the earth full steepe
> And low, where dawning day doth never peepe,
> His dwelling is. There Tethys[11] his wet bed
> Doth ever wash; and Cynthia[12] still doth steepe
> In silver dew his ever-drouping head,
> Whiles sad Night over him her mantle black doth spred.
>
> "And more to lull him in his slumber soft
> A trickling streame from high rocke tumbling downe,
> And ever-drizzling rain upon the loft,
> Mixed with a murmuring winde, much like the soune
> Of swarming bees, did cast him in a swoune.
> No other noise, nor people's troublous cryes,
> As still are wont to annoy the walled towne,
> Might there be heard; but careless Quiet lyes,
> Wrapt in eternall silence, far from enimyes."

Chaucer has drawn the cave of the same god with greater simplicity[13]; but nothing can have a more deep and sullen effect than his cliffs and cold running waters. It seems as real as an actual solitude, or some quaint old picture in a book of travels in Tartary[14]. He is telling the story of Ceyx and Alcyone[15] in the poem called his ***Dream***. Juno tells a messenger to go to Morpheus and "bid him creep into the body" of the drowned king, to let his wife know the fatal event by his apparition.

> "This messenger tooke leave, and went
> Upon his way; and never he stent[16]
> Till he came to the dark valley,
> That stant betweene rockes twey.
> There never yet grew corne, ne gras.
> Ne tree, ne nought, that aught was.
> Beast, ne man, ne naught else;
> Save that there were a few wells
> Came running fro the cliffs adowne,
> That made a deadly sleeping soune,
> And runnen downe right by a cave,
> That was under a rocky grave,
> Amid the valley, wonder-deepe.
> There these goddis lay asleepe,
> Morpheus and Eclympasteire,
> That was the god of Sleepis heire,
> That slept and did none other worke."

Where the credentials of this new son and heir, Eclympasteire, are to be found, we know not; but he acts very much, it must be allowed, like an heir-presumptive, in sleeping and doing "none other work".

We dare not trust ourselves with many quotations upon sleep from the poets; they are so numerous as well as beautiful. We must content ourselves with mentioning that our two most favourite passages are one in the **Philoctetes** of Sophocles[17], admirable for its contrast to a scene of terrible agony, which it closes; and the other the following address in Beaumont and Fletcher's tragedy of **Valentinian**[18], the hero of which is also a sufferer under bodily torment. He is in a chair, slumbering; and these most exquisite lines are gently sung with music:

> "Care-charming Sleep, thou easer of all woes,
> Brother to Death, sweetly thyself dispose
> On this afflicted prince. Fall like a cloud
> In gentle showers: give nothing that is loud
> Or painful to his slumbers: easy, sweet,
> And as a purling stream, thou son of Night,
> Pass by his troubled senses; sing his pain
> Like hollow murmuring wind, or silver rain:
> Into this prince, gently, oh gently slide,
> And kiss him into slumbers, like a bride."

How earnest and prayer-like are these pauses! How lightly sprinkled, and yet how deeply settling, like rain, the fancy! How quiet, affectionate, and perfect the conclusion!

Sleep is most graceful in an infant, soundest in one who has been tired in the open air, completest to the seaman after a hard voyage, most welcome to the mind haunted with one idea, most touching to look at in the parent that has wept, lightest in the playful child, proudest in the bride adored.

NOTES

1. **Sancho:** the squire of Don Quixote in ***Don Quixote***
2. **Blessings on him that first invented sleep!...:** See ***Don Quixote,*** Part II , Chapter 68.
3. **t'other doze:** the other doze, another short light sleep
4. **the black:** the negro servant
5. **upon the rack:** under torture
6. **limb-twisting fool:** clown, harlequin
7. **the Graces:** (Gr. myth.) the three daughters of Zeus and Eurynome and attendants of Aphrodite
8. **Morpheus:** the god of dreams
9. **a good description of it in Ovid:** *Metamorphoses,* xi. 592 sqq
10. **Archimago:** the great enchanter symbolizing Hypocrisy

11. **Tethys:** (Gr. myth.) daughter of Uranus and Ge, wife of Oceanus, and mother of the Oceanids and the river-gods
12. **Cynthia:** Diana, goddess of the moon
13. **Chaucer has drawn the cave of the same god with greater simplicity:** *The Book of the Duchess*, 153 sqq
14. **Tartary:** a vast region in East Europe and Central and West Asia under the control of Tartar tribes in the late Middle Ages
15. **Ceyx and Alcyone:** (Gr. myth.) Ceyx was king of Trachis in Thessaly and husband of Alcyone.
16. **stent:** stopped
17. **in the *Philoctetes* of Sophocles:** *Philoctetes*, 827 sqq
18. **in Beaumont and Fletcher's tragedy of *Valentinian*:** *Valentinian*, Act V. Sc. ii. The fifth line of the quoted passage should be "Or painful to his slumbers: easy, light".

THOMAS DE QUINCEY

(1785–1859)

Thomas De Quincey was an English essayist and critic. He was born in Manchester on August 15, 1785, the son of a rich merchant, and educated at Manchester Grammar School (1801–1802) and at Worcester College, Oxford (1803–1808), which he left without taking a degree. From 1809 to 1821 he lived in Grasmere, where he associated with the Lake Poets. He moved to London in 1821, and to Edinburgh in 1828. He died on December 8, 1859.

De Quincey contributed to various periodicals, including **London Magazine** and **Blackwood's Magazine**. He lived by journalism and elevated it to literature. His literary output is voluminous. **Confessions of an English Opium-Eater** (1822), his autobiography, is his most famous book. His other well-known works are: **Suspiria de Profundis** ("Sighs from the Depths", 1845), a sequel to the **Confessions; Recollections of the Lake Poets** (1834–1839), which contains vivid portraits of Coleridge, Southey, William and Dorothy Wordsworth, and sympathetic comments on the work of the three poets; **The English Mail Coach** (1849), a collection of three essays concerning the faculty of dreaming; and "On the Knocking at the Gate in **Macbeth**", a critical essay highly valuable for its psychological insights. As a writer De Quincey made good use of his observant eye, his sensitive imagination, and his wide knowledge of life and literature. He was also an innovator in style. His prose is impassioned, ornate, and poetical.

ON THE KNOCKING AT THE GATE IN *MACBETH*

From my boyish days I had always felt a great perplexity on one point in **Macbeth**. It was this: The knocking at the gate which succeeds to the murder of Duncan[1] produced to my feelings an effect for which I never could account. The effect was that it reflected back upon the murderer a peculiar awfulness and a depth of solemnity; yet, however obstinately I endeavoured with my understanding to comprehend this, for many years I never could see *why* it should produce such an effect.

Here I pause for one moment, to exhort the reader never to pay any attention to his understanding when it stands in opposition to any other faculty of his mind. The mere understanding, however useful and indispensable, is the meanest faculty in the human mind, and the most to be distrusted; and yet the great majority of people trust to nothing else—which may do for ordinary life, but not for philosophical purposes. Of this out of ten thousand instances that I might produce I will cite one. Ask of any person whatsoever who is not previously prepared for the demand by a knowledge of the perspective to draw in the rudest way the commonest appearance which depends upon the laws of that science, —as, for instance, to represent the effect of two walls standing at right angles to each other, or the appearance of the houses on each side of a street as seen by a person looking down the street from one extremity. Now, in all cases, unless the person has happened to observe in pictures how it is that artists produce these effects, he will be utterly unable to make the smallest approximation to it. Yet why? For he has actually seen the effect every day of his life. The reason is that he allows his understanding to overrule his eyes. His understanding, which includes no intuitive knowledge of the laws of vision, can furnish him with no reason why a line which is known and can be proved to be a horizontal line should not *appear* a horizontal line; a line that made any angle with the perpendicular less than a right angle, would seem to him to indicate that his houses were all tumbling down together. Accordingly, he makes the line of his houses a horizontal line, and fails, of course, to produce the effect demanded. Here, then, is one instance out of many in which not only the understanding is allowed to overrule the eyes, but where the understanding is positively allowed to obliterate the eyes, as it were; for not only does the man believe the evidence of his understanding in opposition to that of his eyes, but (what is monstrous!) the idiot is not aware that his eyes ever gave such evidence. He does not know that he has seen (and therefore *quoad*[2] his consciousness has *not* seen) that which he *has* seen every day of his life.

But to return from this digression. My understanding could furnish no reason why the knocking at the gate in *Macbeth* should produce any effect, direct or reflected. In fact, my understanding said positively that it could *not* produce any effect. But I knew better; I felt that it did; and I waited and clung to the problem until further knowledge should enable me to solve it. At length, in 1812, Mr. Williams made his *debut* on the stage of Ratcliffe Highway, and executed those unparalleled murders which have procured for him such a brilliant and undying reputation[3]. On which murders, by the way, I must observe that in one respect they have had an ill effect, by making the connoisseur in murder very fastidious in his taste, and dissatisfied by anything that has been since done in that line. All other murders look pale by the deep crimson of his; and, as an amateur[4] once said to me in a querulous tone, "There has been absolutely nothing *doing* since his time, or nothing that's worth speaking of." But this is wrong; for it is unreasonable to expect all men to be great artists, and born with the genius of Mr. Williams. Now, it will be remembered that in the first of these murders (that of the Marrs) the same incident (of a knocking at the door[5] soon after the work of extermination was complete) did actually occur which the genius of Shakespeare has invented; and all good judges, and the most eminent dilettanti, acknowledged the felicity of Shakespeare's suggestion as soon as it was actually realised. Here, then, was a fresh proof that I was right in relying on my own feeling, in opposition to my understanding; and I again set myself to study the problem. At length I solved it to my own satisfaction; and my solution is this: Murder, in ordinary cases, where the sympathy is wholly directed to the case of the murdered person, is an incident of coarse and vulgar horror; and for this reason—that it flings the interest exclusively upon the natural but ignoble instinct by which we cleave to life; an instinct which, as being indispensable to the primal law of self-preservation, is the same in kind (though different in degree) amongst all living creatures. This instinct, therefore, because it annihilates all distinctions, and degrades the greatest of men to the level of "the poor beetle that we tread on[6]," exhibits human nature in its most abject and humiliating attitude. Such an attitude would little suit the purposes of the poet. What then must he do? He must throw the interest on the murderer. Our sympathy must be with *him* (of course I mean a sympathy of comprehension, a sympathy by which we enter into his feelings, and are made to understand them—not a sympathy of pity or approbation). In the murdered person, all strife of thought, all flux and reflux of passion and of purpose, are crushed by one overwhelming panic; the fear of instant death smites him "with its petrific mace[7]." But in the murderer, such a murderer as a poet will condescend to, there must be raging some great storm of passion-jealousy, ambition, vengeance, hatred-which will create a hell within him; and into this hell we are to look.

In *Macbeth*, for the sake of gratifying his own enormous and teeming faculty of creation, Shakespeare has introduced two murderers; and, as usual in his hands, they are remarkably discriminated; but, —though in Macbeth the strife of mind is greater than in his wife, the tiger spirit not so awake, and his feelings caught chiefly by contagion from her, —yet, as both were finally involved in the guilt of murder, the murderous mind of necessity is finally to be presumed in both. This was to be expressed; and on its own account, as well as to make it a more proportionable antagonist to the unoffending nature of their victim, "the gracious Duncan[8]," and adequately to expound "the deep damnation of his taking off[9]," this was to be expressed with peculiar energy. We were to be made to feel that the human nature, —*i.e.*, the divine nature of love and mercy, spread through the hearts of all creatures, and seldom utterly withdrawn from man, —was gone, vanished, extinct, and that the fiendish nature had taken its place. And, as this effect is marvellously accomplished in the *dialogues* and *soliloquies* themselves, so it is finally consummated by the expedient under consideration; and it is to this that I now solicit the reader's attention. If the reader has ever witnessed a wife, daughter, or sister in a fainting fit, he may chance to have observed that the most affecting moment in such a spectacle is *that* in which a sigh and a stirring announce the recommencement of suspended life. Or, if the reader has ever been present in a vast metropolis on the day when some great national idol was carried in funeral pomp to his grave, and, chancing to walk near the course through which it passed, has felt powerfully, in the silence and desertion of the streets, and in the stagnation of ordinary business, the deep interest which at that moment was possessing the heart of man, —if all at once he should hear the death-like stillness broken up by the sound of wheels rattling away from the scene, and making known that the transitory vision was dissolved, he will be aware that at no moment was his sense of the complete suspension and pause in ordinary human concerns so full and affecting as at that moment when the suspension ceases, and the goings-on of human life are suddenly resumed. All action in any direction is best expounded, measured, and made apprehensible, by reaction. Now, apply this to the case in **Macbeth**. Here, as I have said, the retiring of the human heart and the entrance of the fiendish heart was to be expressed and made sensible. Another world has stepped in; and the murderers are taken out of the region of human things, human purposes, human desires. They are transfigured: Lady Macbeth is "unsexed"[10]; Macbeth has forgot that he was born of woman; both are conformed to the image of devils; and the world of devils is suddenly revealed. But how shall this be conveyed and made palpable? In order that a new world may step in, this world must for a time disappear. The murderers and the murder must be insulated—cut off by an immeasurable gulf from the ordinary tide and succession of human affairs—locked up and sequestered in some deep recess; we must be made sensible that the world of ordinary life is suddenly arrested, laid asleep, tranced, racked into a dread armistice; time must be annihilated, relation to things without abolished; and all must pass self-withdrawn into a deep syncope[11] and suspension of earthly passion. Hence it is that, when the deed is done, when the work of darkness is perfect, then the world of darkness passes away like a pageantry in the clouds: the knocking at the gate is heard, and it makes known audibly that the reaction has commenced; the human has made its reflux upon the fiendish; the pulses of life are beginning to beat again; and the re-establishment of the goings-on of the world in which we live first makes us profoundly sensible of the awful parenthesis that had suspended them.

O mighty poet! Thy works are not as those of other men, simply and merely great works of art, but are also like the phenomena of nature, like the sun and the sea, the stars and the flowers, like frost and snow, rain and dew, hail-storm and thunder, which are to be studied with entire submission of our own faculties, and in the perfect faith that in them there can be no too much or too little, nothing useless or inert, but that, the farther we press in our discoveries, the more we shall see proofs of design and self-supporting arrangement where the careless eye had seen nothing but accident!

NOTES

1. **the knocking at the gate which succeeds to the murder of Duncan:** In *Macbeth*, II. ii, Macbeth and his wife hear a startling knock at the gate just after they have murdered Duncan.
2. *quoad*: (Lat.) as regards
3. **At length, in 1812, Mr. Williams...undying reputation:** In December 1811 (*not* 1812) John Williams, a sailor, committed two horrible murders; he murdered the Marr family and twelve days later the Williamson family.
4. **an amateur:** a connoisseur of an art
5. **a knocking at the door:** a knocking at the door by a maidservant of the Marr family returning from the purchase of some food
6. **the poor beetle that we tread on:** See *Measure for Measure*, III. i. 79.
7. **with its petrific mace:** from *Paradise Lost*, x. 294 ("with his mace petrific")
8. **the gracious Duncan:** See *Macbeth*, III. i. 66.
9. **the deep damnation of his taking off:** See *Macbeth*, I. vii. 20.
10. **Lady Macbeth is "unsexed":** To harden her resolution for the murder of Duncan, Lady Macbeth calls on the spirits of hell to "unsex" her (*Macbeth*, I. v. 42).
11. **syncope:** faint

JOHN GIBSON LOCKHART

(1794–1854)

J. G. Lockhart was a Scottish journalist and biographer. He was born at Cambusnethan and educated at Glasgow University and at Balliol College, Oxford. A man with strong Tory views, he contributed to **Blackwood's Magazine** and edited from 1825 to 1853 **The Quarterly Review**. He was notorious for his wrong-headed attacks on most of the English Romantic writers. His four novels and many other works are now forgotten. He is chiefly remembered for **The Life of Sir Walter Scott** (1837–1838), a story of his father-in-law and one of the best biographies in the English language. The book is not without a partiality for its subject, but it is comprehensive, coherent, and full of intimate detail.

SCOTT'S WAY WITH HIS CHILDREN

Mr. Morritt's[1] mention of the "happy young family clustered round him" at Mr. Laidlaw's[2] *kirn*[3], reminds me that I ought to say a few words on Scott's method of treating his children in their early days. He had now two boys and two girls; —and he never had more. He was not one of those who take much delight in a mere infant; but no father ever devoted more time and tender care to his off-spring than he did to each of his, as they successively reached the age when they could listen to him, and understand his talk. Like their mute playmates, Camp[4] and the greyhounds, they had at all times free access to his study; he never considered their tattle as any disturbance; they went and came as pleased their fancy; he was always ready to answer their questions; and when they, unconscious how he was engaged, entreated him to lay down his pen and tell them a story, he would take them on his knee, repeat a ballad or a legend, kiss them, and set them down again to their marbles or ninepins, and resume his labour as if refreshed by the interruption. From a very early age he made them dine at table, and "to sit up to supper" was the great reward when they had been "very good bairns."[5] In short, he considered it as the highest duty as well as the sweetest pleasure of a parent to be the companion of his children; he partook all their little joys and sorrows, and made his kind unformal instructions to blend so easily and playfully with the current of their own sayings and doings, that so far from regarding him with any distant awe, it was never thought that any sport or diversion could go on in the right way, unless ***papa*** were of the party, or that the rainiest day could be dull, so he were at home.

Of the irregularity of his own education he speaks with considerable regret, in the autobiographical fragment written this year[6] at Ashestiel[7]; yet his practice does not look as if that feeling had been strongly rooted in his mind; —for he never did show much concern about regulating systematically what is usually called ***education*** in the case of his own children. It seemed, on the contrary, as if he attached little importance to anything else, so he could perceive that the young curiosity was excited—the intellect, by whatever springs of interest, set in motion. He detested and despised the whole generation of modern children's books, in which the attempt is made to convey accurate notions of scientific minutiae[8]: delighting cordially, on the other hand, in those of the preceding age, which, addressing themselves chiefly to the imagination, obtain through it, as he believed, the best chance of stirring our graver faculties also. He exercised the memory, by selecting for tasks of recitation passages of popular verse the most likely to catch the fancy of children; and gradually familiarized them with the ancient history of their own country, by arresting attention, in the course of his own oral narrations, on incidents and characters of a similar description. Nor did he neglect to use the same means of quickening curiosity as to the events of sacred history. On Sunday he never rode—at least not until his growing infirmity made his pony almost necessary to him—for it was his principle that all domestic animals have a full right to their Sabbath of rest; but after he had read the church service, he usually walked with his whole family, dogs included, to some favourite spot at a considerable distance from the house—most frequently, the ruined tower of Elibank—and there dined with them in the open air on a basket of cold provisions, mixing his wine with the water of the brook beside which they all were grouped around him on the turf; and here, or at home, if the weather kept them from their ramble, his Sunday talk was just such a series of biblical lessons as that which we have preserved for the permanent use of rising generations, in his Tales of a Grandfather[9], on the early history of Scotland. I wish he had committed that other series to writing too; —how different that would have been from our thousand compilations of dead epitome and imbecile cant! He had his Bible, the Old Testament especially, by heart; and on these days inwove the simple pathos or sublime enthusiasm of Scripture, in whatever story he was telling, with the same picturesque richness as he did, in his week-day tales, the quaint Scotch of Pitscottie[10], or some rude romantic old rhyme from Barbour's Bruce[11] or Blind Harry's Wallace[12].

By many external accomplishments, either in girl or boy, he set little store. He delighted to hear his daughters sing an old ditty, or one of his own framing; but, so the singer appeared to feel the spirit of her ballad, he was not at all critical of the technical execution. There was one thing, however, on which he fixed his heart hardly less than the ancient Persians of *the Cyropaedia*[13]: like them, next to love of truth, he held love of horsemanship for the prime point of education. As soon as his eldest girl could sit a pony, she was made the regular attendant of his mountain rides; and they all, as they attained sufficient strength, had the like advancement. He taught them to think nothing of tumbles, and habituated them to his own reckless delight in perilous fords and flooded streams; and they all imbibed in great perfection his passion for horses—as well, I may venture to add, as his deep reverence for the more important article of that Persian training. "Without courage," he said, "there cannot be truth; and without truth there can be no other virtue."

He had a horror of boarding-schools; never allowed his girls to learn anything out of his own house; and chose their governess—Miss Miller—who about this time was domesticated with them, and never left them while they needed one, — with far greater regard to her kind good temper and excellent moral and religious principles, than to the measure of her attainments in what are called fashionable accomplishments. The admirable system of education for boys in Scotland combines all the advantages of public and private instruction; his carried their satchels to the High-School[14], when the family was in Edinburgh, just as he had done before them, and shared of course the evening society of their happy home. But he rarely, if ever, left them in town, when he could himself be in the country; and at Ashestiel he was, for better or for worse, his eldest boy's daily tutor, after he began Latin.

NOTES

1. **Mr. Morritt:** John B. Saurey Morritt, a friend of Walter Scott
2. **Mr. Laidlaw:** William Laidlaw, a friend of Walter Scott
3. **kirn:** (Scot.) harvest-home, feast to celebrate the end of the harvest
4. **Camp:** the name of a dog
5. **bairns:** (Scot.) children
6. **written this year:** written in 1808

7. **Ashestiel:** a house on the southern bank of the Tweed, a few miles from Selkirk
8. **minutiae:** small details
9. **his Tales of a Grandfather:** Walter Scott's *Tales of a Grandfather* (1827–1829), a history of Scotland
10. **Pitscottie:** the author of *Chronicles of Scotland*
11. **Barbour's Bruce:** John Barbour (1320–1395) was a Scottish poet who wrote *The Bruce* (1376).
12. **Blind Harry's Wallace:** Henry the Minstrel or Blind Harry (1440–1492) wrote *The Wallace* (c. 1460), one of the most famous Scots poems.
13. ***the Cyropaedia*:** Xenophon's work describing the education of the Persian emperor Cyrus
14. **his carried their satchels to the High-School:** his boys carried their satchels to Edinburgh High-School

JOHN KEATS

(1795–1821)

Keats was one of the major poets in the English Romantic Movement. He was born in London on 31st October 1795, the son of a stable-keeper, and was educated at Clarke's School, Enfield. He trained as a medical student, but gave up medicine for poetry. After a brief but glorious poetic career, he died of tuberculosis in Rome on 23rd February 1821.

Keats published his first volume of poems in 1817, which included the ever-pleasing sonnet "On First Looking into Chapman's Homer". In 1818 appeared his long poem **Endymion**, which tells in a rambling way the legendary love-story of Endymion the shepherd and Cynthia the moon-goddess and is rich in imagery and description. He published another volume of poems in his lifetime, in 1820, a collection of such fine works as **Lamia**, **Isabella**, **The Eve of St. Agnes**, **Hyperion**, and the five odes—**To Autumn**, **On a Grecian Urn**, **To a Nightingale**, **To Psyche**, and **On Melancholy**.

Keats was also one of the best English letter-writers. He wrote interesting letters to his friends, his brothers and sister, and Fanny Brawne, the girl he loved. They contained his thoughts on life, love, and poetry, revealing much wit and vivacity.

TO BENJAMIN BAILEY[1]

Burford Bridge, Nov. 22nd, 1817

MY DEAR BAILEY, —I will get over the first part of this (**un**said) letter[2] as soon as possible, for it relates to the affairs of poor Cripps[3]. —To a man of your nature such a letter as Haydon's[4] must have been extremely cutting—What occasions the greater part of the world's quarrels? —simply this—two minds meet, and do not understand each other time enough[5] to prevent any shock or surprise at the conduct of either party—As soon as I had known Haydon three days, I had got enough of his character not to have been surprised at such a letter as he has hurt you with. Nor, when I knew it, was it a principle with me to drop his acquaintance; although with you it would have been an imperious feeling. I wish you knew all that I think about Genius and the Heart—and yet I think that you are thoroughly acquainted with my innermost breast in that respect, or you could not have known me even thus long, and still hold me worthy to be your dear friend. In passing, however, I must say one thing that has pressed upon me lately, and increased my humility and capability of submission—and that is this truth—Men of Genius are great as certain ethereal chemicals operating on the mass of neutral intellect—but they have not any individuality, any determined character—I would call the top and head of those who have a proper self Men of Power.

But I am running my head into a subject which I am certain I could not do justice to under five years' study, and 3 vols. Octavo—and, moreover, I long to be talking about the Imagination—so, my dear Bailey, do not think of this unpleasant affair, if possible do not—I defy any harm to come of it—I defy. I shall write to Cripps this week, and request him to tell me all his goings—on from time to time by letter wherever I may be. It will go on well—so don't because you have suddenly discovered a coldness in Haydon suffer yourself to be teased—Do not my dear fellow—O! I wish I was as certain of the end of all your troubles as that of your momentary start about the authenticity of the Imagination. I am certain of nothing but of the holiness of the heart's affections, and the truth of Imagination. What the Imagination seizes as beauty must be truth[6]—whether it existed before or not,—for I have the same idea of all our passions as of love: they are all, in their sublime, creative of essential beauty. In a word, you may know my favourite speculation by my first book, and the little song I sent in my last, which is a representation from the fancy of the probable mode of operating in these matters. The Imagination may be compared to Adam's dream[7],—he awoke and found it truth: —I am more zealous in this affair, because I have never yet been able to perceive how anything can be known for truth by consecutive reasoning—and yet it must be. Can it be that even the greatest philosopher ever arrived at his goal without putting aside numerous objections? However it may be, O for a life of sensations rather than of thoughts! It is "a vision in the form of youth," a shadow of reality to come—And this consideration has further convinced me, —for it has come as auxiliary to another favourite speculation of mine, —that we shall enjoy ourselves hereafter by having what we call happiness on earth repeated in a finer tone—And yet such a fate can only befall those who delight in sensation, rather than hunger as you do after truth. Adam's dream will do here, and seems to be a conviction that Imagination and its empyreal reflection, is the same as human life and its spiritual repetition. But, as I was saying, the simple imaginative mind may have its rewards in the repetition of its own silent working coming continually on the spirit with a fine suddenness—to compare great things with small, have you never by being surprised with an old melody, in a delicious place by a delicious voice, *felt* over again your very speculations and surmises at the time it first operated on your soul?—do you not remember forming to yourself the singer's face—more beautiful than it was possible, and yet with the elevation of the moment you did not think so? Even then you were mounted on the wings of Imagination, so high that the prototype must be hereafter—that delicious face you will see. What a time! I am continually running away from the subject. Sure this cannot be exactly the case with a complex mind—one that is imaginative, and at the same time careful of its fruits,—who would exist partly on sensation, partly on thought—

to whom it is necessary that years should bring the philosophic mind?[8] Such a one I consider yours, and therefore it is necessary to your eternal happiness that you not only drink this old wine of Heaven, which I shall call the redigestion of your most ethereal musings upon earth, but also increase in knowledge and know all things. I am glad to hear that you are in a fair way for Easter. You will soon get through your unpleasant reading, and then!—but the world is full of troubles, and I have not much reason to think myself pestered with many.

    I think Jane or Marianne[9] has a better opinion of me than I deserve: for, really and truly, I do not think my brother's illness[10] connected with mine—you know more of the real Cause than they do; nor have I any chance of being rack'd as you have been. You perhaps at one time thought there was such a thing as worldly happiness to be arrived at, at certain periods of time marked out,—you have of necessity from your disposition been thus led away—I scarcely remember counting upon any happiness—I look not for it if it be not in the present hour,—nothing startles me beyond the moment. The setting sun will always set me to rights, or if a sparrow come before my window, I take part in its existence and pick about the gravel. The first thing that strikes me on hearing a misfortune having befallen another is this—"Well, it cannot be helped: he will have the pleasure of trying the resources of his spirit"—and I beg now, my dear Bailey, that hereafter should you observe anything cold in me not to put it to the account of heartlessness, but abstraction—for I assure you I sometimes feel not the influence of a passion or affection during a whole week—and so long this sometimes continues, I begin to suspect myself, and the genuineness of my feelings at other times—thinking them a few barren tragedy tears.

    My brother Tom is much improved—he is going to Devonshire[11]—whither I shall follow him. At present, I am just arrived at Dorking[12]—to change the scene—change the air, and give me a spur to wind up my poem[13], of which there are wanting 500 lines. I should have been here a day sooner, but the Reynoldses persuaded me to stop in Town to meet your friend Christie. There were Rice[14] and Martin[15]—we talked about ghosts. I will have some talk with Taylor[16] and let you know,—when please God I come down at Christmas. I will find that Examiner[17] if possible. My best regards to Gleig[18], my brothers', to you and Mrs. Bentley[19].

Your affectionate Friend

John Keats

I want to say much more to you—a few hints will set me going. Direct Burford Bridge near Dorking.

John Keats (1795-1821)

NOTES

1. **Benjamin Bailey:** Benjamin Bailey (1791-1871) was educated at Oxford. He obtained a curacy in the neighbourhood of Carlish at the end of 1817, and became Vicar of Dallington in Northamptonshire in 1819. He was an intimate friend of Keats.
2. **this (*un*said) letter:** this letter (which is just begun and therefore unsaid). ***Unsaid*** is used in playful contrast to *said*; the "said letter" is a legal term.
3. **Cripps:** a student who learnt painting from Haydon
4. **Haydon:** Benjamin Robert Haydon (1786-1846), a historical painter
5. **time enough:** sufficiently long
6. **What the Imagination seizes as beauty must be truth:** Compare this with the close of the "Ode on a Grecian Urn": Beauty is truth, truth beauty—that is all Ye know on earth, and all ye need to know.
7. **Adam's dream:** Adam mentioned his seeing Eve in his dream; see ***Paradise Lost*** viii. 478-484.
8. **it is necessary that years should bring the philosophic mind:** See Wordsworth, "Ode on Intimations of Immortality", l. 186.
9. **Jane or Marianne:** Marianne and Jane were two of John Hamilton Reynolds's three sisters. Reynolds was one of Keats's intimate friends.
10. **my brother's illness:** Keats's brother Tom was ill with T.B.
11. **Devonshire:** a county of Southwest England
12. **Dorking:** a town in Surrey
13. **my poem:** This refers to ***Endymion***.
14. **Rice:** Jame Rice was an office clerk and a witty and generous soul.
15. **Martin:** John Martin (1791-1855), a publisher

16. **Taylor:** John Taylor (1781–1864), a publisher
17. **that Examiner:** *The Examiner* was a radical weekly magazine established by John and Leigh Hunt in 1808.
18. **Gleig:** G. R. Gleig, a clergyman
19. **Mrs. Bentley:** the Keats brothers' landlady in Well Walk, Hampstead

47

THOMAS CARLYLE

(1795–1881)

Thomas Carlyle was a Scottish essayist, critic, and historian. The eldest son of a stonemason, he was born at Ecclefechan, Dumfriesshire, on December 4, 1795, and educated at Annan Academy (1805–1809) and at the University of Edinburgh (1809–1813). He worked as a teacher from 1814 and as a full-time writer from 1824. He moved with his wife to London in 1834 and lived at Chelsea till the end of his life. He died on February 5, 1881, and was buried at Ecclefechan.

Carlyle's **Sartor Resartus** (1836) contains both an attack on shams and the advocacy of hard work. **The French Revolution** (1837), a book full of vivid word pictures, established his reputation. His other major historical writings are **Heroes and Hero-Worship** (1841), **Letters and Speeches of Cromwell** (1845), and **The History of Friedrich II of Prussia** (1858–1865); in all these books he exaggerates the doctrine that human affairs are determined by great men. His **Life of John Stirling** (1851) is a moving biography. In his works dealing with contemporary problems, **Chartism** (1839), **Past and Present** (1843), and **Latter-day Pamphlets** (1850), he shows his hatred for greed of wealth and moral lassitude, and his contempt for scientific pursuits and political oratory. Carlyle writes in idiosyncratic prose style. While it is violent, ironic, and bizarre, it can be ardent, vivid, and forceful.

COLUMBUS

Work is of a religious nature: —work is of a ***brave*** nature; which it is the aim of all religion to be. All work of man is as the swimmer's: a waste ocean[1] threatens to devour him; if he front it not bravely[2], it will keep its word. By incessant wise defiance of it, lusty rebuke and buffet of it, behold how it loyally supports him, bears him as its conqueror along. "It is so," says Goethe[3], "with all things that man undertakes in this world."

Brave Sea-captain, Norse Sea-king, —Columbus[4], my hero, royalest Sea-king of all! it is no friendly environment this of thine, in the waste deep waters; around thee mutinous discouraged souls, behind thee disgrace and ruin, before thee the unpenetrated veil of Night: Brother, these wild water—mountains, bounding from their deep bases (ten miles deep, I am told), are not entirely there on thy behalf! Meseems[5] ***they*** have other work than floating thee forward; —and the huge Winds, that sweep from Ursa Major[6] to the Tropics and Equators, dancing their giant—waltz through the Kingdoms of Chaos and Immensity, they care little about filling rightly or filling wrongly the small shoulder-of-mutton sails[7] in this cockle-skiff[8] of thine! Thou art not among articulate-speaking friends, my brother thou art among immeasurable dumb monsters, tumbling, howling wide as the world here. Secret, far off, invisible to all hearts but thine, there lies a help in them: see how thou wilt get at that. Patiently thou wilt wait till the mad South-wester[9] spend itself, saving thyself by dexterous science of defence, the while; valiantly, with swift decision, wilt thou strike in, when the favouring East, the Possible, springs up. Mutiny of men thou wilt sternly repress; weakness, despondency, thou wilt cheerily encourage: thou wilt swallow down complaint, unreason, weariness, weakness of others and thyself; —how much wilt thou swallow down! There shall be a depth of Silence in thee, deeper than this Sea, which is but ten miles deep: a Silence unsoundable; known to God only. Thou shalt be a Great Man. Yes, my World—Soldier, thou of the World Marine-service, —thou wilt have to be ***greater*** than this tumultuous unmeasured World here round thee is: thou, in thy strong soul, as with wrestler's arms, shalt embrace it, harness it down; and make it bear thee on, —to new Americas, or whither God wills!

NOTES

1. **a waste ocean:** a vast ocean
2. **if he front it not bravely:** if he should not face or confront it bravely
3. **Goethe:** Johann Wolfgang von Goethe (1749−1832), German poet, novelist, and dramatist. His works include ***Götz von Berlichingen*** (1773), the ***Wilhelm Meister*** novels (1796, 1829), and his greatest poetic masterpiece ***Faust*** (1808, 1832).
4. **Columbus:** Christopher Columbus (1451−1506) was an Italian navigator and explorer in the service of Spain, who discovered the New World on October 12, 1492.
5. **Meseems:** (poet.) It seems to me.
6. **Ursa Major:** the Great Bear, a conspicuous constellation in the north hemisphere
7. **small shoulder-of-mutton sails:** small mutton-shoulder-shaped sails, lugsails
8. **cockle-skiff:** small boat
9. **South-wester:** strong wind from the southwest

48

THOMAS BABINGTON MACAULAY

(1800-1859)

T. B. Macaulay was an English historian, essayist, and politician. He was born in Leicestershire on October 25, 1800, the eldest son of Zachary Macaulay, a well-known philanthropist and reformer. Remarkable for precocity and a photographic memory, he began to read at three and had written a compendium of universal history before he was eight years old. He studied at Trinity College, Cambridge, from 1818 to 1822, worked as a Fellow there from 1824 to 1831, and was called to the bar in 1826. He was for many years a Whig M. P. and several times held a high post in the government. In 1857 he was raised to the peerage as Baron Macaulay of Rothley. He died on December 28, 1859.

Macaulay's first important work, the ***Essay on Milton***, created a sensation when it appeared in the ***Edinburgh Review*** in 1825. For twenty years he wrote for this monthly a total of 36 essays on literary and historical subjects. Towards the close of his life he contributed to the ***Encyclopaedia Britannica*** (8th ed., 1852-1860) five biographical articles, articles on Atterbury, Bunyan, Goldsmith, Johnson, and William Pitt. Ably written, his essays and brief lives were very well received. Equally popular was his ***Lays of Ancient Rome*** (1842), a collection of vigorous narrative poems full of action and colour. Macaulay's ***History of England*** (vols 1-2, 1849; vols 3-4, 1855; vol. 5, 1861) is his masterpiece. This is a detailed account of the reigns of James II and William III, a short period from 1685 to 1702. Here he displays to the full his vast learning, thorough research, narrative power, descriptive art, and enthusiastic eloquence. His style is clear, direct, graphic, and lively.

OLIVER GOLDSMITH

OLIVER GOLDSMITH, one of the most pleasing English writers of the eighteenth century. He was of a Protestant and Saxon family which had been long settled in Ireland, and which had, like most other Protestant and Saxon families, been, in troubled times, harassed and put in fear by the native population. His father, Charles Goldsmith, studied in the reign of Queen Anne[1] at the diocesan school at Elphin[2], became attached to the daughter of the schoolmaster, married her, took orders, and settled at a place called Pallas, in the county of Longford. There he with difficulty supported his wife and children on what he could earn, partly as a curate and partly as a farmer.

At Pallas Oliver Goldsmith was born in November 1728[3]. That spot was then, for all practical purposes, almost as remote from the busy and splendid capital in which his later years were passed, as any clearing in Upper Canada or any sheep-walk in Australasia now is. Even at this day those enthusiasts who venture to make a pilgrimage to the birthplace of the poet are forced to perform the latter part of their journey on foot. The hamlet lies far from any highroad on a dreary plain which in wet weather is often a lake. The lanes would break any jaunting-car to pieces; and there are ruts and sloughs through which the most strongly-built wheels cannot be dragged.

While Oliver was still a child, his father was presented to a living worth about 200 pounds a year, in the county of West Meath. The family accordingly quitted their cottage in the wilderness for a spacious house on a frequented road, near the village of Lissoy. Here the boy was taught his letters by a maid-servant, and was sent in his seventh year to a village school kept by an old quarter-master on half-pay, who professed to teach nothing but reading, writing, and arithmetic, but who had an inexhaustible fund of stories about ghosts, banshees[4], and fairies, about the great Rapparee chiefs[5], Baldearg O'Donnell and galloping Hogan, and about the exploits of Peterborough[6] and Stanhope[7], the surprise of Monjuich[8], and the glorious disaster of Briheuga[9]. This man must have been of the Protestant religion; but he was of the aboriginal race, and not only spoke the Irish language, but could pour forth unpremeditated Irish verses. Oliver early became, and through life continued to be, a passionate admirer of the Irish music, and especially of the compositions of Carolan[10], some of the last notes of whose harp he heard. It ought to be added that Oliver, though by birth one of the Englishry[11], and though connected by numerous ties with the Established Church, never showed the least sign of that contemptuous antipathy with which, in his days, the ruling minority in Ireland too generally regarded the subject majority. So far indeed was he from sharing the opinions and feelings of the caste to which he belonged, that he conceived an aversion to the Glorious and Immortal Memory[12], and, even when George the Third was on the throne, maintained that nothing but the restoration of the banished dynasty could save the country.

From the humble academy kept by the old soldier Goldsmith was removed in his ninth year. He went to several grammar-schools, and acquired some knowledge of the ancient languages. His life at this time seems to have been far from happy. He had, as appears from the admirable portrait of him at Knowle[13], features harsh even to ugliness. The small-pox had set its mark on him with more than usual severity. His stature was small, and his limbs ill put together. Among boys little tenderness is shown to personal defects; and the ridicule excited by poor Oliver's appearance was heightened by a peculiar simplicity and a disposition to blunder which he retained to the last. He became the common butt of boys and masters, was pointed at as a fright in the playground, and flogged as a dunce in the schoolroom. When he had risen to eminence, those who had once derided him ransacked their memory for the events of his early years, and recited repartees and couplets which had dropped from him, and which, though little noticed at the time, were supposed a quarter of a century later, to indicate the powers which produced the ***Vicar of Wakefield***[14] and the ***Deserted Village***[15].

In his seventeenth year Oliver went up to Trinity College, Dublin[16], as a sizar. The sizars paid nothing for food and tuition, and very little for lodging; but they had to perform some menial services from which they have long been relieved. They swept the court: they carried up the dinner to the fellows' table, and changed the plates and poured out the ale of the rulers of the society. Goldsmith was quartered, not alone, in a garret, on the window of which his name, scrawled by himself, is still read with interest. From such garrets many men of less parts than his have made their way to the woolsack[17] or to the episcopal bench[18]. But Goldsmith, while he suffered all the humiliations, threw away all the advantages of his situation. He neglected the studies of the place, stood low at the examinations, was turned down to the bottom of his class for playing the buffoon in the lecture-room, was severely reprimanded for pumping on a constable, and was caned by a brutal tutor for giving a ball in the attic story of the college to some gay youths and damsels from the city.

While Oliver was leading at Dublin a life divided between squalid distress and squalid dissipation, his father died, leaving a mere pittance. The youth obtained his bachelor's degree, and left the University. During some time the humble dwelling to which his widowed mother had retired was his home. He was now in his twenty-first year; it was necessary that he should do something; and his education seemed to have fitted him to do nothing but to dress himself in gaudy colours, of which he was as fond as a magpie, to take a hand at cards, to sing Irish airs, to play the flute, to angle in summer, and to tell ghost stories by the fire in winter. He tried five or six professions in turn without success. He applied for ordination; but, as he applied in scarlet clothes, he was speedily turned out of the Episcopal palace. He then became tutor in an opulent family, but soon quitted his situation in consequence of a dispute about play. Then he determined to emigrate to America. His relations, with much satisfaction, saw him set out for Cork[19] on a good horse, with thirty pounds in his pocket. But in six weeks he came back on a miserable hack, without a penny, and informed his mother that the ship in which he had taken his passage, having got a fair wind while he was at a party of pleasure, had sailed without him. Then he resolved to study the law. A generous kinsman advanced fifty pounds. With this sum Goldsmith went to Dublin, was enticed into a gaming-house, and lost every shilling. He then thought of medicine. A small purse was made up; and in his twenty-fourth year he was sent to Edinburgh. At Edinburgh[20] he passed eighteen months in nominal attendance on lectures, and picked up some superficial information about chemistry and natural history. Thence he went to Leyden[21], still pretending to study physic. He left that celebrated university, the third university at which he had resided, in his twenty-seventh year, without a degree, with the merest smattering of medical knowledge, and with no property but his clothes and his flute. His flute, however, proved a useful friend. He rambled on foot through Flanders[22], France, and Switzerland, playing tunes which everywhere set the peasantry dancing, and which often procured for him a supper and a bed. He wandered as far as Italy. His musical performances, indeed, were not to the taste of the Italians, but he contrived to live on the alms which he obtained at the gates of convents. It should, however, be observed that the stories which he told about this part of his life ought to be received with great caution; for strict veracity was never one of his virtues; and a man who is ordinarily inaccurate in narration is likely to be more than ordinarily inaccurate when he talks about his own travels. Goldsmith, indeed, was so regardless of truth as to assert in print that he was present at a most interesting conversation between Voltaire[23] and Fontenelle[24], and that this conversation took place at Paris. Now it is certain that Voltaire never was within a hundred leagues of Paris during the whole time which Goldsmith passed on the Continent.

In 1756 the wanderer landed at Dover[25], without a shilling, without a friend, and without a calling. He had, indeed, if his own unsupported evidence may be trusted, obtained from the University of Padua[26] a doctor's degree; but this dignity proved utterly useless to him. In England his flute was not in request; there were no convents; and he was forced to have recourse to a series of desperate expedients. He turned strolling player; but his face and figure were ill suited to the boards even of the humblest theatre. He pounded drugs and ran about London with phials for charitable chemists. He joined a swarm of beggars, which made its nest in Axe Yard. He was for a time usher of a school, and felt the miseries and humiliations of this situation so keenly that he thought it a promotion to be permitted to earn his bread as a bookseller's hack; but he soon found the new yoke more galling than the old one, and was glad to become an usher again. He obtained a medical appointment in the service of the East India Company[27]; but the appointment was speedily revoked. Why it was revoked we are not told. The subject was one on which he never liked to talk. It is probable that he was incompetent to perform the duties of the place. Then he presented himself at Surgeons' Hall[28] for examination, as mate to a naval hospital. Even to so humble a post he was found unequal. By this time the schoolmaster whom he had served for a morsel of food and the third part of a bed was no more. Nothing remained but to return to the lowest drudgery of literature. Goldsmith took a garret in a miserable court, to which he had to climb from the brink of Fleet Ditch by a dizzy ladder of flagstones called Breakneck Steps. The court and the ascent have long disappeared; but old Londoners will remember both. Here, at thirty, the unlucky adventurer sat down to toil like a galley slave.

In the succeeding six years he sent to the press some things which have survived and many which have perished. He produced articles for reviews, magazines, and newspapers; children's books which, bound in gilt paper and adorned with hideous woodcuts, appeared in the window of the once far-famed shop at the corner of Saint Paul's Churchyard; ***An Enquiry into the State of Polite Learning in Europe***[29], which, though of little or no value, is still reprinted among his works; a ***Life of Beau Nash***[30], which is not reprinted, though it well deserves to be so; a superficial and incorrect, but very readable, ***History of England***[31], in a series of letters purporting to be addressed by a nobleman to his son; and some lively and amusing ***Sketches of London Society***, in a series of letters purporting to be addressed by a Chinese traveller to his friends[32]. All these works were anonymous; but some of them were well known to be Goldsmith's; and he gradually rose in the estimation of the booksellers for whom he drudged. He was, indeed, emphatically a popular writer. For accurate research or grave disquisition he was not well qualified by nature or by education. He knew nothing accurately: his reading had been desultory; nor had he meditated deeply on what he had read. He had seen much of the world; but he had noticed and retained little more of what he had seen than some grotesque incidents and characters which had happened to strike his fancy. But, though his mind was very scantily stored with materials, he used what materials he had in such a way as to produce a wonderful effect. There have been many greater writers; but perhaps no writer was ever more uniformly agreeable. His style was always pure and easy, and, on proper occasions, pointed and energetic. His narratives were always amusing, his descriptions always picturesque, his humour rich and joyous, yet not without an occasional tinge of amiable sadness. About everything that he wrote, serious or sportive, there was a certain natural grace and decorum, hardly to be expected from a man a great part of whose life had been passed among thieves and beggars, streetwalkers, and merry-andrews, in those squalid dens which are the reproach of great capitals.

As his name gradually became known, the circle of his acquaintance widened. He was introduced to Johnson, who was then considered as the first of living English writers; to Reynolds, the first of English painters; and to Burke, who had not yet entered Parliament, but who had distinguished himself greatly by his writings and by the eloquence of his conversation. With these eminent men Goldsmith became intimate. In 1763 he was one of the nine original members of that celebrated fraternity[33] which has sometimes been called the Literary Club, but which has always disclaimed that epithet, and still glories in the simple name of The Club.

By this time Goldsmith had quitted his miserable dwelling at the top of Breakneck Steps, and had taken chambers in the more civilised region of the Inns of Court. But he was still often reduced to pitiable shifts. Towards the close of 1764 his rent was so long in arrear that his landlady one morning called in the help of a sheriff's officer. The debtor, in great perplexity, dispatched a messenger to Johnson; and Johnson, always friendly, though often surly, sent back the messenger with a guinea, and promised to follow speedily. He came, and found that Goldsmith had changed the guinea, and was railing at the landlady over a bottle of Madeira. Johnson put the cork into the bottle, and entreated his friend to consider calmly how money was to be procured. Goldsmith said that he had a novel ready for the press. Johnson glanced at the manuscript, saw that there were good things in it, took it to a bookseller, sold it for 60 pounds, and soon returned with the money. The rent was paid; and the sheriff's officer withdrew. According to one story, Goldsmith gave his landlady a sharp reprimand for her treatment of him: according to another, he insisted on her joining him in a bowl of punch. Both stories are probably true. The novel which was thus ushered into the world was the *Vicar of Wakefield*.

But, before the *Vicar of Wakefield* appeared in print, came the great crisis of Goldsmith's literary life. In Christmas week, 1764, he published a poem entitled the *Traveller*. It was the first work to which he had put his name; and it at once raised him to the rank of a legitimate English classic. The opinion of the most skilful critics was, that nothing finer had appeared in verse since the fourth book of the ***Dunciad***[34]. In one respect the *Traveller* differs from all Goldsmith's other writings. In general his designs were bad, and his execution good. In the *Traveller*, the execution, though deserving of much praise, is far inferior to the design. No philosophical poem, ancient or modern, has a plan so noble, and at the same time so simple. An English wanderer, seated on a crag among the Alps, near the point where three great countries meet, looks down on the boundless prospect, reviews his long pilgrimage, recalls the varieties of scenery, of climate, of government, of religion, of national character, which he has observed, and comes to the conclusion, just or unjust, that our happiness depends little on political institutions, and much on the temper and regulation of our own minds.

While the fourth edition of the *Traveller* was on the counters of the booksellers, the *Vicar of Wakefield* appeared, and rapidly obtained a popularity which has lasted down to our own time, and which is likely to last as long as our language. The fable is indeed one of the worst that ever was constructed. It wants, not merely that probability which ought to be found in a tale of common English life, but that consistency which ought to be found even in the wildest fiction about witches, giants, and fairies. But the earlier chapters have all the sweetness of pastoral poetry, together with all the vivacity of comedy. Moses and his spectacles, the vicar and his monogamy, the sharper and his cosmogony, the squire proving from Aristotle that relatives are related, Olivia preparing herself for the arduous task of converting a rakish lover by studying the controversy between Robinson Crusoe and Friday, the great ladies with their scandal about Sir Tomkyn's amours and Dr. Burdock's verses, and Mr. Burchell with his "Fudge," have caused as much harmless mirth as has ever been caused by matter packed into so small a number of pages. The latter part of the tale is unworthy of the beginning. As we approach the catastrophe, the absurdities lie thicker and thicker; and the gleams of pleasantry become rarer and rarer.

The success which had attended Goldsmith as a novelist emboldened him to try his fortune as a dramatist. He wrote the ***Goodnatured Man***[35], a piece which had a worse fate than it deserved. Garrick refused to produce it at Drury Lane. It was acted at Covent Garden in 1768, but was coldly received. The author, however, cleared by his benefit nights, and by the sale of the copyright, no less than 500 pounds, five times as much as he had made by the ***Traveller*** and the ***Vicar of Wakefield*** together. The plot of the ***Goodnatured Man*** is, like almost all Goldsmith's plots, very ill constructed. But some passages are exquisitely ludicrous; much more ludicrous, indeed, than suited the taste of the town at that time. A canting, mawkish play, entitled ***False Delicacy***[36], had just had an immense run. Sentimentality was all the mode. During some years, more tears were shed at comedies than at tragedies; and a pleasantry which moved the audience to anything more than a grave smile was reprobated as low. It is not strange, therefore, that the very best scene in the ***Goodnatured Man***, that in which Miss Richland finds her lover attended by the bailiff and the bailiff's follower in full court dresses, should have been mercilessly hissed, and should have been omitted after the first night.

In 1770 appeared the ***Deserted Village***. In mere diction and versification this celebrated poem is fully equal, perhaps superior, to the ***Traveller***, and it is generally preferred to the ***Traveller*** by that large class of readers who think, with Bayes in the ***Rehearsal***[37], that the only use of a plan is to bring in fine things. More discerning judges, however, while they admire the beauty of the details, are shocked by one unpardonable fault which pervades the whole. The fault we mean is not that theory about wealth and luxury which has so often been censured by political economists. The theory is indeed false; but the poem, considered merely as a poem, is not necessarily the worse on that account. The finest poem in the Latin language[38], indeed the finest didactic poem in any language, was written in defence of the silliest and meanest of all systems of natural and moral philosophy. A poet may easily be pardoned for reasoning ill; but he cannot be pardoned for describing ill, for observing the world in which he lives so carelessly that his portraits bear no resemblance to the originals, for exhibiting as copies from real life monstrous combinations of things which never were and never could be found together. What would be thought of a painter who should mix August and January in one landscape, who should introduce a frozen river into a harvest scene? Would it be a sufficient defence of such a picture to say that every part was exquisitely coloured, that the green hedges, the apple-trees loaded with fruit, the wagons reeling under the yellow sheaves, and the sunburned reapers wiping their foreheads, were very fine, and that the ice and the boys sliding were also very fine? To such a picture the ***Deserted Village*** bears a great resemblance. It is made up of incongruous parts. The village in its happy days is a true English village. The village in its decay is an Irish village. The felicity and the misery which Goldsmith has brought close together belong to two different countries, and to two different stages in the progress of society. He had assuredly never seen in his native island such a rural paradise, such a seat of plenty, content, and tranquillity, as his "Auburn." He had assuredly never seen in England all the inhabitants of such a paradise turned out of their homes in one day and forced to emigrate in a body to America. The hamlet he had probably seen in Kent; the ejectment he had probably seen in Munster; but, by joining the two, he has produced something which never was and never will be seen in any part of the world.

In 1773 Goldsmith tried his chance at Covent Garden with a second play, ***She Stoops to Conquer***[39]. The manager was not without great difficulty induced to bring this piece out. The sentimental comedy still reigned; and Goldsmith's comedies were not sentimental. The ***Goodnatured Man*** had been too funny to succeed; yet the mirth of the ***Goodnatured Man*** was sober when compared with the rich drollery of ***She Stoops to Conquer***, which is, in truth, an incomparable farce in five acts. On this occasion, however, genius triumphed. Pit, boxes, and galleries were in a constant roar of laughter. If any bigoted admirer of Kelly[40] and Cumberland[41] ventured to hiss or groan, he was speedily silenced by a general cry of "Turn him out," or "Throw him over." Two generations have since confirmed the verdict which was pronounced on that night.

While Goldsmith was writing the **Deserted Village** and **She Stoops to Conquer**, he was employed in works of a very different kind, works from which he derived little reputation but much profit. He compiled for the use of schools a **History of Rome**, by which he made 300 pounds; a **History of England**, by which he made 600 pounds; a **History of Greece**, for which he received 250 pounds; a **Natural History**, for which the booksellers covenanted to pay him 800 guineas. These works he produced without any elaborate research, by merely selecting, abridging, and translating into his own clear, pure, and flowing language what he found in books well known to the world, but too bulky or too dry for boys and girls. He committed some strange blunders; for he knew nothing with accuracy. Thus in his **History of England** he tells us that Naseby[42] is in Yorkshire; nor did he correct this mistake when the book was reprinted. He was very nearly hoaxed into putting into the **History of Greece** an account of a battle between Alexander the Great[43] and Montezuma[44]. In his **Animated Nature** he relates, with faith and with perfect gravity, all the most absurd lies which he could find in books of travels about gigantic Patagonians[45], monkeys that preach sermons, nightingales that repeat long conversations. "If he can tell a horse from a cow," said Johnson, "that is the extent of his knowledge of zoology." How little Goldsmith was qualified to write about the physical sciences is sufficiently proved by two anecdotes. He on one occasion denied that the sun is longer in the northern than in the southern signs. It was in vain to cite the authority of Maupertuis[46]. "Maupertuis!" he cried; "I understand those matters better than Maupertuis." On another occasion he, in defiance of the evidence of his own senses, maintained obstinately, and even angrily, that he chewed his dinner by moving his upper jaw.

Yet, ignorant as Goldsmith was, few writers have done more to make the first steps in the laborious road to knowledge easy and pleasant. His compilations are widely distinguished from the compilations of ordinary bookmakers. He was a great, perhaps an unequalled, master of the arts of selection and condensation. In these respects his histories of Rome and of England, and still more his own abridgments of these histories, well deserve to be studied. In general nothing is less attractive than an epitome; but the epitomes of Goldsmith, even when most concise, are always amusing; and to read them is considered by intelligent children, not as a task, but as a pleasure.

Goldsmith might now be considered as a prosperous man. He had the means of living in comfort, and even in what to one who had so often slept in barns and on bulks must have been luxury. His fame was great and was constantly rising. He lived in what was intellectually far the best society of the kingdom, in a society in which no talent or accomplishment was wanting, and in which the art of conversation was cultivated with splendid success. There probably were never four talkers more admirable in four different ways than Johnson, Burke, Beauclerk, and Garrick; and Goldsmith was on terms of intimacy with all the four. He aspired to share in their colloquial renown; but never was ambition more unfortunate. It may seem strange that a man who wrote with so much perspicuity, vivacity, and grace should have been, whenever he took a part in conversation, an empty, noisy, blundering rattle. But on this point the evidence is overwhelming. So extraordinary was the contrast between Goldsmith's published works and the silly things which he said, that Horace Walpole described him as an inspired idiot. "Noll," said Garrick, "wrote like an angel, and talked like poor Poll." Chamier declared that it was a hard exercise of faith to believe that so foolish a chatterer could have really written the ***Traveller***. Even Boswell could say, with contemptuous compassion, that he liked very well to hear honest Goldsmith run on. "Yes, sir," said Johnson; "but he should not like to hear himself." Minds differ as rivers differ. There are transparent and sparkling rivers from which it is delightful to drink as they flow; to such rivers the minds of such men as Burke and Johnson may be compared. But there are rivers of which the water when first drawn is turbid and noisome, but becomes pellucid as crystal, and delicious to the taste, if it be suffered to stand till it has deposited a sediment; and such a river is a type of the mind of Goldsmith. His first thoughts on every subject were confused even to absurdity; but they required only a little time to work themselves clear. When he wrote they had that time; and therefore his readers pronounced him a man of genius; but when he talked he talked nonsense, and made himself the laughing-stock of his hearers. He was painfully sensible of his inferiority in conversation; he felt every failure keenly; yet he had not sufficient judgment and self-command to hold his tongue. His animal spirits and vanity were always impelling him to try to do the one thing which he could not do. After every attempt he felt he had exposed himself, and writhed with shame and vexation; yet the next moment he began again.

His associates seem to have regarded him with kindness, which, in spite of their admiration of his writings, was not unmixed with contempt. In truth, there was in his character much to love, but very little to respect. His heart was soft, even to weakness; he was so generous that he quite forgot to be just; he forgave injuries so readily that he might be said to invite them; and was so liberal to beggars that he had nothing left for his tailor and his butcher. He was vain, sensual, frivolous, profuse, improvident. One vice of a darker shade was imputed to him, envy. But there is not the least reason to believe that this bad passion, though it sometimes made him wince and utter fretful exclamations, ever impelled him to injure by wicked arts the reputation of any of his rivals. The truth probably is, that he was not more envious, but merely less prudent than his neighbours. His heart was on his lips. All those small jealousies, which are but too common among men of letters, but which a man of letters who is also a man of the world does his best to conceal, Goldsmith avowed with the simplicity of a child. When he was envious instead of affecting indifference, instead of damning with faint praise, instead of doing injuries slily and in the dark, he told everybody that he was envious. "Do not, pray, do not talk of Johnson in such terms," he said to Boswell; "you harrow up my very soul." George Steevens and Cumberland were men far too cunning to say such a thing. They would have echoed the praises of the man they envied, and then have sent to the newspapers anonymous libels upon him. Both what was good and what was bad in Goldsmith's character was to his associates a perfect security that he would never commit such villainy. He was neither ill-natured enough, nor long-headed enough to be guilty of any malicious act which required contrivance and disguise.

Goldsmith has sometimes been represented as a man of genius, cruelly treated by the world, and doomed to struggle with difficulties which at last broke his heart. But no representation can be more remote from the truth. He did, indeed, go through much sharp misery before he had done anything considerable in literature. But, after his name had appeared on the title-page of the ***Traveller***, he had none to blame but himself for his distresses. His average income during the last seven years of his life certainly exceeded 400 pounds a year; and 400 pounds a year ranked, among the incomes of that day, at least as high as 800 pounds a year would rank at present. A single man living in the Temple[47] with 400 pounds a year might then be called opulent. Not one in ten of the young gentlemen of good families who were studying the law there had so much. But all the wealth which Lord Clive[48] had brought from Bengal, and Sir Lawrence Dundas[49] from Germany, joined together would not have sufficed for Goldsmith. He spent twice as much as he had. He wore fine clothes, gave dinners of several courses, paid court to venal beauties. He had also, it should be remembered, to the honour of his heart, though not of his head, a guinea, or five, or ten, according to the state of his purse, ready for any tale of distress, true or false. But it was not in dress or feasting, in promiscuous amours or promiscuous charities, that his chief expense lay. He had been from boyhood a gambler, and at once the most sanguine and the most unskilful of gamblers. For a time he put off the day of inevitable ruin by temporary expedients. He obtained advances from booksellers, by promising to execute works which he never began. But at length this source of supply failed. He owed more than 2000 pounds; and he saw no hope of extrication from his embarrassments. His spirits and health gave way. He was attacked by a nervous fever[50], which he thought himself competent to treat. It would have been happy for him if his medical skill had been appreciated as justly by himself as by others. Notwithstanding the degree which he pretended to have received at Padua, he could procure no patients. "I do not practise," he once said; "I make it a rule to prescribe only for my friends." "Pray, dear Doctor," said Beauclerk, "alter your rule, and prescribe only for your enemies." Goldsmith now, in spite of this excellent advice, prescribed for himself. The remedy aggravated the malady. The sick man was induced to call in real physicians; and they at one time imagined that they had cured the disease. Still his weakness and restlessness continued. He could get no sleep, he could take no food. "You are worse," said one of his medical attendants, "than you should be from the degree of fever which you have. Is your mind at ease?" "No, it is not," were the last recorded words of Oliver Goldsmith. He died on the 3rd of April 1774, in his forty-sixth year. He was laid in the churchyard of the Temple; but the spot was not marked by any inscription, and is now forgotten. The coffin was followed by Burke and Reynolds. Burke, when he heard of Goldsmith's death, had burst into a flood of tears. Reynolds had been so much moved by the news that he had flung aside his brush and palette for the day.

A short time after Goldsmith's death, a little poem[51] appeared, which will, as long as our language lasts, associate the names of his two illustrious friends with his own. It has already been mentioned that he sometimes felt keenly the sarcasm which his wild blundering talk brought upon him. He was, not long before his last illness, provoked into retaliating. He wisely betook himself to his pen; and at that weapon he proved himself a match for all his assailants together. Within a small compass he drew with a singularly easy and vigorous pencil the characters of nine or ten of his intimate associates. Though this little work did not receive his last touches, it must always be regarded as a masterpiece. It is impossible, however, not to wish that four or five likenesses which have no interest for posterity were wanting to that noble gallery, and that their places were supplied by sketches of Johnson and Gibbon, as happy and vivid as the sketches of Burke and Garrick.

Some of Goldsmith's friends and admirers honoured him with a cenotaph in Westminster Abbey. Nollekens[52] was the sculptor; and Johnson wrote the inscription. It is much to be lamented that Johnson did not leave to posterity a more durable and a more valuable memorial of his friend. A life of Goldsmith would have been an inestimable addition to the Lives of the Poets. No man appreciated Goldsmith's writings more justly than Johnson; no man was better acquainted with Goldsmith's character and habits; and no man was more competent to delineate with truth and spirit the peculiarities of a mind in which great powers were found in company with great weaknesses. But the list of poets to whose works Johnson was requested by the booksellers to furnish prefaces ended with Lyttleton[53], who died in

1773. The line seems to have been drawn expressly for the purpose of excluding the person whose portrait would have most fitly closed the series. Goldsmith, however, has been fortunate in his biographers. Within a few years his life has been written by Mr. Prior[54], by Mr. Washington Irving[55], and by Mr. Forster[56]. The diligence of Mr. Prior deserves great praise; the style of Mr. Washington Irving is always pleasing; but the highest place must, in justice, be assigned to the eminently interesting work of Mr. Forster.

NOTES

1. **Queen Anne:** Queen Anne (1665-1714) was queen of Great Britain and Ireland (1702-1714).
2. **Elphin:** a town in County Roscommon
3. **Oliver Goldsmith was born in November 1728:** Goldsmith was probably born in 1730 rather than 1728.
4. **banshees:** female fairies and spirits in Irish folklore, whose wailing warns of impending death
5. **Rapparee chiefs:** wild Irish bandit leaders
6. **Peterborough:** Charles Mordaunt, third Earl of Peterborough (1658-1735),was a commander of the English forces in the War of the Spanish Succession (1705-1707).
7. **Stanhope:** James Stanhope, first Earl of Stanhope (1673-1721), was made commander-in-chief of the English forces in the War of the Spanish Succession in 1708.
8. **Monjuich:** the castle on the south of Barcelona. Peterborough took it by storm.
9. **Brihuega:** Brihuega is forty miles northeast of Madrid. The English under Stanhope surrendered there.
10. **Carolan:** Turlogh Carolan (1670-1738) was an Irish wandering minstrel.
11. **Englishry:** (chiefly hist.) people of English descent especially in Ireland
12. **the Glorious and Immortal Memory:** the formula used in the Whig toast to the late King William III. Goldsmith hated the phrase because he favoured the Jacobite dynasty.
13. **the admirable portrait of him at Knowle:** The portrait was by Sir Joshua Reynolds.
14. *Vicar of Wakefield*: a novel by Goldsmith, written in 1761-1762 and published in 1766
15. *Deserted Village*: a poem by Goldsmith, published in 1770

16. **Dublin:** the capital of the Republic of Ireland and formerly of all Ireland
17. **the woolsack:** the seat of Lord Chancellor in the House of Lords
18. **the episcopal bench:** the bench on which bishops sit in the House of Lords
19. **Cork:** a county in Southwest Ireland
20. **Edinburgh:** the University of Edinburgh in Scotland
21. **Leyden:** the University of Leyden in the West Netherlands
22. **Flanders:** a medieval principality in the southwest part of the Low Countries, now divided between Belgium, France, and Holland
23. **Voltaire:** the name assumed by François Marie Arouet (1694–1778). He was a famous French writer and the embodiment of the 18th-century Enlightenment. His major works include *Letters Philosophiques* (1734), the satire *Candide* (1759), and the play *Zaire* (1732).
24. **Fontenelle:** Bernard le Bovier de Fontenelle (1657–1757), French philosopher and writer
25. **Dover:** a seaport in east Kent on the Strait of Dover
26. **Padua:** a city in Northeast Italy
27. **the East India Company:** the company chartered in 1660 by the British government to trade with the East Indies and dissolved in 1874
28. **Surgeons' Hall:** the Royal College of Surgeons
29. *An Inquiry into the State of Polite Learning in Europe*: This was in fact Goldsmith's first considerable work (1759).
30. *Life of Beau Nash*: Richard Nash (1674–1761) was a leader of fashion. The *Life* was published in 1762.
31. *History of England*: The work was published in 1764.
32. **a series of letters purporting to be addressed by a Chinese traveller to his friends:** The "Chinese Letters" first appeared in *The Public Ledger* for 1760 and were republished in 1762 as *The Citizen of the World*.
33. **the nine original members of that celebrated fraternity:** The Club or the Literary Club was formed in 1764. Its nine original members, according to Boswell's record, were: "Sir Joshua Reynolds, Dr. Johnson, Mr. Edmund Burke, Dr. Nugent, Mr. Beauclerk, Mr. Langton, Dr. Goldsmith, Mr. Channer, and Sir John Hawkins." Those

elected later included Thomas Percy (1765), David Garrick and James Boswell (1773), C. J. Fox and George Steevens (1774), Adam Smith (1775), Joseph Banks (1778), and Edmond Malone (1782).

34. ***Dunciad***: a satirical poem by Pope (Books I - III , 1728; Book IV , 1742)
35. ***Goodnatured Man***: a comedy by Goldsmith, produced at Covent Garden in 1768
36. ***False Delicacy***: a comedy by Hugh Kelly (1739-1777)
37. ***Rehearsal***: a farcical comedy by George Villiers, Duke of Buckingham, in 1672. Bayes is the chief character in the play.
38. **the finest poem in the Latin language:** Lucretius' long poem ***De Rerum Natura*** ("On the Nature of Things"), based on the philosophy of Epicurus
39. ***She Stoops to Conquer***: a comedy by Goldsmith, produced at Covent Garden in 1773
40. **Kelly:** Hugh Kelly (1739-1777) was the author of ***False Delicacy*** (1768), a sentimental comedy.
41. **Cumberland:** Richard Cumberland (1732-1811) wrote sentimental comedies, such as ***The West Indian*** and ***The Brothers***.
42. **Naseby:** Naseby is in Northamptonshire.
43. **Alexander the Great:** Alexander the Great (356-323 B.C.) was king of Macedon.
44. **Montezuma:** Montezuma II (1466-1520) was the last Aztec emperor of Mexico (1502-1520).
45. **gigantic Patagonians:** a tribe of tall American Indians
46. **Maupertuis:** Pierre Louis Maupertuis (1695-1759), a French mathematician and astronomer
47. **the Temple:** Inner Temple and Middle Temple, two of the four inns of court in London, the other two being Lincoln's Inn and Gray's Inn
48. **Lord Clive:** Robert Clive (1725-1774), British general and statesman, who became Governor of Bengal in 1758.
49. **Sir Lawrence Dundas:** He was a contractor to the English army in Germany during the early part of the Seven Years' War.
50. **a nervous fever:** a fever caused by a nervous strain
51. **a little poem:** Goldsmith's ***Retaliation*** (1774)
52. **Nollekens:** Joseph Nollekens (1737-1832) was a Belgian artist who lived in England.

53. **Lyttelton:** George Lyttelton (1709-1773), a politician and poet
54. **Mr. Prior:** James Prior (1790-1869) published his *Life of Goldsmith* in 1837.
55. **Washington Irving:** Washington Irving (1783-1859) was an American writer. His most famous works are *The Sketch Book* (1819-1820) and *The Life of George Washington* (1855-1859). His *Oliver Goldsmith* appeared in 1840.
56. **Mr. Forster:** John Forster (1812-1876) was a biographer; he wrote on Goldsmith, Landor, Dickens, and Swift. His *Life and Adventures of Oliver Goldsmith* appeared in 1848.

LONDON COFFEE-HOUSES

The coffee-house must not be dismissed with a cursory mention. It might indeed at that time[1] have been not improperly called a most important political institution. No Parliament had sat for years. The municipal council of the City had ceased to speak the sense of the citizens. Public meetings, harangues, resolutions, and the rest of the modern machinery of agitation had not yet come into fashion. Nothing resembling the modern newspaper existed. In such circumstances the coffee-houses were the chief organs through which the public opinion of the metropolis vented itself.

The first of these establishments had been set up, in the time of the Commonwealth[2], by a Turkey merchant, who had acquired among the Mahometans a taste for their favourite beverage. The convenience of being able to make appointments in any part of the town, and of being able to pass evenings socially at a very small charge, was so great that the fashion spread fast. Every man of the upper or middle class went daily to his coffee-house to learn the news and to discuss it. Every coffee-house had one or more orators to whose eloquence the crowd listened with admiration, and who soon became, what the journalists of our own time have been called, a fourth Estate of the realm. The court had long seen with uneasiness the growth of this new power in the state. An attempt had been made, during Danby's[3] administration, to close the coffee-houses. But men of all parties missed their usual places of resort so much that there was an universal outcry. The government did not venture, in opposition to a feeling so strong and general, to enforce a regulation of which the legality might well be questioned. Since that time ten years had elapsed, and during those years the number and influence of the coffee-houses had been constantly increasing. Foreigners remarked that the coffee-house was that which especially distinguished London from all other cities; that the coffee-house was the Londoner's home, and that those who wished to find a gentleman commonly asked, not whether he lived in Fleet

Street or Chancery Lane, but whether he frequented the Grecian[4] or the Rainbow[5]. Nobody was excluded from these places who laid down his penny at the bar. Yet every rank and profession, and every shade of religious and political opinion, had its own headquarters. There were houses near Saint James's Park where fops congregated, their heads and shoulders covered with black or flaxen wigs, not less ample than those which are now worn by the Chancellor and by the Speaker of the House of Commons. The wig came from Paris; and so did the rest of the fine gentleman's ornaments, his embroidered coat, his fringed gloves, and the tassel which upheld his pantaloons. The conversation was in that dialect which, long after it had ceased to be spoken in fashionable circles, continued, in the mouth of Lord Foppington[6], to excite the mirth of theatres. The atmosphere was like that of a perfumer's shop. Tobacco in any other form than that of richly scented snuff was held in abomination. If any clown, ignorant of the usages of the house, called for a pipe, the sneers of the whole assembly and the short answers of the waiters soon convinced him that he had better go somewhere else. Nor, indeed, would he have had far to go. For, in general, the coffee-rooms reeked with tobacco like a guard-room; and strangers sometimes expressed their surprise that so many people should leave their own firesides to sit in the midst of eternal fog and stench. Nowhere was the smoking more constant than at Will's. That celebrated house, situated between Covent Garden and Bow Street[7], was sacred to polite letters. There the talk was about poetical justice and the unities of place and time. There was a faction for Perrault[8] and the moderns, a faction for Boileau[9] and the ancients. One group debated whether **Paradise Lost** ought not to have been in rhyme. To another an envious poetaster demonstrated that **Venice Preserved**[10] ought to have been hooted from the stage. Under no roof was a greater variety of figures to be seen. There were Earls in stars and garters, clergymen in cassocks and bands, pert Templars, sheepish lads from the Universities, translators and index makers in ragged coats of frieze. The great press was to get near the chair where John Dryden[11] sat. In winter that chair was always in the warmest nook by the fire; in summer it stood in the balcony. To bow to the Laureate, and to hear his opinion of Racine's[12] last tragedy or of Bossu's treatise on epic poetry[13], was thought a privilege. A pinch from his snuffbox was an honour sufficient to turn the head of a young enthusiast. There were coffee-houses where the first medical men might be consulted. Doctor John Radcliffe, who, in the year 1685, rose to the largest practice in London, came daily, at the hour when the Exchange was full, from his house in Bow Street, then a fashionable part of the capital, to Garraway's[14], and was to be found, surrounded by surgeons and apothecaries, at a particular table. There were Puritan coffee-houses where no oath was heard, and where lank-haired men discussed election and reprobation through their noses; Jews' coffee-houses where dark-eyed money-changers from Venice and from Amsterdam greeted each other; and Popish coffee-houses where, as good Protestants believed, Jesuits planned, over their cups, another great fire, and cast silver bullets to shoot the King.

NOTES

1. **at that time:** during the reign of Charles II (1660–1685)
2. **the Commonwealth:** the republican government of England between the execution of Charles I in 1649 and the Restoration in 1660
3. **Danby:** Thomas Osborne (1631–1712), first Earl of Danby, was Lord High Treasurer (1673–1678) and Lord President of Council (1689–1699).
4. **the Grecian:** a coffee-house in the Strand
5. **the Rainbow:** a coffee-house in Fleet Street
6. **Lord Foppington:** a character in Vanbrugh's comedy *The Relapse* (1696)
7. **That celebrated house, situated between Covent Garden and Bow Street:** Will's coffee-house
8. **Perrault:** Charles Perrault (1628–1703), a French poet, critic, and fairy-tale writer
9. **Boileau:** Nicolas Boileau-Despreaux (1636–1711) was a French critic and poet and the author of ***L'Art Poetique*** (1674) etc.
10. ***Venice Preserved***: a tragedy in blank verse by Thomas Otway, produced in 1682
11. **John Dryden:** John Dryden (1631–1700) was an English poet, dramatist, and critic; the author of ***Absalom and Achitophel*** (1681), ***All for Love*** (1677), ***An Essay of Dramatic Poesy*** (1668), etc.
12. **Racine:** Jean Baptiste Racine (1639–1699) was a French dramatist and poet and the

author of *Andromaque* (1667), ***Phèdre*** (1677), etc.
13. **Bossu's treatise on epic poetry:** The French critic René le Bossu (1631-1680) set forth rules for epic-writing in his ***Traité du poème épique*** (1675), a neo-classical work much admired in the late 17th and the early 18th century. The book was translated into English in 1695.
14. **Garraway's:** a coffee-house in Exchange Alley, Cornhill

JOHN HENRY CARDINAL NEWMAN

(1801–1890)

John Henry Newman was an English theologian and writer. He was born in London on February 21, 1801, the eldest son of an evangelical banker. Educated at Trinity College, Oxford, he became a Fellow of Iriel College in 1822, was ordained in the Church of England in 1824, and took a leading part in the Oxford Movement from 1833 to 1841. He joined the Roman Catholic Church in 1845, served as rector of the new Catholic University of Dublin for the period 1854–1858, was created a cardinal in 1879, and died in Birmingham, on August 11, 1890.

Newman's complete works fill more than forty volumes. To the general reader he is best known as the author of **Apologia pro Vita Sua** (1864), a spiritual autobiography, and **The Idea of a University Defined and Illustrated** (1873), a thought-provoking book on higher education. He is noted for a lucid, supple, and elegant style.

THE VALUE OF A UNIVERSITY EDUCATION

But I must bring these extracts[1] to an end. Today I have confined myself to saying that that training of the intellect, which is best for the individual himself, best enables him to discharge his duties to society. The Philosopher, indeed, and the man of the world differ in their very notion, but the methods, by which they are respectively formed, are pretty much the same. The Philosopher has the same command of matters of thought, which the true citizen and gentleman has of matters of business and conduct. If then a practical end must be assigned to a University course, I say it is that of training good members of society. Its art is the art of social life, and its end is fitness for the world. It neither confines its views to particular professions on the one hand, nor creates heroes or inspires genius on the other. Works indeed of genius fall under no art; heroic minds come under no rule; a University is not a birthplace of poets or of immortal authors, of founders of schools, leaders of colonies, or conquerors of nations. It does not promise a generation of Aristotles[2] or Newtons[3], of Napoleons[4] or Washingtons[5], or Raphaels[6] or Shakespeares, though such miracles of nature[7] it has before now contained within its precincts. Nor is it content on the other hand with forming the critic or the experimentalist, the economist or the engineer, though such too it includes within its scope. But a University training is the great ordinary means to a great but ordinary end; it aims at raising the intellectual tone of society, at cultivating the public mind, at purifying the national taste, at supplying true principles to popular enthusiasm and fixed aims to popular aspiration, at giving enlargement and sobriety to the ideas of the age, at facilitating the exercise of political power, and refining the intercourse of private life. It is the education which gives a man a clear conscious view of his own opinions and judgments, a truth in developing them, an eloquence in expressing them, and a force in urging them. It teaches him to see things as they are, to go right to the point, to disentangle a skein of thought, to detect what is sophistical, and to discard what is irrelevant. It prepares him to fill any post with credit, and to master any subject with facility. It shows him how to accommodate himself to others, how to throw himself into their state of mind, how to bring before them his own, how to influence them, how to come to an understanding with them, how to bear with them. He is at home in any society, he has common ground with every class; he knows when to speak and when to be silent; he is able to converse, he is able to listen; he can ask a question pertinently, and gain a lesson seasonably, when he has nothing to impart himself; he is ever ready, yet never in the way; he is a pleasant companion, and a comrade you can depend upon; he knows when to be serious and when to trifle, and he has a sure tact which enables him to trifle with gracefulness and to be serious with effect. He has the repose of a mind which lives in itself, while it lives in the world, and which has resources for its happiness at home when it cannot go abroad. He has a gift which serves him in public, and supports him in retirement, without which good fortune is but vulgar, and with which failure and disappointment have a charm. The art which tends to make a man all this is in the object which it pursues, as useful as the art of wealth or the art of health, though it is less susceptible of method, and less tangible, less certain, less complete in its result.

NOTES

1. **these extracts:** the extracts from other authorities on education
2. **Aristotle:** Aristotle (384–322 B.C.) was a Greek philosopher, pupil of Plato, and tutor of Alexander the Great. He conducted the Peripatetic school at Athens, and wrote books on logic, metaphysics, ethics, politics, poetics, rhetoric, biology, etc.
3. **Newton:** Isaac Newton (1642–1727) was an English mathematician, physicist, and astronomer; the formulator of the law of gravitation, three laws of motion, and the elements of differential calculus; and the author of *Principia Mathematica* (1687) and *Opticks* (1704).
4. **Napoleon:** Napoleon I, Napoleon Bonaparte (1769–1821), was a French military leader, the First Consul of France (1799–1804), and the Emperor of France (1804–1815).
5. **Washington:** George Washington (1732–1799), U.S. general and statesman, first

president of the United States
6. **Raphael:** Raffaello Santi or Sanzio (1483−1520), an Italian painter and architect, was one of the great artists of the Renaissance.
7. **miracles of nature:** geniuses

50

GEORGE HENRY BORROW

(1803–1881)

George Henry Borrow was an English writer of travel literature. The son of a recruiting officer, he was born in Norfolk and educated at Edinburgh High School and Norwich Grammar School. He was articled to a solicitor but took to writing. Having travelled widely in England, France, Germany, Spain, Russia, and the East, he married a rich lady in 1840 and lived a landed proprietor in Norfolk until his death.

In Borrow's original writings fact and fiction are blended, and his personality is projected. His major works are **The Bible in Spain** (1843), an account of his adventures in that country as a distributor of Bibles; **Lavengro** (1851), the story of his life among the gipsies; **The Romany Rye** (1857), a sequel to **Lavengro**; and **Wild Wales** (1862), a description of a walking holiday. They reveal the author's sympathetic understanding of offbeat people, his fine love of the open road, and his natural shrewdness and sly humour. Borrow has a good, lively narrative style.

AT AN INN

"YOUNG gentleman," said the huge fat landlord, "you are come[1] at the right time; dinner will be taken up in a few minutes, and such a dinner," he continued, rubbing his hands, "as you will not see every day in these times."

"I am hot and dusty," said I, " and should wish to cool my hands and face."

"Jenny!" said the huge landlord, with the utmost gravity, "show the gentleman into number seven, that he may wash his hands and face."

"By no means," said I, "I am a person of primitive habits, and there is nothing like the pump in weather like this."

"Jenny!" said the landlord, with the same gravity as before, "go with the young gentleman to the pump in the back kitchen, and take a clean towel along with you."

Thereupon the rosy-faced clean-looking damsel went to a drawer, and producing a large, thick, but snowy-white towel, she nodded to me to follow her; whereupon I followed Jenny through a long passage into the back kitchen.

And at the end of the back kitchen there stood a pump; and going to it I placed my hands beneath the spout, and said, "Pump, Jenny;" and Jenny incontinently, without laying down the towel, pumped with one hand, and I washed and cooled my heated hands.

And, when my hands were washed and cooled, I took off my neckcloth, and unbuttoning my shirt collar, I placed my head beneath the spout of the pump, and I said unto Jenny, "Now, Jenny, lay down the towel, and pump for your life[2]."

Thereupon Jenny, placing the towel on a linen-horse[3], took the handle of the pump with both hands and pumped over my head as handmaid had never pumped before; so that the water poured in torrents from my head, my face, and my hair down upon the brick floor.

And after the lapse of somewhat more than a minute, I called out with a half-strangled voice, "Hold, Jenny!" and Jenny desisted. I stood for a few moments to recover my breath, then taking the towel which Jenny proffered, I dried composedly my hands and head, my face and hair; then, returning the towel to Jenny, I gave a deep sigh and said, "Surely this is one of the pleasant moments of life."

Then, having set my dress to rights, and combed my hair with a pocket comb, I followed Jenny, who conducted me back through the long passage, and showed me into a neat sanded parlour on the ground floor.

I sat down by a window which looked out upon the dusty street; presently in came the handmaid, and commenced laying the table-cloth. "Shall I spread the table for one, sir," said she, "or do you expect anybody to dine with you?"

"I can't say that I expect anybody," said I, laughing inwardly to myself; "however, if you please you can lay for two, so that if any acquaintance of mine should chance to step in, he may find a knife and fork ready for him."

So I sat by the window, sometimes looking out upon the dusty street, and now glancing at certain old-fashioned prints which adorned the wall over against me. I fell into a kind of doze, from which I was almost instantly awakened by the opening of the door. Dinner, thought I; and I sat upright in my chair. No, a man of the middle age, and rather above the middle height, dressed in a plain suit of black, made his appearance, and sat down in a chair at some distance from me, but near to the table, and appeared to be lost in thought[4].

"The weather is very warm, sir," said I.

"Very," said the stranger laconically, looking at me for the first time.

"Would you like to see the newspaper?" said I, taking up one which lay upon the window seat.

"I never read newspapers," said the stranger, "nor indeed—" Whatever it might be that he had intended to say he left unfinished. Suddenly he walked to the mantel-piece at the farther end of the room, before which he placed himself with his back towards me. There he remained motionless for some time; at length, raising his hand, he touched the corner of the mantel-piece with his finger, advanced towards the chair which he had left, and again seated himself.

"Have you come far?" said he, suddenly looking towards me, and speaking in a frank and open manner, which denoted a wish to enter into conversation. "You do not seem to be of this place."

"I come from some distance," said I; "indeed I am walking for exercise, which I find as necessary to the mind as to the body. I believe that by exercise people would escape much mental misery."

Scarcely had I uttered these words when the stranger laid his hand, with seeming carelessness, upon the table, near one of the glasses; after a moment or two he touched the glass as if inadvertently, then, glancing furtively at me, he withdrew his hand and looked towards the window.

"Are you from these parts?" said I at last, with apparent carelessness.

"From this vicinity," replied the stranger. "You think, then, that it is as easy to walk off the bad humours of the mind as of the body."

"I, at least, am walking in that hope," said I.

"I wish you may be successful," said the stranger; and here he touched one of the forks which lay on the table near him.

Here the door, which was slightly ajar, was suddenly pushed open with some fracas, and in came the stout landlord, supporting with some difficulty an immense dish, in which was a mighty round mass of smoking meat, garnished all round with vegetables; so high was the mass that it probably obstructed his view, for it was not until he had placed it upon the table that he appeared to observe the stranger; he almost started, and quite out of breath exclaimed, "God bless me, your honour; is your honour the acquaintance that the young gentleman was expecting?"

"Is the young gentleman expecting an acquaintance?" said the stranger.

There is nothing like putting a good face upon these matters, thought I to myself; and, getting up, I bowed to the unknown. "Sir," said I, "when I told Jenny that she might lay the table-cloth for two, so that in the event of any acquaintance dropping in he might find a knife and fork ready for him, I was merely jocular, being an entire stranger in these parts, and expecting no one. Fortune, however, it would seem, has been unexpectedly kind to me; I flatter myself, sir, that since you have been in this room I have had the honour of making your acquaintance; and in the strength of that hope I humbly entreat you to honour me with your company to dinner, provided you have not already dined."

The stranger laughed outright.

"Sir," I continued, "the round of beef is a noble[5] one, and seems exceedingly well boiled, and the landlord was just right when he said I should have such a dinner as is not seen every day. A round of beef, at any rate such a round of beef as this, is seldom seen smoking upon the table in these degenerate times. Allow me, sir," said I, observing that the stranger was about to speak, "allow me another remark. I think I saw you just now touch the fork, I venture to hail it as an omen that you will presently seize it, and apply it to its proper purpose, and its companion the knife also."

The stranger changed colour, and gazed upon me in silence.

"Do, sir," here put in the landlord; "do, sir, accept the young gentleman's invitation. Your honour has of late been looking poorly, and the young gentleman is a funny young gentleman, and a clever young gentleman; and I think it will do your honour good to have a dinner's chat with the young gentleman."

"It is not my dinner-hour," said the stranger; "I dine considerably later; taking anything now would only discompose me; I shall, however, be most happy to sit down with the young gentleman; reach me that paper, and, when the young gentleman has satisfied his appetite, we may perhaps have a little chat together."

The landlord handed the stranger the newspaper, and, bowing, retired with his maid Jenny. I helped myself to a portion of the smoking round, and commenced eating with no little appetite. The stranger appeared to be soon engrossed with the newspaper. We continued thus a considerable time—the one reading and the other dining. Chancing suddenly to cast my eyes upon the stranger, I saw his brow contract; he gave a slight stamp with his foot, and flung the newspaper to the ground, then stooping down he picked it up, first moving his forefinger along the floor, seemingly slightly scratching it with his nail.

"Do you hope, sir," said I, "by that ceremony with the finger to preserve yourself from the evil chance?"

The stranger started; then, after looking at me for some time in silence, he said, "Is it possible that you—?"

"Ay, ay," said I, helping myself to some more of the round, "I have touched myself in my younger days, both for the evil chance and the good. Can't say, though, that I ever trusted much in the ceremony."

The stranger made no reply, but appeared to be in deep thought; nothing further passed between us until I had concluded the dinner, when I said to him, "I shall now be most happy, sir, to have the pleasure of your conversation over a pint of wine."

The stranger rose; "No, my young friend," said he, smiling, "that would scarce be fair. It is my turn now—pray do me the favour to go home with me, and accept what hospitality my poor roof can offer; to tell you the truth, I wish to have some particular discourse with you which would hardly be possible in this place. As for wine, I can give you some much better than you can get here; the landlord is an excellent fellow, but he is an inn-keeper, after all. I am going out for a moment, and will send him in, so that you may settle your account; I trust you will not refuse me, I only live about two miles from here."

I looked in the face of the stranger—it was a fine intelligent face, with a cast of melancholy in it. "Sir," said I, "I would go with you though you lived four miles instead of two."

"Who is that gentleman?" said I to the landlord, after I had settled his bill; "I am going home with him."

"I wish I were going too," said the fat landlord, laying his hand upon his stomach. "Young gentleman, I shall be a loser by his honour's taking you away; but, after all, the truth is the truth—there are few gentlemen in these parts like his honour, either for learning or welcoming his friends. Young gentleman, I congratulate you."

NOTES

1. **you are come:** you have come
2. **for your life:** (colloq.) vigorously
3. **a linen-horse:** a frame on which laundered linen is hung for drying or airing
4. **lost in thought:** engrossed in thought
5. **noble:** grand, excellent

51

ELIZABETH CLEGHORN GASKELL

(1810–1865)

Mrs. Elizabeth Cleghorn Gaskell was an English novelist and biographer. The daughter of William Stevenson, a Unitarian minister, she was born in London, brought up by her aunt in Cheshire, and educated at Miss Byerley's school in Stratford-upon-Avon. She married the Unitarian minister William Gaskell in 1832 and lived in Manchester henceforward.

In her first novel, **Mary Barton** (1848), she reflected the outlook of contemporary mill-hands. Her best-known work is **Cranford** (1853), a series of sketches of life in a quiet country town in the 1830's. Her other novels are **Ruth** (1853), **North and South** (1855), **Sylvia's Lovers** (1863), and **Wives and Daughters** (1866). Mrs. Gaskell was a discerning observer, a fair-minded social critic, and a delightful story-teller. The main interest of her novels lies in the charming character-sketches, the kindly humour, and the clear and terse narrative style. Mrs. Gaskell met Charlotte Brontë in 1850 and wrote **The Life of Charlotte Brontë** (1857), which is accounted one of the best biographies in English.

A PETITION

For three years past[1] trade had been getting worse and worse, and the price of provisions higher and higher. This disparity between the amount of the earnings of the working classes and the price of their food, occasioned, in more cases than could well be imagined, disease and death. Whole families went through a gradual starvation. They only wanted a Dante[2] to record their sufferings. And yet even his words would fall short of the awful truth; they could only present an outline of the tremendous facts of the destitution that surrounded thousands upon thousands in the terrible years 1839, 1840, and 1841. Even philanthropists who had studied the subject, were forced to own themselves perplexed in their endeavour to ascertain the real causes of the misery; the whole matter was of so complicated a nature, that it became next to impossible to understand it thoroughly. It need excite no surprise, then, to learn that a bad feeling between working men and the upper classes became very strong in this season of privation. The indigence and sufferings of the operatives induced a suspicion in the minds of many of them, that their legislators, their magistrates, their employers, and even the ministers of religion, were, in general, their oppressors and enemies; and were in league for their prostration and enthralment. The most deplorable and enduring evil that arose out of the period of commercial depression to which I refer, was this feeling of alienation between the different classes of society. It is so impossible to describe, or even faintly to picture, the state of distress which prevailed in the town[3] at that time, that I will not attempt it; and yet I think again that surely, in a Christian land, it was not known even so feebly as words could tell it, or the more happy and fortunate would have thronged with their sympathy and their aid. In many instances the sufferers wept first, and then they cursed. Their vindictive feelings exhibited themselves in rabid politics. And when I hear, as I have heard, of the sufferings and privations of the poor, of provision shops where ha'porths[4] of tea, sugar, butter, and even flour, were sold to accommodate the indigent, —of parents sitting in their clothes by the fireside during the whole night for seven weeks together, in order that their only bed and bedding might be reserved for the use of their large family, —of others sleeping upon the cold hearthstone for weeks in succession, without adequate means of providing themselves with food or fuel (and this in the depth of winter), —of others being compelled to fast for days together, uncheered by any hope of better fortune, living, moreover, or rather starving, in a crowded garret, or damp cellar, and gradually sinking under the pressure of want and despair into a premature grave; and when this has been confirmed by the evidence of their careworn looks, their excited feelings, and their desolate homes, —can I wonder that many of them, in such times of misery and destitution, spoke and acted with ferocious precipitation?

An idea was now springing up among the operatives, that originated with the Chartists[5], but which came at last to be cherished as a darling child by many and many a one. They could not believe that Government knew of their misery; they rather chose to think it possible that men could voluntarily assume the office of legislators for a nation who were ignorant of its real state; as who should make domestic rules for the pretty behaviour of children without caring to know that those children had been kept for days without food. Besides, the starving multitudes had heard, that the very existence of their distress had been denied in Parliament; and though they felt this strange and inexplicable, yet the idea that their misery had still to be revealed in all its depths, and that then some remedy would be found, soothed their aching hearts, and kept down their rising fury.

So a petition was framed, and signed by thousands in the bright spring days of 1839, imploring Parliament to hear witnesses who could testify to the unparalleled destitution of the manufacturing districts. Nottingham, Sheffield, Glasgow, Manchester, and many other towns, were busy appointing delegates to convey this petition, who might speak, not merely of what they had seen, and had heard, but from what they had borne and suffered. Life-worn, gaunt, anxious, hunger-stamped men, were those delegates.

One of them was John Barton[6]. He would have been ashamed to own the flutter of spirits his appointment gave him. There was the childish delight of seeing London—that went a little way, and but a little way. There was the vain idea of speaking out his notions before so many grand folk—that went a little further; and last, there was the really pure gladness of heart arising from the idea that he was one of those chosen to be instruments in making known the distresses of the people, and consequently in procuring them some grand relief, by means of which they should never suffer want or care any more. He hoped largely, but vaguely, of the results of his expedition. An argosy of the precious hopes of many otherwise despairing creatures, was that petition to be heard concerning their sufferings.

NOTES

1. **For three years past:** for the period 1839-1841
2. **Dante:** Dante Alighieri (1265-1321) was the greatest of Italian poets. His masterpiece was *The Divine Comedy* (*La Divina Commedia*) (?1307-?1320), an account of his imaginary journey through Hell, Purgatory and Paradise. In the first part of his epic, Dante describes the sufferings of people in hell.
3. **in the town:** in Manchester
4. **ha'porths:** halfpennyworths
5. **the Chartists:** those who participated in or supported the revolutionary working-class movement commonly called Chartism (1837-1848)
6. **John Barton:** a major character in the novel *Mary Barton*—an active and clear-sighted worker

52

WILLIAM MAKEPEACE THACKERAY

(1811–1863)

W. M. Thackeray was an English novelist. The only son of an English officer in the East India Company's service, he was born in Calcutta on July 18, 1811, sent to England in 1817, and educated at Charterhouse, London, and at Trinity College, Cambridge. He intended to become an artist but was compelled by circumstances to adopt literature as a profession. He wrote from 1833 until his death, which occurred suddenly on Christmas Eve, 1863.

Thackeray is renowned for his *Vanity Fair* (in monthly parts, 1847–1848) a novel presenting a panorama of the English upper-class society and satirizing its hypocrisy and pretentiousness and his *The History of Henry Esmond* (1852), a historical novel re-creating the style and atmosphere of early 18th century English aristocratic and literary society and exploring the relation between public appearances and private reality. Some of his other novels are *Pendennis* (1848–1850), *The Newcomes* (1853–1855), and *The Virginians* (1857–1859). He delivered two series of lectures mainly on the 18th century, *The English Humourists of the 18th Century* (1851) and *The Four Georges* (1855–1857). His major novels are noted for their social comment, their convincing characters, and their unobtrusive and flexible style.

THE BATTLE OF WATERLOO

All that day[1], from morning until past sunset, the cannon never ceased to roar. It was dark when the cannonading stopped all of a sudden.

All of us have read of what occurred during that interval. The tale is in every Englishman's mouth; and you and I, who were children when the great battle was won and lost, are never tired of hearing and recounting the history of that famous action. Its remembrance rankles still in the bosoms of millions of the countrymen of those brave men who lost the day. They pant for an opportunity of revenging that humiliation; and if a contest, ending in a victory on their part, should ensue, elating them in their turn, and leaving its cursed legacy of hatred and rage behind to us, there is no end to the so-called glory and shame, and to the alternations of successful and unsuccessful murder, in which two high-spirited nations might engage. Centuries hence, we Frenchmen and Englishmen might be boasting and killing each other still, carrying out bravely the Devil's code of honour.

All our friends took their share and fought like men in the great field. All day long, whilst the women were praying ten miles away, the lines of the dauntless English infantry were receiving and repelling the furious charges of the French horsemen. Guns which were heard at Brussels were ploughing up their ranks, and comrades falling, and the resolute survivors closing in. Towards evening, the attack of the French, repeated and resisted so bravely, slackened in its fury. They had other foes besides the British to engage, or were preparing for a final onset. It came at last: the columns of the Imperial Guard marched up the hill of Saint Jean, at length and at once to sweep the English from the height which they had maintained all day, and spite of all. Unscared by the thunder of the artillery, which hurled death from the English line, the dark rolling column pressed on and up the hill. It seemed almost to crest the eminence, when it began to wave and falter. Then it stopped, still facing the shot. Then at last the English troops rushed from the post from which no enemy had been able to dislodge them, and the Guard turned and fled.

No more firing was heard at Brussels—the pursuit rolled miles away. Darkness came down on the field and city; and Amelia was praying for George[2], who was lying on his face, dead, with a bullet through his heart. —*Vanity Fair*

NOTES

1. **All that day:** On (Sunday) 18 June 1815—the British and Prussian forces under the Duke of Wellington and Blücher fought with and routed the French under Napoleon at Waterloo, a village south of Brussels, Belgium. Napoleon was thus finally defeated.
2. **Amelia was praying for George:** Amelia Sedley and George Osborne, two major characters in the novel *Vanity Fair*, had been married only a few weeks before George's death.

THE DUKE OF MARLBOROUGH

And now, having seen a great military march through a friendly country; the pomps and festivities of more than one German court; the severe struggle of a hotly contested battle, and the triumph of victory, Mr. Esmond beheld another part of military duty: our troops entering the enemy's territory, and putting all around them to fire and sword; burning farms, wasted fields, shrieking women, slaughtered sons and fathers, and drunken soldiery, cursing and carousing in the midst of tears, terror, and murder. Why does the stately Muse of History, that delights in describing the valour of heroes and the grandeur of conquest, leave out these scenes, so brutal, mean, and degrading, that yet form by far the greater part of the drama of war? You, gentlemen of England, who live at home at ease, and compliment yourselves in the songs of triumph with which our chieftains are bepraised—you, pretty maidens, that come tumbling down the stairs when the fife and drum call you, and huzzah for the British Grenadiers—do you take account that these items go to make up the amount of the triumph you admire, and form part of the duties of the heroes you fondle? Our chief[1], whom England and all Europe, saving only the Frenchman, worshipped almost, had this of the godlike in him, that he was impassable before victory, before danger, before defeat. Before the greatest obstacle or the most trivial ceremony; before a hundred thousand men drawn in battalia[2], or a peasant slaughtered at the door of his burning hovel; before a carouse of drunken German lords, or a monarch's court, or a cottage table where his plans were laid, or an enemy's battery, vomiting flame and death, and strewing corpses round about him; —he was always cold, calm, resolute, like fate. He performed a treason or a court—bow, he told a falsehood as black as Styx[3], as easily as he paid a compliment or spoke about the weather. He took a mistress, and left her; he betrayed his benefactor, and supported him, or would have murdered him, with the same calmness always, and having no more remorse than Clotho when she weaves the thread, or Lachesis[4] when she cuts it. In the hour of battle I have heard the

Prince of Savoy's[5] officers say, the Prince became possessed with a sort of warlike fury; his eyes lighted up; he rushed hither and thither, raging; he shrieked curses and encouragement, yelling and harking his bloody war-dogs on, and himself always at the first point of the hunt. Our Duke was as calm at the mouth of the cannon as at the door of a drawing-room. Perhaps he could not have been the great man he was, had he had a heart either for love or hatred, or pity or fear, or regret or remorse. He achieved the highest deed of daring, or deepest calculation of thought, as he performed the very meanest action of which a man is capable; told a lie, or cheated a fond woman, or robbed a poor beggar of a halfpenny, with a like awful serenity and equal capacity of the highest and lowest acts of our nature.

His qualities were pretty well known in the army, where there were parties of all politics, and of plenty of shrewdness and wit; but there existed such a perfect confidence in him, as the first captain of the world, and such a faith and admiration in his prodigious genius and fortune, that the very men whom he notoriously cheated of their pay, the chiefs whom he used and injured—for he used all men, great and small, that came near him, as his instruments alike, and took something of theirs, either some quality or some property—the blood of a soldier, it might be, or a jewelled hat, or a hundred thousand crowns from a king, or a portion out of a starving sentinel's three-farthings; or (when he was young) a kiss from a woman, and the gold chain off her neck, taking all he could from woman or man, and having, as I have said, this of the godlike in him, that he could see a hero perish or a sparrow fall, with the same amount of sympathy for either. Not that he had no tears: he could always order up this reserve at the proper moment to battle; he could draw upon tears or smiles alike, and whenever need was for using this cheap coin. He would cringe to a shoeblack, as he would flatter a minister or a monarch; be haughty, be humble, threaten, repent, weep, grasp your hand (or stab you whenever he saw occasion) —But yet those of the army, who knew him best and had suffered most from him, admired him most of all; and as he rode along the lines to battle or galloped up in the nick of time to a battalion reeling from before the enemy's charge or shot, the fainting men and officers got new courage as they saw the splendid calm of his face, and felt that his will made them irresistible.

After the great victory of Blenheim⁶ the enthusiasm of the army for the Duke, even of his bitterest personal enemies in it, amounted to a sort of rage—nay, the very officers who cursed him in their hearts were among the most frantic to cheer him. Who could refuse his meed⁷ of admiration to such a victory and such a victor? Not he who writes: a man may profess to be ever so much a philosopher; but he who fought on that day must feel a thrill of pride as he recalls it.

NOTES

1. **Our chief:** John Churchill (1650–1722), the first Duke of Marlborough, was commander of the British forces in the War of the Spanish Succession (1701–1714). He defeated the French and their allies at Blenheim (1704), Ramillies (1706), Oudenaarde (1708), and Malplaquet (1709).
2. **battalia:** (arch.) battle order
3. **Styx:** (Gr. myth.) the black river in Hades
4. **Clotho...Lachesis:** Clotho, Lachesis, and Atropos were the three Fates in Greek mythology.
5. **the Prince of Savoy's:** Prince Eugene (1663–1736), Austrian general who associated with Marlborough in the War of the Spanish Succession.
6. **the great victory of Blenheim:** On 13 August 1704 Marlborough and Prince Eugene won their victory over the French and Bavarians at Blenheim, a village in West Bavaria, Germany.
7. **meed:** (poet.) reward

53

CHARLES DICKENS

(1812-1870)

Charles Dickens was an English novelist. He was born near Portsmouth on February 7, 1812, the second child of a government clerk. His family moved to Chatham, Kent, in 1816, and then to London in 1821. Largely self-educated, he engaged in journalistic work, and became a full-time writer in 1836. Besides writing, he was interested in amateur theatricals and in reading his works to an audience. He died on June 9, 1870, and was buried in Westminster Abbey.

All of Dickens's novels were first published serially in periodicals, especially in **Household Words** (1849-1859) and **All the Year Round** (1859-1870), two weeklies edited by himself. He made his name with **The Posthumous Papers of the Pickwick Club** (1836-1837), the supreme comic story of Mr. Pickwick and his companions. This was followed by **Oliver Twist** (1837-1838), a protest against society's harsh treatment of poor children; **Nicholas Nickleby** (1838-1839), a protest against bad schools and their proprietors; **The Old Curiosity Shop** (1840-1841), a book containing a number of pathetic scenes and striking characters; **Barnaby Rudge** (1841), a historical novel set in the troubled London of 1780; **Martin Chuzzlewit** (1843-1844), an exposure of selfishness; and several popular Christmas books including **A Christmas Carol** (1843) and **The Cricket on the Hearth** (1846). Then came a succession of great novels: **Dombey and Son** (1846–1848), a satire on business ambitions that sacrifice family love; **David Copperfield** (1849–1850), an autobiographical novel; **Bleak House** (1852–1853), an attack on legal obfuscation; **Hard Times** (1854), an investigation into the ills of industrialized society; **Little Dorrit** (1855–1857), an exposure of the destructive power of money; **A Tale of Two Cities** (1859), a historical novel of the French Revolution; **Great Expectations** (1860–1861), an exposure of greed and hypocrisy; **Our Mutual Friend** (1864–1865), a severe criticism of the love of money; and **Edwin Drood** (1870), an unfinished work. In his novels Dickens is famous for his extraordinary character creation, his attacks on the social evils of his time, and his humour and pathos. He has more than one style; he is often clear, fluent, and lively, but sometimes rhetorical and circumlocutory.

THE ROAD TO DOVER

My box was at my old lodging over the water, and I had written a direction for it on the back of one of our address cards that we nailed on the casks: "Master David, to be left till called for, at the Coach Office, David." This I had in my pocket ready to put on the box, after I should have got it out of the house; and as I went towards my lodging, I looked about me for someone who would help me to carry it to the booking-office.

There was a long-legged young man, with a very little empty donkey-cart, standing near the Obelisk[1], in the Blackfriars Road, whose eye I caught as I was going by, and who, addressing me as "Sixpenn' orth of bad ha 'pence," hoped "I should know him agin to swear to" —in allusion, I have no doubt, to my staring at him. I stopped to assure him that I had not done so in bad manner, but uncertain whether he might or might not like a job.

"Wot job?" said the long-legged young man.

"To move a box," I answered.

"Wot box?" said the long-legged young man.

I told him mine, which was down that street there, and which I wanted him to take to the Dover coach office for sixpence. "Done with you for a tanner!" said the long-legged young man, and directly got upon his cart, which was nothing but a large wooden tray on wheels, and rattled away at such a rate, that it was as much as I could do to keep pace with the donkey.

There was a defiant manner about this young man, and particularly about the way in which he chewed straw as he spoke to me, that I did not much like; as the bargain was made, however, I took him upstairs to the room I was leaving and we brought the box down, and put it on his cart. Now, I was unwilling to put the direction-card on there, lest any of my landlord's family should fathom what I was doing, and detain me; so I said to the young man that I would be glad if he would stop for a minute, when he came to the dead-wall of the King's Bench prison. The words were no sooner out of my mouth, than he rattled away as if he, my box, the cart, and the donkey, were all equally mad; and I was quite out of breath with running and calling after him, when I caught him at the place appointed.

Being much flushed and excited, I tumbled my half-guinea out of my pocket in pulling the card out. I put it in my mouth for safety, and though my hands trembled a good deal, had just tied the card on very much to my satisfaction, when I felt myself violently chucked under the chin by the long-legged young man, and saw my half-guinea fly out of my mouth into his hand.

"Wot!" said the young man, seizing me by my jacket collar, with a frightful grin. "This is a pollis[2] case, is it? You're a-going to bolt, are you? Come to the pollis, you your warmin[3], come to the pollis!"

"You give me my money back, if you please," said I, very much frightened; "and leave me alone."

"Come to the pollis!" said the young man. "You shall prove it yourn[4] to the pollis."

"Give me my box and money, will you?" I cried, bursting into tears.

The young man still replied: "Come to the pollis!" and was dragging me against the donkey in a violent manner, as if there were any affinity between that animal and a magistrate, when he changed his mind, jumped into the cart, sat upon my box, and, exclaiming that he would drive to the pollis straight, rattled away harder than ever.

I ran after him as fast as I could, but I had no breath to call out with, and should not have dared to call out, now, if I had. I narrowly escaped being run over, twenty times at least, in half a mile. Now I lost him, now I saw him, now I lost him, now I was cut at with a whip, now shouted at, now down in the mud, now up again, now running into somebody's arms, now running headlong at a post. At length, confused by fright and heat, and doubting whether half London might not by this time be turning out for my apprehension, I left the young man to go where he would with my box and money; and, panting and crying, but never stopping, faced about for Greenwich[5], which I had understood was on the Dover Road: taking very little more out of the world, towards the retreat of my aunt,

Miss Betsey, than I had brought into it, on the night when my arrival gave her so much umbrage.

. . . .

My bed at night was under another haystack, where I rested comfortably, after having washed my blistered feet in a stream, and dressed them as well as I was able, with some cool leaves. When I took the road again next morning, I found that it lay through a succession of hop-grounds and orchards. It was sufficiently late in the year for the orchards to be ruddy with ripe apples; and in a few places the hop-pickers were already at work. I thought it all extremely beautiful, and made up my mind to sleep among the hops that night: imagining some cheerful companionship in the long perspective of poles, with the graceful leaves twining round them.

The trampers were worse than ever that day, and inspired me with a dread that is yet quite fresh in my mind. Some of them were most ferocious-looking ruffians, who stared at me as I went by; and stopped, perhaps, and called after me to come back and speak to them, and when I took to my heels, stoned me. I recollect one young fellow—a tinker, I suppose, from his wallet and brazier—who had a woman with him, and who faced about and stared at me thus; and then roared at me in such a tremendous voice to come back, that I halted and looked round.

"Come here, when you're called," said the tinker, "or I'll rip your young body open."

I thought it best to go back. As I drew nearer to them, trying to propitiate the tinker by my looks, I observed that the woman had a black eye.

"Where are you going?" said the tinker, gripping the bosom of my shirt with his blackened hand.

"I am going to Dover," I said.

"Where do you come from?" asked the tinker, giving his hand another turn in my shirt, to hold me more securely.

"I come from London," I said.

"What lay are you upon?" asked the tinker. "Are you a prig?"

"N—no," I said.

"Ain't you, by G—? If you make a brag of your honesty to me," said the tinker, "I'll knock your brains out."

With his disengaged hand he made a menace of striking me, and then looked at me from head to foot.

"Have you got the price of a pint of beer about you?" said the tinker, "If you have, out with it, afore I take it away!"

I should certainly have produced it, but that I met the woman's look, and saw her very slightly shake her head, and form "No!" with her lips.

"I am very poor," I said, attempting to smile, "and have got no money."

"Why, what do you mean?" said the tinker, looking so sternly at me, that I almost feared he saw the money in my pocket.

"Sir!" I stammered.

"What do you mean," said the tinker, "by wearing my brother's silk handkercher! Give it over here!" And he had mine off my neck in a moment, and tossed it to the woman.

The woman burst into a fit of laughter, as if she thought this a joke, and tossed it back to me, nodded once, as slightly as before, and made the word "Go!" with her lips. Before I could obey, however, the tinker seized the handkerchief out of my hand with a roughness that threw me away like a feather, and putting it loosely round his own neck, turned upon the woman with an oath, and knocked her down....

[On the sixth day.]

When I came, at last, upon the bare wide downs near Dover, it [David's fanciful picture of his mother in her youth] relieved the solitary aspect of the scene with hope; and not until I reached that first great aim of my journey, and actually set foot in the town itself, on the sixth day of my flight, did it desert me. But then, strange to say, when I stood with my ragged shoes, and my dusty, sunburnt, half-clothed figure, in the place so long desired, it seemed to vanish like a dream, and to leave me helpless and dispirited.

53. CHARLES DICKENS (1812–1870)

I inquired about my aunt among the boatmen first, and received various answers. One said she lived in the South Foreland Light, and had singed her whiskers by doing so; another, that she was made fast to the great buoy outside the harbour, and could only be visited at half-tide; a third, that she was locked up in Maidstone Jail for child-stealing; a fourth, that she was seen to mount a broom, in the last high wind, and make direct for Calais. The fly-drivers, among whom I inquired next, were equally jocose and equally disrespectful; and the shopkeepers, not liking my appearance, generally replied, without hearing what I had to say, that they had got nothing for me. I felt more miserable and destitute than I had done at any period of my running away. My money was all gone. I had nothing left to dispose of; I was hungry, thirsty, and worn out; and seemed as distant from the end as if I had remained in London.

The morning had worn away in these inquiries, and I was sitting on the step of an empty shop at a street corner, near the market-place, deliberating upon wandering towards those other places which had been mentioned, when a fly-driver, coming by with his carriage, dropped a horsecloth. Something good-natured in the man's face, as I handed it up, encouraged me to ask him if he could tell me where Miss Trotwood lived; though I had asked the question so often, that it almost died upon my lips.

"Trotwood," said he. "Let me see. I know the name, too. Old lady?"

"Yes," I said, "rather."

"Pretty stiff in the back?" said he, making himself upright.

"Yes," I said. "I should think it very likely."

"Carries a bag?" said he; "bag with a good deal of room in it: is gruffish, and comes down upon you sharp?"

My heart sank within me as I acknowledged the undoubted accuracy of this description.

"Why then, I tell you what," said he. "If you go up there," pointing with his whip towards the heights, "and keep right on till you come to some houses facing the sea, I think you'll hear of her. My opinion is, she won't stand anything, so here's a penny for you."

I accepted the gift thankfully, and bought a loaf with it. Dispatching this refreshment by the way, I went in the direction my friend had indicated, and walked on a good distance without coming to the houses he had mentioned. At length I saw some before me; and approaching them, went into a little shop (it was what we used to call a general shop, at home), and inquired if they could have the goodness to tell me where Miss Trotwood lived. I addressed myself to a man behind the counter, who was weighing some rice for a young woman; but the latter, taking the inquiry to herself, turned round quickly.

"My mistress?" she said. "What do you want with her, boy?"

"I want," I replied, "to speak to her, if you please"….

…I followed the young woman, and we soon came to a very neat little cottage with cheerful bow-windows; in front of it, a small square gravelled court or garden full of flowers, carefully tended, and smelling deliciously.

"This is Miss Trotwood's," said the young woman. "Now you know; and that's all I have got to say." With which words she hurried into the house, as if to shake off the responsibility of my appearance; and left me standing at the garden-gate, looking disconsolately over the top of it towards the parlour-window, where a muslin curtain partly undrawn in the middle, a large round green screen or fan fastened on to the window-sill, a small table, and a great chair, suggested to me that my aunt might be at that moment seated in awful state.

My shoes were by this time in a woeful condition. The soles had shed themselves bit by bit, and the upper leathers had broken and burst until the very shape and form of shoes had departed from them. My hat (which had served me for a night-cap, too) was so crushed and bent, that no old battered handleless saucepan on a dunghill need have been ashamed to vie with it. My shirt and trousers, stained with heat, dew, grass, and the Kentish[6] soil on which I had slept—and torn besides—might have frightened the birds from my aunt's garden as I stood at the gate. My hair had known no comb or brush since I left London. My face, neck, and hands, from unaccustomed exposure to the air and sun, were burnt to a berry-brown. From head to foot I was powdered almost as white with chalk and dust, as if I had come out of a lime-kiln. In this plight, and with a strong consciousness of it, I waited to introduce myself to, and make my first impression on, my formidable aunt.

The unbroken stillness of the parlour-window leading me to infer, after a while, that she was not there, I lifted up my eyes to the window above it, where I saw a florid, pleasant-looking gentleman, with a grey head, who shut up one eye in a grotesque manner, nodded his head at me several times, shook it at me as often, laughed, and went away.

I had been discomposed enough before; but I was so much the more discomposed by this unexpected behaviour, that I was on the point of slinking off, to think how I had best proceed, when there came out of the house a lady with her handkerchief tied over her cap, and a pair of gardening gloves on her hands, wearing a gardening pocket like a tollman's apron, and carrying a great knife. I knew her immediately to be Miss Betsey, for she came stalking out of the house exactly as my poor mother had so often described her stalking up our garden at Blunderstone Rookery[7].

"Go away!" said Miss Betsey, shaking her head, and making a distant chop in the air with her knife. "Go along! No boys here!"

I watched her, with my heart at my lips, as she marched to a corner of her garden, and stopped to dig up some little root there. Then, without a scrap of courage, but with a great deal of desperation, I went softly in and stood beside her, touching her with my finger.

"If you please, ma'am," I began.

She started and looked up.

"If you please, aunt."

"Eh?" exclaimed Miss Betsey, in a tone of amazement I have never heard approached.

"If you please, aunt, I am your nephew."

"Oh, Lord!" said my aunt. And sat flat down in the garden-path.

"I am David Copperfield, of Blunderstone, in Suffolk[8]—where you came, on the night when I was born, and saw my dear mama. I have been very unhappy since she died. I have been slighted, and taught nothing, and thrown upon myself, and put to work not fit for me. It made me run away to you. I was robbed at first setting out, and have walked all the way, and have never slept in a bed since I began the journey." Here my self-support gave way all at once; and with a movement of my hands, intended to show her my ragged state, and call it to witness that I had suffered something, I broke into a passion of crying, which I suppose had been pent up within me all the week.

My aunt, with every sort of expression but wonder discharged from her countenance, sat on the gravel, staring at me, until I began to cry; when she got up in a great hurry, collared me, and took me into the parlour. Her first proceeding there was to unlock a tall press, bring out several bottles, and pour some of the contents of each into my mouth. I think they must have been taken out at random, for I am sure I tasted aniseed water, anchovy sauce, and salad dressing. When she had administered these restoratives, as I was still quite hysterical, and unable to control my sobs, she put me on the sofa, with a shawl under my head, and the handkerchief from her own head under my feet, lest I should sully the cover; and then, sitting herself down behind the green fan or screen I have already mentioned, so that I could not see her face, ejaculated at intervals, "Mercy on us!" letting those exclamations off like minute guns.

After a time she rang the bell. "Janet," said my aunt, when her servant came in. "Go upstairs, give my compliments to Mr. Dick[9], and say I wish to speak to him."

Janet looked a little surprised to see me lying stiffly on the sofa (I was afraid to move lest it should be displeasing to my aunt), but went on her errand. My aunt, with her hands behind her, walked up and down the room, until the gentleman who had squinted at me from the upper window came in laughing.

"Mr. Dick," said my aunt, "don't be a fool, because nobody can be more discreet than you can, when you choose. We all know that. So don't be a fool, whatever you are."

The gentleman was serious immediately, and looked at me, I thought, as if he would entreat me to say nothing about the window.

"Mr. Dick," said my aunt, "you have heard me mention David Copperfield? Now don't pretend not to have a memory, because you and I know better."

"David Copperfield?" said Mr. Dick, who did not appear to me to remember much about it. "David Copperfield? Oh yes, to be sure. David, certainly."

"Well," said my aunt, "this is his boy, his son. He would be as like his father as it's possible to be, if he was not so like his mother, too."

"His son?" said Mr. Dick. "David's son. Indeed!"

...

"Well then," returned my aunt, softened by the reply, "how can you pretend to be wool-gathering, Dick, when you are as sharp as a surgeon's lancet? Now, here you see young David Copperfield, and the question I put to you is, what shall I do with him?"

"What shall you do with him?" said Mr. Dick, feebly scratching his head. "Oh! do with him?"

"Yes," said my aunt, with a grave look, and her forefinger held up. "Come! I want some very sound advice."

"Why, if I was you," said Mr. Dick, considering, and looking vacantly at me, "I should—" The contemplation of me seemed to inspire him with a sudden idea, and he added, briskly, "I should wash him!"

"Janet," said my aunt, turning round with a quiet triumph, which I did not then understand, "Mr. Dick sets us all right. Heat the bath!"

NOTES
1. **the Obelisk:** Cleopatra's Needle on the Thames Embankment
2. **pollis:** (corrupt. for) police
3. **warmin:** (corrupt. for) vermin
4. **yourn:** (sl.) yours
5. **Greenwich:** a metropolitan borough of Southeast London
6. **Kentish:** of Kent, a county southeast of London
7. **Blunderstone Rookery:** the place where young Mrs. Copperfield had lived and given birth to David
8. **Suffolk:** a county in East England
9. **Mr. Dick:** a half-witted gentleman protected by Miss Trotwood

MR. PICKWICK AND HIS FRIENDS ON THE ICE

"WELL, Sam," said Mr. Pickwick[1] as that favoured servitor entered his bed-chamber with his warm water, on the morning of Christmas Day, "Still frosty?"

"Water in the wash-hand basin's a mask o' ice, sir," responded Sam.

"Severe weather, Sam," observed Mr. Pickwick.

"Fine time for them as is well wropped up, as the Polar Bear said to himself, ven he was practising his skating," replied Mr. Weller[2].

"I shall be down in a quarter of an hour, Sam," said Mr. Pickwick, untying his nightcap.

"Very good, sir," replied Sam. "There's a couple o' Sawbones down-stairs."

"A couple of what!" exclaimed Mr. Pickwick, sitting up in bed.

"A couple o' Sawbones," said Sam.

"What's a Sawbones?" inquired Mr. Pickwick, not quite certain whether it was a live animal, or something to eat.

"What! Don't you know what a Sawbones is, sir?" inquired Mr. Weller. "I thought everybody know'd as a Sawbones was a Surgeon."

"Oh, a Surgeon, eh?" said Mr. Pickwick, with a smile.

"Just that, sir," replied Sam. "These here ones as is below, though, ain't reg'lar thorough-bred Sawbones; they're only in trainin'."

"In other words they're Medical Students, I suppose?" said Mr. Pickwick.

Sam Weller nodded assent.

"I am glad of it," said Mr. Pickwick, casting his nightcap energetically on the counterpane, "They are fine fellows; very fine fellows; with judgments matured by observation and reflection; tastes refined by reading and study. I am very glad of it."

"They're a smokin' cigars by the kitchen fire," said Sam.

"Ah!" observed Mr. Pickwick, rubbing his hands, "overflowing with kindly feelings and animal spirits. Just what I like to see."

"And one on 'em," said Sam, not noticing his master's interruption, "one on 'em's got his legs on the table, and is a drinkin' brandy neat, vile the t'other one—him in the barnacles—has got a barrel o' oysters atween his knees, wich he's a opening like steam, and as fast as he eats 'em, he takes a aim with the shells at young dropsy, who's a sittin' down fast asleep, in the chimbley corner."

"Eccentricities of genius, Sam," said Mr. Pickwick. "You may retire."

Sam did retire accordingly; Mr. Pickwick, at the expiration of the quarter of an hour, went down to breakfast.

"Here he is at last!" said old Mr. Wardle[3]. "Pickwick, this is Miss Allen's brother, Mr. Benjamin Allen. Ben we call him, and so may you if you like. This gentleman is his very particular friend, Mr. —"

"Mr. Bob Sawyer[4]," interposed Mr. Benjamin Allen[5]; whereupon Mr. Bob Sawyer and Mr. Benjamin Allen laughed in concert.

Mr. Pickwick bowed to Bob Sawyer and Bob Sawyer bowed to Mr. Pickwick; Bob and his very particular friend then applied themselves most assiduously to the eatables before them; and Mr. Pickwick had an opportunity of glancing at them both.

Mr. Benjamin Allen was a coarse, stout, thick-set young man, with black hair cut rather short, and a white face cut rather long. He was embellished with spectacles, and wore a white neckerchief. Below his single-breasted black surtout, which was buttoned up to his chin, appeared the usual number of pepper-and-salt coloured legs, terminating in a pair of imperfectly polished boots. Although his coat was short in the sleeves, it disclosed no vestige of a linen wristband; and although there was quite enough of his face to admit of the encroachment of a shirt collar, it was not graced by the smallest approach to that appendage. He presented, altogether, rather a mildewy appearance, and emitted a fragrant odour of full-flavoured Cubas.

Mr. Bob Sawyer, who was habited in a coarse blue coat, which, without being either a great-coat of a surtout, partook of the nature and qualities of both, had about him that sort of slovenly smartness, and swaggering gait, which is peculiar to young gentlemen who smoke in the streets by day, shout and scream in the same by night, call waiters by their Christian names, and do various other acts and deeds of an equally facetious description. He wore a pair of plaid trousers, and a large rough double-breasted waistcoat; out of doors, he carried a thick stick with a big top. He eschewed gloves, and looked, upon the whole, something like a dissipated Robinson Crusoe.

Such were the two worthies to whom Mr. Pickwick was introduced, as he took his seat at the breakfast table on Christmas morning.

"Splendid morning, gentlemen," said Mr. Pickwick.

Mr. Bob Sawyer slightly nodded his assent to the proposition, and asked Mr. Benjamin Allen for the mustard.

"Have you come far this morning, gentlemen?" inquired Mr. Pickwick.

"Blue Lion at Muggleton," briefly responded Mr. Allen.

"You should have joined us last night," said Mr. Pickwick.

"So we should," replied Bob Sawyer, "but the brandy was too good to leave in a hurry: wasn't it, Ben?"

"Certainly," said Mr. Benjamin Allen; "and the cigars were not bad, or the pork chops either: were they, Bob?"

"Decidedly not," said Bob. The particular friends resumed their attack upon the breakfast, more freely than before, as if the recollection of last night's supper had imparted a new relish to the meal.

"Peg away, Bob," said Mr. Allen to his companion, encouragingly.

"So I do," replied Bob Sawyer. And so, to do him justice, he did.

"Nothing like dissecting, to give one an appetite," said Mr. Bob Sawyer, looking round the table.

Mr. Pickwick slightly shuddered.

"By the bye, Bob," said Mr. Allen, "have you finished that leg yet?"

"Nearly," replied Sawyer, helping himself to half a fowl as he spoke. "It's a very muscular one for a child's."

"Is it?" inquired Mr. Allen, carelessly.

"Very," said Bob Sawyer, with his mouth full.

"I've put my name down for an arm, at our place," said Mr. Allen. "We're clubbing for a subject, and the list is nearly full, only we can't get hold of any fellow that wants a head. I wish you'd take it."

"No," replied Bob Saywer; "can't afford expensive luxuries."

"Nonsense!" said Allen.

"Can't indeed," rejoined Bob Sawyer. "I wouldn't mind a brain, but I couldn't stand a whole head."

"Hush, hush, gentlemen, pray," said Mr. Pickwick, "I hear the ladies."

As Mr. Pickwick spoke, the ladies, gallantly escorted by Messrs. Snodgrass[6], Winkle[7], and Tupman[8], returned from an early walk.

"Why, Ben!" said Arabella[9], in a tone which expressed more surprise than pleasure at the sight of her brother.

"Come to take you home to-morrow," replied Benjamin.

Mr. Winkle turned pale.

"Don't you see Bob Sawyer, Arabella?" inquired Mr. Benjamin Allen, somewhat reproachfully. Arabella gracefully held out her hand, in acknowledgment of Bob Sawyer's presence. A thrill of hatred struck to Mr. Winkle's heart, as Bob Sawyer inflicted on the proffered hand a perceptible squeeze.

"Ben, dear!" said Arabella, blushing; "have—have—you been introduced to Mr. Winkle?"

"I have not been, but I shall be very happy to be, Arabella," replied her brother gravely. Here Mr. Allen bowed grimly to Mr. Winkle, while Mr. Winkle and Mr. Bob Sawyer glanced mutual distrust out of the corners of their eyes.

The arrival of the two new visitors, and the consequent check upon Mr. Winkle and the young lady with the fur round her boots, would in all probability have proved a very unpleasant interruption to the hilarity of the party, had not the cheerfulness of Mr. Pickwick, and the good humour of the host, been exerted to the very utmost for the common weal. Mr. Winkle gradually insinuated himself into the good graces of Mr. Benjamin Allen, and even joined in a friendly conversation with Mr. Bob Sawyer; who, enlivened with the brandy, and the breakfast, and the talking, gradually ripened into a state of extreme facetiousness, and related with much glee an agreeable anecdote, about the removal of a tumour on some gentleman's head; which he illustrated by means of an oyster-knife and a half-quartern loaf, to the great edification of the assembled company. Then, the whole train went to church, where Mr. Benjamin Allen fell fast asleep; while Mr. Bob Sawyer abstracted his thoughts from worldly matters, by the ingenious process of carving his name on the seat of the pew, in corpulent letters of four inches long.

"Now," said Wardle, after a substantial lunch, with the agreeable items of strong beer and cherry—brandy, had been done ample justice to; "what say you to an hour on the ice? We shall have plenty of time."

"Capital!" said Mr. Benjamin Allen.

"Prime!" ejaculated Mr. Bob Sawyer.

"You skate, of course, Winkle?" said Wardle.

"Ye—yes; oh, yes," replied Mr. Winkle. "I—I—am ***rather*** out of practice."

"Oh, ***do*** skate, Mr. Winkle," said Arabella. "I like to see it so much."

"Oh, it is ***so*** graceful," said another young lady.

A third young lady said it was elegant, and a fourth expressed her opinion that it was "swan-like."

"I should be very happy, I'm sure," said Mr. Winkle, reddening; "but I have no skates."

This objection was at once overruled. Trundle[10] had a couple of pair, and the fat boy announced that there were half-a-dozen more down-stairs: whereat Mr. Winkle expressed exquisite delight, and looked exquisitely uncomfortable.

Old Wardle led the way to a pretty large sheet of ice; and the fat boy and Mr. Weller, having shovelled and swept away the snow which had fallen on it during the night, Mr. Bob Sawyer adjusted his skates with a dexterity which to Mr. Winkle was perfectly marvellous and described circles with his left leg, and cut figures of eight, and inscribed upon the ice, without once stopping for breath, a great many other pleasant and astonishing devices, to the excessive satisfaction of Mr. Pickwick, Mr. Tupman, and the ladies: which reached a pitch of positive enthusiasm, when old Wardle and Benjamin Allen, assisted by the aforesaid Bob Sawyer, performed some mystic evolutions[11], which they called a reel.

All this time, Mr. Winkle, with his face and hands blue with the cold, had been forcing a gimlet into the soles of his feet, and putting his skates on, with the points behind, and getting the straps into a very complicated and entangled state, with the assistance of Mr. Snodgrass, who knew rather less about skates than a Hindoo. At length, however, with the assistance of Mr. Weller, the unfortunate skates were firmly screwed and buckled on, and Mr. Winkle was raised to his feet.

"Now, then, sir," said Sam, in an encouraging tone; "off vith you[12], and show 'em how to do it."

"Stop, Sam, stop!" said Mr. Winkle, trembling violently, and clutching hold of Sam's arms with the grasp of a drowning man. "How slippery it is, Sam!"

"Not an uncommon thing upon ice, sir," replied Mr. Weller. "Hold up, sir!"

This last observation of Mr. Weller's bore reference to a demonstration Mr. Winkle made at the instant, of a frantic desire to throw his feet in the air, and dash the back of his head on the ice.

"These—these—are very awkward skates; ain't they, Sam?" inquired Mr. Winkle, staggering.

"I'm afeerd there's a orkard gen 'l' m'n in 'em[13], sir," replied Sam.

"Now, Winkle," cried Mr. Pickwick, quite unconscious that there was anything the matter. "Come; the ladies are all anxiety."

"Yes, yes," replied Mr. Winkle, with a ghastly smile, "I'm coming."

"Just a goin' to begin," said Sam, endeavouring to disengage himself. "Now, sir, start off!"

"Stop an instant, Sam," gasped Mr. Winkle, clinging most affectionately to Mr. Weller. "I find I've got a couple of coats at home that I don't want, Sam. You may have them, Sam."

"Thank'ee, sir," replied Mr. Weller.

"Never mind touching your hat, Sam," said Mr. Winkle, hastily. "You needn't take your hand away to do that. I meant to have given you five shillings this morning for a Christmas-box, Sam. I'll give it you this afternoon, Sam."

"You're very good, sir," replied Mr. Weller.

"Just hold me at first, Sam; will you?" said Mr. Winkle. "There—that's right. I shall soon get in the way of it, Sam. Not too fast, Sam; not too fast."

Mr. Winkle stooping forward, with his body half doubled up, was being assisted over the ice by Mr. Weller, in a very singular and un-swan-like manner, when Mr. Pickwick most innocently shouted from the opposite bank:

"Sam!"

"Sir?"

"Here. I want you."

"Let go[14], sir," said Sam. "Don't you hear the governor a callin'? Let go, sir."

With a violent effort, Mr. Weller disengaged himself from the grasp of the agonised Pickwickian, and, in so doing, administered a considerable impetus to the unhappy Mr. Winkle. With an accuracy which no degree of dexterity or practice could have insured, that unfortunate gentleman bore swiftly down into the centre of the reel, at the very moment when Mr. Bob Sawyer was performing a flourish of unparalleled beauty. Mr. Winkle struck wildly against him, and with a loud crash they both fell heavily down. Mr. Pickwick ran to the spot. Bob Sawyer had risen to his feet, but Mr. Winkle was far too wise to do anything of the kind, in skates. He was seated on the ice, making spasmodic efforts to smile; but anguish was depicted of every lineament of his countenance.

"Are you hurt?" inquired Mr. Benjamin Allen, with great anxiety.

"Not much," said Mr. Winkle, rubbing his back very hard.

"I wish you'd let me bleed you," said Mr. Benjamin, with great eagerness.

"No, thank you," replied Mr. Winkle hurriedly.

"I really think you had better," said Allen.

"Thank you," replied Mr. Winkle; "I'd rather not."

"What do *you* think, Mr. Pickwick?" inquired Bob Sawyer.

Mr. Pickwick was excited and indignant. He beckoned to Mr. Weller, and said in a stern voice, "Take his skates off."

"No; but really I had scarcely begun," remonstrated Mr. Winkle.

"Take his skates off," repeated Mr. Pickwick firmly.

The command was not to be resisted. Mr. Winkle allowed Sam to obey it in silence.

"Lift him up," said Mr. Pickwick. Sam assisted him to rise.

Mr. Pickwick retired a few paces apart from the bystanders; and, beckoning his friend to approach, fixed a searching look upon him, and uttered in a low, but distinct and emphatic tone, these remarkable words:

"You're a humbug, sir."

"A what?" said Mr. Winkle, starting.

"A humbug, sir. I will speak plainer, if you wish it. An impostor, sir."

With those words, Mr. Pickwick turned slowly on his heel, and rejoined his friends.

While Mr. Pickwick was delivering himself of the sentiment just recorded, Mr. Weller and the fat boy, having by their joint endeavours cut out a slide, were exercising themselves thereupon, in a very masterly and brilliant manner. Sam Weller, in particular, was displaying that beautiful feat of fancy-sliding which is currently denominated "knocking at the cobbler's door," and which is achieved by skimming over the ice on one foot, and occasionally giving a postman's knock upon it with the other. It was a good long slide, and there was something in the motion which Mr. Pickwick, who was very cold with standing still, could not help envying.

"It looks a nice warm exercise that, doesn't it?" he inquired of Wardle, when that gentleman was thoroughly out of breath, by reason of the indefatigable manner in which he had converted his legs into a pair of compasses, and drawn complicated problems on the ice.

"Ah, it does indeed," replied Wardle. "Do you slide?"

"I used to do so, on the gutters, when I was a boy," replied Mr. Pickwick.

"Try it now," said Wardle.

"Oh do please, Mr. Pickwick!" cried all the ladies.

"I should be very happy to afford you any amusement," replied Mr. Pickwick, "but I haven't done such a thing these thirty years."

"Pooh! pooh! Nonsense!" said Wardle, dragging off his skates with the impetuosity which characterised all his proceedings. "Here; I'll keep you company; come along!" And away went the good-tempered old fellow down the slide, with a rapidity which came very close upon Mr. Weller, and beat the fat boy all to nothing.

Mr. Pickwick paused, considered, pulled off his gloves and put them in his hat: took two or three short runs, baulked himself as often, and at last took another run, and went slowly and gravely down the slide, with his feet about a yard and a quarter apart, amidst the gratified shouts of all the spectators.

"Keep the pot a bilin'[15], sir!" said Sam; and down went Wardle again, and then Mr. Pickwick, and then Sam, and then Mr. Winkle, and then Mr. Bob Sawyer, and then the fat boy, and then Mr. Snodgrass, following closely upon each other's heels, and running after each other with as much eagerness as if all their future prospects in life depended on their expedition.

It was the most intensely interesting thing, to observe the manner in which Mr. Pickwick performed his share in the ceremony; to watch the torture of anxiety with which he viewed the person behind, gaining upon him at the imminent hazard of tripping him up; to see him gradually expend the painful force he had put on at first, and turn slowly round on the slide, with his face towards the point from which he had started; to contemplate the playful smile which mantled on his face when he had accomplished the distance, and the eagerness with which he turned round when he had done so, and ran after his predecessor: his black gaiters tripping pleasantly through the snow, and his eyes beaming cheerfulness and gladness through his spectacles. And when he was knocked down (which happened upon the average every third round), it was the most invigorating sight that can possibly be imagined, to behold him gather up his hat, gloves, and handkerchief, with a glowing countenance, and resume his station in the rank, with an ardour and enthusiasm that nothing could abate.

The sport was at its height, the sliding was at the quickest, the laughter was at the loudest, when a sharp smart crack was heard. There was a quick rush towards the bank, a wild scream from the ladies, and a shout from Mr. Tupman. A large mass of ice disappeared; the water bubbled up over it; Mr. Pickwick's hat, gloves, and handkerchief were floating on the surface; and this was all of Mr. Pickwick that anybody could see.

Dismay and anguish were depicted on every countenance, the males turned pale, and the females fainted, Mr. Snodgrass and Mr. Winkle grasped each other by the hand, and gazed at the spot where their leader had gone down, with frenzied eagerness; while Mr. Tupman, by way of rendering the promptest assistance, and at the same time conveying to any persons who might be within hearing, the clearest possible notion of the catastrophe, ran off across the country at his utmost speed, screaming "Fire!" with all his might.

It was at this moment, when old Wardle and Sam Weller were approaching the hole with cautious steps, and Mr. Benjamin Allen was holding a hurried consultation with Mr. Bob Sawyer, on the advisability of bleeding the company generally, as an improving little bit of professional practice—it was at this very moment, that a face, head, and shoulders, emerged from beneath the water, and disclosed the features and spectacles of Mr. Pickwick.

"Keep yourself up for an instant—for only one instant!" bawled Mr. Snodgrass.

"Yes, do; let me implore you—for my sake!" roared Mr. Winkle, deeply affected. The adjuration was rather unnecessary; the probability being, that if Mr. Pickwick had declined to keep himself up for anybody else's sake, it would have occurred to him that he might as well do so, for his own.

"Do you feel the bottom there, old fellow?" said Wardle.

"Yes, certainly," replied Mr. Pickwick, wringing the water from his head and face, and gasping for breath. "I feel upon my back. I couldn't get on my feet at first."

The clay upon so much of Mr. Pickwick's coat as was yet visible, bore testimony to the accuracy of this statement; and as the fears of the spectators were still further relieved by the fat boy's suddenly recollecting that the water was nowhere more than five feet deep, prodigies of valour were performed to get him out. After a vast quantity of splashing, and cracking, and struggling, Mr. Pickwick was at length fairly extricated from his unpleasant position, and once more stood on dry land.

"Oh, he'll catch his death of cold," said Emily[16].

"Dear old thing!" said Arabella. "Let me wrap this shawl round you, Mr. Pickwick."

"Ah, that's the best thing you can do," said Wardle; "and when you've got it on, run home as fast as your legs can carry you, and jump into bed directly."

A dozen shawls were offered on the instant. Three or four of the thickest having been selected, Mr. Pickwick was wrapped up, and started off, under the guidance of Mr. Weller; presenting the singular phenomenon of an elderly gentleman, dripping wet, and without a hat, with his arms bound down to his sides, skimming over the ground, without any clearly defined purpose, at the rate of six good English miles an hour.

But Mr. Pickwick cared not for appearances in such an extreme case, and urged on by Sam Weller, he kept at the very top of his speed until he reached the door of Manor Farm, where Mr. Tupman had arrived some five minutes before, and had frightened the old lady into palpitations of the heart by impressing her with the unalterable conviction that the kitchen chimney was on fire—a calamity which always presented itself in glowing colours to the old lady's mind, when anybody about her evinced the smallest agitation.

Mr. Pickwick paused not an instant until he was snug in bed. Sam Weller lighted a blazing fire in the room, and took up his dinner; a bowl of punch was carried up afterwards, and a grand carouse held in honour of his safety. Old Wardle would not hear of his rising, so they made the bed the chair, and Mr. Pickwick presided. A second and a third bowl were ordered in; and when Mr. Pickwick awoke next morning, there was not a symptom of rheumatism about him; which proves, as Mr. Bob Sawyer very justly observed, that there is nothing like hot punch in such cases; and that if ever hot punch did fail to act as a preventive, it was merely because the patient fell into the vulgar error of not taking enough of it.

The jovial party broke up next morning. Breakings up are capital things in our school days, but in after life they are painful enough. Death, self-interest, and fortune's changes, are every day breaking up many a happy group, and scattering them far and wide; and the boys and girls never come back again. We do not mean to say that it was exactly the case in this particular instance; all we wish to inform the reader is, that the different members of the party dispersed to their several homes; that Mr. Pickwick and his friends once more took their seats on the top of the Muggleton coach; and that Arabella Allen repaired to her place of destination, wherever it might have been—we daresay Mr. Winkle knew; but we confess we don't—under the care and guardianship of her brother Benjamin, and his most intimate and particular friend, Mr. Bob Sawyer.

Before they separated, however, that gentleman and Mr. Benjamin Allen drew Mr. Pickwick aside with an air of some mystery; and Mr. Bob Sawyer thrusting his forefinger between two of Mr. Pickwick's ribs, and thereby displaying his native drollery, and his knowledge of the anatomy of the human frame, at one and the same time, inquired:

"I say, old boy, where do you hang out?"

Mr. Pickwick replied that he was at present suspended at the George and Vulture.

"I wish you'd come and see me," said Bob Sawyer.

"Nothing would give me greater pleasure," replied Mr. Pickwick.

"There's my lodgings," said Mr. Bob Sawyer, producing a card. "Lant Street, Borough; it's near Guy's, and handy for me, you know. Little distance after you've passed Saint George's Church—turns out of the High Street on the right hand side the way."

"I shall find it," said Mr. Pickwick.

"Come on Thursday fortnight, and bring the other chaps with you," said Mr. Bob Sawyer, "I'm going to have a few medical fellows that night."

Mr. Pickwick expressed the pleasure it would afford him to meet the medical fellows; and after Mr. Bob Sawyer had informed him that he meant to be very cosy, and that his friend Ben was to be one of the party, they shook hands and separated.

We feel that in this place we lay ourself open to the inquiry whether Mr. Winkle was whispering, during this brief conversation, to Arabella Allen; and if so, what he said; and furthermore, whether Mr. Snodgrass was conversing apart with Emily Wardle; and if so, what *he* said. To this, we reply, that whatever they might have said to the ladies, they said nothing at all to Mr. Pickwick or Mr. Tupman for eight-and-twenty miles, and that they sighed very often, refused ale and brandy, and looked gloomy. If our observant lady readers can deduce any satisfactory inferences from these facts, we beg them by all means to do so.

NOTES

1. **Mr. Pickwick:** Samuel Pickwick was chairman of the Pickwick Club in the novel ***Pickwick Papers***.
2. **Mr. Weller:** Sam Weller, servant to Mr. Pickwick
3. **Mr. Wardle:** a hospitable old gentleman living at Dingley Dell
4. **Mr. Bob Sawyer:** a medical student
5. **Mr. Benjamin Allen:** a medical student
6. **Snodgrass:** Augustus Snodgrass, a member of the Pickwick Club
7. **Winkle:** Nathaniel Winkle, a member of the Pickwick Club
8. **Tupman:** Tracy Tupman, a member of the Pickwick Club
9. **Arabella:** Arabella Allen, Benjamin's sister
10. **Trundle:** Mr. Trundle and Bella Wardle (Mr. Wardle's daughter) were married at Dingley Dell.
11. **mystic evolutions:** strange movements
12. **off vith you:** off with you
13. **I'm afeerd there's a orkard gen 'l'm'n in 'em:** I'm afraid there's an awkward gentleman in them.
14. **Let go:** release
15. **Keep the pot a bilin':** keep the pot a boiling; continue the fun
16. **Emily:** Emily Wardle, Mr. Wardle's daughter

CHARLOTTE BRONTË

(1816–1855)

Charlotte Brontë was an English novelist. A clergyman's daughter, she was born at Thornton, Yorkshire, on April 21, 1816. Educated at home and at two schools, she worked as a teacher and as a governess. She became a successful novelist in 1847, married the Reverend A. B. Nicholls in 1854, and died on March 31, 1855. Her younger sisters, Emily Brontë (1818–1848) and Anne Brontë (1820–1849) were also novelists.

Charlotte Brontë's fame rests on four major novels: ***The Professor*** (written in 1846 and published posthumously in 1857), a story of love between a school-master and his pupil; ***Jane Eyre*** (1847), the story of a governess going through all kinds of trials; ***Shirley*** (1849), the story of two pairs of lovers against the background of bad labour relations in the early 19th century; and ***Villette*** (1853), a work mainly concerned with the relationship between the young teacher Lucy Snowe and her colleague Paul Emanuel. Charlotte Brontë's novels are strongly autobiographical; their plots are woven out of her practical experiences and her imaginative experiences as well. Her writing is marked by an intensity of vision and an intensity of feeling. She excels in depicting emotional states of mind and stern phases of nature.

SHIRLEY AND CAROLINE[1]

"...By-the-way, you must miss that Cousin Robert[2] of yours very much, now that you and he never meet?"

"I do."

"And he must miss you?"

"That he does not."

"I cannot imagine," pursued Shirley, who had lately got a habit of introducing Moore's name into the conversation, even when it seemed to have no business there, — "I cannot imagine but that he was fond of you, since he took so much notice of you, talked to you, and taught you so much."

"He never was fond of me; he never professed to be fond of me. He took pains to prove that he only just tolerated me."

Caroline, determined not to err on the flattering side in estimating her cousin's regard for her, always now habitually thought of it and mentioned it in the most scanty measure. She had her own reasons for being less sanguine than ever in hopeful views of the future; less indulgent to pleasurable retrospections of the past.

"Of course, then," observed Miss Keeldar, "you only just tolerated him, in return?"

"Shirley, men and women are so different; they are in such a different position. Women have so few things to think about—men so many; you may have a friendship for a man, while he is almost indifferent to you. Much of what cheers your life may be dependent on him, while not a feeling or interest of moment in his eyes may have reference to you. Robert used to be in the habit of going to London, sometimes for a week or a fortnight together; well, while he was away, I found his absence a void; there was something wanting; Briarfield[3] was duller. Of course, I had my usual occupations; still I missed him. As I sat by myself in the evenings, I used to feel a strange certainty of conviction I cannot describe; that if a magician or a genius had, at that moment, offered me Prince Ali's tube[4] (you remember it in *The Arabian Nights*?), and if, with its aid, I had been enabled to take a view of Robert—to see where he was, how occupied—I should have learned, in a startling manner, the width of the chasm which gaped between such as he and such as I. I knew that, however my thoughts might adhere to him, his were effectually sundered from me."

"Caroline," demanded Miss Keeldar, abruptly, "don't you wish you had a profession—a trade?"

"I wish it fifty times a day. As it is, I often wonder what I came into the world for. I long to have something absorbing and compulsory to fill my head and hands, and to occupy my thoughts."

"Can labour alone make a human being happy?"

"No; but it can give varieties of pain, and prevent us from breaking our hearts with a single tyrant master—torture. Besides, successful labour has its recompense; a vacant, weary, lonely, hopeless life has none."

"But hard labour and learned professions, they say, make women masculine, coarse, unwomanly."

"And what does it signify, whether unmarried and never-to-be-married women are unattractive and inelegant, or not?—provided only they are decent, decorous, and neat, it is enough. The utmost which ought to be required of old maids, in the way of appearance, is that they should not absolutely offend men's eyes as they pass them in the street; for the rest, they should be allowed, without too much scorn, to be as absorbed, grave, plain-looking, and plain-dressed as they please."

"You might be an old maid yourself, Caroline, you speak so earnestly."

"I shall be one; it is my destiny. I will never marry a Malone[5] or a Sykes[6]—and no one else will ever marry me."

Here fell a long pause; Shirley broke it. Again the name by which she seemed bewitched was almost the first on her lips.

"Lina—did not Moore call you Lina sometimes?"

"Yes; it is sometimes used as the abbreviation of Caroline in his native country."

"Well, Lina, do you remember my one day noticing an inequality in your hair—a curl wanting on that right side—and your telling me that it was Robert's fault, as he had once cut therefrom a long lock?"

"Yes."

"If he is, and always was, as indifferent to you as you say, why did he steal your hair?"

"I don't know—yes, I do; it was my doing, not his. Everything of that sort always was my doing. He was going from home to London, as usual; and the night before he went, I had found in his sister's work—box a lock of black hair—a short, round curl; Hortense told me it was her brother's and a keepsake. He was sitting near the table; I looked at his head—he has plenty of hair; on the temples were many such round curls. I thought he could spare me one; I knew I should like to have it, and I asked for it. He said, on condition that he might have his choice of a tress from my head; so he got one of my long locks of hair, and I got one of his short ones. I keep his, but, I dare say, he has lost mine. It was my doing, and one of those silly deeds it distresses the heart and sets the face on fire to think of; one of those small but sharp recollections that return, lacerating your self-respect like tiny pen-knives, and forcing from your lips, as you sit alone, sudden, insane—sounding interjections."

"Caroline!"

"I *do* think myself a fool, Shirley, in some respects; I *do* despise myself. But I said I would not make you my confessor, for you cannot reciprocate foible for foible; you are not weak. How steadily you watch me now! turn aside your clear, strong she—eagle eye; it is an insult to fix it on me thus."

"What a study of character you are! Weak, certainly; but not in the sense you think.—Come in!"

This was said in answer to a tap at the door. Miss Keeldar happened to be near it at the moment, Caroline at the other end of the room; she saw a note put into Shirley's hands, and heard the words—

"From Mr. Moore, Ma'am."

"Bring candles," said Miss Keeldar.

Caroline sat expectant.

"A communication on business," said the heiress; but when candles were brought, she neither opened nor read it. The Rector's[7] Fanny[8] was presently announced, and the Rector's niece went home.

NOTES

1. **Shirley and Caroline:** Shirley Keelder and Caroline Helstone are the two heroines of the novel ***Shirley***. Shirley is a young lady of wealth and high spirit, while Caroline is a gentle and retiring girl.
2. **Robert:** Robert Moore, a mill-owner in Yorkshire, is Caroline's cousin.
3. **Briarfield:** Caroline lives with her uncle in the Rectory of Briarfield.
4. **Prince Ali's tube:** In a story in ***The Arabian Nights***, Prince Ali acquired an ivory tube through which he could see whatever he wished to see.
5. **a Malone:** a man like Malone, who is curate of Briarfield
6. **a Sykes:** a man like Sykes, who works at Robert's mill
7. **the Rector:** Mr. Helstone, Rector of Briarfield
8. **Fanny:** a maid in Helstone's house

GEORGE ELIOT

(1819–1880)

George Eliot, whose real name was Mary Ann Evans, was an English novelist. She was born in Warwickshire on November 22, 1819, the daughter of a land-agent. Privately educated, she took charge of her father's household after her mother's death in 1836. After her father's death in Coventry in 1849, she travelled extensively, settled in London, and devoted herself to literary work. She died on December 22, 1880.

George Eliot's first fictional work, **Scenes of Clerical Life** (1858), was a collection of three tales. Her first full-length novel was **Adam Bede** (1859), the story of a village carpenter, a young man of stern morals and strong character. This was followed by **The Mill on the Floss** (1860), the story of Maggie Tulliver, a miller's daughter, and her brother Tom; and **Silas Marner** (1861), the story of a linen-weaver in a Midland village. Then came four more ambitious works: **Romola** (1863), a scholarly historical novel about the society of Florence at the end of the 15th century; **Felix Holt, The Radical** (1866), the story of a passionate political reformer; **Middlemarch** (1872), a powerful study of life in a provincial town and George Eliot's highest achievement in fiction; and **Daniel Deronda** (1876), a combination of the story of a self-willed girl and the story of an idealistic young man. George Eliot's choice of subject matter broadened the scope of fiction, and her psychological insights deepened the art of characterization. In her best work she kept an adequate balance between intellect and imagination, and made penetrating studies of her people and their feelings, morals, and motives. Her prose style is precise, clear, and vivid. She is accounted one of the greatest Victorian novelists.

EPPIE REJECTS GODFREY'S OFFER

Between eight and nine o'clock that evening Eppie and Silas were seated alone in the cottage. After the great excitement[1] the weaver had undergone from the events of the afternoon, he had felt a longing for this quietude, and had even begged Mrs. Winthrop and Aaron[2], who had naturally lingered behind every one else, to leave him alone with the child. The excitement had not passed away; it had only reached that stage when the keenness of the susceptibility makes external stimulus intolerable—when there is no sense of weariness, but rather an intensity of inward life under which sleep is an impossibility. Any one who has watched such moments in other men remembers the brightness of the eyes and the strange definiteness that comes over coarse features from that transient influence. It is as if a new fineness of ear for all spiritual voices had sent wonder-working vibrations through the heavy mortal frame—as if "beauty born of murmuring sound"[3] had passed into the face of the listener.

Silas's face showed that sort of transfiguration as he sat in his armchair and looked at Eppie. She had drawn her own chair towards his knees, and leaned forward, holding both his hands, while she looked up at him. On the table near them, lit by a candle lay the recovered gold—the old long-loved gold, ranged in orderly heaps, as Silas used to range it in the days when it was his only joy. He had been telling her how he used to count it every night, and how his soul was utterly desolate till she was sent to him.

"At first I'd a sort o'feeling come across me now and then," he was saying in a subdued tone,"as if you might be changed into the gold again; for sometimes, turn my head which way I would[4], I seemed to see the gold; and I thought I should be glad if I could feel it, and find it was come back. But that didn't last long. After a bit I should have thought it was a curse come again if it had drove you from me, for I'd got to feel the need o' your looks,and your voice and the touch o' your little fingers. You didn't know then, Eppie, when you were such a little un—you didn't know what your old father Silas felt for you."

"But I know now, father," said Eppie. "If it hadn't been for you, they'd have taken me to the workhouse, and there'd have been nobody to love me."

"Eh, my precious child, the blessing was mine. If you hadn't been sent to save me, I should ha' gone to the grave in my misery. The money was taken away from me in time; and you see it's been kept—kept till it was wanted for you. It's wonderful—our life is wonderful."

Silas sat in silence a few minutes. looking at the money. "It takes no hold of me now," he said ponderingly— "the money doesn't. I wonder if it ever could again—I doubt it might if I lost you, Eppie. I might come to think I was forsaken again, and lose the feeling that God was good to me."

At that moment there was a knocking at the door; and Eppie was obliged to rise without answering Silas. Beautiful she looked, with the tenderness of gathering tears in her eyes and a slight flush on her cheeks as she stepped to open the door. The flush deepened when she saw Mr. and Mrs. Godfrey Cass. She made her little rustic curtsy, and held the door wide for them to enter.

"We're disturbing you very late, my dear," said Mrs. Cass, taking Eppie's hand and looking in her face with an expression of anxious interest and admiration. Nancy[5] herself was pale and tremulous.

Eppie, after placing chairs for Mr. and Mrs. Cass, went to stand against Silas, opposite to them.

"Well, Marner," said Godfrey, trying to speak with perfect firmness, "it's a great comfort to me to see you with your money again, that you've been deprived of so many years. It was one of my family did you the wrong—the more grief to me—and I feel bound to make up to you for it in every way. Whatever I can do for you will be nothing but paying a debt, even if I looked no further than the robbery. But there are other things I'm beholden—shall be beholden to you for, Marner."

Godfrey checked himself. It had been agreed between him and his wife that the subject of his fatherhood should be approached very carefully, and that, if possible, the disclosure should be reserved for the future, so that it might be made to Eppie gradually. Nancy had urged this, because she felt strongly the painful light in which Eppie must inevitably see the relation between her father and mother.

Silas, always ill at ease when he was being spoken to by "betters," such as Mr. Cass—tall, powerful, florid men, seen chiefly on horseback—answered with some constraint,—

"Sir, I've a deal to thank you for a'ready. As for the robbery, I count it no loss to me. And if I did, you couldn't help it; you aren't answerable for it."

"You may look at it in that way, Marner, but I never can; and I hope you'll let me act according to my own feeling of what's just. I know you're easily contented; you've been a hard-working man all your life."

"Yes, sir, yes," said Marner meditatively. "I should ha' been bad off without my work; it was what I held by when everything else was gone from me."

"Ah," said Godfrey, applying Marner's words simply to his bodily wants, "it was a good trade for you in this country, because there's been a great deal of linen-weaving to be done. But you're getting rather past such close work, Marner; it's time you laid by and had some rest. You look a good deal pulled down, though you're not an old man, *are* you?"

"Fifty-five, as near as I can say, sir," said Silas.

"Oh, why, you may live thirty years longer-look at old Macey[6]! And that money on the table, after all, is but little. It won't go far either way—whether it's put out to interest, or you were to live on it as long as it would last; it wouldn't go far if you'd nobody to keep but yourself, and you've had two to keep for a good many years now."

"Eh, sir," said Silas, unaffected by anything Godfrey was saying, "I'm in no fear o'want. We shall do very well—Eppie and me 'ull do well enough. There's few working-folks have got so much laid by as that. I don't know what it is to gentlefolks, but I look upon it as a deal—almost too much. And as for us, it's little we want."

"Only the garden, father," said Eppie, blushing up to the ears the moment after.

"You love a garden, do you, my dear?" said Nancy, thinking that this turn in the point of view might help her husband. "We should agree in that; I give a deal of time to the garden."

"Ah, there's plenty of gardening at the Red House[7]," said Godfrey, surprised at the difficulty he found in approaching a proposition which had seemed so easy to him in the distance. "You've done a good part by Eppie, Marner, for sixteen years. It 'ud be a great comfort to you to see her well provided for, wouldn't it? She looks blooming and healthy, but not fit for any hardships; she doesn't look like a strapping girl come of working parents. You'd like to see her taken care of by those who can leave her well off, and make a lady of her; she's more fit for it than for a rough life, such as she might come to have in a few years' time."

A slight flush came over Marner's face, and disappeared, like a passing gleam. Eppie was simply wondering Mr. Cass should talk so about things that seemed to have nothing to do with reality, but Silas was hurt and uneasy.

"I don't take your meaning, sir," he answered, not having the words at command to express the mingled feelings with which he had heard Mr. Cass's words.

"Well, my meaning is this, Marner," said Godfrey, determined to come to the point. "Mrs. Cass and I, you know, have no children—nobody to be the better for our good home and everything else we have—more than enough for ourselves. And we should like to have somebody in the place of a daughter to us—we should like to have Eppie, and treat her in every way as our own child. It 'ud be a great comfort to you in your old age, I hope, to see her fortune made in that way, after you've been at the trouble of bringing her up so well. And it's right you should have every reward for that. And Eppie, I'm sure, will always love you and be grateful to you; she'd come and see you very often, and we should all be on the lookout to do everything we could towards making you comfortable."

A plain man like Godfrey Cass, speaking under some embarrassment, necessarily blunders on words that are coarser than his intentions, and that are likely to fall gratingly on susceptible feelings. While he had been speaking, Eppie had quietly passed her arm behind Silas's head, and let her hand rest against it caressingly; she felt him trembling violently. He was silent for some moments when Mr. Cass had ended—powerless under the conflict of emotions, all alike painful. Eppie's heart was swelling at the sense that her father was in distress; and she was just going to lean down and speak to him, when one struggling dread at last gained the mastery over every other in Silas, and he said faintly,—

"Eppie, my child, speak. I won't stand in your way. Thank Mr. and Mrs. Cass."

Eppie took her hand from her father's head, and came forward a step. Her cheeks were flushed, but not with shyness this time; the sense that her father was in doubt and suffering banished that sort of self-consciousness. She dropped a low curtsy, first to Mrs. Cass and then to Mr. Cass, and said,—

"Thank you, ma'am—thank you, sir. But I can't leave my father, nor own anybody nearer than him. And I don't want to be a lady—thank you all the same" (here Eppie dropped another curtsy). "I couldn't give up the folks I've been used to."

Eppie's lip began to tremble a little at the last words. She retreated to her father's chair again, and held him round the neck; while Silas, with a subdued sob, put up his hand to grasp hers.

The tears were in Nancy's eyes, but her sympathy with Eppie was naturally divided with distress on her husband's account. She dared not speak, wondering what was going on in her husband's mind.

Godfrey felt an irritation inevitable to almost all of us when we encounter an unexpected obstacle. He had been full of his own penitence and resolution to retrieve his error as far as the time was left to him. He was possessed with all-important feelings, that were to lead to a predetermined course of action which he had fixed on as the right, and he was not prepared to enter with lively appreciation into other people's feelings counteracting his virtuous resolves. The agitation with which he spoke again was not quite unmixed with anger.

"But I've a claim on you, Eppie—the strongest of all claims. It's my duty, Marner, to own Eppie as my child, and provide for her. She's my own child; her mother was my wife. I've a natural claim on her that must stand before every other."

Eppie had given a violent start, and turned quite pale. Silas, on the contrary, who had been relieved by Eppie's answer from the dread lest his mind should be in opposition to hers, felt the spirit of resistance in him set free, not without a touch of parental fierceness. "Then, sir," he answered with an accent of bitterness that had been silent in him since the memorable day when his youthful hope had perished— "then, sir, why didn't you say so sixteen year ago, and claim her before I'd come to love her, i'stead o' coming to take her from me now, when you might as well take the heart out o' my body? God gave her to me because you turned your back upon her, and He looks upon her as mine. You've no right to her! When a man turns a blessing from his door, it falls to them as take it in[8]."

"I know that, Marner. I was wrong. I've repented of my conduct in that matter," said Godfrey, who could not help feeling the edge of Silas's words.

"I'm glad to hear it, sir," said Marner with gathering excitement; "but repentance doesn't alter what's been going on for sixteen year. Your coming now and saying

"I'm her father, doesn't alter the feelings inside us. It's me she's been calling her father ever since she could say the word."

"But I think that you might look at the thing more reasonably, Marner," said Godfrey, unexpectedly awed by the weaver's direct truth-speaking. "It isn't as if she was to be taken quite away from you, so that you'd never see her again. She'll be very near you, and come to see you very often. She'll feel just the same towards you."

"Just the same?" said Marner, more bitterly than ever. "How'll she feel just the same for me as she does now, when we eat o' the same bit and drink o' the same cup, and think o' the same things from one day's end to another? Just the same? That's idle talk. You'd cut us i' two."

Godfrey, unqualified by experience to discern the pregnancy of Marner's simple words, felt rather angry again. It seemed to him that the weaver was very selfish (a judgment readily passed by those who have never tested their own power of sacrifice) to oppose what was undoubtedly for Eppie's welfare; and he felt himself called upon, for her sake, to assert his authority.

"I should have thought, Marner," he said severely— "I should have thought your affection for Eppie would make you rejoice in what was for her good, even if it did call upon you to give up something. You ought to remember your own life's uncertain, and she's at an age now when her lot may soon be fixed in a way very different from what it would be in her father's home—she may marry some low working-man, and then, whatever I might do for her, I couldn't make her well-off. You're putting yourself in the way of her welfare; and though I'm sorry to hurt you after what you've done, and what I've left undone, I feel now it's my duty to insist on taking care of my own daughter. I want to do my duty."

It would be difficult to say whether it were Silas or Eppie that was more deeply stirred by this last speech of Godfrey's. Thought had been very busy in Eppie as she listened to the contest between her old, long-loved father and this new, unfamiliar father who had suddenly come to fill the place of that black, featureless shadow which had held the ring and placed it on her mother's finger. Her imagination had darted backward in conjectures, and forward in previsions, of what this revealed fatherhood implied; and there were words in Godfrey's last speech which helped to make the previsions especially definite. Not that these thoughts, either of past or future, determined her resolution—that was determined by the feelings which vibrated to every word Silas had uttered; but they raised, even apart from these feelings, a repulsion towards the offered lot and the newly-revealed father.

Silas, on the other hand, was again stricken in conscience, and alarmed lest Godfrey's accusation should be true—lest he should be raising his own will as obstacle to Eppie's good. For many moments he was mute, struggling for the self-conquest necessary to the uttering of the difficult words. They came out tremulously.

"I'll say no more. Let it be as you will. Speak to the child. I'll hinder nothing."

Even Nancy, with all the acute sensibility of her own affections, shared her husband's view that Marner was not justifiable in his wish to retain Eppie after her real father had avowed himself. She felt that it was a very hard trial for the poor weaver, but her code allowed no question that a father by blood must have a claim above that of any foster-father. Besides, Nancy, used all her life to plenteous circumstances and the privileges of "respectability," could not enter into the pleasures which early nurture and habit connect with all the little aims and efforts of the poor who are born poor; to her mind, Eppie, in being restored to her birthright, was entering on a too long withheld but unquestionable good. Hence she heard Silas's last words with relief, and thought, as Godfrey did, that their wish was achieved.

"Eppie, my dear," said Godfrey—looking at his daughter, not without some embarrassment under the sense that she was old enough to judge him—"it'll always be our wish that you should show your love and gratitude to one who's been a father to you so many years, and we shall want to help you to make him comfortable in every way. But we hope you'll come to love us as well; and though I haven't been what a father should ha' been to you all these years, I wish to do the utmost in my power for you for the rest of my life, and provide for you as my only child. And you'll have the best of mothers in my wife—that'll be a blessing you haven't known since you were old enough to know it."

"My dear, you'll be a treasure to me," said Nancy in her gentle voice. "We shall want for nothing when we have our daughter."

Eppie did not come forward and curtsy as she had done before. She held Silas's hand in hers, and grasped it firmly—it was a weaver's hand, with a palm and finger—tips that were sensitive to such pressure—while she spoke with colder decision than before.

"Thank you, ma'am—thank you, sir, for your offers—they're very great, and far above my wish. For I should have no delight i' life any more if I was forced to go away from my father, and knew he was sitting at home, a-thinking of me and feeling lone. We've been used to be happy together every day, and I can't think o' no happiness without him. And he says he'd nobody i' the world till I was sent to him, and he'd have nothing when I was gone. And he's took care of me and loved me from the first, and I'll cleave to him as long as he lives, and nobody shall ever come between him and me."

"But you must make sure, Eppie," said Silas, in a low voice—"you must make sure as you won't ever be sorry, because you've made your choice to stay among poor folks, and with poor clothes and things, when you might ha' had everything o' the best."

His sensitiveness on this point had increased as he listened to Eppie's words of faithful affection.

"I can never be sorry, father," said Eppie. "I shouldn't know what to think on or to wish for with fine things about me, as I haven't been used to. And it 'ud be poor work for me to put on things, and ride in a gig, and sit in a place at church, as 'ud make them as I'm fond of think me unfitting company for 'em. What could *I* care for then?"

Nancy looked at Godfrey with a pained, questioning glance. But his eyes were fixed on the floor, where he was moving the end of his stick, as if he were pondering on something absently. She thought there was a word which might perhaps come better from her lips than from his.

"What you say is natural, my dear child; it's natural you should cling to those who've brought you up," she said mildly; "but there's a duty you owe to your lawful father. There's perhaps something to be given up on more sides than one. When your father opens his home to you, I think it's right you shouldn't turn your back on it."

"I can't feel as I've got any father but one," said Eppie impetuously, while the tears gathered. "I've always thought of a little home where he'd sit i' the corner, and I should fend and do everything for him. I can't think o' no other home. I wasn't brought up to be a lady, and I can't turn my mind to it. I like the working-folks and their victuals and their ways. And," she ended passionately, while the tears fell, "I'm promised to marry a working-man, as 'll live with father, and help me to take care of him."

Godfrey looked up at Nancy with a flushed face and smarting, dilated eyes. This frustration of a purpose towards which he had set out under the exalted consciousness that he was about to compensate in some degree for the greatest demerit of his life made him feel the air of the room stifling.

"Let us go," he said in an undertone.

"We won't talk of this any longer now," said Nancy, rising. "We're your well-wishers, my dear—and yours too, Marner. We shall come and see you again. It's getting late now."

In this way she covered her husband's abrupt departure, for Godfrey had gone straight to the door, unable to say more.

NOTES

1. **the great excitement:** an incident mentioned at the beginning of Chapter 18 of ***Silas Marner***: The draining of a pond near Silas Marner's door revealed the body of Dunstan Cass with the gold he had stolen from Silas's cottage sixteen years before. The gold was then restored to Silas.
2. **Mrs. Winthrop and Aaron:** Mrs. Winthrop was Silas Marner's neighbour. Her son Aaron and Marner's daughter Eppie were engaged.
3. **beauty born of murmuring sound:** from Wordsworth, ***Three Years She Grew***, line 29
4. **turn my head which way I would:** in whichever way I would turn my head
5. **Nancy:** Nancy Cass, Godfrey Cass's wife
6. **old Macey:** Old Mr. Macey was a tailor and parish clerk of Raveloe.
7. **the Red House:** the home of Mr. and Mrs. Cass
8. **it falls to them as take it in:** it belongs to them who take it in

JOHN RUSKIN

(1819–1900)

John Ruskin was an English art and social critic. The only son of a prosperous wine merchant, he was born in London on February 8, 1819, and educated privately and at Christ Church, Oxford. After leaving the University in 1842, he settled down to a literary career and gradually developed advanced ideas on art, politics, and economics. Frequent foreign travels gave him the opportunity to observe and study European painting and architecture. He served as Slade Professor of Art at Oxford from 1869 to 1879 and again in 1883–1884. He retired to Coniston in Lancashire, and died on January 20, 1900.

Ruskin held that great art is moral and advocated "art for the spiritual health of man". He had great sympathy for working men and advocated social reform. His major works on art are: **Modern Painters** (5 vols, 1843–1860), in which he champions the English landscape painter J. M. W. Turner and discusses art in its many aspects; **The Seven Lamps of Architecture** (1849), in which he sets the criterion for rating architecture; and **The Stones of Venice** (3 vols, 1851–1853), in which he explains the beauty of Gothic architecture and comments on Renaissance architectural history. His principal books of social criticism are: **Unto This Last** (1862), a collection of articles on a new political economy which emphasizes human welfare and disapproves of commercialism;

The Crown of Wild Olive (1866), three lectures on work, traffic, and wars; and ***Fors Clavigera*** (1871–1884), 96 letters to the workmen and labourers of Great Britain preaching a happy and noble way of living. His other famous works are: ***The King of the Golden River*** (written in 1841 and published in 1851), a remarkable fairy tale; ***Sesame and Lilies*** (1865), two lectures, the first on what to read and how to read, and the second on the education and duties of women; and ***Praeterita*** (1885–1889), a celebrated autobiography. Ruskin writes, especially in his earlier books, a heightened prose style; it is ornate and sonorous, sumptuous and delicate.

THE TREASURES HIDDEN IN BOOKS

But, granting that we had both the will and the sense to choose our friends well, how few of us have the power! or, at least, how limited, for most, is the sphere of choice! Nearly all our associations are determined by chance, or necessity; and restricted within a narrow circle. We cannot know whom we would; and those whom we know, we cannot have at our side when we most need them. All the higher circles of human intelligence are, to those beneath, only momentarily and partially open. We may, by good fortune, obtain a glimpse of a great poet, and hear the sound of his voice; or put a question to a man of science, and be answered good-humouredly. We may intrude ten minutes' talk on a cabinet minister, answered probably with words worse than silence, being deceptive; or snatch, once or twice in our lives, the privilege of throwing a bouquet in the path of a Princess, or arresting the kind glance of a Queen. And yet these momentary chances we covet; and spend our years, and passions, and powers in pursuit of little more than these; while, meantime, there is a society continually open to us, of people who will talk to us as long as we like, whatever our rank or occupation; —talk to us in the best words they can choose, and with thanks if we listen to them. And this society, because it is so numerous and so gentle, —and can be kept waiting round us all day long, not to grant audience[1], but to gain it; —kings and statesmen lingering patiently in those plainly furnished and narrow anterooms, our bookcase shelves, —we make no account of[2] that company, —perhaps never listen to a word they would say, all day long!

You may tell me, perhaps, or think within yourselves, that the apathy with which we regard this company of the noble, who are praying us to listen to them, and the passion with which we pursue the company, probably of the ignoble, who despise us, or who have nothing to teach us, are grounded in this, —that we can see the faces of the living men, and it is themselves, and not their sayings, with which we desire to become familiar. But it is not so. Suppose you never were to see their faces; —suppose you could be put behind a screen in the statesman's cabinet, or the prince's chamber, would you not be glad to listen to their words, though you were forbidden to advance beyond the screen? And when the screen is only a little less, folded in two, instead of four, and you can be hidden behind the cover of the two boards that bind a book, and listen, all day long, not to the casual talk, but to the studied, determined, chosen addresses of the wisest of men; —this station of audience, and honourable privy council, you despise!

But perhaps you will say that it is because the living people talk of things that are passing, and are of immediate interest to you, that you desire to hear them. Nay; that cannot be so, for the living people will themselves tell you about passing matters, much better in their writings than in their careless talk. But I admit that this motive does influence you, so far as you prefer those rapid and ephemeral writings to slow and enduring writings-books, properly so called. For all books are divisible into two classes, the books of the hour, and the books of all time. Mark this distinction—it is not one of quality only. It is not merely the bad book that does not last, and the good one that does. It is a distinction of species. There are good books for the hour, and good ones for all time; bad books for the hour, and bad ones for all time. I must define the two kinds before I go farther.

The good book of the hour, then, —I do not speak of the bad ones—is simply the useful or pleasant talk of some person whom you cannot otherwise converse with, printed for you. Very useful often, telling you what you need to know; very pleasant often, as a sensible friend's present talk would be. These bright accounts of travels; good-humoured and witty discussions of question; lively or pathetic story-telling in the form of novel; firm fact-telling, by the real agents concerned in the events of passing history; —all these books of the hour, multiplying among us as education becomes more general, are a peculiar characteristic and possession of the present age; we ought to be entirely thankful for them, and entirely ashamed of ourselves if we make no good use of them. But we make the worst possible use, if we allow them to usurp the place of true books; for, strictly speaking, they are not books at all, but merely letters or newspapers in good print. Our friend's letter may be delightful, or necessary, to-day; whether worth keeping or not, is to be considered. The newspaper may be entirely proper at breakfast time, but assuredly it is not reading for all day. So, though bound up in a volume, the long letter which gives you so pleasant an account of the inns, and roads, and weather last year at such a place, or which tells you that amusing story, or gives you the real circumstances of such and such events, however valuable for occasional reference, may not be, in the real sense of the word, a "book" at all, nor, in the real sense, to be "read." A book is essentially not a talked thing, but a written thing; and written, not with the view of mere communication, but of permanence. The book of talk is printed only because its author cannot speak to thousands of people at once; if he could, he would—the volume is mere ***multiplication*** of his voice. You cannot talk to your friend in India; if you could, you would; you write instead; that is mere ***conveyance*** of voice. But a book is written, not to multiply the voice merely, not to carry it merely, but to preserve it. The author has something to say which he perceives to be true and useful, or helpfully beautiful. So far as he knows, no one has yet said it; so far as he knows, no one else can say it. He is bound to say it, clearly and melodiously if he may; clearly, at all events. In the sum of his life he finds this to be the thing, or group of things, manifest to him; —this the piece of true knowledge, or sight, which his share of sunshine and earth[3] has permitted him to seize. He would fain[4] set it down for ever; engrave it on rock, if he could; saying, "This is the best of me; for the rest, I ate, and drank, and slept, loved, and hated, like another; my life was as the vapour, and is not; but this I saw and knew; this, if anything of mine, is worth your memory." That is his "writing;" it is, in his small human way, and with whatever degree of true inspiration is in him, his inscription, or scripture[5]. That is a "Book."

Perhaps you think no books were ever so written?

But, again, I ask you, do you at all believe in honesty, or at all in kindness? or do you think there is never any honesty or benevolence in wise people? None of us, I hope, are so unhappy as to think that. Well, whatever bit of a wise man's work is honestly and benevolently done, that bit is his book, or his piece of art. It is mixed always with evil fragments-ill-done, redundant, affected work. But if you read rightly, you will easily discover the true bits, and those ***are*** the book.

Now books of this kind have been written in all ages by their greatest men: — by great leaders, great statesmen, and great thinkers. These are all at your choice; and life is short. You have heard as much before; —yet have you measured and mapped out this short life and its possibilities? Do you know, if you read this, that you cannot read that—that what you lose to-day you cannot gain to-morrow? Will you go and gossip with your housemaid, or your stable-boy, when you may talk with queens and kings; or flatter yourselves that it is with any worthy consciousness of your own claims to respect that you jostle with the common crowd for ***entrée***[6] here, and audience there, when all the while this eternal court is open to you, with its society wide as the world, multitudinous as its days, the chosen, and the mighty, of every place and time? Into that you may enter always; in that you may take fellowship and rank according to your wish; from that, once entered into it, you can never be outcast but by your own fault; by your aristocracy of companionship there, your own inherent aristocracy will be assuredly tested, and the motives with which you strive to take high place in the society of the living, measured, as to all the truth and sincerity that are in them, by the place you desire to take in this company of the Dead.

"The place you desire," and the place you ***fit yourself for***, I must also say; because, observe, this court of the past differs from all living aristocracy in this:— it is open to labour and to merit, but to nothing else. No wealth will bribe, no name overawe, no artifice deceive, the guardian of those Elysian gates[7]. In the deep sense, no vile or vulgar person ever enters there. At the portières[8] of that silent Faubourg St. Germain[9], there is but brief question, "Do you deserve to enter? Pass. Do you ask to be the companion of nobles? Make yourself noble, and you shall be. Do you long for the conversation of the wise? Learn to understand it, and you shall hear it. But on other terms? —no. If you will not rise to us, we cannot stoop to you. The living lord may assume courtesy, the living philosopher explain his thought to you with considerate pain; but here we neither feign nor interpret; you must rise to the level of our thoughts if you would be gladdened by them, and share our feelings, if you would recognise our presence."

This, then, is what you have to do, and I admit that it is much. You must, in a word, love these people, if you are to be among them. No ambition is of any use. They scorn your ambition. You must love them, and show your love in these two following ways.

I.—First, by a true desire to be taught by them, and to enter into their thoughts. To enter into theirs, observe; not to find your own expressed by them. If the person who wrote the book is not wiser than you, you need not read it; if he be, he will think differently from you in many respects.

Very ready we are to say of a book, "How good this is—that's exactly what I think!" But the right feeling is, "How strange that is! I never thought of that before, and yet I see it is true; or if I do not now, I hope I shall, some day." But whether thus submissively or not, at least be sure that you go to the author to get at *his* meaning, not to find yours. Judge it afterwards, if you think yourself qualified to do so; but ascertain it first. And be sure also, if the author is worth anything, that you will not get at his meaning all at once; —nay, that at his whole meaning you will not for a long time arrive in any wise. Not that he does not say what he means, and in strong words too; but he cannot say it all; and what is more strange, will not, but in a hidden way and in parables[10], in order that he may be sure you want it. I cannot quite see the reason of this, nor analyse that cruel reticence in the breasts of wise men which makes them always hide their deeper thought. They do not give it you by way of help, but of reward, and will make themselves sure that you deserve it before they allow you to reach it. But it is the same with the physical type of wisdom, gold. There seems, to you and me, no reason why the electric forces of the earth should not carry whatever there is of gold within it at once to the mountain tops, so that kings and people might know that all the gold they could get was there; and without any trouble of digging, or anxiety, or chance, or waste of time, cut it away, and coin as much as they needed. But Nature does not manage it so. She puts it in little fissures in the earth, nobody knows where: you may dig long and find none; you must dig painfully to find any.

And it is just the same with men's best wisdom. When you come to a good book, you must ask yourself, "Am I inclined to work as an Australian miner[11] would? Are my pickaxes and shovels in good order, and am I in good trim myself, my sleeves well up to the elbow, and my breath good, and my temper?" And, keeping the figure[12] a little longer, even at cost of tiresomeness, for it is a thoroughly useful one, the metal you are in search of being the author's mind or meaning, his words are as the rock which you have to crush and smelt in order to get at it. And your pickaxes are your own care, wit, and learning; your smelting furnace is your own thoughtful soul. Do not hope to get at any good author's meaning without those tools and that fire; often you will need sharpest, finest chiselling, and patientest fusing, before you can gather one grain of the metal.

...

II. Having then faithfully listened to the great teachers, that you may enter into their Thoughts, you have yet this higher advance to make; —you have to enter into their Hearts. As you go to them first for clear sight, so you must stay with them that you may share at last their just and mighty Passion. Passion, or "sensation." I am not afraid of the word; still less of the thing. You have heard many outcries against sensation lately; but, I can tell you, it is not less sensation we want, but more. The ennobling difference between one man and another, —between one animal and another, —is precisely in this, that one feels more than another. If we were sponges, perhaps sensation might not be easily got for us; if we were earthworms, liable at every instant to be cut in two by the spade, perhaps too much sensation might not be good for us. But being human creatures, it is good for us; nay, we are only human in so far as we are sensitive, and our honour is precisely in proportion to our passion.

NOTES

1. **grant audience:** grant an audience, give an interview
2. **make no account of:** take no account of
3. **his share of sunshine and earth:** his life
4. **would fain:** (arch.) would gladly
5. **scripture:** authoritative piece of writing
6. *entrée*: entrance
7. **those Elysian gates:** the gates of Elysium, the abode of the blest after death

8. **portières:** (Fr.) door curtain; (here) entrances
9. **Faubourg St. Germain:** a fashionable quarter of Paris in which the nobility resided
10. **in parables:** See *Matthew* xiii. 10-13.
11. **an Australian miner:** a miner digging for gold in Australia
12. **the figure:** the figurative comparison

57

MATTHEW ARNOLD

(1822–1888)

Matthew Arnold was an English poet, critic, and educator. The eldest son of Thomas Arnold, headmaster of Rugby, he was born at Laleham, Surrey, on December 24, 1822. Educated at Winchester School, Rugby School, and at Balliol College, Oxford, he became a school teacher and then a private secretary to a statesman. He served as an inspector of schools for 35 years (1851–1886) and as Professor of Poetry at Oxford for ten years (1857–1867). Both jobs prompted much of his critical writing. He went to live at Harrow in 1867 and moved to Cobham in 1873, where he remained for the rest of his life. He died of a heart attack in Liverpool on April 15, 1888.

Arnold as a poet was representative of the mid-19th century. His best-known poems are: *Sohrab and Rustum* (1853), a narrative in blank verse adorned with epic similes; *The Scholar-Gipsy* (1853), a reflective piece; *Thyrsis* (1867), a pastoral elegy; and *Dover Beach* (1867), a short lyric. As a critic, he has greatly influenced later critical thought. His best-known critical works are: *On Translating Homer* (1861), *Essays in Criticism, First Series* (1865), and *Essays in Criticism, Second Series* (1888). He attacks the narrow and shallow philistines of England, defines literature as "a criticism of life", and considers "truth and seriousness" the standards by which to judge literary works. His *Culture and Anarchy* (1869) is a book of social criticism in which he advocates culture, i. e. the pursuit of "sweetness and light". Arnold's prose style is clear, forceful, and vivacious.

CULTURE AND PERFECTION

If culture, then, is a study of perfection, and of harmonious perfection, general perfection, and perfection which consists in becoming something rather than in having something, in an inward condition of the mind and spirit, not in an outward set of circumstances, —it is clear that culture, instead of being the frivolous and useless thing which Mr. Bright[1], and Mr. Frederic Harrison[2], and many other Liberals are apt to call it, has a very important function to fulfil for mankind. And this function is particularly important in our modern world, of which the whole civilisation is, to a much greater degree than the civilisation of Greece and Rome, mechanical and external, and tends constantly to become more so. But above all in our own country has culture a weighty part to perform, because here that mechanical character, which civilisation tends to take everywhere, is shown in the most eminent degree. Indeed nearly all the characters of perfection, as culture teaches us to fix them, meet in this country with some powerful tendency which thwarts them and sets them at defiance. The idea of perfection as an ***inward*** condition of the mind and spirit is at variance with the mechanical and material civilisation in esteem with us, and nowhere, as I have said, so much in esteem as with us. The idea of perfection as a ***general*** expansion of the human family is at variance with our strong individualism, our hatred of all limits to the unrestrained swing of the individual's personality, our maxim of "every man for himself." Above all the idea of perfection as a ***harmonious*** expansion of human nature is at variance with our want of flexibility, with our inaptitude for seeing more than one side of a thing, with our intense energetic absorption in the particular pursuit we happen to be following. So culture has a rough task to achieve in this country. Its preachers have, and are likely long to have, a hard time of it, and they will much oftener be regarded, for a great while to come, as elegant or spurious Jeremiahs[3], than as friends and benefactors. That, however, will not prevent their doing in the end good service if they persevere. And meanwhile, the mode of action they have to pursue, and the sort of habits they must fight against, ought to be made quite clear for every one to see who may be willing to look at the matter attentively and dispassionately.

Faith in machinery[4] is, I said, our besetting danger; often in machinery most absurdly disproportioned to the end which this machinery, if it is to do any good at all, is to serve; but always in machinery, as if it had a value in and for itself. What is freedom but machinery? what is population but machinery? what is coal but machinery? what are railroads but machinery? what is wealth but machinery? what are, even, religious organisations but machinery? Now almost every voice in England is accustomed to speak of these things as if they were precious ends in themselves, and therefore had some of the characters of perfection indisputably joined to them. I have before now noticed Mr. Roebuck's[5] stock argument for proving the greatness and happiness of England as she is, and for quite stopping the mouths of all gainsayers. Mr. Roebuck is never weary of reiterating this argument of his, so I do not know why I should be weary of noticing it. "May not every man in England say what he likes?" —Mr. Roebuck perpetually asks; and that, he thinks, is quite sufficient, and when every man may say what he likes, our aspirations ought to be satisfied. But the aspirations of culture, which is the study of perfection, are not satisfied, unless what men say, when they may say what they like, is worth saying, —has good in it, and more good than bad. In the same way the ***Times***[6], replying to some foreign strictures on the dress, looks, and behaviour of the English abroad, urges that the English ideal is that every one should be free to do and to look just as he likes. But culture indefatigably tries, not to make what each raw person may like, the rule by which he fashions himself; but to draw ever nearer to a sense of what is indeed beautiful, graceful, and becoming, and to get the raw person to like that.

And in the same way with respect to railroads and coal. Every one must have observed the strange language current during the late discussions as to the possible failure of our supplies of coal. Our coal, thousands of people were saying, is the real basis of our national greatness; if our coal runs short, there is an end of the greatness of England. But what is greatness?—culture makes us ask. Greatness is a spiritual condition worthy to excite love, interest, and admiration; and the outward proof of possessing greatness is that we excite love, interest, and admiration. If England were swallowed up by the sea to-morrow, which of the two, a hundred years hence, would most excite the love, interest, and admiration of mankind, —would most, therefore, show the evidences of having possessed greatness, —the England of the last twenty years, or the England of Elizabeth, of a time of splendid spiritual effort, but when our coal, and our industrial operations depending on coal, were very little developed? Well, then, what an unsound habit of mind it must be which makes us talk of things like coal or iron as constituting the greatness of England, and how salutary a friend is culture, bent on seeing things as they are, and thus dissipating delusions of this kind and fixing standards of perfection that are real!

Wealth, again, that end to which our prodigious works for material advantage are directed,—the commonest of commonplaces tells us how men are always apt to regard wealth as a precious end in itself; and certainly they have never been so apt thus to regard it as they are in England at the present time. Never did people believe anything more firmly, than nine Englishmen out of ten at the present day believe that our greatness and welfare are proved by our being so very rich. Now, the use of culture is that it helps us, by means of its spiritual standard of perfection, to regard wealth as but machinery, and not only to say as a matter of words that we regard wealth as but machinery, but really to perceive and feel that it is so. If it were not for this purging effect wrought upon our minds by culture, the whole world, the future as well as the present, would inevitably belong to the Philistines[7]. The people who believe most that our greatness and welfare are proved by our being very rich, and who most give their lives and thoughts to becoming rich, are just the very people whom we call Philistines. Culture says: "Consider these people, then, their way of life, their habits, their manners, the very tones of their voice; look at them attentively; observe the literature they read, the things which give them pleasure, the words which come forth out of their mouths, the thoughts which make the furniture[8] of their minds; would any amount of wealth be worth having with the condition that one was to become just like these people by having it?" And thus culture begets a dissatisfaction which is of the highest possible value in stemming the common tide of men's thoughts in a wealthy and industrial community, and which saves the future, as one may hope, from being vulgarised, even if it cannot save the present.

NOTES
1. **Mr. Bright:** John Bright (1811–1889), an English Liberal statesman and economist
2. **Mr. Frederic Harrison:** Frederic Harrison (1831–1923) was an English positivist philosopher and critic.
3. **Jeremiah:** Jeremiah (c.650–c.570 B.C.), the Hebrew prophet; a person pessimistic about the future
4. **machinery:** combined means for producing a desired result; mechanism
5. **Mr. Roebuck:** J. A. Roebuck (1801–1879), a radical politician of the Benthamite school
6. **the *Times*:** an influential English newspaper founded under the name of "The Daily Universal Register" in 1785 and renamed *The Times* in 1788
7. **the Philistines:** the uncultured, commonplace, materialistic persons
8. **furniture:** equipment

THOMAS HENRY HUXLEY

(1825–1895)

T. H. Huxley was an English biologist. He was born at Ealing, Middlesex, and educated at London University. After studying medicine at Charing Cross Hospital, he became a surgeon in the navy. He was elected an F.R.S. in 1851 and became in 1854 Professor of Natural History at the Royal School of Mines. He wrote extensively on technical and non-technical subjects. Huxley defended Darwin's ***The Origin of Species*** (1859) vigorously against Gladstone and other critics. His most famous works are: ***Man's Place in Nature*** (1863), ***The Physical Basis of Life*** (1868), ***Science and Culture*** (1881), and ***Evolution and Ethics*** (1893). He has a clear and eloquent prose style.

LEARNING THE LAWS OF NATURE

Suppose it were perfectly certain that the life and fortune of every one of us would, one day or other, depend upon his winning or losing a game of chess. Don't you think that we should all consider it to be a primary duty to learn at least the names and the moves of the pieces; to have a notion of a gambit, and a keen eye for all the means of giving and getting out of check? Do you not think that we should look with a disapprobation amounting to scorn, upon the father who allowed his son, or the state which allowed its members, to grow up without knowing a pawn from a knight?

Yet it is a very plain and elementary truth that the life, the fortune, and the happiness of every one of us, and, more or less, of those who are connected with us, do depend upon our knowing something of the rules of a game infinitely more difficult and complicated than chess. It is a game which has been played for untold ages, every man and woman of us being one of the two players in a game of his or her own. The chessboard is the world, the pieces are the phenomena of the universe, the rules of the game are what we call the laws of Nature. The player on the other side is hidden from us. We know that his play is always fair, just, and patient. But also we know, to our cost, that he never overlooks a mistake, or makes the smallest allowance for ignorance. To the man who plays well, the highest stakes are paid, with that sort of overflowing generosity with which the strong shows delight in strength. And one who plays ill is checkmated—without haste, but without remorse.

My metaphor will remind some of you of the famous picture in which Retzsch[1] has depicted Satan playing at chess with man for his soul. Substitute for the mocking fiend in that picture a calm, strong angel who is playing for love, as we say, and would rather lose than win—and I should accept it as an image of human life.

Well, what I mean by Education is learning the rules of this mighty game. In other words, education is the instruction of the intellect in the laws of Nature, under which name I include not merely things and their forces, but men and their ways; and the fashioning of the affections and of the will into an earnest and loving desire to move in harmony with those laws. For me, education means neither more nor less than this. Anything which professes to call itself education must be tried by this standard, and if it fails to stand the test, I will not call it education, whatever may be the force of authority, or of numbers, upon the other side.

It is important to remember that, in strictness, there is no such thing as an uneducated man. Take an extreme case. Suppose that an adult man, in the full vigour of his faculties, could be suddenly placed in the world, as Adam[2] is said to have been, and then left to do as he best might. How long would he be left uneducated? Not five minutes. Nature would begin to teach him, through the eye, the ear, the touch, the properties of objects. Pain and pleasure would be at his elbow telling him to do this and avoid that; and by slow degrees the man would receive an education which, if narrow, would be thorough, real, and adequate to his circumstances, though there would be no extras and very few accomplishments.

And if to this solitary man entered a second Adam or, better still, an Eve[3], a new and greater world, that of social and moral phenomena, would be revealed. Joys and woes, compared with which all others might seem but faint shadows, would spring from the new relations. Happiness and sorrow would take the place of the coarser monitors, pleasure and pain; but conduct would still be shaped by the observation of the natural consequences of actions; or, in other words, by the laws of the nature of man.

To every one of us the world was once as fresh and new as to Adam. And then, long before we were susceptible of any other mode of instruction, Nature took us in hand, and every minute of waking life brought its educational influence, shaping our actions into rough accordance with Nature's laws, so that we might not be ended untimely by too gross disobedience. Nor should I speak of this process of education as past for anyone, be he as old as he may. For every man the world is as fresh as it was at the first day, and as full of untold novelties for him who has the eyes to see them. And Nature is still continuing her patient education of us in that great university, the universe, of which we are all members—Nature having no Test Acts[4].

Those who take honours in Nature's university, who learn the laws which govern men and things and obey them, are the really great and successful men in this world. The great mass of mankind are the "Poll,"[5] who pick up just enough to get through without much discredit. Those who won't learn at all are plucked[6]; and then you can't come up again. Nature's pluck means extermination.

Thus the question of compulsory education is settled so far as Nature is concerned. Her bill on that question was framed and passed long ago. But, like all compulsory legislation, that of Nature is harsh and wasteful in its operation. Ignorance is visited as sharply as willful disobedience—incapacity meets with the same punishment as crime. Nature's discipline is not even a word and a blow, and the blow first; but the blow without the word. It is left to you to find out why your ears are boxed.

The object of what we commonly call education—that educatiom in which man intervenes and which I shall distinguish as artificial education—is to make good these defects in Nature's methods; to prepare the child to receive Nature's education, neither incapably nor ignorantly, nor with wilful disobedience; and to understand the preliminary symptoms of her pleasure, without waiting for the box on the ear. In short, all artificial education ought to be an anticipation of natural education. And a liberal education is an artificial education which has not only prepared a man to escape the great evils of disobedience to natural laws, but has trained him to appreciate and to seize upon the rewards which Nature scatters with as free a hand as her penalties.

That man, I think, has had a liberal education who has been so trained in youth that his body is the ready servant of his will, and does with ease and pleasure all the work that, as a mechanism, it is capable of; whose intellect is a clear, cold, logic engine, with all its parts of equal strength, and in smooth working order; ready, like a steam engine, to be turned to any kind of work, and spin the gossamers as well as forge the anchors of the mind; whose mind is stored with a knowledge of the great and fundamental truths of Nature and of the laws of her operations; one who, no stunted ascetic, is full of life and fire, but whose passions are trained to come to heel by a vigorous will, the servant of a tender conscience; who has learned to love all beauty, whether of Nature or of art, to hate all vileness, and to respect others as himself.

Such a one and no other, I conceive, has had a liberal education; for he is, as completely as a man can be, in harmony with Nature. He will make the best of her, and she of him. They will get on together rarely; she as his ever beneficent mother; he as her mouthpiece, her conscious self, her minister and interpreter.

NOTES

1. **Retzsch:** Friedrich A. M. Retzsch (1779−1857) was a German painter.
2. **Adam:** the first man in the Old Testament (Genesis ii.-iii.)
3. **Eve:** the first woman and the wife of Adam (Genesis iii. 20)
4. **Test Acts:** The Test Act passed in 1672 required all holders of office to profess faith in the Church of England. Accordingly, scholars who applied for admission to Oxford or Cambridge were required to do the same.
5. **the "Poll":** (sl.) the students who get through college with very low (but passing) grades
6. **plucked:** rejected

59

FRANCIS KILVERT

(1840–1879)

Francis Kilvert was an English cleric and diarist. He grew up in Wiltshire, and was curate at Clyro in Radnorshire (1865–1872), curate at Langley Burrell in Wiltshire (1872–1876), and then vicar of Bredwardine in Herefordshire (1877–1879). He is remembered for his diary, kept from 1870 to 1879, a valuable record of his life and experience, and of the people and landscape that he observed closely. His prose is clear and vivid. *Kilvert's Diary* was first published in 1938–1940, edited by William Plomer.

EXTRACTS FROM *KILVERT'S DIARY*

MARCH 19, 1871 (Radnorshire[1])

The sun was almost overpowering. Heavy black clouds drove up and rolled round the sky without veiling the hot sunshine, black clouds with white edges they were, looking suspiciously like thunder clouds. Against these black clouds the sunshine showed the faint delicate green and pink of the trees thickening with bursting buds.

JULY 29, 1871 (Radnorshire—Breconshire[2])

Torrents of lashing and streaming rain all the morning, a thunderstorm without thunder breaking into a beautiful sunny afternoon. I went to Hay to pay some bills. On the crest of the hill above Hay I met a tall woman smoking a clay pipe and driving a black donkey.

DECEMBER 31, 1871 (Wiltshire[3])

At five minutes to midnight the bells of Chippenham[4] church pealed out loud and clear in the frosty air. We opened a shutter and stood around listening. It was a glorious moonlit night.

JANUARY 21, 1872 (Radnorshire)

Sunday. A cold raw frost fog, dark and dreary…the Chapel bell tolled out sharp and sudden through the white mist to give notice of the service a quarter of an hour beforehand. The hedges were hoary with rime and frost and the trees were hailing large pieces of ice down into the road.

Few people in Chapel…. I thought the markers[5] in Bible and Prayers[6] had suddenly become very short, and after service Wilding the Clerk told me the church mice had eaten them off.

FEBRUARY 4, 1872 (Radnorshire)

The coloured primroses were in full bloom in the little round garden plots under the windows. As I came down the hill the air was cold, it had turned cold suddenly, and I noticed that the sky was wild and stormy, bright and tumbled.

MAY 11, 1872 (Radnorshire)

This is the bitterest May I ever saw.... A black bitter wind violent and piercing drove from the east with showers of snow. The mountains and Clyro Hill and Cusop Hill were quite white with snow. The hawthorn bushes are white with may[7] and snow at the same time.

JUNE 7, 1874 (Wiltshire)

Another glowing glorious day of sunshine and unclouded blue. But every day the drought grows drier and the predicted water famine is stealing upon us. Every day the pasture grows whiter and more bare and slippery.... Later the warm soft night was laden with perfume and the sweet scent of the syringa[8].

SEPTEMBER 24, 1874 (Wiltshire)

A day of exceeding and almost unmatched beauty.... A warm delicious calm and sweet peace brooded breathless over the mellow sunny autumn afternoon and the happy stillness was broken only by the voices of children blackberry gathering in an adjoining meadow and the sweet solitary singing of a robin.... Near the entrance to the village of kington St. Michael I fell in with a team of red oxen, harnessed coming home from plough with chains rattling and the old ploughman riding the fore ox....

When I returned home at night the good Vicar accompanied me as far as the Plough Inn. The moon was at the full. The night was sweet and quiet. Overhead was the vast fleecy sky[9] in which the moon was riding silently and the stillness was broken only by the occasional pattering of an acorn or a chestnut through the leaves to the ground.

OCTOBER 25, 1874 (Wiltshire)

A damp warm morning steaming with heat, the outer air like a hothouse, the inner air colder, and in consequence the old thick panelled walls of the front rooms streaming with the warm air condensed on the cold walls.... The afternoon was so gloomy that I was obliged for the first time to have lights in the pulpit.

NOVEMBER 6, 1874 (Wiltshire)

A lovely afternoon of the Martinmas[10] summer.... On all sides the green meadows were illuminated by the golden light of the yellow elms and red beeches.... The old grey manor house and the church tower stood framed as in a picture by the golden elms. It was a beautiful pastoral scene, calm and peaceful. Suddenly someone began playing a beautiful air upon a horn in front of Langley House.

AUGUST 25, 1875 (Wiltshire)

Late in the evening we loitered down into the water meads. The sun was setting in stormy splendour behind Salisbury[11] and the marvellous aerial spire rose against the yellow glare like Ithuriel's spear[12], while the last gleams[13] of the sunset flamed down the long lines of the water carriages making them shine and glow like canals of molten gold.

APRIL 18, 1876 (Wiltshire)

This morning I married John Knight and Elizabeth Austin at Langley Burrell Church. It was April weather with showers and gleams by whiles[14].... Rice and flowers were showered upon the bride in the porch and churchyard. There were three carriages with greys[15] and postilions in scarlet.

NOTES

1. **Radnorshire:** a former county of South Wales, now (since 1974) part of Powys
2. **Breconshire:** or Brecknockshire, a former county of South Wales, now (since 1974) part of Powys
3. **Wiltshire:** a county of Southwest England

4. **Chippenham:** a market town in Wiltshire
5. **markers:** book markers
6. **Prayers:** *The Book of Common Prayer* (first published in 1549 and revised in 1662)
7. **may:** hawthorn flower(s)
8. **syringa:** lilac
9. **the vast fleecy sky:** the sky covered with fleece-like clouds
10. **Martinmas:** the mass or feast of St. Martin on November 11
11. **Salisbury:** a city in the southwest of Wiltshire
12. **Ithuriel's spear:** Ithuriel is an angel character in *Paradise Lost*. A touch of his spear would expose deceit.
13. **gleams:** small beams
14. **by whiles:** by turns
15. **greys:** grey horses

THOMAS HARDY

(1840–1928)

Thomas Hardy was an English novelist and poet. He was born at Upper Bockhampton, Dorset, on June 2, 1840, the son of a stonemason. After attending school in Dorchester for several years, he was articled to an ecclesiastical architect in 1856. He went to London in 1862 to pursue his profession, and returned to Dorset in 1867 to carry on his architectural work. In 1874, after he had published a few notable novels, he abandoned architecture for literature and got married. He continued to write fiction up to 1895, when he began to devote himself to poetry. Honours came to him in succession, including an Order of Merit in 1910. He died on January 11, 1928.

Hardy wrote more than a dozen novels and over forty short stories. His bestknown novels are the following: **Under the Greenwood Tree** (1872), **Far from the Madding Crowd** (1874), **The Return of the Native** (1878), **The Mayor of Casterbridge** (1886), **The Woodlanders** (1887), **Tess of the D'Urbervilles** (1887) and **Jude the Obscure** (1896). Hardy discerned the intimate relationship between character and environment and found life often made unhappy by "blind circumstances". He has given us a sympathetic and convincing gallery of people coming from what he calls "Wessex", the six southwestern counties of England. His humour is delicate and acute; his pathos is deep and strong. His narrative style is stilted but dignified and forceful. Hardy wrote only poetry after 1895. His poetic output is prodigious. Among his most admired poems are those to his dead first wife. ***The Dynasts*** (1903–1908), his most ambitious work, is an epic drama dealing with the Napoleonic wars and taking all Europe as its scene.

HARVESTING

It was a hazy sunrise in August. The denser nocturnal vapours, attacked by the warm beams, were dividing and shrinking into isolated fleeces within hollows and coverts, where they waited till they should be dried away to nothing.

The sun, on account of the mist, had a curious sentient, personal look, demanding the masculine pronoun for its adequate expression. His present aspect, coupled with the lack of all human forms in the scene, explained the old-time heliolatries[1] in a moment. One could feel that a saner religion had never prevailed under the sky. The luminary[2] was a golden-haired, beaming, mild-eyed, God-like creature, gazing down in the vigour and intentness of youth upon an earth that was brimming with interest for him.

His light, a little later, broke through chinks of cottage shutters, throwing stripes like red-hot pokers upon cupboards, chests of drawers, and other furniture within; and awakening harvesters who were not already astir.

But of all ruddy things that morning the brightest were two broad arms of painted wood, which rose from the margin of a yellow cornfield hard by Marlott village. They, with two others below, formed the revolving Maltese cross of the reaping-machine, which had been brought to the field on the previous evening to be ready for operations this day. The paint with which they were smeared, intensified in hue by the sunlight, imparted to them a look of having been dipped in liquid fire.

The field had already been "opened"; that is to say, a lane a few feet wide had been hand-cut through the wheat along the whole circumference of the field, for the first passage of the horses and machine.

Two groups, one of men and lads, the other of women, had come down the lane just at the hour when the shadows of the eastern hedge-top struck the west hedge midway, so that the heads of the groups were enjoying sunrise while their feet were still in the dawn. They disappeared from the lane between the two stone posts which flanked the nearest field-gate.

Presently there arose from within a ticking like the love-making of the grasshopper. The machine had begun, and a moving concatenation of three horses and the aforesaid long rickety machine was visible over the gate, a driver sitting upon one of the hauling horses, and an attendant on the seat of the implement. Along one side of the field the whole wain[3] went, the arms of the mechanical reaper revolving slowly, till it passed down the hill quite out of sight. In a minute it came up on the other side of the field at the same equable pace; the glistening brass star in the forehead of the fore horse first catching the eye as it rose into view over the stubble, then the bright arms, and then the whole machine.

The narrow lane of stubble encompassing the field grew wider with each circuit, and the standing corn was reduced to smaller area as the morning wore on. Rabbits, hares, snakes, rats, mice, retreated inwards as into a fastness[4], unaware of the ephemeral nature of their refuge, and of the doom that awaited them later in the day when, their covert shrinking to a more and more horrible narrowness, they were huddled together, friends and foes, till the last few yards of upright wheat fell also under the teeth of the unerring reaper, and they were every one put to death by the sticks and stones of the harvesters.

The reaping-machine left the fallen corn behind it in little heaps, each heap being of the quantity for a sheaf; and upon these the active binders in the rear laid their hands—mainly women, but some of them men in print shirts, and trousers supported round their waists by leather straps, rendering useless the two buttons behind, which twinkled and bristled with sunbeams at every movement of each wearer, as if they were a pair of eyes in the small of his back.

But those of the other sex were the most interesting of this company of binders, by reason of the charm which is acquired by woman when she becomes part and parcel of outdoor nature, and is not merely an object set down therein as at ordinary times. A field-man is a personality afield; a field-woman is a portion of the field; she has somehow lost her own margin, imbibed the essence of her surroundings, and assimilated herself with it.

NOTES

1. **heliolatry:** sun-worship
2. **the luminary:** the sun
3. **wain:** (arch.) waggon for farm use
4. **fastness:** stronghold

A FACE ON WHICH TIME MAKES BUT LITTLE IMPRESSION

A Saturday afternoon in November was approaching the time of twilight, and the vast tract of unenclosed wild known as Egdon Heath[1] embrowned[2] itself moment by moment. Overhead the hollow stretch of whitish cloud shutting out the sky was as a tent which had the whole heath for its floor.

The heaven being spread with this pallid screen and the earth with the darkest vegetation, their meeting-line at the horizon was clearly marked. In such contrast the heath wore the appearance of an instalment of night which had taken up its place before its astronomical hour was come; darkness had to a great extent arrived hereon, while day stood distinct in the sky. Looking upwards, a furze-cutter would have been inclined to continue work; looking down, he would have decided to finish his faggot and go home. The distant rims of the world and of the firmament seemed to be a division in time no less than a division in matter. The face of the heath by its mere complexion added half an hour to evening; it could in like manner retard the dawn, sadden noon, anticipate the frowning of storms scarcely generated, and intensify the opacity of a moonless midnight to a cause of shaking and dread.

In fact, precisely at this transitional point of its nightly roll into darkness the great and particular glory of the Egdon waste began, and nobody could be said to understand the heath who had not been there at such a time. It could best be felt when it could not clearly be seen, its complete effect and explanation lying in this and the succeeding hours before the next dawn; then, and only then, did it tell its true tale. The spot was, indeed, a near relation of night, and when night showed itself an apparent tendency to gravitate together could be perceived in its shades and the scene. The sombre stretch of rounds and hollows seemed to rise and meet the evening gloom in pure sympathy, the heath exhaling darkness as rapidly as the heavens precipitated it. And so the obscurity in the air and the obscurity in the land closed together in a black fraternization towards which each advanced half-way.

The place became full of a watchful intentness now; for when other things sank brooding to sleep the heath appeared slowly to awake and listen. Every night its Titanic form seemed to await something; but it had waited thus, unmoved, during so many centuries, through the crises of so many things, that it could only be imagined to await one last crisis—the final overthrow.

It was a spot which returned upon the memory of those who loved it with an aspect of peculiar and kindly congruity. Smiling champaigns[3] of flowers and fruit hardly do this, for they are permanently harmonious only with an existence of better reputation as to its issues than the present. Twilight combined with the scenery of Egdon Heath to evolve a thing majestic without severity, impressive without showiness, emphatic in its admonitions, grand in its simplicity. The qualifications which frequently invest the façade of a prison with far more dignity than is found in the façade of a palace double its size lent to this heath a sublimity in which spots renowned for beauty of the accepted kind are utterly wanting. Fair prospects wed happily with fair times; but alas, if times be not fair! Men have oftener suffered from the mockery of a place too smiling for their reason than from the oppression of surroundings oversadly tinged. Haggard Egdon appealed to a subtler and scarcer instinct, to a more recently learnt emotion, than that which responds to the sort of beauty called charming and fair.

Indeed, it is a question if the exclusive reign of this orthodox beauty is not approaching its last quarter. The new Vale of Tempe[4] may be a gaunt waste in Thule[5]: human souls may find themselves in closer and closer harmony with external things wearing a sombreness distasteful to our race when it was young. The time seems near, if it has not actually arrived, when the chastened sublimity of a moor, a sea, or a mountain will be all of nature that is absolutely in keeping with the moods of the more thinking among mankind. And ultimately, to the commonest tourist, spots like Iceland may become what the vineyards and myrtle—gardens of South Europe are to him now; and Heidelberg[6] and Baden[7] be passed unheeded as he hastens from the Alps[8] to the sand-dunes of Scheveningen[9].

The most thorough-going ascetic could feel that he had a natural right to wander on Egdon: he was keeping within the line of legitimate indulgence when he laid himself open to influences such as these. Colours and beauties so far subdued were, at least, the birthright of all. Only in summer days of highest feather[10] did its mood touch the level of gaiety. Intensity was more usually reached by way of the solemn than by way of the brilliant, and such a sort of intensity was often arrived at during winter darkness, tempests, and mists. Then Egdon was aroused to reciprocity; for the storm was its lover, and the wind its friend. Then it became the home of strange phantoms; and it was found to be the hitherto unrecognized original of those wild regions of obscurity which are vaguely felt to be compassing us about in midnight dreams of flight and disaster, and are never thought of after the dream till revived by scenes like this.

It was at present a place perfectly accordant with man's nature—neither ghastly, hateful, nor ugly; neither commonplace, unmeaning, nor tame; but, like man, slighted and enduring; and withal singularly colossal and mysterious in its swarthy monotony. As with some persons who have long lived apart, solitude seemed to look out of its countenance. It had a lonely face, suggesting tragical possibilities.

This obscure, obsolete, superseded country figures in Domesday[11]. Its condition is recorded therein as that of heathy, furzy, briary wilderness—"Bruaria". Then follows the length and breadth in leagues; and, though some uncertainty exists as to the exact extent of this ancient lineal measure, it appears from the figures that the area of Egdon down to the present day has but little diminished. "Turbaria Bruaria"—the right of cutting heath-turf-occurs in charters relating to the district. "Overgrown with heth and mosse," says Leland[12] of the same dark sweep of the country.

Here at least were intelligible facts regarding landscape-far-reaching proofs productive of genuine satisfaction. The untameable, Ishmaelitish[13] thing that Egdon now was it always had been. Civilization was its enemy; and ever since the beginning of vegetation its soil had worn the same antique brown dress, the natural and invariable garment of the particular formation. In its venerable one coat lay a certain vein of satire on human vanity in clothes. A person on a heath in raiment of modern cut and colours has more or less an anomalous look. We seem to want the oldest and simplest human clothing where the clothing of the earth is so primitive.

　　To recline on a stump of thorn in the central valley of Egdon, between afternoon and night, as now, where the eye could reach nothing of the world outside the summits and shoulders of heathland which filled the whole circumference of its glance, and to know that everything around and underneath had been from prehistoric times as unaltered as the stars overhead, gave ballast to the mind adrift on change, and harassed by the irrepressible New. The great inviolate place had an ancient permanence which the sea cannot claim. Who can say of a particular sea that it is old? Distilled by the sun, kneaded by the moon, it is renewed in a year, in a day, or in an hour. The sea changed, the fields changed, the rivers, the villages, and the people changed, yet Egdon remained. Those surfaces were neither so steep as to be destructible by weather, nor so flat as to be the victims of floods and deposits. With the exception of an aged highway, and a still more aged barrow presently to be referred to—themselves almost crystallized to natural products by long continuance—even the trifling irregularities were not caused by pickaxe, plough, or spade, but remained as the very finger-touches of the last geological change.

　　The above-mentioned highway traversed the lower levels of the heath, from one horizon to another. In many portions of its course it overlaid an old vicinal way, which branched from the great Western road of the Romans, the Via Iceniana, or Ikenild Street[14], hard by. On the evening under consideration it would have been noticed that, though the gloom had increased sufficiently to confuse the minor features of the heath, the white surface of the road remained almost as clear as ever.

NOTES

1. **Egdon Heath:** a fictitious name for a composite of the heaths between Bournemouth and Dorchester
2. **embrowned:** turned brown
3. **champaigns:** expanses of open country
4. **Vale of Tempe:** Tempe was a vale in Thessaly with great pastoral beauty.
5. **Thule:** the most northerly and desolate land conceived of by the Greeks

6. **Heidelberg:** a German city on the River Neckar, containing a famous castle and an old university
7. **Baden:** Baden-Baden, a city in the southwest of West Germany, well known for its mineral springs
8. **the Alps:** a mountain range in South Central Europe, its highest peak being Mont Blanc (4807m)
9. **Scheveningen:** a town in the West Netherlands, the chief seaside resort of the country
10. **of highest feather:** in finest feather, in best form
11. **Domesday:** The Domesday or Doomsday Book was the record of a survey of the lands of England carried out by order of William Ⅰ in 1086.
12. **Leland:** John Leland (c.1506–1552) was King's Antiquary to Henry Ⅷ.
13. **Ishmaelitish:** characteristic of Ishmael's descendants; outcast
14. **the Via Iceniana, or Ikenild Street:** The Icknield Way is an ancient road from Norfolk via Stonehenge to Dorset.

61

WILLIAM HENRY HUDSON

(1841–1922)

W. H. Hudson was a British naturalist and writer. He was born near Buenos Aires, Argentina, on August 4, 1841, of American parents. His schooling was haphazard, but he cherished an intense interest in birds from his boyhood. He emigrated to London in 1869, became a British subject in 1900, and was granted a Civil List pension in 1901. He died on August 18, 1922, and three years later a bird sanctuary was erected in his memory in Hyde Park, London.

Hudson's books on natural history include: *Argentine Ornithology* (with P. L. Sclater, 1888–1889); *The Naturalist in La Plata* (1892); *Birds in a Village* (1893); *Idle Days in Patagonia* (1893); *British Birds* (with Frank E. Beddark, 1895); *Birds in London* (1895); *Birds and Man* (1901); *Afoot in England* (1909); *Adventures among Birds* (1913); and *Birds in Town and Village* (1919). Among his literary works are: *The Purple Land* (1885), a narrative of revolution in Uruguay; *A Crystal Age* (1887), an account of a Utopian land; *El Ombú* (1902), a series of tales of the pampas in South America; *Green Mansions* (1904), a haunting romance about the jungles in Venezuela with Ryma, half maiden and half dryad, as its heroine; *A Shepherd's Life* (1910), a fine book which describes Caleb Bawcombe, a Wiltshire shepherd; and *Far Away and Long Ago* (1918), a joyful reminiscence of his boyhood on the pampas of Argentina. Hudson's prose is limpid and natural, simple and moving.

HER OWN VILLAGE

One afternoon when cycling among the limestone hills of Derbyshire[1] I came to an unlovely dreary-looking little village named Chilmorton. It was an exceptionally hot June day and I was consumed with thirst; never had I wanted tea so badly. Small gritstone-built houses and cottages of a somewhat sordid aspect stood on either side of the street, but there was no shop of any kind and not a living creature could I see. It was like a village of the dead or sleeping. At the top of the street I came to the church standing in the middle of its churchyard with the public-house for nearest neighbour. Here there was life. Going in I found it the most squalid and evil-smelling village pub I had ever entered. Half a dozen grimy-looking labourers were drinking at the bar, and the landlord was like them in appearance, with his dirty shirt-front open to give his patrons a view of his hairy sweating chest. I asked him to get me tea. "Tea!" he shouted, staring at me as if I had insulted him; "there's no tea here!" A little frightened at his aggressive manner I then meekly asked for soda-water, which he gave me, and it was warm and tasted like a decoction of mouldy straw. After taking a sip and paying for it I went to look at the church, which I was astonished to find open.

It was a relief to be in that cool, twilight, not unbeautiful interior after my day in the burning sun.

After resting and taking a look round I became interested in watching and listening to the talk of two other visitors who had come in before me. One was a slim, rather lean brown-skinned woman, still young but with the incipient crow's-feet[2], the lines on the forehead, the dusty-looking dark hair, and other signs of time and toil which almost invariably appear in the country labourer's wife before she attains to middle age. She was dressed in a black gown, presumably her best although it was getting a little rusty. Her companion was a fat, red-cheeked young girl in a towny[3] costume, a straw hat decorated with bright flowers and ribbons, and a string of big coloured beads about her neck.

In a few minutes they went out, and when going by me I had a good look at the woman's face, for it was turned towards me with an eager questioning look in her dark eyes and a very friendly smile on her lips. What was the attraction I suddenly found in that sunburnt face? —what did it say to me or remind me of? — what did it suggest?

I followed them out to where they were standing talking among the gravestones, and sitting down on a tomb near them spoke to the woman. She responded readily enough, apparently pleased to have someone to talk to, and pretty soon began to tell me the history of their lives. She told me that Chilmorton was her native place, but that she had been absent from it many many years. She knew just how many years because her child was only six months old when she left and was now fourteen though she looked more. She was such a big girl! Then her man took them to his native place in Staffordshire[4], where they had lived ever since. But their girl didn't live with them now. An aunt, a sister of her husband, had taken her to the town where she lived, and was having her taught at a private school. As soon as she left school her aunt hoped to get her a place in a draper's shop. For a long time past she had wanted to show her daughter her native place, but had never been able to manage it because it was so far to come and they didn't have much money to spend; but now at last she had brought her and was showing her everything.

Glancing at the girl who stood listening, but with no sign of interest in her face, I remarked that her daughter would perhaps hardly think the journey had been worth taking.

"Why do you say that?" she quickly demanded.

"Oh, well," I replied, "because Chilmorton can't have much to interest a girl living in a town." Then I foolishly went on to say what I thought of Chilmorton. The musty taste of that warm soda-water was still in my mouth and made me use some pretty strong words.

At that she flared up and desired me to know that in spite of what I thought of it Chilmorton was the sweetest, dearest village in England; that she was born there and hoped to be buried in its churchyard where her parents were lying, and her grand-parents and many others of her family. She was thirty-six years old now, she said, and would perhaps live to be an old woman, but it would make her miserable for all the rest of her life if she thought she would have to lie in the earth at a distance from Chilmorton.

During this speech I began to think of the soft reply it would now be necessary for me to make, when, having finished speaking, she called sharply to her daughter, "Come, we've others to see yet," and, followed by the girl, walked briskly away without so much as a good-bye, or even a glance!

Oh, you poor foolish woman, thought I; why take it to heart like that! and I was sorry and laughed a little as I went back down the street.

It was beginning to wake up now! A man in his shirt-sleeves and without a hat, a big angry man, was furiously hunting a rebellious pig all round a small field adjoining a cottage, trying to corner it; he swore and shouted, and out of the cottage came a frowsy-looking girl in a ragged gown with her hair hanging all over her face, to help him with the pig. A little further on I caught sight of yet another human being, a tall gaunt old woman in cap and shawl, who came out of a cottage and moved feebly towards a pile of faggots a few yards from the door. Just as she got to the pile I passed, and she slowly turned and gazed at me out of her dim old eyes. Her wrinkled face was the colour of ashes and was like the face of a corpse, still bearing on it the marks of suffering endured for many miserable years. And these three were the only inhabitants I saw on my way down the street.

At the end of the village the street broadened to a clean white road with high ancient hedgerow elms on either side, their upper branches meeting and forming a green canopy over it. As soon as I got to the trees I stopped and dismounted to enjoy the delightful sensation the shade produced; there out of its power I could best appreciate the sun shining in splendour on the wide green hilly earth and in the green translucent foliage above my head. In the upper branches a blackbird was trolling out his music in his usual careless leisurely manner; when I stopped under it the singing was suspended for half a minute or so, then resumed, but in a lower key, which made it seem softer, sweeter, inexpressibly beautiful.

There are beautiful moments in our converse with nature when all the avenues by which nature comes to our souls seem one, when hearing and seeing and smelling and feeling are one sense, when the sweet sound that falls from a bird is but the blue of heaven, the green of earth, and the golden sunshine made audible.

　　Such a moment was mine as I stood under the elms listening to the blackbird. And looking back up the village street I thought of the woman in the churchyard, her sun-parched eager face, her questioning eyes and friendly smile: what was the secret of its attraction? —what did that face say to me or remind me of? —what did it suggest?

　　Now it was plain enough. She was still a child at heart, in spite of those marks of time and toil on her countenance, still full of wonder and delight at this wonderful world of Chilmorton set amidst its lime-stone hills, under the wide blue sky—this poor squalid little village where I couldn't get a cup of tea!

　　It was the child surviving in her which had attracted and puzzled me; it does not often shine through the dulling veil of years[5] so brightly. And as she now appeared to me as a child in heart I could picture her as a child in years, in her little cotton frock and thin bare legs, a sun-burnt little girl of eight, with the wide-eyed, eager, half-shy, half-trustful look, asking you, as the child ever asks, what you think? —what you feel? It was a wonderful world, and the world was the village, its streets of gritstone houses, the people living in them, the comedies and tragedies of their lives and deaths, and burials in the churchyard with grass and flowers to grow over them by-and-by. And the church; —I think its interior must have seemed vaster, more beautiful and sublime to her wondering little soul than the greatest cathedral can be to us. I think that our admiration for the loveliest blooms—the orchids and roses and chrysanthemums at our great annual shows—is a poor languid feeling compared to what she experienced at the sight of any common flower of the field. Best of all perhaps were the elms at the village end, those mighty rough-barked trees that had their tops "so close against the sky."[6] And I think that when a blackbird chanced to sing in the upper branches it was as if some angelic being had dropped down out of the sky into that green translucent cloud of leaves, and seeing the child's eager face looking up had sung a little song of his own celestial country to please her.

NOTES

1. **Derbyshire:** a county of North Central England
2. **incipient crow's-feet:** first wrinkles
3. **towny:** characteristic of a town, fashionable
4. **Staffordshire:** a county of Central England
5. **the dulling veil of years:** the obliterating effect of time
6. **so close against the sky:** Thomas Hood's poem "I Remember, I Remember" contains the line, "Were close against the sky" (l. 28).

ROBERT LOUIS STEVENSON

(1850–1894)

R. L. Stevenson was a Scottish novelist and essayist. He was born in Edinburgh on November 13, 1850, the son of an engineer. He studied engineering at the University of Edinburgh, and then studied law in a law office. Though he was called to the Scottish bar in 1875, he never practised but took to writing. He travelled much, and when his respiratory illness became severe he went to live in Samoa in 1888, finding its climate salutary. His death came prematurely on December 3, 1894.

Stevenson's fame rests on four or five of his fictional works, two travel books, and two volumes of essays. His novels include: ***Treasure Island*** (1883), a fine adventure story; ***The Strange Case of Dr. Jekyll and Mr. Hyde*** (1886), a macabre tale of divided personality; ***Kidnapped*** (1886), ***The Master of Ballantrae*** (1889) and ***Weir of Hermiston*** (1896, unfinished), three historical romances set in 18th-century Scotland. ***An Inland Voyage*** (1878) and ***Travels with a Donkey in the Cevennes*** (1879) are two of his engaging travel books. ***Virginibus Puerisque*** (1881) and ***Familiar Studies of Men and Books*** (1882) are two volumes of his agreeably mannered essays. Stevenson was self-conscious in style; it is precise, careful, and delicate.

THE OLD SEA DOG[1] AT THE *ADMIRAL BENBOW*

Squire Trelawney, Dr. Livesey[2], and the rest of these gentlemen having asked me[3] to write down the whole particulars about Treasure Island, from the beginning to the end, keeping nothing back but the bearings[4] of the island, and that only because there is still treasure not yet lifted, I take up my pen in the year of grace 17— and go back to the time when my father kept the "Admiral Benbow" inn, and the brown old seaman, with the saber cut, first took up his lodging under our roof.

I remember him as if it were yesterday, as he came plodding to the inn door, his sea chest following behind him in a hand-barrow; a tall, strong, heavy, nut-brown man; his tarry pigtail[5] falling over the shoulders of his soiled blue coat; his hands ragged and scarred, with black, broken nails; and the saber cut across one cheek, a dirty, livid white. I remember him looking round the cove and whistling to himself as he did so, and then breaking out in that old sea song that he sang so often afterwards: —

"Fifteen men on the Dead Man's Chest—
Yo-ho-ho, and a bottle of rum!"

in the high old tottering voice that seemed to have been tuned and broken at the capstan bars. Then he rapped on the door with a bit of stick like a handspike that he carried, and when my father appeared, called roughly for a glass of rum. This, when it was brought to him, he drank slowly, like a connoisseur, lingering on the taste, and still looking about him at the cliffs and up at our signboard.

"This is a handy cove," says he, at length; "and a pleasant sittyated[6] grogshop. Much company, mate?"

My father told him no, very little company, the more was the pity.

"Well, then," said he, "this is the berth for me. Here you, matey," he cried to the man who trundled the barrow; "bring up alongside and help up my chest. I'll stay here a bit," he continued. "I'm a plain man; rum and bacon and eggs is what I want, and that head up there[7] for to watch ships off. What you mought[8] call me? You mought call me captain. Oh, I see what you're at-there;" and he threw down three or four gold pieces on the threshold. "You can tell me when I've worked through that," says he, looking as fierce as a commander.

And, indeed, bad as his clothes were, and coarsely as he spoke, he had none of the appearance of a man who sailed before the mast[9]; but seemed like a mate or skipper, accustomed to be obeyed or to strike. The man who came with the barrow told us the mail had set him down the morning before at the "Royal George;" that he had inquired what inns there were along the coast, and hearing ours well spoken of, I suppose, and described as lonely, had chosen it from the others for his place of residence. And that was all we could learn of our guest.

He was a very silent man by custom. All day he hung round the cove, or upon the cliffs, with a brass telescope; all evening he sat in a corner of the parlor next to the fire, and drank rum and water very strong. Mostly he would not speak when spoken to; only look up sudden and fierce, and blow through his nose like a foghorn; and we and the people who came about our house soon learned to let him be. Every day, when he came back from his stroll, he would ask if any seafaring men had gone by along the road? At first we thought it was the want of company of his own kind that made him ask this question; but at last we began to see he was desirous to avoid them. When a seaman put up at "Admiral Benbow" (as now and then some did, making by the coast road for Bristol), he would look in at him through the curtained door before he entered the parlor; and he was always sure to be as silent as a mouse when any such was present. For me, at least, there was no secret about the matter; for I was, in a way, a sharer in his alarms. He had taken me aside one day, and promised me a silver fourpenny on the first of every month if I would only keep my "weather eye open for a seafaring man with one leg," and let him know the moment he appeared. Often enough, when the first of the month came round, and I applied to him for my wage, he would only blow through his nose at me, and stare me down; but before the week was out he was sure to think better of it, bring me my fourpenny piece, and repeat his orders to look out for "the seafaring man with one leg."

How that personage haunted my dreams, I need scarcely tell you. On stormy nights, when the wind shook the four corners of the house, and the surf roared along the cove and up the cliffs, I would see him in a thousand forms, and with a thousand diabolical expressions. Now the leg would be cut off at the knee, now at the hip; now he was a monstrous kind of a creature who had never had but the one leg, and that in the middle of his body. To see him leap and run and pursue me over hedge and ditch was the worst of nightmares. And altogether I paid pretty dear for my monthly fourpenny piece, in the shape of these abominable fancies.

But though I was so terrified by the idea of the seafaring man with one leg, I was far less afraid of the captain himself than anybody else who knew him. There were nights when he took a deal more rum and water than his head would carry; and then he would sometimes sit and sing his wicked, old, wild sea songs, minding nobody; but sometimes he would call for glasses round, and force all the trembling company to listen to his stories or bear a chorus to his singing. Often I have heard the house shaking with "Yo-ho-ho, and a bottle of rum;" all the neighbors joining in for dear life[10], with the fear of death upon them, and each singing louder than the other, to avoid remark. For in these fits he was the most overriding companion ever known; he would slap his hand on the table for silence all round; he would fly up in a passion of anger at a question, or sometimes because none was put, so he judged the company was not following his story. Nor would he allow any one to leave the inn till he had drunk himself sleepy and reeled off to bed.

His stories were what frightened people worst of all. Dreadful stories they were; about hanging, and walking the plank[11], and storms at sea, and the Dry Tortugas[12], and wild deeds and places on the Spanish Main[13]. By his own account he must have lived his life among some of the wickedest men that God ever allowed upon the sea; and the language in which he told these stories shocked our plain country people as much as the crimes that he described. My father was always saying the inn would be ruined, for people would soon cease coming there to be tyrannized over and put down, and sent shivering to their beds; but I really believe his presence did us good. People were frightened at the time, but on looking back they rather liked it; it was a fine excitement in a quiet country life; and there was even a party of the younger men who pretended to admire him, calling him a "true sea dog," and a "real old salt[14]," and such like names, and saying there was the sort of man that made England terrible at sea.

In one way, indeed, he bade fair to ruin us; for he kept on staying week after week, and at last month after month, so that all the money had been long exhausted, and still my father never plucked up the heart to insist on having more. If ever he mentioned it, the captain blew through his nose so loudly, that you might say he roared, and stared my poor father out of the room. I have seen him wringing his hands after such a rebuff, and I am sure the annoyance and the terror he lived in must have greatly hastened his early and unhappy death.

All the time he lived with us the captain made no change whatever in his dress but to buy some stockings from a hawker. One of the cocks of his hat[15] having fallen down, he let it hang from that day forth, though it was a great annoyance when it blew. I remember the appearance of his coat, which he patched himself upstairs in his room, and which, before the end, was nothing but patches. He never wrote or received a letter, and he never spoke with any but the neighbors, and with these, for the most part, only when drunk on rum. The great sea chest none of us had ever seen open.

He was only once crossed, and that was towards the end, when my poor father was far gone in a decline[16] that took him off. Dr. Livesey came late one afternoon to see the patient, took a bit of dinner from my mother, and went into the parlor to smoke a pipe until his horse should come down from the hamlet, for we had no stabling at the old "Benbow." I followed him in, and I remember observing the contrast the neat, bright doctor, with his powder[17] as white as snow, and his bright, black eyes and pleasant manners, made with the coltish country folk, and above all, with that filthy, heavy, bleared scarecrow of a pirate of ours, sitting far gone in rum, with his arms on the table. Suddenly he—the captain, that is—began to pipe up his eternal song: —

"Fifteen men on the Dead Man's Chest—

Yo-ho-ho, and a bottle of rum!
Drink and the devil had done for the rest—
Yo-ho-ho, and a bottle of rum!"

At first I had supposed "the dead man's chest" to be that identical big box of his upstairs in the front room, and the thought had been mingled in my nightmares with that of the one-legged seafaring man. But by this time we had all long ceased to pay any particular notice to the song; it was new, that night, to nobody but Dr. Livesey, and on him I observed it did not produce an agreeable effect, for he looked up for a moment quite angrily before he went on with his talk to old Taylor, the gardener, on a new cure for the rheumatics. In the meantime, the captain gradually brightened up at his own music, and at last flapped his hand upon the table before him in a way we all knew to mean-silence. The voices stopped at once, all but Dr. Livesey's; he went on as before, speaking clear and kind, and drawing briskly at his pipe between every word or two. The captain glared at him for a while, flapped his hand again, glared still harder, and at last broke out with a villainous, low oath: "Silence, there, between decks!"

"Were you addressing me, sir?" says the doctor; and when the ruffian had told him, with another oath, that this was so, "I have only one thing to say to you, sir," replies the doctor, "that if you keep on drinking rum, the world will soon be quit of a very dirty scoundrel!"

The old fellow's fury was awful. He sprang to his feet, drew and opened a sailor's clasp knife[18], and, balancing it open on the palm of his hand, threatened to pin the doctor to the wall.

The doctor never so much as moved. He spoke to him, as before, over his shoulder, and in the same tone of voice; rather high, so that all the room might hear, but perfectly calm and steady: —

"If you do not put that knife this instant in your pocket, I promise, upon my honor, you shall hang at next assizes."

Then followed a battle of looks between them; but the captain soon knuckled under, put up his weapon, and resumed his seat, grumbling like a beaten dog.

"And now, sir," continued the doctor, "since I now know there's such a fellow in my district, you may count I'll have an eye upon you day and night. I'm not a doctor only; I'm a magistrate; and if I catch a breath of complaint against you, if it's only for a piece of incivility like to-night's, I'll take effectual means to have you hunted down and routed out of this. Let that suffice."

Soon after Dr. Livesey's horse came to the door, and he rode away; but the captain held his peace that evening, and for many evenings to come.

NOTES

1. **sea dog:** experienced sailor
2. **Squire Trelawney, Dr. Livesey:** two of the major characters in *Treasure Island*
3. **asked me:** i.e. asked Jim Hawkins, the central character and narrator of *Treasure Island*
4. **bearings:** the position
5. **his tarry pigtail:** Sailors in the 18th century liked to wear their hair in a pigtail.
6. **sittyated:** (dial. phon. sp.) situated
7. **that head up there:** that promontory there
8. **mought:** (dial. phon. sp.) might
9. **a man who sailed before the mast:** an ordinary seaman
10. **for dear life:** as if life were at stake
11. **walking the plank:** walking along a plank out overboard
12. **the Dry Tortugas:** a group of coral keys in the Gulf of Mexico
13. **the Spanish Main:** the northern part of South America, Central America, and the nearby seas under Spanish control
14. **old salt:** sailor of long experience
15. **the cocks of his hat:** the upturned parts (brims) of his three-cornered hat
16. **in a decline:** in the loss of strength; on the decline
17. **powder:** hair-powder
18. **clasp knife:** large knife with one or more blades folding into the handle

EL DORADO[1]

It seems as if a great deal were attainable in a world where there are so many marriages and decisive battles, and where we all, at certain hours of the day, and with great gusto and despatch, stow a portion of victuals finally and irretrievably into a bag which contains us. And it would seem also, on a hasty view, that the attainment of as much as possible was the one goal of man's contentious life. And yet, as regards the spirit, this is but a semblance. We live in an ascending scale when we live happily, one thing leading to another in an endless series. There is always a new horizon for onward-looking men, and although we dwell on a small planet, immersed in petty business and not enduring beyond a brief period of years, we are so constituted that our hopes are inaccessible, like stars, and the term of hoping is prolonged until the term of life. To be truly happy is a question of how we begin and not of how we end, of what we want and not of what we have. An aspiration is a joy for ever, a possession as solid as a landed estate, a fortune which we can never exhaust and which gives us year by year a revenue of pleasurable activity. To have many of these is to be spiritually rich. Life is only a very dull and ill-directed theatre unless we have some interests in the piece; and to those who have neither art nor science, the world is a mere arrangement of colours, or a rough footway where they may very well break their shins. It is in virtue of his own desires and curiosities that any man continues to exist with even patience, that he is charmed by the look of things and people, and that he wakens every morning with a renewed appetite for work and pleasure. Desire and curiosity are the two eyes through which he sees the world in the most enchanted colours; it is they that make women beautiful or fossils interesting; and the man may squander his estate and come to beggary, but if he keeps these two amulets he is still rich in the possibilities of pleasure. Suppose he could take one meal so compact and comprehensive that he should never hunger any more; suppose him, at a glance, to take in all the features of the world and allay the desire for knowledge; suppose him to do the like in any province of experience—would not that man be in a poor way for amusement ever after?

One who goes touring on foot with a single volume in his knapsack reads with circumspection, pausing often to reflect, and often laying the book down to contemplate the landscape or the prints in the inn parlour; for he fears to come to an end of his entertainment, and be left companionless on the last stages of his journey. A young fellow recently finished the works of Thomas Carlyle, winding up, if we remember aright, with the ten note-books upon Frederick the Great[2]. "What!" cried the young fellow, in consternation, "is there no more Carlyle? Am I left to the daily papers?" A more celebrated instance is that of Alexander[3], who wept bitterly because he had no more worlds to subdue. And when Gibbon had finished the **Decline and Fall**, he had only a few moments of joy; and it was with a "sober melancholy" that he parted from his labours.

Happily we all shoot at the moon with ineffectual arrows; our hopes are set on inaccessible EL Dorado; we come to an end of nothing here below. Interests are only plucked up to sow themselves again, like mustard. You would think, when the child was born, there would be an end to trouble; and yet it is only the beginning of fresh anxieties; and when you have seen it through its teething and its education, and at last its marriage, alas! it is only to have new fears, new quivering sensibilities, with every day; and the health of your children's children grows as touching a concern as that of your own. Again, when you have married your wife, you would think you were got upon a hilltop, and might begin to go downward by an easy slope. But you have only ended courting to begin marriage. Falling in love and winning love are often difficult tasks to overbearing and rebellious spirits; but to keep in love is also a business of some importance, to which both man and wife must bring kindness and goodwill. The true love story commences at the altar, when there lies before the married pair a most beautiful contest of wisdom and generosity, and a life-long struggle towards an unattainable ideal. Unattainable! Ay, surely unattainable, from the very fact that they are two instead of one.

"Of making books there is no end[4]," complained the Preacher[5]; and did not perceive how highly he was praising letters as an occupation. There is no end, indeed, to make books or experiments, or to travel, or to gathering wealth. Problem gives rise to problem. We may study for ever, and we are never as learned as we would. We have never made a statue worthy of our dreams. And when we have discovered a continent, or crossed a chain of mountains, it is only to find another ocean or another plain upon the further side. In the infinite universe there is room for our swiftest diligence and to spare. It is not like the works of Carlyle, which can be read to an end. Even in a corner of it, in a private park, or in the neighbourhood of a single hamlet, the weather and the seasons keep so deftly changing that although we walk there for a lifetime there will be always something new to startle and delight us.

There is only one wish realisable on the earth; only one thing that can be perfectly attained: Death. And from a variety of circumstances we have no one to tell us whether it be worth attaining.

A strange picture we make on our way to our chimaeras, ceaselessly marching, grudging ourselves the time for rest; indefatigable, adventurous pioneers. It is true that we shall never reach the goal; it is even more than probable that there is no such place; and if we lived for centuries and were endowed with the powers of a god, we should find ourselves not much nearer what we wanted at the end. O toiling hands of mortals! O unwearied feet, travelling ye know not whither! Soon, soon, it seems to you, you must come forth on some conspicuous hilltop, and but a little way further, against the setting sun, descry the spires of EL Dorado. Little do ye know your own blessedness; for to travel hopefully is a better thing than to arrive, and the true success is to labour.

NOTES

1. **EL Dorado:** (Span.) the Land of Gold; the legendary city of great wealth supposed during the 16th-18th centuries to exist in the north part of South America
2. **the ten note-books upon Frederick the Great:** Carlyle's biographical work, *The History of Friedrick II of Prussia called Frederick the Great* (6 vols.,1858-1865)
3. **Alexander:** Alexander the Great (356-323 B.C.), King of Macedonia
4. **Of making books there is no end:** See Ecclesiastes xii. 12.
5. **the Preacher:** a translation of the title Ecclesiastes

63

LADY GREGORY

(1852–1932)

Lady Gregory, née Isabella Augusta Persse, was an Irish dramatist. She was born in County Galway and educated privately. She married Sir William Gregory in 1880 and was widowed in 1892. Then she pursued a literary career, became a leading figure in the Irish Revival, and helped W. B. Yeats and Edward Martyn to found in 1899 the Irish Literary Theatre, which developed into the Abbey Theatre in 1904. For this famous theatre she wrote many lively one-act plays, mostly about peasant life, including **Spreading the News** (1904), **Hyacinth Halvey** (1906), **The Gaol Gate** (1906), **The Rising of the Moon** (1907), and **The Workhouse Ward** (1908).

THE RISING OF THE MOON

CHARACTERS. Sergeant, Policeman X, Policeman B, A Ragged Man.

SCENE. Side of a quay in a seaport town. Some posts and chains. A large barrel. Enter three policemen. Moonlight.

Sergeant, who is older than the others, crosses the stage to right and looks down steps. The others put down a pastepot and unroll a bundle of placards.

Policeman B. I think this would be a good place to put up a notice.

(*He points to barrel.*)

Policeman X. Better ask him. (*Calls to Sergeant.*) Will this be a good place for a placard?

(*No answer.*)

Policeman B. Will we put up a notice here on the barrel?

(*No answer.*)

Sergeant. There's a flight of steps here that leads to the water. This is a place that should be minded well. If he got down here, his friends might have a boat to meet him; they might send it in here from outside.

Policeman B. Would the barrel be a good place to put a notice up?

Sergeant. It might; you can put it there.

(*They paste the notice up.*)

Sergeant. (*Reading it.*) Dark hair-dark eyes, smooth face, height five feet five—there's not much to take hold of in that[1]—it's a pity I had no chance of seeing him before he broke out of jail. They say he's a wonder, that it's he makes all the plans[2] for the whole organization. There isn't another man in Ireland would have broken jail the way he did. He must have some friends among the jailers.

Policeman B. A hundred pounds is little enough for the Government to offer for him. You may be sure any man in the force[3] that takes him will get promotion.

Sergeant. I'll mind this place myself. I wouldn't wonder at all if he came this way. He might come slipping along there (*points to side of quay*), and his friends might be waiting for him there (*points down steps*), and once he got away it's little chance we'd have of finding him; it's maybe under a load of kelp[4] he'd be in a fishing boat, and not one to help a married man that wants it to the reward.

Policeman X. And if we get him itself[5], nothing but abuse on our heads for it from the people, and maybe from our own relations.

Sergeant. Well, we have to do our duty in the force. Haven't we the whole country depending on us to keep law and order? It's those that are down would be up and those that are up would be down, if it wasn't for us. Well, hurry on, you have plenty of other places to placard yet, and come back here then to me. You can take the lantern. Don't be too long now. It's very lonesome here with nothing but the moon.

Policeman B. It's a pity we can't stop with you. The Government should have brought more police into the town, with him in jail, and at assize time[6] too. Well, good luck to your watch.

(***They go out.***)

Sergeant. (***Walks up and down once or twice and looks at placard.***) A hundred pounds and promotion sure. There must be a great deal of spending in a hundred pounds. It's a pity some honest man not to be the better of that[7]. (***A ragged man appears at left and tries to slip past. Sergeant suddenly turns.***)

Sergeant. Where are you going?

Man. I'm a poor ballad-singer, your honour. I thought to sell some of these (***holds out bundle of ballads***) to the sailors.

(***He goes on.***)

Sergeant. Stop! Didn't I tell you to stop? You can't go on there.

Man. Oh, very well. It's a hard thing to be poor. All the world's against the poor!

Sergeant. Who are you?

Man. You'd be as wise as myself if I told you, but I don't mind. I'm one Jimmy Walsh, a ballad-singer.

Sergeant. Jimmy Walsh? I don't know that name.

Man. Ah, sure, they know it well enough in Ennis[8]. Were you ever in Ennis,

Sergeant?

Sergeant. What brought you here?

Man. Sure, it's to the assizes I came, thinking I might make a few shillings here or there. It's in the one train with the judges I came.

Sergeant. Well, if you came so far, you may as well go farther, for you'll walk out of this.

Man. I will, I will; I'll just go on where I was going.

(*Goes towards steps.*)

Sergeant. Come back from those steps; no one has leave to pass down them[9] to-night.

Man. I'll just sit on the top of the steps till I see will some sailor buy a ballad[10] off me that would give me my supper. They do be late[11] going back to the ship. It's often I saw them in Cork[12] carried down the quay in a hand-cart.

Sergeant. Move on, I tell you. I won't have any one lingering about the quay to-night.

Man. Well, I'll go. It's the poor have the hard life! Maybe yourself might like one, Sergeant. Here's a good sheet now. (***Turns one over.***) **Content and a Pipe**—that's not much. **The Peeler**[13] **and the Goat**—you wouldn't like that. **Johnny Hart**—that's a lovely song.

Sergeant. Move on.

Man. Ah, wait till you hear it. (*Sings*):

> "There was a rich farmer's daughter lived near the town of Ross[14];
> She courted a Highland soldier, his name was Johnny Hart;
> Says the mother to her daughter, 'I'll go distracted mad
> If you marry that Highland soldier dressed up in Highland plaid.'"

Sergeant. Stop that noise.

(***Man wraps up his ballads and shuffles towards the steps.***)

Sergeant. Where are you going?

Man. Sure, you told me to be going, and I am going.

Sergeant. Don't be a fool. I didn't tell you to go that way; I told you to go back to the town.

Man. Back to the town, is it?

Sergeant. (*Taking him by the shoulder and shoving him before him.*) Here, I'll show you the way. Be off with you. What are you stopping for?

Man. (*Who has been keeping his eye on the notice, points to it.*) I think I know what you're waiting for, Sergeant.

Sergeant. What's that to you?

Man. And I know well the man you're waiting for—I know him well—I'll be going. (*He shuffles on.*)

Sergeant. You know him? Come back here. What sort is he?

Man. Come back is it, Sergeant? Do you want to have me killed?

Sergeant. Why do you say that?

Man. Never mind. I'm going. I wouldn't be in your shoes if the reward was ten times as much. (*Goes off stage to left.*) Not if it was ten times as much.

Sergeant. (*Rushing after him.*) Come back here, come back. (*Drags him back.*) What sort is he? Where did you see him?

Man. I saw him in my own place, in the County Clare. I tell you you wouldn't like to be looking at him. You'd be afraid to be in the one place with him. There isn't a weapon he doesn't know the use of, and as to strength, his muscles are as hard as that board. (*Slaps barrel.*)

Sergeant. Is he as bad as that?

Man. He is then.

Sergeant. Do you tell me so?

Man. There was a poor man in our place, a sergeant from Ballyvaughan[15].—It was with a lump of stone he did it.

Sergeant. I never heard of that.

Man. And you wouldn't, Sergeant. It's not everything that happens gets into the papers. And there was a policeman in plain clothes, too… It is in Limerick[16] he was… It was after the time of the attack on the police barrack at Kilmallock[17]… Moonlight…just like this…waterside. Nothing was known for certain.

Sergeant. Do you say so? It's a terrible country to belong to.

Man. That's so, indeed! You might be standing there, looking out that way, thinking you saw him coming up this side of the quay (*points*) and he might be coming up this other side (*points*) and he'd be on you before you knew where you were.

Sergeant. It's a whole troop of police they ought to put here to stop a man like that.

Man. But if you'd like me to stop with you, I could be looking down this side. I could be sitting up here on this barrel.

Sergeant. And you know him well, too?

Man. I'd know him a mile off, Sergeant.

Sergeant. But you wouldn't want to share the reward?

Man. Is it a poor man like me, that has to be going the roads and singing in fairs, to have the name on him that he took a reward? But you don't want me. I'll be safer in the town.

Sergeant. Well, you can stop.

Man. (*Getting up on barrel.*) All right, Sergeant. I wonder, now, you're not tired out, Sergeant. walking up and down the way you are.

Sergeant. If I'm tired I'm used to it.

Man. You might have hard work before you to-night yet. Take it easy while you can. There's plenty of room up here on the barrel, and you see farther when you're higher up.

Sergeant. Maybe so. (*Gets up beside him on barrel, facing right. They sit back to back, looking different ways.*) You made me feel a bit queer with the way you talked.

Man. Give me a match, Sergeant. (*He gives it and Man lights pipe.*) Take a draw yourself? It'll quiet you. Wait now till I give you a light, but you needn't turn round. Don't take your eye off the quay for the life of you.

Sergeant. Never fear, I won't. (*Lights pipe. They both smoke.*) Indeed it's a hard thing to be in the force, out at night and no thanks for it, for all the danger we're in. And it's little we get but abuse from the people, and no choice but to obey our orders, and never asked when a man is sent into danger, if you are a married man with a family.

Man. (*Sings*):

"As through the hills I walked to view the hills and shamrock plain,
I stood awhile where nature smiles to view the rocks and streams,
On a matron fair I fixed my eyes beneath a fertile vale,
As she sang her song it was on the wrong of poor old Granuaile."

Sergeant. Stop that; that's no song to be singing in these times.

Man. Ah, Sergeant, I was only singing to keep my heart up. It sinks when I think of him. To think of us two sitting here, and he creeping up the quay, maybe, to get to us.

Sergeant. Are you keeping a good look-out?

Man. I am; and for no reward too. Amn't I the foolish man? But when I saw a man in trouble, I never could help trying to get him out of it. What's that? Did something hit me? (***Rubs his heart.***)

Sergeant. (***Patting him on the shoulder.***) You will get your reward in heaven.

Man. I know that, I know that, Sergeant, but life is precious.

Sergeant. Well, you can sing if it gives you more courage.

Man. (*Sings*):

"Her head was bare, her hands and feet with iron bands were bound,
Her pensive strain and plaintive wail mingled with the evening gale,
And the song she sang with mournful air, I am old Granuaile,[18]
Her lips so sweet that monarchs kissed..."

Sergeant. That's not it... "Her gown she wore was stained with gore." ... That's it—you missed that.

Man. You're right, Sergeant, so it is; I missed it. (***Repeats line.***) But to think of a man like you knowing a song like that.

Sergeant. There's many a thing a man might know and might not have any wish for.

Man. Now, I dare say, Sergeant, in your youth, you used to be sitting up on a wall, the way you are sitting up on this barrel now, and the other lads beside you, and you singing *Granuaile*? ...

Sergeant. I did then.

Man. And the *Shan Bhean Bhocht*[19]? ...

Sergeant. I did then.

Man. And *the Green on the Cape?*

Sergeant. That was one of them.

Man. And maybe the man you are watching for to-night used to be sitting on the wall, when he was young, and singing those same songs... It's a queer world...

Sergeant. Whisht[20]!... I think I see something coming... It's only a dog.

Man. And isn't it a queer world?... Maybe it's one of the boys you used to be singing with that time you will be arresting to-day or to-morrow, and sending into the dock. ...

Sergeant. That's true indeed.

Man. And maybe one night, after you had been singing, if the other boys had told you some plan they had, some plan to free the country, you might have joined with them...and maybe it is you might be in trouble now.

Sergeant. Well, who knows but I might? I had a great spirit in those days.

Man. It's a queer world, Sergeant, and it's little any mother knows when she sees her child creeping on the floor what might happen to it before it has gone through its life, or who will be who in the end.

Sergeant. That's a queer thought now, and a true thought. Wait now till I think it out... If it wasn't for the sense I have, and for my wife and family, and for me joining the force the time I did, it might be myself now would be after breaking jail and hiding in the dark, and it might be him that's hiding in the dark and that got out of jail would be sitting up where I am on this barrel.... And it might be myself would be creeping up trying to make my escape from himself, and it might be himself would be keeping the law, and myself would be breaking it, and myself would be trying maybe to put a bullet in his head, or to take up a lump of a stone the way you said he did...no, that myself did... Oh! (*Gasps. After a pause.*) What's that?

(*Grasps Man's arm.*)

Man. (*Jumps off barrel and listens, looking out over water.*) It's nothing, Sergeant.

Sergeant. I thought it might be a boat. I had a notion there might be friends of his coming about the quays with a boat.

Man. Sergeant, I am thinking it was with the people you were, and not with the law you were, when you were a young man.

Sergeant. Well, if I was foolish then, that time's gone.

Man. Maybe, Sergeant, it comes into your head sometimes, in spite of your belt and your tunic[21], that it might have been as well for you to have followed Granuaile.

Sergeant. It's no business of yours what I think.

Man. Maybe, Sergeant, you'll be on the side of the country yet.

Sergeant. (*Gets off barrel.*) Don't talk to me like that. I have my duties and I know them. (*Looks round.*) That was a boat; I hear the oars.

(*Goes to the steps and looks down.*)

Man. (*Sings*):

"O, then, tell me Shawn O'Farrell[22],
where the gathering is to be.
In the old spot by the river
Right well known to you and me!"

Sergeant. Stop that! Stop that, I tell you!

Man. (*Sings louder*):

"One word more, for signal token,
Whistle up the marching tune,

With your pike upon your shoulder,
At the Rising of the Moon[23]."

Sergeant. If you don't stop that, I'll arrest you. (*A whistle from below answers, repeating the air.*)

Sergeant. That's a signal. (*Stands between him and steps.*) You must not pass this way... Step farther back... Who are you? You are no ballad-singer.

Man. You needn't ask who I am; that placard will tell you.

(*Points to placard.*)

Sergeant. You are the man I am looking for.

Man. (*Takes off hat and wig. Sergeant seizes them.*) I am. There's a hundred pounds on my head. There is a friend of mine below in a boat. He knows a safe place to bring me to.

Sergeant. (*Looking still at hat and wig.*) It's a pity! It's a pity. You deceived me. You deceived me well.

Man. I am a friend of Granuaile. There is a hundred pounds on my head.

Sergeant. It's a pity, it's a pity!

Man. Will you let me pass, or must I make you let me?

Sergeant. I am in the force. I will not let you pass.

Man. I thought to do it with my tongue. (*Puts hand in breast.*) What is that? (*Voice of Policeman X outside.*) Here, this is where we left him.

Sergeant. It's my comrades coming.

Man. You won't betray me...the friend of Granuaile.

(*Slips behind barrel.*)

(*Voice of Policeman B.*) That was the last of the placards.

Policeman X. (*As they come in.*) If he makes his escape, it won't be unknown he'll make it.

(*Sergeant puts hat and wig behind his back.*)

Policeman B. Did any one come this way?

Sergeant. (*After a pause.*) No one.

Policeman B. No one at all?

Sergeant. No one at all.

Policeman B. We had no orders to go back to the station; we can stop along with you.

Sergeant. I don't want you. There is nothing for you to do here.

Policeman B. You bade us to come back here and keep watch with you.

Sergeant. I'd sooner be alone. Would any man come this way and you making all that talk? It is better the place to be quiet.

Policeman B. Well, we'll leave you the lantern anyhow.

(*Hands it to him.*)

Sergeant. I don't want it. Bring it with you.

Policeman B. You might want it. There are clouds coming up and you have the darkness of the night before you yet. I'll leave it over here on the barrel.

(*Goes to barrel.*)

Sergeant. Bring it with you, I tell you. No more talk.

Policeman B. Well, I thought it might be a comfort to you. I often think when I have it in my hand and can be flashing it about into every dark corner (*doing so*) that it's the same as being beside the fire at home, and the bits of bogwood blazing up now and again.

(*Flashes it about, now on the barrel. Now on Sergeant.*)

Sergeant. (*Furious.*) Be off, the two of you, yourselves and your lantern!

(*They go out. Man comes from behind barrel. He and Sergeant stand looking at one another.*)

Sergeant. What are you waiting for?

Man. For my hat, of course, and my wig. You wouldn't wish me to get my death of cold?

(*Sergeant gives them.*)

Man. (*Going towards steps.*) Well, good night, comrade, and thank you. You did me a good turn to-night, and I'm obliged to you. Maybe I'll be able to do as much for you when the small rise up and the big fall down… when we all change places at the Rising (*waves his hand and disappears*) of the Moon.

Sergeant. (*Turning his back to audience and reading placard.*) A hundred pounds reward! A hundred pounds! (***Turns towards audience.***) I wonder, now, am I as great a fool as I think I am?

NOTES

1. **there's not much to take hold of in that:** there is not much to grasp in the description of the wanted man
2. **it's he makes all the plans:** it is he that makes all the plans
3. **the force:** the police force
4. **kelp:** large seaweed
5. **if we get him itself:** if we get him himself
6. **at assize time:** during the session of a mobile court
7. **some honest man not to be the better of that:** some honest man may not be the better for that
8. **Ennis:** the county town of County Clare in Munster Province, Ireland (the Republic of Ireland since 1922)
9. **no one has leave to pass down them:** no one is permitted to pass down those steps
10. **till I see will some sailor buy a ballad:** till I see whether some sailor will buy a ballad
11. **They do be late:** They are really late.
12. **Cork:** a county of SW Ireland, in Munster Province
13. *Peeler*: policeman
14. **Ross:** a county of NW Scotland
15. **Ballyvaughan:** a town in W Ireland
16. **Limerick:** a county in SW Ireland
17. **Kilmallock:** a town in Limerick
18. **Granuaile:** a personage in Irish folk-songs symbolizing Ireland
19. *Shan Bhean Bhocht*: an Irish folk-song with that title (which means Poor Old Woman)
20. **Whisht:** (Ir.) hush
21. **your belt and your tunic:** your police uniform
22. **Shawn O'Farrell:** an Irish revolutionary, the Man's comrade
23. **the Rising of the Moon:** the title of a revolutionary song; a symbolic expression for the independence of Ireland

OSCAR WILDE

(1854–1900)

Oscar Wilde was an Irish dramatist and prose-writer. He was born in Dublin, the son of a surgeon whose wife was well known as a writer and literary hostess, and educated at Trinity College, Dublin, and at Magdalen College, Oxford. His dandyism and aestheticism attracted attention in London society. He was imprisoned for homosexual offences in 1895, and after his release in 1897 he went to France. He died in Paris three years later.

Oscar Wilde's fame rests on the following works: ***The Happy Prince and Other Tales*** (1888), a volume of fairy tales; ***The Picture of Dorian Gray*** (1890), a novel about a hedonist who embodies the aesthetic way of life; ***Lady Windermere's Fan*** (1892), ***A Woman of No Importance*** (1893), ***An Ideal Husband*** (1895), and above all ***The Importance of Being Earnest*** (1895), four social plays; ***Intentions*** (1891), a volume of social essays; and ***The Ballad of Reading Gaol*** (1898), a poem inspired by his prison experience. His prose is highly wrought and glitteringly witty.

THE HAPPY PRINCE

High above the city, on a tall column, stood the statue of the Happy Prince. He was gilded all over with thin leaves of fine gold, for eyes he had two bright sapphires, and a large red ruby glowed on his sword-hilt.

He was very much admired indeed. "He is as beautiful as a weathercock," remarked one of the Town Councillors who wished to gain a reputation for having artistic tastes; "only not quite so useful," he added, fearing lest people should think him unpractical, which he really was not.

"Why can't you be like the Happy Prince?" asked a sensible mother of her little boy who was crying for the moon. "The Happy Prince never dreams of crying for anything."

"I am glad there is someone in the world who is quite happy," muttered a disappointed man as he gazed at the wonderful statue.

"He looks just like an angel," said the Charity Children[1] as they came out of the cathedral in their bright scarlet cloaks and their clean white pinafores.

"How do you know?" said the Mathematical Master, "you have never seen one."

"Ah! but we have, in our dreams," answered the children; and the Mathematical Master frowned and looked very severe, for he did not approve of children dreaming.

One night there flew over the city a little Swallow. His friends had gone away to Egypt six weeks before, but he had stayed behind, for he was in love with the most beautiful Reed. He had met her early in the spring as he was flying down the river after a big yellow moth, and had been so attracted by her slender waist that he had stopped to talk to her.

"Shall I love you?" said the Swallow, who liked to come to the point at once, and the Reed made him a low bow. So he flew round and round her, touching the water with his wings, and making silver ripples. This was his courtship, and it lasted all through the summer.

"It is a ridiculous attachment," twittered the other Swallows; "she has no money, and far too many relations;" and indeed the river was quite full of Reeds. Then, when the autumn came they all flew away.

After they had gone he felt lonely, and began to tire of his lady-love. "She has no conversation," he said, "and I am afraid that she is a coquette, for she is always flirting with the wind." And certainly, whenever the wind blew, the Reed made the most graceful curtseys. "I admit that she is domestic," he continued, "but I love travelling, and my wife, consequently, should love travelling also."

"Will you come away with me?" he said finally to her, but the Reed shook her head, she was so attached to her home.

"You have been trifling with me," he cried. "I am off to the Pyramids. Good-bye!" and he flew away.

All day long he flew, and at night-time he arrived at the city. "Where shall I put up?" he said; "I hope the town has made preparations."

Then he saw the statue on the tall column.

"I will put up there," he cried; "it is a fine position, with plenty of fresh air." So he alighted just between the feet of the Happy Prince.

"I have a golden bedroom," he said softly to himself as he looked round, and he prepared to go to sleep; but just as he was putting his head under his wing a large drop of water fell on him. "What a curious thing!" he cried; "there is not a single cloud in the sky, the stars are quite clear and bright, and yet it is raining. The climate in the north of Europe is really dreadful. The Reed used to like the rain, but that was merely her selfishness."

Then another drop fell.

"What is the use of a statue if it cannot keep the rain off?" he said; "I must look for a good chimney-pot," and he determined to fly away.

But before he had opened his wings, a third drop fell, and he looked up, and saw—Ah! what did he see?

The eyes of the Happy Prince were filled with tears, and tears were running down his golden cheeks. His face was so beautiful in the moonlight that the little

Swallow was filled with pity.

"Who are you?" he said.

"I am the Happy Prince."

"Why are you weeping then?" asked the Swallow; "you have quite drenched me."

"When I was alive and had a human heart," answered the statue, "I did not know what tears were, for I lived in the Palace of Sans-Souci[2], where sorrow is not allowed to enter. In the daytime I played with my companions in the garden, and in the evening I led the dance in the Great Hall. Round the garden ran a very lofty wall, but I never cared to ask what lay beyond it, everything about me was so beautiful. My courtiers called me the Happy Prince, and happy indeed I was, if pleasure be happiness. So I lived, and so I died. And now that I am dead they have set me up here so high that I can see all the ugliness and all the misery of my city, and though my heart is made of lead yet I cannot choose but weep."

"What! is he not solid gold?" said the Swallow to himself. He was too polite to make any personal remarks out loud.

"Far away," continued the statue in a low musical voice, "far away in a little street there is a poor house. One of the windows is open, and through it I can see a woman seated at a table. Her face is thin and worn, and she has coarse, red hands, all pricked by the needle, for she is a seamstress. She is embroidering passion-flowers[3] on a satin gown for the loveliest of the Queen's maids-of-honour to wear at the next Court ball. In a bed in the corner of the room her little boy is lying ill. He has a fever, and is asking for oranges. His mother has nothing to give him but river water, so he is crying. Swallow, Swallow, little Swallow, will you not take her the ruby out of my sword-hilt? My feet are fastened to this pedestal and I cannot move."

"I am waited for in Egypt," said the Swallow. "My friends are flying up and down the Nile, and talking to the large lotus flowers. Soon they will go to sleep in the tomb of the great King. The King is there himself in his painted coffin. He is wrapped in yellow linen, and embalmed with spices. Round his neck is a chain of pale green jade, and his hands are like withered leaves."

"Swallow, Swallow, little Swallow," said the Prince, "will you not stay with me for one night, and be my messenger? The boy is so thirsty, and the mother so sad."

"I don't think I like boys," answered the Swallow. "Last summer, when I was staying on the river, there were two rude boys, the miller's sons, who were always throwing stones at me. They never hit me, of course; we swallows fly far too well for that, and besides, I come of a family famous for its agility; but still, it was a mark of disrespect."

But the Happy Prince looked so sad that the little Swallow was sorry. "It is very cold here," he said; "but I will stay with you for one night, and be your messenger."

"Thank you, little Swallow," said the Prince.

So the Swallow picked out the great ruby from the Prince's sword, and flew away with it in his beak over the roofs of the town.

He passed by the cathedral tower, where the white marble angels were sculptured. He passed by the palace and heard the sound of dancing. A beautiful girl came out on the balcony with her lover. "How wonderful the stars are," he said to her, "and how wonderful is the power of love!"

"I hope my dress will be ready in time for the State ball," she answered; "I have ordered passion-flowers to be embroidered on it; but the seamstresses are so lazy."

He passed over the river, and saw the lanterns hanging to the masts of the ships. He passed over the Ghetto[4], and saw the old Jews bargaining with each other, and weighing out money in copper scales. At last he came to the poor house and looked in. The boy was tossing feverishly on his bed, and the mother had fallen asleep, she was so tired. In he hopped, and laid the great ruby on the table beside the woman's thimble. Then he flew gently round the bed, fanning the boy's forehead with his wings. "How cool I feel!" said the boy, "I must be getting better;" and he sank into a delicious slumber.

Then the Swallow flew back to the Happy Prince, and told him what he had done. "It is curious," he remarked, "but I feel quite warm now, although it is so cold."

"That is because you have done a good action," said the Prince. And the little Swallow began to think, and then he fell asleep. Thinking always made him sleepy.

When day broke he flew down to the river and had a bath. "What a remarkable phenomenon[5]!" said the Professor of Ornithology as he was passing over the bridge. "A swallow in winter!" And he wrote a long letter about it to the local newspaper. Everyone quoted it, it was full of so many words that they could not understand.

"To-night I go to Egypt," said the Swallow, and he was in high spirits at the prospect. He visited all the public monuments, and sat a long time on top of the church steeple. Wherever he went the Sparrows chirruped, and said to each other, "What a distinguished stranger!" so he enjoyed himself very much.

When the moon rose he flew back to the Happy Prince. "Have you any commissions for Egypt?" he cried; "I am just starting."

"Swallow, Swallow, little Swallow," said the Prince, "will you not stay with me one night longer?"

"I am waited for in Egypt," answered the Swallow. "To-morrow my friends will fly up to the Second Cataract. The river-horse[6] couches there among the bulrushes, and on a great granite throne sits the God Memnon[7]. All night long he watches the stars, and when the morning star shines he utters one cry of joy, and then he is silent. At noon the yellow lions come down to the water's edge to drink. They have eyes like green beryls, and their roar is louder than the roar of the cataract."

"Swallow, Swallow, little Swallow," said the Prince, "far away across the city I see a young man in a garret. He is leaning over a desk covered with papers, and in a tumbler by his side there is a bunch of withered violets. His hair is brown and crisp, and his lips are red as a pomegranate, and he has large and dreamy eyes. He is trying to finish a play for the Director of the Theatre, but he is too cold to write any more. There is no fire in the grate, and hunger has made him faint."

"I will wait with you one night longer," said the Swallow, who really had a good heart. "Shall I take him another ruby?"

"Alas! I have no ruby now," said the Prince; "my eyes are all that I have left. They are made of rare sapphires, which were brought out of India a thousand years ago. Pluck out one of them and take it to him. He will sell it to the jeweller, and buy firewood, and finish his play."

"Dear Prince," said the Swallow, "I cannot do that;" and he began to weep.

"Swallow, Swallow, little Swallow," said the Prince, "do as I command you."

So the Swallow plucked out the Prince's eye, and flew away to the student's garret. It was easy enough to get in, as there was a hole in the roof. Through this he darted, and came into the room. The young man had his head buried in his hands, so he did not hear the flutter of the bird's wings, and when he looked up he found the beautiful sapphire lying on the withered violets.

"I am beginning to be appreciated," he cried; "this is from some great admirer. Now I can finish my play," and he looked quite happy.

The next day the Swallow flew down to the harbour. He sat on the mast of a large vessel and watched the sailors hauling big chests out of the hold with ropes. "Heave a-hoy!"[8] they shouted as each chest came up. "I am going to Egypt!" cried the Swallow, but nobody minded, and when the moon rose he flew back to the Happy Prince.

"I am come to bid you good-bye," he cried.

"Swallow, Swallow, little Swallow," said the Prince, "will you not stay with me one night longer?"

"It is winter," answered the Swallow, "and the chill[9] snow will soon be here. In Egypt the sun is warm on the green palm trees, and the crocodiles lie in the mud and look lazily about them. My companions are building a nest in the Temple of Baalbec[10], and the pink and white doves are watching them, and cooing to each other. Dear Prince, I must leave you, but I will never forget you, and next spring I will bring you back two beautiful jewels in place of those you have given away. The ruby shall be redder than a red rose, and the sapphire shall be as blue as the great sea."

"In the square below," said the Happy Prince, "there stands a little match-girl. She has let her matches fall in the gutter, and they are all spoiled. Her father will beat her if she does not bring home some money, and she is crying. She has no shoes or stockings, and her little head is bare. Pluck out my other eye, and give it to her, and her father will not beat her."

"I will stay with you one night longer," said the Swallow, "but I cannot pluck out your eye. You would be quite blind then."

"Swallow, Swallow, little Swallow," said the Prince, "do as I command you."

So he plucked out the Prince's other eye, and darted down with it. He swooped past the match-girl, and slipped the jewel into the palm of her hand. "What a lovely bit of glass!" cried the little girl; and she ran home, laughing.

Then the Swallow came back to the Prince. "You are blind now," he said, "so I will stay with you always."

"No, little Swallow," said the poor Prince, "you must go away to Egypt."

"I will stay with you always," said the Swallow, and he slept at the Prince's feet.

All the next day he sat on the Prince's shoulder, and told him stories of what he had seen in strange lands. He told him of the red ibises[11], who stand in long rows on the banks of the Nile, and catch goldfish in their beaks; of the Sphinx, who is as old as the world itself, and lives in the desert, and knows everything; of the merchants, who walk slowly by the side of their camels and carry amber beads in their hands; of the King of the Mountains of the Moon, who is as black as ebony, and worships a large crystal; of the great green snake that sleeps in a palm tree, and has twenty priests to feed it with honeycakes; and of the pygmies who sail over a big lake on large flat leaves, and are always at war with the butterflies.

"Dear little Swallow," said the Prince, "you tell me of marvellous things, but more marvellous than anything is the suffering of men and of women. There is no Mystery so great as Misery. Fly over my city, little Swallow, and tell me what you see there."

So the Swallow flew over the great city, and saw the rich making merry in their beautiful houses, while the beggars were sitting at the gates. He flew into dark lanes, and saw the white faces of starving children looking out listlessly at the black streets. Under the archway of a bridge two little boys were lying in one another's arms to try and keep themselves warm. "How hungry we are!" they said. "You must not lie here," shouted the watchman, and they wandered out into the rain.

Then he flew back and told the Prince what he had seen.

"I am covered with fine gold," said the Prince, "you must take it off, leaf by leaf, and give it to my poor; the living always think that gold can make them happy."

Leaf after leaf of the fine gold the Swallow picked off, till the Happy Prince looked quite dull and grey. Leaf after leaf of the fine gold he brought to the poor, and the children's faces grew rosier, and they laughed and played games in the street. "We have bread now!" they cried.

Then the snow came, and after the snow came the frost. The streets looked as if they were made of silver, they were so bright and glistening; long icicles like crystal daggers hung down from the eaves of the houses, everybody went about in furs, and the little boys wore scarlet caps and skated on the ice.

The poor little Swallow grew colder and colder, but he would not leave the Prince, he loved him too well. He picked up crumbs outside the baker's door when the baker was not looking, and tried to keep himself warm by flapping his wings.

But at last he knew that he was going to die. He had just enough strength to fly up to the Prince's shoulder once more. "Good-bye, dear Prince!" he murmured, "will you let me kiss your hand?"

"I am glad that you are going to Egypt at last, little Swallow," said the Prince, "you have stayed too long here; but you must kiss me on the lips, for I love you."

"It is not to Egypt that I am going," said the Swallow. "I am going to the House of Death. Death is the brother of Sleep, is he not?"

And he kissed the Happy Prince on the lips, and fell down dead at his feet.

At that moment a curious crack sounded inside the statue, as if something had broken. The fact is that the leaden heart had snapped right in two. It certainly was a dreadfully hard frost.

Early the next morning the Mayor was walking in the square below in company with the Town Councillors. As they passed the column he looked up at the statue: "Dear me! how shabby the Happy Prince looks!" he said.

"How shabby, indeed!" cried the Town Councillors, who always agreed with the Mayor; and they went up to look at it.

"The ruby has fallen out of his sword, his eyes are gone, and he is golden no longer," said the Mayor; "in fact, he is little better than a beggar!"

"Little better than a beggar," said the Town Councillors.

"And here is actually a dead bird at his feet!" continued the Mayor. "We must really issue a proclamation that birds are not to be allowed to die here." And the Town Clerk made a note of the suggestion.

So they pulled down the statue of the Happy Prince. "As he is no longer beautiful he is no longer useful," said the Art Professor at the University.

Then they melted the statue in a furnace, and the Mayor held a meeting of the Corporation to decide what was to be done with the metal. "We must have another statue, of course," he said, "and it shall be a statue of myself."

"Of myself," said each of the Town Councillors, and they quarrelled. When I last heard of them they were quarrelling still.

"What a strange thing!" said the overseer of the workmen at the foundry. "This broken lead heart will not melt in the furnace. We must throw it away." So they threw it on a dust-heap where the dead Swallow was also lying.

"Bring me the two most precious things in the city," said God to one of His Angels; and the Angel brought Him the leaden heart and the dead bird.

"You have rightly chosen," said God, "for in my garden of Paradise this little bird shall sing for evermore[12], and in my city of gold the Happy Prince shall praise me."

NOTES
1. **Charity Children:** children of a charity school
2. **Sans-Souci:** (Fr.) without care
3. **passion-flowers:** instruments of crucification flowers of *Passiflora* plants suggesting
4. **the Ghetto:** the Jewish quarter in a city
5. **remarkable phenomenon:** striking occurrence

6. **river-horse:** hippopotamus
7. **the God Memnon:** (Gr. myth.) an Ethiopian king killed by Achilles and made immortal by Zeus
8. **"Heave a-hoy!":** a call by sailors when hauling up something
9. **chill:** (adj.) chilly
10. **the Temple of Baalbec:** Baalbec was an ancient city of Syria and a centre of the worship of Baal as sun god.
11. **ibises:** wading birds of the family *Threskiornithida*
12. **for evermore:** (a more emphatic term for) for ever

GEORGE BERNARD SHAW

(1856–1950)

Bernard Shaw was an Irish dramatist, critic, and social thinker. He was born in Dublin on July 26, 1856, left school in 1870 to work as a land-agent's junior clerk, and moved to London in 1876 to begin a literary career. He joined the newly formed Fabian Society in 1884 and served on its executive committee from 1885 to 1911. He published a large amount of art, music, and drama criticism. His work as a playwright began in 1892 and lasted till his advanced age. He lived at Ayot St. Lawrence, Hertfordshire, from 1906 and died there on November 2, 1950. Shaw wrote over fifty plays, including **Widowers' Houses** (1892), **Mrs. Warren's Profession** (1893), **Arms and the Man** (1894), **The Devil's Disciple** (1897), **Candida** (1898), **You Never Can Tell** (1898), **Caesar and Cleopatra** (1901), **Man and Superman** (1903), **John Bull's Other Island** (1904), **Major Barbara** (1905), **The Doctor's Dilemma** (1906), **Androcles and the Lion** (1912), **Pigmalion** (1913), **Heartbreak House** (1919), **Back to Methuselah** (1921), and **Saint Joan** (1923). Among his other works may be mentioned **The Quintessence of Ibsenism** (1891), **Common Sense About the War** (1914), **The Intelligent Woman's Guide to Socialism and Capitalism** (1928), and **Everybody's Political What's What** (1944). Shaw was awarded the Nobel Prize in 1925. In Shaw's plays, it is the ideas that matter rather than the characters, who are but mouthpieces for the author's views. He believes in Fabian socialism and in the "Life Force", and treats social issues with realism. He is well versed in stagecraft and achieves good theatrical effect. He writes in a terse, precise, fluent, and witty style.

THE OPENING SCENE OF *MAJOR BARBARA*

So ends the prologue. The story begins some weeks later in her boudoir upstairs, where Lady Britomart Undershaft[1] *sits at her writing table after dinner. A large and comfortable settee is in the middle of the room with a copy of The Speaker, a Liberal weekly*[2] *journal, on it. A person sitting on it (it is vacant at present) would have, on his right, the writing table, with the lady herself busy at it; the heavily curtained windows on his left with a smaller writing-table and an armchair near them; the door behind him towards his right; and additional sitting accommodation for half a dozen persons.*

Lady Britomart is a mature governing class aristocrat, well dressed and yet careless of her dress, well bred and quite reckless of her breeding, well mannered and yet appallingly outspoken and indifferent to the opinion of her interlocutors, amiable and yet peremptory, arbitrary, and high-tempered to the last bearable degree, and withal a very typical managing matron of the upper class, treated as a naughty child until she grew into a scolding mother, and finally settling down with plenty of practical ability and worldly experience, limited in the oddest way with domestic and class limitations, conceiving the universe exactly as if it were a large house in Wilton Crescent[3]*, though handling her corner of it very effectively on that assumption, and being quite enlightened and liberal as to the books in the library, the pictures on the walls, the music in the portfolios, and the articles in the papers.*

Her son Stephen comes in. He is a gravely correct young man, taking himself very seriously, and, though still in some awe of his mother from childish habit and bachelor shyness, quite untroubled by doubts or diffidence.

STEPHEN. What's the matter?

LADY BRITOMART. Presently[4], Stephen.

Stephen submissively walks to the settee and sits down. He takes The Speaker.

LADY BRITOMART. Dont begin to read, Stephen. I shall require all your attention.

STEPHEN. It was only while I was waiting—

LADY BRITOMART. Dont make excuses, Stephen. *[He puts down The Speaker]*. Now! *[She finishes her writing; rises; and comes to the settee]*. I have not kept you waiting very long, I think.

STEPHEN. Not at all, mother.

LADY BRITOMART. Bring me my cushion. *[He takes the cushion from the chair at the desk and arranges it for her as she sits down on the settee]*. Sit down. *[He sits down and fingers his tie nervously]*. Dont fiddle with your tie, Stephen: there is nothing the matter with it.

STEPHEN. I beg your pardon. *[He fiddles with his watch chain instead]*.

LADY BRITOMART. Now are you attending to me, Stephen?

STEPHEN. Of course, mother.

LADY BRITOMART. No: it's not of course. I want something much more than your everyday matter-of-course attention. I am going to speak to you very seriously, Stephen. I wish you would let that chain alone.

STEPHEN. *[hastily relinquishing the chain]* Have I done anything to annoy you, mother? If so, it was quite unintentional.

LADY BRITOMART. *[astonished]* Nonsense! *[With some remorse]* My poor boy, did you think I was angry with you?

STEPHEN. What is it, then, mother? You are making me very uneasy.

LADY BRITOMART. *[squaring herself at him rather aggressively]* Stephen: may I ask how soon you intend to realize that you are a grown-up man, and that I am only a woman?

STEPHEN. *[amazed]* Only a—

LADY BRITOMART. Dont repeat my words, please: it is a most aggravating habit. You must learn to face life seriously, Stephen. I really cannot bear the whole burden of our family affairs any longer. You must advise me: you must assume the responsibility.

STEPHEN. I!

LADY BRITOMART. Yes, you, of course. You were twenty-four last June. Youve been at Harrow and Cambridge[5]. Youve been to India and Japan. You must know a lot of things, now; unless you have wasted your time most scandalously. Well, advise me.

STEPHEN. *[much perplexed]* You know I have never interfered in the household—

LADY BRITOMART. No: I should think not. I dont want you to order the dinner.

STEPHEN. I mean in our family affairs.

LADY BRITOMART. Well, you must interfere now; for they are getting quite beyond me[6].

STEPHEN. *[troubled]* I have thought sometimes that perhaps I ought; but really, mother, I know so little about them; and what I do know is so painful! it is so impossible to mention some things to you—[he stops, ashamed].

LADY BRITOMART. I suppose you mean your father.

STEPHEN. *[almost inaudibly]* Yes.

LADY BRITOMART. My dear: we cant go on all our lives not mentioning him. Of course you were quite right not to open the subject until I asked you to; but you are old enough now to be taken into my confidence, and to help me to deal with him about the girls.

STEPHEN. But the girls are all right. They are engaged.

LADY BRITOMART. *[complacently]* Yes: I have made a very good match for Sarah. Charles Lomax will be a millionaire when he is thirty-five. But in the meantime his trustees cannot under the terms of his father's will allow him more than £800 a year.

STEPHEN. But the will says also that if he increases his income by his own exertions, they may double the increase.

LADY BRITOMART. Charles Lomax's exertions are much more likely to decrease his income than to increase it. Sarah will have to find at least another £800 a year for the next ten years; and even then they will be as poor as church mice. And what about Barbara? I thought Barbara was going to make the most brilliant career of all of you. And what does she do? Joins the Salvation Army[7]; discharges her maid; lives on a pound a week; and walks in one evening with a professor of Greek whom she has picked up in the street, and who pretends to be a Salvationist, and actually plays the big drum for her in public because he has fallen head over ears in love with her.

STEPHEN. I was certainly rather taken aback when I heard they were engaged. Cusins is a very nice fellow, certainly: nobody would ever guess that he was born in Australia; but—

LADY BRITOMART. Oh, Adolphus Cusins will make a very good husband. After all, nobody can say a word against Greek: it stamps a man at once as an educated gentleman. And my family, thank Heaven, is not a pig-headed Tory one. We are Whigs, and believe in liberty. Let snobbish people say what they please: Barbara shall marry, not the man they like, but the man *I* like.

STEPHEN. Of course I was thinking only of his income. However, he is not likely to be extravagant.

LADY BRITOMART. Dont be too sure of that, Stephen. I know your quiet, simple, refined, poetic people like Adolphus: quite content with the best of every thing! They cost more than your extravagant people, who are always as mean as they are second rate. No: Barbara will need at least £2000 a year. You see it means two additional households. Besides, my dear, you must marry soon. I dont approve of the present fashion of philandering bachelors and late marriages; and I am trying to arrange something for you.

STEPHEN. It's very good of you, mother; but perhaps I had better arrange that for myself.

LADY BRITOMART. Nonsense! you are much too young to begin matchmaking: you would be taken in by some pretty little nobody. Of course I dont mean that you are not to be consulted: you know that as well as I do. *[Stephen closes his lips and is silent].* Now dont sulk, Stephen.

STEPHEN. I am not sulking, mother. What has all this got to do with—with—with my father?

LADY BRITOMART. My dear Stephen: where is the money to come from? It is easy enough for you and the other children to live on my income as long as we are in the same house; but I cant keep four families in four separate houses. You know how poor my father is: he has barely seven thousand a year now; and really, if he were not the Earl of Stevenage, he would have to give up society. He can do nothing for us. He says, naturally enough, that it is absurd that he should be asked to provide for the children of a man who is rolling in money[8]. You see Stephen, your father must be fabulously wealthy, because there is always a war going on somewhere.

STEPHEN. You need not remind me of that, mother. I have hardly ever opened a newspaper in my life without seeing our name in it. The Undershaft torpedo! The Undershaft quick firers! The Undershaft ten inch! The Undershaft disappearing rampart gun! The Undershaft submarine! And now the Undershaft aerial battleship! At Harrow they called me the Woolwich Infant[9]. At Cambridge it was the same. A little brute at King's who was always trying to get up revivals, spoilt my Bible—your first birthday present to me—by writing under my name, "Son and heir to Undershaft and Lazarus[10], Death and Destruction Dealers: address, Christendom and Judea." But that was not so bad as the way I was kowtowed to[11] everywhere because my father was making millions by selling cannons.

LADY BRITOMART. It is not only the cannons, but the war loans that Lazarus arranges under cover of giving credit for the cannons. You know, Stephen, it's perfectly scandalous. Those two men, Andrew Undershaft and Lazarus, positively have Europe under their thumbs. That is why your father is able to behave as he does. He is above the law. Do you think Bismarck[12] or Gladstone[13] or Disraeli[14] could have openly defied every social and moral obligation all their lives as your father has? They simply wouldnt have dared. I asked Gladstone to take it up. I asked The Times to take it up. I asked the Lord Chamberlain to take it up. But it was just like asking them to declare war on the Sultan. They wouldnt. They said they couldnt touch him. I believe they were afraid.

STEPHEN. What could they do? He does not actually break the law.

LADY BRITOMART. Not break the law! He is always breaking the law. He broke the law when he was born: his parents were not married.

STEPHEN. Mother! Is that true?

LADY BRITOMART. Of course it's true: that was why we separated.

STEPHEN. He married without letting you know this!

LADY BRITOMART. *[rather taken aback by this inference]* Oh no. To do Andrew justice, that was not the sort of thing he did. Besides, you know the Undershaft motto: Unashamed. Everybody knew.

STEPHEN. But you said that was why you separated.

LADY BRITOMART. Yes, because he was not content with being a foundling himself: he wanted to disinherit you for another foundling. That was what I couldn't, stand.

STEPHEN. *[ashamed]* Do you mean for—for—for—

LADY BRITOMART. Dont stammer, Stephen. Speak distinctly.

STEPHEN. But this is so frightful to me, mother. To have to speak to you about such things!

LADY BRITOMART. It's not pleasant for me, either, especially if you are still so childish that you must make it worse by a display of embarrassment. It is only in the middle classes, Stephen, that people get into a state of dumb helpless horror when they find that there are wicked people in the world. In our class, we have to decide what is to be done with wicked people; and nothing should disturb our self-possession. Now ask your question properly.

STEPHEN. Mother: have you no consideration for me? For Heaven's sake either treat me as a child, as you always do, and tell me nothing at all; or tell me everything and let me take it as best I can.

LADY BRITOMART. Treat you as a child! What do you mean? It is most unkind and ungrateful of you to say such a thing. You know I have never treated any of you as children. I have always made you my companions and friends, and allowed you perfect freedom to do and say whatever you liked, so long as you liked what I could approve of.

STEPHEN. *[desperately]* I daresay we have been the very imperfect children of a very perfect mother; but I do beg you to let me alone for once, and tell me about this horrible business of my father wanting to set me aside for another son.

LADY BRITOMART. *[amazed]* Another son! I never said anything of the kind. I never dreamt of such a thing. This is what comes of interrupting me.

STEPHEN. But you said—

LADY BRITOMART. *[cutting him short]* Now be a good boy, Stephen, and listen to me patiently. The Undershafts are descended from a foundling in the parish of St. Andrew Undershaft in the city[15]. That was long ago, in the reign of James the First. Well, this foundling was adopted by an armorer and gun-maker. In the course of time the foundling succeeded to the business; and from some notion of gratitude, or some vow or something, he adopted another foundling, and left the business to him. And that foundling did the same. Ever since that, the cannon business has always been left to an adopted foundling named Andrew Undershaft.

STEPHEN. But did they never marry? Were there no legitimate sons?

LADY BRITOMART. Oh yes: they married just as your father did; and they were rich enough to buy land for their own children and leave them well provided for. But they always adopted and trained some foundling to succeed them in the business; and of course they always quarrelled with their wives furiously over it. Your father was adopted in that way; and he pretends to consider himself bound to keep up the tradition and adopt somebody to leave the business to. Of course I was not going to stand that. There may have been some reason for it when the Undershafts could only marry women in their own class, whose sons were not fit to govern great estates. But there could be no excuse for passing over my son.

STEPHEN. *[dubiously]* I am afraid I should make a poor hand of managing a cannon foundry.

LADY BRITOMART. Nonsense! you could easily get a manager and pay him a salary.

STEPHEN. My father evidently had no great opinion of my capacity.

LADY BRITOMART. Stuff, child![16] you were only a baby: it had nothing to do with your capacity. Andrew did it on principle, just as he did every perverse and wicked thing on principle. When my father remonstrated, Andrew actually told him to his face that history tells us of only two successful institutions: one the Undershaft firm, and the other the Roman Empire under the Antonines[17]. That was because the Antonine emperors all adopted their successors. Such rubbish! The

Stevenages are as good as the Antonines, I hope; and you are a Stevenage. But that was Andrew all over. There you have the man! Always clever and unanswerable when he was defending nonsense and wickedness: always awkward and sullen when he had to behave sensibly and decently!

STEPHEN. Then it was on my account that your home life was broken up, mother. I am sorry.

LADY BRITOMART. Well, dear, there were other differences. I really cannot bear an immoral man. I am not a Pharisee, I hope; and I should not have minded his merely doing wrong things: we are none of us perfect. But your father didnt exactly do wrong things: he said them and thought them: that was what was so dreadful. He really had a sort of religion of wrongness. Just as one doesnt mind men practising immorality so long as they own that they are in the wrong by preaching morality; so I couldnt forgive Andrew for preaching immorality while he practised morality. You would all have grown up without principles, without any knowledge of right and wrong, if he had been in the house. You know, my dear, your father was a very attractive man in some ways. Children did not dislike him; and he took advantage of it to put the wickedest ideas into their heads, and make them quite unmanageable. I did not dislike him myself: very far from it; but nothing can bridge over moral disagreement.

STEPHEN. All this simply bewilders me, mother. People may differ about matters of opinion, or even about religion; but how can they differ about right and wrong? Right is right; and wrong is wrong; and if a man cannot distinguish them properly, he is either a fool or a rascal: thats all.

LADY BRITOMART. *[touched]* Thats my own boy *[she pats his cheek]*! Your father never could answer that: he used to laugh and get out of it under cover of some affectionate nonsense. And now that you understand the situation, what do you advise me to do?

STEPHEN. Well, what can you do?

LADY BRITOMART. I must get the money somehow.

STEPHEN. We cannot take money from him. I had rather go and live in some cheap place like Bedford Square[18] or even Hampstead[19] than take a farthing of his money.

LADY BRITOMART. But after all, Stephen, our present income comes from Andrew.

STEPHEN. *[shocked]* I never knew that.

LADY BRITOMART. Well, you surely didnt suppose your grandfather had anything to give me. The Stevenages could not do everything for you. We gave you social position. Andrew had to contribute something. He had a very good bargain, I think.

STEPHEN. *[bitterly]* We are utterly dependent on him and his cannons, then?

LADY BRITOMART. Certainly not: the money is settled. But he provided it. So you see it is not a question of taking money from him or not: it is simply a question of how much. I dont want any more for myself.

STEPHEN. Nor do I.

LADY BRITOMART. But Sarah does; and Barbara does. That is, Charles Lomax and Adolphus Cusins will cost them more. So I must put my pride in my pocket[20] and ask for it, I suppose. That is your advice, Stephen, is it not?

STEPHEN. No.

LADY BRITOMART. *[sharply]* Stephen!

STEPHEN. Of course if you are determined—

LADY BRITOMART. I am not determined: I ask your advice; and I am waiting for it. I will not have all the responsibility thrown on my shoulders.

STEPHEN. *[obstinately]* I would die sooner than ask him for another penny.

LADY BRITOMART. *[resignedly]* You mean that I must ask him. Very well. Stephen: it shall be as you wish. You will be glad to know that your grandfather concurs. But he thinks I ought to ask Andrew to come here and see the girls. After all, he must have some natural affection for them.

STEPHEN. Ask him here!!!

LADY BRITOMART. Do not repeat my words, Stephen. Where else can I ask him?

STEPHEN. I never expected you to ask him at all.

LADY BRITOMART. Now dont tease, Stephen. Come! you see that it is necessary that he should pay us a visit, dont you?

STEPHEN. *[reluctantly]* I suppose so, if the girls cannot do without his money.

LADY BRITOMART. Thank you, Stephen: I knew you would give me the right advice when it was properly explained to you. I have asked your father to come this evening. *[Stephen bounds from his seat]* Dont jump, Stephen: it fidgets me.

STEPHEN. *[in utter consternation]* Do you mean to say that my father is coming here tonight—that he may be here at any moment?

LADY BRITOMART. *[looking at her watch]* I said nine. *[He gasps. She rises].* Ring the bell, please. *[Stephen goes to the smaller writing table: presses a button on it; and sits at it with his elbows on the table and his head in his hands, outwitted and overwhelmed].* It is ten minutes to nine yet; and I have to prepare the girls. I asked Charles Lomax and Adolphus to dinner on purpose that they might be here. Andrew had better see them in case he should cherish any delusions as to their being capable of supporting their wives. *[The butler enters: Lady Britomart goes behind the settee to speak to him].* Morrison: go up to the drawing room and tell everybody to come down here at once. *[Morrison withdraws. Lady Britomart turns to Stephen].* Now remember, Stephen: I shall need all your countenance and authority. *[He rises and tries to recover some vestige of these attributes].* Give me a chair, dear. *[He pushes a chair forward from the wall to where she stands, near the smaller writing table. She sits down; and he goes to the armchair, into which he throws himself].* I dont know how Barbara will take it. Ever since they made her a major in the Salvation Army she has developed a propensity to have her own way and order people about which quite cows me sometimes. It's not ladylike: I'm sure I dont know where she picked it up. Anyhow, Barbara shant bully me; but still it's just as well that your father should be here before she has time to refuse to meet him or make a fuss. Dont look nervous, Stephen: it will only encourage Barbara to make difficulties. I am nervous enough, goodness knows; but I dont shew it.

......

NOTES

1. **Lady Britomart**: She lives in Wilton Crescent with her son Stephen and two daughters, Barbara and Sarah.
2. **a Liberal weekly**: a weekly magazine favouring the Liberal Party
3. **Wilton Crescent**: a crescent-shaped street near Belgrave Square, London
4. **Presently:** (I'll tell you) soon.
5. **Harrow and Cambridge:** Harrow School and Cambridge University. Stephen has had an upper-class education.
6. **they are getting quite beyond me:** they are becoming more than I can cope with
7. **the Salvation Army:** a Christian body founded in 1865 by William Booth to combine missionary work with social welfare work among the poor
8. **a man who is rolling in money:** This refers to Andrew Undershaft, the wealthy manufacturer of armaments.
9. **the Woolwich Infant:** the name of a cannon
10. **Undershaft and Lazarus:** the Undershaft and Lazarus munitions factory
11. **was kowtowed to:** was shown excessive respect
12. **Bismarck:** Otto Eduard Leopold von Bismarck, first chancellor of the German Empire from 1871 to 1890
13. **Gladstone:** William Ewart Gladstone (1809–1898), British Liberal statesman and Prime Minister (1868–1874, 1880–1885, 1886, 1892–1894)
14. **Disraeli:** Benjamin Disraeli (1804–1881), British Tory statesman and Prime Minister (1867–1868, 1874–1880)
15. **the parish of St. Andrew Undershaft in the city:** The old church of St. Andrew Undershaft is in the City of London
16. **Stuff, child!:** Stuff and nonsense, child!
17. **the Antonines:** a group of Roman Emperors related to one another by adoption, namely Nerva (96–98), Trajan (98–117), Hadrian (117–138), Antoninus Pius (138–161) and Marcus Aurelius Antoninus (161–180)
18. **Bedford Square:** a fine square close by Bloomsbury Street, London
19. **Hamstead:** a fine residential suburb of London
20. **put my pride in my pocket:** suppress my pride

SORROWS OF THE MILLIONAIRE

The millionaire class, a small but growing one into which any of us may be flung tomorrow by the accidents of commerce, is perhaps the most neglected in the community. As far as I know, this is the first tract that has ever been written for millionaires.

In the advertisements of the manufacturers of the country, I find that everything is produced for the million[1] and nothing for the millionaire. Children, boys, youths, "gents"[2], ladies, artisans, professional men. Even peers, and kings, are catered for; but the millionaire's custom is evidently not worth having; there are too few of him. Whilst the poorest have their Rag Fair[3], a duly organized and busy market in Houndsditch[4], where you can buy a boot for a penny, you may search the world in vain for the market where the £50 boot, the special dear line of hats at forty guineas, the cloth of gold bicycling suit[5], and the Cleopatra claret, four pearls to the bottle[6], can be purchased wholesale.

Thus the unfortunate millionaire has the responsibility of prodigious wealth without the possibility of enjoying himself more than any ordinary rich man. Indeed, in many things he cannot enjoy himself more than many poor men do, nor even so much; for a drum major[7] is better dressed; a trainer's stable lad often rides a better horse; the first-class carriage is shared by office boys taking their young ladies out for the evening; everybody who goes down to Brighton[8] for Sunday rides in the Pullman car; and of what use is it to be able to pay for a peacock's brain sandwich[9] when there is nothing to be had but ham or beef?

The injustice of this state of things has not been sufficiently considered. A man with an income of £25 a year can multiply his comfort beyond all calculation by doubling his income. A man with £50 a year can at least quadruple his comfort by doubling his income. Probably up to even £250 a year doubled income means doubled comfort. After that the increment of comfort grows less in proportion to the increment of income until a point is reached at which the victim is satiated and even surfeited with everything that money can procure. To expect him to enjoy another hundred thousand pounds because men like money, is exactly as if you were to expect a confectioner's shopboy to enjoy two hours more work a day because boys are fond of sweets. What can the wretched millionaire do that needs a million? Does he want a fleet of yachts, a Rotten Row[10] full of carriages, an army of servants, a whole city of town houses, or a continent for a game preserve? Can he attend more than one theatre in one evening, or wear more than one suit at a time, or digest more meals than his butler? Is it a luxury to have more money to take care of, more begging letters to read, and to be cut off from those delicious Alnaschar dreams[11] in which the poor man, sitting down to consider what he will do in the always possible event of some unknown relative leaving him a fortune, forgets his privation.

And yet there is no sympathy for this hidden sorrow of Plutocracy. The poor alone are pitied. Societies spring up in all directions to relieve all sorts of comparatively happy people, from discharged prisoners in the first rapture of their regained liberty to children reveling in the luxury of an unlimited appetite; but no hand is stretched out to the millionaire, except to beg. In all our dealing with him lies implicit the delusion that he has nothing to complain of, and that he ought to be ashamed of rolling in wealth whilst others are starving.

NOTES

1. **the million:** the common people
2. **gents:** (colloq.) gentlemen
3. **Rag Fair:** old-clothes market
4. **Houndsditch:** a district in the east of London
5. **bicycling suit:** cycling suit
6. **Cleopatra claret, four pearls to the bottle:** a very luxurious drink
7. **drum major:** non-commissioned officer commanding the drummers of a regiment
8. **Brighton:** a seaside resort in East England
9. **peacock's brain sandwich:** a very luxurious food
10. **Rotten Row:** the wide track in Hyde Park, London, for horse-riders
11. **Alnaschar dreams:** visionary projects

GEORGE GISSING

(1857–1903)

George Gissing was an English novelist. He was born at Wakefield, Yorkshire, the son of a pharmacist, and educated at a Quaker boarding school in Cheshire and at Owens College, Manchester. He struggled against poverty by writing and teaching for most of his life. His last three years were passed happily in the south of France.

Gissing wrote about twenty novels, of which the best-known is **New Grub Street** (1891), a powerful study of literary life in late-19th-century London with a protest against the demoralizing commercialized culture. His **Charles Dickens: A Critical Study** (1898) is among the best works in Dickens criticism. **By the Ionian Sea: Notes of a Ramble in Southern Italy** (1901) is a fine record of his trips to Italy with his friend H. G. Wells in 1897. **The Private Papers of Henry Ryecroft** (1903), his most happy book, is a fictional and partly autobiographical journal describing the quiet, bookish life of a man no longer in financial worry. Gissing's works impress people by his intense sincerity. His prose style is simple and neat.

EXTRACTS FROM
THE PRIVATE PAPERS OF HENRY RYECROFT

SPRING

For more than six years I trod the pavement never stepping once upon mother earth—for the parks are but pavement disguised with a growth of grass. Then the worst was over. Say I the worst? No, no; things far worse were to come; the struggle against starvation has its cheery side when one is young and vigorous. But at all events I had begun to earn a living; I held assurance of food and clothing for half a year at a time; granted health, I might hope to draw my not insufficient wages for many a twelvemonth. And they were the wages of work done independently, when and where I would. I thought with horror of lives spent in an office, with an employer to obey. The glory of the career of letters was its freedom, its dignity!

The fact of the matter was, of course, that I served, not one master, but a whole crowd of them. Independence, forsooth! If my writing failed to please editor, publisher, public, where was my daily bread? The greater my success, the more numerous my employers. I was the slave of a multitude. By heaven's grace I had succeeded in pleasing (that is to say, in making myself a source of profit to) certain persons who represented this vague throng; for the time, they were gracious to me; but what justified me in the faith that I should hold the ground I had gained? Could the position of any toiling man be more precarious than mine? I tremble now as I think of it, tremble as I should in watching some one who walked carelessly on the edge of an abyss. I marvel at the recollection that for a good score of years this pen and a scrap of paper clothed and fed me and my household, kept me in physical comfort, held at bay all those hostile forces of the world ranged against one who has no resource save in his own right hand.

But I was thinking of the year which saw my first exodus[1] from London. On an irresistible impulse, I suddenly made up my mind to go into Devon[2], a part of

England I had never seen. At the end of March I escaped from my grim lodgings, and, before I had time to reflect on the details of my undertaking, I found myself sitting in sunshine at a spot very near to where I now dwell-before me the green valley of the broadening Exe[3] and the pine-clad ridge of Haldon[4]. That was one of the moments of my life when I have tasted exquisite joy. My state of mind was very strange. Though as boy and youth I had been familiar with the country, had seen much of England's beauties, it was as though I found myself for the first time before a natural landscape. Those years of London had obscured all my earlier life; I was like a man town-born and bred, who scarce knows anything but street vistas. The light, the air, had for me something of the supernatural—affected me, indeed, only less than at a later time did the atmosphere of Italy. It was glorious spring weather; a few white clouds floated amid the blue, and the earth had an intoxicating fragrance. Then first did I know myself for a sun-worshipper. How had I lived so long without asking whether there was a sun in the heavens or not? Under that radiant firmament, I could have thrown myself upon my knees in adoration. As I walked, I found myself avoiding every strip of shadow; were it but that of a birch trunk, I felt as if it robbed me of the day's delight. I went bare-headed, that the golden beams might shed upon me their unstinted blessing. That day I must have walked some thirty miles, yet I knew not fatigue. Could I but have once more the strength which then supported me!

I had stepped into a new life. Between the man I had been and that which I now became there was a very notable difference. In a single day I had matured astonishingly; which means, no doubt, that I suddenly entered into conscious enjoyment of powers and sensibilities which had been developing unknown to me. To instance only one point: till then I had cared very little about plants and flowers, but now I found myself eagerly interested in every blossom, in every growth of the wayside. As I walked I gathered a quantity of plants. Promising myself to buy a book on the morrow and identify them all. Nor was it a passing humour[5]; never since have I lost my pleasure in the flowers of the field, and my desire to know them all. My ignorance at the time of which I speak seems to me now very shameful; but I was merely in the case of ordinary people[6], whether living in town or country. How many could give the familiar name of half a dozen plants plucked at random from beneath the hedge in springtime? To me the flowers became symbolical of a great release, of a wonderful awakening. My eyes had all at once been opened; till then I had walked in darkness, yet knew it not.

Well do I remember the rambles of that springtide[7]. I had a lodging in one of those outer streets of Exeter[8] which savour more of country than of town, and every morning I set forth to make discoveries. The weather could not have been more kindly; I felt the influences of a climate I had never known; there was a balm in the air which soothed no less than it exhilarated me. Now inland, now seaward, I followed the windings of the Exe. One day I wandered in rich, warm valleys, by orchards bursting into bloom, from farmhouse to farmhouse, each more beautiful than the other, and from hamlet to hamlet bowered amid dark evergreens; the next, I was on pine-clad heights, gazing over moorland brown with last year's heather, feeling upon my face a wind from the white-flecked Channel. So intense was my delight in the beautiful world about me that I forgot even myself; I enjoyed without retrospect or forecast; I, the egoist in grain[9], forgot to scrutinize my own emotions, or to trouble my happiness by comparison with others' happier fortune. It was a healthful time; it gave me a new lease of life, and taught me—in so far as I was teachable—how to make use of it.

SUMMER

To-day, as I was reading in the garden, a waft of summer perfume—some hidden link of association in what I read—I know not what it may have been—took me back to school-boy holidays; I recovered with strange intensity that lightsome[10] mood of long release from tasks, of going away to the seaside, which is one of childhood's blessings. I was in the train; no rushing express, such as bears you great distances; the sober train which goes to no place of importance, which lets you see the white steam of the engine float and fall upon a meadow ere you pass. Thanks to a good and wise father, we youngsters saw nothing of seaside places where crowds assemble; I am speaking, too, of a time more than forty years ago, when it was still possible to find on the coasts of northern England, east or west, spots known only to those who loved the shore for its beauty and its solitude. At every station the train stopped; little stations, decked with beds of flowers, smelling warm in the sunshine where country-folk got in with baskets, and talked in an unfamiliar dialect, an English which to us sounded almost like a foreign tongue. Then the first glimpse of the sea; the excitement of noting whether tide was high or low-stretches of sand and weedy pools, or halcyon wavelets frothing at their furthest reach, under the sea-banks starred with convolvulus. Of a sudden, our station!

Ah, that taste of the brine on a child's lips! Nowadays, I can take holiday[11] when I will, and go whithersoever it pleases me; but that salt kiss of the sea air I shall never know again. My senses are dulled; I cannot get so near to Nature; I have a sorry dread of her clouds, her winds, and must walk with tedious circumspection where once I ran and leapt exultingly. Were it possible, but for one half-hour, to plunge and bask in the sunny surf, to roll on the silvery sand-hills, to leap from rock to rock on shining sea-ferns, laughing if I slipped into the shallows among starfish and anemones! I am much older in body than in mind; I can but look at what I once enjoyed.

AUTUMN

The characteristic motive of English poetry is love of nature, especially of nature as seen in the English rural landscape. From the "Cuckoo Song"[12] of our language in its beginnings to the perfect loveliness of Tennyson's[13] best verse, this note is ever sounding. It is persistent even amid the triumph of the drama. Take away from Shakespeare all his bits of natural description, all his casual allusions to the life and aspects of the country, and what a loss were there! The reign of the iambic couplet confined, but could not suppress, this native music; Pope[14] notwithstanding, there came the "Ode to Evening"[15] and that "Elegy"[16] which, unsurpassed for beauty of thought and nobility of utterance in all the treasury of our lyrics, remains perhaps the most essentially English poem ever written.

This attribute of our national mind availed even to give rise to an English school of painting. It came late; that it ever came at all is remarkable enough. A people apparently less apt for that kind of achievement never existed. So profound is the English joy in meadow and stream and hill, that, unsatisfied at last with vocal expression, it took up the brush, the pencil, the etching tool, and created a new form of art. The National Gallery[17] represents only in a very imperfect way the richness and variety of our landscape work. Were it possible to collect, and suitably to display, the very best of such work in every vehicle, I know not which would be the stronger emotion in an English heart, pride or rapture.

One obvious reason for the long neglect of Turner[18] lies in the fact that his genius does not seem to be truly English. Turner's landscape, even when it presents familiar scenes, does not show them in the familiar light. Neither the artist nor the intelligent layman is satisfied. He gives us glorious visions; we admit the glory—but we miss something which we deem essential. I doubt whether Turner tasted rural England; I doubt whether the spirit of English poetry was in him; I doubt whether the essential significance of the common things which we call beautiful was revealed to his soul. Such doubt does not affect his greatness as a poet in colour and in form, but I suspect that it has always been the cause why England could not love him. If any man whom I knew to be a man of brains confessed to me that he preferred Birket Foster[19], I should smile—but I should understand.

WINTER

It is a pleasant thing enough to be able to spend a little money without fear when the desire for some indulgence is strong upon one; but how much pleasanter the ability to give money away! Greatly as I relish the comforts of my wonderful new life, no joy it has brought me equals that of coming in aid to another's necessity. The man for ever pinched in circumstances can live only for himself. It is all very well to talk about doing moral good; in practice, there is little scope or hope for anything of that kind in a state of material hardship. To-day I have sent S— a cheque for fifty pounds; it will come as a very boon of heaven, and assuredly blesseth him that gives as much as him that takes. A poor fifty pounds, which the wealthy fool throws away upon some idle or base fantasy, and never thinks of it; yet to S— it will mean life and light. And I, to whom this power of benefaction is such a new thing, sign the cheque with a hand trembling, so glad and proud I am. In the days gone by, I have sometimes given money, but with trembling of another kind; it was as likely as not that I myself, some black foggy morning, might have to go begging for my own dire needs. That is one of the bitter curses of poverty; it leaves no right to be generous. Of my abundance—abundance to me, though starveling[20] pittance in the view of everyday prosperity—I can give with happiest freedom; I feel myself a man, and no crouching slave with his back ever ready for the lash of circumstance. There are those, I know, who thank the gods amiss, and most easily does this happen in the matter of wealth. But oh, how good it is to desire little, and to have a little more than enough!

NOTES

1. **exodus:** departure
2. **Devon:** a county of Southwest England, between the Bristol Channel and the English Channel
3. **the Exe:** a river in Devon
4. **Haldon:** a hill
5. **a passing humour:** a transient mood or whim
6. **I was merely in the case of ordinary people:** I behaved only like ordinary people.
7. **springtide:** springtime
8. **Exeter:** a city of Devon
9. **in grain:** by nature, in temperament
10. **lightsome:** merry
11. **take holiday:** have a holiday
12. **the "Cuckoo Song":** a Middle English lyric of 12 lines
13. **Tennyson:** Alfred Tennyson (1809–1892) was an English poet, the Poet Laureate from 1850, and the author of ***The Princess*** (1847), ***In Memoriam*** (1850), ***Maud*** (1855), ***Idylls of the King*** (1859–1885), ***Enoch Arden*** (1864), etc.

14. **Pope:** Alexander Pope (1688–1744) was an English poet and the author of *An Essay on Criticism* (1714), *The Rape of the Lock* (1714), *The Dunciad* (1728), *An Essay on Man* (1733–1734), etc.
15. **the "Ode to Evening":** a poem (1746) by William Collins (1721–1759)
16. **that "Elegy":** the "Elegy Written in a Country Church-yard" (1751) by Thomas Gray (1716–1771)
17. **the National Gallery:** an art gallery in Trafalgar Square, London
18. **Turner:** Joseph Mallord William Turner (1779–1851), English landscape painter
19. **Birket Foster:** Myles Birket Foster (1825–1899), English painter and engraver
20. **starveling:** meagre

JOSEPH CONRAD

(1857–1924)

Joseph Conrad was a British novelist. He was born near Berdichev, Poland on December 3, 1857, his real name being Teodor Josef Konrad Korzeniowski. He was educated in Cracow, pursued a sailor's career from 1874, became a British subject in 1886, and settled in England in 1894 to devote himself to writing. He knew hardly any English when he was twenty, yet he published his first novel, ***Almayer's Folly***, in English at the age of 38, and eventually established himself as one of the major modern English writers. He died at his home in Ashford, Kent, on August 3, 1924.

Conrad's most famous novels (and novellas) are: ***The Nigger of the "Narcissus"*** (1897), ***Lord Jim*** (1900), ***Heart of Darkness*** (1902), ***Typhoon*** (1902), ***Nostromo*** (1904), ***The Secret Agent*** (1907), ***Under Western Eyes*** (1911), ***Chance*** (1913), ***Victory*** (1915), and ***The Shadow Line*** (1917). Many of his novels are based on his knowledge of the sea and seafarers. The story is told by a complex narrative technique, with psychological insights, and for a particular atmosphere or mood. The people in the story are often tested in extreme situations; they fight their own weakness as well as external forces. Conrad's men characters are much more convincing than his women characters. His prose is sensuously rich, strangely beautiful, and amazingly forceful.

CAPTAIN MACWHIRR

Captain MacWhirr[1], of the steamer "Nan-Shan," had a physiognomy that, in the order of[2] material appearances, was the exact counterpart of his mind: it presented no marked characteristics of firmness or stupidity; it had no pronounced characteristics whatever; it was simply ordinary, irresponsive, and unruffled.

The only thing his aspect might have been said to suggest, at times, was bashfulness; because he would sit, in business offices ashore, sunburnt and smiling faintly, with downcast eyes. When he raised them, they were perceived to be direct in their glance and of blue colour. His hair was fair and extremely fine, clasping from temple to temple the bald dome of his skull in a clamp as of fluffy silk. The hair of his face, on the contrary, carroty[3] and flaming, resembled a growth of copper wire clipped short to the line of the lip; while, no matter how close he shaved, fiery metallic gleams passed, when he moved his head, over the surface of his cheeks. He was rather below the medium height, a bit round-shouldered, and so sturdy of limb that his clothes always looked a shade too tight for his arms and legs. As if unable to grasp what is due to the difference of latitudes, he wore a brown bowler hat[4], a complete suit of a brownish hue, and clumsy black boots. These harbour togs[5] gave to his thick figure an air of stiff and uncouth smartness. A thin silver watch-chain looped his waistcoat, and he never left his ship for the shore without clutching in his powerful, hairy fist an elegant umbrella of the very best quality, but generally unrolled. Young Jukes, the chief mate[6], attending his commander to the gangway, would sometimes venture to say, with the greatest gentleness, "Allow me, sir" —and possessing himself of the umbrella deferentially, would elevate the ferrule, shake the folds, twirl a neat furl in a jiffy[7], and hand it back; going through the performance with a face of such portentous gravity, that Mr. Solomon Rout, the chief engineer, smoking his morning cigar over the skylight, would turn away his head in order to hide a smile. "Oh! aye! The blessed gamp.... Thank 'ee, Jukes, thank 'ee," would mutter Captain MacWhirr, heartily, without looking up.

Having just enough imagination to carry him through each successive day, and no more, he was tranquilly sure of himself; and from the very same cause he was not in the least conceited. It is your imaginative superior who is touchy, overbearing, and difficult to please; but every ship Captain MacWhirr commanded was the floating abode of harmony and peace. It was, in truth, as impossible for him to take a flight of fancy[8] as it would be for a watchmaker to put together a chronometer with nothing except a two-pound hammer and a whip-saw in the way of tools. Yet the uninteresting lives of men so entirely given to the actuality of the bare existence have their mysterious side. It was impossible in Captain MacWhirr's case, for instance, to understand what under heaven could have induced that perfectly satisfactory son of a petty grocer in Belfast[9] to run away to sea. And yet he had done that very thing at the age of fifteen. It was enough, when you thought it over, to give you the idea of an immense, potent, and invisible hand thrust into the ant-heap of the earth, laying hold of shoulders, knocking heads together, and setting the unconscious faces of the multitude towards inconceivable goals and in undreamt-of directions.

His father never really forgave him for this undutiful stupidity. "We could have got on without him", he used to say later on, "but there's the business. And he an only son, too!" His mother wept very much after his disappearance. As it had never occurred to him to leave word behind, he was mourned over for dead till, after eight months, his first letter arrived from Talcahuano[10]. It was short, and contained the statement: "We had very fine weather on our passage out." But evidently, in the writer's mind, the only important intelligence was to the effect that his captain had, on the very day of writing, entered him regularly on the ship's articles[11] as Ordinary Seaman[12]. "Because I can do the work," he explained. The mother again wept copiously, while the remark, "Tom's an ass," expressed the emotions of the father. He was a corpulent man, with a gift for sly chaffing, which to the end of his life he exercised in his intercourse with his son, a little pityingly, as if upon a half-witted person.

MacWhirr's visits to his home were necessarily rare, and in the course of years he despatched other letters to his parents, informing them of his successive promotions and of his movements upon the vast earth. In these missives could be found sentences like this: "The heat here is very great." Or: "On Christmas Day at 4 p.m. we fell in with some icebergs." The old people ultimately became acquainted with a good many names of ships, and with the names of the skippers who commanded them—with the names of Scots and English shipowners—with the names of seas, oceans, straits, promontories—with outlandish names of lumber-ports, of rice-ports, of cotton-ports—with the names of islands—with the name of their son's young woman. She was called Lucy. It did not suggest itself to him to mention whether he thought the name pretty. And then they died.

The great day of MacWhirr's marriage came in due course, following shortly upon the great day when he got his first command.

All these events had taken place many years before the morning when, in the chart-room[13] of the steamer "Nan-Shan," he stood confronted by the fall of a barometer he had no reason to distrust. The fall-taking into account the excellence of the instrument, the time of the year, and the ship's position on the terrestrial globe—was of a nature ominously prophetic; but the red face of the man betrayed no sort of inward disturbance. Omens were as nothing to him, and he was unable to discover the message of a prophecy till the fulfilment had brought it home to his very door[14]. "That's a fall, and no mistake," he thought. "There must be some uncommonly dirty weather knocking about."

NOTES

1. **Captain MacWhirr:** a character in the story *Typhoon*
2. **in the order of:** in the way of
3. **carroty:** (sl.) (of a person or his hair) red
4. **bowler hat:** bowler, hard round felt hat
5. **togs:** (sl.) clothes
6. **the chief mate:** the first mate, an officer second in command of a merchant ship
7. **in a jiffy:** (inf.) in a jiff, in a very short time
8. **a flight of fancy:** a sally of fancy
9. **Belfast:** a seaport and the capital of Northern Ireland

10. **Talcahuano:** a seaport in South Central Chile
11. **the ship's articles:** the ship's document or contract
12. **Ordinary Seaman:** ordinary sailor as distinguished from an **able seaman**
13. **the chart-room:** the room where maps and graphs of navigation are kept
14. **had brought it home to his very door:** had made it very clear to him

68

HENRY WATSON FOWLER

(1858–1933)

H. W. Fowler was an English lexicographer and grammarian. He was born at Tonbridge, Kent, and educated at Rugby School, Warwickshire, and at Balliol College, Oxford. For many years he worked as a teacher and an essayist. Then he wrote, in collaboration with his brother Francis George Fowler (1870–1918), *The King's English* (1906 etc.), *The Concise Oxford Dictionary of Current English* (1911 etc.), and *The Pocket Oxford Dictionary of Current English* (1924 etc.), all influential books. After his brother's death, H. W. Fowler wrote *A Dictionary of Modern English Usage* (1926; revised by Ernest Gowers, 1965), an enlightening and entertaining treatise enthusiastically received by the reading public. His prose style is terse, precise, and witty.

EXTRACTS FROM
A DICTIONARY OF MODERN ENGLISH USAGE

1. **broad, wide.** Both words have general currency; their existence side by side is not accounted for by one's being more appropriate to any special style; what difference there is must be in meaning; yet how close they are in this respect is shown by their both having *narrow* as their usual opposite, & both standing in the same relation, if in any at all, to *long*. Nevertheless, though they may often be used indifferently (*a b.* or *a w. road; three feet w.* or *b.*), there are (1) many words with which one may be used & not the other, (2) many with which one is more idiomatic than the other though the sense is the same, (3) many with which either can be used, but not with precisely the same sense as the other; these numbered points are illustrated below.

The explanation seems to be that *wide* refers to the distance that separates the limits, & *broad* to the amplitude of what connects them. When it does not matter which of these is in our minds, either word does equally well; if the hedges are far apart, we have a w. road; if there is an apple surface, we have a b. road; it is all one. But (1) backs, shoulders, chests, bosoms, are b., not w., whereas eyes & mouths are w., not b.; *at w. intervals, give a w. berth*[1], *a w. ball*[2], *w. open,* in all of which *b.* is impossible, have the idea of separation strongly; & *w. trousers, w. sleeves, w. range, w. influence, w. favour, w. distribution, the w. world,* where *b.* is again impossible, suggest the remoteness of the limit. Of the words that admit *b.* but refuse *w.* some are of the simple kind (*b. blades, spearheads, leaves; the b. arrow*[3]), but with many some secondary notion such as generosity or downrightness or neglect of the petty is the representative of the simple idea of amplitude (*b. daylight, B. Church*[4], *b. jests, b. farce, b. hint, b. Scotch*[5], *b. facts, b. outline*).

(2) Some words with which one of the two is idiomatic, but the other not impossible, are: —(preferring *broad*) *expanse, brow, forehead, lands, estates, acres, brim, mind, gauge*; (preferring *wide*) *opening, gap, gulf, culture.*

(3) Some illustrations of the difference in meaning between **broad** & **wide** with the same word; the first two may be thought fanciful, but hardly the others: *A w. door* is one that gives entrance to several abreast, *a b. door* one of imposing dimensions; *a w. river* takes long to cross, *a b. river* shows a fine expanse of water; *a w. generalization* covers many particulars, *a b. generalization* disregards unimportant exceptions; a page has *a b. margin*, i. e. a fine expanse of white, but we allow *a w. margin*[6] for extras, i. e. a great interval between the certain & the possible costs; *a w. distinction* or *difference* implies that the things are very far from identical, but *a b. distinction* or *difference* is merely one that requires no subtlety for its appreciation.

2. FALSE SCENT. The laying of false scent, i. e., the causing of a reader to suppose that a sentence or part of one is taking a certain course, which he afterwards finds to his confusion that it does not take, is an obvious folly—so obvious that no-one commits it wittingly except when surprise is designed to amuse. But writers are apt to forget that, if the false scent is there, it is no excuse to say they did not intend to lay it; it is their business to see that it is not there, & this requires more care than might be supposed. The reader comes to a sentence not knowing what it is going to contain; the writer knows; consequently what seems to the latter, owing to his private information, to bear unquestionably one sense & no other may present to the former, with his open mind, either a choice of meaning or even a different one only. Nor has the writer even the satisfaction of calling his reader a fool for misunderstanding him, since he seldom hears of it; it is the reader who calls the writer a fool for not being able to express himself.

The possibilities of false scent are too miscellaneous to be exhaustively tabulated; the image of the reader with the open mind, ready to seize every chance of going wrong, should be always present to the inexperienced writer. A few examples, however, may suggest certain constructions in which special care is necessary: —*It was only after Mr Buckmaster, Lord Wodehouse, & Mr Freake, finding that they were unable to go, that the England team as now constituted, but with Major Hunter in the place of Captain Cheape, was decided on.* The writer knew that *after* was to be a preposition governing *Mr B. & c. finding*; but the reader takes it for a conjunction with a verb yet to come, & is angry at having to reconsider. Such things happen with the FUSED PARTICIPLE./*Four years, the years that followed her marriage, suffice Lady Younghusband for her somewhat elaborate study,* "*Marie Antoinette: Her Early Youth, 1770-1774*" (*Macmillan & Co.,15s. net*). The reader does not dream of jumping over Lady Y. to get at the owner of *her* (marriage) till *1770-1774* at the end throws a new light on the four years. See PRONOUNS for more such false scent./*The official announcement at Rome that the Ottoman Government[7], having failed to meet Italy's demands, Italy & Turkey were in a state of war from 2.30 yesterday afternoon,was promptly followed by hostilities.* The punctuation (see ABSOLUTE CONSTRUCTION) deludes us into expecting a verb for *the Ottoman Government*, instead of which comes a new subject./*The influences of that age, his open, kind, susceptible nature, to say nothing of his highly untoward situation, made it more than usually difficult for him to cast aside or rightly subordinate.* Only the end of the sentence reveals that we were wrong in guessing the influences & his nature to be parts of a compound subject.

3. idiom. This dictionary being much concerned with idiom & the idiomatic, some slight explanation of the terms may perhaps be expected. For some synonyms, see JARGON. "A manifestation of the peculiar" is the closest possible translation of the Greek word[8]. In the realm of speech this may be applied to a whole language as peculiar to a people, to a dialect as peculiar to a district, to a technical vocabulary as peculiar to a profession, & so forth. In this book, "an idiom" is any form of expression that, as compared with other forms in which the principles of abstract grammar, if there is such a thing, would have allowed the idea in question to be clothed, has established itself as the particular way preferred by Englishmen & therefore presumably characteristic of them. "Idiom" is the sum total of such forms of expression, & is consequently the same as natural or racy or unaffected English; that is idiomatic which it is natural for a normal Englishman to say or write; to suppose that grammatical English is either all idiomatic or all unidiomatic would be as far from the truth as that idiomatic English is either all grammatical or all ungrammatical; grammar & idiom are independent categories;

being applicable to the same material, they sometimes agree & sometimes disagree about particular specimens of it; the most that can be said is that what is idiomatic is far more often grammatical than ungrammatical; but that is worth saying, because grammar & idiom are sometimes treated as incompatibles; the fact is that they are distinct, but usually in alliance. To give a few illustrations: *You would not go for to do it* is neither grammatical nor idiomatic English: *I doubt that they really mean it*[9]. *The distinction leaps to the eyes*[10], & *A hardly earned income,* are all grammatical, but all for different reasons unidiomatic; *It was not me, Who do you take me for? There is heaps of material,* are idiomatic but ungrammatical; *He was promoted captain, She all but capsized, Were it true,* are both grammatical & idiomatic. For examples of special idioms see CASTIRON IDIOM.

NOTES

1. *give a wide berth (to)*: avoid coming into contact (with), keep clear (of)
2. *a wide ball*: (in cricket) a ball bowled outside the batman's reach and scoring a run from the batting side
3. *the broad arrow*: the mark like an upward-pointing arrowhead designating British government property and formerly used on prison clothing
4. **Broad Church**: a section within the Church of England favouring a liberal interpretation of Anglican formularies and rubrics
5. *broad Scotch*: broad Scots, older or dialectal Scottish forms of English
6. *a wide margin*: a considerable additional amount beyond the minimum or necessary
7. *the Ottoman Government*: the Government of the Ottoman Empire—the Turkish Empire lasting from about 1300 till 1919
8. **the Greek word:** i.e. the Greek word *idios*
9. *I doubt that they really mean it*: This sentence goes against British idiom. In Britain people say: I doubt whether they really mean it. I don't doubt that they really mean it. Do you doubt that they really mean it?
10. *The distinction leaps to the eyes*: *To leap (or jump) to the eye(s)* is a bad Gallicism and an unidiomatic phrase.

JEROME KLAPKA JEROME

(1859–1927)

Jerome K. Jerome was an English novelist and playwright. He was born at Walsall, Staffordshire, and educated at Marylebone Grammar School, London. He worked as a railway clerk, schoolmaster, actor, and journalist. **The Idle Thoughts of an Idle Fellow** (1886), a collection of his light essays, was well received. He earned enduring fame with **Three Men in a Boat** (1889), the humorous story of three young men taking a rowing holiday on the Thames. His **Three Men on the Bummel** (1900), a worthy sequel, describes a tour in Germany. His **Paul Klever** (1902) is an excellent autobiographical novel. He wrote many plays, including **The Passing of the Third Floor Back** (1908), a memorable work.

A FISHY STORY

We stayed two days at Streatley, and got our clothes washed. We had tried washing them ourselves, in the river under George's superintendence, and it had been a failure. Indeed, it had been more than a failure, because we were worse off after we had washed our clothes than we were before. Before we had washed them, they had been very, very dirty, it is true; but they were just wearable. *After* we had washed them—well, the river between Reading and Henley was much cleaner, after we had washed our clothes in it, than it was before. All the dirt contained in the river between Reading and Henley we collected, during that wash, and worked it into our clothes.

The washerwoman at Streatley said she felt she owed it to herself to charge us just three times the usual prices for that wash. She said it had not been like washing, it had been more in the nature of excavating.

We paid the bill without a murmur.

The neighbourhood of Streatley and Goring is a great fishing centre. There is some excellent fishing to be had here. The river abounds in pike, roach, dace, gudgeon, and eels, just here; and you can sit and fish for them all day.

Some people do. They never catch them. I never knew anybody catch anything up the Thames, except minnows and dead cats, but that has nothing to do, of course, with fishing! The local fisherman's guide doesn't say a word about catching anything. All it says is the place is "a good station for fishing"; and, from what I have seen of the district, I am quite prepared to bear out this statement.

There is no spot in the world where you can get more fishing, or where you can fish for a longer period. Some fishermen come here and fish for a day, and others stop and fish for a month. You can hang on and fish for a year, if you want to: it will be all the same.

The *Angler's Guide to the Thames* says that "jack and perch are also to be had about here," but there the *Angler's Guide* is wrong. Jack and perch may *be* about there. Indeed, I know for a fact that they are. You can *see* them there in shoals, when you are out for a walk along the banks: they come and stand half out of the water with their mouths open for biscuits. And, if you go for a bathe, they crowd round, and get in your way and irritate you. But they are not to be "had" by a bit of worm on the end of a hook, nor anything like it—not they!

I am not a good fisherman myself. I devoted a considerable amount of attention to the subject at one time, and was getting on, as I thought, fairly well; but the old hands told me that I should never be any real good at it, and advised me to give it up. They said that I was an extremely neat thrower, and that I seemed to have plenty of gumption for the thing, and quite enough constitutional laziness. But they were sure I should never make anything of a fisherman. I had not got sufficient imagination.

They said that as a poet, or a shilling shocker, or a reporter, or anything of that kind, I might be satisfactory, but that, to gain any position as a Thames angler, would require more play of fancy, more power of invention than I appeared to possess.

Some people are under the impression that all that is required to make a good fisherman is the ability to tell lies easily and without blushing; but this is a mistake. Mere bald fabrication is useless; the veriest tyro can manage that. It is in the circumstantial detail, the embellishing touches of probability, the general air of scrupulous—almost of pedantic—veracity, that the experienced angler is seen.

Anybody can come in and say, "Oh, I caught fifteen dozen perch yesterday evening;" or "Last Monday I landed a gudgeon, weighing eighteen pounds, and measuring three feet from the tip to the tail."

There is no art, no skill, required for that sort of thing. It shows pluck, but that is all.

No; your accomplished angler would scorn to tell a lie that way. His method is a study in itself.

He comes in quietly with his hat on, appropriates the most comfortable chair, lights his pipe, and commences to puff in silence. He lets the youngsters brag away for a while, and then, during a momentary lull, he removes the pipe from his mouth, and remarks, as he knocks the ashes out against the bars:

"Well, I had a haul on Tuesday evening that it's not much good my telling anybody about."

"Oh! why's that?" they ask.

"Because I don't expect anybody would believe me if I did," replies the old fellow calmly, and without even a tinge of bitterness in his tone, as he refills his pipe, and requests the landlord to bring him three of Scotch, cold.

There is a pause after this, nobody feeling sufficiently sure of himself to contradict the old gentleman. So he has to go on by himself without any encouragement.

"No," he continues thoughtfully; "I shouldn't believe it myself if anybody told it to me, but it's a fact, for all that. I had been sitting there all the afternoon and had caught literally nothing—except a few dozen dace and a score of jack and I was just about giving it up as a bad job when I suddenly felt a rather smart pull at the line. I thought it was another little one, and I went to jerk it up. Hang me, if I could move the rod! It took me half an hour—half an hour, sir! —to land that fish; and every moment I thought the line was going to snap! I reached him at last, and what do you think it was? A sturgeon! a forty-pound sturgeon! taken on a line, sir! Yes, you may well look surprised—I'll have another three of Scotch, landlord, please."

And then he goes on to tell of the astonishment of everybody who saw it; and what his wife said, when he got home, and of what Joe Buggles thought about it.

I asked the landlord of an inn up the river once, if it did not injure him, sometimes, listening to the tales that the fishermen about there told him; and he said:

"Oh, no; not now, sir. It did used to knock me over a bit at first, but, lord love you! me and the missus we listens to 'em all day now. It's what you're used to, you know. It's what you're used to."

I knew a young man once, he was a most conscientious fellow, and, when he took to fly-fishing, he determined never to exaggerate his hauls by more than twenty-five per cent.

"When I have caught forty fish," said he, "then I will tell people that I have caught fifty, and so on. But I will not lie any more than that, because it is sinful to lie."

But the twenty-five per cent plan did not work well at all. He never was able to use it. The greatest number of fish he ever caught in one day was three, and you can't add twenty-five per cent to three—at least, not in fish.

So he increased his percentage to thirty-three and a third, but that, again, was awkward, when he had only caught one or two; so, to simplify matters, he made up his mind to just double the quantity.

He stuck to this arrangement for a couple of months, and then he grew dissatisfied with it. Nobody believed him when he told them that he only doubled, and he, therefore, gained no credit that way whatever, while his moderation put him at a disadvantage among the other anglers. When he had really caught three small fish, and said he had caught six, it used to make him quite jealous to hear a man, whom he knew for a fact had only caught one, going about telling people he had landed two dozen.

So, eventually he made one final arrangement with himself, which he has religiously held to ever since, and that was to count each fish that he caught as ten, and to assume ten to begin with. For example, if he did not catch any fish at all, then he said he had caught ten fish—you could never catch less than ten fish by his system; that was the foundation of it. Then, if by any chance he really did catch one fish, he called it twenty, while two fish would count thirty, three forty, and so on.

It is a simple and easily worked plan, and there has been some talk lately of its being made use of by the angling fraternity in general. Indeed, the Committee of the Thames Anglers' Association did recommend its adoption about two years ago, but some of the older members opposed it. They said they would consider the idea if the number were doubled, and each fish counted as twenty.

If ever you have an evening to spare, up the river, I should advise you to drop into one of the little village inns, and take a seat in the tap-room. You will be nearly sure to meet one or two old rodmen, sipping their toddy there, and they will tell you enough fishy stories in half-an-hour to give you indigestion for a month.

George and I—I don't know what had become of Harris; he had gone out and had a shave, early in the afternoon, and had then come back and spent full forty minutes in pipe-claying[1] his shoes, we had not seen him since—George and I, therefore, and the dog, left to ourselves, went for a walk to Wallingford[2] on the second evening, and, coming home, we called in at a little river-side inn, for a rest, and other things.

We went into the parlour and sat down. There was an old fellow there, smoking a long clay pipe, and we naturally began chatting.

He told us that it had been a fine day to-day, and we told him that it had been a fine day yesterday, and then we all told each other that we thought it would be a fine day to-morrow, and George said the crops seemed to be coming up nicely.

After that it came out, somehow or other, that we were strangers in the neighbourhood, and that we were going away the next morning.

Then a pause ensued in the conversation, during which our eyes wandered round the room. They finally rested upon a dusty old glass-case, fixed very high up above the chimney-piece[3], and containing a trout. It rather fascinated me, that trout; it was such a monstrous fish. In fact, at first glance, I thought it was a cod.

"Ah!" said the old gentleman, following the direction of my gaze, "fine fellow that, ain't he?[4]"

"Quite uncommon," I murmured; and George asked the old man how much he thought it weighed.

"Eighteen pounds six ounces," said our friend, rising and taking down his coat. "Yes," he continued, "it wur sixteen year ago[5], come the third o'next month, that I landed him. I caught him just below the bridge with a minnow. They told me he wur in the river, and I said I'd have him, and so I did. You don't see many fish that size about here now, I'm thinking. Good night, gentlemen, good night."

And out he went, and left us alone.

We could not take our eyes off the fish after that. It really was a remarkably fine fish. We were still looking at it, when the local carrier[6], who had just stopped at the inn, came to the door of the room with a pot of beer in his hand, and he also looked at the fish.

"Good-sized trout, that," said George, turning round to him.

"Ah! you may well say that, sir," replied the man; and then, after a pull at his beer, he added, "Maybe you wasn't⁷ here, sir, when that fish was caught?"

"No," we told him. We were strangers in the neighbourhood.

"Ah!" said the carrier, "then, of course, how should you? It was nearly five years ago that I caught that trout."

"Oh! was it you who caught it, then?" said I.

"Yes, sir," replied the genial old fellow. "I caught him just below the lock—leastways⁸, what was the lock then—one Friday afternoon; and the remarkable thing about it is that I caught him with a fly. I'd gone out pike fishing⁹, bless you, never thinking of a trout, and when I saw that whopper on the end of my line, blest if it didn't quite take me aback¹⁰. Well, you see, he weighed twenty-six pound. Good night, gentlemen, good night."

Five minutes afterwards, a third man came in, and described how he had caught it early one morning, with bleak; and then he left, and a stolid, solemn-looking, middle-aged individual came in, and sat down over by the window.

None of us spoke for a while; but, at length, George turned to the new-comer, and said:

"I beg your pardon, I hope you will forgive the liberty that we—perfect strangers in the neighbourhood—are taking, but my friend here and myself would be so much obliged if you would tell us how you caught that trout up there."

"Why, who told you I caught that trout?" was the surprised query.

We said that nobody had told us so, but somehow or other we felt instinctively that it was he who had done it.

"Well, it's a most remarkable thing—most remarkable," answered the stolid stranger, laughing; "because, as a matter of fact, you are quite right. I did catch it. But fancy your guessing it like that. Dear me, it's really a most remarkable thing."

And then he went on, and told us how it had taken him half-an-hour to land it, and how it had broken his rod. He said he had weighed it carefully when he reached home, and it had turned the scale at thirty-four pounds.

He went in his turn, and when he was gone, the landlord came in to us. We told him the various histories we had heard about his trout, and he was immensely amused, and we all laughed very heartily.

"Fancy Jim Bates and Joe Muggles and Mr. Jones and old Billy Maunders all telling you that they had caught it. Ha! ha! ha! Well, that is good," said the honest old fellow, laughing heartily.

"Yes, they are the sort to give it to *me*, to put up in my parlour, if ***they*** had caught it, they are! Ha! ha! ha!"

And then he told us the real history of the fish. It seemed that he had caught it himself, years ago, when he was quite a lad; not by any art or skill, but by that unaccountable luck that appears to always wait upon a boy when he plays the wag from school, and goes out fishing on a sunny afternoon, with a bit of string tied on to the end of a tree.

He said that bringing home that trout had saved him from a whacking, and that even his schoolmaster had said it was worth the rule of three[11] and practice put together.

He was called out of the room at this point, and George and I again turned our gaze upon the fish.

It really was a most astonishing trout. The more we looked at it, the more we marvelled at it.

It excited George so much that he climbed up on the back of a chair to get a better view of it.

And then the chair slipped, and George clutched wildly at the trout-case to save himself, and down it came with a crash, George and the chair on top of it.

"You haven't injured the fish, have you?" I cried in alarm, rushing up.

"I hope not," said George, rising cautiously and looking about.

But he had. That trout lay shattered into a thousand fragments—I say a thousand, but they may have only been nine hundred. I did not count them.

We thought it strange and unaccountable that a stuffed trout should break up into little pieces like that.

And so it would have been strange and unaccountable, if it had been a stuffed trout, but it was not.

That trout was plaster-of-Paris[12].

NOTES

1. **pipe-claying:** whitening with pipe-clay
2. **Wallingford:** town of Berkshire on the River Thames in South England
3. **chimney-piece:** mantel
4. **ain't he:** isn't he
5. **it wur sixteen year ago:** (dial.) it was sixteen years ago
6. **carrier:** one hired to carry parcels
7. **you wasn't:** (vulg.) you weren't
8. **leastways:** (inf.) or at least, or rather
9. **pike fishing:** fishing pike
10. **blest if it didn't quite take me aback:** I was blest if it didn't quite take me aback; it quite took me aback
11. **the rule of three:** a method of finding the fourth number from three given numbers
12. **plaster-of-Paris:** fine white plaster used to make sculptures or casts

LOGAN PEARSALL SMITH

(1865–1946)

Logan Pearsall Smith was a British essayist and critic. He was born in the United States, studied at Harvard and Oxford, lived in England from 1888, and became a naturalized British subject in 1913. He is well known for his *Trivia* (1902), *More Trivia* (1921), *Afterthoughts* (1931), and *Last Words* (1933). These volumes of essays and aphorisms were collected in *All Trivia* (1933). They reflect the moods of a scholar who enjoyed life in a detached and self-mocking manner. He also published valuable linguistic and critical works, such as *The English Language* (1912), *Words and Idioms* (1925), *On Reading Shakespeare* (1933), and *Milton and His Modern Critics* (1940). *Unforgotten Years* (1938) is his autobiography. His prose is clear, neat, and elegant.

THE ROSE

    The old lady had always been proud of the great rose-tree in her garden, and was fond of telling how it had grown from a cutting she had brought years before from Italy, when she was first married. She and her husband had been travelling back in their carriage from Rome (it was before the time of railways), and on a bad piece of road south of Siena[1] they had broken down[2], and had been forced to pass the night in a little house by the roadside. The accommodation was wretched of course; she had spent a sleepless night, and rising early had stood, wrapped up, at her window, with the cool air blowing on her face, to watch the dawn. She could still, after all these years, remember the blue mountains with the bright moon above them, and how a far-off town on one of the peaks had gradually grown whiter and whiter, till the moon faded, the mountains were touched with the pink of the rising sun, and suddenly the town was lit as by an illumination[3], one window after another catching and reflecting the sun's beams, till at last the whole little city twinkled and sparkled up in the sky like a nest of stars.

    That morning, finding they would have to wait while their carriage was being repaired, they had driven in a local conveyance up to the city on the mountain, where they had been told they would find better quarters[4]; and there they had stayed two or three days. It was one of the miniature Italian cities with a high church, a pretentious piazza[5], a few narrow streets and little palaces, perched, all compact and complete, on the top of a mountain, within an enclosure of walls hardly larger than an English kitchen garden. But it was full of life and noise, echoing all day and all night with the sounds of feet and voices.

    The cafe of the simple inn where they stayed was the meeting-place of the notabilities of the little city; the ***Sindaco***[6], the ***avvocato***[7], the doctor, and a few others; and among them they noticed a beautiful, slim, talkative old man, with bright black eyes and snow-white hair—tall and straight and still with the figure of a youth, although the waiter told them with pride that the ***Conte***[8] was ***molto***

vecchio*^{9}**—would in fact be eighty in the following year. He was the last of his family, the waiter added—they had once been great and rich people—but he had no descendants; in fact the waiter mentioned with complacency, as if it were a story on which the locality prided itself, that the ***Conte had been unfortunate in love, and had never married.

The old gentleman, however, seemed cheerful enough; and it was plain that he took an interest in the strangers, and wished to make their acquaintance. This was soon effected by the friendly waiter; and after a little talk the old man invited them to visit his villa and garden which were just outside the walls of the town. So the next afternoon, when the sun began to descend, and they saw in glimpses through doorways and windows, blue shadows beginning to spread over the brown mountains, they went to pay their visit. It was not much of a place^{10}, a small, modernized, stucco villa, with a hot pebbly garden, and in it a stone basin with torpid gold fish, and a statue of Diana^{11} and her hounds against the wall. But what gave a glory to it was a gigantic rose-tree which clambered over the house, almost smothering the windows, and filling the air with the perfume of its sweetness. Yes, it was a fine rose, the ***Conte*** said proudly when they praised it, and he would tell the ***Signora***^{12} about it. And as they sat there, drinking the wine he offered them, he alluded with the cheerful indifference of old age to his love affair, as though he took for granted that they had heard of it already.

"The lady lived across the valley there beyond that hill. I was a young man then, for it was many years ago. I used to ride over to see her; it was a long way, but I rode fast, for young men, as no doubt the ***Signora*** knows, are impatient. But the lady was not kind, she would keep me waiting, oh, for hours; and one day when I had waited very long I grew very angry, and as I walked up and down in the garden where she had told me she would see me, I broke one of her roses, broke a branch from it; and when I saw what I had done, I hid it inside my coat—so—; and when I came home I planted it, and the ***Signora*** sees how it has grown. If the ***Signora*** admires it, I must give her a cutting to plant also in her garden; I am told the English have beautiful gardens that are green, and not burnt with the sun like ours."

The next day, when their mended carriage had come up to fetch them, and they were just starting to drive away from the inn, the ***Conte***'s old servant appeared with the rose-cutting neatly wrapped up, and the compliments and wishes for a ***buon viaggio***[13] from her master. The town collected to see them depart, and the children ran after their carriage through the gate of the little city. They heard a rush of feet behind them for a few moments, but soon they were far down toward the valley; the little town with all its noise and life was high above them on its mountain peak.

She had planted the rose at home, where it had grown and flourished in a wonderful manner; and every June the great mass of leaves and shoots still broke out into a passionate splendour of scent and crimson colour, as if in its root and fibres there still burnt the anger and thwarted desire of that Italian lover. Of course, the old ***Conte*** must have died many years ago; she had forgotten his name, and had even forgotten the name of the mountain city that she had stayed in, after first seeing it twinkling at dawn in the sky, like a nest of stars.

NOTES

1. **Siena:** a city in Tuscany, Italy
2. **they had broken down:** they had suffered a breakdown of their carriage
3. **an illumination:** a flood of light
4. **quarters:** lodgings
5. **piazza:** public square or market place
6. ***Sindaco*:** (It.) Mayor
7. ***avvocato*:** (It.) advocate, barrister
8. ***Conte*:** (It.) Count
9. ***molto vecchio*:** (It.) very old
10. **not much of a place:** not a large place
11. **Diana:** Roman goddess of hunting
12. ***Signora*:** (It.) Madam
13. ***buon viaggio*:** (It.) good journey

71

HERBERT GEORGE WELLS

(1866–1946)

H. G. Wells was an English novelist, journalist, and social reformer. He was born at Bromley, Kent, on September 21, 1866, the son of an unsuccessful shopkeeper. He received an elementary education at Bromley, was apprenticed to a draper, worked as an assistant teacher, and then studied at the Normal School of Science (later renamed the Imperial College of Science and Technology) in London, taking his B.Sc. in 1890. After teaching in several schools he became a professional writer in 1893. In the same year he joined the Fabian Society. He died in London on August 13, 1946.

Wells wrote about a hundred and twenty books and half of them were fictional works. A pioneer in science fiction, he remains unsurpassed in this field. His scientific romances include *The Time Machine* (1895), *The Invisible Man* (1897), *The War of the Worlds* (1898), and *The First Men in the Moon* (1901). He deals with the lower-middle-class world in his comic novels. These include *Love and Mr Lewisham* (1900), the story of a young teacher; *Kipps* (1905), the story of a draper's assistant; and *The History of Mr Polly* (1910), the story of a shopkeeper. He produced a third group of novels—novels of ideas. Didactic and satirical, they include: *Tono-Bungay* (1909), about English society in dissolution; *Ann Veronica* (1909), about a girl of the "New Woman" type; *The New*

Machiavelli (1911), about a politician; and ***Mr Britling Sees It Through*** (1916), about the question of war. Wells advocated scientific progress and Fabian socialism. He was not a deep thinker, but a great popularizer. He wrote several influential encyclopaedic books: ***The Outline of History*** (1920), ***The Science of Life*** (with Julian Huxley and G. P. Wells, 1929), and ***The Work, Wealth, and Happiness of Mankind*** (1932). His ***Experiment in Autobiography*** (1934) is a charming portrait of himself, his society and his times. Wells's prose style is simple and unadorned but evocative.

A DAY IN THE COUNTRY

There is no countryside like the English countryside for those who have learned to love it; its firm yet gentle lines of hill and dale, its ordered confusion of features, its deer parks and downland[1], its castles and stately houses, its hamlets and old churches, its farms and ricks and great barns and ancient trees, its pools and ponds and shining threads of rivers, its flower-starred[2] hedgerows, its orchards and woodland patches, its village greens and kindly inns. Other countrysides have their pleasant aspects, but none such variety, none that shine so steadfastly throughout the year. Picardy[3] is pink and white and pleasant in the blossom time; Burgundy[4] goes on with its sunshine and wide hillsides and cramped vineyards, a beautiful tune repeated and repeated; Italy gives salitas[5] and wayside chapels, and chestnuts and olive orchards; the Ardennes[6] has its woods and gorges—Touraine[7] and the Rhineland[8], the wide Campagna[9] with its distant Apennines[10], and the neat prosperity and mountain backgrounds of South Germany all clamour their especial merits at one's memory. And there are the hills and fields of Virginia[11], like an England grown very big and slovenly, the woods and big river sweeps of Pennsylvania[12], the trim New England[13] landscape, a little bleak and rather fine, like the New England mind, and the wide rough country roads and hills and woodland of New York State[14]. But none of these change scene and character in three miles of walking, nor have so mellow a sunlight nor so diversified a cloudland[15] nor confess the perpetual refreshment of the strong soft winds that blow from off the sea, as our mother England does.

It was good for the three P's[16] to walk through such a land and forget for a time that indeed they had no footing in it all, that they were doomed to toil behind counters in such places as Port Burdock[17] for the better part of their lives. They would forget the customers and shopwalkers[18] and department buyers[19] and everything, and become just happy wanderers in a world of pleasant breezes and songbirds and shady trees.

The arrival at the inn was a great affair. No one, they were convinced, would take them for drapers, and there might be a pretty serving-girl or a jolly old landlady, or what Parsons called a "bit of character" drinking in the bar.

There would always be weighty inquiries as to what they could have, and it would work out always at cold beef and pickles, or fried ham and eggs and shandygaff[20], two pints of beer and two bottles of ginger-beer foaming in a huge round-bellied jug.

The glorious moment of standing lordly in the inn doorway and staring out at the world, the swinging sign, the geese upon the green, the duckpond, a waiting wagon, the church tower, a sleepy cat, the blue heavens, with the sizzle of the frying audible behind one! The keen smell of the bacon! The trotting of feet bearing the repast; the click and clatter as the table ware is finally arranged! A clean white cloth! "Ready Sir!" or "Ready, Gentlemen!" Better hearing that than "Forward, Polly! Look sharp!"

The going in! The sitting down! The falling to[21]!

"Bread, O' Man[22]?"

"Right O! Don't bag[23] all the crust, O' Man."

Once a simple-mannered girl in a pink print dress stayed and talked with them as they ate; led by the gallant Parsons they professed to be all desperately in love with her, and courted her to say which she preferred of them, it was so manifest she did prefer one and so impossible to say which it was held her there, until a distant maternal voice called her away. Afterwards, as they left the inn, she waylaid them at the orchard corner and gave them, a little shyly, three yellow-green apples—and wished them to come again some day, and vanished, and reappeared looking after them as they turned the corner, waving a white handkerchief. All the rest of that day they disputed over the signs of her favour, and the next Sunday they went there again.

But she had vanished, and a mother of forbidding aspect[24] afforded no explanations.

If Platt and Parsons and Mr. Polly live to be a hundred, they will none of them forget that girl as she stood with a pink flush upon her, faintly smiling and yet earnest, parting the branches of the hedgerows and reaching down, apple in hand....

NOTES
1. **downland:** downs, areas of low chalk hills in the south of England
2. **flower-starred:** adorned with flowers
3. **Picardy:** a region of North France
4. **Burgundy:** a region of East France
5. **salitas:** small hills
6. **the Ardennes:** the wooded district including parts of Belgium, Luxemburg, and North France
7. **Touraine:** a region of Northwest Central France
8. **the Rhineland:** the region of Germany west of the Rhine
9. **Campagna:** the level district surrounding Rome
10. **[the] Apennines:** a mountain range running down the length of Italy
11. **Virginia:** a state of the Eastern U.S. on the Atlantic
12. **Pennsylvania:** a state of the Northeastern U.S.
13. **New England:** the northeastern part of the U.S.
14. **New York State:** a state of the Northeastern U.S.
15. **cloudland:** fanciful land, visionary realm
16. **the three P's:** the three friends, namely Parsons, Platt, and Polly (in *The History of Mr. Polly*)
17. **Port Burdock:** the town where the three P's worked in a department store
18. **shopwalkers:** persons employed in a department store to direct customers, supervise sales, etc.
19. **department buyers:** persons employed to buy goods from the manufacturers for a large department store
20. **shandygaff:** (old-fashioned) shandy
21. **The falling to!:** The beginning to eat!
22. **O' Man:** old fellow
23. **bag:** take
24. **forbidding aspect:** repellent appeareance

THE LITERARY RENAISSANCE

A great outbreak of creative literature is associated with this general reawakening of the Western European intelligence. We have already noted the appearance of literature in Italian under the initiatives of the Emperor Frederick Ⅱ. Simultaneously the Troubadours[1] in both Northern France and in Provence[2] were setting people to the making of verse in the northern and southern dialects, love songs, narrative songs and the like. These things broke out, so to speak, beneath a general disposition to write and read Latin. They came from the popular mind and the relaxed mind and not from the learned. In Florence[3] in 1265 was born Dante Alighieri[4], who, after vehement political activities, became an exile and wrote, among other works, an elaborate poem in rhymed Italian verse, the **Commedia**, a tapestry of allegory and sporadic incident and religious disquisition. It describes a visit to Hell, Purgatory and Paradise. Its relationship to the ancestral Latin literature is suggested by the fact that Dante's guide in the lower regions is Virgil. In its various English translations it makes extremely dull reading, but those who are best qualified to speak in the matter are scarce able to express their perception of the exquisite beauty, interest and wisdom of the original. Dante also wrote in Latin upon political questions and upon the claims of the Italian tongue to be considered a literary language. He was severely criticized for his use of Italian and accused of an incapacity for Latin verse.

A little later Petrarch[5] (1304-1374) was also writing sonnets and odes in Italian which arouse the enthusiasm of all who have been sufficiently cultivated to respond to them. For example, John Addington Symonds[6] wrote: "***The Rime in Vita e Morte di Madonna Laura*** cannot become obsolete, for perfectly metrical form has here been married to language of the choicest and purest." The poems leave us doubtful if Madonna Laura ever existed. Petrarch was one of the group of Italians who were strenuous to restore the glories of the Latin literature. In an *Outline of History* these glories are not perhaps so supreme as they seemed to be to a generation of Italians reawakening to the charms and excitement of literary beauty. Writing in Italian waned for a time before a revival of Latin authorship. Petrarch wrote an epic in Latin, *Africa*. There was a considerable output of pseudo-classical writing, epics and sham tragedies and sham comedies in Latin, no doubt very like the poems and rhetorical prose one receives in English from gifted young Indians. It was only later with Boiardo[7] and Ariosto (1475-1533) that Italian poetry emerges again to distinction. Ariosto's ***Orlando Furioso*** was only the crowning specimen of a great multitude of romantic narrative poems that delighted the less erudite readers of the Renaissance. These narrative poems always paid the tribute of more or less allusion and imitation to the traditions of the artificial Virgilian epic, itself an imitative and scholarly exploit. Comedy and the narrative poem, shorter poems in various forms, constitute the bulk of this literature. Prose was not sufficiently artificial and genteel for critical approval.

The reawakening of literary life in the French-speaking community was also dominated by memories of the Latin literature. There was already a literature of merry songs in mediaeval Latin in France, songs of the tavern and the road (the Goliardic[8] poetry of the thirteenth century), and the spirit of this authentic writing lived in such true and native verse as that of Villon (1431-1463), but the revival of Latin studies flowed in from Italy and imposed artificiality upon all but the sturdiest minds. An elaborate style was established, with something of the dignity of monumental masonry, and splendid poems and classical plays were erected for the admiration rather than the pleasure of posterity. Yet the genius of French life was not altogether confined to these noble exercises; a fine and flexible prose appeared. Montaigne (1533-1592), the first of essayists, wrote pleasantly of life and unpleasantly about the learned, and Rabelais (1490?-1553), like a torrent of burning, shouting, laughing lava, burst through all the dignitaries and decencies of the pedants.

In Germany and in Holland the new intellectual impulses were more nearly simultaneous with the immense political and religious stresses of the Reformation[9], and they produced less purely artistic forms. Erasmus, says J. Addington Symonds, is the great representative in Holland of the Renaissance as Luther[10] was in

Germany, but he wrote not in Dutch but Latin.

There was an outbreak of literary activity in England as early as the fourteenth century. Geoffrey Chaucer (1340?-1400) produced delightful narrative poetry that derived very obviously from Italian models, and there was much pre-existing romantic narrative verse. But the Civil Wars, the Wars of the Roses[11], pestilence, and religious conflicts damped down this first beginning, and it was only with the sixteenth century and after the reign of Henry VIII that English literature broke into vigorous life. There was first a rapid spread of classical learning and a fertilizing torrent of translations from Latin, Greek and Italian. There came a sudden harvest of fine English writing. English was played with, tested, elaborated. Spenser wrote his *Faerie Queen*, a tedious allegorical work of great decorative beauty. But it was in the drama, in the days of Queen Elizabeth, that the English genius found its best expression. It never succumbed to the classical tradition; the Elizabethan drama was a new and fuller and looser, more vigorous and altogether more natural, literary form. It found its extreme exponent in Shakespeare (1564-1616), a man happily with "little Latin and less Greek," whose richest, subtlest passages are drawn from homely and even vulgar life. He was a man of keen humour and great sweetness of mind, who turned every sentence he wrote into melody. Eight years before the death of Shakespeare, Milton (1608-1674) was born. Early classical studies gave both his prose and verse a proud and pompous gait from which they never completely recovered. He went to Italy and saw the glories of Renaissance painting. He translated the paintings of Raphael[12] and Michael Angelo into superb English verse in his great epics of *Paradise Lost* and *Paradise Regained*. It is well for English literature that Shakespeare lived to counter-balance Milton and save so much of its essential spirit from the classical obsession.

Portugal, at the touch of the literary Renaissance, produced an epic, the *Lusiad* of Camoens (1524-1580); but Spain, like England, was so fortunate as to find a man of supreme genius, unembarrassed by an excess of learning, to express its spirit. Cervantes (1547-1616) seized upon the humours and absurdities of a conflict between the mediæval tradition of chivalry in possession of the imagination of a lean, poor, half-crazy gentleman, and the needs and impulses of the vulgar life. His Don Quixote and Sancho Panza, like Shakespeare's Sir John Falstaff, Chaucer's wife of Bath, and Rabelais' Gargantua break through the dignity and heroics of formal literature to let in freedom and laughter. They break through as Roger Bacon[13] and the scientific men broke through the bookish science of the scholars, and as the painters and sculptors we have next to tell about broke through the decorative restraints and religious decorum of mediaeval art. The fundamental fact of the Renaissance was not classicism but release. The revival of Latin and Greek learning only contributed to the positive values of the Renaissance by their corrosive influence upon the Catholic, Gothic and Imperial traditions.

NOTES

1. **the Troubadours:** a class of lyric poets of the 11th-13th centuries living in South France, East Spain, and North Italy and singing of chivalry and gallantry in Provencal
2. **Provence:** a district—formerly a province—of Southeast France
3. **Florence:** the chief city of Tuscany, Italy
4. **Dante Alighieri:** Dante Alighieri (1265-1321) was the Italian poet who wrote **La Vita Nuova** and **La Divina Commedia**.
5. **Petrarch:** Francesco Petrarca (1304-1374), Italian poet and humanist
6. **John Addington Symonds:** John Addington Symonds (1840-1893) was an English poet, essayist and literary historian, who was the author of **A History of the Renaissance in Italy** (1875-1886), **Studies of the Greek Poets** (1873), etc.
7. **Boiardo:** Matteo Mario Boiardo (1434-1494) was an Italian poet and the author of **Orlando Innamorato**.
8. **Goliardic:** pertaining to a class of wandering students, chiefly of the 12th and 13th centuries, who composed loose and satirical Latin verse
9. **the Reformation:** the religious movement in Western Christendom beginning early in the 16th century and resulting in the formation of the Protestant churches
10. **Luther:** Martin Luther (1483-1546), leader of the Protestant Reformation in Germany
11. **the Wars of the Roses:** a series of civil wars in England that lasted thirty years (1455-1485), between the followers of the house of York (**White Rose**) and those of the house of Lancaster (**Red Rose**)

12. **Raphael:** Raffaello Santi or Sanzio (1483–1520) was an Italian painter and architect, regarded as one of the greatest artists of the Renaissance.
13. **Roger Bacon:** Roger Bacon (1214–1294) was an English Franciscan monk, philosopher, and student of experimental science.

ARNOLD BENNETT

(1867–1931)

Arnold Bennett was an English novelist and playwright. He was born at Henley, Staffordshire, on May 27, 1867, the eldest of six children of a solicitor. Educated at Burslem and Newcastle-under-Lyme, he worked as a clerk, for three years in his father's office and five years in a London law firm. He was a free-lance journalist till 1900 when he became a full-time writer. He lived in Paris from 1902 to 1912, did voluntary propaganda work for the British Government during the First World War, and lived in London from 1919 till his death, which occurred on March 27, 1931.

Bennett's fame rests chiefly on six of his novels: ***Anna of the Five Towns*** (1902), the story of a miser's daughter; ***The Old Wives' Tale*** (1908), the story of fly-away Sophia Baines and her stay-at-home sister Constance; the ***Clayhanger*** trilogy, namely ***Clayhanger*** (1910), ***Hilda Lessways*** (1911), and ***These Twain*** (1916); and ***Riceman Steps*** (1923), the story of a miserly bookseller. These novels, except ***Riceman Steps*** which is set in East London, deal with life in the industrial Five Towns of the northwest Midlands (the Potteries). Bennett saw the influence of environment and created a number of memorable characters. He is remembered for his realistic portrayal of ordinary people and their ordinary life. Bennett also wrote several successful plays, including ***Milestones*** (with Edward Knoblock, 1912) and ***The Great Adventure*** (1913). His ***Journal***, begun in 1896, is a striking record of his working life and literary ideas. His prose is clear and careful.

ST. LUKE'S SQUARE

Those two girls, Constance and Sophia Baines, paid no heed to the manifold interest of their situation, of which, indeed, they had never been conscious. They were, for example, established almost precisely on the fifty-third parallel of latitude. A little way to the north of them, in the creases of a hill famous for its religious orgies, rose the River Trent[1], the calm and characteristic stream of middle England. Somewhat further northwards, in the near neighbourhood of the highest public-house in the realm, rose two lesser rivers, the Dane and the Dove, which, quarrelling in early infancy, turned their backs on each other, and, the one by favour of the Weaver and the other by favour of the Trent, watered between them the whole width of England, and poured themselves respectively into the Irish Sea[2] and the German Ocean[3]. What a county of modest, unnoticed rivers! What a natural, simple county, content to fix its boundaries by these tortuous island brooks, with their comfortable names—Trent, Mease, Dove, Tern, Dane, Mees, Stour, Tame, and even hasty Severn[4]! Not that the Severn is suitable to the county! In the county excess is deprecated. The county is happy in not exciting remark. It is content that Shropshire should possess that swollen bump, the Wrekin[5], and that the exaggerated wildness of the Peak should lie over its border. It does not desire to be a pancake like Cheshire[6]. It has everything that England has, including thirty miles of Watling Street[7]; and England can show nothing more beautiful and nothing uglier than the works of nature and the works of man to be seen within the limits of the county. It is England in little, lost in the midst of England, unsung by searchers after the extreme; perhaps occasionally somewhat sore at this neglect, but how proud in the instinctive cognizance of its representative features and traits!

Constance and Sophia, busy with the intense preoccupations of youth, recked not of such matters. They were surrounded by the county. On every side the fields and moors of Staffordshire[8], intersected by roads and lanes, railways, watercourses, and telegraph-lines, patterned by hedges, ornamented and made respectable by halls and genteel parks, enlivened by villages at the intersections, and warmly surveyed by the sun, spread out undulating. And trains were rushing round curves in deep cuttings, and carts and wagons trotting and jingling on the yellow roads, and long, narrow boats passing in a leisure majestic and infinite over the surface of the stolid canals; the rivers had only themselves to support, for Staffordshire rivers have remained virgin of keels to this day. One could imagine the messages concerning prices, sudden death, and horses, in their flight through the wires under the feet of birds. In the inns Utopians were shouting the universe into order over beer, and in the halls and parks the dignity of England was being preserved in a fitting manner. The villages were full of women who did nothing but fight against dirt and hunger, and repair the effects of friction on clothes. Thousands of labourers were in the fields, but the fields were so broad and numerous that this scattered multitude was totally lost therein. The cuckoo was much more perceptible than man, dominating whole square miles with his resounding call. And on the airy moors heath-larks played in the ineffaceable mule-tracks that had served centuries before even the Romans thought of Watling Street. In short, the usual daily life of the county was proceeding with all its immense variety and importance; but though Constance and Sophia were in it they were not of it.

The fact is, that while in the county[9] they were also in the district[10]; and no person who lives in the district, even if he should be old and have nothing to do but reflect upon things in general, ever thinks about the county. So far as the county goes, the district might almost as well be in the middle of the Sahara. It ignores the county, save that it uses it nonchalantly sometimes as leg-stretcher on holiday afternoons, as a man may use his back garden. It has nothing in common with the county; it is richly sufficient to itself. Nevertheless, its self-sufficiency and the true salt savour of its life can only be appreciated by picturing it hemmed in by the county. It lies on the face of the county like an insignificant stain, like a dark Pleiades in a green and empty sky. And Hanbridge has the shape of a horse and its rider, Bursley of half a donkey, Knype of a pair of trousers, Longshaw of an octopus, and little Turnhill of a beetle. The Five Towns seem to cling together for safety. Yet the idea of clinging together for safety would make them laugh. They are unique and indispensable. From the north of the county right down to the south they alone stand for civilization, applied science, organized manufacture, and the century—until you come to Wolverhampton[11]. They are unique and indispensable because you cannot drink tea out of a teacup without the aid of the Five Towns; because you cannot eat a meal in decency without the aid of the Five Towns. For this the architecture of the Five Towns is an architecture of ovens and chimneys; for this its atmosphere is as black as its mud; for this it burns and smokes all night, so that Longshaw has been compared to hell; for this it is unlearned in the ways of agriculture, never having seen corn except as packing straw and in quartern loaves; for this, on the other hand, it comprehends the mysterious habits of fire and pure, sterile earth; for this it lives crammed together in slippery streets where the housewife must change white window-curtains at least once a fortnight if she wishes to remain respectable; for this it gets up in the mass at six a.m., winter and summer, and goes to bed when the public-houses close; for this it exists—that you may drink tea out of a teacup and toy with a chop on a plate. All the everyday crockery used in the kingdom is made in the Five Towns—all, and much besides. A district capable of such gigantic manufacture, of such a perfect monopoly—and which finds energy also to produce coal and iron and great men—may be an insignificant stain on a county, considered geographically, but it is surely well justified in treating the county as its back garden once a week, and in blindly ignoring it the rest of the time.

Even the majestic thought that whenever and wherever in all England a woman washes up, she washes up the product of the district; that whenever and wherever in all England a plate is broken the fracture means new business for the district—even this majestic thought had probably never occurred to either of the girls. The fact is, that while in the Five Towns they were also in the Square, Bursley, and the Square ignored the staple manufacture as perfectly as the district ignored the county. Bursley has the honours of antiquity in the Five Towns. No industrial development can ever rob it of its superiority in age, which makes it absolutely sure in its conceit. And the time will never come when the other towns—let them swell and bluster as they may—will not pronounce the name of

Bursley as one pronounces the name of one's mother. Add to this that the Square was the centre of Bursley's retail trade (which scorned the staple as something wholesale, vulgar, and assuredly filthy), and you will comprehend the importance and the self-isolation of the Square in the scheme of the created universe. There you have it, embedded in the district, and the district embedded in the county, and the county lost and dreaming in the heart of England!

The Square was named after St. Luke. The evangelist might have been startled by certain phenomena in his square, but, except in Wakes Week[12], when the shocking always happened, St. Luke's Square lived in a manner passably saintly— though it contained five public-houses. It contained five public-houses, a bank, a barber's, a confectioner's, three grocers', two chemists', an iron-monger's, a clothier's, and five drapers'. These were all the catalogue. St. Luke's Square had no room for minor establishments. The aristocracy of the Square undoubtedly consisted of the drapers (for the bank was impersonal); and among the five the shop of Baines stood supreme. No business establishment could possibly be more respected than that of Mr. Baines was respected. And though John Baines had been bedridden for a dozen years, he still lived on the lips of admiring, ceremonious burgesses as "our honoured fellow-townsman." He deserved his reputation.

The Baineses' shop, to make which three dwellings had at intervals been thrown into one, lay at the bottom of the Square. It formed about one-third of the south side of the Square, the remainder being made up of Critchlow's (chemist), the clothier's, and the Hanover Spirit Vaults. ("Vaults" was a favourite synonym of the public-house in the Square. Only two of the public-houses were crude public-houses: the rest were "vaults.") It was a composite building of three stories, in blackish-crimson brick, with a projecting shop-front and, above and behind that, two rows of little windows. On the sash of each window was a red cloth roll stuffed with sawdust, to prevent draughts; plain white blinds descended about six inches from the top of each window. There were no curtains to any of the windows save one; this was the window of the drawing-room, on the first floor at the corner of the Square and King Street. Another window, on the second story, was peculiar, in that it had neither blind nor pad, and was very dirty; this was the window of an unused room that had a separate staircase to itself, the staircase being barred by a door always locked. Constance and Sophia had lived in continual expectation of the abnormal issuing from that mysterious room, which was next to their own. But they were disappointed. The room had no shameful secret except the incompetence of the architect who had made one house out of three; it was just an empty, unemployable room. The building had also a considerable frontage on King Street, where, behind the shop, was sheltered the parlour, with a large window and a door that led directly by two steps into the street. A strange peculiarity of the shop was that it bore no signboard. Once it had had a large signboard which a memorable gale had blown into the Square. Mr. Baines had decided not to replace it. He had always objected to what he called "puffing[13]," and for this reason would never hear of such a thing as a clearance sale. The hatred of "puffing" grew on him until he came to regard even a sign as "puffing." Uninformed persons who wished to find Baines's must ask and learn. For Mr. Baines, to have replaced the sign would have been to condone, yea, to participate in, the modern craze for unscrupulous self-advertisement. This abstention of Mr. Baines's from indulgence in signboards was somehow accepted by the more thoughtful members of the community as evidence that the height of Mr. Baines's principles was greater even than they had imagined.

Constance and Sophia were the daughters of this credit to human nature[14]. He had no other children.

NOTES

1. **the River Trent:** a river in Central England, flowing from Staffordshire northeast into the North Sea by the Humber
2. **the Irish Sea:** the sea between Ireland and England
3. **the German Ocean:** the North Sea
4. **[the] Severn:** a river in East Wales and West England, the longest river in Great Britain
5. **the Wrekin:** a hill in the English Midlands
6. **Cheshire:** a county of Northwest England
7. **Watling Street:** one of the main Roman roads running from Kent through London to Shropshire

8. **Staffordshire:** a county of Central England
9. **the county:** i.e. the county of Staffordshire
10. **the district:** i.e. the district of the Five Towns. The towns of Longton, Stoke, Hanley, Burslem, and Tunstall are situated in the industrial area known as the Potteries in Northern Staffordshire. They appear respectively as Longshaw, Hanbridge, Bursley, Knype, and Turnhill in Arnold Bennett's novels and stories.
11. **Wolverhampton:** a county in the West Midlands
12. **Wakes Week:** an annual holiday in several towns of Northern England
13. **puffing:** extolling in dishonest advertisement
14. **this credit to human nature:** this man of fine character

73

JOHN GALSWORTHY

(1867–1933)

John Galsworthy was an English novelist and dramatist. He was born at Coombe, Surrey, on August 14, 1867, the son of a lawyer. Educated at Harrow and New College, Oxford, he entered Lincoln's Inn, London, in 1889 and was called to the bar in 1890. He travelled widely, practised law for a short time, and turned to writing in about 1895. He was awarded the Order of Merit in 1929 and the Nobel Prize for Literature in 1932, and died on January 31, 1933.

As a novelist, Galsworthy is remembered chiefly for his trilogy **The Forsyte Saga** (complete version, 1922), consisting of **The Man of Property** (1906), **In Chancery** (1920), and **To Let** (1921), with two interludes—"Indian Summer of a Forsyte" (1918) and "Awakening" (1920). These books are novels of the upper middle class. They contain many lifelike characters against the background of changing English society during the period 1886–1920, and make an attack on commercialism. His study of the Forsytes is continued in his second trilogy, **A Modern Comedy** (1929), comprising **The White Monkey** (1924), **The Silver Spoon** (1926), and **Swan Song** (1928), with the two interludes "A Silent Wooing" (1927) and "Passers By" (1927). His last trilogy, **The End of the Chapter** (1934), composed of **Maid in Waiting** (1931), **Flowering Wilderness** (1932), and **Over the River** (1933), is devoted to the Charwells, cousins of the younger Forsytes. Galsworthy's plays are mostly on social and moral themes. The best-known of them are: ***The Silver Box*** (1906), ***Strife*** (1909), ***Justice*** (1910), ***The Skin Game*** (1920), and ***Loyalties*** (1922). His prose is close to the language of real life.

ENCOUNTER

Arriving at the Gallery off Cork Street, however, he paid his shilling, picked up a catalogue, and entered. Some ten persons were prowling round. Soames[1] took steps and came on what looked to him like a lamp-post bent by collision with a motor omnibus. It was advanced some three paces from the wall, and was described in his catalogue as "Jupiter"[2]. He examined it with curiosity, having recently turned some of his attention to sculpture. "If that's Jupiter," he thought, "I wonder what Juno's[3] like." And suddenly he saw her, opposite. She appeared to him like nothing so much as a pump with two handles, lightly clad in snow. He was still gazing at her, when two of the prowlers halted on his left. "*Épatant!*[4]" he heard one say.

"Jargon!" growled Soames to himself.

The other boyish voice replied:

"Missed it[5], old bean[6]; he's pulling your leg. When Jove[7] and Juno created he them[8], he was saying: 'I'll see how much these fools will swallow.' And they've lapped up the lot[9]."

"You young duffer[10]! Vospovitch is an innovator. Don't you see that he's brought satire into sculpture? The future of plastic art, of music, painting, and even architecture, has set in satiric[11]. It was bound to. People are tired—the bottom's tumbled out of sentiment[12]."

"Well, I'm quite equal to taking a little interest in beauty. I was through the War. You've dropped your handkerchief, sir."

Soames saw a handkerchief held out in front of him. He took it with some natural suspicion, and approached it to his nose. It had the right scent—of distant Eau de Cologne—and his initials in a corner. Slightly reassured, he raised his eyes to the young man's face. It had rather fawn-like ears, a laughing mouth, with half a toothbrush growing out of it on each side, and small lively eyes above a normally dressed appearance.

"Thank you," he said; and moved by a sort of irritation, added: "Glad to hear you like beauty; that's rare, nowadays."

"I dote on it," said the young man; "but you and I are the last of the old Guard[13], sir."

Soames smiled.

"If you really care for pictures," he said, "here's my card. I can show you some quite good ones any Sunday, if you're down the river and care to look in."

"Awfully nice of you, sir. I'll drop in like a bird[14]. My name's Mont-Michael." And he took off his hat.

Soames, already regretting his impulse, raised his own slightly in response, with a downward look at the young man's companion, who had a purple tie, dreadful little sluglike whiskers, and a scornful look—as if he were a poet!

It was the first indiscretion he had committed for so long that he went and sat down in an alcove. What had possessed him to give his card to a rackety young fellow, who went about with a thing like that? And Fleur[15], always at the back of his thoughts, started out like a filigree figure from a clock when the hour strikes. On the screen opposite the alcove was a large canvas with a great many square tomato-coloured blobs on it, and nothing else, so far as Soames could see from where he sat. He looked at his catalogue: "No. 32 — 'The Future Town' — Paul Post." "I suppose that's satiric too," he thought. "What a thing!" But his second impulse was more cautious. It did not do to condemn hurriedly. There had been those stripey, streaky creations of Monet's[16], which had turned out such trumps; and then the stippled school[17], and Gauguin[18]. Why, even since the Post-Impressionists there had been one or two painters not to be sneezed at. During the thirty-eight years of his connoisseur's life, indeed, he had marked so many "movements", seen the tides of taste and technique so ebb and flow, that there was really no telling anything except that there was money to be made out of every change of fashion. This too might quite well be a case where one must subdue primordial instinct, or lose the market. He got up and stood before the picture, trying hard to see it with the eyes of other people. Above the tomato blobs was what he took to be a sunset, till some one passing said: "He's got the airplanes wonderfully, don't you think!" Below the tomato blobs was a band of white with vertical black stripes, to which he could assign no meaning whatever, till some one else came by, murmuring: "What expression he gets with his foreground!" Expression? Of what? Soames went back to his seat. The thing was "rich", as his father would have said, and he wouldn't give a damn for it. Expression! Ah! they were all Expressionists[19] now, he had heard, on the Continent. So it was coming here too, was it? He remembered the first wave of influenza in 1887—or 8—[20] hatched in China, so they said. He wondered where this—this Expressionism—had been hatched. The thing was a regular disease!

NOTES

1. **Soames:** Soames Forsyte in the ***Forsyte Saga***
2. **Jupiter:** (Rom. myth.) the chief of the gods, identified with the Greek Zeus
3. **Juno:** Jupiter's queen, identified with the Greek Hera
4. ***Épatant*:** (Fr.) thrilling
5. **Missed it:** You have missed or misunderstood it.
6. **old bean:** (sl.) old friend
7. **Jove:** (another name for) Jupiter
8. **When Jove and Juno created he them:** cf. "Male and female created he them" (Genesis i. 27)
9. **they've lapped up the lot:** they have eaten or drunk the whole lot; they have taken in everything
10. **duffer:** (sl.) simpleton, fool
11. **The future of plastic art...has set in satiric:** Plastic art in future...will certainly be satirical.
12. **the bottom's tumbled out of sentiment:** sentiment is eliminated
13. **the old Guard:** the established conservative group
14. **like a bird:** (sl.) with alacrity
15. **Fleur:** Soames's daughter
16. **Monet:** Claude Monet (1840–1926), French impressionist painter
17. **the stippled school:** the painters who paint in dots and flecks
18. **Gauguin:** Paul Gauguin (1848–1903), French post-impressionist painter
19. **Expressionists:** artists who seek to express emotions rather than external reality
20. **in 1887—or 8—:** in 1887—or 1888—

ACME

In these days no man of genius need starve. The following story of my friend Bruce may be taken as proof of this assertion. Nearly sixty when I first knew him, he must have written already some fifteen books, which had earned him the reputation of "a genius" with the few who know. He used to live in York Street, Adelphi[1], where he had two rooms up the very shaky staircase of a house chiefly remarkable for the fact that its front door seemed always open. I suppose there never was a writer more indifferent to what people thought of him. He profoundly neglected the Press—not with one of those neglects which grow on writers from reading reviews of their own works—he seemed never to read criticism, but with the basic neglect of "an original[2]," a nomadic spirit, a stranger in modern civilization, who would leave his attics for long months of wandering and come back there to hibernate and write a book. He was a tall, thin man, with a face rather like Mark Twain's, black eyebrows which bristled and shot up, a bitten, drooping grey moustache, and fuzzy grey hair; but his eyes were like owl's eyes, piercing, melancholy, dark brown, and gave to his rugged face the extraordinary expression of a spirit remote from the flesh which had captured it. He was a bachelor, who seemed to avoid women; perhaps they had "learned" him that; for he must have been very attractive to them.

The year of which I write had been to my friend Bruce the devil[3], monetarily speaking. With his passion for writing that for which his age had no taste—what could he expect? His last book had been a complete frost. He had undergone, too, an operation which had cost him much money and left him very weak. When I went to see him that October I found him stretched out on two chairs, smoking the Brazilian cigarettes which he affected[4]—and which always affected me[5], so black and strong they were, in their yellow maize-leaf coverings. He had a writing-pad on his knee, and sheets of paper scattered all around. The room had a very meager look. I had not seen him for a year and more, but he looked up at me as if I'd been in yesterday.

"Hallo!" he said. "I went into a thing they call a cinema last night. Have you ever been?"

"Ever been? Do you know how long the cinema has been going? Since about 1900."

"Well! What a *thing*! I'm writing a skit on it!"

"How—a skit?"

"Parody—wildest yarn you ever read."

He took up a sheet of paper and began chuckling to himself.

"My heroine," he said, "is an Octoroon[6]. Her eyes swim, and her lovely bosom heaves. Everybody wants her, and she's more virtuous than words can say. The situations she doesn't succumb to would freeze your blood; they'd roast your marrow. She has a perfect devil of a brother, with whom she was brought up, and who knows her deep dark secret and wants to trade her off to a millionaire who also has a deep dark secret. Altogether there are four deep dark secrets in my yarn. It's a corker[7]."

"What a waste of your time!" I said.

"My time!" he answered fiercely. "What's the use of my time? Nobody buys my books."

"Who's attending you?"

"Doctors! They take your money, that's all. I've got no money. Don't talk about me!" Again he took up a sheet of manuscript; and chuckled.

"Last night—at that place—they had—good God![8]—a race between a train and a motor-car. Well, I've got one between a train, a motor-car, a flying machine, and a horse."

I sat up.

"May I have a look at your skit," I said, "when you've finished it?"

"It is finished. Wrote it straight off. D'you think I could stop and then go on again with a thing like that?" He gathered the sheets and held them out to me. "Take the thing—it's amused me to do it. The heroine's secret is that she isn't an Octoroon at all; she's a De La Casse—purest Creole blood of the South; and her villainous brother isn't her brother; and the bad millionaire isn't a millionaire; and her penniless lover is. It's rich, I tell you!"

"Thanks," I said dryly, and took the sheets.

I went away concerned about my friend, his illness, and his poverty, especially his poverty, for I saw no end to it.

After dinner that evening I began languidly to read his skit. I had not read two pages of the thirty-five before I started up, sat down again, and feverishly read on. Skit! By George[9]! He had written a perfect scenario—or, rather, that which wanted the merest professional touching-up to be perfect. I was excited. It was a little gold-mine if properly handled. Any good film company, I felt convinced, would catch at it. Yes! But how to handle it? Bruce was such an unaccountable creature, such a wild old bird[10]! Imagine his having only just realised the cinema! If I told him his skit was a serious film, he would say: "Good God!" and put it in the fire, priceless though it was. And yet, how could I market it without **carte blanche**[11], and how get **carte blanche** without giving my discovery away? I was deathly[12] keen on getting some money for him; and this thing, properly worked, might almost make him independent. I felt as if I had a priceless museum piece which a single stumble might shatter to fragments. The tone of his voice when he spoke of the cinema—"What a *thing*!" —kept coming back to me. He was prickly[13] proud, too—very difficult about money. Could I work it without telling him anything? I knew he never looked at a newspaper. But should I be justified in taking advantage of that—in getting the thing accepted and produced without his knowing? I revolved the question for hours, and went to see him again next day.

He was reading.

"Hallo! You again? What do you think of this theory—that the Egyptians derive from a Saharan[14] civilisation?"

"I don't think," I said.

"It's nonsense. This fellow—"

I interrupted him.

"Do you want that skit back, or can I keep it?"

"Skit? What skit?"

"The thing you gave me yesterday."

"That! Light your fire with it. This fellow— "

"Yes," I said; "I'll light a fire with it. I see you're busy."

"Oh, no! I'm not," he said. "I've nothing to do. What's the good of my writing? I earn less and less with every book that comes out. I'm dying of poverty."

"That's because you won't consider the Public."

"How can I consider the Public when I don't know what they want?"

"Because you won't take the trouble to find out. If I suggested a way to you of pleasing the Public and making money you'd kick me out of the room."

And the words, "For instance, I've got a little gold-mine of yours in my pocket," were on the tip of my tongue, but I choked them back. "Daren't risk it!" I thought. "He's given you the thing. *Carte blanche—cartes serrées*[15]!"

I took the gold mine away and promptly rough-shaped it for the film. It was perfectly easy, without any alteration of the story. Then I was faced with the temptation to put his name to it. The point was this: If I took it to a film company as an authorless scenario I should only get authorless terms; whereas, if I put his name to it, with a little talking I could double the terms at least. The film public didn't know his name, of course, but the inner literary public did, and it's wonderful how you can impress the market with the word "genius" judiciously used. It was too dangerous, however; and at last I hit on a middle course. I would take it to them with no name attached, but tell them it was by "a genius," and suggest that they could make capital out of[16] the incognito. I knew they would feel it was by a genius.

I took it to an excellent company next day with a covering note saying: "The author, a man of recognised literary genius, for certain reasons prefers to remain unknown." They took a fortnight in which to rise, but they rose. They had to. The thing was too good in itself. For a week I played them over terms. Twice I delivered an ultimatum—twice they surrendered: they knew too well what they had got. I could have made a contract with £2,000 down[17] which would have brought at least another £2,000 before the contract term closed; but I compounded for one that gave me £3,000 down as likely to lead to less difficulty with Bruce. The terms were not a whit too good for what was really the "acme" of scenarios. If I could have been quite open I could certainly have done better. Finally, however, I signed the contract, delivered the manuscript, and received a cheque for the price. I was elated, and at the same time knew that my troubles were just beginning. With Bruce's feeling about the film how the deuce[18] should I get him to take the money? Could I go to his publishers and conspire with them to trickle it out to him gradually as if it came from his books? That meant letting them into the secret; besides, he was too used to receiving practically nothing from his books; it would lead him to make enquiry, and the secret was bound to come out. Could I get a lawyer to spring an inheritance on him[19]? That would mean no end of lying and elaboration, even if a lawyer would consent. Should I send him the money in Bank of England notes with the words: "From a lifelong admirer of your genius?" I was afraid he would suspect a trick, or stolen notes, and go to the police to trace them. Or should I just go, put the cheque on the table and tell him the truth?

The question worried me terribly, for I didn't feel entitled to consult others who knew him. It was the sort of thing that, if talked over, would certainly leak out. It was not desirable, however, to delay cashing a big cheque like that. Besides, they had started on the production. It happened to be a slack time, with a dearth of good films, so that they were rushing it on. And in the meantime there was Bruce—starved of everything he wanted, unable to get away for want of money, depressed about his health and his future. And yet so completely had he always seemed to me different, strange, superior to this civilization of ours, that the idea of going to him and saying simply: "This is yours, for the film you wrote," scared me. I could hear his: "I? Write for cinema? What do you mean?"

When I came to think of it, I had surely taken an extravagant liberty in marketing the thing without consulting him. I felt he would never forgive that, and my feeling towards him was so affectionate, even reverential, that I simply hated the idea of being wiped out of his good books. At last I hit on a way that by introducing my own interest might break my fall. I cashed the cheque, lodged the money at my bank, drew my own cheque on it for the full amount, and, armed with that and the contract, went to see him.

He was lying on two chairs smoking his Brazilians[20] and playing with a stray cat which had attached itself to him. He seemed rather less prickly than usual, and, after beating about the bushes of his health and other matters, I began:

"I've got a confession to make, Bruce."

"Confession!" he said. "What confession?"

"You remember that skit on the film you wrote and gave me about six weeks ago?"

"No."

"Yes, you do—about an Octoroon."

He chuckled. "Oh! Ah! That!"

I took a deep breath, and went on:

"Well, I sold it; and the price of course belongs to you."

"What? Who'd print a thing like that?"

"It isn't printed. It's been made into a film—superfilm, they call it."

His hand came to a pause on the cat's back, and he glared at me. I hastened on:

"I ought to have told you what I was doing, but you're so prickly, and you've got such confounded superior notions. I thought if I did, you'd be biting off your nose to spite your own face[21]. The fact is it made a marvellous scenario. Here's the contract, and here's a cheque on my bank for the price—£3,000. If you like to treat me as your agent, you owe me £300. I don't expect it, but I'm not proud like you, and I shan't sneeze[22]."

"Good God!" he said.

"Yes, I know. But it's all nonsense, Bruce. You can carry scruples to altogether too great length. Tainted source! Everything's tainted, if you come to that. The film's a quite justified expression of modern civilization—a natural outcome of the age. It gives amusement; it affords pleasure. It may be vulgar, it may be cheap, but we are vulgar, we are cheap, and it's no use pretending we're not—not you, of course, Bruce, but people at large. A vulgar age wants vulgar amusement, and if we can give it that amusement we ought to; life's not too cheery, anyway."

The glare in his eyes was almost paralising me, but I managed to stammer on.

"You live out of the world—you don't realise what humdrum people want; something to balance the greyness, the—the banality of their lives. They want blood, thrill, sensation of all sorts. You didn't mean to give it them, but you have, you've done them a benefit, whether you wish to or not, and the money's yours and you've got to take it."

The cat suddenly jumped down. I waited for the storm to burst.

"I know," I dashed on, "that you hate and despise the film— "

Suddenly his voice boomed out:

"Bosh[23]! What are you talking about? Film! I go there every other night."

It was my turn to say "Good God!" And ramming contract and cheque into his empty hand, I bolted, closely followed by the cat.

NOTES

1. **Adelphi:** a section of West Central London
2. **original:** (n.) eccentric person
3. **had been...the devil:** had been...something difficult; had been...very bad
4. **which he affected:** which he liked
5. **which always affected me:** which always influenced me in an adverse way
6. **Octoroon:** person with one-eighth negro blood
7. **corker:** (sl.) remarkable or excellent thing
8. **good God!:** Good heavens! (an exclamation of surprise)
9. **By George:** an exclamation of mild surprise
10. **old bird:** (sl.) experienced person
11. *carte blanche*: (Fr.) free hand
12. **deathly:** (sl.) extremely
13. **prickly:** (sl., adj.) easily irritated; (here adv.) irritably
14. **Saharan:** relating to the Sahara desert
15. *cartes serrées*: (Fr.) careful play
16. **make capital out of:** make use of to one's own advantage

17. **with two thousand pounds down:** with 2,000 pounds paid at the time of purchase
18. **how the deuce...:** (sl.) how the devil...
19. **to spring an inheritance on him:** to give him an inheritance suddenly
20. **his Brazilians:** (here) his Brazilian cigarettes
21. **biting off your nose to spite your own face:** damaging yourself by a vengeful action
22. **I shan't sneeze:** I shan't despise it
23. **Bosh:** (sl.) nonsense

74

ROBERT FALCON SCOTT

(1868–1912)

Captain Robert Falcon Scott was a British naval officer and explorer. He commanded the national antarctic expeditions of 1900–1904 and 1910–1912. He published an account of his first exploration in *The Voyage of the Discovery* (1905). His remarkable journal, issued after his death as **Scott's Last Expedition** (2 vols, 1913), describes his second exploration. He and four companions reached the South Pole in January 1912, but on the return journey they all died heroically in March 1912.

THE END OF THE STORY

Friday, March 16 or Saturday 17.— Lost track of dates, but think the last correct. Tragedy all along the line[1]. At lunch, the day before yesterday, poor Titus Oates said he couldn't go on; he proposed we should leave him in his sleeping-bag. That we could not do, and we induced him to come on, on the afternoon march. In spite of its awful nature for him he struggled on and we made a few miles. At night he was worse and we knew that the end had come.

Should this be found, I want these facts recorded. Oates' last thoughts were of his mother, but immediately before, he took pride in thinking that his regiment would be pleased with the bold way in which he met his death. We can testify to his bravery. He has borne intense suffering for weeks without complaint, and to the very last was able and willing to discuss outside subjects[2]. He did not—would not—give up hope till the very end. He was a brave soul. This was the end. He slept through the night before last, hoping not to wake, but he woke in the morning—yesterday. It was blowing a blizzard. He said, "I am just going outside and may be some time." He went out to the blizzard and we have not seen him since.

I take this opportunity of saying that we have stuck to our sick companions to the last. In the case of Edgar Evans, when absolutely out of food[3] and he lay insensible, the safety of the remainder seemed to demand his abandonment, but Providence mercifully removed him at this moment. He died a natural death, and we did not leave him till two hours after his death. We knew that poor Oates was walking to his death, but though we tried to dissuade him, we knew it was the act of a brave man and an English gentleman. We all hope to meet the end with a similar spirit, and assuredly the end is not far.

I can only write at lunch, and then only occasionally. The cold is intense, –40 ℃ at midday. My companions are unendingly cheerful, but we are all on the verge of serious frost-bites, and though we constantly talk of fetching through[4], I don't think any one of us believes it in his heart.

Thursday, March 29. —Since the 21st we have had a continuous gale from W.S.W. and S.W. We had fuel to make two cups of tea apiece and bare food for two days on the 20th. Every day we have been ready to start for our depot 11 miles away, but outside the door of the tent it remains a scene of whirling drift. I do not think we can hope for any better things now. We shall stick it out[5] to the end, but we are getting weaker, of course, and the end cannot be far.

It seems a pity, but I do not think I can write more.

R. Scott

Last entry:

For God's sake look after our people.

NOTES

1. **all along the line:** at every point, in every way
2. **outside subjects:** topics remote from the current situation
3. **out of food:** without food
4. **fetching through:** (colloq.) eventually arriving at a destination
5. **stick it out:** (colloq.) endure something unpleasant

75

ARTHUR CLUTTON-BROCK

(1868–1924)

Arthur Clutton-Brock was an English essayist and critic. He was born at Weybridge, Surrey, educated at Eton and New College, Oxford, and called to the bar in 1895. After he practised law for several years, he began to contribute to periodicals in 1904. He wrote, among other books, **Shelley**: **The Man and the Poet** (1909); **William Morris: His Work and Influence** (1914); **Essays on Art** (1918); and **Essays on Books** (1920).

SUNDAY BEFORE THE WAR

On Sunday, in a remote valley in the West of England, where the people are few and scattered and placid, there was no more sign among them than among the quiet hills of the anxiety that holds the world. They had no news and seemed to want none. The postmaster had been ordered to stay all day in his little post-office, and that was something unusual that interested them, but only because it affected the postmaster.

It rained in the morning, but the afternoon was clear and glorious and shining, with all the distances revealed far into the heart of Wales and to the high ridges of the Welsh mountains. The cottages of that valley are not gathered into villages, but two or three together or lonely among their fruit-trees on the hill-side; and the cottagers, who are always courteous and friendly, said a word or two as one went by, but just what they would have said on any other day and without any question about the war. Indeed, they seemed to know, or to wish to know, as little about that as the earth itself, which, beautiful there at any time, seemed that afternoon to wear an extreme and pathetic beauty. The country, more than any other in England, has the secret of peace. It is not wild, though it looks into the wildness of Wales; but all its cultivation, its orchards and hop-yards[1] and fields of golden wheat, seem to have the beauty of time upon them, as if men there had long lived happily upon the earth with no desire for change nor fear of decay. It is not the sad beauty of a past cut off from the present, but a mellowness that the present inherits from the past; and in the mellowness all the hill-side seems a garden to the spacious farm-houses and the little cottages; each led up to by its own narrow, flowery lane. There the meadows are all lawns with the lustrous green of spring even in August, and often over-shadowed by old fruit-trees—cherry, or apple or pear; and on Sunday after the rain there was an April glory and freshness added to the quiet of the later summer.

Nowhere and never in the world can there have been a deeper peace; and the bells from the little red church down by the river seemed to be the music of it, as the song of birds is the music of spring. There one saw how beautiful the life of man can be, and how men by the innocent labours of many generations can give to the earth a beauty it has never known in its wildness. And all this peace, one knew, was threatened; and the threat came into one's mind as if it were a soundless message from over the great eastward plain[2]; and with it the beauty seemed unsubstantial and strange, as if it were sinking away into the past, as if it were only a memory of childhood.

So it is always when the mind is troubled among happy things, and then one almost wishes they could share one's troubles and become more real with it. It seemed on that Sunday that a golden age had lasted till yesterday, and that the earth had still to learn the news of its ending. And this change had come, not by the will of God, not even by the will of man, but because some few men far away were afraid to be open and generous with each other. There was a power in their hands so great that it frightened them. There was a spring[3] that they knew they must not touch, and, like mischievous and nervous children, they had touched it at last, and now all the world was to suffer for their mischief.

So the next morning one saw a reservist[4] in his uniform saying good-bye to his wife and children at his cottage-gate and then walking up the hill that leads out of the valley with a cheerful smile still on his face. There was the first open sign of trouble, a very little one, and he made the least of it; and, after all, this valley is very far from any possible war, and its harvest and its vintage of perry[5] and cider will surely be gathered in peace.

But what happiness can there be in that peace, or what security in the mind of man, when the madness of war is let loose in so many other valleys? Here there is a beauty inherited from the past, and added to the earth by man's will; but the men here are of the same nature and subject to the same madness as those who are gathering to fight on the frontiers. We are all men with the same power of making and destroying, with the same divine foresight mocked by the same animal blindness. We ourselves may not be in fault[6] today, but it is human beings in no way different from us who are doing what we abhor and they abhor even while they do it. There is a fate, coming from the beast in our own past, that the present man in us has not yet mastered, and for the moment that fate seems a malignity in the nature of the universe that mocks us even in the beauty of these lonely hills. But it is not so, for we are not separate and indifferent like the beasts; and if one nation for the moment forgets our common humanity and its future, then another must take over that sacred charge and guard it without hatred or fear until the madness is passed. May that be our task now, so that we may wage war only for the future peace of the world and with the lasting courage that needs no stimulant of hate.

NOTES
1. **hop-yards:** hop gardens, fields of hops
2. **the great eastward plain:** the mainland of Europe
3. **a spring:** an elastic contrivance
4. **reservist:** member of reserve forces
5. **perry:** wine made from pears
6. **in fault:** (arch.) blameworthy

EDWARD VERRALL LUCAS

(1868–1938)

E. V. Lucas was an English journalist and essayist. He was born at Eltham, Kent, educated in Brighton, and apprenticed to a bookseller there. He began journalism early in life and was for some time on the staff of **Punch**. Lucas wrote prolifically on various subjects. Representative volumes of his familiar essays are: ***Fireside and Sunshine*** (1906), ***Character and Comedy*** (1907), ***Loiterer's Harvest*** (1913), ***Adventures and Enthusiasms*** (1920), ***Events and Embroideries*** (1926), and ***Adventures and Misgivings*** (1938). The best of his novels is ***Over Bemerton's*** (1908). He brought out a dozen travel books, e.g. ***Highways and Byways in Sussex*** (1904) and ***A Wanderer in London*** (1906). He compiled anthologies, such as ***The Open Road*** (1899) and ***The Gentlest Art*** (a selection of letters, 1907). He edited ***The Works of Charles and Mary Lamb*** (1903–1905). His ***Reading, Writing, and Remembering*** (1932) is an engaging autobiography. Lucas's prose style is lucid, simple, and witty.

MEDITATIONS AMONG THE CAGES

Drifting somewhat aimlessly about the Zoo on Sunday afternoon, I came suddenly upon the hippopotamus's vast and homely countenance peering round the corner of its stockade. It is the hugest, most incredible thing—just for an instant a little like the late Herbert Campbell carried out to the highest power—and I felt for the moment as if I were in another world, a kind of impossible pantomime land[1]. There was nothing frightening about it; it was more companionable than many faces that sit opposite one in a bus; and yet it was repellent, unnegotiable, absurd. It is not a thing to see suddenly.

This hippopotamus, who is now thirty years or more old, shows signs of age. Her feet are sore, her eyes are scaly, her teeth are few and awry and very brown. In bulk she is immense, of a rotund solidity unequalled in my experience. The Great Tun, filled with its gallons, would, one feels, be light compared with her. I could not help wondering what will happen when she dies, as die she must before very long: how her gigantic carcase will be moved, how dealt with, how eliminated. I am sure her lifeless form will be the heaviest thing in London—heavier than any girder, heavier than any gun. One has this impression, I suppose, because one knows something of the weight of an ordinary body, and one's mind multiplies that, whereas a girder or a gun conveys no distinct impression. Even the baby hippopotami, in the next cage, ridiculous little pigs of hippos, fresh from their packing-case and the voyage from Africa, are probably each heavier than four aldermen; but the old one is fifty times heavier than the baby, and might easily, such is the consistency of her alarming barrel, be full of lead. When her tottering legs at length give way and she falls to rise no more, may I not be there to see!

Standing before this ridiculous mammoth, so useless and unwieldy, I failed utterly to understand the feelings of the big-game hunter who could deliberately shoot it. If ever there was an animal that should inculcate or encourage the maxim "Live and let live," it is the hippopotamus. I cannot understand how a man can dare to be responsible for adding so much mortality to this already encumbered earth. And yet there are members of West End clubs sipping their coffee at this moment who have probably shot many. To kill a lion or tiger, or any of the active, dangerous beasts: I can understand that, although I wish never to do it; but to interrupt the already stagnant life of one of these gentle mountains—*that* I could never bring myself to do. How can one kill a creature that wallows?

Falling in later with a zoological Fellow[2], with a head full of Greek and a pocket full of apples and onions, without which he never visits these friends, I learned many curious facts. Among other things, I learned that the hornbill, who looks a desperately fierce biped, prepared at a second's notice to stab one with his iron beak, even in the back, is really the kindliest and most companionable of birds, ready and eager for any amount of petting. He is also, perhaps, the best short-slip[3] in the Gardens, for unwieldy as his beak looks to be, he can catch anything, throw it how you may. Albert Trott has hitherto been my ideal, but he reigns in my mind no more. *Le roi est mort; vive l'hornbill.*

I cannot get over my surprise about the hornbill, whose favorite food, it ought to be known, is grapes. No animal looks much less tractable and nursable; yet as a matter of fact the hornbill is as anxious to be noticed as a spoiled dog, and as full of sentimentality. Best of all—even more than grapes—he likes to be scratched under the chin, and he leans his head farther and farther back in the enjoyment of this ecstasy, until his bill points into the sky like the spire of a village church.

In close proximity to the hornbills live the boatbill, who is as lovely as a Japanese print, and Pel's Owl, who has perhaps the richest eyes in the whole Zoo, and not the least melancholy life; for he, accustomed to fly lightly and noiselessly over the surface of African rivers, catching unwary fish in his claws as he flies, is now confined to a cage within a cage, a few feet square. What must be his thoughts as he watches the sight-seers go by! What must be the thoughts of all these caged aliens! The seals and sea-lions, one can believe, are not unhappy; the otter is in his element; the birds in the large aviaries, the monkeys, the snakes—these, one feels, are not so badly off. But the beasts and birds of a higher spirit, a mounting ambition—the eagles and hawks and lions and tigers, and Pel's Owl—what a destiny! What a future! I would not think their thoughts.

I learned also from my instructive Fellow that one of the llamas can expectorate with more precision and less warning than any American described by the old satirists; that the Bird of Paradise, exquisite and beautiful though he is, with every right to be disdainful and eremitic, will yet cling to the sides of the cage to eat a piece of apple from the hand, and, having taken it, swallow it whole; that the most westerly owl in the owl house will say "woof-woof" after anyone that it esteems; that eagles like having their heads stroked, and that there is one of them who, if you give it a lead, will crow like a cock. I doubt if such things should be. I like to think of the eagle as soaring into the face of the sun with an unwinking eye, and allowing no liberties. But in Regent's Park....I suppose we must make allowances. Does not the rhinoceros eat biscuits?

I learned also that the thar[4] loves orange-peel above all delicacies, and that the mountain goat who possesses the biggest horns can bring them down on the railings with a thwack that, if your finger chanced to be there, as it easily might, would assuredly cut it in two; but, on the other hand, that the slender, graceful deer in the pen near the elephants, who has lately lost one horn, is as gentle as a spaniel and greatly in need of sympathy.

I learned, also, that the baby elephant eats Quaker oats; and that there are keepers in the Gardens who have never yet seen the beaver, not because they keep looking the opposite way, but because that creature is so unaccountably shy. The only chance one has of catching a glimpse of him is at sunset.

But the introduction to Delia was the crown of the morning—the coping-stone of my good fortune in meeting this zoological friend. We spent an hour in her company, while she toyed with an assorted fruitarian dinner. I should not call her a slave to her palate; I never remember seeing a non-human animal (is she a non-human animal, I wonder?) so willing to drop a delicacy and turn to other things. She turned with chief interest to my walking-stick; but now and then the trapeze caught her restless eye, and she was on it; and now and then it seemed to be time to embrace or to be embraced. A very simple, loving soul, this Delia (is she a soul, has she a soul, I wonder?), with the prettiest little thumb imaginable—for an ourang-outang, and, so far as I could observe, no *arrières pensées*. Clean, too. In fact, quite one of us.

Delia is the first ape I ever saw that did not make me uneasy. So many monkeys—especially the larger apes—are such travesties of ourselves—and not only such travesties, but now and then such reminders of our worse selves—that one regards them with an increased scepticism as to man's part not only in this life, but in the next. But Delia is winsome; Delia has the virtues. She is kind, and gentle, and quiet. All her movements are deliberate and well thought out. She has none of the dreadful furtive suspiciousness of the smaller monkeys; so far as I could see, no pettiness at all. And the hair that serves her also for clothes, like Lady Godiva[5], is a very beautiful rich auburn. I cherish her memory.

It was the more pleasant to come under Delia's fascination, because I had just seen that horrible sight, the feeding of the diving birds. Here, at the most, one said in Delia's warm basement-room—here, at the most, is only mischief and want of thought; here are no cruel predatory jaws pursuing their living prey. The diving birds give one, indeed, a new symbol for rapacity and relentlessness, partly because the victims which they catch with such accuracy and ferocity, are so exquisitely made for joy and life. Can there be anything more beautiful than a slender diaphanous fish, gliding through the water with the light of day inhabiting its fragile body? The movements of a fish are in themselves grace incarnate. The keeper flings a dozen of these little miracles into the tank, and straightway they begin their magical progress through the green water. He then opens a cage, and a huge black and white bird, all cruel eye and snapping beak, plunges in, and in two minutes it has seized and swallowed every fish. The spectacle appeared to be very popular; but I came away sick.

I walked from Delia's boudoir to the lions, and from the lions to the sea-lions, by way of the long row of sheds where the nilghais[6] and hartebeests and elands dwell, and found that the real interest of this house lay, not in those aliens, but in a domestic creature which, common though it be in English homes, is yet not too easy to observe—the mouse. If you want to see the mouse at ease, confidently moving hither and thither, and taking its meals with a mind secure from danger, go to the Zoo, nominally to study the eland. It is no injustice to the eland, who cares nothing for notice, therein differing completely from the male giraffe, who looks after his departing friends with a moist and wistful eye and a yearning extension of neck that only the stony-hearted can resist. The eland is less affectionate; he has no timidity, and he has no vanity. He does not mind what you look at, and therefore you may lavish all your attention on the mice that move about among his legs like the shadows of little racing clouds on a windy April day.

And so I came away, having seen everything in the Zoo except the most advertised animal of all—the pickpocket. To see so many visitors to the cages wearing a patronizing air, and to hear their remarks of condescension or dislike, as animal after animal is passed under review, has a certain piquancy in the contiguity of this ever present notice, "Beware of Pickpockets," warning man against—what? —man. Lions, at any rate, one feels (desirable as it may be to capture their skins for hearthrugs), pick no pockets.

NOTES

1. **pantomime land:** fairyland
2. **Fellow:** research fellow from a university
3. **short-slip:** catcher in cricket
4. **thar:** Himalayan wild goat
5. **Lady Godiva:** a legendary lady of early Saxon history, who was made to ride naked through the streets of Coventry and whose long hair covered her body
6. **nilghais:** or nilgais, large short-horned Indian antelopes

RIVALRY

From Mrs. Horace Spong to the Rev. Samson Spong

Dear Samson, —I was so glad to hear from Lydia that you are better. We have been rather nervous about you, for a cold at this time of year is often difficult to throw off. Horace is better too, and we are making our plans for Mentone[1] as usual. I don't pretend to care much for this annual exile from home, but Horace counts on it.

I am,
Your affectionate Sister,
Grace Spong

The Rev. Samson Spong to Mrs. Horace Spong

Dear Grace, —I can't think what Lydia was about, to tell you that I am better. I am not better. If anything[2] I am worse. Indeed it is within the bounds of probability that I shall never be anything but a wreck, for this cold is the most malignant that I ever had and gives me no peace. I am miserable all day and at night unable to sleep. Either I am coughing or I have the feeling of being smothered.

Tell Horace that I envy him his recovery: he was always so much stronger than I. In fact, our dear mother often expressed surprise that as an infant I survived at all.

You are fortunate in being able to get to the South of France and avoid this terrible climate. I should like nothing better, but I dread the journey too much; nor would my straitened means[3], much depleted by excessive taxation, permit it. Horace has always been so richly blessed in worldly goods.

Your affectionate Brother,
Samson Spong

Mrs. Samson Spong to Mrs. Horace Spong

My Dear Grace, —Please don't write to Samson again about his condition. He much resented my telling you that he was better, although as a matter of fact he is—much better. He eats better, is more cheerful, except when he recollects that he is an invalid, and sleeps well. He may not always sleep right through the night, but like all men, if he is awake five minutes he thinks it is two hours.

Yours,

Lydia

Mr. Horace Spong to the Rev. Samson Spong

Dear Samson, —Grace has given me your message about my recovery. I only wish I had earned it; but, alas! I feel anything but a convalescent. In fact, in confidence, for I should not like every one to know, I am conscious of increasing weakness daily, I have even kept it a secret from Grace. There are some colds that seem to strike deeper the more you nurse them[4], and mine is one of them.

I am sorry for the pessimistic tone of your letter, but I feel sure that things are not so bad with you as you say. It is possible to take too gloomy a view of oneself, especially when one is weak, and I have discounted your remarks in consequence. You are a strong man ***au fond***[5] and you will shake this off very soon, I am convinced.

We are off to Mentone next week. It is a dreary business, but Grace likes it there, and what she likes is law with me.

Yours,

Horace

The Rev. Samson Spong to Mr. Horace Spong

Dear Horace, —I wish you wouldn't write nonsense about my being strong. I am not strong and never was. I was always delicate, even before cold after cold enfeebled me, and now I am a wreck. Surely I am the best judge as to how ill I am! Now you, I consider, really are strong, though you may not look it. Only a strong man could undertake a journey to Mentone at this time of year.

I will say good-bye, my dear brother, as it is exceedingly unlikely that you will find me here when you return in the spring.

Yours,
Samson

Miss Hilda Spong to the Rev. Samson Spong

Dear Uncle Samson, —I was very glad to hear the other day from mother that you are better. I send you a little present now as at Christmas I shall be far away in Switzerland with a Winter Sports party. We are going to some place thousands of feet up, where skating and skiing and bob-sleighing are a cert[6]. I will send you a card from there.

Your affectionate Niece,
Hilda

The Rev. Samson Spong to Mrs. Horace Spong

Dear Grace, —If you are writing to Hilda you might give her a hint that it would be kinder not to send me a card as she has undertaken to do. I feel sure it would suggest snow and be harmful to me in my present delicate state. She is a dear girl, but her letter about those Alpine heights, although meant, I am sure, in all good faith[7], gave me a severe shock. I have just now to be very, very careful.

Your affectionate Brother,
Samson

P.S. —Tell Horace that what he wants is more employment. It is when one is idle that one broods on one's health. He should take up some hobby.

Mr. Horace Spong to the Rev. Samson Spong

My dear Samson, —I really must protest against the suggestion in your letter to Grace that I am a ***malade imaginaire***[8]. Fortunately Grace and I understand one another and there is no fear of any mishap; but I can believe that there are households which might be undermined by such insinuations. So far from being idle, as you put it, I am continually busy. There is not a penny spent in this establishment[9], indoors or out[10], that I am unaware of: I see all the tradesmen's books; I know exactly how much petrol the car uses from day to day; in fact, I am constantly vigilant and interested. Please do not again refer to the matter.

While on this subject, let me say that it is increasingly borne in upon me that[11] you made a terrible mistake when you gave up your living[12]. You were far less faddy about[13] yourself when you had your duties to perform. You were also more considerate for others. Your very gloomy reference in your last letter to your imminent decease might have caused me a really serious relapse, had I not just run into Corder in our London hotel and had a talk with him about you. But from what he says you are getting along famously[14].

My love to Lydia.

Yours,
Horace

The Rev. Samson Spong to Richard Corder, M.D.

Dear Corder, —I am sorry that after all these years we should have to part, but I must ask you for your account. I cannot continue with a medical man who gossips about his patient. I was much distressed this morning to learn from my brother that you had told him I was better. Apart from the fact that I am not, I hold that a doctor's first duty is not to tell. You have greatly shaken me.

I am,
Yours sincerely,
Samson Spong

NOTES

1. **Mentone:** Menton, a town and winter resort in Southeast France
2. **If anything:** If there is any difference
3. **straitened means:** inadequate income
4. **nurse them:** try to cure the colds
5. *au fond*: (Fr.) at bottom, in the main

6. **cert:** (sl.) certainty, some event certain to happen
7. **in all good faith:** with great honesty and sincerity
8. *malade imaginaire*: (Fr.) imaginary invalid
9. **this establishment:** this household
10. **indoors or out:** indoors or outdoors
11. **it is...borne in upon me that...:** it makes an impression on me that...
12. **your living:** your benefice
13. **faddy about:** crazy about
14. **famously:** (colloq.) satisfactorily

A FUNERAL

It was in a Surrey[1] churchyard on a grey, damp afternoon—all very solitary and quiet, with no alien spectators and only a very few mourners; and no desolating[2] sense of loss, although a very true and kindly friend was passing from us. A football match was in progress in a field adjoining the churchyard, and I wondered, as I stood by the grave, if, were I the schoolmaster, I would stop the game just for the few minutes during which a body was committed to the earth; and I decided that I would not. In the midst of death we are in life, just as in the midst of life we are in death; it is all as it should be in this bizarre, jostling world. And he whom we had come to bury would have been the first to wish the boys to go on with their sport.

He was an old scholar—not so very old, either—whom I had known for some five years, and had many a long walk with: a short and sturdy Irish gentleman, with a large, genial grey head stored with odd lore and the best literature; and the heart of a child. I never knew a man of so transparent a character. He showed you all his thoughts: as some one once said, his brain was like a beehive under glass—you could watch all its workings. And the honey in it! To walk with him at any season of the year was to be reminded or newly told of the best that the English poets have said on all the phenomena of wood and hedgerow, meadow and sky. He had the more lyrical passages of Shakespeare at his tongue's end, and all Wordsworth and Keats. These were his favourites; but he had read everything that has the true rapturous note[3], and had forgotten none of its spirit.

His life was divided between his books, his friends, and long walks. A solitary man, he worked at all hours without much method, and probably courted his fatal illness in this way. To his own name there is not much to show; but such was his liberality that he was continually helping others, and the fruits of his erudition are widely scattered, and have gone to increase many a comparative stranger's reputation. His own ***magnum opus***[4] he left unfinished; he had worked at it for years, until to his friends it had come to be something of a joke. But though still shapeless, it was a great feast, as the world, I hope, will one day know. If, however, this treasure does not reach the world, it will not be because its worth was insufficient, but because no one can be found to decipher the manuscript; for I may say incidentally that our old friend wrote the worst hand in London, and it was not an uncommon experience of his correspondents to carry his missives from one pair of eyes to another, seeking a clue; and I remember on one occasion two such inquirers meeting unexpectedly, and each simultaneously drawing a letter from his pocket and uttering the request that the other should put everything else on one side in order to solve the enigma.

Lack of method and a haphazard and unlimited generosity were not his only Irish qualities. He had a quick, chivalrous temper, too, and I remember the difficulty I once had in restraining him from leaping the counter of a small tobacconist's in Great Portland Street[5], to give the man a good dressing[6] for an imagined rudeness—not to himself, but to me. And there is more than one bus conductor in London who has cause to remember this sturdy Quixotic passenger's championship of a poor woman to whom insufficient courtesy seemed to him to have been shown. Normally kindly and tolerant, his indignation on hearing of injustice was red hot. He burned at a story of meanness. It would haunt him all the evening. "Can it really be true?" he would ask, and burst forth again to flame.

Abstemious himself in all things, save reading and writing and helping his friends and correspondents, he mixed excellent whisky punch, as he called it. He brought to this office all the concentration which he lacked in his literary labours. It was a ritual with him; nothing might be hurried or left undone, and the result, I might say, justified the means. His death reduces the number of such convivial alchemists to one only, and he is in Tasmania[7], and, so far as I am concerned, useless.

His avidity as a reader—his desire to master his subject—led to some charming eccentricities, as when, for a daily journey between Earl's Court Road and Addison Road stations, he would carry a heavy hand-bag filled with books, "to read in the train." This was no satire on the railway system, but pure zeal. He had indeed no satire in him; he spoke his mind and it was over.

It was a curious little company that assembled to do honour to this old kindly bachelor—the two or three relatives that he possessed, and eight of his literary friends, most of them of a good age, and for the most part men of intellect, and in one or two cases of world-wide reputation, and all a little uncomfortable in unwonted formal black. We were very grave and thoughtful, but it was not exactly a sad funeral, for we knew that had he lived longer—he was sixty-three—he would certainly have been an invalid, which would have irked his active, restless mind and body almost unbearably; and we knew, also, that he had died in his first real illness after a very happy life. Since we knew this, and also that he was a bachelor and almost alone, those of us who were not his kin were not melted and unstrung by that poignant sense of untimely loss and irreparable removal that makes some funerals so tragic; but death, however it come, is a mystery before which one cannot stand unmoved and unregretful; and I, for one, as I stood there, remembered how easy it would have been oftener to have ascended to his eyrie[8] and lured him out into Hertfordshire[9] or his beloved Epping[10], or even have dragged him away to dinner and whisky punch; and I found myself meditating, too, as the profoundly impressive service rolled on, how melancholy it was that all that storied brain[11], with its thousands of exquisite phrases and its perhaps unrivalled knowledge of Shakespearean philology, should have ceased to be. For such a cessation, at any rate, say what one will of immortality, is part of the sting of death, part of the victory of the grave, which St. Paul[12] denied with such magnificent irony.

And then we filed out into the churchyard, which is a new and very large one, although the church is old, and at a snail's pace, led by the clergyman, we crept along, a little black company, for, I suppose, nearly a quarter of a mile, under the cold grey sky. As I said, many of us were old, and most of us were indoor men, and I was amused to see how close to the head some of us held our hats—the merest barleycorn of interval being maintained for reverence' sake; whereas the sexton and the clergyman had slipped on those black velvet skull-caps which God, in His infinite mercy, either completely overlooks, or seeing, smiles at. And there our old friend was committed to the earth, amid the contending shouts of the football players, and then we all clapped our hats on our heads with firmness (as he would have wished us to do long before), and returned to the town to drink tea in an ancient hostelry[13], and exchange memories, quaint, and humorous, and touching, and beautiful, of the dead.

NOTES

1. **Surrey:** a county of Southeast England
2. **desolating:** grieving
3. **the true rapturous note:** the real delightful characteristic
4. *magnum opus*: (Lat.) great work
5. **Great Portland Street:** a thoroughfare running south to Oxford Street
6. **a good dressing:** (sl.) a dressing down; a severe reprimand
7. **Tasmania:** an island south of Australia
8. **eyrie:** high isolated house
9. **Hertfordshire:** a county in West England
10. **Epping:** Epping Forest, a forest in East England
11. **that storied brain:** that interesting brain of his which held many stories
12. **St. Paul:** an early Christian missionary who died a martyr in Rome (? 67 A.D.)
13. **hostelry:** (arch.) inn

ROBERT TRESSELL

(1870–1911)

Robert Tressell, whose real name was Robert Noonan, was a British worker-novelist. He was born in London on December 5, 1870, of Irish parents, was educated at a grammar school, and began to earn a living when he was fourteen. He was employed as a house-painter and sign-writer in Johannesburg, South Africa, in 1897–1899, lived and worked in Hastings from 1902 to 1910, and died of tuberculosis in a Liverpool hospital on February 3, 1911. He is remembered for his novel *The Ragged Trousered Philanthropists*, composed in 1906–1910. A much reduced edition of the work appeared in 1914, and a still shorter version in 1918. The full text, edited by F. C. Ball, was published in 1955. *The Ragged Trousered Philanthropists* is the first English novel about working-class life written by a worker. The story, told with genuine realism, is a bitter attack on the greed and hypocrisy of the employers and also a satire on the gullibility of the workmen. It is enlivened by the author's comic irony.

PREFACE TO
THE RAGGED TROUSERED PHILANTHROPISTS

In writing this book my intention was to present, in the form of an interesting story, a faithful picture of working-class life—more especially of those engaged in the Building trades—in a small town in the south of England[1].

I wished to describe the relations existing between the workmen and their employers, the attitude and feelings of these two classes towards each other; the condition of the workers during the different seasons of the year, their circumstances when at work and when out of employment: their pleasures, their intellectual outlook, their religious and political opinions and ideals.

The action of the story covers a period of only a little over twelve months, but in order that the picture might be complete it was necessary to describe how the workers are circumstanced at all periods of their lives, from the cradle to the grave. Therefore the characters include women and children, a young boy—the apprentice—some improvers[2], journeymen in the prime of life, and worn-out old men.

I designed to show the conditions resulting from poverty and unemployment: to expose the futility of the measures taken to deal with them and to indicate what I believe to be the only real remedy, namely—Socialism. I intended to explain what Socialists understand by the word "Poverty": to define the Socialist theory of the causes of poverty, and to explain how Socialists propose to abolish poverty.

It may be objected that, considering the number of books dealing with these subjects already existing, such a work as this was uncalled for. The answer is that not only are the majority of people opposed to Socialism, but a very brief conversation with an average anti-socialist is sufficient to show that he does not know what Socialism means. The same is true of all the anti-socialist writers and the "great statesmen" who make anti-socialist speeches: unless we believe that they are all deliberate liars and impostors, who to serve their own interests labour to mislead other people, we must conclude that they do not understand Socialism. There is no other possible explanation of the extraordinary things they write and say. The thing they cry out against is not Socialism but a phantom of their own imagining.

Another answer is that "The Philanthropists" is not a treatise or essay, but a novel. My main object was to write a readable story full of human interest and based on the happenings of everyday life, the subject of Socialism being treated incidentally.

This was the task I set myself. To what extent I have succeeded is for others to say; but whatever their verdict, the work possesses at least one merit—that of being true. I have invented nothing. There are no scenes or incidents in the story that I have not either witnessed myself or had conclusive evidence of. As far as I dared I let the characters express themselves in their own sort of language and consequently some passages may be considered objectionable. At the same time I believe that—because it is true—the book is not without its humorous side.

The scenes and characters are typical of every town in the South of England and they will be readily recognised by those concerned. If the book is published I think it will appeal to a very large number of readers. Because it is true it will probably be denounced as a libel on the working classes and their employers, and upon the religious-professing section of the community. But I believe it will be acknowledged as true by most of those who are compelled to spend their lives amid the surroundings it describes, and it will be evident that no attack is made upon sincere religion....

NOTES

1. **a small town in the south of England:** The place is called Mugsborough in the novel.
2. **improvers:** those who work at low wages to improve their skill

78

SAKI

(PSEUDONYM OF HECTOR HUGH MUNRO, 1870–1916)

Hugh Munro, who used the pen-name of "Saki", was an English short-story writer. He was born at Akyab, Burma, on December 18, 1870, the son of an English senior officer in the Burma Police, and educated at Exmouth and Bedford, Devonshire, from 1882 to 1887. After travelling widely in Europe, he joined the Military Police of Burma in 1893, but ill-health compelled him to resign from it the next year. He settled in London in 1896 as a professional writer. During World War I , he enlisted as a trooper in 1914 and was killed in action in France on November 13, 1916.

Saki is known principally for his witty, bizarre, and satirical short stories collected in such volumes as **Reginald** (1904), **Reginald in Russia and Other Sketches** (1910), **The Chronicles of Clovis** (1911), and **Beasts and Super-Beasts** (1914). His other works include two novels, **The Unbearable Bassington** (1912) and **When William Came** (1913).

THE OPEN WINDOW

"My aunt will be down presently, Mr. Nuttel," said a very self-possessed young lady of fifteen; "in the meantime you must put up with me."

Framton Nuttel endeavoured to say the correct something which should duly flatter the niece of the moment without unduly discounting the aunt that was to come. Privately he doubted more than ever whether these formal visits on a succession of total strangers would do much towards helping the nerve cure[1] which he was supposed to be undergoing.

"I know how it will be," his sister had said when he was preparing to migrate to this rural retreat[2]; "you will bury yourself down there and not speak to a living soul, and your nerves will be worse than ever from moping. I shall just give you letters of introduction to all the people I know there. Some of them, as far as I can remember, were quite nice."

Framton wondered whether Mrs. Sappleton, the lady to whom he was presenting one of the letters of introduction, came into the nice division.[3]

"Do you know many of the people round here?" asked the niece, when she judged that they had had sufficient silent communion.

"Hardly a soul," said Framton. "My sister was staying here, at the rectory you know, some four years ago, and she gave me letters of introduction to some of the people here."

He made the last statement in a tone of distinct regret.

"Then you know practically nothing about my aunt?" pursued the self-possessed young lady.

"Only her name and address," admitted the caller. He was wondering whether Mrs. Sappleton was in the married or widowed state. An undefinable something about the room seemed to suggest masculine habitation.

"Her great tragedy happened just three years ago," said the child; "that would be since your sister's time."

"Her tragedy?" asked Framton; somehow in this restful country spot tragedies seemed out of place.

"You may wonder why we keep that window wide open on an October afternoon," said the niece, indicating a large French window[4] that opened on to a lawn.

"It is quite warm for the time of the year," said Framton; "but has that window got anything to do with the tragedy?"

"Out through that window, three years ago to a day[5], her husband and her two young brothers went off for their day's shooting. They never came back. In crossing the moor to their favourite snipe-shooting ground they were all three engulfed in a treacherous piece of bog[6]. It had been that dreadful wet summer, you know, and places that were safe in other years gave way suddenly without warning. Their bodies were never recovered. That was the dreadful part of it." Here the child's voice lost its self-possessed note and became falteringly human. "Poor aunt always thinks that they will come back some day, they and the little brown spaniel that was lost with them, and walk in at that window just as they used to do. That is why the window is kept open every evening till it is quite dusk. Poor dear aunt, she has often told me how they went out, her husband with his white waterproof coat over his arm, and Ronnie, her youngest brother, singing, 'Bertie, why do you bound?' as he always did to tease her, because she said it got on her nerves. Do you know, sometimes on still, quiet evenings like this, I almost get a creepy feeling that they will all walk in through that window— "

She broke off with a little shudder. It was a relief to Framton when the aunt bustled into the room with a whirl of apologies for being late in making her appearance.

"I hope Vera has been amusing you?" she said.

"She has been very interesting," said Framton.

"I hope you don't mind the open window," said Mrs. Sappleton briskly; "my husband and brothers will be home directly from shooting and they always come in this way. They've been out for snipe in the marshes today, so they'll make a fine mess over my poor carpets. So like you menfolk, isn't it?"

She rattled on cheerfully about the shooting and the scarcity of birds, and the prospects for duck in the winter. To Framton it was all purely horrible. He made a desperate but only partially successful effort to turn the talk on to a less ghastly topic; he was conscious that his hostess was giving him only a fragment of her attention, and her eyes were constantly straying past him to the open window and the lawn beyond. It was certainly an unfortunate coincidence that he should have paid his visit on this tragic anniversary.

"The doctors agree in ordering me a complete rest, an absence of mental excitement, and avoidance of anything in the nature of violent physical exercise," announced Framton, who laboured under the tolerably wide-spread delusion[7] that total strangers and chance acquaintances are hungry for the least detail of one's ailments and infirmities, their cause and cure. "On the matter of diet they are not so much in agreement," he continued.

"No?" said Mrs. Sappleton, in a voice which only replaced a yawn at the last moment. Then she suddenly brightened into alert attention—but not to what Framton was saying.

"Here they are at last!" she cried. "Just in time for tea, and don't they look as if they were muddy up to the eyes!"

Framton shivered slightly and turned towards the niece with a look intended to convey sympathetic comprehension. The child was staring out through the open window with dazed horror in her eyes. In a chill shock of nameless fear Framton swung round in his seat and looked in the same direction.

In the deepening twilight three figures were walking across the lawn towards the window; they all carried guns under their arms, and one of them was additionally burdened with a white coat hung over his shoulders. A tired brown spaniel kept close at their heels. Noiselessly they neared the house, and then a hoarse young voice chanted out of the dusk: "I said, Bertie, why do you bound?"

Framton grabbed wildly at his stick and hat; the hall-door, the gravel-drive, and the front gate were dimly noted stages in his headlong retreat. A cyclist coming along the road had to run into the hedge to avoid imminent collision.

"Here we are, my dear," said the bearer of the white mackintosh coming in through the window; "fairly muddy, but most of it's dry. Who was that who bolted out as we came up?"

"A most extraordinary man, a Mr. Nuttel," said Mrs. Sappleton, "could only talk about his illnesses, and dashed off without a word of good-bye or apology when you arrived. One would think he had seen a ghost."

"I expect it was the spaniel," said the niece calmly; "He told me he had a horror of dogs. He was once hunted into a cemetery somewhere on the banks of the Ganges[8] by a pack of pariah dogs[9], and had to spend the night in a newly dug grave with the creatures snarling and grinning and foaming just above him. Enough to make any one lose their nerve."

Romance at short notice was her specialty.

NOTES

1. **the nerve cure:** the treatment for his nerves
2. **rural retreat:** place of seclusion in the country
3. **came into the nice division:** belonged to the group of nice people
4. **French window:** glazed door serving as both door and window
5. **three years ago to a day:** exactly three years ago
6. **engulfed in a treacherous piece of bog:** swallowed up in a swamp
7. **laboured under the tolerably wide-spread delusion:** suffered from the pretty common false belief
8. **the Ganges:** the great river of North India and Central Bangladesh
9. **pariah dog:** pye-dog or pie-dog, vagabond half-wild dog in India

79

HILAIRE BELLOC

(1870–1953)

Hilaire Belloc was a British essayist, historian, and poet. He was born at Saint-Cloud, near Paris, on July 28, 1870, of a French father and an English mother. Educated at Newman's Oratory School, Birmingham, and at Balliol College, Oxford, he moved to London in 1899 and became a naturalized British citizen in 1902. His literary output was vast and prodigious. He died at Guildford, Surrey, on July 16, 1953.

Some of Belloc's famous works are: ***The Path to Rome*** (1902), an account of a journey undertaken largely on foot; ***The Cruise of the "Nona"*** (1925), an account of a voyage containing many personal reflections; ***Cautionary Tales*** (1907) and ***Sonnets and Verse*** (1924), collections of poetry; ***On Something*** (1911), ***A Conversation with an Angel*** (1928), and ***A Conversation with a Cat*** (1931), collections of essays; ***Belinda*** (1928), a romantic and ironic love story; ***Napoleon*** (1932) and ***Cromwell*** (1934), biographies. Belloc's earlier prose is lucid; his later prose is rhetorical.

ON THINKING

Canon Dimnet[1] of Cambrai lately wrote a little book upon the Art of Thinking. He wrote it, I believe, in the English tongue; but whether it be a translation or from his own pen (which is the more likely, for he writes English like an Englishman), it is a book without the mark of a foreign origin; and perhaps he chose English for his medium on the consideration that thinking had often been condemned during the last century and even lately in the English tongue as a solvent of judgment and instinctive power. I desire to take the title of this book for a text, and to affirm that the business of Thinking has been somewhat under-estimated of late: I desire to proclaim its modest value; to urge its use (in moderation, of course), and to say, even though I must say it timidly, a word in its favour. Come, let us take up the unpopular side, play the devil's advocate[2], and write a cautious brief in defence of this half-forgotten exercise, Thinking.

It was said some months ago by a witty Englishman, in praise of his own people, on returning from some foreign conference or other, that there was written up in flaming red letters upon the cliffs of Dover[3], for all returning men to read:

> Thou shalt not Think.
> Thought is the foe of action.
> Therefore by Thinking men and nations perish.

It is a precept which has been repeated in various forms a thousand times. I doubt its soundness. It still seems to me that Thinking must have some good about it, and that those who decry Thinking are misled by an abuse of terms: an ambiguity. For the word "thinking" is used of musing, as when we say of a man run over by a motor car that he was plunged in thought: and it is used of doubt, as when one says: "I don't think the earth is flat: I know it"; it is used of vain illusion, as of Algernon, who thought himself the hell of a fellow[4]; but it should more properly be used of discernment, so that by thought we see clearly the consequence of things, and by intelligence decide affairs and reach success in conclusions.

I have noticed not infrequently upon my rambles through this world that men (my brethren and similars) would order animals about: great strong animals, such as horned beeves, fierce dogs, and nervous horses: and that they were able so to do (it seemed to me) was due to their superior power of Thought. Observing this result, I have ever felt a certain anxiety lest, if we give up Thinking altogether, we may not become the prey of other nations more exercised in the practice.

Then, also, I have noticed that fame (which we all desire) is not unattached to this art of Thinking. Of close and clear thinkers there occur to me—Euclid[5], Descartes[6], Aquinas, even Cicero, and no one can say that they will be easily forgotten. Newton, by the way, should be added, and Locke, and John Stuart Mill; three prominent men who seemed to have rebelled against the patriotic order emblazoned on the cliffs of Dover.

But, talking of patriotism, there have been other rebels. For instance, not only was political economy founded here in England, where we are told no man should be allowed to Think, but the inferences and deductions of geology as well; for beginnings of Geology are English. Then there is the whole science and practice of the Law, wherein I admit men will continually protest they prefer good honest sense to thinking, but wherein also I notice there is quite a lot of Thinking done, sometimes a little too finely.

Then there are all those of the delicate profession, if I may use that term. I mean, the careers in which men advance by a certain light dexterity in appreciation of others and by the laying of subtle plans. Such are promoters, share-shufflers, big business men, money dealers, sharpers, those of the three-card trick and the great army of snatchers and lifters. Which of them would survive if he did not think—rapidly, clearly, and continually?

When, therefore, I hear the phrase that what is of importance to mortals is character, not intellect, I am so moved that I fall into verse—a thing habitual with versifiers when their emotions are stirred—and on this very matter have I composed a short epic, the first lines of which I will now humbly put before you, reminding you, however, that they are copyright, and reserving the sequel that I may sell it again later:

> I knew a man who used to say
> (Not once, but twenty times a day)
> That in the turmoil and the strife—
> His very phrase—of human life,
> The thing of ultimate effect
> Was character not intellect.
> He therefore was at constant pains
> To atrophy his puny brains,
> And registered success in this
> Beyond the dreams of avarice.

The epic goes on to describe his career, how, when he had become completely imbecile, he was selected for the highest posts in the land, and died—for even such men must die at last—saturated with glory, rolling in money and a model for all of us.

But this poem, I must warn you, was by way of satire, or something the opposite of what it plainly states. It was malicious. It was not to be taken literally, for within my own great soul I knew well that some measure of intellect was essential, even to public life, let alone to the running of a whelk stall[7].

I fancy that those who decry the ancient and honorable practice of Thinking are mixing it up with two things very different, which are called Deduction from Insufficient Premises, and Deduction from False Premises; or perhaps they are mixing it up with Argufying[8]—which of all the detestable habits of man is perhaps the most intolerable—unless, indeed, it be set to work upon matters wholly undiscoverable, wherein it is a very tolerable pastime. Indeed, you may note that men in their cups[9] generally talk metaphysics. And this, let me tell you, is not particularly true of the over-educated, but of all men whatsoever. It was but the other day I heard two men, with no pretence to any excess of culture, shouting at each other in the bar of an inn close against the shores of the Southern Sea, and one of them kept on saying, "How d'you know that what you saw was Bill's ketch, anyhow?" And the other kept on replying, "Why, it stands to reason that if I saw the thing it was there." Wherein was developed all the quarrel of Kant[10] and the sceptics with the peripatetics[11], and of sophists with common sense from the beginning of time; also the dear little fuss about phenomena.

And as for Thinking interfering with action, that is using one word in two senses. It is not Thinking that interferes with action; Thinking decides action. It is hesitation in Thought that interferes with action, it is paralysis in Thought that interferes with action, like that weariness of mind wherein a tune goes on buzzing in one's head. The man who keeps on saying, "Shall I? Shall I not?" is not Thinking, he is cutting the nerve of Thought. And even if Thinking have no practical value (though I stoutly maintain it has), at the least it is an absorbing exercise, bridging over those empty moments when we have neither scandal to talk against our neighbors, nor money to filch from them, nor vapid books to read.

Therefore do I think that I shall continue to think; and whether you think I think right in so thinking I care not, for I think so.

NOTES

1. **Dimnet:** Ernest Dimnet (1866–1954), French author
2. **the devil's advocate:** literally, one who speaks in favour of the devil; here, one who tries to say something good about what is generally unfavourably regarded
3. **Dover:** a seaport of Kent, Southeast England
4. **the hell of a fellow:** (sl.) an excellent fellow
5. **Euclid:** Greek methematician of Alexandria (3rd century B.C.)
6. **Descartes:** René Descartes (1596–1650), French mathematician, physicist, and philosopher
7. **whelk stall:** food stall where whelks are sold
8. **Argufying:** arguing
9. **in their cups:** drunk
10. **Kant:** Immanuel Kant (1724–1804), the great German philosopher, was the founder of the school of transcendental philosophy.
11. **peripatetics:** disciples of Aristotle

AN EXTRACT FROM *THE PATH TO ROME*

At three o'clock the guide knocked at my door, and I rose and came out to him. We drank coffee and ate bread. We put into our sacks ham and bread, and he white wine and I brandy. Then we set out. The rain had dropped to a drizzle, and there was no wind. The sky was obscured for the most part, but here and there was a star. The hills hung awfully above us in the night as we crossed the spongy[1] valley. A little wooden bridge took us over the young Rhône[2], here only a stream, and we followed a path up into the tributary ravine which leads to the Nufenen[3] and the Gries[4]. In a mile or two it was a little lighter, and this was as well, for some weeks before a great avalanche had fallen, and we had to cross it gingerly. Beneath the wide cap of frozen snow ran a torrent roaring. I remembered Colorado[5], and how I had crossed the Arkansaw[6] on such a bridge as a boy. We went on in the uneasy dawn. The woods began to show, and there was a cross where a man had slipped from above that very April and been killed. Then, most ominous and disturbing, the drizzle changed to a rain, and the guide shook his head and said it would be snowing higher up. We went on, and it grew lighter. Before it was really day (or else the weather confused and darkened the sky), we crossed a good bridge, built long ago, and we halted at a shed where the cattle lie in the late summer when the snow is melted. There we rested a moment.

But on leaving its shelter we noticed many disquieting things. The place was a hollow, the end of the ravine—a bowl, as it were; one way out of which is the Nufenen, and the other the Gries.

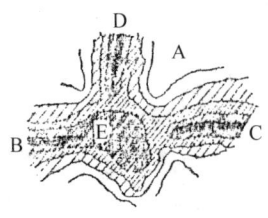

Here it is in a sketch map. The heights are marked lighter and lighter, from black in the valleys to white in the impassable mountains. E is where we stood, in a great cup or basin, having just come up the ravine B. C is the Italian valley of the Tosa, and the neck between it and E is the Gries. D is the valley of the

Ticino, and the neck between E and it is the Nufenen. A is the Crystal Mountain. You may take the necks or passes to be about 8,000, and the mountains 10,000 or 11,000 feet above the sea.

We noticed, I say, many disquieting things. First, all that bowl or cup below the passes was a carpet of snow, save where patches of black water showed, and all the passes and mountains, from top to bottom, were covered with very thick snow; the deep surface of it soft and fresh fallen. Secondly, the rain had turned into snow. It was falling thickly all around. Nowhere have I more perceived the immediate presence of great Death. Thirdly, it was far colder, and we felt the beginning of a wind. Fourthly, the clouds had come quite low down.

The guide said it could not be done, but I said we must attempt it. I was eager, and had not yet felt the awful grip of the cold. We left the Nufenen on our left, a hopeless steep of new snow buried in fog, and we attacked the Gries. For half an hour we plunged on through snow above our knees, and my thin cotton clothes were soaked. So far the guide knew we were more or less on the path, and he went on and I panted after him. Neither of us spoke, but occasionally he looked back to make sure I had not dropped out.

The snow began to fall more thickly, and the wind had risen somewhat. I was afraid of another protest from the guide, but he stuck to it well, and I after him, continually plunging through soft snow and making yard after yard upwards. The snow fell more thickly and the wind still rose.

We came to a place which is, in the warm season, an alp[7]; that is, a slope of grass, very steep but not terrifying; having here and there sharp little precipices of rock breaking it into steps, but by no means (in summer) a matter to make one draw back. Now, however, when everything was still Arctic[8] it was a very different matter. A sheer steep of snow whose downward plunge ran into the driving storm and was lost, whose head was lost in the same mass of thick cloud above, a slope somewhat hollowed and bent inwards, had to be crossed if we were to go any further; and I was terrified, for I knew nothing of climbing. The guide said there was little danger, only if one slipped one might slide down to safety, or one might (much less probably) get over rocks and be killed. I was chattering a little with cold; but as he did not propose a return, I followed him. The surface was alternately slabs of frozen snow and patches of soft new snow. In the first he cut steps, in the second we plunged, and once I went right in and a mass of snow broke off beneath me and went careering[9] down the slope. He showed me how to hold my staff backwards as he did his alpenstock[10]; and use it as a kind of brake in case I slipped.

We had been about twenty minutes crawling over that wall of snow and ice; and it was more and more apparent that we were in for danger[11]. Before we had quite reached the far side, the wind was blowing a very full gale and roared past our ears. The surface snow was whirring furiously like dust before it, past our faces and against them drove the snow-flakes, cutting the air: not falling, but making straight darts and streaks. They seemed like the form of the whistling wind; they blinded us. The rocks on the far side of the slope, rocks which had been our goal when we set out to cross it, had long ago disappeared in the increasing rush of the blizzard. Suddenly as we were still painfully moving on, stooping against the mad wind, these rocks loomed up over as large as houses, and we saw them through the swarming snow-flakes as great hulls are seen through a fog at sea. The guide crouched under the lee of the nearest[12]; I came up close to him and he put his hands to my ear and shouted to me that nothing further could be done—he had so to shout because in among the rocks the hurricane made a roaring sound, swamping the voice.

I asked how far we were from the summit. He said he did not know where we were exactly, but that we could not be more than eight hundred feet from it. I was but that from Italy[13] and I would not admit defeat. I offered him all I had in money to go on, but it was folly in me, because if I had had enough to tempt him and if he had yielded we should both have died. Luckily it was but a little sum. He shook his head. He would not go on, he broke out, for all the money there was in the world. He shouted me to eat and drink, and so we both did.

Then I understood his wisdom, for in a little while the cold began to seize me in my thin clothes. My hands were numb, my face already gave me intolerable pain, and my legs suffered and felt heavy. I learnt another thing (which had I been used to mountains I should have known), that it was not a simple thing to return. The guide was hesitating whether to stay in this rough shelter, or to face the chances of the descent. This terror had not crossed my mind, and I thought as little of it as I could, needing my courage, and being near to breaking down from the intensity of the cold.

It seems that in a ***tourmente*** (for by that excellent name do the mountain people call such a storm) it is always a matter of doubt whether to halt or to go back. If you go back through it and lose your way, you are done for. If you halt in some shelter, it may go on for two or three days, and then there is an end of you.

After a little he decided for a return, but he told me honestly what the chances were, and my suffering from cold mercifully mitigated my fear. But even in that moment, I felt in a confused but very conscious way that I was defeated. I had crossed so many great hills and rivers, and pressed so well on my undeviating arrow-line to Rome, and I had charged this one great barrier manfully where the straight path of my pilgrimage crossed the Alps—and I had failed! Even in that fearful cold I felt it, and it ran through my doubt of return like another and deeper current of pain. Italy was there, just above, right to my hand. A lifting of a cloud, a little respite, and every downward step would have been towards the sunlight. As it was, I was being driven back northward, in retreat and ashamed. The Alps had conquered me.

Let us always after this combat their immensity and their will, and always hate the inhuman guards that hold the gates of Italy, and the powers that lie in wait for men on those high places. But now I know that Italy will always stand apart. She is cut off by no ordinary wall, and Death has all his army on her frontiers.

Well, we returned. Twice the guide rubbed my hands with brandy, and once I had to halt and recover for a moment, failing and losing my hold. Believe it or not, the deep footsteps of our ascent were already quite lost and covered by the new snow since our halt, and even had they been visible, the guide would not have retraced them. He did what I did not at first understand, but what I soon saw to be wise. He took a steep slant downward over the face of the snow-slope, and though such a pitch of descent a little unnerved me, it was well in the end. For when we had gone down perhaps nine hundred feet, or a thousand, in perpendicular distance, even I, half numb and fainting, could feel that the storm was less violent. Another two hundred, and the flakes could be seen not driving in flashes past, but separately falling. Then in some few minutes we could see the slope for a very long way downwards quite clearly; then, soon after, we saw far below us the place where the mountain-side merged easily into the plain of that cup or basin whence we had started.

When we saw this, the guide said to me: "Hold your stick thus, if you are strong enough, and let yourself slide." I could just hold it, in spite of the cold. Life was returning to me with intolerable pain. We shot down the slope almost as quickly as falling, but it was evidently safe to do so, as the end was clearly visible, and had no break or rock in it.

So we reached the plain below, and entered the little shed, and thence looking up, we saw the storm above us; but no one could have told it for what it was. Here, below, was silence, and the terror and raging above seemed only a great trembling cloud occupying the mountain. Then we set our faces down the ravine by which we had come up, and so came down to where the snow changed to rain. When we got right down into the valley of the Rhône, we found it all roofed with cloud, and the higher trees were white with snow, making a line like a tide mark on the slopes of the hills.

I re-entered "The Bear[14]," silent and angered, and not accepting the humiliation of that failure. Then, having eaten, I determined in equal silence to take the road like any other fool; to cross the Furka[15] by a fine high road, like any tourist, and to cross the St. Gothard[16] by another fine high road, as millions had done before me, and not to look heaven in the face again till I was back after my long detour, on the straight road again for Rome.

But to think of it! I who had all that planned out, and had so nearly done it! I who had cut a path across Europe like a shaft, and seen so many strange places!—now to have to recite all the litany of the vulgar; Bellinzona[17], Lugano[18], and this and that, which any railway travelling fellow can tell you. Not till Como[19] should I feel a man again....

Indeed it is a bitter thing to have to give up one's sword.

·   ·   ·   ·   ·   ·   ·

At the foot of the hill I prepared to enter the city, and I lifted up my heart. There was an open space; a tramway; a tram upon it about to be drawn by two lean and tired horses whom in the heat many flies disturbed. There was dust on everything around.

A bridge was immediately in front. It was adorned with statues in soft stone, half-eaten away, but still gesticulating in corruption, after the manner of the seventeenth century. Beneath the bridge there tumbled and swelled and ran fast a great confusion of yellow water: it was the Tiber[20]. Far on the right were white barracks of huge and of hideous appearance; over these the Dome of St. Peter's[21] rose and looked like something newly built. It was of a delicate blue, but made a metallic contrast against the sky.

Then (along a road perfectly straight and bounded by factories, mean houses and distempered walls: a road littered with many scraps of paper, bones, dirt, and refuse) I went on for several hundred yards, having the old wall of Rome before me all the time, till I came right under it at last; and with the hesitation that befits all great actions I entered, putting the right foot first[22] lest I should bring further misfortune upon that capital of all our fortunes.

And so the journey ended.

NOTES

1. **spongy:** wet and soft
2. **the Rhône:** a river in West Europe
3. **the Nufenen:** a mountain pass
4. **the Gries:** a mountain pass
5. **Colorado:** a state of the Central U. S.
6. **the Arkansaw:** a river in the West Central U. S.
7. **alp:** mountain pasture
8. **Arctic:** intensely cold
9. **careering:** moving swiftly along

10. **alpenstock:** staff with an iron tip used by mountain climbers
11. **were in for danger:** were certain to meet with danger
12. **under the lee of the nearest:** under the shelter side of the nearest rock
13. **I was but that from Italy:** I was only that distance (eight hundred feet) from Italy.
14. **The Bear:** a little inn
15. **the Furka:** a mountain pass
16. **the St. Gothard:** a mountain pass
17. **Bellinzona:** a town in South Switzerland
18. **Lugano:** a town in South Switzerland
19. **Como:** a city in Northwest Italy
20. **the Tiber:** a river of Central Italy, upon which Rome stands, flowing 405 km westward from the Tuscan Appenines to the Mediterranean Sea at Ostia
21. **St. Peter's:** the basilica of St. Peter in the Vatican City, the largest church in the world
22. **putting the right foot first:** Some westerners think it unlucky to enter or leave a house with the left foot foremost.

80

MAX BEERBOHM
(1872–1956)

Max Beerbohm was an English essayist, critic, and caricaturist. He was born in London on August 24, 1872, the son of a corn-merchant. Educated at Charterhouse School, London, and at Merton College, Oxford, he pursued a writing career. He lived in Rapallo, Italy, from 1911. When the Second World War broke out, he returned to England and did broadcasting on the B.B.C. He was knighted in 1939, and died on May 20, 1956.

Beerbohm's novel ***Zuleika Dobson*** (1911) is a fanciful burlesque of student life at Oxford in the 1890s. ***A Christmas Garland*** (1912) contains his expert parodies of leading contemporary writers, such as James, Wells, Bennett, and Conrad. His essays were collected in several volumes including ***And Even Now*** (1920), and his broadcast commentaries on England were posthumously published as ***Mainly on the Air*** (1957). ***Around Theatres*** (1953) and ***More Theatres*** (1969) are collections of dramatic criticism. ***Caricatures of Twenty-Five Gentlemen*** (1896), ***The Poets' Corner*** (1904), and ***Rossetti and His Circle*** (1922) are collections of his dexterous and witty cartoons. Max Beerbohm has a cultivated prose style.

SEEING PEOPLE OFF

I am not good at it. To do it well seems to me one of the most difficult things in the world, and probably seems so to you, too.

To see a friend off from Waterloo to Vauxhall[1] were easy enough[2]. But we are never called on to perform that small feat. It is only when a friend is going on a longish[3] journey, and will be absent for a longish time, that we turn up at the railway station. The dearer the friend, and the longer the journey, and the longer the likely absence, the earlier do we turn up, and the more lamentably do we fail. Our failure is in exact ratio to the seriousness of the occasion, and to the depth of our feeling.

In a room, or even on a doorstep, we can make the farewell quite worthily. We can express in our faces the genuine sorrow we feel. Nor do words fail us. There is no awkwardness, no restraint, on either side. The thread of our intimacy has not been snapped. The leave-taking is an ideal one. Why not, then, leave the leave-taking at that? Always, departing friends implore us not to bother to come to the railway station next morning. Always, we are deaf to these entreaties, knowing them to be not quite sincere. The departing friends would think it very odd of us if we took them at their word. Besides, they really do want to see us again. And that wish is heartily reciprocated. We duly turn up. And then, oh then, what a gulf yawns![4] We stretch our arms vainly across it. We have utterly lost touch. We have nothing at all to say. We gaze at each other as dumb animals gaze at human beings. We "make conversation" —and *such* conversation! We know that these friends are the friends from whom we parted overnight. They know that we have not altered. Yet, on the surface, everything is different; and the tension is such that we only long for the guard to blow his whistle and put an end to the farce.

On a cold grey morning of last week I duly turned up at Euston[5], to see off an old friend who was starting for America.

Overnight, we had given him a farewell dinner, in which sadness was well mingled with festivity. Years probably would elapse before his return. Some of us might never see him again. Not ignoring the shadow of the future, we gaily celebrated the past. We were as thankful to have known our guest as we were grieved to lose him; and both these emotions were made manifest. It was a perfect farewell.

And now, here we were, stiff and self-conscious on the platform; and framed in the window of the railway-carriage was the face of our friend; but it was as the face of a stranger—a stranger anxious to please, an appealing stranger, an awkward stranger. "Have you got everything?" asked one of us, breaking the silence. "Yes, everything," said our friend, with a pleasant nod. "Everything," he repeated, with the emphasis of an empty brain. "You'll be able to lunch on the train," said I, though the prophecy had already been made more than once. "Oh, yes," he said with conviction. He added that the train went straight through to Liverpool[6]. This fact seemed to strike us as rather odd. We exchanged glances. "Doesn't it stop at Crewe[7]?" asked one of us. "No," said our friend, briefly. He seemed almost disagreeable. There was a long pause. One of us, with a nod and a forced smile at the traveller, said "Well!" The nod, the smile and the unmeaning monosyllable were returned conscientiously. Another pause was broken by one of us with a fit of coughing. It was an obviously assumed fit, but it served to pass the time. The bustle of the platform was unabated. There was no sign of the train's departure. Release —ours, and our friend's —was not yet.

My wandering eye alighted on a rather portly middle-aged man who was talking earnestly from the platform to a young lady at the next window but one to ours. His fine profile was vaguely familiar to me. The young lady was evidently American, and he was evidently English; otherwise I should have guessed from his impressive air that he was her father. I wished I could hear what he was saying. I was sure he was giving the very best advice; and the strong tenderness of his gaze was really beautiful. He seemed magnetic, as he poured out his final injunctions. I could feel something of his magnetism even where I stood. And the magnetism, like the profile, was vaguely familiar to me. Where had I experienced it?

In a flash I remembered. The man was Hubert Le Ros. But how changed since last I saw him! That was seven or eight years ago, in the Strand[8]. He was then (as usual) out of an engagement⁹, and borrowed half-a-crown¹⁰. It seemed a privilege to lend anything to him. He was always magnetic. And why his magnetism had never made him successful on the London stage was always a mystery to me. He was an excellent actor, and a man of sober habit. But, like many others of his kind, Hubert Le Ros (I do not, of course, give the actual name by which he was known) drifted speedily away into the provinces; and I, like every one else, ceased to remember him.

It was strange to see him, after all these years, here on the platform of Euston, looking so prosperous and solid. It was not only the flesh that he had put on, but also the clothes, that made him hard to recognise. In the old days, an imitation fur coat had seemed to be as integral a part of him as were his ill-shorn¹¹ lantern jaws¹². But now his costume was a model of rich and sombre moderation, drawing, not calling, attention to itself. He looked like a banker. Any one would have been proud to be seen off by him.

"Stand back, please!" The train was about to start, and I waved farewell to my friend. Le Ros did not stand back. He stood clasping in both hands the hands of the young American. "Stand back, sir, please!" He obeyed, but quickly darted forward again to whisper some final word. I think there were tears in her eyes. There certainly were tears in his when, at length, having watched the train out of sight, he turned round. He seemed, nevertheless, delighted to see me. He asked me where I had been hiding all these years; and simultaneously repaid me the half-crown as though it had been borrowed yesterday. He linked his arm in mine, and walked with me slowly along the platform, saying with what pleasure he read my dramatic criticisms every Saturday.

I told him, in return, how much he was missed on the stage. "Ah, yes," he said, "I never act on the stage nowadays." He laid some emphasis on the word "stage," and I asked him where, then, he did act. "On the platform," he answered. "You mean," said I, "that you recite at concerts?" He smiled. "This," he whispered, striking his stick on the ground, "is the platform I mean." Had his mysterious prosperity unhinged¹³ him? He looked quite sane. I begged him to be more explicit.

"I suppose," he said presently, giving me a light for the cigar which he had offered me, "you have been seeing a friend off?" I assented. He asked me what I supposed he had been doing. I said that I had watched him doing the same thing. "No," he said gravely. "That lady was not a friend of mine. I met her for the first time this morning, less than half an hour ago, **here**," and again he struck the platform with his stick.

I confessed that I was bewildered. He smiled. "You may," he said, "have heard of the Anglo-American Social Bureau?" I had not. He explained to me that of the thousands of Americans who annually pass through England there are many hundreds who have no English friends. In the old days they used to bring letters of introduction. But the English are so inhospitable that these letters are hardly worth the paper they are written on. "Thus," said Le Ros, "the A. A. S. B. supplies a long-felt want. Americans are a sociable people, and most of them have plenty of money to spend. The A. A. S. B. supplies them with English friends. Fifty per cent of the fees is paid over to the friends. The other fifty is retained by the A. A. S. B. I am not, alas! a director. If I were, I should be a very rich man indeed. I am only an employé. But even so I do very well. I am one of the seers-off."

Again I asked for enlightenment. "Many Americans," he said, "cannot afford to keep friends in England. But they can all afford to be seen off. The fee is only five pounds (twenty-five dollars) for a single traveller; and eight pounds (forty dollars) for a party of two or more. They send that in to the Bureau, giving the date of their departure, and a description by which the seer-off can identify them on the platform. And then—well, then they are seen off."

"But is it worth it?" I exclaimed. "Of course it is worth it," said Le Ros. "It prevents them from feeling 'out of it.'[14] It earns them the respect of the guard. It saves them from being despised by their fellow-passengers—the people who are going to be on the boat. It gives them a ***footing*** for the whole voyage. Besides, it is a great pleasure in itself. You saw me seeing that young lady off. Didn't you think I did it beautifully?" "Beautifully," I admitted. "I envied you. There was I—" "Yes, I can imagine. There were you, shuffling from head to foot, staring blankly at your friend, trying to make conversation. I know. That's how I used to be myself, before I studied, and went into the thing professionally. I don't say

I'm perfect yet. I'm still a martyr to platform fright. A railway station is the most difficult of all places to act in, as you have discovered for yourself." "But," I said with resentment, "I wasn't trying to act. I really *felt*." "So did I, my boy," said Le Ros. "You can't act without feeling. What's-his-name, the Frenchman—Diderot, yes—said you could; but what did *he* know about it? Didn't you see those tears in my eyes when the train started? I hadn't forced them. I tell you I was **moved**. So were you, I dare say. But you couldn't have pumped up a tear to prove it. You can't express your feelings. In other words, you can't act. At any rate," he added kindly, "not in a railway station." "Teach me!" I cried. He looked thoughtfully at me. "Well," he said at length, "the seeing-off season is practically over. Yes, I'll give you a course. I have a good many pupils on hand already; but yes," he said, consulting an ornate notebook, "I could give you an hour on Tuesdays and Fridays."

His terms, I confess, are rather high. But I don't grudge the investment.

NOTES

1. **from Waterloo to Vauxhall:** Waterloo Station and Vauxhall Station are both on the south bank of the Thames, about two kilometres from each other.
2. **were easy enough:** would be quite easy
3. **longish:** somewhat long
4. **what a gulf yawns:** what a chasm gapes between us
5. **Euston:** Euston Station in London
6. **Liverpool:** a city in Northwest England
7. **Crewe:** a town in Cheshire in Northwest England
8. **the Strand:** a street in West Central London
9. **out of an engagement:** out of a job
10. **half-a-crown:** half-crown, a silver coin worth formerly 2 shillings and 6 pence. It was taken out of circulation in 1970.
11. **ill-shorn:** badly shaven
12. **lantern jaws:** long thin jaws that give a hollow look to the face
13. **unhinged:** deranged or disordered
14. **feeling "out of it":** feeling forlorn, feeling at a loss

81

HENRY MAJOR TOMLINSON

(1873–1958)

H. M. Tomlinson was an English novelist and essayist. He was born in London, the son of a foreman at West India Dock. On the death of his father in 1886 he began to work in an office. He joined the staff of the **Morning Leader** in 1904, wrote for the **Daily News** during World War I, and was literary editor of **The Nation** from 1917 to 1923. He is well remembered for his sea stories. Among his writings may be mentioned: **The Sea and the Jungle** (1912), an account of a voyage up the Amazon River; **London River** (1921) and **A Mingled Yarn** (1953), collections of essays; **Gallions Reach** (1927) and **All Our Yesterdays** (1930), novels.

THE MASTER

This master of a ship I remember first as a slim lad, with a shy smile, and hands that were lonely beyond his outgrown reefer jacket[1]. His cap was always too small for him, and the soiled frontal badge of his line became a coloured button beyond his forelock. He used to come home occasionally—and it was always when we were on the point of forgetting him altogether. He came with a huge bolster in a cab, as though out of the past and nowhere. There is a tradition, a book tradition, that the boy apprenticed to the sea acquires saucy eyes, and a self-reliance always ready to dare to that bleak extreme the very thought of which horrifies those who are lawful and cautious. They know better who live where the ships are. He used to bring his young shipmates to see us, and they were like himself. Their eyes were downcast. They showed no self-reliance. Their shyness and politeness, when the occasion was quite simple, were absurdly incommensurate even with modesty. Their sisters, not nearly so polite, used to mock them.

As our own shy lad was never with us for long, his departure being as abrupt and unannounced as his appearance, we could willingly endure him. But he was extraneous to the household. He had the impeding nature of a new and superfluous piece of furniture which is in the way, yet never knows it, and placidly stays where it is, in its wooden manner, till it is placed elsewhere. There was a morning when, as he was leaving the house, I noticed to my astonishment that he had grown taller than myself. How had that happened? And where? I had followed him to the door that morning because, looking down at his cap which he was nervously handling, he had told me he was going then to an examination. About a week later he announced, in a casual way, that he had got his master's ticket[2]. After the first shock of surprise, caused by the fact that this information was an unexpected warning of our advance in years, we were amused, and we congratulated him. Naturally he had got his certificate as master mariner. Why not? Nearly all the mates we knew got it, sooner or later. That was bound to come. But very soon after that he gave us a genuine surprise, and made us anxious. He informed us, as casually, that he had been appointed master to a ship; a very different matter from merely possessing the licence to command.

We were even alarmed. This was serious. He could not do it. He was not the man to make a command for anything. A fellow who, not so long ago, used to walk a mile with a telegram because he had not the strength of character to face the lady clerk in the post office round the corner, was hardly the man to overawe a crowd of hard characters gathered by chance from Tower Hill[3], socialize them, and direct them successfully in subduing the conflicting elements of a difficult enterprise. Not he. But we said nothing to discourage him.

Of course, he was a delightful fellow. He often amused us, and he did not always know why. He was frank, he was gentle, but that large vacancy, the sea, where he had spent most of his young life, had made him—well, slow. You know what I mean. He was curiously innocent[4] of those dangers of great cities which are nothing to us because we know they are there. Yet he was always on the alert for thieves and parasites. I think he enjoyed his belief in their crafty omnipresence ashore. Proud of his alert and knowing intelligence, he would relate a long story of the way he had not only frustrated an artful shark[5], but had enjoyed the process in perfect safety. That we, who rarely went out in London, never had such adventures, did not strike him as worth a thought or two. He never paused in his merriment to consider the strange fact that to him, alone of our household, such wayside adventures fell. With a shrewd air he would inform us that he was about to put the savings of a voyage into an advertised trap[6] which a country parson would have stepped over without a second contemptuous glance.

He took his ship away. The affair was not discussed at home, though each of us gave it some private despondency. We followed him silently, apprehensively, through the reports in the ***Shipping Gazette***. He made point after point safely—St. Vincent[7], Gibralter, Suez, Aden—after him we went across to Colombo, Singapore, and at length we learned that he was safe at Batavia[8]. He had got that steamer out all right. He got her home again, too. After his first adventure as master he made voyage after voyage with no more excitement in them than you would find in Sunday walks in a suburb. It was plain luck; or else navigation and seamanship were greatly overrated arts.

A day came when he invited me to go with him part of his voyage. I could leave the ship at Bordeaux. I went. You must remember that we had never seen his ship. And there he was, walking with me to the dock from a Welsh railway station, a man in a cheap macintosh, with an umbrella I will not describe, and he was carrying a brown paper parcel. He was appropriately crowned with a bowler hat several sizes too small for him. Glancing up at his profile, I actually wondered whether the turmoil was now going on in his mind over that confession which now he was bound to make: that he was not the master of a ship, and never had been.

There she was, a bulky modern freighter, full of derricks and time-saving appliances, and her funnel lording it over the neighborhood. The man with the parcel under his arm led me up the gangway. I was not yet convinced. I was, indeed, less sure than ever that he could be master of this huge community of engines and men. He did not accord with it.

We were no sooner on deck than a man in uniform, grey-haired, with a seamed and resolute face, which anyone would have recognized at once as a sailor's, approached us. He was introduced as the chief officer. He had a tale of woe: trouble with the dockmaster, with the stevedores, with the cargo, with many things. He did not appear to know what to do with them. He was asking this boy of ours.

The skipper began to speak. At that moment I was gazing at the funnel, trying to decipher a monogram upon it; but I heard a new voice, rapid and incisive, sure of its subject, resolving doubts, and making the crooked straight. It was the man with the brown paper parcel. It was still under his arm—in fact, the parcel contained pink pyjamas, and there was hardly enough paper. The respect of the mate was not lessened by this.

The skipper went to gaze down a hatchway. He walked to the other side of the ship, and inspected something there. Conned her length, called up in a friendly but authoritative way to an engineer standing by an amidship rail above. He came back to the mate, and with an easy precision directed his will on others, through his deputy, up to the time of sailing. He beckoned to me, who also, apparently, was under his august orders, and turned, as though perfectly aware that in this place I should follow him meekly, in all obedience.

Our steamer moved out at midnight, in a drive of wind and rain. There were bewildering and unrelated lights about us. Peremptory challenges were shouted to us from nowhere. Sirens blared out of dark voids. And there was the skipper on the bridge, the lad who caused us amusement at home, with this confusion in the dark about him, and an immense insentient mass moving with him at his will, and he had his hands in his pockets, and turned to tell me what a cold night it was. The pier-head searchlight showed his face, alert, serene, with his brows knitted in a little frown, and his underlip projecting as the sign of the pride of those who look direct into the eyes of an opponent, and care not at all. In my berth that night I searched for a moral for this narrative, but went to sleep before I found it.

NOTES

1. **reefer jacket:** reefing jacket, short thick double-breasted jacket as worn by a sailor
2. **master's ticket:** captain's certificate
3. **Tower Hill:** the hill to the northwest of the Tower of London
4. **innocent:** (here) ignorant
5. **shark:** swindler
6. **an advertised trap:** a fraudulent or risky business
7. **St. Vincent:** a British Associated State in the Caribbean
8. **Batavia:** (a former name for) Djakarta

82

GILBERT KEITH CHESTERTON

(1874–1936)

G. K. Chesterton was an English essayist, novelist, and poet. He was born in London on May 29, 1874, the son of an estate agent, and educated at St. Paul's School and the Slade School of Art, London. He made a reputation for his fecund work in journalism and literature. He died at Beaconsfield on June 14, 1936.

Chesterton contributed weekly essays to **The Illustrated London News** for 25 years from 1905 to 1930. These and other essays from his pen were collected in many volumes, e.g. **All Things Considered** (1908), **Tremendous Trifles** (1909), **A Miscellany of Men** (1912), and **Generally Speaking** (1928). He impresses the reader with his range of interests, his love of argument, his touch of robust humour, and his manipulation of paradox. His most notable works in fiction are **The Man Who Was Thursday** (1908), a rollicking fantasy, and such volumes of detective stories as **The Innocence of Father Brown** (1926). His poetry is various in moods. Some of his critical works—**Robert Browning** (1903), **Charles Dickens** (1906), **Thackeray** (1909), **Bernard Shaw** (1909), **Chaucer** (1932), and **The Victorian Age in Literature** (1913)—are still valuable guides. His prose style is fresh and piquant.

WHAT I FOUND IN MY POCKET

Once when I was very young I met one of those men who have made the Empire what it is[1]—a man in an astracan coat, with an astracan moustache—a tight, black, curly moustache. Whether he put on the moustache with the coat or whether his Napoleonic will enabled him not only to grow a moustache in the usual place, but also to grow little moustaches all over his clothes, I do not know. I only remember that he said to me the following words: "A man can't get on nowadays by hanging about with his hands in his pockets." I made reply with the quite obvious flippancy that perhaps a man got on by having his hands in other people's pockets; whereupon he began to argue about Moral Evolution, so I suppose what I said had some truth in it. But the incident now comes back to me, and connects itself with another incident—if you can call it an incident—which happened to me only the other day.

I have only once in my life picked a pocket, and then (perhaps through some absent-mindedness) I picked my own. My act can really with some reason be so described. For in taking things out of my own pocket I had at least one of the more tense, and quivering emotions of the thief; I had a complete ignorance and a profound curiosity as to what I should find there. Perhaps it would be the exaggeration of eulogy to call me a tidy person. But I can always pretty satisfactorily account for all my possessions. I can always tell where they are, and what I have done with them, so long as I can keep them out of my pockets. If once anything slips into those unknown abysses, I wave it a sad Virgilian farewell[2]. I suppose that the things that I have dropped into my pockets are still there; the same presumption applies to the things that I have dropped into the sea. But I regard the riches stored in both these bottomless chasms with the same reverent ignorance. They tell us that on the last day the sea will give up its dead; and I suppose that on the same occasion long strings of extraordinary things will come running out of my pockets. But I have quite forgotten what any of them are; and there is really nothing (excepting the money) that I shall be at all surprised at finding among them.

 Such at least has hitherto been my state of innocence. I here only wish briefly to recall the special, extraordinary, and hitherto unprecedented circumstances which led me in cold blood, and being of sound mind, to turn out my pockets. I was locked up in a third-class carriage for a rather long journey. The time was towards evening, but it might have been anything, for everything resembling earth or sky or light or shade was painted out as if with a great wet brush by an unshifting sheet of quite colourless rain. I had no books or newspapers. I had not even a pencil and a scrap of paper with which to write a religious epic. There were no advertisements on the walls of the carriage, otherwise I could have plunged into the study of them, for any collection of printed words is quite enough to suggest infinite complexities of mental ingenuity. When I find myself opposite the words "Sunlight Soap" I can exhaust all the aspects of Sun Worship, Apollo, and Summer poetry before I go on to the less congenial subject of soap. But there was no printed word or picture anywhere; there was nothing but blank wood inside the carriage and blank wet without. Now I deny most energetically that anything is, or can be, uninteresting. So I stared at the joints of the walls and seats, and began thinking hard on the fascinating subject of wood. Just as I had begun to realize why, perhaps, it was that Christ was a carpenter, rather than a bricklayer, or a baker, or anything else, I suddenly started upright, and remembered my pockets. I was carrying about with me an unknown treasury. I had a British Museum[3] and a South Kensington[4] collection of unknown curios hung all over me in different places. I began to take the things out.

 The first thing I came upon consisted of piles and heaps of Battersea tram tickets. There were enough to equip a paper chase[5]. They shook down in showers like confetti. Primarily, of course, they touched my patriotic emotions, and brought tears to my eyes; also they provided me with the printed matter I required, for I found on the back of them some short but striking little scientific essays about some kind of pill. Comparatively speaking, in my then destitution, those tickets might be regarded as a small but well-chosen scientific library. Should my railway journey continue (which seemed likely at the time) for a few months longer, I could imagine myself throwing myself into the controversial aspects of the pill, composing replies and rejoinders pro and con upon the data furnished to me. But after all it was the symbolic quality of the tickets that moved me most. For as certainly as the cross of St. George[6] means English patriotism, those scraps of paper meant all that municipal patriotism which is now, perhaps, the greatest hope of England.

The next thing that I took out was a pocket-knife. A pocket-knife, I need hardly say, would require a thick book full of moral meditations all to itself. A knife typifies one of the most primary of those practical origins upon which as upon low, thick pillows all our human civilization reposes. Metals, the mystery of the thing called iron and of the thing called steel, led me off half-dazed into a kind of dream. I saw into the entrails of dim, damp wood, where the first man among all the common stones found the strange stone. I saw a vague and violent battle, in which stone axes broke and stone knives were splintered against something shining and new in the hand of one desperate man. I heard all the hammers on all the anvils of the earth. I saw all the swords of Feudal[7] and all the weals of Industrial war[8]. For the knife is only a short sword and the pocket-knife is a secret sword. I opened it and looked at that brilliant and terrible tongue which we call a blade; and I thought that perhaps it was the symbol of the oldest of the needs of man. The next moment I knew that I was wrong; for the thing that came next out of my pocket was a box of matches. Then I saw fire, which is stronger even than steel, the old, fierce female thing, the thing we all love, but dare not touch.

The next thing I found was a piece of chalk; and I saw in it all the art and all the frescoes of the world. The next was a coin of a very modest value; and I saw in it not only the image and superscription of our own Caesar[9], but all government and order since the world began. But I have not space to say what were the items in the long and splendid procession of poetical symbols that came pouring out. I cannot tell you all the things that were in my pocket. I can tell you one thing, however, that I could not find in my pocket. I allude to my railway ticket.

NOTES

1. **one of those men who have made the Empire what it is:** a British statesman
2. **wave it a sad Virgilian farewell:** bid a sad farewell in the manner of Virgil as to the dead
3. **British Museum:** The British Museum in London contains rich collections of antiquities and the British national library.
4. **South Kensington:** the Victoria and Albert Museum at South Kensington in London
5. **paper chase:** cross-country race in which a runner lays a trail of torn-up paper for others to follow
6. **the cross of St. George:** St. George's Cross, a red cross on a white background. St. George was the patron saint of England.
7. **all the swords of Feudal:** all the weapons of feudal war
8. **all the weals of Industrial war:** all the welfare brought about by the Industrial Revolution
9. **Caesar:** monarch

THE WORSHIP OF THE WEALTHY

There has crept, I notice, into our literature and journalism a new way of flattering the wealthy and the great. In more straightforward times flattery itself was more straightforward; falsehood itself was more true. A poor man wishing to please a rich man simply said that he was the wisest, bravest, tallest, strongest, most benevolent and most beautiful of mankind; and as even the rich man probably knew that he wasn't that, the thing did the less harm. When courtiers sang the praises of a king they attributed to him things that were entirely improbable as that he resembled the sun at noonday, that they had to shade their eyes when he entered the room, that his people could not breathe without him, or that he had with his single sword conquered Europe, Asia, Africa, and America. The safety of this method was its artificiality; between the king and his public image there was really no relation. But the moderns have invented a much subtler and more poisonous kind of eulogy. The modern method is to take the prince or rich man, to give a credible picture of his type of personality, as that he is businesslike, or a sportsman, or fond of art, or convivial, or reserved; and then enormously exaggerate the value and importance of these natural qualities. Those who praise Mr. Carnegie[1] do not say that he is as wise as Solomon and as brave as Mars[2]; I wish they did. It would be the next most honest thing to giving their real reason for praising him, which is simply that he has money. The journalists who write about Mr. Pierpont Morgan[3] do not say that he is as beautiful as Apollo; I wish they did. What they do is to take the rich man's superficial life and manner, clothes, hobbies, love of cats, dislike of doctors, or what not; and then with the assistance of this realism make the man out to be a prophet and a saviour of his kind, whereas he is merely a private and stupid man who happens to like cats or to dislike doctors. The old flatterer took for granted that the king was an ordinary man, and set to work to make him out extraordinary. The newer and cleverer flatterer takes for granted that he is extraordinary, and that therefore even ordinary things about him will be of interest.

I have noticed one very amusing way in which this is done. I notice the method applied to about six of the wealthiest men in England in a book of interviews published by an able and well-known journalist. The flatterer contrives to combine strict truth of fact with a vast atmosphere of awe and mystery by the simple operation of dealing almost entirely in negatives. Suppose you are writing a sympathetic study of Mr. Pierpont Morgan. Perhaps there is not much to say about what he does think, or like, or admire; but you can suggest whole vistas of his taste and philosophy by talking a great deal about what he does not think, or like, or admire. You say of him—"But little attracted to the most recent schools of German philosophy, he stands almost as resolutely aloof from the tendencies of transcendental Pantheism as from the narrower ecstasies of Neo-Catholicism." Or suppose I am called upon to praise the charwoman who has just come into my house, and who certainly deserves it much more. I say:—"It would be a mistake to class Mrs. Higgs among the followers of Loisy[4]; her position is in many ways different; nor is she wholly to be identified with the concrete Hebraism of Harnack[5]." It is a splendid method as it gives the flatterer an opportunity of talking about something else besides the subject of the flattery, and it gives the subject of the flattery a rich, if somewhat bewildered, mental glow, as of one who has somehow gone through agonies of philosophical choice of which he was previously unaware. It is a splendid method; but I wish it were applied sometimes to charwomen rather than only to millionaires.

There is another way of flattering important people which has become very common, I notice, among writers in the newspapers and elsewhere. It consists in applying to them the phrases "simple," or "quiet," or "modest," without any sort of meaning or relation to the person to whom they are applied. To be simple is the best thing in the world; to be modest is the next best thing. I am not so sure about being quiet. I am rather inclined to think that really modest people make a great deal of noise. It is quite self-evident that really simple people make a great deal of noise. But simplicity and modesty, at least, are very rare and royal human virtues, not to be lightly talked about. Few human beings, and at rare intervals, have really risen into being modest; not one man in ten or in twenty has by long wars become simple, as an actual old soldier does by long wars become simple. These virtues are not things to fling about as mere flattery; many prophets and righteous men have desired to see these things and have not seen them. But in the description of the births, lives, and deaths of very luxurious men they are used incessantly and quite without thought. If a journalist has to describe a great politician or financier (the things are substantially the same) entering a room or walking down a thoroughfare, he always says, "Mr. Midas[6] was quietly dressed in a black frock coat, a white waistcoat, and light grey trousers, with a plain green tie and simple flower in his button-hole." As if any one would expect him to have a crimson frock coat or spangled trousers. As if any one would expect him to have a burning Catherine wheel[7] in his button-hole.

But this process, which is absurd enough when applied to the ordinary and external lives of worldly people, becomes perfectly intolerable when it is applied, as it always is applied, to the one episode which is serious even in the lives of politicians. I mean their death. When we have been sufficiently bored with the account of the simple costume of the millionaire, which is generally about as complicated as any that he could assume without being simply thought mad; when we have been told about the modest home of the millionaire, a home which is generally much too immodest to be called a home at all; when we have followed him through all these unmeaning eulogies, we are always asked last of all to admire his quiet funeral. I do not know what else people think a funeral should be except quiet. Yet again and again, over the grave of every one of those sad rich men, for whom one should surely feel, first and last, a speechless pity—over the grave of Beit[8], over the grave of Whiteley[9]—this sickening nonsense about modesty and simplicity has been poured out. I well remember that when Beit was buried, the papers said that the mourning-coaches contained everybody of importance, that the floral tributes were sumptuous, splendid, intoxicating; but, for all that, it was a simple and quiet funeral. What, in the name of Acheron[10], did they expect it to be? Did they think there would be human sacrifice—the immolation of Oriental slaves upon the tomb? Did they think that long rows of Oriental dancing-girls would sway hither and thither in an ecstasy of lament? Did they look for the funeral games of Patroclus[11]? I fear they had no such splendid and pagan meaning. I fear they were only using the words "quiet" and "modest" as words to fill up a page—a mere piece of the automatic hypocrisy which does become too common among those who have to write rapidly and often. The word "modest" will soon become like the word "honourable," which is said to be employed by the Japanese before any word that occurs in a polite sentence, as "Put honourable umbrella in honourable umbrella-stand"; or "condescend to clean honourable boots." We shall read in the future that the modest king went out in his modest crown, clad from head to foot in modest gold and attended with his ten thousand modest earls, their swords modestly drawn. No! if we have to pay for splendour let us praise it as splendour, not as simplicity. When next I meet a rich man I intend to walk up to him in the street and address him with Oriental hyperbole. He will probably run away.

NOTES

1. **Mr. Carnegie:** Andrew Carnegie (1835–1919), the Scottish-born American millionaire and philanthropist
2. **Mars:** Roman god of war
3. **Pierpont Morgan:** Pierpont Morgan (1837–1913) was an American banker and millionaire.
4. **Loisy:** Alfred Firmin Loisy (1857–1940), French biblical critic
5. **Harnack:** Adolf von Harnack (1851–1930), German theologian and church historian
6. **Midas:** (Gr. legend) the Phrygian king with the golden touch
7. **Catherine wheel:** a circular firework
8. **Beit:** Otto Beit (1865–1930), a British financier and art collector
9. **Whiteley:** William Whiteley (1831–1907), a big English merchant
10. **Acheron:** (Gr. myth.) a river in the lower world; also Hades itself
11. **Patroclus:** Achilles' friend in the *Iliad* who was slain by Hector

WILLIAM SOMERSET MAUGHAM

(1874-1965)

W. Somerset Maugham was an English novelist, short-story writer, and playwright. He was born in Paris on January 25, 1874, of English parents, and educated at King's School, Canterbury, 1887-1891, and at Heidelbery University, 1891-1892. He studied medicine at St. Thomas's Hospital, London, from 1892 to 1897, and was qualified as a surgeon in 1897, but never practised. Instead he turned to writing as a career. He served with the Red Cross Ambulance Unit and later with the British Intelligence Corps during World War II, was created a Companion of Honour in 1954, and died at his home in the southeast of France on December 16, 1965.

Maugham's novels include **Liza of Lambeth** (1897), a realistic account of life in the London slums; **Of Human Bondage** (1915), his masterpiece and a semi-autobiographical novel about Philip Carey's lonely boyhood and subsequent adventures; **The Moon and Sixpence** (1919), a narrative of Gauguin's career; **Cakes and Ale** (1930), a tale about a famous novelist and his young wife; and **The Razor's Edge** (1944), the story of an American's experience in India. Maugham excels especially in the short-story form. His short stories were collected in several volumes such as **Orientations** (1899) and **The Trembling of a Leaf** (1921). They are often tightly knit, sharply characterized, and peculiarly realistic. He wrote more than thirty plays. Among his successful plays were ***Lady Frederick*** (1907), a comedy of marriage and money; ***Our Betters*** (1917), a satire on title-hunting; ***The Circle*** (1921), about a romantic young wife; and ***The Constant Wife*** (1926), about a woman's revenge on her unfaithful husband. His ***On a Chinese Screen*** (1922) and ***The Gentleman in the Parlour*** (1930) are entertaining travel books. ***The Summing Up*** (1938) and ***A Writer's Notebook*** (1949) are two of his interesting personal books. His prose style is lucid and terse.

THE LUNCHEON

I caught sight of her at the play, and in answer to her beckoning I went over during the interval and sat down beside her. It was long since I had last seen her, and if someone had not mentioned her name I hardly think I would have recognised her. She addressed me brightly.

"Well, it's many years since we first met. How time does fly! We're none of us getting any younger. Do you remember the first time I saw you? You asked me to luncheon."

Did I remember?

It was twenty years ago and I was living in Paris. I had a tiny apartment in the Latin quarter[1] overlooking a cemetery, and I was earning barely enough money to keep body and soul together. She had read a book of mine and had written to me about it. I answered, thanking her, and presently I received from her another letter saying that she was passing through Paris and would like to have a chat with me; but her time was limited, and the only free moment she had was on the following Thursday; she was spending the morning at the Luxembourg[2] and would I give her a little luncheon at Foyot's afterwards? Foyot's is a restaurant at which the French senators eat, and it was so far beyond my means that I had never even thought of going there. But I was flattered, and I was too young to have learned to say no to a woman. (Few men, I may add, learn this until they are too old to make it of any consequence to a woman what they say.) I had eighty francs (gold francs) to last me the rest of the month, and a modest luncheon should not cost more than fifteen. If I cut out coffee for the next two weeks I could manage well enough.

I answered that I would meet my friend—by correspondence—at Foyot's on Thursday at half-past twelve. She was not so young as I expected and in appearance imposing rather than attractive. She was, in fact, a woman of forty (a charming age, but not one that excites a sudden and devastating passion at first sight), and she gave me the impression of having more teeth, white and large and even, than were necessary for any practical purpose. She was talkative, but since she seemed inclined to talk about me I was prepared to be an attentive listener.

I was startled when the bill of fare was brought, for the prices were a great deal higher than I had anticipated. But she reassured me.

"I never eat anything for luncheon," she said.

"Oh, don't say that!" I answered generously.

"I never eat more than one thing. I think people eat far too much nowadays. A little fish, perhaps. I wonder if they have any salmon."

Well, it was early in the year for salmon and it was not on the bill of fare[3], but I asked the waiter if there was any. Yes, a beautiful salmon had just come in, it was the first they had had. I ordered it for my guest. The waiter asked her if she would have something while it was being cooked.

"No," she answered, "I never eat more than one thing. Unless you have a little caviare. I never mind caviare."

My heart sank a little. I knew I could not afford caviare, but I could not very well tell her that. I told the waiter by all means bring caviare. For myself I chose the cheapest dish on the menu and that was a mutton chop.

"I think you are unwise to eat meat," she said. "I don't know how you can expect to work after eating heavy things like chops. I don't believe in overloading my stomach."

Then came the question of drink.

"I never drink anything for luncheon," she said.

"Neither do I," I answered promptly.

"Except white wine," she proceeded as though I had not spoken. "These French white wines are so light. They're wonderful for the digestion."

"What would you like?" I asked, hospitable still, but not exactly effusive.

She gave me a bright and amicable flash of her white teeth.

"My doctor won't let me drink anything but champagne."

I fancy I turned a trifle pale. I ordered half a bottle. I mentioned casually that my doctor had absolutely forbidden me to drink champagne.

"What are you going to drink, then?"

"Water."

She ate the caviare and she ate the salmon. She talked gaily of art and literature and music. But I wondered what the bill would come to. When my mutton chop arrived she took me quite seriously to task.

"I see that you're in the habit of eating a heavy luncheon. I'm sure it's a mistake. Why don't you follow my example and just eat one thing? I'm sure you'd feel ever so much better for it."

"I am only going to eat one thing," I said, as the waiter came again with the bill of fare.

She waved him aside with an airy gesture.

"No, no, I never eat anything for luncheon. Just a bite, I never want more than that, and I eat that more as an excuse for conversation than anything else. I couldn't possibly eat anything more unless they had some of those giant asparagus. I should be sorry to leave Paris without having some of them."

My heart sank. I had seen them in the shops, and I knew that they were horribly expensive. My mouth had often watered at the sight of them.

"Madame wants to know if you have any of those giant asparagus," I asked the waiter.

I tried with all my might to will him to say no[4]. A happy smile spread over his broad, priest-like face, and he assured me that they had some so large, so splendid, so tender, that it was a marvel.

"I'm not in the least hungry," my guest sighed, "but if you insist I don't mind having some asparagus."

I ordered them.

"Aren't you going to have any?"

"No, I never eat asparagus."

"I know there are people who don't like them. The fact is, you ruin your palate by all the meat you eat."

We waited for the asparagus to be cooked. Panic seized me. It was not a question now how much money I should have left over for the rest of the month, but whether I had enough to pay the bill. It would be mortifying to find myself ten francs short and be obliged to borrow from my guest. I could not bring myself to do that. I knew exactly how much I had, and if the bill came to more I made up my mind that I would put my hand in my pocket and with a dramatic cry start up and say it had been picked. Of course, it would be awkward if she had not money enough either to pay the bill. Then the only thing would be to leave my watch and say I would come back and pay later.

The asparagus appeared. They were enormous, succulent, and appetising. The smell of the melted butter tickled my nostrils as the nostrils of Jehovah[5] were tickled by the burned offerings of the virtuous Semites[6]. I watched the abandoned[7] woman thrust them down her throat in large voluptuous mouthfuls, and in my polite way I discoursed on the condition of the drama in the Balkans. At last she finished.

"Coffee?" I said.

"Yes, just an ice-cream and coffee," she answered.

I was past caring now, so I ordered coffee for myself and an ice-cream and coffee for her.

"You know, there's one thing I thoroughly believe in," she said, as she ate the ice-cream. "One should always get up from a meal feeling one could eat a little more."

"Are you still hungry?" I asked faintly.

"Oh, no, I'm not hungry; you see, I don't eat luncheon. I have a cup of coffee in the morning and then dinner, but I never eat more than one thing for luncheon. I was speaking for you."

"Oh, I see!"

Then a terrible thing happened. While we were waiting for the coffee the head waiter, with an ingratiating smile on his false face, came up to us bearing a large basket full of huge peaches. They had the blush of an innocent girl; they had the rich tone of an Italian landscape. But surely peaches were not in season then? Lord knew what they cost. I knew too—a little later, for my guest, going on with her conversation, absentmindedly took one.

"You see, you've filled your stomach with a lot of meat" —my one miserable little chop— "and you can't eat any more. But I've just had a snack and I shall enjoy a peach."

The bill came, and when I paid it I found that I had only enough for a quite inadequate tip. Her eyes rested for an instant on the three francs I left for the waiter, and I knew that she thought me mean. But when I walked out of the restaurant I had the whole month before me and not a penny in my pocket.

"Follow my example," she said as we shook hands, "and never eat more than one thing for luncheon."

"I'll do better than that," I retorted. "I'll eat nothing for dinner to-night."

"Humorist!" she cried gaily, jumping into a cab. "You're quite a humorist!"

But I have had my revenge at last. I do not believe that I am a vindictive man, but when the immortal gods take a hand in the matter it is pardonable to observe the result with complacency. To-day she weighs twenty-one stone[8].

NOTES

1. **the Latin quarter:** the district of Paris where students and artists live
2. **the Luxembourg:** a palace south of the Seine in Paris
3. **bill of fare:** menu
4. **to will him to say no:** to wish him to say no
5. **Jehovah:** Yahweh, name of God in the Old Testament
6. **Semites:** people speaking a Semitic language; Jews, Arabs, Assyrians, and Phoenicians
7. **abandoned:** unrestrained, excessively extravagant
8. **twenty-one stone:** In Britain a stone (pl. unchanged) is a unit of weight equal to 14 pounds or 6.35 kilograms, used especially of human body weight. 21 stone = 294 pounds.

LUCIDITY, SIMPLICITY, EUPHONY

I have never had much patience with the writers who claim from the reader an effort to understand their meaning. You have only to go to the great philosophers to see that it is possible to express with lucidity the most subtle reflections. You may find it difficult to understand the thought of Hume[1], and if you have no philosophical training its implications will doubtless escape you; but no one with any education at all can fail to understand exactly what the meaning of each sentence is. Few people have written English with more grace than Berkeley[2]. There are two sorts of obscurity that you find in writers. One is due to negligence and the other to wilfulness. People often write obscurely because they have never taken the trouble to learn to write clearly. This sort of obscurity you find too often in modern philosophers, in men of science, and even in literary critics. Here it is indeed strange. You would have thought that men who passed their lives in the study of the great masters of literature would be sufficiently sensitive to the beauty of language to write if not beautifully at least with perspicuity. Yet you will find in their works sentence after sentence that you must read twice to discover the sense. Often you can only guess at it, for the writers have evidently not said what they intended.

Another cause of obscurity is that the writer is himself not quite sure of his meaning. He has a vague impression of what he wants to say, but has not, either from lack of mental power or from laziness, exactly formulated it in his mind and it is natural enough that he should not find a precise expression for a confused idea. This is due largely to the fact that many writers think, not before, but as they write. The pen originates the thought. The disadvantage of this, and indeed it is a danger against which the author must be always on his guard, is that there is a sort of magic in the written word. The idea acquires substance by taking on a visible nature, and then stands in the way of its own clarification. But this sort of obscurity merges very easily into the wilful. Some writers who do not think clearly are inclined to suppose that their thoughts have a significance greater than at first sight appears. It is flattering to believe that they are too profound to be expressed so clearly that all who run may read[3], and very naturally it does not occur to such writers that the fault is with their own minds which have not the faculty of precise reflection. Here again the magic of the written word obtains. It is very easy to persuade oneself that a phrase that one does not quite understand may mean a great deal more than one realizes. From this there is only a little way to go to fall into the habit of setting down one's impression in all their original vagueness. Fools can always be found to discover a hidden sense in them. There is another form of willful obscurity that masquerades as aristocratic exclusiveness. The author wraps his meaning in mystery so that the vulgar shall not participate in it. His soul is a secret garden into which the elect[4] may penetrate only after overcoming a number of perilous obstacles. But this kind of obscurity is not only pretentious; it is short-sighted. For time plays it an odd trick. If the sense is meagre time reduces it to a meaningless verbiage that no one thinks of reading. This is the fact that has befallen the lucubrations of those French writers who were seduced by the example of Guillaume Apollinaire[5]. But occasionally it throws a sharp cold light on what had seemed profound and thus discloses the fact that these contortions of language disguised very commonplace notions. There are few of Mallarmé's[6] poems now that are not clear; one cannot fail to notice that his thought singularly lacked originality. Some of his phrases were beautiful; the materials of his verse were the poetic platitudes of his day.

Simplicity is not such an obvious merit as lucidity. I have aimed at it because I have no gift for richness. Within limits I admire richness in others, though I find it difficult to digest in quantity. I can read one page of Ruskin with delight, but twenty only with weariness. The rolling period[7], the stately epithet, the noun rich in poetic associations, the subordinate clauses that give the sentence weight and magnificence, the grandeur like that of wave following wave in the open sea; there is no doubt that in all this there is something inspiring. Words thus strung together fall on the ear like music. The appeal is sensuous rather than intellectual, and the beauty of the sound leads you easily to conclude that you need not bother about the meaning. But words are tyrannical things, they exist for their meanings, and if you will not pay attention to these, you cannot pay attention at all. Your mind wanders. This kind of writing demands a subject that will suit it. It is surely out of place to write in the grand style[8] of inconsiderable things. No one wrote in this manner with greater success than Sir Thomas Browne, but even he did not always escape this pitfall. In the last chapter of **Hydriotaphia** the matter, which is the destiny of man, wonderfully fits the baroque splendour of the language, and here the Norwich doctor produced a piece of prose that has never been surpassed in our literature; but when he describes the finding of his urns in the same splendid manner the effect (at least to my taste) is less happy. When a modern writer is grandiloquent to tell you whether or no a little trollop shall hop into bed with a commonplace young man you are right to be disgusted.

But if richness needs gifts with which everyone is not endowed, simplicity by no means comes by nature. To achieve it needs rigid discipline. So far as I know ours is the only language in which it has been found necessary to give a name to the piece of prose which is described as the purple patch[9], it would not have been necessary to do so unless it were characteristic. English prose is elaborate rather than simple. It was not always so. Nothing could be more racy, straightforward and alive than the prose of Shakespeare; but it must be remembered that this was dialogue written to be spoken. We do not know how he would have written if like Corneille[10] he had composed prefaces to his plays. It may be that they would have been as euphuistic as the letters of Queen Elizabeth. But earlier prose, the prose of Sir Thomas More[11], for instance, is neither ponderous, flowery nor oratorical. It smacks of the English soil. To my mind King James's Bible[12] has been a very harmful influence on English prose. I am not so stupid as to deny its great beauty. It is majestical. But the Bible is an oriental book. Its alien imagery has nothing to do with us.

Those hyperboles, those luscious metaphors, are foreign to our genius. I cannot but think that not the least of the misfortunes that the Secession from Rome[13] brought upon the spiritual life of our country is that this work for so long a period became the daily, and with many the only, reading of our people. Those rhythms, that powerful vocabulary, that grandiloquence, became part and parcel of the national sensibility. The plain, honest English speech was overwhelmed with ornament. Blunt Englishmen twisted their tongues to speak like Hebrew prophets. There was evidently something in the English temper to which this was congenial, perhaps a native lack of precision in thought, perhaps a naive delight in fine words for their own sake, an innate eccentricity and love of embroidery, I do not know; but the fact remains that ever since, English prose has had to struggle against the tendency to luxuriance. When from time to time the spirit of the language has reasserted itself, as it did with Dryden and the writers of Queen Anne, it was only to be submerged once more by the pomposities of Gibbon and Dr. Johnson. When English prose recovered simplicity with Hazlitt, the Shelley[14] of the letters and Charles Lamb at his best, it lost it again with De Quincey, Carlyle, Meredith[15] and Walter Pater[16]. It is obvious that the grand style is more striking than the plain. Indeed many people think that a style that does not attract notice is not style. They will admire Walter Pater's, but will read an essay by Matthew Arnold without giving a moment's attention to the elegance, distinction and sobriety with which he set down what he had to say.

The dictum that the style is the man[17] is well known. It is one of those aphorisms that say too much to mean a great deal. Where is the man in Goethe[18], in his birdlike lyrics or in his clumsy prose? And Hazlitt? But I suppose that if a man has a confused mind he will write in a confused way, if his temper is capricious his prose will be fantastical, and if he has a quick, darting intelligence that is reminded by the matter in hand of a hundred things, he will, unless he has great self-control, load his pages with metaphor and simile. There is a great difference between the magniloquence of the Jacobean writers[19], who were intoxicated with the new wealth that had lately been brought into the language, and the turgidity of Gibbon and Dr. Johnson, who were the victims of bad theories. I can read every word that Dr. Johnson wrote with delight, for he had good sense, charm and wit. No one could have written better if he had not wilfully set himself to write in the grand style. He knew good English when he saw it. No critic has praised Dryden's prose more aptly. He said of him that he appeared to have no art other than that of expressing with clearness what he thought with ***vigour***. And one of his ***Lives*** he finished with the words: "Whoever wishes to attain an English style, familiar but not coarse, and elegant but not ostentatious, must give his days and nights to the volumes of Addison." But when he himself sat down to write it was with a very different aim. He mistook the orotund for the dignified. He had not the good breeding to see that simplicity and naturalness are the truest marks of distinction.

    For to write good prose is an affair of good manners. It is, unlike verse, a civil art. Poetry is baroque[20]. Baroque is tragic, massive and mystical. It is elemental. It demands depth and insight. I cannot but feel that the prose writers of the baroque period, the authors of King James's Bible, Sir Thomas Browne, Glanville[21], were poets who had lost their way. Prose is a rococo art. It needs taste rather than power, decorum rather than inspiration and vigour rather than grandeur. Form for the poet is the bit and the bridle without which (unless you are an acrobat) you cannot ride your horse; but for the writer of prose it is the chassis without which your car dose not exist. It is not an accident that the best prose was written when rococo[22] with its elegance and moderation, at its birth attained its greatest excellence. For rococo was evolved when baroque had become declamatory and the world, tired of the stupendous, asked for restraint. It was the natural expression of persons who valued a civilized life. Humour, tolerance and horse sense made the great tragic issues that had preoccupied the first half of the seventeenth century seem excessive. The world was a more comfortable place to live in and perhaps for the first time in centuries the cultivated classes could sit back and enjoy their leisure. It has been said that good prose should resemble the conversation of a well-bred man. Conversation is only possible when men's minds are free from pressing anxieties. Their lives must be reasonably secure and they must have no grave concern about their souls. They must attach importance to the refinements of civilization. They must value courtesy, they must pay attention to their persons (and have we not also been told that good prose should be like the clothes of a well-dressed man, appropriate but unobtrusive?), they must fear to bore, they must be neither flippant nor solemn, but always apt; and they must look upon "enthusiasm" with a critical glance. This is a soil very suitable for prose. It is not to be wondered at that it gave a fitting opportunity for the appearance of the best writer of prose that our modern world has seen, Voltaire. The writers of English, perhaps owing to the poetic nature of the language, have seldom reached the excellence that seems to have come so naturally to him. It is in so far as they have approached the ease, sobriety and precision of the great French masters that they are admirable.

Whether you ascribe importance to euphony, the last of the three characteristics that I mentioned, must depend on the sensitiveness of your ear. A great many readers, and many admirable writers, are devoid of this quality. Poets as we know have always made a great use of alliteration. They are persuaded that the repetition of a sound gives an effect of beauty. I do not think it does so in prose. It seems to me that in prose alliteration should be used only for a special reason; when used by accident it falls on the ear very disagreeably. But its accidental use is so common that one can only suppose that the sound of it is not universally offensive. Many writers without distress will put two rhyming words together, join a monstrous long adjective to a monstrous long noun, or between the end of one word and the beginning of another have a conjunction of consonants that almost breaks your jaw. These are trivial and obvious instances. I mention them only to prove that if careful writers can do such things it is only because they have no ear. Words have weight, sound and appearance; it is only by considering these that you can write a sentence that is good to look at and good to listen to.

I have read many books on English prose, but have found it hard to profit by them; for the most part they are vague, unduly theoretical, and often scolding. But you cannot say this of Fowler's ***Dictionary of Modern English Usage***. It is a valuable work. I do not think anyone writes so well that he cannot learn much from it. It is lively reading. Fowler liked simplicity, straightforwardness and common sense. He had no patience with pretentiousness. He had a sound feeling that idiom was the backbone of a language and he was all for the racy phrase. He was no slavish admirer of logic and was willing enough to give usage right of way through the exact demesnes of grammar. English grammar is very difficult and few writers have avoided making mistakes in it. So heedful a writer as Henry James[23], for instance, on occasion wrote so ungrammatically that a schoolmaster, finding such errors in a schoolboy's essay, would be justly indignant. It is necessary to know grammar, and it is better to write grammatically than not, but it is well to remember that grammar is common speech formulated. Usage is the only test. I would prefer a phrase that was easy and unaffected to a phrase that was grammatical. One of the differences between French and English is that in French you can be grammatical with complete naturalness, but in English not invariably. It is a difficulty in writing English that the sound of the living voice dominates the look of the printed word. I have given the matter of style a great deal of thought and have taken great pains. I have written few pages that I feel I could not improve and far too many that I have left with dissatisfaction because, try as I would, I could do no better. I cannot say of myself what Johnson said of Pope: "He never passed a fault unamended by indifference, nor quitted it by despair." I do not write as I want to; I write as I can.

But Fowler had no ear. He did not see that simplicity may sometimes make concessions to euphony. I do not think a far-fetched, an archaic or even an affected word is out of place when it sounds better than the blunt, obvious one or when it gives a sentence a better balance. But, I hasten to add, though I think you may without misgiving make this concession to pleasant sound, I think you should make none to what may obscure your meaning. Anything is better than not to write clearly. There is nothing to be said against lucidity, and against simplicity only the possibility of dryness. This is a risk that is well worth taking when you reflect how much better it is to be bald than to wear a curly wig. But there is in euphony a danger that must be considered. It is very likely to be monotonous. When George Moore[24] began to write, his style was poor; it gave you the impression that he wrote on wrapping paper with a blunt pencil. But he developed gradually a very musical English. He learnt to write sentences that fall away on the ear with a misty languor and it delighted him so much that he could never have enough of it. He did not escape monotony. It is like the sound of water lapping a shingly beach, so soothing that you presently cease to be sensible of it. It is so mellifluous that you hanker for some harshness, for an abrupt dissonance, that will interrupt the silky concord. I do not know how one can guard against this. I suppose the best chance is to have a more lively faculty of boredom than one's readers so that one is wearied before they are. One must always be on the watch for mannerisms and when certain cadences come too easily to the pen ask oneself whether they have not become mechanical. It is very hard to discover the exact point where the idiom one has formed to express oneself has lost its tang. As Dr. Johnson said: "He that has once studiously formed a style, rarely writes afterwards with complete ease." Admirably as I think Matthew Arnold's style was suited to his particular purposes, I must admit that his mannerisms are often irritating. His style was an instrument that he had forged once for all; it was not like the human hand capable of performing a variety of actions.

If you could write lucidly, simply, euphoniously and yet with liveliness you would write perfectly; you would write like Voltaire. And yet we know how fatal the pursuit of liveliness may be; it may result in the tiresome acrobatics of Meredith. Macaulay and Carlyle were in their different ways arresting but at the heavy cost of naturalness. Their flashy effects distract the mind. They destroy their persuasiveness; you would not believe a man was very intent on ploughing a furrow if he carried a hoop with him and jumped through it at every other step. A good style should show no sign of effort. What is written should seem a happy accident. I think no one in France now writes more admirably than Colette[25], and such is the ease of her expression that you cannot bring yourself to believe that she takes any trouble over it. I am told that there are pianists who have a natural technique so that they can play in a manner that most executants can achieve only as the result of unremitting toil, and I am willing to believe that there are writers who are equally fortunate. Among them I was much inclined to place Colette. I asked her. I was exceedingly surprised to hear that she wrote everything over and over again. She told me that she would often spend a whole morning working upon a single page. But it does not matter how one gets the effect of ease. For my part, if I get it at all, it is only by strenuous effort. Nature seldom provides me with the word, the turn of phrase, that is appropriate without being far-fetched or commonplace.

NOTES

1. **Hume:** David Hume (1711-1776) was a Scottish philosopher and historian. His

works include *A Treatise of Human Nature* (1739), *An Enquiry Concerning Human Understanding* (1748), *An Enquiry Concerning the Principles of Morals* (1751), and *A History of Great Britain* (1754–1762).

2. **Berkeley:** George Berkeley (1685–1753) was an Irish bishop and philosopher. His main works include *An Essay Towards a New Theory of Vision* (1709) and *A Treatise Concerning the Principles of Human Knowledge* (1710).

3. **all who run may read:** all people may read and understand while running; all hasty readers may understand

4. **the elect:** the persons who are chosen for excellence

5. **Guillaume Apollinaire:** Guillaume Apollinaire (1880–1918) was a French prose writer, art critic, and poet.

6. **Mallarmé's:** Stéphane Mallarmé (1842–1898), French poet

7. **The rolling period:** the long complex sentence

8. **the grand style:** an elevated style adapted to lofty or sublime subjects

9. **the purple patch:** the incongruously ornate passage

10. **Corneille:** Pierre Corneille (1606–1684), a French dramatist, was noted for his tragedies including *Le Cid* (late 1636 or early 1637).

11. **Sir Thomas More:** Thomas More (1478–1535) was an English statesman and humanist and the author of *Utopia* (1516), a Latin work describing an ideal state.

12. **King James's Bible:** an English translation of the Bible published in 1611 under James I. It is also called the Authorized Version (A. V.) of the Bible, or "The King James Bible".

13. **the Secession from Rome:** the English Reformation in the 16th century

14. **Shelley:** Percy Bysshe Shelley (1792–1822) was an English romantic poet. His works include the long poems *Queen Mab* (1813), *The Revolt of Islam* (1817), and *Adonais* (1821), the verse dramas *The Cenci* (1819) and *Prometheus Unbound* (1820), and such lyrics as *Ode to the West Wind*, *To a Skylark*, and *The Cloud*.

15. **Meredith:** George Meredith (1828–1909) was an English novelist and poet, and the author of *Diana of the Crossways* (1885), *The Ordeal of Richard Feverel* (1859), *The Egoist* (1879), and the long tragic poem *Modern Love*.

16. **Walter Pater:** Walter Horatio Pater (1839–1894), an English essayist and critic, was

noted for his ***Studies in the History of the Renaissance*** (1873) and for his ornate prose style.

17. **the style is the man:** a saying of Georges-Louis Leclerc Buffon (1707–1788), French scientist and writer
18. **Goethe:** Johann Wolfgang von Goethe (1749–1832), Germany's greatest poet. He wrote lyric poems, dramas, and novels. His major works include ***Faust*** (1808, 1832), ***The Sorrows of Young Werther*** (1774), and ***Wilhelm Meister*** (1829).
19. **the Jacobean writers:** the writers of the period of James I (1603–1625), the writers of the early 17th century
20. **baroque:** ornate or sumptuous (style of art and literature in the 17th century)
21. **Glanville:** Joseph Glanville (1636–1680) was an English writer on philosophy and religion. His first book, ***The Vanity of Dogmatizing*** (1661), was written in an image-laden style. His prose became plainer in his later works.
22. **rococo:** light, gay, and graceful (style of art and literature in the 18th century)
23. **Henry James:** Henry James (1843–1916) was an American novelist, short-story writer, and critic. He settled in Europe from 1875 and was naturalized as a British subject in 1915. Among his novels are ***The Portrait of a Lady*** (1881), ***The Wings of the Dove*** (1902), ***The Ambassadors*** (1903), and ***The Golden Bowl*** (1904).
24. **George Moore:** George Moore (1852–1933) was an Irish novelist and the author of ***Esther Waters*** (1894), ***The Brook Kerith*** (1916), etc.
25. **Colette:** Sidonie Gabrielle Colette (1873–1954), French novelist

84

WINSTON LEONARD SPENCER CHURCHILL

(1874–1965)

Winston L. S. Churchill was a British statesman, journalist, and historian. He was born at Blenheim Palace, Oxfordshire, on November 30, 1874, the eldest son of Lord Randolph Churchill. Educated at Harrow and Sandhurst, he entered the army in 1895, and saw several campaigns for the next few years. His political career began in 1900, and he was a Conservative M. P. for about sixty years. For half a century he held various ministerial and cabinet offices, culminating in being Prime Minister from 1940 to 1945 and from 1951 to 1953. During the Second World War, Britain, led by Churchill, and her allies fought against Hitler and won ultimate victory. In 1953 he was created a Knight of the Garter and awarded the Nobel Prize for Literature. He died on January 24, 1965.

Among Churchill's numerous works should be mentioned: **Lord Randolph Churchill** (1906–1907), a life of his father; **My Early Life** (1930), his autobiography; **Marlborough** (4 vols, 1933–1938), a life of his ancestor; **War Speeches, 1940–1945** (1946), moving documents; **The Second World War** (6 vols, 1948–1954), his masterpiece; and **A History of the English-Speaking Peoples** (4 vols, 1956–1958), a book covering a wide stretch of time and space. His prose often shows a florid and picturesque style, but it is sometimes eloquently simple.

THE NORMAN CONQUEST

William the Conqueror's[1] invasion of England was planned like a business enterprise. The resources of Normandy[2] were obviously unequal to the task; but the Duke's name was famous throughout the feudal world, and the idea of seizing and dividing England commended itself to the martial nobility of many lands. The barons of Normandy had refused to countenance the enterprise officially. It was the Duke's venture, and not that of Normandy. But the bulk[3] of them hastened to subscribe their quota of knights and ships. Brittany[4] sent a large contingent. It must be remembered that some of the best stocks from Roman Britain had found refuge there, establishing a strong blood strain which had preserved a continuity with the Classic Age and with the British race. But all France was deeply interested. Mercenaries came from Flanders[5], and even from beyond the Alps; Normans from South Italy and Spain, nobles and knights, answered the advertisement.

The shares in this enterprise were represented by knights or ships, and it was plainly engaged that the lands of the slaughtered English would be divided in proportion to the contributions, subject, of course, to a bonus for good work in the field. During the summer of 1066, this great gathering of audacious buccaneers—land-hungry, war-hungry[6]—assembled in a merry company around St. Valéry[7], at the mouth of the Somme[8]. Ships had been built in all the French ports from the spring onwards, and by the beginning of August nearly seven hundred vessels and about seven thousand men, of whom the majority were persons of rank and quality, were ready to follow the renowned Duke and share the lands and wealth of England.

But the winds were contrary. For six whole weeks there was no day when the south wind blew. The heterogeneous army, bound by no tie of feudal allegiance, patriotism, or moral theme, began to bicker and grumble. Only William's repute as a managing director and the rich pillage to be expected held them together.

At length extreme measures had to be taken with the weather. The bones of St. Edmund[9] were brought from the church of St. Valéry and carried with military and religious pomp along the seashore. This proved effective, for the very next day the wind changed, not indeed to the south, but to the southwest. William thought this sufficient, and gave the signal.

The whole fleet put to sea[10], with all their stores, weapons, coats of mail, and great numbers of horses. Special arrangements were made to keep the fleet together. From the point of rendezvous at the mouth of the Somme, the Duke kept a lamp of special brilliancy upon the masthead of his ship that night. The next morning all steered towards the English coast. The Duke, who had a faster vessel, soon found himself alone in mid-Channel. He hove to[11] and breakfasted with his staff "as if he had been in his own hall." Wine was not lacking, and after the meal he expressed himself in enthusiastic terms upon his great undertaking and the prizes and profit it would bring to all engaged therein.

On September 28, the fleet hove in sight[12], and all came safely to anchor in Pevensey Bay[13]. There was no opposition to the landing. The local fyrd[14] had been called out this year four times already to watch the coast, and having, in true English style, come to the conclusion that the danger was past because it had not yet arrived, had gone back to their homes. William landed, as the tale goes, and fell flat on his face as he stepped out of the boat. "See," he said, turning the omen into a favorable channel, "I have taken England with both my hands." He occupied himself with organizing his army, raiding for supplies in Sussex[15], and building some defensive works for the protection of his fleet and base. Thus a fortnight passed.

Meanwhile in London, King Harold[16] gathered all the forces he could, and most of the principal persons in Wessex and Kent hastened to join his standard, bringing their retainers and local militia with them. Harold marched towards Pevensey[17], and in the evening of October 13, took up his position upon the slope of a hill which barred the direct march upon the capital.

The military opinion of those as of these days has criticized his staking all upon an immediate battle. Some have suggested that he should have used the tactics which eleven hundred years before the ancient Britons had employed against Caesar. But these critics overlook the fact that whereas the Roman army consisted only of infantry, and the British only of charioteers and horsemen, Duke William's was essentially a cavalry force assisted by archers, while Harold had nothing but foot soldiers who used horses only as transport. It is one thing for mounted forces to hover round and harry an infantry army, and the opposite for bands of foot soldiers to use these tactics against cavalry.

King Harold had great confidence in his redoubtable axe-men[18], and it was in good heart that he formed his shield-wall on the morning of October 14. There is a great dispute about the numbers engaged. Some modern authorities suppose the battle was fought by five or six thousand Norman knights and men-at-arms[19], with a few thousand archers, against eight to ten thousand axe- and spearmen, and the numbers on both sides may have been fewer. However it may be, at the first streak of dawn William set out from his camp at Pevensey, resolved to put all to the test; and Harold, eight miles away, awaited him in resolute array.

As the battle began, Ivo Taillefer, the minstrel knight who had claimed the right to make the first attack, advanced up the hill on horseback, throwing his lance and sword into the air and catching them before the astonished English. He then charged deep into the English ranks, and was slain. The cavalry charges of William's mail-clad knights, cumbersome in maneuvre, beat in vain upon the dense, ordered masses of the English. Neither the arrow hail[20] nor the assaults of the horsemen could prevail against them. William's left wing of cavalry was thrown into disorder, and retreated rapidly down the hill. On this the troops on Harold's right, who were mainly the local fyrd, broke their ranks in eager pursuit. William, in the centre, turned his disciplined squadrons upon them and cut them to pieces. The Normans then re-formed their ranks and began a second series of charges upon the English masses, subjecting them in the intervals to severe archery.

It has often been remarked that this part of the action resembles the afternoon at Waterloo[21], when Ney's [22]cavalry exhausted themselves upon the British squares, torn by artillery in the intervals. In both cases the tortured infantry stood unbroken. Never, it was said, had the Norman knights met foot soldiers of this stubbornness.

They were utterly unable to break through the shield-walls, and they suffered serious losses from deft blows of the axe-men, or from javelins, or clubs hurled from the ranks behind. But the arrow showers took a cruel toll. So closely were the English wedged that the wounded could not be removed, and the dead scarcely found room in which to sink upon the ground.

The autumn afternoon was far spent before any result had been achieved, and it was then that William adopted the time-honoured ruse of a feigned retreat[23]. He had seen how readily Harold's right had quitted their positions in pursuit after the first repulse of the Normans. He now organized a sham retreat in apparent disorder, while keeping a powerful force in his own hands. The housecarls[24] around Harold preserved their discipline and kept their ranks, but the sense of relief to the less trained forces after these hours of combat was such that seeing their enemy in flight proved irresistible.

They surged forward on the impulse of victory, and when halfway down the hill, they were savagely slaughtered by William's horsemen. There remained, as the dusk grew, only the valiant bodyguard who fought round the King and his standard. His brothers, Gyrth and Leofwine, had already been killed. William now directed his archers to shoot high into the air, so that the arrows would fall behind the shield-wall, and one of these pierced Harold in the right eye, inflicting a mortal wound. He fell at the foot of the royal standard, unconquerable except by death, which does not count in honor. The hard-fought battle was now decided. The last formed body of troops was broken, though by no means overwhelmed. They withdrew into the woods behind, and William, who had fought in the foremost ranks and had three horses killed under him, could claim the victory. Nevertheless, the pursuit was heavily checked. There is a sudden deep ditch on the reverse slope of the hill of Hastings[25], into which large numbers of Norman horsemen fell, and in which they were butchered by the infuriated English lurking in the woods.

The dead King's naked body, wrapped only in a robe of purple, was hidden among the rocks of the bay. His mother in vain offered the weight of the body in gold for permission to bury him in holy ground. The Norman Duke's answer was that Harold would be more fittingly laid upon the Saxon shore which he had given his life to defend. The body was later transferred to Waltham Abbey[26], which he had founded. Although here the English once again accepted conquest and bowed in a new destiny, yet ever must the name of Harold be honored in the Island for which he and his famous housecarls fought indomitably to the end.

NOTES

1. **William the Conqueror:** William I (1027–1087), known as William the Conqueror, was Duke of Normandy (1035–1087) and King of England (1066–1087). He invaded England in 1066 and defeated Harold II at Hastings.
2. **Normandy:** a former province of Northwest France, on the English Channel
3. **bulk:** greater part
4. **Brittany:** a region of Northwest France, settled by Celtic refugees from Great Britain during the Anglo-Saxon invasions
5. **Flanders:** a medieval principality in the southwest part of the Low Countries, now divided between Belgium, France, and Holland
6. **land-hungry, war-hungry:** greedy for land and greedy for war
7. **St. Valéry:** St-Valéry-sur-Somme, a town in North France
8. **the Somme:** a river in North France which flows into the English Channel
9. **St. Edmund:** Edmund, Martyr and Saint, was the last King of East Anglia, who began to reign in 855 and was killed by the Danes in 870.
10. **put to sea:** left the port
11. **hove to:** (of a ship) came to a standstill
12. **hove in sight:** (of a ship or ships) became visible
13. **Pevensey Bay:** a small bay in Southeast England
14. **fyrd:** militia of old English times
15. **Sussex:** (in Anglo-Saxon times) the kingdom of the South Saxons in Southeast England
16. **King Harold:** Harold II (1022–1066)
17. **Pevensey:** a small seaport in Southeast England
18. **axe-men:** axe-wielding fighters
19. **men-at-arms:** (arch.) soldiers
20. **the arrow hail:** the shower of arrows

21. **Waterloo:** a village south of Brussels, Belgium, where on 18 June 1815 British and Prussian forces under the Duke of Wellington and Blucher defeated the French under Napoleon
22. **Ney:** Michael Ney (1769−1815), French marshal
23. **the time-honoured ruse of feigned retreat:** the traditional trick of pretended retreat
24. **housecarls:** (in medieval Europe) household warriors
25. **Hastings:** the site of the Battle of Hastings which was fought on 14 October 1066. Hastings is in Southeast England.
26. **Waltham Abbey:** a church in Essex, Southeast England

A FEW HOBBIES

A gifted American psychologist has said, "Worry is a spasm of the emotion[1]; the mind catches hold of something and will not let it go." It is useless to argue with the mind in this condition. The stronger the will, the more futile the task. One can only gently insinuate something else into its convulsive grasp. And if this something else is rightly chosen, if it is really attended by the illumination of another field of interest, gradually, and often quite swiftly, the old undue grip relaxes and the process of recuperation and repair begins.

The cultivation of a hobby and new forms of interest is therefore a policy of first importance to a public man. But this is not a business that can be undertaken in a day or swiftly improvised by a mere command of the will. The growth of alternative mental interests is a long process. The seeds must be carefully chosen; they must fall on good ground; they must be sedulously tended[2], if the vivifying fruits are to be at hand when needed.

To be really happy and really safe, one ought to have at least two or three hobbies, and they must all be real. It is no use starting late in life to say: "I will take an interest in this or that." Such an attempt only aggravates the strain of mental effort. A man may acquire great knowledge of topics unconnected with his daily work, and yet hardly get any benefit or relief. It is no use doing what you like; you have got to like what you do. Broadly speaking, human beings may be divided into three classes: those who are toiled to death, those who are worried to death, and those who are bored to death. It is no use offering the manual labourer, tired out with a hard week's sweat and effort, the chance of playing a game of football or baseball on Saturday afternoon. It is no use inviting the politician or the professional or business man, who has been working or worrying about serious things for six days, to work or worry about trifling things at the week-end.

As for the unfortunate people who can command everything they want, who can gratify every caprice and lay their hands on almost every object of desire—for them a new pleasure, a new excitement is only an additional satiation. In vain they rush frantically round from place to place, trying to escape from avenging boredom by mere clatter and motion. For them discipline in one form or another is the most hopeful path.

It may also be said that rational, industrious, useful human beings are divided into two classes: first, those whose work is work and whose pleasure is pleasure; and secondly, those whose work and pleasure are one. Of these the former are the majority. They have their compensations. The long hours in the office or the factory bring with them as their reward, not only the means of sustenance, but a keen appetite for pleasure even in its simplest and most modest forms. But Fortune's favoured children belong to the second class. Their life is a natural harmony. For them the working hours are never long enough. Each day is a holiday, and ordinary holidays when they come are grudged as enforced interruptions in an absorbing vocation. Yet to both classes the need of an alternative outlook, of a change of atmosphere, of a diversion of effort, is essential. Indeed, it may well be that those whose work is their pleasure are those who most need the means of banishing it at intervals from their minds.

NOTES

1. **a spasm of the emotion:** an emotional convulsion
2. **sedulously tended:** looked after assiduously

85

JAMES JEANS

(1877–1946)

James Jeans was an English mathematician, physicist, and astronomer. A Londoner educated at Merchant Taylors' School and Cambridge University, he worked as Professor of Applied Mathematics at Princeton University, U. S. (1905–1909), Lecturer in Applied Mathematics at Cambridge University (1910–1912), Secretary of the Royal Society (1919–1929), and Professor of Astronomy at the Royal Institution (1935–1946). He contributed to the dynamical theory of gases and the mathematical theory of electricity and magnetism, and developed, with Harold A. Jeffreys, the tidal hypothesis of the origin of the earth. He was knighted in 1928. His numerous books include ***Radiation and the Quantum Theory*** (1914), ***Astronomy and Cosmogony*** (1928), ***The Universe Around Us*** (1929), ***The Mysterious Universe*** (1930), ***The Stars in Their Courses*** (1931), and ***Physics and Philosophy*** (1942). Some of his popular works made an extremely wide appeal. His prose style is attractively lucid.

THE FUTURE OF THE EARTH

Apart from accidents, we have seen that if the solar system is left to the natural course of evolution, the earth is likely to remain a possible abode of life for something of the order of[1] a million million years to come.

This is some five hundred times the past age of the earth, and over three million times the period through which humanity has so far existed on earth. Let us try to see these times in their proper proportion by the help of yet another simple model. Take a postage stamp, and stick it on to a penny. Now climb Cleopatra's Needle[2] and lay the penny flat, postage-stamp uppermost, on top of the obelisk. The height of the whole structure may be taken to represent the time that has elapsed since the earth was born. On this scale, the thickness of the penny and postage-stamp together represents the time that man has lived on earth. The thickness of the postage-stamp represents the time he has been civilised, the thickness of the penny representing the time he lived in an uncivilised state. Now stick another postage-stamp on top of the first to represent the next 5000 years of civilisation, and keep sticking on postage-stamps until you have a pile as high as Mont Blanc[3]. Even now the pile forms an inadequate representation of the length of the future which, so far as astronomy can see, probably stretches before civilised humanity, unless an accident cuts it short. The first postage-stamp was the past of civilisation; the column higher than Mont Blanc is its future. Or, to look at it in another way, the first postage-stamp represents what man has already achieved; the pile which outtops Mont Blanc represents what he may achieve, if his future achievement is proportional to his time on earth.

Yet we have seen that we cannot count on such a length of future with any certainty. Accidents may happen to the race as to the individual. Celestial collisions may occur; shrinking into a white dwarf, the sun may freeze terrestrial life out of existence; bursting out as a nova it may scorch our race to death. Accident may replace our Mont Blanc of postage-stamps by a truncated column of only a fraction of the height of Mont Blanc. Even so, there is a prospect of tens of thousands of millions of years before our race. And the human mind, as apart from the mind of the mathematician, can hardly distinguish clearly between such a period as this and the million million years to which we may look forward if accidents do not overtake us. For all practical purpose the only statement that conveys any real meaning is that our race may look forward to occupying the earth for a time incomparably longer than any we can imagine.

Looked at in terms of space, the message of astronomy is at best one of melancholy grandeur and oppressive vastness. Looked at in terms of time, it becomes one of almost endless possibility and hope. As denizens of the universe we may be living near its end rather than its beginning, for it seems likely that most of the universe had melted into radiation before we appeared on the scene. But as inhabitants of the earth, we are living at the very beginning of time. We have come into being in the fresh glory of the dawn, and a day of almost unthinkable length stretches before us with unimaginable opportunities for accomplishment. Our descendants of far-off ages, looking down this long vista of time from the other end, will see our present age as the misty morning of the world's history; our contemporaries of to-day will appear as dim heroic figures who fought their way through jungles of ignorance, error, and superstition to discover truth, to learn how to harness the forces of Nature, and to make a world worthy for mankind to live in. We are still too much engulfed in the greyness of the morning mists to be able to imagine, however vaguely, how this world of ours will appear to those who will come after us and see it in the full light of day. But by what light we have, we seem to discern that the main message of astronomy is one of hope to the race and of responsibility to the individual—of responsibility because we are drawing plans and laying foundations for a longer future than we can well imagine.

NOTES

1. **something of the order of:** about the size or quantity of
2. **Cleopatra's Needle:** either of the two Egyptian granite obelisks. One was brought to England in 1878 and stood on the Thames Embankment, and the other was moved to Central Park, New York, in 1880.
3. **Mont Blanc:** the highest mountain in the Alps. It is 4810 m. high.

86

ROBERT LYND

(1879–1949)

Robert Lynd was an Irish essayist. He was born in Belfast on April 20, 1879. Educated at Queen's College, Belfast, he migrated to England in 1901 and worked as a journalist. For many years he contributed to *The Daily News* and then *The News Chronicle*. He was especially known for his weekly essays in the *Nation* and then in the *New Statesman*, signed "Y.Y." He died in London on October 6, 1949. His essays were collected in many volumes, such as *The Pleasures of Ignorance* (1921), *Selected Essays* (1923), *The Green Man* (1928), *Books and Authors* (1929), *In Defence of Pink* (1937), and *Life's Little Oddities* (1941). They were personal reflections on life and letters, showing good sense, deep humour, and a limpid, neat style. He could tolerate many things, but detested bunkum and brutality.

BACK TO THE DESK

There is something peculiarly restful in returning to work after a holiday. After the rigours of doing nothing for a month, how peaceful it seems to be sitting once more before a desk in an armchair! Work, I sometimes think, is the ultimate recreation of the really lazy man.

The first thing I do when I return to work after a holiday is to have breakfast sent up to me in bed. How different from all those miseries of early rising which are almost inseparable from a holiday! It may be retorted that it is perfectly easy to arrange to have one's breakfast in bed in any seaside hotel in England; but the fact is, when I am on holiday, my conscience will not permit this. If I lay late in bed at the seaside, I should feel that I was wasting the best part of the day. In London, I am thankful to say, there is no such thing as a best part of the day—or, if there is, it occurs at a much later hour than at the seaside.

Apart from this, the hotel breakfast is a much more formidable affair than breakfast at home. The menu which the waiter hands you is an invitation to gluttony before you are quite awake. If you were in full possession of your senses you would wave the thing away and ask for a kipper or a boiled egg. As it is, your will is so weak as a result of the soporific effects of early rising that you yield to temptation and go through a breakfast that would satisfy Carnera[1] after a week's fasting.

From that point on your troubles multiply. After breakfast, since you are on holiday, you cannot sit down in a chair, like a rational being, and work or otherwise enjoy yourself. Some demon inside you drives you out into the open air. This usually involves walking—one of the most exhausting of exercises, if persisted in by the novice for long periods. The best view of the bay may be from a chair in a window of your hotel; but, when on a holiday, you cannot help believing that it is round the corner, and you set out for it, however steep the local hills may be. The bay was certainly extraordinarily beautiful, with white sails moving across its ruffled surface under the sun, but, as I trudged along its coast road on foot, I could not help wishing at times that some less strenuous form of exercise than walking had been discovered. I reckon that during the first week of the holiday my pedestrian hours were from 10 A.M. to 10 P.M., with intervals for meals and one ride on a merry-go-round.

Professor Julian Huxley[2] has been writing on the necessity of organising leisure, and, no doubt, when this is done, a local committee at every seaside town will take the sedentary visitor in hand and show him how he can enjoy himself without tiring himself. I certainly do not know how. I cannot enjoy myself on a holiday without ending the day as a physical wreck. Golf is an innocent-looking game; but I must say that if I felt as exhausted after a day's work in the office as I did after a day's golf in Cornwall[3] I should denounce my employers as tyrants. You may guess how strenuous the golf was from the fact that on the first morning my opponent and I took two hours and a half to get round nine holes. It was real hammer-and-tongs stuff[4], with no quarter given to the ball, the air, or anything else.

I think the most exhausting part of golf, perhaps, is the stooping required to take the balls out of the hole. This unnatural posture, when practised repeatedly, overworks a number of hitherto unsuspected sinews, which protest at the end of the day by simulating a number of the symptoms of lumbago and sciatica. And the dreadful thing is that, when once one has begun, one cannot stop playing. There is no hope of relief except in a return to work.

Yet there was plenty to occupy an indolent man, if one had had the strength of character to be indolent. There were curlews and sanderlings and ringed plovers on the tide-deserted sands, but it takes a man of powerful will to trouble about curlews when there is a golf-course within reach. Later, in Devonshire[5], there were buzzards mewing overhead and a raven croaking, but who with a wild and never-to-be-fulfilled dream of getting on to the first green in one has time to pay much attention to buzzards and ravens?

I used to be able to take a restful holiday when I was young, but, now that I am middle-aged and believe in the virtue of fresh air and exercise and all that sort of thing, I can no more take a restful holiday than I could swim the Atlantic.

Now that I am back at work, I am beginning to feel much better. Every muscle is already subsiding into a delicious inactivity. I am borne lazily from place to place on the top of a bus instead of working like a navvy in pursuit of a small white ball. I can watch the pink clouds above the setting sun from the office window without regarding them as an invitation to take yet another unnecessary walk. I can do all my work sitting and even with my feet on the table. The only muscles that I need exercise are the muscles of my fingers and my wrist as I guide the pencil across the paper; and a great golfer or oarsman would think nothing of this. A lift is provided to save me from the drudgery of climbing, so common on a holiday. I can go home in the evening and not budge out of the house again till bedtime with a perfectly clear conscience.

Who can deny that there is much to be said for the working life? To have escaped from the tyranny of fresh air and exercise—is not this, perhaps, to have gained something? Once more I am my own master—more or less. More, at least, than during any holiday I have had for years.

NOTES

1. **Carnera:** the name of a heavy-weight boxer
2. **Julian Huxley:** Julian Huxley (1887−1975) was an English biologist.
3. **Cornwall:** a county of Southwest England
4. **hammer-and-tongs stuff:** strenuous activity
5. **Devonshire:** a county of Southwest England

87

LYTTON STRACHEY

(1880–1932)

Lytton Strachey was an English biographer and essayist. He was born in London, the son of a general, and educated at Leamington College, Liverpool University, and at Trinity College, Cambridge. His first book was **Landmarks in French Literature** (1912), written in a flamboyant style but containing illuminating matter. The first work that won him fame was **Eminent Victorians** (1918), a volume of iconoclastic biographical sketches of Cardinal Manning, Florence Nightingale, Dr. Arnold of Rugby, and General Gordon. He wrote the sketches with a cynical irony and made no scruples about defaming the people he portrayed. His **Queen Victoria** (1921) was another highly successful work. His **Elizabeth and Essex** (1928) was less happy. Strachey's prose style is elegant and witty.

GLADSTONE[1]

The old statesman was now entering upon the penultimate period of his enormous career. He who had once been the rising hope of the stern and unbending Tories[2], had at length emerged, after a lifetime of transmutations, as the champion of militant democracy. He was at the apex of his power. His great rival[3] was dead; he stood pre-eminent in the eye of the nation; he enjoyed the applause, the confidence, the admiration, the adoration, even, of multitudes. Yet—such was the peculiar character of the man, and such the intensity of the feelings which he called forth—at this very moment, at the height of his popularity, he was distrusted and loathed; already an unparalleled animosity was gathering its forces against him. For, indeed, there was something in his nature which invited—which demanded—the clashing reactions of passionate extremes. It was easy to worship Mr. Gladstone; to see in him the perfect model of the upright man—the man of virtue and of religion—the man whose whole life had been devoted to the application of high principles to affairs of state—the man, too, whose sense of right and justice was invigorated and ennobled by an enthusiastic heart. It was also easy to detest him as a hypocrite, to despise him as a demagogue, and to dread him as a crafty manipulator of men and things for the purposes of his own ambition. It might have been supposed that one or other of these conflicting judgements must have been palpably absurd, that nothing short of gross prejudice or wilful blindness, on one side or the other, could reconcile such contradictory conceptions of a single human being. But it was not so; "the elements" were "so mixed"[4] in Mr. Gladstone that his bitterest enemies (and his enemies were never mild) and his warmest friends (and his friends were never tepid) could justify, with equal plausibility, their denunciations or their praises. What, then, was the truth? In the physical universe there are no chimeras. But man is more various than Nature; was Mr. Gladstone, perhaps, a chimera of the spirit? Did his very essence lie in the confusion of incompatibles? His very essence? It eludes the hand that seems to grasp it. One is baffled, as his political opponents were baffled fifty years ago. The soft serpent coils harden into quick strength that has vanished, leaving only emptiness and perplexity behind. Speech was the fibre of his being; and, when he spoke, the ambiguity of ambiguity was revealed. The long, winding, intricate sentences, with their vast burden of subtle and complicated qualifications, befogged the mind like clouds, and, like clouds, too, dropped thunderbolts[5]. Could it not then at least be said of him with certainty that his was a complex character? But here also there was a contradiction. In spite of the involutions of his intellect and the contortions of his spirit, it is impossible not to perceive a strain of *naïveté* in Mr. Gladstone. He adhered to some of his principles—that of the value of representative institutions, for instance—with a faith which was singularly literal; his views upon religion were uncritical to crudeness; he had no sense of humour. Compared with Disraeli's, his attitude towards life strikes one as that of an ingenuous child. His very egoism was simple-minded; through all the labyrinth of his passions there ran a single thread. But the centre of the labyrinth? Ah! the thread might lead there, through those wandering mazes, at last. Only, with the last corner turned, the last step taken, the explorer might find that he was looking down into the gulf of a crater. The flame shot out on every side, scorching and brilliant; but in the midst there was a darkness.

NOTES

1. **Gladstone:** William Ewart Gladstone (1809-1898) was a British statesman. He became leader of the Liberal Party in 1867 and was four times Prime Minister (1868-1874, 1880-1885, 1886, 1892-1894).
2. **the rising hope of the stern and unbending Tories:** Gladstone began as a conservative in his political career, but turned a liberal in the mid-century.
3. **His great rival:** Benjamin Disraeli (1804-1881), British Tory statesman and novelist. He was Prime Minister in 1868 and 1874-1880. His novels include ***Coningsby*** (1844) and ***Sybil*** (1845).
4. **"the elements" were "so mixed":** from ***Julius Caesar*** v.

> His life was gentle, and the elements
> So mixed in him, that nature might stand up
> And say to all the world, "This was a man!"

The lines were said of Brutus by Antony.

5. **thunderbolts:** startling or terrible things

VIRGINIA WOOLF

(*NÉE* ADELINE VIRGINIA STEPHEN, 1882–1941)

Virginia Woolf was an English novelist and critic. She was born in London on January 25, 1882, the youngest of eight children of the critic and biographer Leslie Stephen, and was educated at home. When her father died in 1904, she and her sister Vanessa and two brothers settled in Bloomsbury. The four of them formed the nucleus of the "Bloomsbury Group", which included Bertrand Russell, E. M. Forster, J. M. Keynes, Lytton Strachey, Clive Bell, and Roger Fry. Virginia Stephen began to write in 1905, and married the political writer Leonard Woolf in 1912. She and her husband moved out of London to Hogarth House, Richmond in 1915, and founded the Hogarth Press in 1917. During the Second World War, Virginia Woolf became greatly depressed and drowned herself in the River Ouse on March 28, 1941.

Virginia Woolf's first two novels were realistic and technically traditional: *The Voyage Out* (1915), an account of a young girl's voyage to South America, her discovery of love, and her death; *Night and Day* (1919), a story of the intellectual and emotional growing up of a girl from an upper-middle-class family. The author became more and more innovative with the use of "stream-of-consciousness" technique in her four subsequent major novels: *Jacob's Room* (1922), a study of the life of a young man as told about and thought about by his friends; *Mrs*

Dalloway (1925), the story of one day in the heroine's life with her past experience brought in by flashback; *To the Lighthouse* (1927), the story of a voyage to the lighthouse off the Isle of Skye involving the thoughts, moods, and impressions of the Ramsays and their guests; *The Waves* (1931), a study of six characters each of whom tells his own story in monologue. Her other fictional works include *Orlando: A Biography* (1928), a fantastic life of a character through four hundred years; and *The Years* (1937), a more conventional family chronicle. Virginia Woolf was also an original and able critic. Her literary criticism was collected in *The Common Reader* (1925), *The Common Reader, Second Series* (1932), and other volumes. Her feminist criticism is contained in *A Room of One's Own* (1929). Her prose is natural, simple, and rich in imagery.

MY FATHER: LESLIE STEPHEN[1]

By the time that his children were growing up the great days of my father's life were over. His feats on the river and on the mountains[2] had been won before they were born. Relics of them were to be found lying about the house—the silver cup on the study mantelpiece; the rusty alpenstocks that leant against the bookcase in the corner; and to the end of his days he would speak of great climbers and explorers with a peculiar mixture of admiration and envy. But his own years of activity were over, and my father had to content himself with pottering about[3] the Swiss valleys or taking a stroll across the Cornish moors[4].

That to potter and to stroll meant more on his lips than on other people's becoming obvious now that some of his friends have given their own version of those expeditions. He would start off after breakfast alone, or with one companion. Shortly before dinner he would return. If the walk had been successful, he would have out[5] his great map and commemorate a new short cut in red ink. And he was quite capable, it appears, of striding all day across the moors without speaking more than a word or two to his companion. By that time, too, he had written the ***History of English Thought in the Eighteenth Century***, which is said by some to be his masterpiece; and the ***Science of Ethics***—the book which interested him most; and ***The Playground of Europe***, in which is to be found "The Sunset on Mont Blanc"—in his opinion the best thing he ever wrote.

He still wrote daily and methodically, though never for long at a time. In London he wrote in the large room with three long windows at the top of the house. He wrote lying almost recumbent in a low rocking chair which he tipped to and fro as he wrote, like a cradle, and as he wrote he smoked a short clay pipe, and he scattered books round him in a circle. The thud of a book dropped on the floor could be heard in the room beneath. And often as he would burst, not into song, for he was entirely unmusical, but into a strange rhythmical chant, for verse of all kinds, both "utter trash," as he called it, and the most sublime words of Milton and

Wordsworth stuck in his memory, and the act of walking or climbing seemed to inspire him to recite whichever it was that came uppermost or suited his mood.

But it was his dexterity with his fingers that delighted his children before they could potter along the lanes at his heels or read his books. He would twist a sheet of paper beneath a pair of scissors and out would drop an elephant, a stag, or a monkey with trunks, horns, and tails delicately and exactly formed. Or, taking a pencil, he would draw beast after beast—an art that he practised almost unconsciously as he read, so that the fly-leaves of his books swarm with owls and donkeys as if to illustrate the "Oh, you ass!" or "Conceited dunce," that he was wont to scribble impatiently in the margin. Such brief comments, in which one may find the germ of the more temperate statements of his essays, recall some of the characteristics of his talk. He could be very silent, as his friends have testified. But his remarks, made suddenly in a low voice between the puffs of his pipe, were extremely effective. Sometimes with one word—but his one word was accompanied by a gesture of the hand—he would dispose of the tissue of exaggerations[6] which his own sobriety seemed to provoke. "There are 40,000,000 unmarried women in London alone!" Lady Ritchie once informed him. "Oh, Annie, Annie!" my father exclaimed in tones of horrified but affectionate rebuke. But lady Ritchie, as if she enjoyed being rebuked, would pile it up even higher next time she came.

The stories he told to amuse his children of adventures in the Alps—but accidents only happened, he would explain, if you were so foolish as to disobey your guides—or of those long walks, after one of which, from Cambridge to London on a hot day, "I drank, I am sorry to say, rather more than was good for me," were told very briefly, but with a curious power to impress the scene. The things that he did not say were always there in the background. So, too, though he seldom told anecdotes, and his memory for facts was bad, when he described a person—and he had known many people, both famous and obscure—he would convey exactly what he thought of him in two or three words. And what he thought might be the opposite of what other people thought. He had a way of upsetting established reputations and disregarding conventional values that could be disconcerting, and sometimes perhaps wounding, though no one was more respectful of any feeling that seemed to him genuine. But when, suddenly opening his bright blue eyes, and rousing himself from what had seemed complete abstraction, he gave his opinion, it was difficult to disregard it. It was a habit, especially when deafness made him unaware that this opinion could be heard, that had its inconveniences.

"I am the most easily bored of men," he wrote, truthfully as usual; and when, as was inevitable in a large family, some visitor threatened to stay not merely for tea but also for dinner, my father would express his anguish at first by twisting and untwisting a certain lock of hair. Then he would burst out, half to himself, half to the powers above[7], but quite audibly, "Why can't he go? Why can't he go?" Yes such is the charm of simplicity—and did he not say, also truthfully, that "bores are the salt of the earth"?—that the bores seldom went, or, if they did, forgave him and came again.

Too much, perhaps, has been said of his silence; too much stress has been laid upon his reserve. He loved clear thinking; he hated sentimentality and gush[8]; but this by no means meant that he was cold and unemotional, perpetually critical and condemnatory in daily life. On the contrary, it was his power of feeling strongly and of expressing his feeling with vigour that made him sometimes so alarming as a companion. A lady, for instance, complained of the wet summer that was spoiling her tour in Cornwall. But to my father, though he never called himself a democrat, the rain meant that the corn was being laid[9]; some poor man was being ruined; and the energy with which he expressed his sympathy—not with the lady—left her discomfited. He had something of the same respect for farmers and fishermen that he had for climbers and explorers. So, too, he talked little of patriotism, but during the South African War[10]—and all wars were hateful to him—he lay awake thinking that he heard the guns on the battlefield. Again, neither his reason nor his cold common sense helped to convince him that a child could be late for dinner without having been maimed or killed in an accident. And not all his mathematics, together with a bank balance which he insisted must be ample in the extreme, could persuade him, when it came to signing a cheque, that the whole family was not "shooting Niagara to ruin,"[11] as he put it. The pictures that he would draw of old age and the bankruptcy court, of ruined men of letters who have to support large families in small houses at Wimbledon[12] (he owned a very small house at Wimbledon) might have convinced those who complain of his understatements that hyperbole was well within his reach had he chosen.

Yet the unreasonable mood was superficial, as the rapidity with which it vanished would prove. The chequebook was shut; Wimbledon and the workhouse were forgotten. Some thought of a humorous kind made him chuckle. Taking his hat and his stick, calling for his dog and his daughter, he would stride off into Kensington Gardens[13], where he had walked as a little boy, where his brother Fitzjames and he had made beautiful bows to young Queen Victoria[14] and she had swept them a curtsey, and so, round the Serpentine[15], to Hyde Park Corner, where he had once saluted the great Duke[16] himself; and so home. He was not then in the least "alarming"; he was very simple, very confiding; and his silence, though one might last unbroken from the Round Pond[17] to the Marble Arch[18], was curiously full of meaning, as if he were thinking half aloud, about poetry and philosophy and people he had known.

He himself was the most abstemious of men. He smoked a pipe perpetually, but never a cigar. He wore his clothes until they were too shabby to be tolerable; and he held old-fashioned and rather puritanical views as to the vice of luxury and the sin of idleness. The relations between parents and children today have a freedom that would have been impossible with my father. He expected a certain standard of behaviour, even of ceremony, in family life. Yet if freedom means the right to think one's own thoughts and to follow one's own pursuits, then no one respected and indeed insisted upon freedom more completely than he did. His sons, with the exception of the Army and Navy, should follow whatever professions they chose; his daughters, though he cared little enough for the higher education of women, should have the same liberty. If at one moment he rebuked a daughter sharply for smoking a cigarette—smoking was not in his opinion a nice habit in the other sex—she had only to ask him if she took her work seriously he would give her all the help he could. He had no special love for painting; but he kept his word.

Freedom of that sort was worth thousands of cigarettes.

It was the same with the perhaps more difficult problem of literature. Even today there may be parents who would doubt the wisdom of allowing a girl of fifteen the free run of a large and quite unexpurgated library. But my father allowed it. There were certain facts—very briefly, very shyly he referred to them. Yet "Read what you like," he said, and all his books, "mangy[19] and worthless," as he called them, but certainly they were many and various, were to be had without asking. To read what one liked because one liked it, never to pretend to admire what one did not—that was his only lesson in the art of reading. To write in the fewest possibly words, as clearly as possible, exactly what one meant—that was his only lesson in the art of writing. All the rest must be learnt for oneself. Yet a child must have been childish in the extreme not to feel that such was the teaching of a man of great learning and wide experience, though he would never impose his own views or parade his own knowledge. For, as his tailor remarked when he saw my father walk past his shop up Bond Street[20], "There goes a gentleman that wears good clothes without knowing it."

In those last years, grown solitary and very deaf, he would sometimes call himself a failure as a writer; he had been "jack of all trades, and master of none." But whether he failed or succeeded as a writer, it is permissible to believe that he left a distinct impression of himself on the minds of his friends. Meredith[21] saw him as "Phoebus Apollo turned fasting friar" in his earlier days; Thomas Hardy, years later, looked at the "spare and desolate figure" of the Schreckhorn[22] and thought of him,

> Who scaled its horn with ventured life and limb,
> Drawn on by vague imaginings, maybe,
> Of semblance to his personality
> In its quaint glooms, keen lights, and rugged trim.

But the praise he would have valued most, for though he was an agnostic nobody believed more profoundly in the worth of human relationships, was Meredith's tribute after his death: "He was the one man to my knowledge worthy to have married your mother," And Lowell[23], when he called him "L.S., the most lovable of men," has best described the quality that makes him, after all these years, unforgettable.

NOTES

1. **Leslie Stephen:** Leslie Stephen (1832–1904) was an English critic and biographer. He was the editor of the ***Cornhill Magazine*** from 1871 to 1882, the first editor of the ***Dictionary of National Biography*** from 1885 to 1891, and the author of ***Hours in a Library*** (1874–1879), ***History of English Thought in the Eighteenth Century*** (1876), etc.
2. **feats on the river and on the mountains:** boat-racing and mountain-climbing
3. **pottering about:** loitering
4. **Cornish moors:** tracts of waste ground in Cornwall
5. **have out:** take out
6. **the tissue of exaggerations:** the mass of exaggerations
7. **the powers above:** the deities
8. **gush:** affectation
9. **the corn was being laid:** the cereal crop was being beaten down
10. **the South African War:** the Boer War (1899–1902), the war between Britain and two South African republics, the Transvaal and the Orange Free State
11. **shooting Niagara to ruin:** going over the Niagara Falls in a boat with tragical consequences
12. **Wimbledon:** a town near London
13. **Kensington Gardens:** a big park in London, originally the Gardens of Kensington Palace
14. **Queen Victoria:** Victoria (1819–1901), queen of Great Britain and Ireland (1837–1901)
15. **the Serpentine:** an artificial lake in Hyde Park, London
16. **the great Duke:** the Duke of Wellington (1769–1852), victor at the Battle of Waterloo
17. **the Round Pond:** a pond in Hyde Park
18. **the Marble Arch:** an arch skirting the east side of Hyde Park

19. **mangy:** shabby
20. **Bond Street:** a street parallel to the Burlington Arcade in London
21. **Meredith:** George Meredith (1828–1909) was an English novelist and poet, and the author of *The Ordeal of Richard Feverel* (1859), *The Egoist* (1879), and *Modern Love* (1862), the last being a long tragic poem.
22. **Schreckhorn:** one of the chief peaks in Switzerland
23. **Lowell:** James Russell Lowell (1819–1891) was an American poet, essayist, and diplomat.

JAMES JOYCE

(1882–1941)

James Joyce was an Irish novelist and short-story writer. He was born in Dublin on February 2, 1882, and educated at Clongowes Wood College, Belvedere College, and University College, Dublin, from 1888 to 1902. As a teacher of English he lived in Yugoslavia and Switzerland from 1905 to 1920, and as a full-time writer he lived in Paris from 1920 to 1939 and in Zurich from 1939 to 1941. He died on January 13, 1941.

Joyce's first published work was **Chamber Music** (1907), a volume of 36 short and simple lyric poems. His first major work was **Dubliners** (1914), a collection of 15 short stories, which are moral studies of Joyce's fellow citizens from four points of view: childhood, adolescence, maturity, and public life. He followed **Dubliners** with his first novel, ***A Portrait of the Artist as a Young Man*** (1916). This semi-autobiographical work describes how Stephen Dedalus moves from childhood to youth and how he discovers his artistic vocation. The story is told from the view-point of the central character, but not entirely with the "stream-of-consciousness" technique. Joyce's next novel, **Ulysses** (1922), is remarkable both for matter and for manner. It is concerned with a single day—16 June 1904—in the life of three Dubliners: Stephen Dedalus, made to correspond to Telemachus in Homer's ***Odyssey***; Leopold Bloom, to Ulysses; and Molly Bloom, to Penelope. Its 18 episodes are presented with the stream-of-consciousness technique and in a variety of literary styles. It is thus a very difficult book. Even more difficult than **Ulysses** is **Finnegans Wake** (1939), the last book Joyce published. This is concerned with one night in the life of the Dublin pub-keeper, H. C. Earwicker, with his dreams and nightmares. Based on Earwicker's relationships with his family, the story is told with the stream-of-consciousness technique and in a kind of dream language containing words from many languages.

ARABY[1]

North Richmond Street, being blind, was a quiet street except at the hour when the Christian Brothers[2] School set the boys free. An uninhabited house of two storeys stood at the blind end, detached from its neighbours in a square ground. The other houses of the street, conscious of decent lives within them, gazed at one another with brown imperturbable faces.

The former tenant of our house, a priest, had died in the back drawing-room. Air, musty from having been long enclosed, hung in all the rooms, and the waste room behind the kitchen was littered with old useless papers. Among these I found a few paper-covered books, the pages of which were curled and damp: ***The Abbot***[3], by Walter Scott, ***The Devout Communicant***[4] and ***The Memoirs of Vidocq***[5]. I liked the last best because its leaves were yellow. The wild garden behind the house contained a central apple-tree and a few straggling bushes under one of which I found the late tenant's rusty bicycle-pump. He had been a very charitable priest; in his will he had left all his money to institutions and the furniture of his house to his sister.

When the short days of winter came dusk fell before we had well eaten our dinners. When we met in the street the houses had grown sombre. The space of sky above us was the colour of ever-changing violet and towards it the lamps of the street lifted their feeble lanterns. The cold air stung us and we played till our bodies glowed. Our shouts echoed in the silent street. The career of our play brought us through the dark muddy lanes behind the houses where we ran the gauntlet of[6] the rough tribes from the cottages, to the back doors of the dark dripping gardens where odours arose from the ashpits, to the dark odorous stables where a coachman smoothed and combed the horse or shook music from the buckled harness. When we returned to the street light from the kitchen windows had filled the areas. If my uncle was seen turning the corner we hid in the shadow until we had seen him safely housed. Or if Mangan's[7] sister came out on the doorstep to call her brother in to his tea we watched her from our shadow peer up and down the street. We waited to see whether she would remain or go in and, if she remained, we left our shadow and walked up to Mangan's steps resignedly. She was waiting for us, her figure defined by the light from the half-opened door. Her brother always teased her before he obeyed and I stood by the railings looking at her. Her dress swung as she moved her body and the soft rope of her hair tossed from side to side.

　　Every morning I lay on the floor in the front parlour watching her door. The blind was pulled down to within an inch of the sash so that I could not be seen. When she came out on the doorstep my heart leaped. I ran to the hall, seized my books and followed her. I kept her brown figure always in my eye and, when we came near the point at which our ways diverged, I quickened my pace and passed her. This happened morning after morning. I had never spoken to her, except for a few casual words, and yet her name was like a summons to all my foolish blood.

　　Her image accompanied me even in places the most hostile to romance. On Saturday evenings when my aunt went marketing I had to go to carry some of the parcels. We walked through the flaring streets, jostled by drunken men and bargaining women, amid the curses of labourers, the shrill litanies of shop-boys who stood on guard by the barrels of pigs' cheeks, the nasal chanting of street-singers, who sang a *come-all-you* about O'Donovan Rossa[8], or a ballad about the troubles in our native land. These noises converged in a single sensation of life for me; I imagined that I bore my chalice safely through a throng of foes. Her name sprang to my lips at moments in strange prayers and praises which I myself did not understand. My eyes were often full of tears (I could not tell why) and at times a flood from my heart seemed to pour itself out into my bosom. I thought little of the future. I did not know whether I would ever speak to her or not or, if I spoke to her, how I could tell her of my confused adoration. But my body was like a harp and her words and gestures were like fingers running upon the wires.

　　One evening I went into the back drawing-room in which the priest had died. It was a dark rainy evening and there was no sound in the house. Through one of the broken panes I heard the rain impinge upon the earth, the fine incessant needles of water playing in the sodden beds. Some distant lamp or lighted window gleamed below me. I was thankful that I could see so little. All my senses seemed to desire to veil themselves and, feeling that I was about to slip from them, I pressed the palms of my hands together until they trembled, murmuring: "*O love! O love!*" many times.

At last she spoke to me. When she addressed the first words to me I was so confused that I did not know what to answer. She asked me was I going to *Araby*. I forgot whether I answered yes or no. It would be a splendid bazaar, she said she would love to go.

"And why can't you?" I asked.

While she spoke she turned a silver bracelet round and round her wrist. She could not go, she said, because there would be a retreat[9] that week in her convent[10]. Her brother and two other boys were fighting for their caps and I was alone at the railings. She held one of the spikes, bowing her head towards me. The light from the lamp opposite our door caught the white curve of her neck, lit up her hair that rested there and, falling, lit up the hand upon the railing. It fell over one side of her dress and caught the white border of a petticoat, just visible as she stood at ease.

"It's well for you," she said.

"If I go," I said, "I will bring you something."

What innumerable follies laid waste my waking and sleeping thoughts after that evening! I wished to annihilate the tedious intervening days. I chafed against the work of school. At night in my bedroom and by day in the classroom her image came between me and the page I strove to read. The syllables of the word *Araby* were called to me through the silence in which my soul luxuriated and cast an Eastern enchantment over me. I asked for leave to go to the bazaar on Saturday night. My aunt was surprised and hoped it was not some Freemason[11] affair. I answered few questions in class. I watched my master's face pass from amiability to sternness; he hoped I was not beginning to idle. I could not call my wandering thoughts together. I had hardly any patience with the serious work of life which, now that it stood between me and my desire, seemed to me child's play, ugly monotonous child's play.

On Saturday morning I reminded my uncle that I wished to go to the bazaar in the evening. He was fussing at the hallstand, looking for the hatbrush, and answered me curtly:

"Yes, boy, I know."

As he was in the hall I could not go into the front parlour and lie at the window. I left the house in bad humour and walked slowly towards the school. The air was pitilessly raw and already my heart misgave me.

When I came home to dinner my uncle had not yet been home. Still it was early. I sat staring at the clock for some time and, when its ticking began to irritate me, I left the room. I mounted the staircase and gained the upper part of the house. The high cold empty gloomy rooms liberated me and I went from room to room singing. From the front window I saw my companions playing below in the street. Their cries reached me weakened and indistinct and, leaning my forehead against the cool glass, I looked over at the dark house where she lived. I may have stood there for an hour, seeing nothing but the brown-clad figure cast by my imagination, touched discreetly by the lamplight at the curved neck, at the hand upon the railings and at the border below the dress.

When I came downstairs again I found Mrs. Mercer sitting at the fire. She was an old garrulous woman, a pawnbroker's widow, who collected used stamps for some pious purpose. I had to endure the gossip of the tea-table. The meal was prolonged beyond an hour and still my uncle did not come. Mrs. Mercer stood up to go; she was sorry she couldn't wait any longer, but it was after eight o'clock and she did not like to be out late, as the night air was bad for her. When she had gone I began to walk up and down the room, clenching my fists. My aunt said:

"I'm afraid you may put off your bazaar for this night of Our Lord."

At nine o'clock I heard my uncle's latchkey in the halldoor. I heard him talking to himself and heard the hallstand rocking when it had received the weight of his overcoat. I could interpret these signs. When he was midway through his dinner I asked him to give me the money to go to the bazaar. He had forgotten.

"The people are in bed and after their first sleep now," he said.

I did not smile. My aunt said to him energetically:

"Can't you give him the money and let him go? You've kept him late enough as it is."

My uncle said he was very sorry he had forgotten. He said he believed in the old saying: "All work and no play makes Jack a dull boy." He asked me where I was going and, when I had told him a second time he asked me did I know ***The Arab's Farewell to his Steed***[12]. When I left the kitchen he was about to recite the opening lines of the piece to my aunt.

I held a florin tightly in my hand as I strode down Buckingham Street towards the station. The sight of the streets thronged with buyers and glaring with gas recalled to me the purpose of my journey. I took my seat in a third-class carriage of a deserted train. After an intolerable delay the train moved out of the station slowly. It crept onward among ruinous houses and over the twinkling river. At Westland Row Station a crowd of people pressed to the carriage door; but the porters moved them back, saying that it was a special train for the bazaar. I remained alone in the bare carriage. In a few minutes the train drew up beside an improvised wooden platform. I passed out on to the road and saw by the lighted dial of a clock that it was ten minutes to ten. In front of me was a large building which displayed the magical name.

I could not find any sixpenny entrance and, fearing that the bazaar would be closed, I passed in quickly through a turnstile, handing a shilling to a weary-looking man. I found myself in a big hall girdled at half its height by a gallery. Nearly all the stalls were closed and the greater part of the hall was in darkness. I recognised a silence like that which pervades a church after a service. I walked into the centre of the bazaar timidly. A few people were gathered about the stalls which were still open. Before a curtain, over which the words ***Café Chantant***[13] were written in coloured lamps, two men were counting money on a salver. I listened to the fall of the coins.

Remembering with difficulty why I had come I went over to one of the stalls and examined porcelain vases and flowered tea-sets. At the door of the stall a young lady was talking and laughing with two young gentlemen. I remarked their English accents and listened vaguely to their conversation.

"O, I never said such a thing!"

"O, but you did!"

"O, but I didn't!"

"Didn't she say that?"

"Yes. I heard her."

"O, there's a...fib[14]!"

Observing me the young lady came over and asked me did I wish to buy anything. The tone of her voice was not encouraging; she seemed to have spoken to me out of a sense of duty. I looked humbly at the great jars that stood like eastern guards at either side of the dark entrance to the stall and murmured:

"No, thank you."

The young lady changed the position of one of the vases and went back to the two young men. They began to talk of the same subject. Once or twice the young lady glanced at me over her shoulder.

I lingered before her stall, though I knew my stay was useless, to make my interest in her wares seem the more real. Then I turned away slowly and walked down the middle of the bazaar. I allowed the two pennies to fall against the sixpence in my pocket. I heard a voice call from one end of the gallery that the light was out. The upper part of the hall was now completely dark.

Gazing up into the darkness I saw myself as a creature driven and derided by vanity; and my eyes burned with anguish and anger.

NOTES

1. **Araby:** the bazaar
2. **the Christian Brothers:** a teaching order (a Catholic religious community)
3. ***The Abbot:*** *The Abbot* is a historical novel (1820) by Walter Scott. It deals with Mary Queen of Scots and Roland Graeme or Roland Avenel, a romantic youth.
4. ***The Devout Communicant:*** a religious tract (1813) by Pacificus Baker
5. ***The Memoirs of Vidocq:*** François Èugene Vidocq (1775–1857) was a French soldier, thief, and head of the Police. His *Memoirs* was published in France in 1828, and was soon translated into English in the same year.
6. **ran the gauntlet of:** were subjected to criticism

7. **Mangan:** one of the narrator's schoolmates
8. **a *come-all-you* about O'Donovan Rossa:** a street ballad about O'Donovan Rossa, a Fenian nationalist leader (1831–1915)
9. **a retreat:** a period of retirement from ordinary activities for devotion to religious exercises
10. **her convent:** her convent school
11. **Freemason:** The Freemasons were a secret society not tolerated by the Catholic Church.
12. ***The Arab's Farewell to his Steed*:** a sentimental poem by Mrs. Caroline Norton (1807–1877)
13. ***Café Chantant*:** (Fr.) Singing Cafe; a public house selling drinks and providing musical entertainment
14. **fib:** (sl.) a lie

90

ARTHUR STANLEY EDDINGTON

(1882–1944)

Sir A. S. Eddington was an English astronomer, mathematician, and physicist. He was born in Westmorland and educated at Manchester and Cambridge universities. He served as Chief Assistant at the Royal Observatory, Greenwich, Professor of Astronomy at Cambridge, and president of several learned societies. Elected F.R.S. in 1914 and knighted in 1930, he was noted for his researches into the structure, motion, and evolution of stars, and for his exposition of the General Theory of Relativity. His numerous works include **Mathematical Theory of Relativity** (1923), **The Nature of the Physical World** (1928), and **Fundamental Theory** (published posthumously in 1946), all written in lucid prose.

THE MILKY WAY AND BEYOND

In one of Jules Verne's[1] stories the astronomer begins his lecture with the words: "Gentlemen, you have seen the moon—or at least heard tell of it." I think I may in the same way presume that you are acquainted with the Milky Way, which can be seen on any clear dark night as a faintly luminous band forming an arch from horizon to horizon. The telescopes show that it is composed of multitudes of stars. One is tempted to say "countless multitudes"; but it is part of the business of an astronomer to count them, and the number is not uncountable though it amounts to more than ten thousand millions. The number of the stars in the Milky Way is considerably greater than the number of human beings on the earth. Each star, I may remind you, is an immense fiery globe of the same general nature as our sun.

There is no sharp division between the distant stars which form the Milky Way and the brighter stars which we see strewn over the sky. All these stars taken together form one system or galaxy; its extent is enormous but not unlimited. Since we are situated inside it we do not obtain a good view of its form; but we are able to see far away in space other galaxies which also consist of thousands of millions of stars, and presumably if we could see our own galaxy from outside, it would appear like one of them. These other galaxies are known as "spiral nebulae." We believe that our own Milky Way system is more or less like them. If so, the stars form a flat coil—rather like a watch-spring—except that the coil is double.

When we look out in directions perpendicular to the plane of the coil, we soon reach the limit of the system; but in the plane of the coil we see stars behind stars until they become indistinguishable and fade into the hazy light of the Milky Way. It has been ascertained that we are a very long way from the centre of our own galaxy, so that there are many more stars on one side of us than on the other.

Looking at one of these galaxies, it is impossible to resist the impression that it is whirling round—like a Catherine Wheel[2]. It has, in fact, been possible to prove that some of the spiral nebulae are rotating, and to measure the rate of rotation. Also by studying the motions of the stars in our own galaxy, it has been found that it too is rotating about a centre. The centre is situated a long way from us in the constellation Ophiuchus[3] near a particularly bright patch of the Milky Way; the actual centre is, however, hidden from us by a cloud of obscuring matter. My phrase, "whirling round," may possibly give you a wrong impression. With these vast systems we have to think in a different scale of space and time, and the whirling is slow according to our ordinary ideas. It takes about 300 millions years for the Milky Way to turn round once. But after all that is not so very long. Geologists tell us that the older rocks in the earth's crust were formed 1300 million years ago; so the sun, carrying with it the earth and planets, has made four or five complete revolutions round the centre of the galaxy within geological times.

The stars which form our Milky Way system show a very wide diversity. Some give out more than 10,000 times as much light and heat as the sun; others less than 1/100th. Some are extremely dense and compact; others are extremely tenuous. Some have a surface temperature as high as 20,000° or 30,000℃ ; others not more than 3000℃. Some are believed to be pulsating—swelling up and deflating within a period of a few days or weeks; these undergo great changes of light and heat accompanying the expansion and collapse. It would be awkward for us if our sun behaved that way. A considerable proportion (about 1/3 of the whole number) go about in pairs, forming "double stars"; the majority, however, are bachelors like the sun.

But in spite of this diversity, the stars have one comparatively uniform characteristic, namely their mass, that is, the amount of matter which goes to form them. A range from 1/5 to 5 times the sun's mass would cover all but the most exceptional stars; and the general run of the masses is within an even narrower range. Among a hundred stars picked at random the diversity of mass would not be greater proportionately than among a hundred men, women and children picked at random from a crowd.

Broadly speaking, a big star is big, not because it contains an excessive amount of material, but because it is, puffed out like a balloon; and a small star is small because its material is highly compressed. Our sun, which is intermediate in this, as in most respects, has a density rather greater than that of water. (The sun is in every way a typical middle-class star.) The two extremes—the extremely rarefied and the extremely dense stars—are especially interesting. We find stars whose material is as tenuous as a gas. The well-known star Capella[4], for example, has an average density about equal to that of air; to be inside Capella would be like being surrounded by air, as we ordinarily are, except that the temperature (which is about 5,000,000 ℃.) is hotter than we are accustomed to. Still more extreme are the red giant stars Betelgeuse[5] in Orion[6] and Antares[7] in Scorpio[8]. To obtain a star like Betelgeuse, we must imagine the sun swelling out until it has swallowed up Mercury[9], Venus[10] and the Earth, and has a circumference almost equal to the orbit of Mars[11]. The density of this vast globe is that of a gas in rather highly exhausted vessel[12]. Betelgeuse could be described as "a rather good vacuum."

At the other extreme are the "white dwarf" stars, which have extravagantly high density. I must say a little about the way in which this was discovered.

Between 1916 and 1924 I was very much occupied trying to understand the internal constitution of the stars, for example, finding the temperature in the deep interior, which is usually ten million degrees, and making out what sort of properties matter would have at such high temperatures. Physicists had recently been making great advances in our knowledge of atoms and radiation; and the problem was to apply this new knowledge to the study of what was taking place inside a star. In the end I obtained a formula by which, if you knew the mass of a star, you could calculate how bright it ought to be. An electrical engineer will tell you that to produce a certain amount of illumination you must have a dynamo of a size which he will specify; somewhat analogously I found that for a star to give a certain amount of illumination it must have a definite mass which the formula specified. This formula, however, was not intended to apply to all stars, but only to diffuse stars with densities corresponding to a gas, because the problem became too complicated if the material could not be treated as a perfect gas.

Having obtained the theoretical formula, the next thing was to compare it with observation. That is where the trouble often begins. And there was trouble in this case; only it was not of the usual kind. The observed masses and luminosities agreed with the formulae all right; the trouble was that they would not stop agreeing! The dense stars for which the formula was not intended agreed just as well as the diffuse stars for which the formula was intended. This surprising result could only mean that, although their densities were as great as that of water or iron, the stellar material was nevertheless behaving like a gas. In particular, it was compressible like an ordinary gas.

We had been rather blind not to have foreseen this: Why is it that we can compress air, but cannot appreciably compress water? It is because in air the ultimate particles (the molecules) are wide apart, with plenty of empty space between them. When we compress air we merely pack the molecules a bit closer, reducing the amount of vacant space. But in water the molecules are practically in contact and cannot be packed any closer. In all substances the ordinary limit of compression is when the molecules jam in contact; after that we cannot appreciably increase the density. This limit corresponds approximately to the density of the solid or liquid state. We had been supposing that the same limit would apply in the interior of a star. We ought to have remembered that at the temperature of millions of degrees there prevailing the atoms are highly ionized, i.e. broken up. An atom has a heavy central nucleus surrounded by a widely extended but insubstantial structure of electrons—a sort of crinoline[13]. At the high temperature in the stars this crinoline of electrons is broken up. If you are calculating how many dancers can be accommodated in a ballroom, it makes a difference whether the ladies wear crinolines or not. Judging by the crinolined terrestrial atoms we should reach the limit of compression at densities not much greater than water; but the uncrinolined stell atoms can pack much more densely, and do not jam together until densities far beyond terrestrial experience are reached.

This suggested that there might exist stars of density greater than any material hitherto known, which called to mind a mystery concerning the Companion of Sirius[14]. The dog-star Sirius has a faint companion close to it, visible in telescopes of moderate power. There is a method of finding densities of stars which I must not stop to explain. The method is rather tentative; and when it was found to give for the Companion of Sirius a density 50,000 times greater than water, it was naturally assumed that it had gone wrong in its application. But in the light of the foregoing discussion, it now seemed possible that the method had not failed, and that the extravagantly high density might be genuine. So astronomers endeavoured to check the determination of density by another method depending on Einstein's[15] relativity theory. The second method confirmed the high density, and it is now generally accepted. The stuff of the Companion of Sirius is 2000 times as dense as platinum. Imagine a match-box filled with this matter. It would need a crane to lift it—it would weigh a ton.

I am afraid that what I have to say about the stars is largely a matter of facts and figures. There is only one star near enough for us to study its surface, namely our sun. Ordinary photographs of the sun show few features, except the dark spots which appear at times. But much more interesting photographs are obtained by using a spectro-heliograph[16], which is an instrument blind to all light except that of one particular wave length—coming from one particular kind of atom.

Now let us turn to the rest of the universe which lies beyond the Milky Way. Our galaxy is, as it were, an oasis of matter in the desert of emptiness, an island in the boundless ocean of space. From our own island we see in the far distance other islands—in fact a whole archipelago of islands one beyond another till our vision fails. One of the nearest of them can actually be seen with the naked eye; it is in the constellation Andromeda, and looks like a faint, rather hazy, star. The light which we now see has taken 900,000 years to reach us. When we look at that faint object in Andromeda we are looking back 900,000 years into the past. Some of the telescopic spiral nebulae are much more distant. The most remote that has yet been examined is 300,000,000 light-years away.

These galaxies are very numerous. From sample counts it is found that more than a million of them are visible in our largest telescopes; and there must be many more fainter ones which we do not see. Our sun is just one star in a system of thousands of millions of stars; and that whole system is just one galaxy in a universe of thousands of millions of galaxies.

Let us pause to see where we have now got to in a scale of size. The following comparative table of distances will help to show us where we are:

	Kilometres
Distance of the sun	150,000,000
Limit of the solar system (Orbit of Pluto[17])	5,800,000,000
Distance of the nearest star	40,000,000,000,000
Distance of nearest external galaxy	8,000,000,000,000,000,000
Distance of furthest galaxy yet observed	3,000,000,000,000,000,000,000

Some people complain that they cannot realize these figures. Of course they cannot. But that is the last thing one wants to do with big numbers—to "realize" them. In a few weeks' time our finance minister in England will be presenting his annual budget of about £900,000,000. Do you suppose that by way of preparation, he throws himself into a state of trance in which he can visualize the vast pile of coins or notes or commodities that it represents? I am quite sure he can not "realize" £900,000,000. But he can spend it. It is a fallacious idea that these big numbers create a difficulty in comprehending astronomy; they can only do so if you are seeking the wrong sort of comprehension. They are not meant to be gaped at, but to be manipulated and used. It is as easy to use millions and billions and trillions[18] for our counters as ones and twos and threes. What I want to call attention to in the above table is that since we are going out beyond the Milky Way we have taken a very big step up in the scale of distance.

The remarkable thing that has been discovered about these galaxies is that (except three or four of the nearest of them) they are running away from our own galaxy; and the further they are away, the faster they go. The distant ones have very high speeds. On the average the speed is proportional to the distance, so that a galaxy 10 million light-years away recedes at 1500 kilometres per second, one 50 million light-years away recedes at 7500 kilometres per second, and so on. The fastest yet discovered recedes at 42,000 kilometres per second.

Why are they all running away from us? If we think a little, we shall see that the aversion is not especially directed against us; they are running away from us, but they are also running away from each other. If this room were to expand 10 per cent in its dimensions, the seats all separating in proportion, you would at first think that everyone was moving away from you; the man 10 metres away has moved 1 metre further off; the man 20 metres away has moved 2 metres further off; and so on. Just as with the galaxies, the recession is proportional to the distance. This law of proportion is characteristic of a uniform expansion, not directed away from any one centre, but causing a general scattering apart. So we conclude that recession of the nebulae is an effort of uniform expansion.

The system of the galaxies is all the universe we know, and indeed we have strong reason to believe that it is the whole physical universe. The expansion of the system, or scattering apart of the galaxies, is therefore commonly referred to as the expansion of the universe; and the problem which it raises is the problem of the "expanding universe."

The expansion is proceeding so fast that, at the present rate, the nebulae will recede to double their present distances in 1300 million years. Astronomers will have to double the apertures of their telescopes every 1300 million years in order to keep pace with the recession. But seriously, 1300 million years is not a long period of cosmic history; I have already mentioned it as the age of terrestrial rocks. It comes as a surprise that the universe should have doubled its dimensions within geological times. It means that we cannot go back indefinitely in time; and indeed the enormous time-scale of billions of years, which was fashionable ten years ago, must be drastically cut down. We are becoming reconciled to this speeding up of the time-scale of evolution, for various other lines of evidence have convinced us that it is essential. It seems clear now that we must take an upper limit to the age of the stars not greater than 10,000 million years; previously, an age of a thousand times longer was commonly adopted.

For reasons which I cannot discuss fully we believe that along with the expansion of the material universe there is an expansion of space itself. The idea is that the island galaxies are scattered throughout a "spherical space." Spherical space means that if you keep going straight on in any direction you will ultimately find yourself back at your starting point. This is analogous to what happens when you travel straight ahead on the earth; you reach your starting point again, having gone round the world. But here we apply the analogy to an extra dimension—to *space* instead of to a *surface*. I realize, of course, that this conception of a closed spherical space is very difficult to grasp, but really it is not worse than the older conception of infinite open space which no one can properly imagine. No one can conceive infinity; one just uses the term by habit without trying to grasp it. If I may refer to our English expression, "out of the frying-pan into the fire," I suggest that if you feel that in receiving this modern conception of space you are falling into fire, please remember that you are at least escaping from the frying-pan.

Spherical space has many curious properties. I said that if you go straight ahead in any direction you will return to your starting point. So if you look far enough in any direction and there is nothing in the way, you ought to see—the back of your head. Well, not exactly—because light takes at least 6000 million years to travel round the universe and your head was not there when it started. But you will understand the general idea. However, these curiosities do not concern us much. The main point is that if the galaxies are distributed over the spherical space more or less in the same way that human beings are distributed over the earth, they cannot form an expanding system—they cannot all be receding from one another—unless the space itself expands. So the expansion of the material system involves, and is an aspect of, the expansion of space.

This scattering apart of the galaxies was not unforeseen. As far back as 1917, Professor W. de Sitter[19] showed that there was reason to expect this phenomenon and urged astronomers to look for it. But it is only recently that radial velocities of spiral nebulae have been measured in sufficient numbers to show conclusively that the scattering occurs. It is one of the deductions from relativity theory that there must exist a force, known as "cosmical repulsion," which tends to produce this kind of scattering in which every object recedes from every other object. You know the theory of relativity led to certain astronomical consequences—a bending of light near the sun detectable at eclipses, a motion of the perihelion[20] of Mercury, a red-shift of spectral lines—which have been more or less satisfactorily verified. The existence of cosmical repulsion is an equally definite consequence of the theory, though this is not so widely known—partly because it comes from a more difficult branch of the theory and was not noticed so early, and perhaps partly because it is not so directly associated with the magic name of Einstein.

I can see no reason to doubt that the observed recession of the spiral nebulae is due to cosmical repulsion, and is the effect predicted by relativity theory which we were hoping to find. Many other explanations have been proposed—some of them rather fantastic—and there has been a great deal of discussion which seems to me rather pointless. In this, as in other developments of scientific exploration, we must recognize the limitations of our present knowledge and be prepared to consider revolutionary changes. But when, as in this case, observation agrees with what our existing knowledge had led us to expect, it is reasonable to feel encouraged to pursue the line of thought which has proved successful; and there seems little excuse for an outburst of unsupported speculation.

...Now we have been over all the universe. If my survey has been rather inadequate, I might plead that light takes 6000 million years to make the circuit that I have made in an hour. Or rather, that was the original length of the circuit; but the universe is expanding continually, and whist I have been talking the increase of the circuit amounts to one or two more days' journey for the light. Anyhow, the time has come to leave this nightmare of immensity and find again, among the myriads of orbs, the tiny planet which is our home.

NOTES

1. **Jules Verne's:** Jules Verne (1828–1905), French writer of science fiction and author of ***Twenty Thousand Miles Under the Sea*** (1870), ***Around the World in Eighty Days*** (1873), etc.
2. **Catherine Wheel:** a kind of firework that rotates and throws out coloured lights
3. **Ophiuchus:** 蛇夫座 , a large constellation lying between Hercules and Scorpius
4. **Capella:** 御夫座 , the brightest star in the constellation Auriga
5. **Betelgeuse:** the second brightest star in the constellation Orion
6. **Orion:** 猎户座 , a constellation near Canis Major containing the bright stars Rigel and Betelgeuse
7. **Antares:** the brightest star in the constellation Scorpius
8. **Scorpio:** 天蝎座 , or Scorpius, a constellation lying between Libra and Sagittarius
9. **Mercury:** 水星 , the smallest planet of the solar system which is also the nearest to the

sun

10. **Venus:** 金星, the brightest planet which is the second nearest to the sun
11. **Mars:** 火星, the planet fourth in distance from the sun
12. **exhausted vessel:** vessel emptied of its contents
13. **crinoline:** petticoat of a stiff fabric
14. **the Companion of Sirius:** Sirius or Dog Star (天狼星) is the brightest star in the sky, lying in the constellation Canis Major; but its companion, Sirius ß (天狼星伴星), is a very faint star.
15. **Einstein's:** Albert Einstein (1879–1955), the German-born American physicist and mathematician who formulated the Special Theory of Relativity (1905) and the General Theory of Relativity (1916). He is noted not only for his revolutionary scientific principles but also for his contribution to world peace.
16. **spectro-heliograph:** an instrument for making spectro-heliograms or photographs of the sun
17. **Pluto:** 冥王星, a small planet which is the ninth in distance from the sun
18. **billions and trillions:** In British usage, a billion has traditionally meant "a million million" and a trillion "a million million million".
19. **Professor W. de Sitter:** Professor Willem de Sitter (1872–1934), Dutch astronomer
20. **perihelion:** the point nearest to the sun in the orbit of a planet

91

DAVID HERBERT LAWRENCE

(1885-1930)

D. H. Lawrence was an English novelist, poet, and critic. He was born at Eastwood, Nottinghamshire, on September 11, 1885, and educated at Nottingham High School, 1898-1901, and at University College, Nottingham, 1906-1908. He worked as a teacher from 1902 to 1912, and as a full-time writer from 1912 till his death. He lived in Germany in 1912-1914 and in England in 1914-1919; after 1919 he travelled and lived abroad, and died in a sanatorium at Vence, France, on March 2, 1930.

D. H. Lawrence was the author of such famous novels as **Sons and Lovers** (1913), **The Rainbow** (1915), **Women in Love** (1920), and **Lady Chatterley's Lover** (1928). In them he presents working-class life realistically, emphasizes the association of consciousness with feeling and sexuality, repudiates urbanism and industrialism, and yearns for a natural, simple way of life. His description of character and setting is impressive. Sometimes he uses natural surroundings and natural objects as symbols for mental or emotional states. His short stories were collected in volumes like **The Prussian Officer and Other Stories** (1914); **England, My England, and Other Stories** (1922); and **The Lady Bird and Other Tales** (1923). His travel books, **Twilight in Italy** (1916), **Sea and Sardinia** (1921), and **Mornings in Mexico** (1927), make excellent reading. His ***Studies in Classic American Literature*** (1923) is an interesting critical work. His ***Psychoanalysis and the Unconscious*** (1921) and ***Fantasia of the Unconscious*** (1922) are imaginative rather than scientific works. His volumes ***Look! We Have Come Through!*** (1917) and ***Birds, Beasts and Flowers*** (1923) are poems about man and nature. His prose is usually easy and natural, and only occasionally turgid.

PAUL'S FIRST DAY AT JORDAN'S

At eight o'clock he climbed the dismal stairs of Jordan's Surgical Appliance Factory, and stood helplessly against the first great parcel-rack, waiting for somebody to pick him up. The place was still not awake. Over the counters were great dust sheets. Two men only had arrived, and were heard talking in a corner, as they took off their coats and rolled up their shirt-sleeves. It was ten past eight. Evidently there was no rush of punctuality. Paul[1] listened to the voices of the two clerks. Then he heard someone cough, and saw in the office at the end of the room an old, decaying clerk, in a round smoking-cap of black velvet embroidered with red and green, opening letters. He waited and waited. One of the junior clerks went to the old man, greeted him cheerily and loudly. Evidently the old "chief" was deaf. Then the young fellow came striding importantly down to his counter. He spied Paul.

"Hello!" he said. "You the new lad?"

"Yes," said Paul.

"H'm! What's your name?"

"Paul Morel."

"Paul Morel? All right, you come on round here."

Paul followed him round the rectangle of counters. The room was second storey. It had a great hole in the middle of the floor, fenced as with a wall of counters, and down this wide shaft the lifts went, and the light for the bottom storey. Also there was a corresponding big, oblong hole in the ceiling, and one would see above, over the fence of the top floor, some machinery; and right away overhead was the glass roof, and all light for the three storeys came downwards, getting dimmer, so that it was always night on the ground floor and rather gloomy on the second floor. The factory was the top floor, the warehouse the second, the storehouse the ground floor. It was an insanitary, ancient place.

Paul was led round to a very dark corner.

"This is the 'Spiral'[2] corner," said the clerk. "You're Spiral[3], with Pappleworth. He's your boss, but he's not come yet. He doesn't get here till half-past eight. So you can fetch the letters, if you like, from Mr Melling down there."

The young man pointed to the old clerk in the office.

"All right," said Paul.

"Here's a peg to hang your cap on. Here are your entry ledgers. Mr Pappleworth won't be long."

And the thin young man stalked away with long, busy strides over the hollow wooden floor.

After a minute or two Paul went down and stood in the door of the glass office. The old clerk in the smoking-cap[4] looked down over the rim of his spectacles.

"Good morning," he said, kindly and impressively. "You want the letters for the Spiral department, Thomas?"

Paul resented being called "Thomas". But he took the letters and returned to his dark place, where the counter made an angle, where the great parcel-rack came to an end, and where there were three doors in the corner. He sat on a high stool and read the letters—those whose handwriting was not too difficult. They ran as follows:

"Will you please send me at once a pair of lady's silk spiral thigh-hose, without feet, such as I had from you last year; length, thigh to knee, etc." Or "Major Chamberlain wishes to repeat his previous order for a silk non-elastic suspensory bandage."

Many of the letters, some of them in French or Norwegian, were a great puzzle to the boy. He sat on his stool nervously awaiting the arrival of his "boss". He suffered tortures of shyness when, at half-past eight, the factory girls for upstairs trooped past him.

Mr Pappleworth arrived, chewing a chlorodyne gum[5], at about twenty to nine, when all the other men were at work. He was a thin, sallow man with a red nose, quick, staccato, and smartly but stiffly dressed. He was about thirty-six years old. There was something rather "doggy"[6], rather smart, rather 'cute[7] and shrewd, and something warm, and something slightly contemptible about him.

"You my new lad?" he said.

Paul stood up and said he was.

"Fetched the letters?"

Mr Pappleworth gave a chew to his gum.

"Yes."

"Copied 'em?"

"No."

"Well, come on then, let's look slippy[8]. Changed your coat?"

"No."

"You want to bring an old coat[9] and leave it here." He pronounced the last words, with the chlorodyne gum between his side teeth. He vanished into darkness behind the great parcel-rack, reappeared coatless, turning up a smart striped shirt-cuff over a thin and hairy arm. Then he slipped into his coat. Paul noticed how thin he was, and that his trousers were in folds behind. He seized a stool, dragged it beside the boy's, and sat down.

"Sit down," he said.

Paul took a seat.

Mr Pappleworth was very close to him. The man seized the letters, snatched a long entry-book out of a rack in front of him, flung it open, seized a pen, and said:

"Now look here. You want to copy these letters in here." He sniffed twice, gave a quick chew at his gum, stared fixedly at a letter, then went very still and absorbed, and wrote the entry rapidly, in a beautiful flourishing hand. He glanced quickly at Paul.

"See that?"

"Yes."

"Think you can do it all right?"

"Yes."

"All right then, let's see you."

He sprang off his stool. Paul took a pen. Mr Pappleworth disappeared. Paul rather liked copying the letters, but he wrote slowly, laboriously, and exceedingly badly. He was doing the fourth letter, and feeling quite busy and happy, when Mr

Pappleworth reappeared.

"Now then, how'r yer getting on? Done 'em?"

He leaned over the boy's shoulder, chewing, and smelling of chlorodyne[10].

"Strike my bob[11], lad, but you're a beautiful writer!" he exclaimed satirically. "Ne'er mind, how many h'yer done?[12] Only three! I'd a eaten 'em.[13] Get on, my lad, an' put numbers on 'em. Here, look! Get on!"

Paul ground away[14] at the letters. While Mr Pappleworth fussed over various jobs. Suddenly the boy started as a shrill whistle sounded near his ear. Mr Pappleworth came, took a plug out of a pipe, and said, in an amazingly cross and bossy voice:

"Yes?"

Paul heard a faint voice, like a woman's, out of the mouth of the tube. He gazed in wonder, never having seen a speaking-tube[15] before.

"Well," said Mr Pappleworth disagreeably into the tube, "you'd better get some of your back work done, then."

Again the woman's tiny voice was heard, sounding pretty and cross.

"I've not time to stand here while you talk," said Mr Pappleworth, and he pushed the plug into the tube.

"Come, my lad," he said imploringly to Paul, "there's Polly crying out for them orders. Can't you buck up[16] a bit? Here, come out!"

He took the book, to Paul's immense chagrin, and began the copying himself. He worked quickly and well. This done, he seized some strips of long yellow paper, about three inches wide, and made out the day's orders for the work-girls.

"You'd better watch me," he said to Paul, working all the while rapidly. Paul watched the weird little drawings of legs, and thighs, and ankles, with the strokes across and the numbers, and the few brief directions which his chief made upon the yellow paper. Then Mr Pappleworth finished and jumped up.

"Come on with me," he said, and the yellow papers flying in his hands, he dashed through a door and down some stairs, into the basement where the gas was burning. They crossed the cold, damp storeroom, then a long, dreary room with a long table on trestles, into a smaller, cosy apartment, not very high, which had been built on to the main building. In this room a small woman with a red serge blouse, and her black hair done on top of her head, was waiting like a proud little bantam.

"Here y'are!" said Pappleworth.

"I think it is 'here you are!'" exclaimed Polly. "The girls have been here nearly half an hour waiting. Just think of the time wasted!"

"*You* think of getting your work done and not talking so much," said Mr Pappleworth. "You could ha' been finishing off."

"You know quite well we finished everything off on Saturday!" cried Polly, flying at him, her dark eyes flashing.

"Tu-tu-tu-tu-terterter!" he mocked. "Here's your new lad. Don't ruin him as you did the last."

"As we did the last!" repeated Polly. "Yes, *we* do a lot of ruining, we do. My word, a lad would *take* some ruining after he'd been with you."

"It's time for work now, not for talk," said Mr Pappleworth severely and coldly.

"It was time for work some time back," said Polly, marching away with her head in the air. She was an erect little body of forty.

In that room were two round spiral machines on the bench under the window. Through the inner doorway was another longer room, with six more machines. A little group of girls, nicely dressed and in white aprons, stood talking together.

"Have you nothing else to do but talk?" said Mr Pappleworth.

"Only wait for you," said one handsome girl, laughing.

"Well, get on, get on," he said. "Come on, my lad. You'll know your road down here again."

And Paul ran upstairs after his chief. He was given some checking and invoicing to do. He stood at the desk, labouring in his execrable handwriting. Presently Mr Jordan came strutting down from the glass office and stood behind him, to the boy's great discomfort. Suddenly a red and fat finger was thrust on the form he was filling in.

"*Mr* J. A. Bates, Esquire!" exclaimed the cross voice just behind his ear.

Paul looked at "Mr J. A. Bates, Esquire" in his own vile writing, and wondered what was the matter now.

"Didn't they teach you any better than *that* while they were at it? If you put 'Mr' you don't put 'Esquire' —a man can't be both at once."

The boy regretted his too-much generosity in disposing of honours, hesitated, and with trembling fingers, scratched out the "Mr". Then all at once Mr Jordan snatched away the invoice.

"Make another! Are you going to send *that* to a gentleman?" And he tore up the blue form irritably.

Paul, his ears red with shame, began again. Still Mr Jordan watched.

"I don't know what they *do* teach in school. You'll have to write better than that. Lads learn nothing nowadays, but how to recite poetry and play the fiddle. Have you seen his writing?" he asked of Mr Pappleworth.

"Yes; prime[17], isn't it?" replied Mr Pappleworth, indifferently.

Mr Jordan gave a little grunt, not unamiable. Paul divined that his master's bark was worse than his bite. Indeed, the little manufacturer, although he spoke bad English, was quite gentleman enough to leave his men alone and to take no notice of trifles. But he knew he did not look like the boss and owner of the show, so he had to play his role of proprietor at first, to put things on a right footing.

"Let's see, *what's* your name?" asked Mr Pappleworth of the boy.

"Paul Morel."

It is curious that children suffer so much at having to pronounce their own names.

"Paul Morel, is it? All right, you Paul-Morel through them things there, and then—"

Mr Pappleworth subsided on to a stool, and began writing. A girl came up from out of a door just behind, put some newly pressed elastic web appliance on the counter, and returned. Mr Pappleworth picked up the whitey-blue knee-band, examined it and its yellow order-paper quickly, and put it on one side. Next was a flesh-pink "leg". He went through the few things, wrote out a couple of orders, and called to Paul to accompany him. This time they went through the door whence the girl had emerged. There Paul found himself at the top of a little wooden flight of steps, and below him saw a room with windows round two sides, and at the farther end half a dozen girls sitting bending over the benches in the light from the window, sewing. They were singing together "Two Little Girls in Blue". Hearing the door opened, they all turned round, to see Mr Pappleworth and Paul looking down on them from the far end of the room. They stopped singing.

"Can't you make a bit less row?" said Mr Pappleworth. "Folk'll think we keep cats."

A hunchback woman on a high stool turned her long, rather heavy face towards Mr Pappleworth, and said, in a contralto voice:

"They're all tom-cats then."

In vain Mr Pappleworth tried to be impressive for Paul's benefit. He descended the steps into the finishing-off room, and went to the hunchback Fanny. She had such a short body on her high stool that her head, with its great bands of bright brown hair, seemed over large, as did her pale, heavy face. She wore a dress of green-black cashmere, and her wrists, coming out of the narrow cuffs, were thin and flat, as she put down her work nervously. He showed her something that was wrong with a knee-cap.

"Well," she said, "you needn't come blaming it on to me. It's not my fault." Her colour mounted to her cheek.

"I never said it *was* your fault. Will you do as I tell you?" replied Mr Pappleworth shortly.

"You don't say it's my fault, but you'd like to make out as it was," the hunchback woman cried, almost in tears. Then she snatched the knee-cap from her "boss", saying: "Yes, I'll do it for you, but you needn't be snappy."

"Here's your new lad," said Mr Pappleworth.

Fanny turned, smiling very gently on Paul.

"Oh!" she said.

"Yes; don't make a softy[18] of him between you."

"It's not us as 'ud make a softy of him," she said indignantly.

"Come on then, Paul," said Mr Pappleworth.

"*Au revoy*[19], Paul," said one of the girls.

There was a titter of laughter. Paul went out, blushing deeply, not having spoken a word.

The day was very long. All morning the work-people were coming to speak to Mr Papplewort. Paul was writing or learning to make up parcels, ready for the midday post. At one o'clock, or, rather, at a quarter to one, Mr Papplewort disappeared to catch his train: he lived in the suburbs. At one o'clock, Paul, feeling very lost, took his dinner-basket down into the stockroom in the basement, that had the long table on trestles, and ate his meal hurriedly, alone in that cellar of gloom and desolation. Then he went out of doors. The brightness and the freedom of the streets made him feel adventurous and happy. But at two o'clock he was back in the corner of the big room. Soon the work-girls went trooping past, making remarks. It was the commoner girls who worked upstairs at the heavy tasks of truss-making[20] and the finishing of artificial limbs. He waited for Mr Papplewort, not knowing what to do, sitting scribbling on the yellow order-paper. Mr Papplewort came at twenty minutes to three. Then he sat and gossiped with Paul, treating the boy entirely as an equal, even in age.

In the afternoon there was never very much to do, unless it were near the week-end, and the accounts had to be made up. At five o'clock all the men went down into the dungeon with the table on trestles, and there they had tea, eating bread-and-butter on the bare, dirty boards, talking with the same kind of ugly haste and slovenliness with which they ate their meal. And yet upstairs the atmosphere among them was always jolly and clear. The cellar and the trestles affected them.

After tea, when all the gases were lighted, **work** went more briskly. There was the big evening post to get off. The hose came up warm and newly pressed from the workrooms. Paul had made out the invoices. Now he had the packing up and addressing to do, then he had to weigh his stock of parcels on the scales. Everywhere voices were calling weights, there was the chink of metal, the rapid snapping of string, the hurrying to old Mr Melling for stamps. And at last the postman came with his sack, laughing and jolly. Then everything slacked off, and Paul took his dinner-basket and ran to the station to catch the eight-twenty train. The day in the factory was just twelve hours long.

NOTES

1. **Paul:** Paul Morel, the central character of ***Sons and Lovers***
2. **Spiral:** The spiral is connected with the machine for making elastic.
3. **You're Spiral:** You are of the Spiral department.
4. **smoking-cap:** light ornamental cap
5. **chlorodyne gum:** patent medicine in the form of gum that allays pain
6. **doggy:** (sl.) dashing, showy
7. **'cute:** acute; sharp, clever
8. **look slippy:** (sl.) look sharp, make haste
9. **You want to bring an old coat...:** You will or should bring an old coat...
10. **smelling of chlorodyne:** giving off the smell of chlorodyne
11. **Strike my bob:** (sl.) come upon my shilling; dear me!
12. **how many h'yer done:** how many have you done
13. **I'd a eaten 'em:** I would have eaten them; I would have done them quickly.
14. **ground away:** worked continuously
15. **speaking-tube:** tube or pipe for conveying a person's voice from one room or building to another
16. **buck up:** (sl.) hurry
17. **prime:** excellent
18. **softy:** (informal) sentimental or weakly foolish person
19. *Au revoy*: (imitated French phrase) *Au revoir*, good-bye
20. **truss-making:** making trusses or pads for holding hernia in place

92

KATHERINE MANSFIELD
(PSEUDONYM OF KATHLEEN MANSFIELD BEAUCHAMP, 1888–1923)

Katherine Mansfield, the short-story writer, was born in Wellington, New Zealand, on October 14, 1888; studied at Queen's College, London, 1903–1906, and at the Royal Academy of Music, Wellington, 1906–1908; and settled in London in 1908 to embark on a literary career. She lived with John Middleton Murry, the critic, from 1912 and married him in 1918. She died of tuberculosis at Fontainebleau, France, on January 9, 1923.

Katherine Mansfield's stories were collected in five volumes, three in her lifetime and two posthumously: **In a German Pension** (1911), **Bliss and Other Stories** (1920), **The Garden Party and Other Stories** (1922), **The Dove's Nest and Other Stories** (1923), and **Something Childish and Other Stories** (1924). The clarity of detail and atmosphere, the symbolic use of objects and incidents, the presentation of interior monologue and shifting viewpoints, and the selection of significant impressions of life are some special features of her work. Her range of materials is rather narrow, but her art is original and illuminating.

THE GARDEN PARTY

And after all the weather was ideal. They could not have had a more perfect day for a garden party if they had ordered it. Windless, warm, the sky without a cloud. The gardener had been up since dawn cutting the grass and sweeping the lawns until they shone. The roses seemed to understand that they are the only flowers that impress people at garden parties; the only flowers that everybody knows. Hundreds, yes, hundreds had come out in a single night. The green bushes were weighed down with them.

The men came to put up the marquee[1] before breakfast was over.

"Where do you want them to put the marquee, mother?"

"My dear child, it's no use asking me. I'm determined to leave everything to you children this year. Forget I am your mother. Treat me as a guest."

But Meg could not possibly go and tell the men what to do. She had washed her hair before breakfast, and she sat drinking her coffee with a scarf over her head, and a dark, wet curl carefully arranged on each cheek.

"You'll have to go, Laura; you're the artistic one."

Laura ran off, still holding her piece of bread and butter. It was so good to have an excuse for eating outside, and besides, she loved arranging things. She always felt she could do it so much better than anybody else.

Four men stood in a group on the garden path. They carried pieces of wood covered with rolls of canvas, and they had big toolbags on their backs. They looked impressive. Laura wished now that she was not holding that piece of bread and butter, but there was nowhere to put it, and she couldn't possibly throw it away. She blushed and tried to look severe as she came up to them.

"Good morning," she said, copying her mother's voice. But that sounded so unnatural that she felt ashamed, and went on nervously like a little girl, "Oh–er– have you come—is it about the marquee?"

"That's right, miss," said the tallest of the men, and he moved his toolbag slightly, knocked back his straw hat and smiled down at her. "That's it."

His smile was so easy, so friendly, that Laura recovered. What nice eyes he had, small, but such a dark blue! And now she looked at the others, they were smiling too. "Cheer up, we won't bite," their smile seemed to say. How very nice workmen were! And what a beautiful morning! She mustn't mention the morning; she must be businesslike. The marquee.

"Well, what about on the lawn? Would that be suitable?"

And she pointed to the lawn with the hand that didn't hold the bread and butter. They turned, they stared in the direction. A little fat man shook his head, and the tall man looked doubtful.

"I don't think so," he said. "It wouldn't stand out enough. You see, with something like a marquee," and he turned to Laura in his easy way, "you want to put it somewhere where it'll hit you in the eye[2], if you see what I mean."

Because of the way she had been brought up, Laura wondered for a moment whether it was quite respectful of a workman to talk to her like that. But she saw what he meant.

"A corner of the tennis-court," she suggested. "But the band's going to be in one corner."

"H'm, you're going to have a band, are you?" said another of the workmen. He looked pale and tired. What was he thinking?

"Only a very small band," said Laura gently. Perhaps he wouldn't mind so much if the band was quite small. But the tall man interrupted.

"Look miss, that's the place. Against those trees. Over there. That'll be fine."

Against the trees. Then they would be hidden. And they were so lovely, with their broad, shining leaves, and their yellow fruit. Must they be hidden by a marquee?

Yes, they must. Already the men had picked up their things and were walking towards the place. Only the tall man was left. He bent down to one of the rose-bushes and breathed in the scent. When Laura saw that, she was filled with wonder at him caring for things like that—caring for the smell of a rose. How many men that she knew would have done such a thing? Oh, how extraordinarily nice workmen were, she thought. Why couldn't she have workmen for friends rather than the silly boys she danced with, and who came to Sunday night supper? She would get on much better with men like these.

It's all the fault of these stupid class distinctions, she decided, as the tall man drew a diagram on the back of an old envelope. Well, for her part, she didn't feel them. Not a bit, not at all... And now there came the sound of wooden hammers. Someone whistled. someone called out, "Are you all right there?" It all seemed so friendly, so–so–Just to show the tall man how happy she felt, just to prove that she didn't believe in class distinctions, Laura took a big bite of her bread and butter as she stared at the little drawing. She felt just like a workgirl.

"Laura, Laura, where are you? Telephone, Laura!" a voice cried from the house.

"I'm coming!" She ran off, over the lawn, up the path, up the steps and into the house. In the hall her father and her brother Laurie were brushing their hats ready to go to the office.

"Hey, Laura," said Laurie very fast, "could you just have a look at my coat before this afternoon, and see if it needs pressing."

"I will," she said. Suddenly she couldn't stop herself. She ran to Laurie and put her arms round him. "Oh, I love parties, don't you?" she said excitedly.

"I do too," said Laurie's warm voice, and he gave his sister a gentle push. "Run off to the telephone, dear."

The telephone. "Yes, yes; oh yes. Kitty? Hello. Come to lunch? Yes, of course you can. It will only be a very simple meal—just sandwiches and what's left over from the preparations. Yes, isn't it a perfect morning? Your white dress? Yes, you must wear that. One moment—hold the line. Mother's calling." And Laura sat back. "What, mother? I can't hear."

Mrs Sheridan's voice floated down the stairs. "Tell her to wear that sweet hat she had on last Sunday."

"Mother says you must wear that sweet hat you had on last Sunday. Good. I'll see you at one o'clock then. Bye-bye."

Laura put back the receiver, stretched her arms above her head, took a deep breath, and let them fall again.

"Huh," she sighed, and the moment after the sigh she sat up quickly. She was still, listening. All the doors in the house seemed to be open. The house was alive with soft, quick steps and the sound of voices. The door that led to the kitchen swung open and shut. And then came the sound of the heavy piano being moved. The air was wonderful—warm and alive. Was the air always like this, if you stopped to notice it? There were two tiny spots of sunlight, one on the inkpot, one on a silver photograph frame. Lovely little spots. Especially the one on the inkpot. It was quite warm. A warm little silver star. She felt like kissing it.

The front door bell rang and she heard Sadie go and open it. A man's voice said something; Sadie answered, carelessly, "I'm sure I don't know. Wait. I'll ask Mrs Sheridan."

"What is it, Sadie?" Laura came into the hall.

"It's the flowers, Miss Laura."

And so it was. There, just inside the door, stood a wide, shallow tray full of pots of pink lilies. No other kind of flowers. Nothing but lilies, big pink flowers wide open, almost frighteningly alive on bright red stems.

"O—oh, Sadie!" said Laura. She bent down as if to warm herself at a fire. She felt as if the lilies were in her fingers, on her lips, growing in her breast.

"It's a mistake," she said faintly. "Nobody ever ordered so many. Sadie, go and find mother."

But at that moment Mrs Sheridan joined them.

"It's quite right," she said calmly. "Yes, I ordered them. Aren't they lovely?" She pressed Laura's arm. "I was passing the shop yesterday, and I saw them in the window. And I suddenly thought, for once in my life I shall have enough lilies. The garden party will be a good excuse."

"But I thought you said you didn't mean to interfere," said Laura. Sadie had gone. The man from the flower shop was still outside at his van. She put her arm round her mother's neck and gently, very gently, she bit her mother's ear.

"My dear child, you wouldn't like a logical mother, would you? Don't do that. Here's the man."

He carried more lilies still, another whole tray.

"Put them just inside the door, on both sides of the hall, please," said Mrs Sheridan. "Do you agree, Laura?"

"Oh, I do, mother."

In the sitting-room Meg, Jose and good little Hans had at last succeeded in moving the piano.

"Now if we put this couch against the wall and move everything out of the room except the chairs, that'll be best, don't you think?"

"Right."

"Hans, move these tables into the dining-room, and bring a brush to take the dust off the carpet and—one moment, Hans—" Jose loved giving orders to the servants, and they loved obeying her. She always made them feel that they were taking part in a drama. "Tell mother and Miss Laura to come here at once."

"Very good, Miss Jose."

She turned to Meg. "I want to hear what the piano sounds like, just in case I'm asked to sing this afternoon. Let's practise a song."

As the first notes of the piano filled the room Jose's face changed. She looked sorrowfully at her mother and Laura as they came in.

> "A love that changes,
> And then...goodbye!"

But as she sang the word "goodbye", although the piano sounded more sorrowful than ever, she gave them a brilliant, totally unsympathetic smile.

"Isn't my voice good today, mummy?" she said.

But now Sadie interrupted them. "What is it, Sadie?"

"If you please, cook says have you got the flags for the sandwiches?"[3]

"The flags for the sandwiches, Sadie?" repeated Mrs Sheridan dreamily. And the children knew by her face that she hadn't got them. "Let me see." And she said to Sadie firmly, "Tell cook I'll let her have them in ten minutes."

Sadie went.

"Now Laura," said her mother quickly, "come with me into the dining-room. I've got the names somewhere on the back of an envelope. You'll have to write them out for me. Meg, go upstairs this minute and take that wet thing off your head. Jose, run and finish dressing at once. Do you hear me, children, or shall I have to tell your father when he comes home tonight? And—and, Jose, be nice to cook if you go into the kitchen, will you? I'm really frightened of her this morning."

The envelope was found at last behind the dining-room clock, although Mrs Sheridan could not imagine how it had got there.

"One of you children must have stolen it out of my bag, because I remember putting it there quite clearly. Cheese and tomato. Have you written that?"

"Yes."

"Egg and—" Mrs Sheridan held the envelope away from her. "It looks like mice. It can't be mice, can it?"

"Olive, dear," said Laura looking over her shoulder.

"Yes, of course, olive. What an awful combination it sounds. Egg and olive."

The flags were finished at last, and Laura took them off to the kitchen. She found Jose there being nice to cook, who did not look at all frightening.

"I have never seen such wonderful sandwiches before," said Jose. "How many kinds did you say there were, cook? Fifteen?"

"Fifteen, Miss Jose."

"Well, cook, I congratulate you."

Cook put the flags on the plates of sandwiches and smiled broadly.

"Godber's man has come," announced Sadie coming into the kitchen. She had seen the man pass the window.

That meant that the cream cakes had arrived. Godber's the baker's were famous for their cream cakes. Nobody ever made them at home.

"Bring them in and put them on the table, my girl," ordered cook.

Sadie brought in the cakes and went back to the door. Of course Laura and Jose were far too old to care about such things as cream cakes. However they agreed that the cakes looked very attractive. Very. Cook began arranging them, shaking off the extra sugar.

"They remind you of all your parties, don't they?" said Laura.

"I suppose so," said practical Jose, who never liked to be reminded of the past. "They look beautifully light, I must say."

"Have one each, my dears," said cook in her comfortable voice. "Your mother won't know."

Oh, it would be impossible to eat cream cakes so soon after breakfast. No, they really couldn't. However two minutes later Jose and Laura were licking their fingers contentedly.

"Let's go into the garden, out by the back way," suggested Laura. "I want to see how the men are getting on with the marquee. They're very nice men."

But the back door was blocked by cook, Sadie, and Godber's man.

Something had happened.

"Oh dear," cook stood there, slowly shaking her head from side to side. Sadie had her hand over her mouth as if to stop herself from crying out. Only Godber's man seemed to be enjoying himself; it was his story.

"What's the matter? What's happened?"

"There's been a terrible accident," said cook. "A man has been killed."

"A man killed! Where? How? When?"

But Godber's man was determined to tell the story himself.

"You know those little cottages just below here, miss?" Did she know them? Of course she knew them. "Well, there's a young fellow living there called Scott. He was thrown off his horse at the corner of Hawke Street this morning. He fell on the back of his head and was killed."

"Dead!" Laura stared at Godber's man.

"Dead when they picked him up," said Godber's man, enjoying the effect his story was having on them. "They were taking the body home as I came up here." And he said to cook, "He's left a wife and five children."

"Jose, come here." Laura caught hold of her sister's arm and dragged her through the kitchen and into the hall. There she paused. "Jose!" she said in a shocked voice, "however are we going to stop everything?"

"Stop everything, Laura!" cried Jose in astonishment. "What do you mean?"

"Stop the garden party, of course." Why did Jose pretend that she didn't understand?

But Jose was still more surprised. "Stop the garden party? My dear Laura, don't be so silly. Of course we can't stop it. Nobody expects us to. Don't be so stupid."

"But we can't possibly have a garden party with a man dead just outside the front gate."

That really was a stupid thing to say, for the little cottages were in their own street at the bottom of a steep hill that led up to the Sheridans' house. A broad road ran between them. It was true that they were far too near. They were terribly ugly and they had no right to be in that neighbourhood at all. They were poor little houses painted a chocolate brown colour. In the tiny little gardens there was nothing but cabbages, sick hens and empty tins. Even the smoke coming out of their chimneys looked poor. Workmen lived there and there were always crowds of children. When the Sheridans were little they were forbidden to go there in case they caught some awful disease. But since they were older Laura and Laurie sometimes walked through. It was disgusting. But still one must go everywhere; one must see everything. So they went through.

"And just think how terrible the band would sound to that poor woman," said Laura.

"Oh, Laura!" Jose began to be seriously annoyed. "If you're going to stop a band playing every time someone has an accident, you'll lead a very busy life. I'm just as sorry about it as you. I feel just as sympathetic." Her eyes hardened. She looked at her sister just as she used to when they were little and fighting together. "You won't bring a drunk workman back to life by stopping the party," she said softly.

"Drunk! He wasn't drunk!" Laura turned on Jose angrily. "I'm going up to tell mother," she said, just as they used to say when they were little.

"Yes, you do that," said Jose sweetly.

"Mother, can I come into your room?" Laura pushed open the big, heavy door.

"Of course, child. Why, what's the matter? What's made you so pale?" And Mrs Sheridan turned round from her dressing-table. She was trying on a new hat.

"Mother, a man's been killed," began Laura.

"Not in the garden?" interrupted her mother.

"No, no!"

"Oh, what a fright you gave me!" Mrs Sheridan sighed with relief, and took off the big hat and held it on her knees.

"But listen, mother," said Laura, and she told the terrible story. "Of course, we can't have our party, can we?" she begged. "The band and everybody arriving. They'd hear us, mother. They're nearly neighbours!"

To Laura's astonishment her mother behaved just like Jose. It was harder to bear because she seemed to be amused. She refused to take Laura seriously.

"But, my dear child, be sensible. It's only by chance that we've heard about it. If someone had died there normally—and I can't understand how they stay alive in those awful little houses—we would still have our party, wouldn't we?"

Laura had to say "yes" to that, but she felt that it was all wrong. She sat down on her mother's bed and picked up a hair-brush.

"Mother, isn't it really terribly heartless of us?" she asked.

"My dear!" Mrs Sheridan got up and came over to her carrying the hat. Before her daughter could stop her, she had put it on Laura's head. "My child!" said her mother, "the hat is yours. It's made for you. It's much too young for me. I have never seen you look so charming before. Look at yourself!" And she held up her hand-mirror.

"But, mother," Laura began again. She couldn't look at herself; she turned away.

This time Mrs Sheridan lost patience just as Jose had done.

"You are being very stupid Laura," she said coldly. "People of that sort don't expect sacrifices from us. And it's not very sympathetic to spoil everybody's enjoyment as you're doing now."

"I don't understand," said Laura, and she walked quickly out of the room into her own bedroom. There, quite by chance, the first thing she saw was this charming girl in the mirror, in her black hat with gold flowers on it, and a long black ribbon. She had never imagined she could look like that. Is mother right? she thought. And now she hoped her mother was right. Am I being stupid? Perhaps it was stupid. Just for a moment she imagined once again that poor woman and those little children, and the body being carried into the house. But it all seemed far away and unreal, like a picture in the newspaper. I'll remember it again after the party's over, she decided. And somehow that seemed quite the best plan...

Lunch was over by half past one. By half past two they were all ready for the party. The band had arrived, dressed in green coats and had taken up their positions in a corner of the tennis-court.

"My dear!" cried Kitty Maitland, "don't they look just like frogs? You ought to have arranged them round the pond with the conductor in the middle on a leaf."

Laurie arrived and waved to them on his way up to dress. At the sight of him Laura remembered the accident again. She wanted to tell him. If Laurie agreed with the others, then it must be all right. And she followed him into the hall.

"Laurie!"

"Hello!" He was half-way upstairs, but when he turned round and saw Laura he stopped suddenly and stared at her. "Laura, you look absolutely wonderful," said Laurie. "What a beautiful hat!"

Laura said faintly "Is it?" and smiled up at Laurie, and didn't tell him about the accident after all.

Soon after that people started to arrive. The band began to play; the hired waiters ran from the house to the marquee. Wherever you looked there were couples walking, bending to the flowers, greeting each other, moving on over the lawn. They were like bright birds that had paused in the Sheridans' garden for this one afternoon, on their way to—where? Ah, what happiness it is to be with people who are all happy, to press hands, press cheeks, smile into eyes.

"My dear Laura, how well you look!"

"What a beautiful hat. It suits you child!"

"Laura, you look quite Spanish. I've never seen you look so charming."

And Laura, smiling, answered softly, "Have you had tea? Won't you have an ice? They are really rather special." She ran to her father and begged him. "Daddy dear, can't the band have something to drink?"

And, like a flower, the perfect afternoon slowly ripened, slowly faded, slowly its petals closed.

"The most delightful garden-party..."

"The greatest success..."

"Quite the most wonderful afternoon..."

Laura helped her mother with the goodbyes. They stood side by side at the door until it was all over.

"All over, all over, thank heaven," said Mrs Sheridan. "Go and find the others, Laura, and let's have some fresh coffee. I'm so tired. Yes, it was very successful. But oh, these parties! Why must you children give parties!" And they all of them sat down in the empty marquee.

"Have a sandwich, daddy dear. I wrote the name on the flag."

"Thanks." Mr Sheridan took a bite and the sandwich was gone. He took another. "I suppose you didn't hear about an awful accident that happened today?" he said.

"My dear," said Mrs Sheridan, holding up her hand, "we did. It nearly spoilt everything. Laura wanted us to stop the party."

"Oh, mother!" Laura didn't want them to laugh at her.

"It was a terrible affair though," said Mr Sheridan. "The man was married too. He lived just below us in that street of little cottages. He leaves a wife and half a dozen children, so they say."

An awkward little silence fell. Mrs Sheridan picked up her cup, feeling uncomfortable. Really, it was very unkind of father to talk about the accident.

Suddenly she looked up. There on the table were all those sandwiches and cakes, all un-eaten, all going to be wasted. She had one of her brilliant ideas.

"I know," she said. "Let's take her a basket. Let's send that poor woman some of this perfectly good food. It will be a great treat for the children, anyway. Don't you agree? And there are sure to be neighbours calling on her and so on. What an advantage to have some food all ready prepared. Laura!" She jumped up.

"Get me the big basket out of the cupboard under the stairs."

"But, mother, do you really think it's a good idea?" said Laura.

Again, how strange, she seemed to be different from them all. To take leftovers[4] from their party. Would the poor woman really like that?

"Of course! What's the matter with you today? An hour or two ago you were telling us to be sympathetic, and now you've changed your mind."

Oh well! Laura ran for the basket. It was filled, it was heaped by her mother.

"Take it yourself, dear," she said. "Run down there now. Don't change your clothes. No, wait, take the lilies too. People of that class are so impressed by lilies."

"The lilies will ruin her dress," said practical Jose.

"Yes, so they will. Only the basket then. Off you go."

Dusk was falling as Laura shut their garden gates. A big dog ran by like a shadow. The road shone white, and down below in the hollow the little cottages were in deep shade. It seemed so quiet after the afternoon. Now she was going down the hill to somewhere where a man lay dead, and she couldn't realise it. Why couldn't she? She stopped a minute. And it seemed to her that kisses, voices, music, laughter, the smell of crushed grass were somehow inside her. There was no room for anything else in her. How strange! She looked up at the pale sky, and all she thought was, "Yes, it was a most successful party."

Now she had crossed the broad road. The street began smoky and dark. Women in shawls hurried by. Men stood at the doors; children played in the gardens. The sound of voices came from the little cottages. In some of them there was a light, and a shadow moved across the window. Laura bent her head and hurried on. She wished now that she had put on a coat. Her dress shone. And the big hat with the long ribbon—if only it was a different hat! Were the people looking at her? They must be. It was a mistake to have come; she knew all the time that it was a mistake. Should she go back even now?

No, too late. This was the house. It must be. A small group of people stood outside. Beside the gate an old, old woman sat in a chair, watching. She had her feet on a newspaper. The voices stopped as Laura came near. The group made way for her. It was as though she was expected, as though they had known that she was coming here.

Laura was terribly nervous. She said to a woman standing by, "Is this Mrs Scott's house?" and the woman, smiling queerly, said, "It is, my girl."

Oh, if only she was away from all this! She actually said, "Help me, God," as she walked up the tiny path and knocked at the door. To be away from those staring eyes, or to be covered up in anything, even in one of those women's shawls. I'll just leave the basket and go, she decided. I won't even wait for it to be emptied.

Then the door opened. A little woman in black could be seen in the darkness.

Laura said, "Are you Mrs Scott?" But the woman answered, "Walk in, please, miss," and she was shut in the passage.

"No," said Laura, "I don't want to come in. I only want to leave this basket. Mother sent—"

The little woman in the dark passage seemed not to have heard her. "Come this way, please, miss," she said in an oily voice[5], and Laura followed her.

She found herself in a miserable little low kitchen, lighted by a smoky lamp. There was a woman sitting in front of the fire.

"Em," said the little woman who had let her in. "Em! It's a young lady." She turned to Laura. She said, "I'm her sister, miss. You'll excuse her, won't you?"

"Oh, but of course!" said Laura. "Please, please don't disturb her. I—I only want to leave—"

But at that moment the woman at the fire turned round. Her face, red, with swollen eyes and swollen lips looked terrible. She seemed as though she couldn't understand why Laura was there. What did it mean? Why was this stranger standing in the kitchen with a basket? What was it all about? And then she began to cry again.

"All right, my dear," said her sister. "I'll thank the young lady."

And again she began, "You'll excuse her, miss, I'm sure," and her face, swollen too, tried to give an oily smile.

Laura only wanted to get out, to get away. She was back in the passage. The door opened. She walked straight through into the bedroom where the dead man was lying.

"You'd like to look at him, wouldn't you?" said Em's sister, and she went past Laura over to the bed. "Don't be afraid, miss," and now her voice sounded fond and sly[6]. Gently she pulled back the sheet, "He looks lovely. There's nothing to show he's dead. Come along, my dear."

Laura came.

There lay a young man, fast asleep—sleeping so soundly, so deeply, that he was far, far away from them both. So distant, so peaceful. He was dreaming. His head was sunk in the pillow, his eyes were closed; they were blind under the closed eyelids. He was given up to his dream. What did garden parties and baskets and pretty dresses matter to him? He was far from all those things. He was wonderful, beautiful. While they were laughing and while the band was playing, this marvel had come to the little street. Happy... happy... All is well, said that sleeping face. This is just as it should be. I am content.

But still you had to cry, and she couldn't go out of the room without saying something to him. Laura gave a loud childish sob.

"Forgive me for wearing this hat," she said.

And this time she didn't wait for Em's sister. She found her way out of the door, down the path, past all those dark people. At the corner of the street she met Laurie.

He came out of the shadows. "Is that you, Laura?"

"Yes."

"Mother was getting anxious. Was it all right?"

"Yes, quite. Oh, Laurie!" She took his arm, she pressed up against him.

"You're not crying, are you?" asked her brother.

Laura shook her head. But she was crying.

Laurie put his arm round her shoulder. "Don't cry," he said in his warm, loving voice. "Was it awful?"

"No!" cried Laura. "It was simply marvellous. But, Laurie—" She stopped, she looked at her brother. "Isn't life," she said, "isn't life—" But what life was she couldn't explain. It didn't matter. He understood perfectly. "Isn't it, dear?" said Laurie.

NOTES

1. **marquee:** large tent used at fêtes or shows
2. **hit you in the eye:** catch your eye
3. **the flags for the sandwiches:** the labels for the sandwiches
4. **left-overs:** food uneaten at a meal
5. **in an oily voice:** in a fawning or obsequious voice
6. **sly:** with hidden meaning

93

ROBIN GEORGE COLLINGWOOD

(1889–1943)

R. G. Collingwood was an English historian and philosopher. He was born at Cartmel, Lancashire, the son of the artist and antiquarian W. G. Collingwood, and educated at Rugby and Oxford. He served as Professor of Philosophy at Oxford University from 1935 to 1941. He published numerous works on Ancient Britain, including **Roman Britain** (1921) and **Roman Britain and the English Settlements** (with J. N. L. Myers, 1936). In **The Idea of History** (1946), a masterpiece, he combines history with philosophy. **An Essay on Philosophical Method** (1933) is his best-known book on philosophy. **The Principles of Art** (1938) is based on his wide knowledge of the arts and much concerned with the role of art in modern life. **An Autobiography** (1939) is a vigorous account of his life and personality.

THE NATURE, OBJECT AND PURPOSE OF HISTORY

I shall therefore propound answers to my four questions such as I think any present-day historian would accept. Here they will be rough and ready[1] answers, but they will serve for a provisional definition of our subject-matter and they will be defended and elaborated as the argument proceeds.

(a) What is history? Every historian would agree, I think, that history is a kind of research or inquiry. What kind of inquiry it is I do not yet ask. The point is that generically it belongs to what we call the sciences: that is, the forms of thought whereby we ask questions and try to answer them. Science in general, it is important to realize, does not consist in collecting what we already know and arranging it in this or that kind of pattern. It consists in fastening upon something we do not know, and trying to discover it. Playing patience[2] with things we already know may be a useful means towards this end, but it is not the end itself. It is at best only the means. It is scientifically valuable only in so far as the new arrangement gives us the answer to a question we have already decided to ask. That is why all science begins from the knowledge of our own ignorance: not our ignorance of everything, but our ignorance of some definite thing—the origin of parliament, the cause of cancer, the chemical composition of the sun, the way to make a pump work without muscular exertion on the part of a man or a horse or some other docile animal. Science is finding things out: and in that sense history is a science.

(b) What is the object of history? One science differs from another in that it finds out things of a different kind. What kinds of things does history find out? I answer, ***res gestae***[3]: actions of human beings that have been done in the past. Although this answer raises all kinds of further questions many of which are controversial, still, however they may be answered, the answers do not discredit the proposition that history is the science of ***res gestae***, the attempt to answer questions about human actions done in the past.

(c) How does history proceed? History proceeds by the interpretation of evidence: where evidence is a collective name for things which singly are called documents, and a document is a thing existing here and now, of such a kind that the historian, by thinking about it, can get answers to the questions he asks about past events. Here again there are plenty of difficult questions to ask as to what the characteristics of evidence are and how it is interpreted. But there is no need for us to raise them at this stage. However they are answered[4], historians will agree that historical procedure, or method, consists essentially of interpreting evidence.

(d) Lastly, what is history for? This is perhaps a harder question than the others; a man who answers it will have to reflect rather more widely than a man who answers the three we have answered already. He must reflect not only on historical thinking but on other things as well, because to say that something is "for" something implies a distinction between A and B, where A is good for something and B is that for which something is good. But I will suggest an answer, and express the opinion that no historian would reject it, although the further questions to which it gives rise are numerous and difficult.

My answer is that history is "for" human self-knowledge. It is generally thought to be of importance to man that he should know himself: where knowing himself means knowing not his merely personal peculiarities, the things that distinguish him from other men, but his nature as man. Knowing yourself means knowing, first, what it is to be a man; secondly, knowing what it is to be the kind of man you are; and thirdly, knowing what it is to be the man you are and nobody else is. Knowing yourself means knowing what you can do; and since nobody knows what he can do until he tries, the only clue to what man can do is what man has done. The value of history, then, is that it teaches us what man has done and thus what man is.

NOTES

1. **rough and ready:** not elaborate but effective
2. **patience:** a card game for one person with the object of arranging the cards in some systematic order
3. **res gestae:** (Lat.) things done
4. **However they are answered:** No matter how they are answered.

94

JOHN MIDDLETON MURRY
(1889–1957)

J. Middleton Murry was an English critic. He was born in London, of lower-middle-class parents, and educated at Christ's Hospital and Brasenose College, Oxford. After a few years of journalistic work, he served in the War Office from 1916 to 1919, and edited *The Athenaeum* from 1919 to 1921 and *The Adelphi* from 1923 to 1948. He met Katherine Mansfield in 1912 and married her in 1918. His numerous critical works include **Keats and Shakespeare** (1925), **Son of Woman, the Story of D. H. Lawrence** (1931), **William Blake** (1933), and **Jonathan Swift** (1954). In his studies of writers, he relates their lives to the art. **The Problem of Style** (1922) is perhaps his best-known book. **Between Two Worlds** (1935) is his autobiography. He edited the literary remains of Katherine Mansfield, namely her **Journal** (1927), **Novels and Novelists** (1930), **Scrapbook** (1939), and **Letters to John Middleton Murry, 1913–1922** (1951).

THREE MEANINGS OF THE WORD STYLE

We may make a little clearing in the jungle by considering the way in which the word Style is commonly used. I think that I detect at least three fairly distinct meanings; they appear in these three sentences. First, "I know who wrote the article in last week's **Saturday Review**[1]—Mr. Saintsbury[2]. You couldn't mistake the style." Second, "Mr. Wilkinson's ideas are interesting; but he must learn to write; at present he has no style." Third, "You may call Marlowe bombastic; you may even call him farcical; but one quality outweighs his bombast, his savagery, and his farce—he has style."

In the first of these sentences "I know who wrote the article in the **Saturday Review**—Mr. Saintsbury. You couldn't mistake the style", "style" means that personal idiosyncrasy of expression by which we recognize a writer. Many elements go to make up this individuality. One of the best ways of distinguishing them and discovering the order of their importance is to play that excellent game of guessing the authorship of passages. It is easy to guess Dr. Johnson or Gibbon or Meredith[3] or Henry James[4]; it is much harder to guess Tourneur[5] or Webster[6] or Beaumont and Fletcher; you will probably find yourself fathering any half-dozen lines of the **Maid's Tragedy**[7] on to Shakespeare. You may give ten lines of Webster to Shakespeare; in twenty, however, you will know your man. There is a handling of the long rhythmical period in Shakespeare, a subtlety of harmony, a swift superabundance of metaphor, that not even the greatest of his contemporaries could touch. When the writer speaks in his own person, as the essayist or the critic, you look first to his turn of thought, then to his turn of phrase; when you are dealing with the "objective" art of the dramatist or the novelist, you look, perhaps, first to his turn of phrase, then to the peculiarity of his vision. Whatever goes to make a man's writing recognizable is included in his style.

To say that a writer has his style in this sense of idiosyncrasy is by no means necessarily to praise him. The individuality of Meredith's style is undeniable;

there is a growing body of opinion that it was not a good one. The great Doctor's peculiarities have received the irreverent name of Johnsonese. Henry James's later manner was so much his own that it reminded Mr. H.G. Wells of "a hippopotamus trying to pick up a pea". On the other hand, to say that a writer has not a style in this sense is, I think to condemn him; though it would demand much more skill and learning than most of us possess to pronounce positively on the authorship of an unfamiliar piece of English prose written at the end of the seventeenth century. The *sermo communis*[8] of those days had a limpidity which makes it hard to be sure of the personal nuance.

In the second sentence: "Mr. Wilkinson's ideas are interesting; but he must learn to write; at present he has no style", the word is used of the technique of expression. This style is the quality which—it is often said—French journalists do, and English journalists do not, possess by nature; the power of lucid exposition of a sequence of ideas. I think that style in this sense can only be properly applied to the exposition of intellectual ideas. I am suggesting that whereas we may with propriety use the sentence "He has good ideas, but a bad style" of a philosopher or an essayist, it is not applicable to a novelist or a poet. In the first place, novelists and poets, *qua*[9] novelists and poets, do not really have ideas at all, they have perceptions, intuitions, emotional convictions; and secondly, the only evidence that they have true perceptions is the fact that they are conveyed to us in all their particularity. If this is done it is misleading to speak of the style as being good or bad; the novel or the poem has the excellence proper to it. The novel or the poem that is well conceived and badly written is a chimera. "***Tout déroule de la conception***"[10], said Flaubert, unconsciously following Aristotle's words of wisdom about plots. If a story or a poem is really well conceived, it is immune from the danger of being badly written; for to conceive a work of creative literature is to conceive it in its particularity. An argument is a different matter; it is concerned with ideas in the logical sense, and these may be expounded either clearly or obscurely, with economy or waste. Style of this kind may be (to some degree at least) taught, as it is taught in France today, and as it was taught in the old schools of rhetoric.

Of course it is true that there are certain general rules of composition that must be observed: one must not be ambiguous, one must avoid solecisms, one's grammar must be reasonably correct. More offences are actually committed against these elementary rules by reputable writers than is generally supposed; and Shakespeare had a perceptible tendency to override grammar altogether in his latest work. But if it is impossible to hold that offences of this kind are anything but offences, except when committed, as most frequently in Shakespeare, for potent dramatic reasons, it is certain that no amount of correctness in grammar and composition is enough to make a positive style, even in the sense of technique of expression.

In the third sentence: "Marlowe, in spite of his bombast, his savagery and farce, had style", the word is used absolutely. We do not know precisely what it means; but we know that it means generally that Marlowe could write such lines as

See where Christ's blood streams in the firmament[11]...

or,

Sweet Helen, make me immortal with a kiss.[12]

Her lips suck forth my soul: see where it flies.

They are Marlowe's lines. No one else could have written them; not even Shakespeare. When Shakespeare was writing in the style of Marlowe he was incapable of this magnificence; when he became capable of it he had worked out a style of his own, utterly different from Marlowe's. Those lines are recognizably Marlowe's; but when we say that Marlowe had style, we are referring to a quality which transcends all personal idiosyncrasy, yet needs—or seems to need—personal idiosyncrasy in order to be manifested. Style, in this absolute sense, is a complete fusion of the personal and the universal. A great writer is never more intensely and recognizably himself than in his greatest passages; to use a vaguely metaphysical phrase, absolute style is the complete realization of a universal significance in a personal and particular expression.

Here, then, we have three fairly distinct meanings of the word Style disengaged; Style, as personal idiosyncrasy; Style, as technique of exposition; Style, as the highest achievement of literature. The opportunities for confusion are great. We may say that the critic should make clear by his context the sense in which he is using the word; the fact remains that he seldom does—for this reason. The critic, unless he is that very rare and valuable thing, a technical critic, must be to some extent a creative artist in his criticism. The first part of his work is to convey the effect, the whole intellectual and emotional impression made by the work he is criticizing: without this foundation his criticism will be jejune[13] and unsubstantial. In this respect his task is strictly analogous to that of the creative writer. Instead of trying to communicate the emotions liberated in him by a primrose, or life as one mysterious whole, he is trying to recreate in his reader the peculiar emotion aroused in him by a work of literature. He has other things to do besides this, and to do at the same time; but if he is successful in this primary task, it will follow necessary that the general terms he may use to elucidate his impression will have a particular colour and quality, if not a definite sense, given to them. If, for example, a critic has been successful in communicating a sense of the majestical, symphonic effect of Milton's ***Areopagitica***, and he goes on to talk of its style, he will hardly need to define the meaning of the word. He has already given it a fuller content than any definition can convey. And so it might seem that all attempts to analyse a word so Protean[14] are lost labour. They would be, if all critics were perfect, and all criticisms the complete and rounded works of art which they are by intention. But the perfect critic does not exist, and never has existed; critics succeed sometimes and fail at others; the best of them fail more often than they succeed; and when they are failing, their invariable gesture is to use general terms as a prop to their own defective achievement. Instead of giving their general terms a full and particular content, they use them rather to give an appearance of weight and authority to misty and undecided perceptions.

Then the different meanings contained in the word Style work havoc in the mind both of the critic and the reader. The word slips from one sense into another, until the weary Aristaeus[15] has no more strength to grapple with the old man of the sea[16]. The vital relation of style, in any of its sense, to the particularity of the work of which it is predicated, is weakened and finally severed altogether. Then we find style in the first sense of idiosyncrasy used quite indiscriminately as a term of praise, as though it were really a literary merit for an author to be recognizable at all times and all places in his work: on the whole it is far more likely to be an impertinence. In how many novels of recent years is the all-important dialogue carried on between so many obvious hypostatizations[17] of the novelist's self! Or again, the unaccented style ("style" in our second sense) proper to a lucid exposition of intellectual argument, innocent of all distracting metaphor, with the plastic and emotional suggestion of the words reduced to a minimum, will be considered an excellence in a writer whose chief function it is to give the illusion of life. This is one of the most glaring of the false sophistications prevalent in what we may call superior criticism today. A flat style is supposed to have some aristocratic virtue of its own, no matter to what subject-matter it is applied; to be vivid, on the other hand, is to be vulgar. That is pure heresy, and those writers who, through some deficiency in their own creative vitality or some fear of the contempt of the superior person, embrace it, must inevitably become parochial. They will enjoy a languid sequence of *succès d'estime*[18] in their lives and be quietly forgotten after their deaths.

NOTES

1. **Saturday Review:** The *Saturday Review* was an influential periodical (1855–1938).
2. **Saintsbury:** George Edward Bateman Saintsbury (1845–1933) was an English literary critic and historian. He wrote voluminously on English and French literature. At one time (in 1883–1894) he was assistant editor of the *Saturday Review*.
3. **Meredith:** George Meredith (1828–1909) was an English novelist and poet. His novels include *The Ordeal of Richard Feverel* (1859), *Beauchamp's Career* (1876), and *The Egoist* (1879). His poetical works include *Modern Love* (1862).
4. **Henry James:** Henry James (1843–1916) was an American-born British novelist and critic. Among his novels are *Roderick Hudson* (1875), *Daisy Miller* (1879), *The Portrait of a Lady* (1881), *The Wings of the Dove* (1902), *The Ambassadors* (1903), and *The Golden Bowl* (1904).
5. **Tourneur:** Cyril Tourneur (1575?–1626) was an English dramatist. His plays include *The Atheist's Tragedy* (1611) and probably *The Revenger's Tragedy* (1607).
6. **Webster:** John Webster (c.1578–c.1632) was an English dramatist whose two major

works are *The White Devil* (published in 1612), and *The Duchess of Malfi* (written in 1613).

7. **the *Maid's Tragedy*:** a tragedy (1610–1611) by Beaumont and Fletcher, one of their best works
8. ***sermo communis*:** (Lat.) common talk
9. ***qua*:** (Lat.) in the capacity of
10. ***Tout déroule de la conception*:** (Fr.) Everything unfolds from the conception.
11. **See where Christ's blood streams in the firmament:** See *Doctor Faustus*, V. ii. 156.
12. **Sweet Helen, make me immortal with a kiss./Her lips suck forth my soul:** See *Doctor Faustus* V. i. 99-100.
13. **jejune:** dry
14. **Protean:** changeable like Proteus, the Greek prophetic marine demi-god
15. **Aristaeus:** son of Apollo and the Nymph Cyrene. He once consulted Proteus as to how to recover his lost bees.
16. **the old man of the sea:** Proteus
17. **hypostatizations:** embodiments or personifications
18. ***succès d'estime*:** (Fr.) success of esteem, success with more honour than profit

95

ALDOUS LEONARD HUXLEY

(1894-1963)

Aldous L. Huxley was an English novelist and essayist. He was born at Godalming, Surrey, the grandson of T. H. Huxley, and educated at Eton and Oxford. After a year in the War Office (1917) and a year at Eton College (1918), he worked as a literary journalist. He settled in California in 1937.

Huxley's early novels—***Crome Yellow*** (1921), ***Antic Hay*** (1923), and ***Those Barren Leaves*** (1925)—are gay, witty and ironical novels of conversation. His later novels—e.g. ***Point Counter Point*** (1928), ***Brave New World*** (1932), ***Eyeless in Gaza*** (1936), and ***After Many A Summer*** (1939)—are novels of ideas in which characters appear like puppets. His ***Collected Short Stories*** (1957) and ***Collected Essays*** (1960) contain some excellent writing.

GEORGE AND GEORGIANA[1]

"It was in the spring of 1833 that my grandfather, George Wimbush, first made the acquaintance of the 'three lovely Lapiths,' as they were always called. He was then a young man of twenty-two, with curly yellow hair and a smooth pink face that was the mirror of his youthful and ingenuous mind. He had been educated at Harrow[2] and Christ Church[3], he enjoyed hunting and all other field sports, and, though his circumstances were comfortable to the verge of affluence, his pleasures were temperate and innocent. His father, an East Indian merchant, had destined him for a political career, and had gone to considerable expense in acquiring a pleasant little Cornish borough[4] as a twenty-first birthday gift for his son. He was justly indignant when, on the very eve of George's majority, the Reform Bill of 1832[5] swept the borough out of existence. The inauguration of George's political career had to be postponed. At the time he got to know the lovely Lapiths he was waiting; he was not at all impatient.

"The lovely Lapiths did not fail to impress him. Georgiana, the eldest, with her black ringlets, her flashing eyes, her noble aquiline profile, her swan-like neck, and sloping shoulders, was orientally dazzling; and the twins, with their delicately turned-up noses, their blue eyes, and chestnut hair, were an identical pair of ravishingly English charmers.

"Their conversation at this first meeting proved, however, to be so forbidding that, but for the invincible attraction exercised by their beauty, George would never have had the courage to follow up the acquaintance. The twins, looking up their noses at him with an air of languid superiority, asked him what he thought of the latest French poetry and whether he liked the *Indiana* of George Sand[6]. But what was almost worse was the question with which Georgiana opened her conversation with him. 'In music,' she asked, leaning forward and fixing him with her large dark eyes, 'are you a classicist or a transcendentalist?'[7] George did not lose his presence of mind. He had enough appreciation of music to know that he hated anything classical, and so, with a promptitude which did him credit, he replied, 'I am a transcendentalist.' Georgiana smiled bewitchingly. 'I am glad,' she said; 'so am I. You went to hear Paganini[8] last week, of course. 'The Prayer of Moses' —ah!' She closed her eyes. 'Do you know anything more transcendental than that?' 'No,' said George, 'I don't.' He hesitated, was about to go on speaking, and then decided that after all it would be wiser not to say—what was in fact true—that he had enjoyed above all Paganini's Farmyard Imitations. The man had made his fiddle bray like an ass, cluck like a hen, grunt, squeal, bark, neigh, quack, bellow, and growl; that last item, in George's estimation, had almost compensated for the tediousness of the rest of the concert. He smiled with pleasure at the thought of it. Yes, decidedly, he was no classicist in music; he was a thoroughgoing transcendentalist.

"George followed up this first introduction by paying a call on the young ladies and their mother, who occupied, during the season[9], a small but elegant house in the neighbourhood of Berkeley Square[10]. Lady Lapith made a few discreet inquiries, and having found that George's financial position, character, and family were all passably good, she asked him to dine. She hoped and expected that her daughters would all marry into the peerage; but, being a prudent woman, she knew it was advisable to prepare for all contingencies. George Wimbusch, she thought, would make an excellent second string for one of the twins.

"At this first dinner, George's partner was Emmeline. They talked of Nature. Emmeline protested that to her high mountains were a feeling and the hum of human cities torture. George agreed that the country was very agreeable, but held that London during the season also had its charms. He noticed with surprise and a certain solicitous distress that Miss Emmeline's appetite was poor, that it didn't, in fact, exist. Two spoonfuls of soup, a morsel of fish, no bread, no meat, and three grapes—that was her whole dinner. He looked from time to time at her two sisters; Georgiana and Caroline seemed to be quite as abstemious. They waved away whatever was offered them with an expression of delicate disgust, shutting their eyes and averting their faces from the proffered dish, as though the lemon sole, the duck, the loin of veal, the trifle, were objects revolting to the sight and smell. George, who thought the dinner capital, ventured to comment on the sisters' lack of appetite.

"'Pray, don't talk to me of eating,' said Emmeline, drooping like a sensitive plant. 'We find it so coarse, so unspiritual, my sisters and I. One can't think of one's soul while one is eating.'

"George agreed; one couldn't. 'But one must live,' he said.

"'Alas!' Emmeline sighed. 'One must. Death is very beautiful, don't you think?' She broke a corner off a piece of toast and began to nibble at it languidly. 'But since, as you say, one must live...' She made a little gesture of resignation. 'Luckily a very little suffices to keep one alive.' She put down her corner of toast half eaten.

"George regarded her with some surprise. She was pale, but she looked extraordinarily healthy, he thought; so did her sisters. Perhaps if you were really spiritual you needed less food. He, clearly, was not spiritual.

"After this he saw them frequently. They all liked him, from Lady Lapith downwards. True, he was not very romantic or poetical; but he was such a pleasant, unpretentious, kind-hearted young man, that one couldn't help liking him. For his part, he thought them wonderful, wonderful, especially Georgiana. He enveloped them all in a warm, protective affection. For they needed protection; they were altogether too frail, too spiritual for this world. They never ate, they were always pale, they often complained of fever, they talked much and lovingly of death, they frequently swooned. Georgiana was the most ethereal of all; of the three she ate least, swooned most often, talked most of death, and was the palest—with a pallor that was so startling as to appear positively artificial. At any moment, it seemed, she might loose her precarious hold on this material world and become all spirit. To George the thought was a continual agony. If she were to die...

"She contrived, however, to live through the season, and that in spite of the numerous balls, routs[11], and other parties of pleasure which, in company with the rest of the lovely trio, she never failed to attend. In the middle of July the whole household moved down to the country. George was invited to spend the month of August at Crome[12].

"The house-party was distinguished; in the list of visitors figured the names of two marriageable young men of title. George had hoped that country air, repose, and natural surroundings might have restored to the three sisters their appetites and the roses of their cheeks. He was mistaken. For dinner, the first evening, Georgiana ate only an olive, two or three salted almonds, and half a peach. She was as pale as ever. During the meal she spoke of love.

"'True love,' she said, 'being infinite and eternal, can only be consummated in eternity. Indiana and Sir Rodolphe[13] celebrated the mystic wedding of their souls by jumping into Niagara. Love is incompatible with life. The wish of two people who truly love one another is not to live together but to die together.'

"'Come, come, my dear,' said Lady Lapith, stout and practical. 'What would become of the next generation, pray if all the world acted on your principles?'

"'Mamma!...' Georgiana protested, and dropped her eyes.

"'In my young days,' Lady Lapith went on, 'I should have been laughed out of countenance if I'd said a thing like that. But then in my young days souls weren't as fashionable as they are now and we didn't think death was at all poetical. It was just unpleasant.'

"'Mamma!...' Emmeline and Caroline implored in unison.

"'In my young days—' Lady Lapith was launched into her subject; nothing, it seemed, could stop her now. 'In my young days, if you didn't eat, people told you you needed a dose of rhubarb. Nowadays...'

"There was a cry; Georgiana had swooned sideways on to Lord Timpany's shoulder. It was a desperate expedient; but it was successful. Lady Lapith was stopped.

"The days passed in an uneventful round of pleasures. Of all the gay party George alone was unhappy. Lord Timpany was paying his court to Georgiana, and it was clear that he was not unfavourably received. George looked on, and his soul was a hell of jealousy and despair. The boisterous company of the young men became intolerable to him; he shrank from them, seeking gloom and solitude. One morning, having broken away from them on some vague pretext, he returned to the house alone. The young men were bathing in the pool below; their cries and laughter floated up to him, making the quiet house seem lonelier and more silent. The lovely sisters and their mamma still kept their chambers; they did not customarily make their appearance till luncheon, so that the male guests had the morning to themselves. George sat down in the hall and abandoned himself to thought.

"At any moment she might die; at any moment she might become Lady Timpany. It was terrible, terrible. If she died, then he would die to; he would go to seek her beyond the grave. If she became Lady Timpany...ah, then! The solution of the problem would not be so simple. If she became Lady Timpany: it was a horrible thought. But then suppose she were in love with Timpany—though it seemed incredible that anyone could be in love with Timpany—suppose her life depended on Timpany, suppose she couldn't live without him? He was fumbling his way along this clueless labyrinth of suppositions when the clock struck twelve. On the last stroke, like an automaton released by the turning clockwork, a little maid, holding a large covered tray, popped out of the door that led from the kitchen regions into the hall. From his deep arm-chair George watched her (himself, it was evident, unobserved) with an idle curiosity. She pattered across the room and came to a halt in front of what seemed a blank expanse of panelling. She reached out her hand and, to George's extreme astonishment, a little door swung open, revealing the foot of a winding staircase. Turning sideways in order to get her tray through the narrow opening, the little maid darted in with a rapid crablike motion. The door closed behind her with a click. A minute later it opened again and the maid, without her tray hurried back across the hall and disappeared in the direction of the kitchen. George tried to recompose his thoughts, but an invincible curiosity drew his mind towards the hidden door, the staircase, the little maid. It was in vain he told himself that the matter was none of his business, that to explore the secrets of that surprising door, that mysterious staircase within, would be a piece of unforgivable rudeness and indiscretion. It was in vain; for five minutes he struggled heroically with his curiosity, but at the end of that time he found himself standing in front of the innocent sheet of panelling through which the little maid had disappeared. A glance sufficed to show him the position of the secret door—secret, he perceived, only to those who looked with a careless eye. It was just an ordinary door let in flush with the panelling. No latch nor handle betrayed its position, but an unobtrusive catch sunk in the wood invited the thumb. George was astonished that he had not noticed it before; now that he had seen it, it was so obvious, almost as obvious as the cupboard door in the library with its lines of imitation shelves and its dummy books. He pulled back the catch and peeped inside. The staircase, of which the degrees were made not of stone but of blocks of ancient oak, wound up and out of sight. A slit-like window admitted the day-light; he was at the foot of the central tower, and the little window looked out over the terrace; they were still shouting and splashing in the pool below.

"George closed the door and went back to his seat. But his curiosity was not satisfied. Indeed, this partial satisfaction had but whetted its appetite. Where did the staircase lead? What was the errand of the little maid? It was no business of his, he kept repeating—no business of his. He tried to read, but his attention wandered. A quarter-past twelve sounded on the harmonious clock. Suddenly determined, George rose, crossed the room, opened the hidden door, and began to ascend the stairs. He passed the first window, corkscrewed round, and came to another. He paused for a moment to look out; his heart beat uncomfortably, as though he were affronting some unknown danger. What he was doing, he told himself, was extremely ungentlemanly, horribly underbred. He tiptoed onward and upward. One turn more, then half a turn, and a door confronted him. He halted before it, listened; he could hear no sound. Putting his eye to the keyhole, he saw nothing but a stretch of white sunlit wall. Emboldened, he turned the handle and stepped across the threshold. There he halted, petrified by what he saw, mutely gaping.

"In the middle of a pleasantly sunny little room— 'it is now Priscilla's boudoir,' Mr. Wimbush remarked parenthetically—stood a small circular table of mahogany. Crystal, porcelain, and silver—all the shining apparatus of an elegant meal—were mirrored in its polished depths. The carcase of a cold chicken, a bowl of fruit, a great ham, deeply gashed to its heart of tenderest white and pink, the brown cannon ball of a cold plum-pudding, a slender Hock bottle, and a decanter of claret jostled one another for a place on this festive board. And round the table sat the three sisters, the three lovely Lapiths—eating!

"At George's sudden entrance they had all looked towards the door, and now they sat, petrified by the same astonishment which kept George fixed and staring. Georgiana, who sat immediately facing the door, gazed at him with dark, enormous eyes. Between the thumb and forefinger of her right hand she was holding a drumstick of the dismembered chicken; her little finger, elegantly crooked, stood apart from the rest of her hand. Her mouth was open, but the drumstick had never reached its destination; it remained, suspended, frozen, in mid-air. The other two sisters had turned round to look at the intruder. Caroline still grasped her knife and fork; Emmeline's fingers were round the stem of her claret glass. For what seemed a very long time, George and the three sisters stared at one another in silence. They were a group of statues. Then suddenly there was movement. Georgiana dropped her chicken bone, Caroline's knife and fork clattered on her plate. The movement propagated itself, grew more decisive; Emmeline sprang to her feet, uttering a cry. The wave of panic reached George; he turned and, mumbling something unintelligible as he went, rushed out of the room and down the winding stairs. He came to a standstill in the hall, and there, all by himself in the quiet house, he began to laugh.

"At luncheon it was noticed that the sisters ate a little more than usual. Georgiana toyed with some French beans and a spoonful of calves'-foot jelly. 'I feel a little stronger to-day,' she said to Lord Timpany, when he congratulated her on this increase of appetite; 'a little more material,' she added, with a nervous laugh. Looking up, she caught George's eye; a blush suffused her cheeks and she looked hastily away.

"In the garden that afternoon they found themselves for a moment alone.

"'You won't tell anyone, George? Promise you won't tell anyone,' she implored. 'It would make us look so ridiculous. And besides, eating *is* unspiritual, isn't it? Say you won't tell anyone.'

"'I will,' said George brutally. 'I'll tell everyone, unless...'

"'It's blackmail.'

"'I don't care,' said George. 'I'll give you twenty-four hours to decide.'

"Lady Lapith was disappointed, of course; she had hoped for better things—for Timpany and a coronet. But George, after all, wasn't so bad. They were married at the New Year."

NOTES

1. **George and Georgiana:** This story of George Wimbush and Georgiana Lapith is told by a character in the novel ***Crome Yellow***.
2. **Harrow:** Harrow School, a boys' public school at Harrow-on-the-Hill in London
3. **Christ Church:** one of the colleges of Oxford University
4. **acquiring a pleasant little Cornish borough:** acquiring the power to control the election of an M. P. for the pleasant little borough in Cornwall
5. **the Reform Bill of 1832:** the Third Reform Bill Act passed in 1832 to reform the representation of the people in Parliament
6. **the *Indiana* of George Sand:** *Indiana* (1832) was the first successful novel by the French romantic writer George Sand (1804–1876). The heroine of the novel struggles for her right to love and independence.
7. **transcendentalist:** one whose philosophy emphasizes intuition as a means to knowledge
8. **Paganini:** Niccolò Paganini (1782–1840), Italian violinist and composer
9. **during the season:** during the time from May to July when fashionable society is assembled in London
10. **Berkeley Square:** a fashionable quarter in London
11. **routs:** (arch.) large parties or social gatherings
12. **Crome:** Crome Yellow in the novel bearing its name is the family home of Henry and Priscilla Wimbush and was formerly the country house of the Lapiths.
13. **Sir Rodolphe:** Sir Rodolphe Brown is Indiana's cousin and lover in the novel ***Indiana***.

GEORGE ORWELL

(1903–1950)

George Orwell (pseudonym of Eric Blair) was an English novelist and essayist. He was born in Bengal on 25th June 1903, the son of an English official in the Indian Civil Service, and was educated in England at a private school and at Eton College. His service with the Burma Police from 1922 to 1927 resulted in a hatred of colonialism and imperialist oppression. He returned and lived in Paris and then in London, doing ill-paid jobs. In December 1936 he went to Spain to fight for the Republican cause in the Civil War, and was severely wounded five months later. During the Second World War he wrote a large amount of journalism. He believed in what he termed democratic socialism, but never joined any political party. He died of tuberculosis on 21st January 1950.

Orwell's general works include ***Down and Out in Paris and London*** (1933), ***The Road to Wigan Pier*** (1937), and ***Homage to Catalonia*** (1938). His collections of essays include ***Inside the Whale*** (1940), ***Critical Essays*** (1946), and ***Shooting an Elephant*** (1950). Among his earlier novels may be mentioned ***Burmese Days*** (1934), ***Keep the Aspidistra Flying*** (1936), and ***Coming Up for Air*** (1939). His later novels, ***Animal Farm*** (1945) and ***Nineteen Eighty-four*** (1949), both satires against tyranny, are his most popular books. His lucid, colloquial prose style is widely acclaimed.

WHY I WRITE

From a very early age, perhaps the age of five or six, I knew that when I grew up I should be a writer. Between the ages of about seventeen and twenty-four I tried to abandon this idea, but I did so with the consciousness that I was outraging my true nature and that sooner or later I should have to settle down and write books.

I was the middle child of three, but there was a gap of five years on either side, and I barely saw my father before I was eight. For this and other reasons I was somewhat lonely, and I soon developed disagreeable mannerisms which made me unpopular throughout my schooldays. I had the lonely child's habit of making up stories and holding conversations with imaginary persons, and I think from the very start my literary ambitions were mixed up with the feeling of being isolated and undervalued. I knew that I had a facility with words and a power of facing unpleasant facts, and I felt that this created a sort of private world in which I could get my own back[1] for my failure in everyday life. Nevertheless the volume of serious—i.e. seriously intended—writing which I produced all through my childhood and boyhood would not amount to half a dozen pages. I wrote my first poem at the age of four or five, my mother taking it down to dictation. I cannot remember anything about it except that it was about a tiger and the tiger had "chair-like teeth"—a good enough phrase, but I fancy the poem was a plagiarism of Blake's "Tiger, Tiger". At eleven, when the war of 1914–1918 broke out, I wrote a patriotic poem which was printed in the local newspaper, as was another, two years later, on the death of Kitchener[2]. From time to time, when I was a bit older, I wrote bad and usually unfinished "nature poems" in the Georgian style[3]. I also, about twice, attempted a short story which was a ghastly failure. That was the total of the would-be serious work that I actually set down on paper during all those years.

However, throughout this time I did in a sense engage in literary activities.

To begin with there was the made-to-order stuff which I produced quickly, easily and without much pleasure to myself. Apart from school work, I wrote ***vers d'occasion***[4], semi-comic poems which I could turn out at what now seems to me astonishing speed—at fourteen I wrote a whole rhyming play, in imitation of Aristophanes, in about a week—and helped to edit school magazines, both printed and in manuscript. These magazines were the most pitiful burlesque stuff that you could imagine, and I took far less trouble with them than I now would with the cheapest journalism. But side by side with all this, for fifteen years or more, I was carrying out a literary exercise of a quite different kind: this was the making up of a continuous "story" about myself, a sort of diary existing only in the mind. I believe this is a common habit of children and adolescents. As a very small child I used to imagine that I was, say, Robin Hood[5], and picture myself as the hero of thrilling adventures, but quite soon my "story" ceased to be narcissistic in a crude way and became more and more a mere description of what I was doing and the things I saw. For minutes at a time this kind of thing would be running through my head: "He pushed the door open and entered the room. A yellow beam of sunlight, filtering through the muslin curtains, slanted on to the table, where a matchbox, half open, lay beside the inkpot. With his right hand in his pocket he moved across to the window. Down in the street a tortoise-shell cat[6] was chasing a dead leaf," etc. etc. This habit continued till I was about twenty-five, right through my non-literary years. Although I had to search, and did search, for the right words, I seemed to be making this descriptive effort almost against my will, under a kind of compulsion from outside. The "story" must, I suppose, have reflected the styles of the various writers I admired at different ages, but so far as I remember it always had the same meticulous descriptive quality.

When I was about sixteen I suddenly discovered the joy of mere words, i.e. the sounds and associations of words. The lines from ***Paradise Lost***,

>So hee with difficulty and labour hard
>Moved on: with difficulty and labour hee[7],

which do not now seem to me so very wonderful, sent shivers down my backbone; and the spelling "hee" for "he" was an added pleasure. As for the need to describe things, I knew all about it already. So it is clear what kind of books I wanted to write, in so far as I could be said to want to write books at that time. I wanted to write enormous naturalistic novels with unhappy endings, full of detailed descriptions and arresting similes, and also full of purple passages in which words were used partly for the sake of their sound. And in fact my first completed novel, **Burmese Days**, which I wrote when I was thirty but projected much earlier, is rather that kind of book.

I give all this background information because I do not think one can assess a writer's motives without knowing something of his early development. His subject matter will be determined by the age he lives in—at least this is true in tumultuous, revolutionary ages like our own—but before he ever begins to write he will have acquired an emotional attitude from which he will never completely escape. It is his job, no doubt, to discipline his temperament and avoid getting stuck at some immature stage, or in some perverse mood: but if he escapes from his early influences altogether, he will have killed his impulse to write. Putting aside the need to earn a living, I think there are four great motives for writing, at any rate for writing prose. They exist in different degrees in every writer, and in any one writer the proportions will vary from time to time, according to the atmosphere in which he is living. They are:

1. Sheer egoism. Desire to seem clever, to be talked about, to be remembered after death, to get your own back on grown-ups who snubbed you in childhood, etc. etc. It is humbug to pretend that this is not a motive, and a strong one. Writers share this characteristic with scientists, artists, politicians, lawyers, soldiers, successful businessmen—in short, with the whole top crust of humanity. The great mass of human beings are not acutely selfish. After the age of about thirty they abandon individual ambition—in many cases, indeed, they almost abandon the sense of being individuals at all—and live chiefly for others, or are simply smothered under drudgery. But there is also the minority of gifted, wilful people who are determined to live their own lives to the end, and writers belong in this

class. Serious writers, I should say, are on the whole more vain and self-centered than journalists, though less interested in money.

2. Aesthetic enthusiasm. Perception of beauty in the external world, or, on the other hand, in words and their right arrangement. Pleasure in the impact of one sound on another, in the firmness of good prose or the rhythm of a good story. Desire to share an experience which one feels is valuable and ought not to be missed. The aesthetic motive is very feeble in a lot of writers, but even a pamphleteer or a writer of textbooks will have pet words and phrases which appeal to him for non-utilitarian reasons; or he may feel strongly about typography, width of margins, etc. Above the level of a railway guide, no book is quite free from aesthetic considerations.

3. Historical impulse. Desire to see things as they are, to find out true facts and store them up for the use of posterity.

4. Political purpose—using the word "political" in the widest possible sense. Desire to push the world in a certain direction, to alter other people's idea of the kind of society that they should strive after. Once again, no book is genuinely free from political bias. The opinion that art should have nothing to do with politics is itself a political attitude.

It can be seen how these various impulses must war against one another, and how they must fluctuate from person to person and from time to time. By nature—taking your "nature" to be the state you have attained when you are first adult—I am a person in whom the first three motives would outweigh the fourth. In a peaceful age I might have written ornate or merely descriptive books, and might have remained almost unaware of my political loyalties. As it is I have been forced into becoming a sort of pamphleteer. First I spent five years in an unsuitable profession (the Indian Imperial Police, in Burma), and then I underwent poverty and the sense of failure. This increased my natural hatred of authority and made me for the first time fully aware of the existence of the working classes, and the job in Burma had given me some understanding of the nature of imperialism: but these experiences were not enough to give me an accurate political orientation. Then came Hitler, the Spanish civil war[8], etc. By the end of 1935 I had still failed to reach a firm decision. I remember a little poem that I wrote at that date, expressing my dilemma:

> A happy vicar I might have been
> Two hundred years ago,
> To preach upon eternal doom
> And watch my walnuts grow;
>
> But born, alas, in an evil time,
> I missed that pleasant haven,
> For the hair has grown on my upper lip
> And the clergy are all clean-shaven.
>
> And later still the times were good,
> We were so easy to please,
> We rocked our troubled thoughts to sleep
> On the bosoms of the trees.
>
> All ignorant we dared to own
> The joys we now dissemble;
> The greenfinch on the apple bough
> Could make my enemies tremble.
>
> But girls' bellies and apricots,
> Roach in a shaded stream,
> Horses, ducks in flight at dawn,
> All these are a dream.
>
> It is forbidden to dream again;
> We maim our joys or hide them;
> Horses are made of chromium steel

And little fat men shall ride them.

I am the worm who never turned,
The eunuch without a harem;
Between the priest and the commissar
I walk like Eugene Aram;

And the commissar is telling my fortune
While the radio plays,
But the priest has promised an Austin Seven,
For Duggie always pays.

I dreamed I dwelt in marble halls,
And woke to find it true;
I wasn't born for an age like this;
Was Smith? Was Jones? Were you?

The Spanish war and other events in 1936-1937 turned the scale and thereafter I knew where I stood. Every line of serious work that I have written since 1936 has been written, directly or indirectly, ***against*** totalitarianism and ***for*** democratic Socialism, as I understand it. It seems to me nonsense, in a period like our own, to think that one can avoid writing of such subjects. Everyone writes of them in one guise or another. It is simply a question of which side one takes and what approach one follows. And the more one is conscious of one's political bias, the more chance one has of acting politically without sacrificing one's aesthetic and intellectual integrity.

What I have most wanted to do throughout the past ten years is to make political writing into an art. My starting point is always a feeling of partisanship, a sense of injustice. When I sit down to write a book, I do not say to myself, "I am going to produce a work of art." I write it because there is some lie that I want to expose, some fact to which I want to draw attention, and my initial concern is to get a hearing. But I could not do the work of writing a book, or even a long magazine article, if it were not also an aesthetic experience. Anyone who cares to examine my work will see that even when it is downright propaganda it contains much that a full-time politician would consider irrelevant. I am not able, and I do not want, completely to abandon the world-view that I acquired in childhood. So long as I remain alive and well I shall continue to feel strongly about prose style, to love the surface of the earth, and to take pleasure in solid objects and scraps of useless information. It is no use trying to suppress that side of myself. The job is to reconcile my ingrained likes and dislikes with the essentially public, non-individual activities that this age forces on all of us.

It is not easy. It raises problems of construction and of language, and it raises in a new way the problem of truthfulness. Let me give just one example of the cruder kind of difficulty that arises. My book about the Spanish civil war, **Homage to Catalonia**, is, of course, a frankly political book, but in the main it is written with a certain detachment and regard for form. I did try very hard in it to tell the whole truth without violating my literary instincts. But among other things it contains a long chapter, full of newspaper quotations and the like, defending the Trotskyists[9] who were accused of plotting with Franco[10]. Clearly such a chapter, which after a year or two would lose its interest for any ordinary reader, must ruin the book. A critic whom I respect read me a lecture about it. "Why did you put in all that stuff?" he said. "You've turned what might have been a good book into journalism." What he said was true, but I could not have done otherwise. I happened to know, what very few people in England had been allowed to know, that innocent men were being falsely accused. If I had not been angry about that I should never have written the book.

In one form or another this problem comes up again. The problem of language is subtler and would take too long to discuss. I will only say that of late years I have tried to write less picturesquely and more exactly. In any case I find that by the time you have perfected any style of writing, you have always outgrown it. **Animal Farm** was the first book in which I tried, with full consciousness of what I was doing, to fuse political purpose and artistic purpose into one whole. I have not written a novel for seven years, but I hope to write another fairly soon. It is bound to be a failure, every book is a failure, but I know with some clarity what kind of book I want to write.

Looking back through the last page or two, I see that I have made it appear as though my motives in writing were wholly public-spirited. I don't want to leave that as the final impression. All writers are vain, selfish and lazy, and at the very bottom of their motives there lies a mystery. Writing a book is a horrible, exhausting struggle, like a long bout of some painful illness. One would never undertake such a thing if one were not driven on by some demon whom one can neither resist nor understand. For all one knows that demon is simply the same instinct that makes a baby squall for attention. And yet it is also true that one can write nothing readable unless one constantly struggles to efface one's own personality. Good prose is like a window pane. I cannot say with certainty which of my motives are the strongest, but I know which of them deserve to be followed. And looking back through my work, I see that it is invariably where I lacked a *political* purpose that I wrote lifeless books and was betrayed into purple passages, sentences without meaning, decorative adjectives and humbug generally.

NOTES

1. **get my own back:** (colloq.) get revenge
2. **Kitchener:** Horatio Herbert or Earl Kitchener of Khartoum (1850–1916), who was British field marshal and Secretary of State for War (1914–1916)
3. **the Georgian style:** the style of poetry written during the reign of George V (1910–1936)
4. *vers d'occasion*: (Fr.) occasional verse
5. **Robin Hood:** a legendary outlaw and the hero of many English ballads. He is said to have lived in the latter part of the 12th century and the early part of the 13th, and to have robbed the rich and helped the poor.
6. **a tortoise-shell cat:** a yellowish brown cat
7. **So hee with difficulty and labour hard/Moved on: with difficulty and labour hee:**

So he moved on with difficulty and hard labour (***Paradise Lost*** II. 1021-1022).

8. **the Spanish civil war:** the struggle between the Falangists and the Republican government from 1936 to 1939
9. **Trotskyists:** followers of Leon Trotsky (1877–1940), a leader of the October Revolution (1917)
10. **Franco:** Francisco Franco Bahamonde (1892–1975), a Spanish military leader and right-wing politician, who commanded the Falangists in the Civil War and established a dictatorship in 1939.

后 记

本书的原始依据是鲍屡平教授的自编教材《英国散文选》。这是他为杭州大学外语系第一、二届英语研究生讲授英国散文时编写的。而后鲍屡平教授对其进行补充、加深并完成了这份书稿的全部选注工作。惜后因病未能整理成书。

近年来，姚祖培教授、王锦副教授和孙玲副教授对鲍屡平教授上述那份遗稿进行了整理。在整理过程中，三位同志不顾年老体弱，按照鲍屡平教授的意愿，坚持工作。感人的情景充分体现了师生间情谊之深。现书稿基本整理成书，或可献给读者应用了。（注：①姚祖培教授1951年毕业于浙江大学外文系英语专业，是当年班上的优等生。他在杭州大学外语系任教时，教授高年级英语专业课程及研究生"英国诗歌"等课程。②王锦副教授是杭州大学外语系英语专业首届研究生，毕业后留校任教，主要教授英语精读、泛读等专业课程。他对英语词典、词汇、惯用法等深有研究。③孙玲副教授1956年毕业于北京大学西语系英语专业，毕业后一直在杭州大学外语系任教，"文革"前教授"英国文学史"课程，之后教授公共英语课程，兼任教学组长。）

本书提供了自16世纪至20世纪中期约400年之间英国近百位散文名家和他们的百余篇散文名作。这些作品的可读性、实用性和鉴赏性较强。为此，本书可用作英语专业高年级学生的教材，也可用作英语爱好者的自学读物或研究对象，更多的读者还可从本书中获得各种美的享受，本书甚至还可起到传承的作用。在国内，类似本书这样较全面、较系统、较完整地反映上述期间英国散文名家名作各方面情况的英国散文名篇选注，至今似乎还不多见。

上世纪末，北京大学英语教授李赋宁老师来杭时，闲谈中他热情地提出今后由他为本书写序，但时机错失。今日，赋宁老师不在了，我们不禁无限惋惜，也无限怀念他。现在，本书的"前言"用了鲍屡平教授所写的《谈英文散文阅读》一文中的第一部分"多读英文散文佳作"。其中较详尽地介绍了散文的含义、范围、类别、主要名家名作等情况，既有助于增强读者对散文的认识和理解，还能有效地指导读者阅读本书的百余篇英文散文佳作。读者不妨细阅一下。（注：《谈英文散文阅读》一文的全文刊登于1983年12月《杭州大学学报》第13卷第4期。）

在整理本书的过程中，不少亲朋好友和同志们给予了亲切的关怀和帮助。黄敬先、王欧文、温时幸等在美国的亲友也不辞辛劳，想方设法代查阅或核对有关资料，以保证本书质量。任绍曾、殷企平、方凡、王小潞四位教授对本书给予了极大关注。曹国忠、孙仁昌等同志帮助处理较多的具体事项。谨此一并致谢。

本书虽经多次校对，在质量方面会更有所保证，但这些年来因我多病，在校阅本书时恐难避免有错漏之处，还请读者见谅。

在上述亲友们的大力相助下，鲍屡平教授的一个遗愿——将他所选注的《英国散文名篇选注》献给读者——终于得以实现。在此，我代他向大家致以最衷心的感谢。

最后，本书来之不易，且均为名家名作，愿读者喜欢。

孙玲

2016年10月　浙江　杭州